THE MESSIANIC IDEA IN ISRAEL

THE MESSIANIC IDEA IN ISRAEL

From Its Beginning

to the Completion of the Mishnah

by JOSEPH KLAUSNER, Ph.D.
PROFESSOR EMERITUS OF HEBREW LITERATURE AND JEWISH HISTORY
IN THE HEBREW UNIVERSITY, JERUSALEM

TRANSLATED FROM THE THIRD HEBREW EDITION
by W. F. STINESPRING, Ph.D.
PROFESSOR OF OLD TESTAMENT, DUKE UNIVERSITY

WIPF & STOCK · Eugene, Oregon

Wipf and Stock Publishers
199 W 8th Ave, Suite 3
Eugene, OR 97401

The Messianic Idea in Israel
From Its Beginning to the Completion of the Mishnah
By Klausner, Joseph and Stinespring, W. F.
Softcover ISBN-13: 979-8-3852-2342-8
Hardcover ISBN-13: 979-8-3852-2343-5
eBook ISBN-13: 979-8-3852-2344-2
Publication date 4/9/2024
Previously published by The Macmillan Company, 1955

This edition is a scanned facsimile of the original edition published in 1955.

TO THE MEMORY OF
THE FIRST HEAD OF THE
HEBREW UNIVERSITY IN JERUSALEM

Dr. Judah L. Magnes

ALL OF WHOSE DEEDS WERE FOR THE
GLORY OF GOD

Translator's Preface

THIS WORK is the third of a trilogy by Professor Klausner in the field of the relations between Judaism and Christianity at the time of the rise of the latter. The first work, *Jesus of Nazareth,* was translated by the late Professor Herbert Danby of Oxford and appeared in 1925. The second, *From Jesus to Paul,* was rendered by the present translator and appeared in 1943. The reader is asked to reread the translators' prefaces of the two earlier books for an understanding of the problems of translating modern Hebrew into English.

In presenting quotations from ancient works I have relied mainly on *The Holy Scriptures* [Old Testament] of the Jewish Publication Society, Charles's edition of the Apocrypha and Pseudepigrapha, Danby's translation of the Mishnah, the Soncino editions of the Babylonian Talmud and the Midrash Rabbah, and Lauterbach's edition of the Mekhilta. But in a number of cases these translations have had to be modified to conform to Dr. Klausner's interpretation, or to achieve a greater clarity of style. It should be noted here that explanatory remarks of the author are enclosed within parentheses, while similar remarks of the translator appear within square brackets.

From Jesus to Paul was translated during World War II, when it was impossible to communicate with the author. Fortunately, Dr. B. Netanyahu, a pupil and associate of Dr. Klausner, was available in this country and I was able to go over the manuscript of the translation with him. In the case of the present work, I have been more fortunate in being able to send chapters as they were translated to the author for his corrections and suggestions. Dr. Netanyahu, by assisting the author in the process of reading, has again been helpful. I am deeply grateful to both men for their co-operative attitude.

On Part III I had two additional aids: the author's Heidelberg doctoral dissertation of 1902, written in the German language under the title of *Die messianischen Vorstellungen des jüdischen Volkes im Zeitalter der Tannaiten;* and a rough-draft English translation of Part III of the second Hebrew edition [1927] of the present work by Professor Danby, who before his lamented death freely turned this material over to me upon hearing that I contemplated translating the whole book. However, the translation of Part III appearing herewith is an entirely new rendering of the author's third Hebrew edition to conform with the similar rendering of Parts I and II.

Acknowledgment of courtesy is also due to Dr. H. Leo Eddleman, President of Georgetown College, Kentucky, who withdrew his own plan to translate the present work when he learned that I was engaged in a similar project.

August 15, 1954, was the eightieth birthday of Professor Klausner. It is thus a happy coincidence that this translation of his favorite work should appear at this time.

W. F. STINESPRING

Durham, N.C.
September 1, 1954

Preface to the Second Edition

THE THREE PARTS included in the present book were not written at one time. The last part in order, the third, is the first in time. It was written in German as a doctoral dissertation at the University of Heidelberg in the year 1902, but was not translated into Hebrew until 1923. Next, the first part was composed at intervals in the year 1903 and in the years 1907–08 (being first published in *Ha-Shiloah*, Vols. 12, 16 and 18), and appeared as a separate book in Cracow in 1909. The second part was written and printed in Jerusalem in 1921.

The intermittent writing and printing caused a certain incompleteness in the different parts of the book. This fact has forced me to make radical changes in style and, more particularly, in content. I have incorporated all the copious material on this subject which has accumulated in my hands during the course of twenty-five years; I have made rearrangements and have introduced whole new sections and chapters. It is my hope that my extensive and difficult labor on this book will not have been in vain and that the book will find readers attentive to the subjects incorporated in it, and that scholars will be interested in the problems raised by it.

I was very young when the last and first parts of the book were written, and now old age has come upon me. During the twenty-five years which have passed since the first and third parts of the book were printed, the idea of redemption in Israel has spread and overflowed into many hearts like a flood of mighty waters. And to this idea there has become attached another idea, which has an organic connexion with it: *viz.*, the idea of social equality and righteousness. For the idea of redemption is impossible without the positive element of the eternal vision of the prophets of truth and righteousness—the Messianic idea, the idea of the knowledge of God as revealed in the prophetic ethic, the idea of the brotherhood of man and the rule of righteousness in the world.

But alas! it is not the Hebraic, the prophetic, the Messianic-Israelitic social conception which has become a basis for bringing about redemption in the land of vision and promise, but a foreign social conception, linked up with economic and historical materialism, to which the prophetic idealism is a mockery. All this is not Jewish, not Palestinian, and therefore is not truly humanitarian either. Zionist social policy cannot be based on an authoritarian materialism, which brings about equality by deeds of violence; it must be prophetic, saturated with the Jewish Messianic idea, or else not be at all. If this book can succeed in giving an idea of the close connexion between the political redemption of Israel in its own land and the ideal of righteousness, peace, and brotherhood among all peoples; and if a prophetic social outlook can be gained from this idea, and can be laid as a foundation stone in the building of our politico-spiritual National Home, I shall know that my labor of many years has not been in vain.

J. K.

Jerusalem-Talpioth
The day after Passover, 5687 [1927]

To the Third Edition

TWENTY-THREE years have passed since the second edition of the present work appeared, and during that time many matters with which this book is concerned have received new scholarly treatment. As far as it was in my power, I have taken into account the new opinions and have called attention to the new works touching upon the main theme. At the end of the book I have included an article which sums up the differences between "The Jewish and the Christian Messiah." Thus the book in its new form has been made much more complete. Moreover, as a summary of the book and at the same time a supplement to it, there is now to be seen the article "The Prophets and Prophetic Socialism," which was printed in my *Philosophers and Thinkers* [in Hebrew], Vol. II, Jerusalem 1941, pp. 1–22.

The present book in its second edition was dedicated to Dr. Judah Leon Magnes upon his having reached the age of fifty years. I had hoped that I would be privileged to gladden him with the third edition. I was not so privileged. On the 24th of Tishri, 5709 [October 27, 1948], Dr. Magnes, of blessed memory, went to his eternal reward. Therefore, may the new edition of the book which Dr. Magnes loved so much be a monument to his noble spirit! For, in spite of all the differences of opinion between us, I learned to honor his nobility of soul and to value highly his splendid deeds, in all of which his intention was for the glory of God.

J. K.

Jerusalem
Hanukkah 5710 [December, 1949]

Contents

TRANSLATOR'S PREFACE	vii
PREFACE TO THE SECOND EDITION	ix
PREFACE TO THE THIRD EDITION	xi

PART I *THE MESSIANIC IDEA IN THE PERIOD OF THE PROPHETS*

	Introduction	2
I.	Belief in the Messiah and the Messianic Expectation	7
II.	The Source and Beginnings of the Messianic Idea	13
III.	Allusions to the Messianic Idea in the Pentateuch and Former Prophets	26
IV.	Amos and Hosea	36
V.	Isaiah	52
VI.	Micah and Nahum	72
VII.	Zephaniah and Habakkuk	82
VIII.	Jeremiah	88
IX.	Ezekiel	108
X.	Obadiah	135
XI.	Hymns of the Exile in the Book of Psalms	140
XII.	Deutero-Isaiah	143
XIII.	Haggai and Zechariah	185
XIV.	Joel and Malachi	206
XV.	Psalms from the Period of the Second Temple	217
XVI.	Daniel	222
XVII.	General Survey	237

CONTENTS

PART II *THE MESSIANIC IDEA IN THE BOOKS OF THE APOCRYPHA AND PSEUDEPIGRAPHA*

    General Note   246

A. The Messianic Idea in the Apocrypha   248
    I. Ben-Sira   252
    II. I Maccabees   259
    III. II Maccabees   262
    IV. Judith   264
    V. Tobit   265
    VI. The Apocryphal Baruch   267
    VII. The Wisdom of Solomon   270

B. The Messianic Idea in the Pseudepigrapha   272
    I. The "Ethiopic" Book of Enoch   277
    II. The Book of Jubilees   302
    III. The Testament of the Twelve Tribes   310
    IV. The Psalms of Solomon   317
    V. The Assumption of Moses   325
    VI. The Syriac Book of Baruch   330
    VII. The Pseudepigraphic (Fourth) Book of Ezra   349
    VIII. The Biblical Antiquities   366
    IX. The Sibylline Oracles   370
    X. The Greek Book of Baruch   382
    XI. The Slavonic Book of Enoch   383

C. General Survey   384

PART III *THE MESSIANIC IDEA IN THE PERIOD OF THE TANNAIM*

    General Note   388
    I. The Messianic Idea in the Tannaitic and Post-Tannaitic Periods (Introduction)   391

	CONTENTS	
II.	The Messianic Age and the World to Come	408
III.	The "End" and the Messianic Age	420
IV.	The Prerequisites of Messiah's Coming	427
V.	The Birth Pangs of Messiah	440
VI.	Elijah, the Forerunner of the Messiah	451
VII.	The Name and Personality of the Messiah	458
VIII.	The Ingathering of the Exiles and the Reception of Proselytes	470
IX.	Messiah ben Joseph and the War with Gog and Magog	483
X.	The Messianic Age and the Signs of the Messiah	502
APPENDIX:	The Jewish and the Christian Messiah	519
INDEX		533

PART I

THE MESSIANIC IDEA IN THE PERIOD OF THE PROPHETS

Introduction

EVEN IN my early youth, the greatness and loftiness of the Messianic idea, that *original* Hebrew idea which has influenced all humanity so much, thrilled my soul; and I vowed in my heart to dedicate to it the labor of years, in order to examine it from every side and to grasp its essence. As early as the year 1900 I approached the work of collecting the abundant material necessary for a complete book embracing "The Messianic Idea in Israel from Its Beginning to the Present Time." To the best of my knowledge, no such book then existed in any language on earth except the Italian, in which the Jewish scholar David Castelli, of Florence, had written a splendid work entitled *The Messiah According to the Jews*.[1] In other languages there are many books on the Messianic idea in the period of the prophets;[2] there are also monographs which span the period of the Second Temple;[3] others treat the Talmudic period in relation to some more or less important *detail* of the Messianic idea.[4] But there

---

[1] David Castelli, *Il Messia secondo gli Ebrei*, Florence, 1874. Only three years after these words were printed in *Ha-Shiloah* (Vol. 12, Cracow, 1903-1904), there was published the book of J. H. Greenstone, *The Messiah Idea in Jewish History*, Philadelphia, 1906.

[2] Most of the works of this kind are listed in the book of Castelli (mentioned in the preceding note), p. 32, in the foreword of P. Schmiedel to the book of Eugen Hühn, *Die messianischen Weissagungen des israelitisch-jüdischen Volkes bis zu den Targumim*, I, Freiburg, 1899, p. vi, and in the book of E. Koenig, *Die messianischen Weissagungen des Alten Testaments*, Stuttgart, 1923, p. 72.

[3] Such is the book of Maurice Vernes, *Histoire des idées messianique depuis Alexandre jusqu'à l'empereur Hadrien*, Paris, 1874; P. Volz, *Jüdische Eschatologie von Daniel bis Akiba*, Tübingen, 1903 (in the second edition the book was called *Die Eschatologie der jüdischen Gemeinde im neutestamentlichen Zeitalter*, Tübingen, 1934).

[4] Such are the books of August Wünsche, *Die Leiden des Messias*, Leipzig, 1870; G. H. Dalman, *Der leidende und sterbende Messias der Synagoge im ersten*

is not even one book which encompasses the Messianic hope in all its periods "from its beginning to the present time." The English book of Drummond, which bears the inclusive title *The Jewish Messiah*,[5] and therefore makes the reader hope to find in it the Jewish Messianic ideas in all times, is most concerned with those Messianic ideas found in the Apocryphal and Pseudepigraphical books. The Messianic ideas in the Talmud are regarded in this work as mere supplements to the conceptions in the aforesaid books. Moreover, the author (a learned Christian), confesses that in everything having to do with the Talmud he was forced to depend upon what was transmitted to him by a Jewish scholar in England. From books later than the Talmud Drummond does not present anything. Thus do all Christian theologians. And no wonder; for they investigate the Messianic ideas of the Jews not as a scientific end in itself, but as a means of becoming acquainted with the Messianic ideas which prevailed in the time of the rise of Christianity. Naturally, from this point of view, the ideas of Messianism in Jewish works later than the completion of the Talmud have no value whatever.

The book of Greenstone [6] is too brief and summarizing. That of Castelli is far superior. In it, scientific accuracy and seriousness are combined with reflection and broad philosophy, as well as with a profound historical discernment. Yet it has two fundamental shortcomings. The first is the product of the time and place of the author. Castelli was an Italian Jew of the 1870's. It is well known that the Messianic idea became in the hands of the Jews of the West a sharp weapon with which to fight against Jewish nationalism. Castelli's book is filled with an anti-national spirit. Castelli is, to be sure, as objective as possible; but after all, the cosmopolitan intention which is in him bubbles up and appears in every chapter of his excellent book. The whole Messianic idea appears to him at times completely spiritual and humanitarian. In any place where the political and national coloring of this idea stands out too much, he apologizes for this and, as it were,

---

nachchristlichen Jahrtausend, Berlin, 1888; P. M. Lagrange, *Le Messianisme chez les Juifs*, Paris, 1909; M. Rabinsohn, *Le Messianisme dans le Talmud et les Midraschim*, Paris, 1907.

[5] James Drummond, *The Jewish Messiah*, London, 1877.
[6] See Note 1, above.

seeks an excuse for the fact that the Jewish people could not raise itself up to the level of a spiritual and all-embracing Messiah. In the body of the present book, the reader will see that I have endeavored to bring into relief the *universalistic* (which is still very far from cosmopolitan) and the spiritual part of the Messianic idea; but along with this I have found it right, for the sake of scientific objectivity, to emphasize also the national and political part. As it seems to me, no unscientific inclination has blinded my eyes; the *facts* have demanded that I show the duality and two-sidedness of the Messianic idea. One does not need to apologize for scientific truth.

But there is still another great lack in Castelli's book. In spite of all his freedom of view, in spite of the fact that it is difficult to label him a "rationalist" in the exact sense of that word, in the last analysis he is filled with the dogmatic spirit of his age. The idea of evolution had not yet (in 1874) sufficiently permeated historical science. Beliefs and opinions were still considered as more or less standing above time and place. Therefore, when a scholar came to describe the beliefs and opinions of any nation, he would attempt to organize them only according to their logical relationship. This method was called "schematic arrangement." The *historical* relationship of beliefs and opinions, the fact that they depend upon historical events and upon changes of the times—this was still hazy in the minds of scholars. Likewise, this historical relationship is hazy in Castelli's book, although he points it out in a few places.[7] Not without cause is he disturbed because there is no *accepted* Jewish system of doctrine such as the system of Catholic doctrine.[8] He, to be sure, arranges the Messianic beliefs and opinions of the prophetic period in chronological order, and sometimes sheds light on them by means of historical events. But when he approaches the period after the prophets, the period of the Talmud and the Midrashim, he arranges the Messianic beliefs only according to their content and logical relationship, without taking into account that between the Book of Ben-Sira, for example, and the Babylonian Amoraim there lies a long period of *seven centuries;* that between the "Tannaitic Midrashim" (Mekhilta, Siphra,

---

[7] See, e.g., *Il Messia*, p. 33.
[8] *Op. cit.*, Introduzione, pp. 6–30.

Siphre) and Midrash Konen, Midrash Vayyosha, Otot ha-Mashiah (Signs of the Messiah), and the rest of the smaller Midrashim, which were first published by A. Jellinek in his *Beth ha-Midrash*, a millennium passed by. And how manifold were the political and cultural changes which took place in the life of the Jewish people in the course of this long and productive period! To all this Castelli paid no attention; likewise, the Christian scholar Gfroerer failed to take it into account.[9] The Messianic opinions of the Tannaim, the Amoraim, and the authors of the later Midrashim here come side by side, as though they all belonged to one period.

A book which arranges the Messianic beliefs and opinions in all times and periods according to historical evolution, and shows their connexion with and attachment to historical events, has not yet been written. Therefore it occurred to me almost fifty years ago to write such a book.

One part of this book of mine, that which comprises the Messianic ideas in the period of the Tannaim, I wrote originally in the German language,[10] and only a few years ago translated it into Hebrew (it is the third part of the present work). I wrote it in German because about Messianism in the Tannaitic period specifically—in spite of all its great importance for the understanding of the development of Christianity—no *specialized* book had yet been written at a time when in German there was a multitude of works on the Messianic ideas of the period of the prophets and the period of the Apocrypha and Pseudepigrapha. I wish to give, in the Hebrew language, a complete picture of the development of the Messianic idea *from its beginning to the present time*. For the time being I have gone as far as the end of the Mishnah; but this is the foundation for all the rest. I think that if we explore and search into this *original Hebrew* idea, into its formation, its evolution, and its different forms during the course of the three thousand years of its development as they were determined by the unique history of the people Israel—then there will be revealed to us many new horizons in the entire history of Israel, and no less

[9] See A. Fr. Gfroerer, *Das Jahrhundert des Heils* (oder *Geschichte des Urchristenthums*), Stuttgart, 1838, II, 195-444.

[10] Joseph Klausner, *Die messianischen Vorstellungen des jüdischen Volkes im Zeitalter der Tannaiten*, Cracow, 1903 (Berlin, 1904).

in human history as a whole. We shall recognize the spirit of our people in one of its most original revelations, we shall know the *indispensable* element in the work of the prophets and in the Jewish Aggadah, and we shall observe one of the most important causes of the rise of Christianity, the very name of which (from *Christos*, "Messiah") means "Messianism" and remains to this day. Moreover, we shall get before our minds the future of our Jewish people and of all humanity; for Messianism, whose origin is from the ancient past, is the summation of the most exalted hopes for a shining future, which our greatest and most venerated dreamers await.

Warsaw, in the month of Tammuz 5663 [June–July, 1903].
Jerusalem, in the month of Kislev 5687 [November–December, 1926].

CHAPTER I

Belief in the Messiah and the Messianic Expectation

THE HEBREW word *Māshîaḥ* (in Aramaic *Meshîḥa*, in Greek *Christos*, and from the Aramaic is derived the Greek form Messias [whence the English "Messiah"]) is an adjective formed like *tsāʿîr* (young), *nāʿîm* (pleasant), *ʿāshîr* (rich), and the like; its meaning is "anointed" (with oil). In the Holy Scriptures kings, Israelite and foreign, and high priests are described by this word, for all of these were anointed with oil.[1] Saul, the first Israelite king, is already called "the Lord's anointed" (I Sam. 24:7 [24:6 in English *]). But the foreign king, Cyrus the Persian, is also so called (Isa. 45:1). Likewise, the high priest is called "the anointed priest" (Lev. 4:3 and 5:16). But other men also, among the greatest and most renowned in Israel, of whom we do not ever hear that they were actually anointed, are called by this name. In the verse "Touch not mine anointed," which occurs twice (Ps. 105:15 and I Chron. 16:22), the word "anointed" signifies the Patriarchs. In other places (Ps. 89:39 and 52 [Eng. 38 and 51], and apparently also Ps. 84:10 [Eng. 9]), this word designates the whole people, Israel.

From these examples we see that the word *Māshîaḥ*, which was originally only another term for "anointed with oil," gradually became a title of honor signifying "chosen," because the act of anoint-

* Hereafter abbreviated "Eng."
[1] From what is written in I Kings (19:16), it appears that the prophets also were anointed with oil, but we do not find that the prophet would be called by the name *Māshîaḥ*.

ing with oil was the sign of choice and elevation. This is, undoubtedly, an extension of meaning that came about at a later time, not before the Babylonian Exile; for Psalm 105 and I Chronicles, in all probability, are not from a time before the First Destruction [586 B.C.]. This extension of meaning apparently contributed to the fact that the expected redeemer, the king of the future, the one chosen of God from birth, was also called "Messiah." Yet the word "Messiah," to designate the expected redeemer, *does not occur either in the Holy Scriptures* [Old Testament] *or in the books of the Apocrypha.* We find it in this sense for the first time in the Book of Enoch, and precisely in that part of this Pseudepigraphic book which was composed, in the opinion of all the best scholars, in the time of Herod the Great.[2] The word "Messiah" in that special and consistent meaning which was employed in the Tannaitic period and afterward is, therefore, from a much later time even than that in which the verse "Touch not mine anointed" was written. Thus we can determine with certainty that the idea of the savior and redeemer was not originally connected at all with the idea of "anointing," but with the idea of king and high priest.

In fact, the idea of political and spiritual redemption was not always connected with the idea of a *personal Messiah.* This expectation—redemption without a human redeemer—resides in the nature of the Jewish view of the Deity and the control of the world. "For unto me the children of Israel are servants; they are my servants" (Lev. 25:55)—is written in the Torah. "Ye said unto me, Nay; but a king shall reign over us—when the LORD your God was your king" (I Sam. 12:12), cries out Samuel the Ramathite. It is no wonder, therefore, if a nation which had a religio-national view like this was looking for unmediated redemption, which would come directly from God, without any need for a human redeemer. Hence we find in the period of the prophets many words of prophecy which without any doubt refer to the expected redemption, yet contain *no hint* of a personal Messiah. Thus the matter also in all the books of the Apocrypha, though to be sure in some of them (Ben-Sira 47:11; I

---

[2] See Emil Schürer, *Geschichte des jüdischen Volkes im Zeitalter Jesu Christi,* II⁴, 613; III⁴, 279, 280.

Macc. 2:57) there is mention of a kingdom of the house of David, which shall rule in the future, but concerning the individual personality of any particular Messiah there is to be found not even a hint. Likewise, in some of the Pseudepigrapha there is no mention of a personal Messiah.

In addition, the late Talmudic saying of the Amora R. Hillel, "There shall be no Messiah for Israel, because they have already enjoyed him in the days of Hezekiah" (Sanhedrin 99*a*), is interpreted by Rashi—and his words are reasonable—in the same sense, that R. Hillel did not deny the Messianic hope in general: he did not believe in a *human* Messiah for the Time to Come, but was expecting that the Holy One, blessed be He, would Himself come and deliver His people (see Rashi, Sanhedrin 99*a*). But it is worth while to note that in the period of the Amoraim the belief in a human Messiah was already so firmly rooted in the nation that the Amora R. Joseph was incensed at these words of R. Hillel, and said, "May the LORD forgive R. Hillel!"[3] For, as I have remarked in another place, it is impossible to find in the Talmud any saying of a Tanna that could prove that the Tannaim believed in the possibility of future redemption without the mediation of a human redeemer.[4]

Accordingly, a distinction must be made between the vague *Messianic expectation* and the more explicit *belief in the Messiah*. The definition of the Messianic expectation is: *The prophetic hope for the end of this age, in which there will be political freedom, moral perfection, and earthly bliss for the people Israel in its own land, and also for the entire human race.* But the definition of belief in the Messiah is: *The prophetic hope for the end of this age, in which a strong redeemer, by his power and his spirit, will bring complete redemption, political and spiritual, to the people Israel, and along with this, earthly bliss and moral perfection to the entire human race.*

Everything which there is in the Messianic expectation is also contained in the belief in the Messiah. But in the latter, redemption from

---

[3] See J. Drummond, *The Jewish Messiah*, London, 1877. In a special chapter entitled "Conception of Ideal Kingdom Without a Messiah" (pp. 226–277), he shows that according to most of the books of Scripture and the Apocrypha, and many of the Pseudepigrapha, redemption is possible without a Messiah.

[4] See below, Part III, beginning of Chap. VII.

national subjugation and the great importance of a very lofty and exalted political and spiritual personality are more emphasized.

The different elements of the belief in the Messiah—in which are included parts of the nationalistic expectation—were continually changing, above all, under the influence of historical events, though the emphasis upon one element or the other was more or less dependent upon the individual character of the proclaimers of the expectations. In those periods in which the people Israel was still living an independent political life in its own land, ethical perfection and earthly bliss were more emphasized; but in the period of subjugation and exile the yearning for *political* freedom took first place. In times of national freedom, the world-wide, universalistic part of the Messianic hopes was the basic element in the Messianic idea; but in times of trouble and distress for the people Israel the nationalistic element was stressed much more. But this much we can determine with complete confidence: in the belief in the Messiah of the people Israel, *the political part goes arm in arm with the ethical part, and the nationalistic with the universalistic*.[5] It is Christianity which has attempted to remove the political and nationalistic part which is there, and leave only the ethical and spiritual part. Yet the influence of Judaism on the first Christians was so strong, that the "chiliasts" (those early Christians who believed that Jesus the Messiah would return, coming down to earth and setting up the millennial kingdom) pictured to themselves the Kingdom of Heaven filled with bodily and earthly pleasure, precisely as did the Jews.

· For the kingdom of the Jewish Messiah was never pictured as "a kingdom not of this world" (John 18:36). The Jewish Messiah also comes to prepare a world for the Almighty's kingdom, but the world to be prepared is *this world*. The Jewish Messianic world becomes ethical, is idealistic and exalted, but it remains terrestrial. The Kingdom of Heaven of the Jewish Messiah is not only within the soul of man, but also upon the earth.· This "dualism" of the Jewish belief in the Messiah was the direct result of the character of the Jewish people, which does not carry its spirituality to extremes: it does not ever

---

[5] See Ahad Ha-Am, '*Al Parashat-Derakhim* [At the Parting of the Ways], Part III, p. 68.

do away with the earthly ground which is under its feet. Hence the Jewish people did not separate faith, which is spiritual, from social life, which is practical and political. Hence Israel was not able to imagine a man who had attained a *completely* divine stage. And hence its Messiah was not *entirely spiritual:* he was *spiritual and political at the same time.*

As we shall see in the next chapter, the historical development of the Messianic idea was one of the fundamental causes of its being composed both of political and of spiritual longings, which blended and became a unity. And in the course of the present book, the reader will see that the dualism mentioned above had to create, under certain historical circumstances, a twofold Messiah: *Messiah ben Joseph*, an earthly Messiah, who fights against Gog and Magog and falls in battle; and *Messiah ben David*, a spiritual Messiah, who prepares the world for the Kingdom of God.[6]

The political part of the belief in the Messiah took in ancient times, as said above, first place during periods of trouble and distress precisely because it proclaimed comfort and the hope that political freedom would return to the Jewish people. But, of course, in the Middle Ages it declined more and more, because then the hope that Israel would again be a political people in its own land appeared in the nature of things impossible. The expectation of a miraculous redemption strangled the political yearning that is included in the Messianic hope. Yet a certain political coloring remained even in the numerous Messianic movements of the Middle Ages; even the "false Messiahs" like David Alroy and Shabbatai Zevi, who strove to attain the Kingdom of God by means of mysticism and ceremonial kabbalism, wished in the last analysis that their kingdom might be earthly and actually develop in the land of the Patriarchs.

And in our own times and before our very eyes, the politico-national part which is in the hope for redemption has returned to life together with the spiritual-universalistic element which is in the Messianic expectation. The dualism of the Jewish belief in the Messiah, as described above, gives a fundamental authority to these two currents in the idea of redemption. Only when the two of them flow

[6] See below, Part III, Chaps. I and IX.

together to make one mighty stream can the most important Jewish movement, Zionism, consider itself to have come into possession of the inheritance of the Messianic idea. This idea, to be sure, did change its form according to events and circumstances; but always at the base of it was one great longing: to redeem Israel from its servitude and from all its tribulations and to bring salvation to all humanity through the salvation of Israel, which should precede and make straight the highway before it.

CHAPTER II

The Source and Beginnings of the Messianic Idea

TO THE three good gifts which the people Israel have left as an inheritance to the entire world: monotheism, refined morality, and the prophets of truth and righteousness—a fourth gift must be added: *belief in the Messiah*.

No other nation in the world knew a belief like this. To be sure, various Christian theologians, and likewise a number of other independent scholars, have attempted to rob Israel of its prior right to the belief in the Messiah, and to confer it upon the Assyrians, the Egyptians, or the Persians.[1] But even those who defend the cause of

[1] See on this, first of all, in the important book of H. Gressmann, *Der Ursprung der israelitisch-jüdischen Eschatologie*, Göttingen, 1905, pp. 36, 160, 190, 206, 215, 245, 247, Note 2; A. Jeremias, *Handbuch der altorientalischen Geisteskultur*, Leipzig, 1913, pp. 205-225; E. Sellin, *Die israelitisch-jüdische Heilandserwartung*, Berlin, 1909, pp. 38-46. Wilhelm Bousset (*Die jüdische Apokalyptik*, 1903; Bousset-Gressmann, *Die Religion des Judentums im Neutestamentlichen Zeitalter*, 3rd ed., 1926, p. 226) attempted to prove that the Jewish Messiah of the period of the Second Temple resembles the Persian "Saoshyant"; and P. Volz (*Die vorexilische Jahveprophetie und der Messias*, Göttingen, 1897) supposes that the prophets had no ideal of a King-Messiah until Ezekiel. Against Gressmann in particular see Nathanael Schmidt, "The Origin of Jewish Eschatology" (*Journal of Biblical Literature*, XLI [1922], 102-114). Against Gressmann, Jeremias, Sellin, *et al.*, see E. Koenig, *Die messianischen Weissagungen des Alten Testaments*, Stuttgart, 1923, pp. 20-25; and against Volz even Gressmann himself has come out (in his book mentioned above, pp. 238-250). Rudolf Kittel, who inclines toward early Babylonian-Egyptian influence, limits it strictly, seeing it only as a *possibility*, since the *essential* marks of the Hebrew Messianic expectation are lacking in both the Babylonian and the Egyptian literature (see R. Kittel, *Geschichte des Volkes Israel*, 5th ed., Gotha, 1922, II, 256-257, note 3). See also G. Kittel, *Die Probleme des palaestinischen Spätjudentums und das Urchristentum*, Stuttgart, 1926, pp. 75-85.

Babylonian influence are forced to confess that in the Sumero-Babylonian literature there is no "clear expectation of the restoration of the good conditions of Paradise, by which history might be consummated." [2] And those who insist that the first ancient stimulus came to the Hebrew Messianic idea from the Egyptians, the Persians, or the Babylonians also see the exceedingly great advantage of the Jewish Messianic ideals.[3] The most original people in the world—the Greek people—did not have any real Messianic expectation; and the *Fourth Eclogue* of Vergil is so late that there can be no doubt of the influence of the ancient Jewish Sibyl upon this Roman poet, or even of the influence—direct or indirect—of the prophets of Israel in Greek translation. Moreover, the threefold Persian Saoshyant is also completely remote from the Jewish Messiah, for Zoroaster lived at a time so late (*c.* 660–583 B.C.E.*) that it is hard to believe that the three "Messiahs" (Saoshyants), all of whom had to be sons of Zoroaster, were the ones who brought into being the Hebrew Messianic expectation, which we see already fully developed in the time of Isaiah and even before.[4]

How is it possible to explain this wonderful phenomenon: the marvelous development of the Messianic idea in the midst of a unique people, Israel, to such a degree that there is nothing like it in any other nation?

The answer to this question is to be sought in the ancient history of the Israelite people.

The Messianic expectation is the *Golden Age in the future.* But all the ancient peoples except Israel could tell only of a *Golden Age in the past.* Many philosophers and students of religions have been amazed at the marvelous fact that all ancient peoples praised and exalted the Age of Gold which is already past, but only the people Israel related wonders about the Golden Age *which is still to come.* The happy state of the first man in the Garden of Eden was so short

---

* Before the Christian Era.

[2] See W. Eichrodt, *Die Hoffnung des ewigen Friedens in alten Israel,* Gütersloh, 1920, p. 155 (also p. 142).

[3] See A. Jeremias, *op. cit.,* p. 225; Sellin, *op. cit.,* pp. 42–43, 44–45.

[4] See J. Scheftelowitz, *Die altpersische Religion und das Judentum,* Giessen, 1920, pp. 197, 202–203.

that it is difficult to call it an "Age." The cause of this difference between Israel and the other peoples is made understandable to us when we consider the ancient historical traditions of the people Israel.

The ancient, primitive history of every people is regularly pictured in its imagination as a period of happiness and tranquillity, as is pictured the period of childhood in the mind of every person whose childhood was not most unfortunate. Not so the ancient history of the people Israel. Dark was the childhood of this people destined for tribulation. The Patriarchs were forced to move from country to country time after time because of severe famine in their homeland. While they were wandering in foreign lands, they suffered from the insolence and tyranny of the kings of those lands (Pharaoh, Abimelech, Shechem son of Hamor). A short time after the death of the Patriarchs began the Egyptian bondage, with all its terrible oppressions. No nation on earth knew such sufferings in its early youth. Israelite history in its earliest time became a history of afflictions. The people Israel did not have a *glorious past*, hence it was forced to direct its gaze toward a *glorious future*. It longed for one to ransom and deliver it from its afflictions and troubles. It yearned for a *redeemer and savior*. And such a savior appeared in the form of *Moses*.

The name Moses [Heb. *Mosheh*] itself, according to popular etymology, indicates one who brings out or ransoms.[5] The Talmud calls him "savior of Israel." [6] It is not our concern here to investigate whether there is a historical kernel in the stories about the Patriarchs, nor whether the oppression in Egypt is entirely or only partly historical and whether the exodus from Egypt under the leadership of Moses is historical fact or only legend. Sufficient here is the fact that at a very early time, relatively speaking, the traditions about the Egyptian captivity and the Exodus were very well established in the nation. In the mind of the nation, therefore, its whole childhood was considered, at a relatively early time, as having been filled with af-

---

[5] Therefore he is not called Mashui ["drawn," passive voice], as the phrase "Because I drew him out of the water" (Exod. 2:10) would require; this was already noted by the ancient interpreters. Actually, of course, Mosheh is thought to be an Egyptian word, which is a part of the names of a number of Egyptian kings (Thutmose, Ahmose, *et al.*).

[6] Sotah 12*b* (see also 11*b* and 13*a*); Sanhedrin 101*b*.

flictions, oppression, and servitude. It was inevitable that the stories of oppression, as we find them in the first sections of the Book of Exodus, should make a strong impression on the entire people Israel. It was also inevitable that the people should feel compelled to accord the very greatest glory and honor to the exalted and grandiose personality of *the first deliverer*. This was the man Moses, this the great deliverer, who not only ransomed Israel from all its *material* troubles and from *political* servitude, but also redeemed it from its ignorance and its spiritual bondage. He was not only a guide and leader of the Israelite people; he was also a lawgiver and prophet. The exalted picture of Moses necessarily, therefore, impressed itself upon the spirit of the nation and became a symbol of the redeemer in general. Political salvation and spiritual redemption of necessity were combined in the consciousness of the nation to become one great work of redemption. Thus was born the redemptive dualism which necessarily put its stamp upon the redeemer of the future, *the expected Messiah*.

Various scholars assert that the Messianic idea could have been born only after kings ruled in Israel, since the prophets portrayed the Messiah as a mighty king and an exalted ruler.[7] But they forget, first, that the prophets do not call the redeemer by the name "Messiah," [8] and hence in the time of the prophets the "anointing" of the kings was not a clear sign of the redeemer; and secondly, that the spiritual-ethical characteristics of the Messiah, which in the last analysis are fundamental in the prophetic portrayal of the Messiah—precisely these characteristics are hard to find not only in the kings of Israel but also in the kings of Judah. Yet precisely these characteristics were found in Moses.

Moreover, in Moses were embodied not only the spiritual characteristics of the Messiah but also his political characteristics. Moses was not only a lawgiver; he was also a leader of the nation, over the fate of which the Most High had made him ruler. He fought the people's wars against Amalek, against Sihon and Og, and against the kings of Midian. Though he himself did not command the army in

---

[7] See F. Giesebrecht, *Beiträge zur Jesajakritik*, 1890, p. 26. Cf. also *Dor Dor ve-Doreshav* by I. H. Weiss, I, 28–34.

[8] See above, Chap. I, p. 8.

the war against Amalek and Midian, nevertheless Joshua, the son of Nun, and Phinehas, the son of Eleazar, fought according to his directions and under his supervision. In the Talmud and Midrash he is called "king" a number of times.[9] The designation "warrior" fits him no less than that of "sage."[10] He would impose the death sentence upon those meriting judicial death; he was the head of the nation in times of peace and its commander-in-chief in times of war. To be sure, these were not the main characteristics of Moses. And so it is with the characteristics of the Messiah: the ethico-spiritual characteristics are the principal ones, but the political characteristics are not lacking.

The authors of the Talmud and Midrash, with their fine national feeling, perceived the relation and connexion between the Messianic expectation and the exodus from Egypt, between the Messiah and Moses. They name Moses "the first redeemer"[11] in contrast to the Messiah, who is "the last redeemer."[12] They compare Moses to the Messiah in various phraseology:[13] for example, just as Moses brought redemption to his people, so also will Messiah bring redemption;[14] just as Moses was brought up in the house of Pharaoh among the enemies of his people, so also will Messiah dwell in the city of Rome, among the destroyers of his land;[15] just as Moses, after revealing himself to his brethren in Egypt and announcing to them that deliverance was near, was forced to go into hiding for a time, so also will Messiah be forced to hide himself after the first revelations;[16] just as Moses crossed from Midian to Egypt riding on an ass (Exod. 4:20), so also will Messiah come riding on an ass; just as Moses caused manna to

[9] See, e.g., Zebahim 102b; Seder Olam Rabbah, Chap. 4.
[10] See Nedarim 38a and Shabbath 92a.
[11] Ruth Rabbah 2:14 on the text "And Boaz said unto her."
[12] Genesis Rabbah, Chap. 85.
[13] "Rab said: The world was created only on David's account. Samuel said: On *Moses'* account; R. Johanan said: For the sake of *the Messiah*" (Sanhedrin 98b).
[14] Genesis Rabbah, Chap. 85; Exodus Rabbah, Chap. 1; Tanhuma, Shemoth, 8.
[15] Exodus Rabbah, Chap. 1; Tanhuma, Shemoth, 8, and Tazri'a, 8. Cf. also Sanhedrin 19b.
[16] Numbers Rabbah, Chap. 11; Song of Songs Rabbah, on the text "My beloved is like a gazelle" (2:9); Pesiḳta Rabbathi, Chap. 36 (ed. M. Friedmann, pp. 161–162).

rain from the sky, so will Messiah bring forth different kinds of food in a miraculous way; and just as Moses gave to the children of Israel wells and springs of water in the wilderness, so also will Messiah make streams of water flow in the desert.[17] Not only this, but the acceptance of suffering because of the iniquities of others, which late Jewish legend attributes to the Messiah, is in the Talmud and is also attributed to our master Moses.[18] (This may be called "suffering for atonement;" Christian scholars call it "vicarious suffering," and in Christianity this idea has become an important article of faith.)

The phrases cited from the Talmud and Midrash, which mostly belong to the Amoraim and were spoken at a very late time, cannot, of course, be used as historical proof that the belief in the Messiah actually sprang from the marvelous traditions about Moses the first redeemer. I have cited them here only to show that these traditions about "the savior of Israel," who brought out his people from the first captivity, comprise the authentic *embryo* from which the Messianic idea of necessity developed. Even at a relatively late time, in the period of the Amoraim, the connexion between the first redeemer and the last redeemer was still felt and recognized by the sages of Israel. The oppression and afflictions in which the first traditions of the history of Israel began inevitably brought forth within Israel the strong yearning for redemption.[19] And the first traditions about the first redeemer necessarily left their stamp upon this yearning, that is to say, upon the ideals of redemption. Thus were brought forth within Israel both the impersonal Messianic expectation and the personal Messiah. For the ideal of redemption is the Messianic expectation, and the *personal* ideal of redemption is the belief in the Messiah.

This lofty ideal, of which Moses inevitably became a symbol,

[17] Koheleth Rabbah 1:9, on the text "That which hath been"; Midrash Shemuel, Chap. 14 (ed. Buber, p. 90). The prophet Elijah, the herald of the coming of the Messiah, is also compared with Moses in a number of ways, because Elijah is also the chosen of the LORD and also in a certain sense a redeemer. See the citation of passages in the Italian work of Castelli, *Il Messia*, pp. 197-198; cf. also pp. 213-214.

[18] See Berakoth 32a, and at length in Sotah, end of Chap. 1 (14a).

[19] This does not exclude the possibility that the element of *retribution* in the Messianic idea has in it some of "the odor of the soil of Palestine," as Gressmann showed in two excellent books. See H. Gressmann, *Eschatologie*, p. 192; *Palaestinas Erdgeruch in der israelitischen Religion*, Berlin, 1909.

SOURCE AND BEGINNINGS OF THE MESSIANIC IDEA 19

owing to the development of events in Israelite history, gained strength and struck deep root in the nation. Never did a young and conquering people endure afflictions and troubles in the land which it had subdued by sword and bow, as endured the people Israel after the death of Joshua. The former inhabitants of the land, who were thought to have been conquered, continued to subdue and oppress different tribes of Israel one after the other. "And the children of Israel cried to the LORD"—we find this expression in the Book of Judges time after time. The period of heroes is the earliest historical period of every people; but not even one other people can tell in its early legends about such numerous afflictions and oppressions as can the people Israel. Now when the cry of the oppressed people would ascend to heaven, "The LORD would raise up a *savior* for the children of Israel"—thus relates the Book of Judges. Redeemer after redeemer helped them. These were the "judges" who did not judge at all, just as the "judges" (*suffetae*) of the Carthaginians, offspring of the Tyrians, did not judge. The "judges" were political saviors: noble fighters, bold heroes, and temporary rulers, mostly in times of war only, but sometimes (as we find in Gideon) also in times of peace. These "saviors" had the political characteristics of Moses and in their prowess in war they even surpassed him; but the spiritual-ethical characteristics of Moses were lacking. Each one of the judges was a temporary "Messiah" of his tribe or of a number of tribes in the political sense but not in the spiritual sense. Each was a kind of little but successful Bar-Cochba. Samuel, the last judge, had all the spiritual characteristics of Moses. It is well known how excessively the men of the Talmud praise him;[20] but the political characteristics were lacking. The first Israelite king, Saul, son of Kish, lacked the spiritual characteristics of a Messiah. To be sure, he is called in the Scriptures "the LORD's anointed"; but I have already said that these words must be understood in their plain meaning: he was the LORD's chosen one and was anointed as king.[21]

The true prototype of the Messiah was the second Israelite king, David, son of Jesse. His great political talents, by means of which he

[20] See, e.g., Nedarim 38a.
[21] See, above, beginning of Chap. I, p. 7.

succeeded in unifying all the tribes of Israel and making them one great and powerful nation according to the conceptions of his time, his marvelous heroism and courage, as revealed in his extensive wars against all the neighbors of Israel, and his glorious victories in which he defeated all those peoples to whom Israel had been subject until his time—all these things were necessary to make him in the eyes of the people the greatest political savior of all those who defended Israel at any time.

But his spiritual characteristics also fitted him to become in the eyes of the people the ideal type of the King-Messiah. In spite of the fact that cruelty is imputed to him with respect to the Moabites and Ammonites, whom he measured with the line and made to pass under saws and axes of iron, or with respect to the sons of Rizpah, daughter of Aiah, whom he commanded to be hanged, and the like; and in spite of the affair of Bath-sheba, which the Scriptures did not cover up, David was in the last analysis—if we judge him according to his time and according to the characteristics of Oriental monarchs—an ideal king. Following the severe words of Ernest Renan about David,[22] it has been in latter years almost a fashion to belittle the importance of David and to diminish his historical stature. How do these scholars support their case? Only from the discreditable deeds which are related about him in the Bible. But, if they give credence to the narratives of the Bible, if they admit that it does not spare even those in whom it delights, telling the "bitter truth" about them, why do they not give credence also to those numerous passages in the Bible in which the figure of David appears before us full of light and splendor? In the Bible we see David doing deeds of cruelty, but we likewise see him confessing his sins and repenting of them, loving even his rebellious son Absalom more than his own life; requiting Saul, who hated him, with mercy when Saul's life was in his hands and lamenting over his death after he was slain; permitting the prophet Nathan to say everything that was on his mind; and wholeheartedly concerning himself about the national religion.

To be sure, popular legend exaggerated too much in praising him and his good qualities, and was not satisfied until it made him the

[22] See *Histoire du peuple d'Israel*, I, 411–451.

author of various hymns in the Book of Psalms. Yet this fact alone, that popular imagination expanded and exalted this national hero not only as a king possessing outstanding political talents but also as the possessor of superior religio-ethical qualities—this fact alone proves that undoubtedly David was a man of the very highest attainments. *Ex nihilo nihil fit*. Outstanding political abilities together with these religio-ethical qualities made David the *authentic* prototype of the redeemer and the founder of that ruling family one of whose descendants the Messiah must be. Not only did the name "son of David" become a standing title of the King-Messiah, but also the name "David" itself. The prophet Hosea says, concerning the Messianic age, "Afterward shall the children of Israel return, and seek the LORD their God, and David their king" (Hos. 3:5). And in the Talmud there is an opinion that the expected Messiah will be David himself or will be called by the name "David." [23]

Meanwhile, prophecy was developing in Israel, and in the kingdoms of Ephraim and Judah arose prophets who broadened and deepened the conceptions of the tribes of Israel. In this process the Messianic expectation received an almost entirely new form.

In fact, *the Messianic expectation is the positive element in the message of the prophets*. As reprovers and preachers, the prophets were by necessity great masters of negation. King Ahab charges one of the prophets of the LORD that "he doth not prophesy good concerning me, but evil" (I Kings 22:8). The whole struggle of the true prophets against the false prophets revolved around this point only, that the false prophets envisioned what the people wanted them to envision: prosperity and happiness and peace in the present. And they praised the deeds of kings, princes, and people at the time when the true prophets were dissatisfied with the present, and were denouncing in very harsh words both the deeds of the people and the deeds of those standing at their head. Before the eyes of these true prophets was hovering a high ideal, from which the forces of the

[23] Yer. Berakoth, Chap. 2, Hal. 1, *in the Baraitha*, which, to be sure, appears to be not very early; cf. the words of R. Judah in the name of Rab and of R. Papa in Sanhedrin 95*b*, and the symbolic saying, "David King of Israel is alive and vigorous," which was transmitted by Rabbi (Rosh Ha-Shanah 25*a*). Below, in Part III, Chap. VII, I have enlarged on this.

time were completely remote, not even attempting or seeking to approach it. The *existing situation* was bad in the eyes of these prophets; only what *should be*—and according to their conviction it also *could be*—was good. The bad, therefore, was in the *present*, and the good in the *future;* the bad was in *actuality*, and the good in the *ideal*.

The hoped-for good, the ideal, which will be the actuality in the future—this is the Messianic expectation in its full depth. Thus the strong contrast between the actual and the ideal deepened and broadened the early Messianic expectation and made it a universal and eternal conception.[24] The more the prophets were dissatisfied with the present, the more they were embittered against conditions existing in their day and were impelled to warn the people, to prophesy an evil day, with troubles and distress, the more would their hearts, crushed and sick at the ruin of their people, seek comfort in visions and imaginings of "the end of [these] days." There, in the world of the future, their imaginations would soar to the skies, and the ideal which was living in their noble hearts would become for them complete actuality. So with this future actuality they would comfort the unhappy people, who had to endure so much from foes and adversaries without and from proclaimers of easy times, deceivers, and false teachers within. The great love and compassion which filled their kindly hearts—though so often they had to harden themselves against their beloved people, to call them all sorts of dishonorable names, and to prophesy all the evils in the world against them—would flood over into the Messianic conceptions and fill them with light and splendor, national power, and spiritual exaltation.

But not only this. The prophets also introduced into the Messianic expectation the humanitarian-universal and spiritual-ethical elements, which at the beginning had made little impression on it. Up to the time of the prophets, the savior was mostly a strong deliverer of his people from political oppression. But the prophets, who sought

---

[24] Gunkel, Gressmann, and Sellin (in their books cited above, p. 13, Note 1) have shown almost certainly that the basic Messianic ideas were long antecedent to the prophets, and it is actually possible that the beginning of these ideas is mythological and comes from Egypt and Babylonia; but what they are now—the hope of the nation and the consolation of humanity—they were made by the prophets. On this no doubt can be cast.

always righteousness and justice and whose wide range of vision took in the whole world, broadened and deepened this idea also. Up to the time of the prophets, the nation had been most conscious of *political wrong*, which had manifested itself in the evils of oppression and captivity. The prophets, who carried the banner of truth and righteousness in their time, were the first in Israel who began to feel that there is in the world a greater evil than this: *personal evil*, that is to say, the wrong which man does to his fellow man. This perception brought them to the conviction that evil is not accidental, and also that it does not pass away when the end of oppression and subjection to another people arrives; and redemption from this personal evil was the chief of all their aspirations. It is no wonder, then, that for the most part the prophets thought of the redemption from personal evil as a *personal redemption*. Thus the man who will bring this redemption, the Messiah, had to be the embodiment of the highest righteousness, which tolerates no evil. Therefore, the Messiah became more and more not only a pre-eminent political ruler, but also a man of pre-eminent moral qualities.

Now, since evil is not political alone and is not accidental and transitory, since it is human, it is thus stamped upon the spirits of all men; therefore it is spiritual and universally human. (Natural catastrophe is not taken into account, since this sort of evil comes from God as a punishment for the evil deeds of men.) Therefore, salvation and redemption from this evil must also be spiritual and universal. In such wise the Messianic idea, without destroying its political attributes, became more and more spiritual, and without destroying its nationalist characteristics became more and more universal. The dreams of the people Israel became at the hands of the prophets the dreams of all humanity. Redemption encompasses not alone the people Israel and its land, but likewise all peoples and all lands. This is the goal of universal righteousness, of which the prophets were the supreme exponents.

The sages of Greece also recognized the evil in the world, and from Socrates to the last of the Stoics, the philosophers longed for redemption from this evil. But since the evil they saw was more the *natural* evil, from which there is no flight or escape and for which no human being is really to be blamed, therefore they sought deliverance in other ways. The Stoics and Cynics taught that salvation from the evil in this world is to be sought and found in *salvation from the world itself*, that is, in flight from the storms and passions of this world. Christianity, which was compounded of Judaism and Greek philosophy, has a redeemer of the world, but along with this there are also ascetics who are saved from the evil in the world by flight from the world to desert places and monasteries. Judaism, seeking redemption from the personal evil in this world, found it in *improvement of the world* by a personal Messiah alone. The personality of the Messiah became more and more elevated in the time of the prophets and the time of the Tannaim, finally reaching tremendous power and eminence. The Messiah had the attributes of a king, inherited from Moses, the judges, and David; to these were added also the attributes of a *prophet*.

Thus the Messiah, as I have said, became a truly pre-eminent man, to the extent that the *Jewish* imagination could picture him: he was supreme in strength and heroism; he was also supreme in moral qualities. A great personality, which is incomparably higher and stronger than ordinary people, a personality to which all very willingly make themselves subject and which can overcome all things, but for these very reasons feeling a very strong sense of obligation—this is the pre-eminent man of Judaism. Of a pre-eminent man like this it is possible to say, "Thou hast made him a little lower than God." For from a pre-eminent man like this to God is but a step. But this step Judaism did *not* take. It formed within the limits of a humanity, which is continually raising itself up, the ideal of flesh and blood, "the idea of the ultimate limit of man" (in the language of Kant), this great personality, only by means of which and by the help of which can redemption and salvation come to humanity—the King-Messiah.

There is yet another great universal conception included in the Messianic expectation.

We have already seen that the Israelite nation, which had a history of afflictions from the beginning of its growth, dreamed about a Golden Age, which was not behind it but before it. This Golden

Age was called "the end of the days" ["latter days," "final days," "final time," and so on]. As long as these "coming days" had not arrived, the development of the nation was still *incomplete;* particularly so after its land, political power, sanctuary, and language had been destroyed. Judaism is, therefore, *imperfect* or, more correctly, lacking completion. And thus it will continue to be until it returns to its own land, until its sanctuary is rebuilt, and until its exiles are gathered in from the four corners of the earth—and until "the earth shall be full of the knowledge of the LORD as the waters cover the sea," and "the wolf shall dwell with the lamb" [Isa. 11:6, 9]. Development and completion, therefore, were laid in the foundation of Judaism by means of the Messianic idea. And since the completion of the Jewish nation is connected with the completion of all humanity which must "be full of the knowledge of the LORD" and cease from wars and oppression, therefore included in the Messianic expectation is that concept of a general going-forward, which neither the Greeks nor any other peoples knew; in other words, the idea of progress in the broadest and most exalted sense.[25]

Truly the Messianic idea is the most glistening jewel in the glorious crown of Judaism!

[25] There are objectors who would argue that this conclusion is the product of the idea of progress in which the liberal nineteenth century believed so completely but which is now difficult to maintain, in view of all that has happened in world history; actually, however, the Messianic idea is an idea of sudden, catastrophic change. These objectors should be reminded of the matter of the *repentance* which precedes the *redemption;* in the repentance required in the Messianic age a basic element is the demand for *moral reform*—and this is the very foundation of the idea of progress.

CHAPTER III

Allusions to the Messianic Idea in the Pentateuch and Former Prophets

JEWISH SCRIPTURAL interpretation and Christian theology join together in one aspiration—to find the Messianic idea in many Biblical passages where in truth there is not even a hint of it. In the very first chapters of the Book of Genesis, ancient Jewish and Christian scholars found such Messianic prophecies. In the curse upon the serpent (Gen. 3:14–15), especially in the words, "They shall bruise thy head and thou shalt bruise their heel," both the Targum attributed to Jonathan ben Uzziel and the Targum Yerushalmi saw an indication that the people Israel would conquer Sammael "in the days of the King-Messiah." Correspondingly, the church father Irenaeus found that these words indicated the Christian redeemer: it is the seed of the woman which is the enemy of the serpent, the serpent being Satan and the impulse to evil ("And I will put enmity between thee and the woman, and between thy seed and her seed"); and if the serpent, that is, Satan, shall bruise man first ("head"), then finally ("heel") man shall bruise him. Also in the blessing by Noah, "Blessed be the LORD, the God of Shem. . . . God shall enlarge Japheth and he shall dwell in the tents of Shem" (Gen. 9:26–27), the theologians have sought to find a hint of the Messiah, who will come forth from Shem and through whom the sons of Japheth also will acknowledge the God of Shem.[1] The Christian theologians actually find a hint like this in

---

[1] See in the book of Castelli, *Il Messia*, pp. 37–38, and especially Note 1 on p. 37.

the promises: "A prophet will the LORD thy God raise up unto thee, from the midst of thee, of thy brethren, like unto me"; and "I will raise them up a prophet from among their brethren, like unto thee, and I will put My words in his mouth" (Deut. 18:15 and 18);[2] also in the "Redeemer" in Job (19:25): "I know that my Redeemer liveth, and at the last He will rise upon the dust."

All these examples, and very many more like them, are theological interpretations, which it is fitting merely to mention before we pass on to the matter of genuinely Messianic Biblical passages. When we reach the Talmudic period, which coincides in time with the rise of Christianity, we shall be forced to concern ourselves again with interpretations like these, since they greatly influenced the people of that period. They had historical value, therefore, only in a very late time. Biblical verses of this kind, which were mistakenly considered to be Messianic, had a significant Messianic influence upon people of later generations; but at the time when they were written they had no Messianic purpose.

However, there are verses which, although considered Messianic only through error and by interpretation, nevertheless have a definite value in the history of the development of the Messianic idea from the beginning. They, likewise, did not exhibit a clear Messianic intent; yet they were the embryonic material from which the Messianic idea was afterward formed, under the influence of historical events. Such are, first of all, the verses containing the blessing of the LORD upon Abraham, Isaac, and Jacob:

And I will make of thee a great nation, and I will bless thee and make thy name great, and be thou a blessing . . . and in thee shall all the families of the earth be blessed (Gen. 12:2-3).

And I will multiply thy seed as the stars of heaven . . . and by thy seed shall all nations of the earth bless themselves (Gen. 26:4).

And thy seed shall be as the dust of the earth. . . . And in thee and in thy seed shall all the families of the earth be blessed (Gen. 28:14).

---

[2] See John 5:46; 6:14; 7:40; Acts 3:22; 7:37. Cf. also Matt. 11:3; 17:5; Luke 7:19, 9:35. For details see Hühn, *Die messian. Weissag.* I, pp. 141-143.

If we find in most of the Messianic expectations of the prophetic period, on the one hand, the prophetic promise that the people Israel will spread and increase and attain earthly happiness, and on the other hand, that Israel will be a light to the nations and from its land will go forth instruction to all peoples—then the *embryonic* material of these Messianic expectations is already to be found in the verses just cited. All the nations of the earth and all the families of mankind will be blessed by Israel—this is the kind of prophetic promise which has a nationalistic and universalistic quality at one and the same time; in other words, that quality which belongs to the Messianic idea in its entirety.

Thus it is also with the verses "Then ye shall be Mine own treasure from among all peoples," and "Ye shall be unto Me a kingdom of priests and a holy nation" (Exodus 19:5-6). This is not the Messianic expectation as it was pictured later, but from expressions like these the national and universal Messianic expectation grew. It is impossible to determine with certainty when these verses were written. But in all probability they preceded the writings of those prophets whose books are preserved to us, since according even to the most extreme Biblical critics the verses quoted belong to the Yahwist (J) and Elohist (E) sources, which preceded by a considerable time Amos and Hosea.[3] Therefore it is possible to see in these verses and verses like them the basis upon which little by little all Jewish Messianism was built. So from this point of view these verses have great importance in the history of the Messianic idea.

Of similar importance also are the well known verses (II Sam. 7:8-16 and I Chron. 17:7-14) in which Nathan the prophet assures David, "Thy throne shall be established forever" and "Thy house and thy kingdom shall be made sure forever." During his discourse the prophet says: "And I will appoint a place for My people Israel, and I will plant them, that they may dwell in their own place . . . neither shall the children of wickedness afflict them any more, as at the first" (II Sam. 7:10). If the Messianic idea in the prophetic period and in all later periods is almost never portrayed without mentioning "the kingdom of the house of David," and the name "son of David"

---

[3] See O. Eissfeldt, *Hexateuch-Synopse*, Leipzig, 1922, pp. 19*, 48*, 52-53*.

ALLUSIONS TO THE MESSIANIC IDEA   29

(or even "David") became almost the essential personal name of the Messiah [4]—then we can see that the belief in the victory of the house of David and in its everlasting sovereignty is already to be found in these verses.[5]

Traces of the belief that the Messiah will come forth from the house of David and that his kingdom will be an everlasting kingdom are also sought by Jewish and Christian theologians in the Blessing of Jacob, as bestowed upon Judah (Gen. 49:10):

> The sceptre shall not depart from Judah,
> Nor the ruler's staff from between his feet,
> Until Shiloh come;
> And unto him shall the obedience of the peoples be.

A whole literature has been written about this verse, and there is even a good-sized book on the different interpretations of the word "Shiloh." [6] Undoubtedly the part of the verse in which this word appears is very difficult to explain. The majority of modern Biblical exegetes read, according to the Targums Onkelos and Yerushalmi, the Syriac Peshitto, the translations of Aquila and Symmachus, and the interpretations of Rashi and Abravanel, not "Shiloh" but "*shello*" (the one to whom), and consider superfluous the words "and unto him" which follow Shiloh; they are only an interpretative addition to the expression "until shall come the one to whom shall be the obedience (that is, submission) of the peoples" ("peoples" meaning, as many times in the Bible, the tribes of Israel). This interpretation is particularly supported by the Septuagint, which translated "until Shiloh come" by ἕως ἂν ἔλθῃ τὰ ἀποκείμενα αὐτῷ.[7] But this interpretation, in spite of the fact that there is a certain scientific foundation for it, is not acceptable.

It is likewise difficult to consider the text in error and to read with Gressmann [8] *mōshelōh* (his ruler) instead of "Shiloh." Nearer the

---
[4] See above, pp. 20–21.
[5] See on this, E. Koenig, *Die messian. Weissag. d. A.T.*, 1923, pp. 132–142.
[6] A. Poznansky, *Schiloh: Ein Beitrag zur Geschichte der Messiaslehre*, Leipzig, 1904.
[7] "Until shall come the things stored up for him." See the book of Stade, *Geschichte des Volkes Israel*, I, 158ff.
[8] H. Gressmann, *Eschatologie*, pp. 263, 287.

truth is another interpretation, according to which the meaning intended in the word "Shiloh" is *Solomon, the son of David*. "Shiloh" is from the root SHLH, which is related both in meaning and in origin to the root SHLM, from which the name "Solomon" (*Shelomoh* in Hebrew) is formed.[9] And since all recent scholars conclude that the Blessing of Jacob was not composed before the period of the monarchy, it may be conjectured that it was composed in the time of Solomon. After the brilliant victories of David, which subdued many peoples, "the kingdom was established in the hand of Solomon," according to the witness of Scripture (I Kings 2:46). He did not have to fight any more; the submission of neighboring peoples was assured (compare "the rod that smote thee," Isa. 14:29). If we remember the promise of Nathan the prophet, mentioned above, the words in this verse will be understood in their plain meaning: "The sceptre shall not depart from Judah, nor the ruler's staff from between his feet, until Shiloh (Solomon) comes, and unto him shall be the obedience (submission) of the peoples." To be sure, Judah, like any of the larger tribes, always had rulers and lawgivers for itself; but the tribe of Judah had "the obedience of the peoples" only in the time of Solomon. There are no Messianic allusions, therefore, in this verse;[10] yet it is one of those Biblical passages upon which were based the Messianic expectations of later times. It, like the words of Nathan the prophet, strengthened the faith that the kingdom of the house of David would endure forever, rising up time after time to return to its pristine glory.[11]

From the same period and of the same nature are the well known verses in the section on Balaam:

> I see him, but not now;
> I behold him, but not nigh;
> There shall step forth [12] a star out of Jacob,
> And a sceptre shall rise out of Israel,
> And shall smite through the corners of Moab,

---

[9] The Christian theologian Hengstenberg has already translated "Shiloh" by the name Friedrich, i.e., man of *peace and security*.

[10] In spite of the opinion of Gressmann (*op. cit.*, p. 288), who thinks the old traditional view—that we have here a Messianic promise—correct.

[11] See also Castelli, *op. cit.*, pp. 38-41.

[12] Wellhausen reads *zāraḥ*, "shine forth."

And break down all the sons of Seth.
And Edom shall be a possession,
Seir also, even his enemies,[13] shall be a possession;
While Israel doeth valiantly.
And out of Jacob shall one have dominion
And shall destroy the remnant from the city.
(Numbers 24:17-19).

All this was interpreted in a Messianic sense by the early Christians.[14] But more especially did the Sages of the Talmud see Messianic indications in them. It is well known that Rabbi Akiba said of Simon ben-Coziba, "A star has gone forth out of Jacob"; from this circumstance, apparently, this Messiah acquired the name Bar-Cochba, "son of a star." [15] But actually, these words refer to David.[16] This is what is called in Latin *vaticinium ex eventu* (prophecy out of the event). David was the first to conquer Edom; he also struck Moab a decisive blow.

In the same passage, a little before the verses just discussed (Num. 24:7), there is mention of Agag ("his king shall be higher than Agag"),[17] who was conquered and all but destroyed by Saul, as is well known. Some verses farther on (Num. 24:20-24), Amalek and its downfall are mentioned ("Amalek was the first of the nations, but his end shall come to destruction"); there is also mention of the victory of Asshur (Assyria) over the Kenites ("Nevertheless the Kenite shall be wasted, until Asshur shall carry thee away captive"); likewise of ships from the island of Cyprus ("Kittim," in Assyrian "Gutium") which shall harass Asshur ("But ships shall come from the coast of Kittim, and shall afflict Asshur"). All this shows that it is

---

[13] In the opinion of many Biblical scholars, the words "his enemies" belong to the end of the verse thus: "from the city of his enemies."

[14] See Matt. 2:2; Luke 1:78; Acts 22:16.

[15] Yer. Taanith, Chap. 4, Hal. 8; Lamentations Rabbah on the text "The LORD hath swallowed up" (2:2). See J. Klausner, *When a Nation Fights for Its Freedom* [in Hebrew], 5th ed., Tel-Aviv, 5707 [1947], pp. 167-169, in contrast to S. Yeivin, *The War of Bar-Cochba* [in Hebrew], Jerusalem, 5706, pp. 54-56.

[16] See Rashi and Ibn-Ezra on this passage; the Christian scholar Grotius also agrees with this view. In the opinion of Sellin (*Heilandserwartung*, 1909, pp. 10-12), this is a Messianic prophecy even earlier than the time of David, since a king is not mentioned in it, and it is very difficult in its idioms.

[17] In the Septuagint "Gog" is written in place of this. But "Gog" came to Ezekiel from an ancient legend (Sellin, *op. cit.*, p. 10).

impossible to date the Balaam passages before the period of David and Solomon.[18] And everything which we find in all these passages was realized in David, as has already been observed by medieval Jewish interpreters. There is no doubt, therefore, that it is impossible to consider these passages as Messianic in themselves. But also there is no doubt, in my opinion, that the exaggerated hopes about the glorious future of the people Israel, its greatness, its power, and its broad area of authority in days to come, as expressed in these verses, are the embryonic material out of which was afterward formed the Messianic idea in all its majesty and splendor.

Also considered as Messianic are those passages in the Books of Leviticus and Deuteronomy which contain the conditional blessing and curse (Lev. 26:3–45; Deut. 28:1–68, also Deut. 30:3–10) and which, according to the opinion of Biblical critics, are later than the first of the writing prophets. The Tannaitic Midrash, *Siphra*, on the section *Behukkothai* ("In My Statutes," beginning at Lev. 26:3), interprets all the words of the blessing as referring to the Messianic age.[19] In a certain sense this is correct. The great good, which God will pour out upon His people in the Messianic age, will come only as a result of the keeping of the statutes. Such was the opinion of the prophets and such is also the opinion of many of the Sages of the Talmud.[20] But still more Messianic is the assurance that comes after the terrific rebuke: "And yet for all that, when they are in the land of their enemies, I will not reject them, neither will I abhor them, to destroy them utterly, and to break my covenant with them; for I am the LORD their God," and so on (Lev. 26:44). This is the great promise, that the people Israel will endure forever, and after all the misery which it will undergo for its iniquities, it will rouse itself and be restored to its pristine glory. This matter is thoroughly explained in the Book of Deuteronomy:

---

[18] Against the opinions of David Kahana in his treatise *Introduction to the Balaam Passage* [in Hebrew] (Lvov, 5643 [1883]), of Sellin (see the preceding note), and of Hommel in his book *Die altisraelitische Ueberlieferung in inschriftlicher Beleuchtung*, München, 1897.
[19] See below, Part II, Chap. X.
[20] See below, Part III, Chap. IV.

Then the LORD thy God will turn thy captivity, and have compassion upon thee, and will return and gather thee from all the peoples, whither the LORD thy God hath scattered thee. If any of thine that are dispersed be in the uttermost parts of heaven, from thence will the LORD thy God gather thee, and from thence will He fetch thee. And the LORD thy God will bring thee into the land which thy fathers possessed, and thou shalt possess it; and He will do thee good, and multiply thee above thy fathers (Deut. 30:3–5).

The idea of "the return to Zion"—that hope of redemption and faith in the return of the natives to their own country, which is the cornerstone of the Jewish Messianic ideal—is found here almost in its entirety. This is not at all surprising. The Book of Deuteronomy is not earlier than the books of those prophets whose prophecies were collected together and preserved to us. Verses such as "The LORD will bring thee, and *thy king* whom thou shalt set over thee, unto a nation that thou hast not known, thou nor thy fathers" (Deut. 28:36) do not allow the possibility of dating the Book of Deuteronomy *in its entirety* before the fall of Samaria (individual elements could be more ancient). In the Book of Leviticus—of which the "rebuke section" is later even than Deuteronomy, in the opinion of Biblical critics (upon which doubt may still be cast), who attribute it to the Priestly Code —the idea of "the return to Zion" is not expressed with complete clarity. Nevertheless, a Messianic expectation is also to be seen in the assurance, "When they are in the land of their enemies, I will not reject them, neither will I abhor them, to destroy them utterly, and to break my covenant with them." Not yet here—nor in the Book of Deuteronomy—is the hope that a period of universal bliss and general ethical perfection will come upon mankind. Also still lacking is any hint of a personal Messiah. But already here *is* a strong hope that the Jewish nation will not sink down in sin and be lost among the Gentile nations.

With a strong hand and an outstretched arm, the LORD will rule over His nation, according to the words of Ezekiel. He will *force* it, by severe troubles and afflictions, to offer complete repentance. Then He will renew His covenant with it, which is to say that He will restore it to its own land and to its pristine glory, and it will again be "a kingdom of priests and a holy nation." This is not only the nucleus from which grew many other Messianic expectations; it is the cornerstone of the hope for revival.[21] Moreover, the well known conception of "the birth pangs of the Messiah," to precede the future redemption, is already embodied in these passages, which are not so early, yet in any case contain an early prophetic deposit.

The fact that we did not find the Messianic idea expressed in all its fullness at a time earlier than the period of the monarchy cannot be considered a contradiction of the opinion expressed above,[22] that the Messianic idea is the result of the history of afflictions which began for Israel in its early youth, and that the personal Messiah is the product of the early traditions about Moses, the first redeemer. The Messianic idea is a complex of hopes for the future; it can, therefore, be embodied only in the words of prophecy. And there are almost no words of prophecy left to us from before the period of the monarchy, in spite of the fact that undoubtedly there were prophets in Israel before this period. In the Pentateuch and in the Former Prophets it is not possible even to seek for hopes for the future based on the Messianic idea, because these books are not collections of prophetic visions, but compilations of popular traditions, histories, and legends. To be sure, in places in the Pentateuch and Former Prophets where prophetic oracles do occur, we have found indications of Messianic expectations.[23]

This and one other thing.

The Messianic idea, whatever its origin, was not created in a day as we have it now. It grew, it developed little by little, while various periods of time passed by. Undoubtedly, in the early period there was yearning for a Messiah—a simple longing to be redeemed from victorious and oppressive enemies; I have already indicated above that every one of the judges was a temporary Messiah for his tribe or for

---

[21] See Castelli, *op. cit.*, pp. 41–43. On the passages wrongly thought to be Messianic, see in general in this book, pp. 34–76; also Hühn, *op. cit.*, I, 134–156. On the Psalms which are wrongly considered to be Messianic, and on "the servant of the LORD" in Isa. 52–53, I shall speak in the following chapters.

[22] See above, Chap. II, pp. 19–22.

[23] Such an indication may *possibly* be found also in the last verse of the prayer of Hannah (I Sam. 2:10).

ALLUSIONS TO THE MESSIANIC IDEA 35

a group of tribes.[24] In the time of David and Solomon this longing was increased and extended. But the Messianic idea did not reach its highest development before the time of Amos and Hosea. This is in the nature of things. The prophets had to reach an exceedingly great height in order that the Messianic ideal might become broad and lofty, spiritual and universal. I have already said that the personal Messiah has in him both kingly and prophetic attributes. Thus the more the prophetic standard was elevated, the more the whole Messianic idea was exalted and ennobled.

I did wish to emphasize one thing at the end of this chapter: if we see that Amos and Hosea—and a little later Isaiah and Micah—already had a very highly developed Messianic ideal, then we *must* suppose that this ideal was not born at one moment, but developed during the course of several generations before the time of Jeroboam II (son of Joash) and Uzziah son of Amaziah. And in at least half of the Messianic verses cited in the present chapter can be seen, in my opinion, those elements from which grew all those lofty Messianic expectations that are the glory and pride of Hebrew prophecy in its golden age.[25]

[24] See above, p. 19.
[25] These ideas, which were completely new when I published them for the first time (in *Ha-Shiloah*, Vol. 12, of the year 1903), have become acceptable views in recent years, owing to the researches of Gunkel, Gressmann, Sellin, Eichrodt, Kittel, *et al.*, who of course, to our sorrow, did not read modern Hebrew.

CHAPTER IV

Amos (c. 760 B.C.E.) and Hosea (c. 750 B.C.E.) [1]

THESE TWO prophets, Amos of Tekoa and Hosea son of Beeri, prophesied before the exile of the Ten Tribes and before the fall of the kingdom of Israel. The former prophesied, according to the witness of the text, upon which there is no occasion to cast doubt, "in the days of Uzziah king of Judah, and in the days of Jeroboam the son of Joash king of Israel, two years before the earthquake" (Amos 1:1). The latter prophesied "in the days of Uzziah, Jotham, Ahaz, and Hezekiah, kings of Judah, and in the days of Jeroboam the son of Joash, king of Israel." The prophetic career of Amos ceased, therefore, some time before that of Hosea; it may also be supposed that the former began to prophesy before the latter. One thing is common to both: most of their prophecies preceded the Assyrian exile.

The victorious chariot of the kings of Assyria had once before passed through "the land of the Hittites," subduing on its way Jehu, king of Israel. Now it was about to come again to the land of Canaan, its purpose being to trample in the dust the kingdom of Samaria. The prophets saw it coming from the first. Yet another fearful enemy, and one even closer to Israel and Judah in those days, was Aram (Syria). In the beginning of the reign of Jeroboam son of Joash, or Jeroboam II (784–744 B.C.E.), the political situation in Judah and

---

[1] From here on to the end of the chapters on the prophets one should also consult M. Z. Segal, *Introduction to the Bible* [in Hebrew], Book II (Latter Prophets), Jerusalem, 5706 [1946].

Israel was very humiliating. The Biblical text bears witness to this in clear and pointed words: "For the LORD saw the affliction of Israel, that it was very bitter; for there was none shut up nor left at large,[2] neither was there any helper for Israel. *And the LORD said not that He would blot out the name of Israel from under heaven*" (II Kings 14:26–27). The last verse shows us clearly what a state affairs had reached in the kingdom of Israel during the early part of the reign of Jeroboam II. But in the period when Amos and Hosea began their prophecy, that is, during the latter part of the reign of Jeroboam II, the condition of the kingdom was very much improved. According to the Biblical text (II Kings 14:25 and 28), Jeroboam restored to the rule of Samaria all the Israelite cities which had been conquered by the Arameans, and also subdued many Aramean cities.

Uzziah, king of Judah (779–739 B.C.E.), a contemporary of Jeroboam son of Joash, in whose time also Amos and Hosea prophesied, was likewise a powerful and victorious king. He decisively defeated the Philistines, also conquered the Ammonites and the Arabians, and in general increased the political power and the economic wealth of the land of Judah. The short-sighted in Israel and Judah, the princes, the rich, and the owners of great possessions, the ones "at ease in Zion" and "secure in the mountain of Samaria"—these believed that Israel and Judah had been saved with an everlasting salvation.

But not so Amos and Hosea. With their seers' eyes they penetrated into the inmost recesses of the apparently happy life, and recognized that its foundations were rotten. The political power, likewise, was transitory. The peoples conquered by Israel and Judah were influencing spiritually their conquerors: after Amaziah, king of Judah, had subdued the Edomites, he set up the gods of the children of Seir to be his own gods (II Chron. 25:14). The economic wealth was given only into the hands of the few property owners, and they, being men

---

[2] I.e., there was no one to exercise authority among the people (cf. "there was none in the land possessing authority," Judges 18:7, or "by oppression [authority?] and judgment he was taken away," Isa. 53:8) or to help his people (cf. "thou shalt surely release it with him," Ex. 23:5); the end of this verse (26) is only an explanatory addition. The passive participle is used here in place of the active, as in "daughter of Babylon, the destroyed" (Ps. 137:8) instead of "the destroyer" [English versions do not agree]; and in the later literature, *māsōr* ("informer") and *lāqōbōt* ("buyers") instead of *mōsēr* and *lōqeḥīm*.

of power, oppressed and crushed the many poor.³ Therefore this wealth could not endure for long. Moral corruption was rife among the people, especially in the kingdom of Israel, and since the God of Israel is a righteous judge it was inevitable that this moral corruption should bring in its wake a severe penalty. Punishment and afflictions, political downfall and exile—these are the fruit and the outcome of sins. But the final outcome of the punishment and afflictions would be—repentance and salvation. This is the common axis upon which the prophecies of both Amos and Hosea revolve. Sin brings punishment, punishment brings repentance, which in turn brings the Days of the Messiah.

All this fits exactly the description of the formation of the Messianic idea as it was presented in Chapter II of the present book. Therefore, all the prophets view the evolution of Messianic events from this clear point of view; and so do Amos and Hosea view it. Yet in details of the Messianic descriptions Amos and Hosea differ from each other; there is no fundamental difference, of course, but enough to be recognized.

The period of affliction and punishment is called by Amos,⁴ along with several other prophets, "the day of the LORD" or "that day." Apparently the Israelites in his time—and even considerably earlier —meant by this name the day of judgment in general, that is, the great day on which the wicked would be punished and the righteous be given a good reward. So, since those swimming with the stream and following the usual customs are always confident of their own integrity and righteousness, therefore all such people wished to attain "the day of the LORD," in order that they might be privileged to eat the fruit of their deeds which were so good in their own eyes. As to this, the prophet says:

> Woe unto you that desire the day of the LORD!
> Wherefore would ye have the day of the LORD?
> It is darkness, and not light.
> As if a man did flee from a lion,

---

³ On this see Franz Walther, *Die Propheten in ihrem sozialen Beruf und das Wirtschaftsleben ihrer Zeit*, Freiburg, 1900.

⁴ On Amos in general and on his Messianic pronouncements in particular, see also J. Klausner, *The Book of Amos* [in Hebrew], Tel-Aviv, 1943.

> And a bear met him;
> And went into the house and leaned his hand on the wall,
> And a serpent bit him.
> Shall not the day of the LORD be darkness, and not light?
> Even very dark, and no brightness in it? (Amos 5:18-20)

The prophet continues to portray the day of the LORD in darkest colors:

> Lamentation shall be in the broad places,
> And they shall say in all the streets: "Alas! alas!"
> And shall call the husbandman to mourning,
> And proclaim lamentation to such as are skilful of wailing.
> And in all the vineyards shall be lamentation;
> For I will pass through the midst of thee,
> Saith the LORD (5:16-17).

Again, Amos prophesies that in that day "the LORD commandeth, and the great house shall be smitten into splinters, and the little house into chips" (6:11). The great majority of the nation will be destroyed from off the face of the earth: "And it shall come to pass, if there remain ten men in one house, that they shall die" (6:9):

> And though they go into captivity before their enemies,
> Thence will I command the sword, and it shall slay them;
> And I will set Mine eyes upon them
> For evil, and not for good (9:4).

> There shall not one of them flee away,
> And there shall not one of them escape (9:1).

For "that day," the day of the LORD, will be "a bitter day": feasts will be turned into mourning and songs into lamentation; all loins will put on sackcloth and baldness will be on every head (8:10). "In that day shall the fair virgins and the young men faint for thirst" (8:13). All who bow down before the calves of Bethel and Dan shall fall and never rise up again (8:14).

Those "that are at ease in Zion" and "that are secure in the mountain of Samaria," that is to say, the princes and notables of Judah and Israel, must now "go captive at the head of them that go captive" (6:7). For the prophet senses a future in which "Israel shall surely be led away captive out of his land" (7:17). In another place the prophet says, "Therefore will I cause you to go into captivity beyond Damascus, saith He, whose name is the LORD God of hosts" (5:27). Here, apparently, the exile to Assyria is indicated. That "the day of the LORD" or "that day" is not yet "the end of days" of the later prophets, that is, a far distant future—of this I am sure. It is proved not only by the verse "I will cause you to go into captivity beyond Damascus," but also by this one:

> And the high places of Isaac shall be desolate,
> And the sanctuaries of Israel shall be laid waste;
> And I will rise against the house of Jeroboam with the sword (7:9).

This characteristic—to prophesy punishments soon to come—remains in almost all the prophets. Nearly all of them cry out, "Near is the day of the LORD." Punishment necessarily follows sin, since sin and punishment are always for the prophets only cause and effect, occasion and realization, as said above. Thus the punishment cannot be long delayed. But *salvation* is not so closely connected with punishment as is sin. Salvation depends upon *repentance*, or it is an act of *grace*, which the LORD performs for his chosen people. Now repentance and grace can delay their coming. Therefore salvation does not appear to the prophet as very near, although he firmly believes that it will surely come, even though it be tardy.

When we recognize to what an extent Amos looks upon "the day of the LORD" as the *necessary* result of the sins of Judah and Israel, it can be thought that we have here before us a completely natural event. But it is not to be forgotten that the prophet believes in the LORD to such a degree that every event that happens in the world appears to him as an act of the LORD; moreover, the prophet is an exalted poet, the flight of whose imagination soars to the skies. Hence we must not be surprised at all, if we find in the words of Amos that not alone will sinful men suffer on "the day of the LORD," but that there will come about in *all nature* great changes for the worse:

> And it shall come to pass in that day,
> Saith the LORD God,
> That I will cause the sun to go down at noon,
> And I will darken the earth in the clear day.

Also, the earth will tremble and quake, "yea it shall rise up wholly like the River, and it shall be troubled and sink down again, like the River of Egypt" (8:8, also 9:5).

All the outlines in the terrible and grandiose picture, fearful in its gloomy splendor, which the Sages of the Talmud call "the birth pangs of Messiah,"[5] are found here almost in their entirety. Also one other feature, which is not clear in the descriptions of the rest of the prophets and the importance of which is so great for the development of Messianism during subsequent generations, is to be found in the words of Amos: among the rest of the punishments that must come upon the people Israel, this prophet numbers also the *cessation of prophecy* or *the Torah's being forgotten* by Israel:

> Behold, the days come, saith the LORD God,
> That I will send a famine in the land,
> Not a famine of bread, nor a thirst for water,
> But of hearing the words of the LORD.
> And they shall wander from sea to sea,
> And from the north even to the east;
> They shall run to and fro to seek the word of the LORD,
> And shall not find it (8:11–12).

On these two verses is based the belief that "Torah is destined to be forgotten by Israel"—a belief found in the most ancient Messianic Baraithas and also in the Mishnah itself.[6]

In Amos's description of "the day of the LORD," we have, therefore, the whole outline of the period which must come before the advent of the Messiah: exile, destruction, slaughter, humiliation, changes in the order of nature, and stoppage of Torah. Not so his description of the redemption: in it are lacking many of the fundamental signs of the Days of the Messiah.

This description begins with a splendid introduction. The Israelites are not more exalted in the eyes of the LORD than other peoples, since all are sinners ("Are ye not as the children of the Ethiopians unto Me, O children of Israel?" and so on). The LORD God will destroy from off the face of the earth "the sinful kingdom" (mean-

---

[5] See on this picture, below, Part III, especially in Chap. V.
[6] See for particulars, below, Part III, Chap. V.

ing, apparently, the house of Jehu), "except"—and here the prophet interrupts himself and shakes off all his pessimism— "that I will not utterly destroy the house of Jacob, saith the LORD" (9:8). "By the sword shall die" only "all the sinners of My people, that say: The evil shall not overtake nor confront us" (9:10); but this evil will not touch at all the good and upright men in the nation.[7] All the exiles and captives will return from the lands of their captivity:

> For, lo, I will command, and I will sift
>   the house of Israel among all the nations,
> Like as corn is sifted in a sieve,
> Yet shall not the least grain fall upon the earth (9:9).[8]

Then the prophet adds:

> In that day I will raise up
>   The tabernacle of David that is fallen, [9]

[7] Cf. "Seek ye Me, and live" (5:4); "Seek the LORD, and live" (5:6); "Seek good, and not evil, that ye may live" (5:14); "Hate the evil, and love the good, and establish justice in the gate; it may be that the LORD, the God of hosts, will be gracious unto *the remnant of Joseph*" (5:15). From this it appears that the idea of "a remnant shall return" and "the remnant of Israel" is not entirely new with Isaiah.

[8] On the basis of this verse, Wellhausen, Marti, and Volz concluded that Verses 9:8-15 do not belong to Amos. The argument is that this prophet, who prophesied well before the Assyrian exile, could not have spoken in such forceful terms of the return of exiles to their own land. According to this opinion, the Book of Amos would be completely lacking in any description of the Messianic deliverance. But it seems to me that there is no substance in this opinion. Did not Israelites go into exile to other lands before they were exiled to the land of Assyria? Several times a certain portion of the kingdom of Israel was taken into exile by the kings of Aram [Syria] (whence the prophet warns that the Israelites will "go into captivity beyond Damascus," 5:27). Even before Verse 9:8 the prophet says, "And though they go into captivity before their enemies, thence will I command the sword, and it shall slay them" (9:4). Dispersion by means of captivity and exile was a common thing in those days, as is shown again by these words of the same prophet: "Because they carried away captive a whole captivity, to deliver them up to Edom" (1:6), and also, "Because they delivered up a whole captivity to Edom" (1:9). This view, which was new in the year 1903, when I first expressed it, is more and more accepted today by the best Biblical scholars even in liberal circles. See, e.g., Sellin, *Heilandserwartung*, p. 23. For a list of scholars who affirm this, see A. Lods, *Les Prophètes d'Israël*, Paris, 1935, p. 97.

[9] Kautzsch, in the German translation of the Old Testament which he edited, reads not "the tabernacle of David that is fallen," but "the tabernacles of David that are fallen," so that these words may agree with the expression "their breaches" [in the next clause, according to the Hebrew]. But in my opinion it is more correct to read "the tabernacle of David that is fallen" as in the text,

And close up the breaches thereof,
And I will raise up his ruins,[10]
And I will build it as in the days of old (9:11).

The kingdom of the house of David, therefore, will be restored to its pristine glory and the kings of the house of David will rule also over the Ten Tribes. Not without reason did Amaziah, priest of Bethel, advise Amos to flee to the land of Judah, to eat bread and to prophesy there (7:12); for Amos, in fact, was not entirely faithful to the house of Jehu.[11]

When the kingdom of the house of David again becomes a powerful dominion, as it was before the Division, all the peoples will return to subservience to the people Israel, as in the time of David ("that they may possess the remnant of Edom, and all the nations, upon whom My name is called").[12] Then shall Israel have not only political power, but also this world's economic wealth. Just as on "the day of the LORD," the day ordained for punishment, the order of nature will be changed for the worse, so in the time of salvation it will be changed for the better:

Behold, the days come, saith the LORD,
That the plowman shall overtake the reaper,
And the treader of grapes him that soweth seed;
And the mountains shall drop sweet wine,

---

but instead of "their breaches" to read "its breaches" in agreement with "I will build *it*."

[10] Apparently we should read "its ruins"; but Kautzsch and Hühn read "his ruins" and think that this pronoun refers to David. Hühn (*Die messian. Weissag.*, I, p. 13, Note 1) proposes to read along with this also "I will build him" instead of "I will build it"; thus half of the verse would refer to the tabernacle and half of it to David.

[11] Smend (*Lehrbuch der alttestamentlichen Religionsgeschichte*, p. 128, note) also concludes that all the Verses 9:11-15, i.e., a very explicit description of the Messianic salvation, do not belong to Amos. His argument is that in another place Amos says "The virgin of Israel is fallen, she shall no more rise" (5:2), even though in 9:11-15 he heralds deliverance and restoration. But just this is the way of the prophet, who always delivers his message under the influence of his strongest emotions, resulting from his observations at that particular time; therefore one should not make difficulties by setting one verse over against another verse in the oracles of the same prophet. Such contradictions can be found in the books of Isaiah and Jeremiah in great number. See on this also J. Klausner, *The Book of Amos*, pp. 22-25.

[12] For the interpretation of the words "upon whom My name is called," see in the book of Hühn, p. 13.

> And all the hills shall melt.
> And I will turn the captivity of My people Israel,
> And they shall build the waste cities, and inhabit them;
> And they shall plant vineyards, and drink the wine thereof;
> They shall also make gardens, and eat the fruit of them.
>
> And I will plant them upon their land,
> And they shall no more be plucked up
> Out of their land which I have given them,
> Saith the LORD thy God (9:13-15).

In these Messianic promises there are many of the political and earthly characteristics belonging to the Messianic idea: the ingathering of exiles, the rule of the kingdom of the house of David over all Israel, the subduing of other peoples, bountiful and miraculous productivity of the soil, and so on—in short, strong political power and great earthly wealth. But the great spiritual-ethical characteristics of the time of redemption, which are found a little later in the lofty prophecies of Isaiah and Micah, are still lacking here. There is no mention of the dissemination of the Torah of Israel throughout all the world; spiritual wealth is not described here in bright colors; righteousness and justice, which must of necessity rule in the midst of the new kingdom, are not stressed here at all; and besides all this, there is here no mention whatever of an *individual Messiah*. Instead, a collective Messiah is indicated—the whole kingdom of the house of David.

We do not know for sure, whether the Messianic idea in the time of Amos had yet reached that high level of development upon which stood Isaiah, who began to prophesy only about twenty years after Amos; or perhaps we simply lack many sections of the prophecies of Amos in which this great prophet spoke about the Messianic idea in more detail. We are more inclined to attribute the paucity of spiritual elements in the Messianic idea of Amos to the first cause. The Israelites preserved the prophetic promises very carefully, and sections of this kind could hardly have been lost. But, however that may be, if we had only the Messianic verses of Amos, the Messianic idea of Israel could not have had so much influence on Jewish history and on the history of all humanity.

The Messianic conceptions of the prophet Hosea, the contemporary of Amos, are more highly developed.

I have already said that in both time and place of activity, as well as in the general flow of his ideas, Hosea is much like Amos. Both of them prophesy in and against the kingdom of Israel, both of them have their visions before the Assyrian exile, and both of them see punishment approaching close on the heels of sin and moral deterioration. But Hosea, the last of the prophets of the kingdom of Ephraim, foresees not only the end of "the house of Jehu," but also the complete end of the Northern Kingdom: "I will cause to cease the kingdom of the house of Israel" (Hosea 1:4), says he without any waver of doubt. He prophesies for Israel exile to Assyria and to Egypt:

> They shall not dwell in the LORD's land;
> But Ephraim shall return to Egypt,
> And they shall eat unclean food in Assyria (9:3).

The disaster will be dreadful:

> They shall fall by the sword:
> Their infants shall be dashed in pieces,
> And their women with child shall be ripped up
> (14:1; Eng. 13:16).

The high places—"the sin of Israel," as the prophet calls them in his pointed metaphor—will all be destroyed, and thorns and thistles will grow up over the altars. The shame will be so great that the Israelites "shall say to the mountains, 'Cover us,' and to the hills, 'Fall on us'" (10:8). Such will be the fate of the sinners—the great majority of the people—on the day of punishment.

In all this description Hosea resembles Amos. But one new idea comes up to the surface from within the prophecies of Hosea: *punishment is not an end in itself as vengeance upon sinners; it is only a means to moral reform.* "The destruction of community life and the devastation of the land are to be regarded less as a punishment than as a means of instruction," says Hühn rightly.[13] "In their trouble they will seek Me earnestly" (5:15), thinks the prophet. The punish-

---

[13] See Hühn, *op. cit.*, I, p. 15.

ment is only a transition to a shining future. To be sure, Israel must endure "the pangs of a woman in childbirth" before the advent of the Messiah (this expression, found in Hosea 13:13, brought about the formulation of the Talmudic expression "the birth pangs of Messiah"); however, these "birth pangs" are not tribulations and afflictions which the LORD will mete out in anger to transgressors, but a means by which to arouse the transgressors to repentance and good deeds. The prophet is certain that through these blows Israel will return to its God, and then the LORD will have mercy on Israel and exalt her in the end:

> Come, and let us return unto the LORD;
> For He hath torn, and He will heal us,
> He hath smitten, and He will bind us up.
> After two days will He revive us,
> On the third day He will raise us up,
>   that we may live in His presence.
> And let us know, eagerly strive to know the LORD,
> His going forth is sure as the morning;
> And He shall come unto us as the rain,
> As the latter rain that watereth [14] the earth (6:1-3).

The direct connexion which exists between chastisement and redemption, we find in these verses:

For the children of Israel shall sit solitary many days without king, and without prince, and without sacrifice, and without pillar, and without ephod or teraphim; afterward shall the children of Israel return, and seek the LORD their God, and David their king; and shall come trembling unto the LORD and to His goodness in the end of days (3:4-5).

The words "in the end of days" allow no doubt to be cast on the fact that here is meant the Messianic redemption. According to the words of the prophet, this redemption will come after a period of tribulations and entire lack of all national privileges. This period will bring about a complete repentance, and through this will lead to the attainment of the hoped-for happiness.

This is a new and beautiful element in the whole great portrayal

---

[14] Apparently it is better to read *yerawweh*.

of the Messianic idea, an element which we did not find in the prophecies of Amos.

We find still another new element here: we have before us the first trace of a *personal* Messiah.

Certainly the words "David their king" cannot be taken in their literal meaning. In other words, it is impossible to conclude that according to Hosea David himself will return to rule over Israel in the final days, or that "David, king of Israel, has come to life," as thought some of the Sages of the Talmud.[15] The name "David" is used here in place of "house of David"; for in the time of Hosea the people Israel did not yet know of the belief in the resurrection of the dead. In the Book of II Kings we find the following words written time after time concerning certain of the later kings of Judah (for example, Ahaz and his son Hezekiah): "He did not that which was right in the eyes of the LORD his God, *like David his father*" (II Kings 16:2), or, "He did that which was right in the eyes of the LORD, according to all that David his father had done" (II Kings 18:3); yet David was not the father of Ahaz or Hezekiah, but their remote ancestor. David was the dynastic progenitor of the kings of Judah, therefore he is considered in the Bible as the "father" of the kings of Judah. Hence also the use of his name in place of "the house of David."

But we find in Hosea also clear indication of *an individual Messiah*. The prophet comforts his people and feels that they have a future, when "the number of the children of Israel shall be as the sands of the sea, which cannot be measured nor numbered"; and instead of their being despised as they have been up to now, "it shall be said unto them, 'Ye are children of the living God.'" Then the prophet adds:

And the children of Judah and the children of Israel shall be gathered together, *and they shall appoint themselves one head, and shall go up out of the land;* for great shall be the day of Jezreel (2:1–2).[16]

[15] See above, Chap. II, p. 21, and below, Part III, Chap. 7.

[16] Hühn (*op. cit.*, I, p. 15) thinks that Hosea means by "the day of Jezreel" what Amos means by "the day of the LORD" or "that day." But from Verse 2:2 we see clearly that the prophet means by "the day of Jezreel" the day of redemption, since it will come after the ingathering of exiles.

The "one head," which the children of Israel will appoint in order to go up from the land of their exile,[17] must be, without doubt, a strong redeemer, a personal Messiah.

This is still not a redeemer in the later sense of this word. He is not *sent* from the LORD, but "appointed," that is, chosen by the children of Judah and the children of Israel. We do not know whether he will have material and spiritual virtues and advantages, and in general we do not know what will be the details of his deeds. We do know only this, that he will be the head, the leader, of those particular parts of the nation that will go up from the land of their exile. Apparently he will conduct them to the land of their fathers. More than this we do not know at all. Yet one thing is clear: Hosea speaks of an individual personality that is exalted above the rest of the nation and becomes head of it; this we have not found in the Scriptures so clearly prior to Hosea. In this Hosea goes beyond Amos. Amos recognizes the Days of the Messiah as a new period, but he does not know a central personality, around which will be gathered the two greatest, yet most separated, parts of the nation.[18]

In most of the rest of his Messianic prophecies, and especially in the portrayal of redemption and the Messianic happiness, Hosea resembles Amos very much. Yet one distinguishing feature is found in Hosea: he prophesies that the future redemption will be like the redemption from the Egyptian bondage:

> Therefore, behold I will allure her,
> And bring her into the wilderness,
> And speak tenderly unto her.
> And I will give her her vineyards from thence,
> And the valley of Achor for a door of hope;
> And she shall respond there as in the days of her youth,
> *As in the day when she came up out of the land of Egypt* (2:16–17).

This strengthens the view which I expressed in the second chapter of this book, that the ancient traditions about the exile in Egypt and the

---

[17] And not in order to go up to battle, as Hühn thinks (*op. cit.*, I, p. 16), without any basis. The comparison with the Egyptian exile and the deliverance from this exile in Hos. 2:16-17 strengthens the validity of my opinion; of this I shall speak again below.

[18] See on this the correct words of Castelli, *Il Messia*, p. 87.

deliverance from this exile were the initial stimulus to the formation of the entire Messianic idea, which is fundamentally the idea of redemption from exile.[19] But this is not found in Amos.

Yet in most Messianic expectations Hosea resembles Amos, as was said before. Like Amos, he also promises that in the Days of the Messiah the produce of the ground will be great and abundant: "the earth shall respond to the corn, and the wine, and the oil" (2:24, Eng. 22). In lofty figures, filled with poetic splendor, and soft beauty and tenderness, the prophet describes the *earthly bliss* of Israel in the Days of the Messiah:

> I will be as the dew unto Israel;
> He shall blossom as the lily,
> And cast forth his roots as Lebanon.
> His branches shall spread,
> And his beauty shall be as the olive tree,
> And his fragrance as Lebanon.
> They that dwell under his shadow shall again
> Make corn to grow,
> And shall blossom as the vine;
> The scent thereof shall be as the wine of Lebanon (14:6-8, Eng. 5-7).

But *spiritual bliss* will also be great. The names of the Baals will be cut off from the mouth of the virgin daughter of Israel "and they shall no more be mentioned by their name," so that she will not call the LORD "Baali" (my Baal) but "Ishi" (my husband).[20] Israel will return to its God, and the LORD will return to His people:

> I will heal their backsliding
> I will love them freely;
> For Mine anger is turned away from him (14:5, Eng. 4).

The virgin daughter of Israel will return and be to her God as a wife of youthful innocence, though now she is a wife of harlotry:

> And I will betroth thee unto Me for ever;
> Yea, I will betroth thee unto Me in righteousness, and in justice,

---

[19] See above, pp. 15-19. It is on this basis that I think that the words "they shall go up out of the land" (2:2) are to be interpreted: they shall go up from the land of their exile; and not according to the opinion of Hühn. See the note before the preceding one.

[20] On this see the book of E. Koenig, *Die Hauptprobleme der altisraelitischen Religionsgeschichte*, 1884, p. 35.

> And in lovingkindness, and in compassion.
> And I will betroth thee unto Me in faithfulness;
> And thou shalt know the LORD (2:21-22, Eng. 19-20).

The exiles and captives will return to their own land willingly or under compulsion:

> They shall walk after the LORD,
> Who shall roar like a lion;
> For He shall roar,
> And the children shall come trembling from the west.
> They shall come trembling as a bird out of Egypt,
> And as a dove out of the land of Assyria;
> And I will make them to dwell in their houses,
> Saith the LORD (2:21-22).

In another place the prophet says in the name of the LORD: "Yea, though they hire among the nations, now will I gather them up" (8:10); which is to say, even if the children of Israel hire lovers and make covenants among the heathen nations (but Duhm reads *yit'u*, "wander" instead of "hire"), the LORD will gather them out by the strength of His hand.

Like Amos, Hosea also prophesies changes in the order of nature; not, however, for the worse, but for the better:

> And in that day will I make a covenant for them
> With the beasts of the field, and with the fowls of heaven,
> And with the creeping things of the ground (2:20).

Here we have already, in undeveloped form, to be sure, the prophecy of "the wolf lying down with the lamb." And the end of the verse is—if we may say so—completely "Isaianic":

And I will break the bow and the sword and the battle out of the land,
And will make them to lie down safely.

This is a new thought, which we do not find in the prophecies of Amos but which became afterward, in the time of Isaiah and Micah, an inseparable part of the Messianic ideal: *perfect peace in the Days of the Messiah*. Not without reason does Hosea refrain from speaking about the subjection of other nations to Israel, as Amos had spoken.[21] If bow and sword and battle pass from the land, obviously

---

[21] See Amos 9:12, and in the present book, above, p. 43.

there will be no place for subjugation. Not for nothing was Hosea the older contemporary of Isaiah. Hosea is the spiritual father of the greatest prophet of the Messianic idea. In the Messianic prophecies of the last prophet of Israel (the Northern Kingdom) are already present the definitely formed embryonic materials of those exalted Messianic ideas which before long were to be made more concrete in all their loftiness and brightness by the two great prophets of Judah, Isaiah the son of Amoz, and Micah the Morashtite. Both of these prophets lived during the time of the fall of Samaria and the reign of Hezekiah; and both of them drew high faith and inspiration from the national disaster, as well as from the glory and honor which the royal pupil of the prophets conferred upon the instruction of his great teachers.

CHAPTER V

Isaiah

(C. 740-700 B.C.E.)

AT THE beginning of the Book of Isaiah (1:1), it is recorded that this great prophet prophesied "in the days of Uzziah, Jotham, Ahaz, and Hezekiah, kings of Judah." But according to Chapter 6 it is to be supposed that the prophetic career of the son of Amoz began only "in the year that King Uzziah died," that is, in 740-739 B.C.E. His prophesying extended, therefore, through the reigns of three kings of Judah: Jotham, Ahaz, and Hezekiah.

According to the Biblical record (II Kings 15:33 and II Chron. 27:1), Jotham reigned sixteen years; but apparently included in these are six or seven years of rule by Jotham during the lifetime of Uzziah his father, after the latter was stricken with leprosy and placed in "a house set apart" (II Kings 15:5 and II Chron. 26:21). We are forced to this conclusion by the "synchronisms" which we find in the lists of Assyrian kings.[1] Jotham reigned alone, therefore, only nine or ten years, or perhaps only five years (739-734, according to Kittel); Ahaz reigned about fifteen years (734-719), and Hezekiah about twenty-nine years (719-691). Even if we assume that Isaiah lived only two or three years after the illness of Hezekiah, who had

[1] On the chronology of the kings of Judah and Israel in the time of Isaiah, see R. Kittel, *Geschichte des Volkes Israel*, 5th ed., 1922, II, 264-271; F. Hommel, *Geschichte des alten Morgenlandes*, 2nd ed., Leipzig, 1898, pp. 123-126, 128-129, 130-131, 135, 137, 139-142; J. Lewy, *Die Chronologie der Koenige von Israel und Juda*, Giessen, 1927; Begrich, *Die Chronologie der Koenige von Israel und Juda*, Tübingen, 1924; E. Auerbach, *Wüste und gelobtes Land*, II (1936), 20-28.

52

ISAIAH 53

fifteen years added to his life (II Kings 20:1–11; Isa. 38:1–8), that is, to the eighteenth year of the reign of Hezekiah, which is the year of the attack of Sennacherib on Jerusalem, 701 B.C.E. according to the cuneiform inscriptions [2]—even so, the prophetic career of Isaiah extended over thirty-eight or forty years (five years of Jotham, fifteen or sixteen of Ahaz, and eighteen of Hezekiah). In the course of a long time like this, it is inevitable that certain changes should take place in the spiritual processes of a man, even though he be the greatest among the great. Moreover, the long period in which Isaiah prophesied was filled with changes and vicissitudes in the life of Israel and Judah beyond anything that had gone before.

Isaiah prophesied in the time of four of the greatest kings of Assyria, whose numerous and frequent victories are now well known to us in almost all their details, thanks to the cuneiform inscriptions. These kings were Tiglath-pileser IV [*] (745–727), Shalmaneser IV [*] (727–722), Sargon (722–705), and Sennacherib (705–681).

Tiglath-pileser IV subdued almost all the kings of Syria with "Ruṣunu" (Rezin), king of Damascus, at their head; also "Menihime (mat)-Samerinai," that is, Menahem, son of Gadi, king of Samaria, became subject to him and brought him forced laborers and tribute.[3] Tribute was also brought to him by an Arabian queen, one Zabibe, and by certain kings of the far distant Sheba. He also fought against Gaza, subdued it, and banished its king, Hanan (734).

Meanwhile, an event of great consequence happened to Israel and Judah: Rezin, king of Aram (Syria), conspired with Pekah the son of Remaliah, king of Israel, and the two of them attacked Judah and Ahaz its king (Isa. 7:1; II Chron. 28:5). The account in II Chronicles (28:6) that Pekah slew in Judah "a hundred and twenty thousand in one day" is certainly exaggerated; likewise greatly exaggerated is the statement (28:8) that the Israelites carried away captive

[*] Most authorities give Tiglath-pileser III and Shalmaneser V.—TRANS.
[2] See II Kings 18:13, and the book of Hommel, p. 137 and also pp. 139–141.
[3] This fact is also mentioned in the Bible, where it is said that Menahem, son of Gadi, sent a thousand talents of silver to Pul, the king of Assyria (II Kings 15:19–20). "Pul" is Tiglath-pileser IV. This is his Babylonian name, whence comes "Poros"—Polos—Pul in the Canon of Ptolemy (see A. Jeremias, *Das Alte Testament im Lichte des alten Orients*, 3rd ed., Leipzig, 1916, p. 520, Note 4).

from Judah "two hundred thousand women, sons, and daughters." In Isaiah (7:1) it is stated that "Rezin the king of Aram, and Pekah the son of Remaliah, king of Israel, went up to Jerusalem to war against it; *but could not prevail against it.*" Yet it also appears from Isaiah that fear of Aram and Israel was great in Judah in general and in the house of David in particular: "And his heart was moved, and the heart of his people, as the trees of the forest are moved with the wind" (7:2). Isaiah tried to allay this fear by prophesying that in a short time Damascus would cease to be a kingdom, and that the kingdom of Ephraim would also be destroyed (7:8; 17:1–3). The prophecy about Damascus was quickly fulfilled. In the year 733, Tiglath-pileser IV made war, apparently at the request of Ahaz (II Kings 16:7-10), against Damascus and Israel; and in 732 Damascus was captured and became "a heap of ruins" (Isa. 17:1). From the king of Israel, Tiglath-pileser in 733 took all the land of Naphtali and many towns in Transjordania (II Kings 15:29; Isa. 8:23). "Ya'uḥazi (mat) Ya'uda'i" (Ahaz the Judean)[4] paid tribute to Tiglath-pileser together with the kings of Ammon, Moab, Ashkelon, and Edom. And when Pekah (Paḳaḥ in Assyrian) was assassinated, Tiglath-pileser placed Hoshea ('Usi'e in Assyrian) son of Elah on the throne in the year 733/2.

Shalmaneser IV "found conspiracy in Hoshea" (II Kings 17:4) and besieged Samaria for three years (725–722). But the beleaguered city fell only after the beginning of the reign of Sargon (722).

Sargon was a great conqueror. All the ancient world felt his impact and was shaken to the depths by him. He subdued Hamath, Arpad, Carchemish, Midian, Kittim (the island of Cyprus), Elam, Babylon, and even the kings of Sheba. He punished Moab, Edom, Philistia and "Ya'adu" (Judah) for sending tribute and bribes to "Pir'u sha-(mat) Muṣur," that is, to Pharaoh, king of Egypt (711).

Sennacherib, the son of Sargon, also made war against "the land of the Hittites," meaning the land of Canaan, and overthrew all the kings of Philistia, the kings of Canaan, and the kings of Ammon, Moab, and Edom. But in particular he fought against "Hazakiya'u

---

[4] "Ahaz" is shortened from "Joahaz" or "Jehoahaz," from which comes the Assyrian form of this name.

(mat) Ya'uda'i" (Hezekiah the Judean), because he had led a great conspiracy in which almost all the kings of Canaan rebelled against the king of Assyria; this war Sennacherib described in all its details in his great inscription.[5]

This was the political and historical milieu in which Isaiah prophesied. All these important political events, happening in rapid succession, took place in his time. In all these events Israel and Judah took an active part. It was inevitable, therefore, that they should touch the heart of the prophet. It was inevitable that these manifold changes and vicissitudes, which made such a deep impression on the spiritual mood of the ancient world in general and on the political situation of Judah and Israel in particular, should influence the spiritual mood of this great seer, who was not only a *preacher* with a religious and social message, but also a *practical politician*. In this Isaiah goes beyond Amos and Hosea and in a certain way comes nearer the pattern of Elijah and Elisha: he is not satisfied with preaching alone, that is, with a *remote* influence, but attempts to influence political policies *directly, frequently, and at close range*. He enters into conversation with Ahaz, and Hezekiah sends messengers to him to ask his advice. A man who is so close to political events will inevitably be more or less changed by their influence. If we could know at what time each chapter of Isaiah was written, we should certainly not find many contradictions in his prophecies. But this knowledge we now lack, and there is almost no hope that we shall have it in the future. Therefore, it is no wonder if many contradictions are found in his prophecies; particularly since the prophet is not a philosopher of *logic*, but a philosopher of *emotion;* in other words, not a philosopher of a system, but a philosopher of life.

Jewish and Christian exegetes attempt to resolve these contradic-

---

[5] On the strategy and particulars of this war, see my detailed article, "Cuneiform Inscriptions and Holy Writ" [in Hebrew], in the introduction to the translation of this great inscription (*Ha-Shiloah*, Vol. 11, pp. 160–162); and for the description of the war itself in Assyrian and in Hebrew translation, see *ibid.*, pp. 240–242 and also pp. 252–259. The article was published fifty years ago (in 1901), and of course it contains things that are antiquated; but it seems to me that it can still be used. See S. I. Feigin, *Missitre he-'Avar* [From the Hidden Places of the Past], New York, 5703 [1943], pp. 88–117; L. L. Honor, *Sennacherib's Invasion of Palestine*, New York, 1926.

tions by finding in each chapter of Isaiah "interpolations," that is, later additions. Sometimes they dissect a chapter, dividing it into a number of parts and attributing each part to a different author; and sometimes they attribute even one verse to several different authors.[6] I do not follow this extreme course. I shall attempt to give a complete portrayal of the Messianic beliefs and opinions of Isaiah according to the *majority* of the chapters that can be attributed to him without any *necessity* of dating them later or of attributing them to other writers. If in this portrayal there should be features that do not fit together perfectly, it is necessary to remember always that certain variations and inconsistencies are inevitable in the collected prophecies proclaimed by a prophet during the course of about forty years rich in changes and vicissitudes.[7]

Before I pass to the essence of the Messianic beliefs and opinions of Isaiah, I find it proper to make an observation about one important matter.

Only a few Messianic prophecies in Isaiah are marked by the words "in the end of days" or "in that day," by which the prophets for the most part indicate that their prophecy is directed "to distant days." For the most part it is possible to say definitely that Isaiah prophesied of days very near at hand: many of the Messianic promises were undoubtedly intended for the time and person of *Hezekiah king of Judah*. Of this kind are even the superb prophecies of the personal Messiah, which begin "for unto us a child is born" (9:5) and "there shall come forth a shoot out of the stock of Jesse" (11:1). The most likely possibility is that the one intended by these prophecies is Hezekiah.[8] Thus arises the question: Is it possible to consider all

[6] The English authority Cheyne has gone particularly far along this line in his well known book *The Prophecies of Isaiah*, London, 1880-1882.

[7] It is self-evident that when I speak of the prophecies of that Isaiah who prophesied in the time of Jotham, Ahaz, and Hezekiah, I exclude Chaps. 40-66 and Chaps. 13-14, which undoubtedly were written at a later time and about which I shall speak only when I reach the period of the Babylonian exile. Likewise, it is practically necessary to exclude Chaps. 24-27 and 34-35 from the prophecies of the original Isaiah, since these chapters are considered by many scholars to be later, for adequate reasons. But where there is no logical *necessity* to assign a later date, it is proper to depend upon the Hebrew tradition.

[8] The Jews in the time of Justin Martyr (*c.* 150 C.E.) still understood these prophecies in this way. See the book of Justin, *Dialogue with Trypho the Jew*,

these prophecies Messianic? Most modern scholars answer this question *in the affirmative;* and in my opinion, correctly. "The prophets hoped," says Castelli, the first of these scholars, "that the Messianic era would not be far distant; as happens to noble hearts in every age of decline (*decadenza*), they take pleasure in the hope of a near-at-hand revival. Thus Hezekiah was considered at one and the same time as the restorer of Hebrew sovereignty and the spiritual head of the other peoples. Therefore I consider these prophecies as an aspiration looking toward a general regeneration of all peoples, which in the imagination of the prophet was not so far away." [9]

When the Messianic expectations were not fulfilled in the time of Hezekiah, the nation—and perhaps also the prophet himself—postponed the fulfillment to a later time. Such postponement was natural and necessary. It was also *proper.* For the basic principle of the Messianic expectation is nothing else than the longing for the Golden Age in the future, whether near or distant—the exact time was not the most important thing in the eyes of the prophet or even in the eyes of his contemporaries and pupils, since fundamentally this was dependent on repentance and good works. And this basic principle is the secret of the eternal endurance of the Messianic expectations. By means of this all Messianism became an everlasting ideal. Gradually there was brought into being the conviction that the *complete* attainment of this ideal is not possible unless "all the peoples of the LORD shall be prophets." And this conviction made that ideal lofty and exalted, holding sway over the best of the human race in all generations.

Therefore I include here all those Messianic prophecies of Isaiah which were not fulfilled in the days of Hezekiah, even if they were intended to apply to that righteous and worthy king. Only those prophecies showing most clearly the influence of the passing events

---

Chaps. 43, 67, 68, 71. An echo of this belief is still heard in the Talmudic saying, "The Holy One, blessed be He, wished to appoint Hezekiah as the Messiah and Sennacherib as Gog and Magog" (Sanhedrin 94*a*); and in the saying of the Amora R. Hillel: "There shall be no Messiah for Israel, because they have already enjoyed him in the days of Hezekiah" (*ibid.,* 98*b* and 99*a*). See below, Part III, Chap. VII.

[9] See Castelli, *Il Messia,* pp. 99–100, 102.

which took place in Judah and Israel in the times of Sargon and Sennacherib—these alone I have not brought at all into the presentation here.

The Messianic chain of causes and effects, known to us from the Messianic prophecies of Amos and Hosea, stands forth strongly also in the prophecies of Isaiah. Sin causes punishment, punishment causes repentance, and repentance brings in its wake redemption, with all its majesty and splendor, with all the earthly and spiritual bliss which is in store for the righteous. About sin Isaiah speaks in the very first chapter of his book in hard and terrifying words, unexampled in all the books of the prophets. He calls the princes of Judah and the people living in Jerusalem "rulers of Sodom" and "people of Gomorrah" (1:10). These rulers do not protect the rights of the weak, they do not defend the cause of the orphan and the widow (1:23). The princes of Judah are "companions of thieves," loving bribes and pursuing rewards (*ibid.*). The hands of the people are full of blood, therefore even their prayer is an abomination and their offerings and feasts are burdensome (1:11–15).

Sin brings after it punishment without let or hindrance; the prophet prophesies a decisive annihilation for all sinners:

> But the destruction of the transgressors and
>   the sinners shall be together,
> And they that forsake the LORD shall be consumed (1:28).

The sacred terebinths which the transgressors and sinners have desired, and the sacred gardens which they have chosen, will become a shame and a reproach to them. They themselves will be as a terebinth whose leaf fades, and as a garden which has no water (1:29–30). God will be avenged of His enemies and adversaries in the midst of His people (1:24).

> The lofty looks of man shall be brought low,
> And the haughtiness of men shall be bowed down,
> And the LORD alone shall be exalted *in that day* (2:11).

"That day" is the day of judgment, the day of punishment. Then will man cast away his idols of silver and gold, and all the idols will utterly pass away (2:18, 20). Then will the LORD arise "to shake mightily the earth," and man will hide "from before the terror of the LORD, and from the glory of His majesty" in "the clefts of the rocks" and "the crevices of the crags" (2:21). But not man alone will be shaken and frightened. *All nature* also will be in terror of the day of the LORD. This should cause us no surprise. We have already seen that natural evil [catastrophe] was in the eyes of the prophets only the result of human evil. God, the creator of nature, cannot be the source of evil: if it were not so, two forces, good and evil, would be used by Him in mixed confusion and His character would not be complete, harmonious, essentially great. The deeds of man are, therefore, the source of evil both in society and in nature. Thus, when the day of judgment comes, nature, together with man, must be judged. And the description, in the Book of Isaiah, of the judgment that must be meted out to nature in the day of the LORD is one of the most lofty descriptions in prophetic literature. Here are those wonderful prophetic verses, perhaps unparalleled in all the world's literature for beauty and majestic power:

> For the LORD of hosts hath a day
> Upon all that is proud and lofty,
> And upon all that is lifted up,
>   and it shall be brought low; [10]
> And upon all the cedars of Lebanon
> That are high and lifted up,
> And upon all the oaks of Bashan;
> And upon all the high mountains,
> And upon all the hills that are lifted up;
> And upon every lofty tower,
> And upon every fortified wall;
> And upon all the ships of Tarshish,
> And upon all delightful imagery (2:12–16).

Such is the power of the Hebrew prophet! He observes nature and loves it; but God is the most powerful and the highest of all, and when He comes into judgment with men He will also judge the powers of nature.

[10] According to the Septuagint, we should read here "and high" ($\mu\varepsilon\tau\dot{\varepsilon}\omega\rho o\nu$) [instead of "and it shall be brought low"].

Fearful will be "that day." The prophet prophesies complete exile for Judah. Famine and thirst will be present (3:1). The captain of fifty will not be there any more; the mighty men and the warrior will be destroyed from the land. Judges, counsellors, prophets will be taken away, likewise sorcerers and enchanters will cease to be (3:2–3). Impudence will increase: "The child will behave insolently against the aged, and the base against the honorable" (3:5). This is the same impudence in which the later sages saw "footsteps of the Messiah." The LORD will enter into judgment with the elders and princes of His people because they crush the lowly among the people and the spoil of the poor is in their houses (3:13–15). Also the haughty daughters of Zion, to whom coquetry and flirtation are main objects and for whom their many various ornaments form the essence of life; also "the women that are at ease" and "the confident daughters," whose hearts are full of deceit, treachery and pursuit of fleshly desires and pleasures—upon these also will the LORD proclaim a severe judgment (3:15–24; 4:4; 32:9–12). The vineyard of the LORD of hosts—the house of Israel—will be laid waste and briers and thorns will come up in it (5:5–6). Many great houses will be desolate, without inhabitant (5:9). The earth will not give its produce: "For ten acres of vineyard shall yield one bath and the seed of a homer shall yield an ephah" (5:10).

As in the time of Amos,[11] most of the wicked in the time of Isaiah were confident and certain that they were thoroughly righteous. Hence they would say:

> "Let Him make speed, let Him hasten His work,
>   That we may see it;
> And let the counsel of the Holy One of Israel
>   draw nigh and come,
> That we may know it!" (5:19).

The prophet indicates to them that soon Assyria will accomplish the LORD's work in Israel and Judah, describing in very strong and beautiful poetic figures the might and speed of the Assyrian army (5:25–30). Fearful despair overtakes the prophet, and it seems to him that the people will not turn from their iniquity nor be willing to hear

---

[11] See Amos 5:18, and above, p. 38.

and understand the word of the LORD "until cities be waste without inhabitant, and houses without man, and the land becomes utterly waste," until "forsaken places be many in the midst of the land" (6:11-12). Even if only a tenth of the people remain, it too must again be "eaten up," that is, from it also must the unworthy part be selected and consumed; and just as there remains from the terebinth and oak at the time of "casting down" (Heb. *shallekheth*—the shedding of the leaves, or, more correctly, the cutting and felling of the trunk) only the stump of the tree, so will remain only the stump of the nation—its holy seed (6:13).

Furthermore, "the LORD standeth up to plead, and standeth to judge the peoples" (3:13), and makes "an extermination wholly determined . . . in the midst of all the earth" (10:23, also 28:22). In particular will He punish Assyria for her haughtiness and arrogance (10:16-19). The prophet feels, of course, that the work of destruction and the act of extermination are a "strange work" and an "alien act" (28:21). But what is to be done? The Israelites themselves are guilty of this: they "make a man an offender by words, and lay a snare for him that reproveth in the gate, and turn aside the just with a thing of nought" (29:21). Sin is the cause.

But terrible punishment will rouse all hearts to complete repentance:

> And it shall come to pass in that day,
> That the remnant of Israel,
> And they that are escaped of the house of Jacob,
> Shall no more again stay upon him that smote them;
> But shall stay upon the LORD,
>   the Holy One of Israel, in truth (10:20).

The remnant of Jacob will return unto God the Mighty (10:21). In that day man will turn to his Maker, the Holy One of Israel, and he will not turn any more to the idols, the work of his hands, nor to the sacred poles and incense altars (17:7-8; see also 27:9). Isaiah does not see, as does Hosea, a complete period of repentance lying in between the period of punishment and the period of redemption,[12] but he is

---

[12] See Hos. 3:4-5; see also the preceding chapter, above, p. 46. This fact is also pointed out by Hühn (*Die messian. Weissag.*, I, p. 20).

convinced that a fundamental spiritual conversion will take place after the punishment and because of it.

Innumerable times the prophet repeated the promise that only a very few, a small remnant and tiny fragment, "gleanings as at the beating of an olive tree" (17:6), would turn about in complete repentance and be saved in the day of the LORD.[13] But these survivors would be materially and spiritually blessed. Among these will be reckoned "every one that is written unto life in Jerusalem"; and each of these will be considered holy (4:3). These survivors will be a "holy seed" (6:13). For the people that dwell in Zion "shall be forgiven their iniquity" (33:24).

Zion will again become "the city of righteousness" (1:26; see also 28:6). She will be redeemed with justice and those returning to her will be redeemed with righteousness (1:27). For judges and counsellors will be righteous as in early times (1:26). Justice will dwell not only in the city of Zion, but also in every place, even in the desert (32:16). For the LORD will be "for a crown of glory, and for a diadem of beauty unto the residue of His people" (28:5).

This will be the *spiritual bliss* of the days of redemption.

But the *material well-being* will also be great. Over the site of Mount Zion there will be a cloud by day and the brightness of a flaming fire by night. A canopy of glory will be spread out over the righteous, and they will have a pavilion as a shade from the heat and a refuge and shelter from storm and rain (4:5-6). The fruitfulness of the ground will be amazingly great: "The growth of the LORD" (that is, the produce of the earth) [14] will be beautiful and glorious, and the fruit of the land excellent and comely for them that are escaped of Israel" (4:2). "Curd and honey shall everyone eat that is left in the midst of the land" (7:22). The LORD will give rain on the earth when needed and in abundance. Bread, a product of the soil, will come forth in great quantity; and the cattle will graze in broad pastures (30:23). Produce will be so abundant that the oxen and

---

[13] See Isa. 4:2-3; 6:13; 10:21-22; 17:4-6, etc. Cf. also 37:31-32.

[14] Contrary to the opinion of Sellin (in *Heilandserwartung*, p. 32), that "the growth [or "shoot," see Zech. 3:8 and 6:12] of the LORD" is a technical term for the savior and redeemer (see on this Gressmann, *Eschatologie*, p. 209).

young asses will eat "savory provender, which hath been winnowed with the shovel and with the fan" (30:24), that is, fodder mixed with sour grasses, from which the thorns are removed by a kind of sieve and winnowing-fork. Even the animals will no longer be forced to seek food anywhere they can find it or to put up with thorns. Upon every lofty mountain and upon every high hill there will be "streams and watercourses" (30:25). The increase in water supply will bring about marvelous fruitfulness of the soil, as described above. And in the matter of commerce, behold the profits and even the harlots' hire of Tyre will be dedicated to the LORD and to those who dwell in His presence, that they may eat their fill and dress in splendid clothing (23:18).[15]

The ingathering of exiles will take place at the time of redemption. From Ethiopia, Elam, Hamath, and the islands of the Mediterranean Sea the LORD will gather the remnant of His people (11:11):

> He will set up an ensign for the nations,
> And will assemble the dispersed of Israel,
> And gather together the scattered of Judah
> From the four corners of the earth (11:12).

Like Hosea (2:16–17), Isaiah also likens the expected redemption to the Egyptian exile (11:15–16). The redeemed and ransomed will sing songs and praises to the LORD (12:1ff.; 26:1ff.).[16] Judah and Ephraim will make peace between themselves (11:13). All the people will have peace round about them: "My people shall abide in a peaceful habitation, and in secure dwellings, and in quiet resting-places" (32:18). Jacob (Judah) will take root in his own land; Israel will blossom and bud, and together they will fill the face of the earth with fruitage (27:6).

---

[15] See *Mishpat ha-Urim* [Biblical dictionary] by Joshua Steinberg, article עתיק, pp. 655–656.
[16] These verses, and also the verse "And He will set up an ensign for the nations and will assemble the dispersed of Israel," etc. (11:12), have caused Biblical interpreters to think that a part of Chap. 11 (11–16) also, and other passages, are later. But I have already observed that exile and captivity, and hence the need for redemption and ransom, long antedated the Babylonian exile, and even the Assyrian exile.

And over these redeemed and blessed ones will rule the King-Messiah, *a personal Messiah*, Messiah *son of David:*

> For a child is born unto us,
> A son is given unto us;
> And the government shall be upon his shoulder;
> And his name shall be called: [17]
> Wonderful in counsel is God the Mighty,[18]
> the Everlasting [19] Father, the Ruler of peace (9:5, Eng. 6).

Authority (that is, the ruler and the government) will be great [20] in his time, yet nevertheless everlasting peace will prevail over them. For he will sit on the throne of David, and establish and uphold this throne "in justice and in righteousness from henceforth even forever" (9:6, Eng. 7).

From the whole content of the first verses of Chap. 9 we see clearly that in all these attributes Isaiah referred to Hezekiah, son of Ahaz, before he ascended the throne of the kingdom. Nevertheless, I, along with most modern scholars, consider this whole prophecy Messianic. The prophet *wished and longed* that Hezekiah would be a "wonderful counsellor" and a "prince of peace"; but Hezekiah was

---

[17] We should point *wayyiqqare'* [passive], since the Septuagint has καλεῖται.
[18] Castelli (*op. cit.*, p. 98) thinks the words "wonderful in counsel" govern "God the Mighty," and translates "mirabile consigliere dell' Iddio onnipotente" (wonderful counsellor *of* almighty God). S. D. Luzzato, in his commentary on Isaiah (*The Book of Isaiah, translated into Italian, and explained in Hebrew*, Padua, 1855, pp. 132–134), considers all these words one name, like "Spoilsoon-plunderquick" [Isa. 8:1], and their interpretation to be: "God the Mighty," who is "the Everlasting Father, the Ruler of peace," is also the "wonderful counsellor"—the deviser of wonderful things; and it is not the "child" and the "son" who is a wonderful counsellor, a mighty God, an everlasting father, and a prince of peace. This is close to the truth.
[19] In spite of all the opposition on the part of modern scholars, it appears reasonable to me to translate the word '*ad* as it was translated by Abravanel in his commentary on Isaiah: "booty." The contradiction between "father of booty" and "prince of peace" should not surprise us: "God the mighty (warrior)" also does not agree with "prince of peace." See in support of this translation Hühn, *op. cit.*, I, p. 21, Note 3; and in support of the translation "everlastingness" and against this translation, Castelli, *op cit.*, pp. 98–99, Note 3.
[20] Graetz has already noted that the final Mem in the word *le-marbeh* comes about because the letters *l-m* in this word were repeated by a scribal error from the preceding word *sh-l-w-m* (defectively written *sh-l-m*), which ends Verse 5. The reading must be, therefore, *rabbah ha-miśrah*, "the authority is great." With this the Septuagint agrees: μεγάλη ἡ ἀρχή.

ISAIAH 65

such a person only in a limited way. Hence the wish and longing of the prophet to see his ideal *completely* realized are his Messianic expectations.²¹

What I have said about this prophecy we must also say about the exalted portrayal of the personal Messiah found in Chapter 11. This is the most exalted portrayal of the personal Messiah which we have in the books of the prophets. Isaiah's Messiah is actually *the supreme man*, politically and spiritually, physically and ethically, alike.²²

A shoot will come forth out of the stem of Jesse, upon whom will rest the spirit of the LORD: the spirit of wisdom and understanding, the spirit of counsel and might, the spirit of knowledge and the fear of the LORD.²³ He will not judge by what his eyes see, nor decide according to what his ears hear. He will judge the needy with righteousness and smite the ruthless ²⁴ with the rod of his mouth. He will not strike with the iron rod or with the sword and spear: "with the breath of his lips shall he slay the wicked" (11:1-4).

> And righteousness shall be the girdle of his loins,
> And faithfulness the girdle of his reins (11:5).

By the righteousness and justice which this Messiah son of David will establish in the world, nature also will be changed for the better. We have already seen this thing in the prophets a number of times. And we already know the reason. The wise men of Israel, contrary to those of Greece, saw natural evil [disaster] not as an independent

---

²¹ Rudolf Kittel (*Die hellenistische Mysterienreligion und das Alte Testament*, Stuttgart, 1924, pp. 1-80) wishes to see in the "child" eating "curds and honey," who is a "mighty god" and an "everlasting father," and in the "young woman with child," and the like, distant echoes of the Egyptian myth about Horus-Osiris, which found its way both to the Canaanites (Adonis) and into the Greek mysteries—but the Hebrew prophet used them *unconsciously*. In my opinion these proposals have no weight.

²² On the details of these verses, which may perhaps actually contain distant echoes from an ancient and partly pagan past, see Sellin, *op. cit.*, pp. 279-286.

²³ These are the seven gifts of the Holy Spirit ($\tau\grave{\alpha}$ $\dot{\epsilon}\pi\tau\grave{\alpha}$ $\pi\nu\epsilon\acute{\upsilon}\mu\alpha\tau\alpha$), about which the early Christians speak. The Talmud (Sanhedrin 93*a* and *b*) calls them "six blessings."

²⁴ So reads Gesenius instead of "the land"; "the ruthless" would be parallel to "the wicked" at the end of the verse ("he shall smite *the ruthless* with the rod of his mouth, and with the breath of his lips shall he slay *the wicked*"). But both the Septuagint and the author of the Psalms of Solomon (17:35) already read "the land" [or "the earth"].

entity, but as the result of human evil [wrongdoing]. Since the prophets believed in a one and only God, not in many gods which embody the powers of nature, good and evil, they were *forced* to conclude that both good and evil proceed from the one and only God. And if good and evil have their source in *one* Supreme Being, whose nature must be absolutely perfect and harmonious (otherwise he would not be *one* and only, and therefore there would be a place for belief in dualism), then the Supreme Being by necessity creates evil *because of* evil persons and *for* evil persons. Thus, if the evil of evil persons, that is, human evil, should come to an end, *all evil* would cease, even natural evil in general. Therefore, Isaiah prophesies that when shall come the King-Messiah of the house of David, filled with the spirit of the LORD, the spirit of wisdom and understanding, the spirit of righteousness and justice, natural evil also shall cease:

> And the wolf shall dwell with the lamb,
> And the leopard shall lie down with the kid;
> And the calf and the young lion and the fatling together;
> And a little child shall lead them.
> And the cow and the bear [25] shall feed;
> Their young ones shall lie down together;
> And the lion shall eat straw like the ox.
> And the sucking child shall play on the hole of the asp,
> And the weaned child shall put his hand on the basilisk's den.
> They shall not hurt nor destroy
> In all My holy mountain;
> For the earth shall be full of the knowledge of the LORD,
> As the waters cover the sea (11:6–9).

Here the lot of man is joined with the lot of the rest of the creatures to such an extent that it is impossible to distinguish between them. But also in the vegetable kingdom and in inanimate nature a great change will take place. Just as they were changed for the worse in the day of judgment, so will they be changed for the better in the time of redemption: Lebanon will be fruitful like garden land [Carmel in Heb.] and the garden land will have numerous trees like a forest

---

[25] The female bear. Cf. "And there came forth two she-bears" (II Kings 2:24).

(29:17); even the desert will be fruitful like garden land (32:15). The heavenly bodies will also experience a profound change:

Moreover the light of the moon shall be as the light of the sun,
And the light of the sun shall be sevenfold, as the light of the seven days,
In the day that the LORD bindeth up the bruise of His people,
And healeth the stroke of their wound (30:26).

Supernatural wonders will happen to man: the deaf will hear the words of a book, and the eyes of the blind will see even—and this is a miracle within a miracle—in gloom and darkness; also the lame man will leap as a hart (29:18; compare also 35:5).

Now, if the redemption will act for good even on wild and domestic animals and on inanimate nature, then it is impossible that it should come to the world for Israel alone. Just as in the day of judgment God will punish all peoples, so will He do good in the day of redemption even to the peoples who afflicted Israel. The envy prevailing between Assyria and Egypt will come to an end, and the striving of both to rule over Judah and Israel will cease. The land of Judah will inspire awe in the hearts of the Egyptians (19:17). There will be five cities in the land of Egypt "that speak the language of Canaan, and swear to the LORD of hosts." [26] In the midst of the land of Egypt there will be an altar to the LORD, and at its border will stand a pillar to the God of Israel; and these will be a sign and a witness to the LORD: when the Egyptians cry out to Him "because of the op-

---

[26] Many Biblical interpreters (led by Duhm in his commentary on Isaiah) have wished to see in this verse [18], and in Verses 19–25 following it, a later addition added to the words of Isaiah by a Jew from Egypt in the second century B.C.E., in the time of the temple of Onias, in order to justify and explain the sanctuary which stood in 'ir ha-ḥeres (in the district of Heliopolis—the City of the Sun). But many exegetes who cannot be suspected of any orthodoxy whatever have risen against this hypothesis (see, e.g., Kuenen, *Einleitung*, 43, Note 5). It is altogether more possible that the words [in verse 18] "one shall be called 'the city of the sun'" [the city of destruction in the Masoretic text] are later. But even they, of course, were not written in so very late a time. If so, we should not have found them in the ancient Palestinian manuscripts of the Septuagint, where "city of righteousness" is written instead of "city of the sun." It is more probable that the Jews of Egypt found support in this verse in the time of Onias and introduced into it an idea that was not originally included in it. On the relation of these verses to the Aramaic documents of the time of Ezra (texts of Syene-Yeb), see the article of S. Daiches in *Ha-Shiloaḥ*, XVII, 507–508. On "the city of destruction," see also Joshua Steinberg, *Mishpaṭ ha-Urim*, Article 'הרס p. 190*b*.

pressors," He will send them a savior, who will defend their cause and deliver them (19:19-20). The Egyptians will know the LORD, they will worship Him with sacrifice and offering, and will make vows in His name. After He smites them, they will turn to Him, and then He will be entreated by them and will heal them (19:21-22). "In that day shall there be a highway out of Egypt to Assyria, and the Assyrian shall come into Egypt, and the Egyptian into Assyria: and the Egyptians shall worship [the LORD] with the Assyrians" (19:23). And the LORD will bless all of them together, saying:

> Blessed be Egypt My people,
> And Assyria the work of My hands,
> And Israel Mine inheritance (19:25).

Here we see the broad historical view of the prophets. The central point of political and cultural life in ancient times was sometimes the land of Assyria and sometimes the land of Egypt. But the prophets felt that their people had become—and must become—the center of gravity of spiritual and ethical life. And with their strong spiritual insight they saw the three great peoples in whom was compressed all the human history of that period united in fruitful co-operative effort in behalf of one great ideal: in behalf of the God of the prophets, the God of justice and righteousness.

But the two most powerful peoples of ancient times would not be the only ones to co-operate in bringing about peace and goodness. The distant land "which is beyond the rivers of Ethiopia" (18:1) would also bring an offering to the LORD: "In that time shall a present be brought unto the LORD of hosts (from) a people [27] tall and of glossy skin, and from a people dreaded near and far,[28] a nation

---

[27] Instead of "a people" we must have "from a people," as it is farther on, "from a people dreaded." So reads Duhm in his commentary on Isaiah, in accordance with the Septuagint; by this means the whole verse takes on a new meaning: the "people tall and of glossy skin," like the "people dreaded near and far," the "nation that is sturdy and treadeth down, whose land the rivers divide," are not the children of Israel, who bring a present, but the tall and glossy-skinned people of Ethiopia, from whom a present for the LORD will be brought to Mount Zion.

[28] I.e., from this place to places remote from here. [So Klausner interprets instead of the usual "from their beginning onward."—TRANS.]

that is sturdy and treadeth down,[29] whose land the rivers divide,[30] to the place of the name of the LORD of hosts, Mount Zion" (18:7).

This great day, in which even the most distant peoples will bring an offering for the LORD of hosts to Mount Zion, will be the great and exalted day of humanity, the day of the brotherhood of all peoples. We have before us the greatest and most exalted dream of peace, which humanity dreamed for "the end of days" through its chosen sons:

And it shall come to pass in the end of days,
That the mountain of the LORD's house shall be established as the top of
    the mountains,
And shall be exalted above the hills;
And all nations shall flow unto it.
And many peoples shall go up and say:
"Come ye, and let us go up to the mountain of the LORD,
To the house of the God of Jacob;
And He will teach us of His ways,
And we will walk in His paths."
For out of Zion shall go forth the law,
And the word of the LORD from Jerusalem.
And He shall judge between the nations,
And shall decide for many peoples;
And they shall beat their swords into plowshares,
And their spears into pruning-hooks;
Nation shall not lift up sword against nation,
Neither shall they learn war any more (2:2–4).[31]

---

[29] I.e., measuring and crushing its enemies. [Klausner interprets this enigmatic phrase as meaning literally "a nation of line and of treading-down."—TRANS.]

[30] Cut through and divide in two. *Baza'* is from the same root as *batsa'* in Hebrew and *b^eza'* in Aramaic.

[31] *The same prophecy is also found in Micah* (4:1–3), and it concludes with this verse, which is lacking in Isaiah: "But they shall sit every man under his vine and under his fig-tree, and none shall make them afraid" (4:4). But immediately afterward comes a verse (4:5) that does not agree with these universalistic ideas. Hence a number of scholars have seen fit to conclude that this prophecy was taken from a later prophet and inserted into the words of both Isaiah and Micah; other scholars conclude that both Isaiah and Micah heard this prophecy from an earlier prophet. But it seems to me that there is no basis for all these conjectures. Every word in this prophecy agrees perfectly with the spirit of most of the prophecies in Isaiah (minor contradictions must *inevitably* be found in the words of every prophet in general, and in particular in the words of a prophet like Isaiah, who prophesied during a long period of about

These words, together with the texts "He shall smite the land [or "the ruthless," see Note 24 above] with the rod of his mouth" and "The wolf shall dwell with the lamb," are one of the miracles of history. Amidst the fearful and cruel wars of the Tiglath-pilesers, the Shalmanesers, the Sargons, and the Sennacheribs, amidst the egoistic and ruthless world of ancient peoples, within little Judah which was then torn to pieces by internal party strife and was in fear and trembling before numerous and powerful enemies from without—there rises up the gigantic figure of the great prophet, who lifts himself above the cruel wars of the bloodthirsty and ruthless ancients, above national and racial hatreds, above partisan controversies, and prophesies of everlasting peace, of the brotherhood of peoples, of righteousness and justice, which get no help from the power of the mailed fist! . . . Isaiah does not prophesy of the abolition of nations: *they will remain nations*, but they will not any longer use armed force one against another. He does not prophesy of the assimilation of Israel in humanity. Israel will remain, *and remain in Zion*, with Jerusalem as the center of its life; but it will be preserved in order to teach righteousness and justice to all mankind, and it will be gathered in to Zion in order to make this place a place of instruction to all peoples.[32] This is the magic dream which the prophet of truth and righteousness dreamed in little Judah 2,600 years ago!

This dream is far from being entirely realized. Yet such is its divine greatness and such its eternal sacredness that it unceasingly continues to achieve a *partial* realization, without attaining *complete* realization. Therefore, it is the "spiritual-absolute" of the people Israel, if we may speak in the language of the Jewish thinker Nahman Krochmal; the "human-eternal" I would call it in my own language.

This charming "human-eternal" dream made the Jewish Messianic idea a world-wide, broadly humanitarian vision. For the quintessence of Jewish Messianism is included in this unique prophecy, and it has

---

forty years, as I have already pointed out in discussing this above, p. 56). Therefore I think that Isaiah was the author of this exalted prophecy and that it passed from the book of his prophecies into the collection of the prophecies of Micah, his younger contemporary.

[32] On this, S. D. Luzzato remarked already in the year 5618 [1858]. See *Iggerot ShaDaL* ("Letters of S. D. Luzzatto"), IX, 1335–1336.

made the Jewish Messianic idea not a national ideal alone, but also a universal ideal: the ideal of unceasing progress, of continuing spiritual increase—of the brotherhood of peoples, and of the Golden Age *in the future.*

CHAPTER VI

Micah (*c.* 723–700 B.C.E.) and Nahum (*c.* 625–610 B.C.E.)

MICAH WAS the contemporary of Isaiah, but apparently he was younger than the son of Amoz. At the beginning of the Book of Isaiah (1:1), it is said that the latter prophesied "in the days of Uzziah, Jotham, Ahaz, and Hezekiah, kings of Judah"; but at the beginning of the Book of Micah (1:1) it is written: "The word of the LORD that came to Micah the Morashtite in the days of Jotham, Ahaz, and Hezekiah, kings of Judah." Here Uzziah is not mentioned at all, and hence the conclusion that Micah was younger than Isaiah. But Micah also began to prophesy before the fall of Samaria: "he saw concerning Samaria and Jerusalem" (1:1; compare also 1:5–6). The historical events which occurred in the time of Micah and the historical environment in which this prophet lived were, therefore, very similar to the events which occurred in the time of Isaiah and to the environment by which this great prophet was surrounded; moreover, the flow of the ideas of Micah is very similar to that of Isaiah.

The sins which the rulers and rich men among the people were committing, and the evil influence of the false prophets, who spoke anything which the powerful put into their mouths, are described by Micah in very dark colors, that are not inferior to the fearful colors of Isaiah (see, for example, 2:1–2; 3:1–5, 9–11). In these passages the words of Micah recall the rebukes of Amos. It is clear that, in spite of all the blows which Judah and Israel were struck after the death of Jeroboam II and Uzziah, they had not improved their ways even a little.

And the prophet is convinced that sin will bring in its wake *punishment*. The LORD will go forth to judge His people, who have betrayed Him. He will come down from His holy habitation and will tread upon the high places of the earth; the mountains will melt under Him like wax before a fire and the valleys will be split open like waters poured down over a steep place (1:3-4). Samaria will be destroyed and become a heap of ruins. The LORD will throw down the stones of its walls into the valley, laying bare the foundations of these walls (1:6).

Zion also will be destroyed, becoming as a plowed field, while Jerusalem will be turned into a ruin, and the temple mountain will become a thicket (3:12). The sinful clan of the ruthless rulers and the powerful rich will have "none that shall cast the line by lot in the congregation of the LORD" (2:5), that is, they will not have a portion and inheritance on the soil of Israel. And the false prophets, who cry, "Peace, peace," preach prosperity, but prepare war against any "who do not put something into their mouths," will become dumb in the darkness along with the diviners and would-be "seers." For then the day will be darkened for Judah and Israel, and night will come upon them; that is, the day of punishment will come to them, and it will be impossible, therefore, to mislead the people with hopes and assurances that soon will come light and an abundance of prosperity (3:6-7). The punishment will be great and fearful: the people will eat but not be satisfied, they will sow but not reap, they will tread the olives but not anoint themselves with oil, and from the newly trodden juice of the grape they will not drink wine (6:15). Even what they remove from the enemy they will not save from capture ("thou shalt take hold, but shalt not deliver"), and what they save will fall by the sword (6:14). The land will be desolate and its inhabitants will perish. This will be the fruit of the deeds of the transgressors and sinners (7:13).

But the punishment will not be prolonged forever: "Though I am fallen, I shall arise," says the nation (7:8). It is bearing the anger of the LORD because it sinned against Him, but finally He will plead its cause and bring it forth to relief, as the measure of His righteousness demands (7:9). For He swore to the fathers of old that He would show mercy and faithfulness to their sons (7:20).

When the LORD again has mercy upon His people and casts all their sins into the depths of the sea (7:19), there will be at the beginning of the redemption an *ingathering of exiles*. The LORD will assemble all of Jacob (Judah) and also collect the remnant of Israel. Then the lands of Judah and Israel will give forth a great noise because of the multitude of people, as does a pasture field filled with flocks of sheep and goats (2:12). The LORD will also gather in the banished, the dispersed, and the oppressed of His people just as a shepherd gathers in the limping, the straying, and the castaway sheep. He will make the dispersed of Israel into a strong nation and He Himself will rule over them on Mount Zion "from henceforth, even for ever" (4:6–7). But they will also have a king, *the King-Messiah*: "their king shall pass on before them, with the LORD at their head" (2:13). For the King-Messiah will feed His people "in the strength of the LORD, in the majesty of the name of his God" (5:3). Likewise, the deliverance from Egypt came at the hands of Moses, yet nevertheless it is considered as though done by the LORD Himself, since Moses did his deeds at the command of the LORD.[1] For, like Hosea (2:15–16), Micah stresses the great similarity between the expected redemption and the exodus from Egypt in the time of Moses: "As in the days of thy coming forth out of the land of Egypt will I show unto him marvellous things" (7:15), says the prophet. So, there is in Micah also convincing proof of the opinion which I expressed in Chapter II of the present book, that the hope of redemption was influenced by the old tradition which Israel had concerning the Egyptian exile and the deliverance from this exile, and that the belief in the Messiah was brought into being by the early portrayal possessed by Israel of the gigantic figure of Moses—"the first redeemer" and "the savior of Israel," according to the Sages of the Talmud.[2]

[1] See Castelli, *Il Messia*, p. 103.
[2] Many scholars deny to Micah the prophecies included in the book bearing his name, from Chap. 4 to the end of the book (see, e.g., K. Budde, *Geschichte der althebräischen Litteratur*, Leipzig, 1906, pp. 86–87), and they assign a num-

In the time of redemption the children of Israel will be strong and courageous, and all the nations will fear them:

> Arise and thresh, O daughter of Zion;
> For I will make thy horn iron,
> And I will make thy hoofs brass;
> And thou shalt beat in pieces many peoples;
> And thou [3] shalt devote their gain unto the LORD,
> And their substance unto the LORD of the whole earth (4:13).

Jacob (Judah) shall be in the midst of the nations

> As a lion among the beasts of the forest,
> As a young lion among the flocks of sheep,
> Who, if he go through, treadeth down and teareth in pieces,
> And there is none to deliver (5:7).

His hand will be lifted above his adversaries and all his enemies will be cut off (5:8). The enemies of Israel will be confounded and put to shame and also "be trodden down as the mire of the streets" (7:10). Foreign nations will cease to despise the name of Israel. "They shall lick the dust like a serpent, like crawling things of the earth," and will fear and tremble before the LORD (7:17). For the LORD Himself will execute vengeance upon the nations which have not hearkened unto His voice (5:14). When the nations see all the great and wonderful things which the LORD will do for His people, they will stand in fear of Him just as Moab, Edom, and Philistia feared and trembled in the time of the exodus from Egypt. That these nations will take upon themselves the yoke of authority of the God of Israel and forsake their idols—such a hope we do not find in the prophecies of Micah. On the contrary, he says:

---

ber of these prophecies to the time of Manasseh (Budde, *ibid.;* J. Wellhausen, *Israelitische und jüdische Geschichte*, 7th ed., Berlin, 1914, p. 126), or even to later times—especially the passages of consolation in Micah. But, *first*, what could have been said in the time of Manasseh could also have been said in the time of his grandfather Ahaz, who was like him in his deeds; *second*, I have already shown above, where I spoke of Amos (p. 43, Note 11), that a prophet must almost inevitably envision both punishment and restoration.

[3] *W^{e}hah^{a}ramti* is not only the form of the first person perfect, but also of the *second person feminine* instead of *w^{e}heh^{e}ramt*, like '*ad shaqqamti D^{e}borah* (Judges 5:7) instead of *shaqqamt*.

For let all the peoples walk each in the name of its god,
But we will walk in the name of the LORD our God for ever and ever (4:5).[4]

Only in Israel will idolatry cease completely; and along with it will cease also false beliefs and wars:

>And it shall come to pass in that day, saith the LORD,
>That I will cut off thy horses out of the midst of thee,
>And will destroy thy chariots;
>And I will cut off the cities of thy land,
>And I will throw down all thy strongholds;
>And I will cut off witchcrafts out of thy hand;
>And thou shalt have no more soothsayers;
>And I will cut off thy graven images and thy pillars
>   out of the midst of thee;
>And thou shalt no more worship the work of thy hands.
>And I will pluck up thy Asherim [sacred poles]
>   out of the midst of thee:
>And I will destroy thy cities [5] (5:9-13).

For there will be peace in the land, hence there will not be any need for horses and war chariots, nor for fortified cities. Every man will sit "under his vine and under his fig-tree," with no one to make him afraid (4:4).

>And the remnant of Jacob shall be in the midst of many peoples,
>As dew from the LORD, as showers upon the grass,

---

[4] On the basis of this verse, which comes in Micah almost immediately after the prophecy, "But in the end of days it shall come to pass" (4:1-3), also found with minor variations in Isaiah (2:2-4)—a verse which obviously contradicts the universalistic ideas in the prophecy, "And all nations shall flow unto it"—a number of scholars conclude that the prophecy, "But in the end of days it shall come to pass," was inserted at a later time into the collection of Micah's prophecies. But, as it seems to me, in the prophecy, "But in the end of days it shall come to pass," there is nothing that would compel us to think that the Gentiles will forsake their gods *completely*. In the prophecy it is said that all nations will come to seek instruction and counsel on the mountain of the LORD; but probably at the same time they would not cease to walk "each one in the name of his [own] god." It must always be remembered that the logical processes of the ancients were very far from our logical processes, and that what we think completely contradictory they did not think contradictory at all. I have already spoken of this whole matter above, at the end of the preceding chapter. See there, Note 31, pp. 69-70.

[5] Our ancient Jewish interpreters regularly translate the expression "thy cities" as "thine enemies." Christian scholars read instead "thine images" or "thine idols" to make parallelism with "thy Asherim" in the first half of the verse.

That are not looked for from man,
Nor awaited at the hands of the sons of men (5:6).

To be sure, the day for building the walls of the nation is far away, but come it will (7:11). "Migdal-eder" (tower of the flock), near Bethlehem (or Ephrathah),[6] where David was born, and "the hill of the daughter of Zion," on which was set up and fortified the royal seat of the house of David—unto them will come "the former dominion," "the kingdom of the daughter of Jerusalem" (4:8). For from "Bethlehem Ephrathah," [7] the city in which lives "the least among the thousands [8] of Judah," will come forth one "that is to be ruler in Israel, whose origins are from of old, from ancient days" (5:1). This will be the *King-Messiah*. It is obvious that here is indicated only a king from the *royal line* of the house of David, which originated in Bethlehem, and there is no need to suppose that this king himself is to be born in Bethlehem. Likewise, the words "from of old, from ancient days" indicate only the antiquity of his origin (since from the time of David to the time of Micah several centuries had passed), but nothing more.[9]

When this Messiah arises, the punishment will cease completely: the LORD will let his people suffer "until the time that she who travaileth hath brought forth" (that is, until the one "that is to be ruler in Israel" is born), "then the residue of his brethren shall return with the children of Israel" (5:2). In other words, the redemption will begin after the Messiah is born and after the return of the Ju-

---

[6] See in Genesis 35:19–21: "And Rachel died, and was buried in the way to *Ephrath(ah)—the same is Bethlehem.* . . . And Israel journeyed, and spread his tent beyond *Migdal-eder.*" The ancient name of Bethelehem was Ephrathah, and Bethlehem Ephrathah and Migdal-eder were near each other.

[7] Ephrathah was the ancient name of Bethlehem (see the preceding note), and therefore there is no need for the emendation of Wellhausen (*Skizzen und Vorarbeiten*, Vol. 5, 2nd ed., p. 104), "Beth-ephrath"; nor for that of Hitzig (in his commentary on Micah), "Ephrath the least." It is to be noted that the Septuagint reads "Beth-lehem Beth-ephrathah," and not "Ephrath" as does Hitzig, nor "Beth-ephrathah" with cancellation of "Bethlehem," as Wellhausen would have it.

[8] I.e., "districts of Judah," like "I will search him out among all the thousands [districts] of Judah" (I Sam. 23:23). The word "to be" ("the least *to be* among the thousands of Judah") has been brought here superfluously (according to the correct opinion of Hitzig) from the end of the verse: "*to be* ruler in Israel").

[9] See Castelli, *op. cit.*, p. 105, Note 1.

dahites (who even at that time were in large measure dispersed) together with the northern Israelites to their land—after the ingathering of exiles or after all return to the LORD in complete repentance. The Messiah will lead his people "in the strength of the LORD, in the majesty of the name of his God, and they shall abide (in safety), for then shall it (the name of the King-Messiah) be great unto the ends of the earth" (5:3). And then will peace be established.

> When the Assyrian shall come into our land,
> And when he shall tread on our soil,[10]
> Then shall we raise against him seven shepherds,
> And eight princes among men.
> And they shall waste the land of Assyria with the sword,
> And the land of Nimrod with the keen-edged sword;[11]
> And he shall deliver us from the Assyrian,
>   when he cometh unto our land,
> And when he treadeth within our border (5:4-5).

The verb "he shall deliver" refers, apparently, to the King-Messiah. In general Micah emphasizes the real personality of the King-Messiah and its great importance no less than Isaiah. In this is to be recognized a sign of an important development going beyond the Messianic conception of the prophets who preceded Isaiah and Micah. But in the Messianic ideas of Micah there are also signs of another conception. Micah speaks a number of times about the vengeance which the LORD will wreak on the nations that persecuted Israel and did not give heed to the word of the LORD; and he prophesies that they will "be trodden down as the mire of the streets," that "they shall lick the dust like a serpent" and be filled with fear and trembling before the remnant of Jacob, which will trample and tear in pieces these nations "as a lion among the beasts of the forest, as a young lion among the flocks of sheep" (see 5:7, 17; also 7:10, 17). The desire for

---

[10] So reads Kautzsch in place of "in our palaces," in accordance with the Septuagint, which has ἐπὶ τὴν χώραν.

[11] Krenkel (in his commentary on Micah) reads, instead of biph^{e}thaḥeha ("in the entrances thereof"), biph^{e}thiḥoth (Ps. 55:22), i.e., "with drawn swords"; but Cheyne (*Jewish Quarterly Review*, 1898, pp. 580 *et sq.*) reads b^{e}thothaḥim ["with javelins"] (Job 41:21, Eng. 41:29), which is *tartaḥu* in Assyrian—a kind of spear (Wurfspiess). See J. Klausner, "The Cuneiform Inscriptions and Holy Writ" [in Hebrew], *Ha-Shiloah*, Vol. 11, p. 556, Note 378.

vengeance of a weak people, downtrodden by all the powerful nations of that time, speaks out from the mouth of the prophet. This is a natural and human feeling. But the real prophetic feeling in Micah comes to light in all those places in which he speaks about universal peace, about the cessation of war and the complete freedom which the peoples will have, each to walk in the name of its own god, and at the same time to find instruction in Zion and the word of the LORD in Jerusalem (4:1–5; 5:6).[12] The prophet here surpasses mere man and lifts himself higher, rising to that ethical height upon which a Jewish prophet of the Isaianic period must stand.

In the three chapters of Nahum's prophecy,[13] Messianic prophecies are very few, and many students of the Messianic idea in Israel conclude that there is nothing Messianic in this prophecy.[14] Actually, it contains some Messianic verses, but from them it is impossible to present a complete picture of the Messianic conception held by Nahum the Elkoshite. The scarcity of Messianic ideas in Nahum's book is explained, in my opinion, not alone by the fact that only three short chapters of this prophet have reached us. I have already pointed out once that I do not believe that many important Messianic prophecies were lost or forgotten in the course of time. The Hebrew people guarded Messianic prophecies of this kind as the apple of its eye, since they were necessary to national existence. Thus it is impossible that the Messianic prophecies of Nahum are few be-

[12] See Castelli, *op. cit.*, p. 107.
[13] It is impossible to determine with complete exactitude the time when Nahum the Elkoshite prophesied. We can only say with confidence that he prophesied not before 662 B.C.E., because he mentions the destruction of No-amon [Thebes] (3:10), which Ashurbanipal plundered in the year 663. Of Nineveh he speaks as of a city about to be destroyed. Nineveh was destroyed, according to the latest revelations of the cuneiform inscriptions, in the month of Ab, 612 (see C. J. Gadd, *The Fall of Nineveh*, London, 1923; J. Klausner, "The Fall of Nineveh in the Light of New Evidence" [in Hebrew], *Ha-Shiloah*, XLIII, 336–342); hence it is impossible to date these prophecies later than about the year 610. It would appear that Nahum prophesied in this year (610), and not in 625, after the death of Ashurbanipal (Budde, *op. cit.*, pp. 89–90). The difficulty of the mention of Egypt (3:9) has been resolved in my article just mentioned, *op. cit.*, p. 338.
[14] See, e.g., Castelli, *op. cit.*, p. 112. Many scholars consider 2:1 and 3 to be later additions (Budde, *op. cit.*, p. 90).

cause some of them were lost. The cause of the phenomenon lies within the book itself: Nahum did not prophesy concerning Judah (Israel had already gone into exile and no longer had sovereignty); he prophesied only concerning the fall of Nineveh, and the end which would soon come to the kingdom of Assyria. It is not surprising, therefore, that he did not have much to say about the national hopes of the people Israel.

But he was not able to omit mention of these hopes entirely. We have already seen that the Messianic prophecies are always connected with and attached to the events of the time, which are always related to the Messianic prophecies in one way or another. Therefore, it was inevitable that it should occur to Nahum, that after the downfall of Assyria, of whose heavy yoke Judah had been in constant fear, salvation would come to the house of Jacob (that is, the kingdom of Judah). For "the LORD is good, a stronghold [15] in the day of trouble, and he knoweth them that take refuge in Him" (1:7). The prophet assures his people that the powerful heathen kingdoms which had fallen upon the land of Judah had passed away and vanished never to return: "And though I have afflicted thee, I will afflict thee no more" (1:12), says the LORD. He will break the yoke of Assyria from off the neck of Judah and will burst her bonds asunder (1:13).[16] The LORD has had pity on both Judah and Israel whom "the emptiers have emptied out;" and He will restore "the pride of Jacob (Judah), as the pride of Israel" (2:3). And the day of redemption is very near:

> Behold upon the mountains the feet of him
> That bringeth good tidings, that announceth peace! [17]

[15] [The Hebrew reads "*to* a stronghold."] According to the Septuagint (τοῖς ὑπομένουσιν αὐτόν), we must read "to those that wait for him" instead of "to a stronghold." Thus the opinion of Wellhausen. However, it is possible that we should read "and a stronghold" instead of "to a stronghold"; then the verse would have a clear meaning. But it is also possible that the Seventy translated "to a stronghold" in the sense of "to those that find strength and hope in the LORD."

[16] Many scholars even consider the whole of Chap. 1 of Nahum as a later addition, a kind of psalm of the alphabetic type, which by much tampering has had its alphabetic form damaged (Budde, *loc. cit.*). This is nothing but conjecture.

[17] Cf. Second Isaiah (52:7): "How beautiful upon the mountains are the feet of the messenger of good tidings, that announceth peace," etc.

Keep thy feasts, O Judah,
Perform thy vows;
For the wicked one shall no more pass through thee;
He is utterly cut off (2:1, Eng. 1:15).

This is all of the Messianic portion of the prophecies of Nahum, who was more of a prophet to Assyria than to Israel. It is fitting to point out that the book of the prophet Jonah, who also is described as a prophet sent to Nineveh, is the one among the Books of the Twelve which contains no Messianic prophecies at all. There is no need for surprise at this. *First*, it is a moralistic story only; *secondly*, from Jonah's prophecies against Nineveh and from the repentance which the inhabitants of the Assyrian royal city manifested, it is possible to conclude that punishment was not necessary, since the repentance was sufficient; and where there is no punishment there is no redemption in the Messianic sense.

CHAPTER VII

Zephaniah (*c.* 630 B.C.E.) and Habakkuk (*c.* 620–610 B.C.E.)

ZEPHANIAH, THE son of Cushi, prophesied "in the days of Josiah the son of Amon, king of Judah" (Zeph. 1:1), and apparently he began to prophesy in the early years of the reign of Josiah. *First,* there was greater and more dreadful moral corruption in these years, before the book of the law was found (in the fifteenth year of his reign) and fundamental changes in the religious life of the nation took place;[1] thus the severe rebukes of Zephaniah would be much more suitable to these years. *Secondly,* Zephaniah uses hard words against "the princes and the king's sons," and this would be more suitable to those years in which the boy-king (Josiah became king at the age of eight years) was surrounded by princes and nobles who followed heathen ways.[2]

The Messianic chain, sin—punishment—repentance—redemption, is discernible also in the Messianic prophecies of Zephaniah.

[1] So, according to the testimony of the Book of Kings (II, 22). According to Chronicles (II, 34:3), Josiah began "to purge Judah and Jerusalem" long before this; but from what is said later in the same book (II Chron. 34:5) it would appear that the author of Chronicles exaggerated this somewhat in his praise of Josiah, as was his custom in everything concerning the good qualities of the kings of Judah.

[2] The reader can examine the events and the historical environment, concerning which and in which Zephaniah prophesied, in the next chapter, when I come to speak of Jeremiah, his great contemporary, who had more influence than Zephaniah, and apparently lived and prophesied for a much longer time than the latter.

The sin is grievous and dreadful. "The oppressing city"—this is the name by which Zephaniah calls Jerusalem (3:1). He says:

> Her princes in the midst of her are roaring lions;
> Her judges are wolves of the desert,
> Her prophets are wanton. . . .
> Her priests have profaned that which is holy (3:3-4).

She has seen all that the LORD has done to the rest of the nations, but has not been dismayed and has not received correction (3:6-7). The inhabitants of Judah have become so insolent and so confident in their own strength that "they say in their hearts: 'The LORD will not do good, neither will He do evil'" (1:12). All their doings are corrupt and abominable (3:7). They have not sought the LORD, they have never inquired after Him, or they knew Him and turned back from following Him (1:6).

Following hard upon the sins comes *the punishment*.

The LORD will stretch out His hand against Judah and Jerusalem and cut off all who are carried away by idolatry, and all those who have sinned against the LORD, who are full of extortion, deceit, and oppression (1:4-6, 8-9, 17). The wealth of the sinful men will become booty and their houses a desolation. They will plant vineyards, but not drink the wine thereof (1:13). Their blood will be poured out at the head of every street, and their corpses will be thrown out like dung (1:17). Even their silver and their gold will not save them in that fearful day (1:18).

But the sons of Judah are not the only ones who have sinned and transgressed: the sons of Moab, Ammon, and Assyria also have done evil in the eyes of the LORD (2:8-10, 13-15). Therefore the punishment will be general, shared by all the nations: "In the day of the LORD's wrath . . . the *whole* earth shall be devoured by the fire of His jealousy; for He will make an end, yea, a terrible end, of *all* them that dwell in the earth" (1:18; see also 3:8). On that day, that is, on the day of punishment, the LORD will destroy *everything* from upon the face of the ground (1:2). For the sins of men all nature will also suffer. This is the common view of the prophets, since natural evil is only the result of human evil:

> I will consume man and beast,
> I will consume the fowls of the heaven,
> > and the fishes of the sea . . .
> And I will cut off man from off the face of the earth (1:3).

Not only one people will suffer, but all peoples, all the sons of man:

> > And I will bring distress upon mankind,
> > That they shall walk like the blind,
> > Because they have sinned against the LORD (1:17).

The land of the Philistines will be destroyed (2:4-7); "Moab shall be as Sodom and the children of Ammon as Gomorrah" (2:9); the LORD will destroy Assyria and Nineveh, making them a desolation (2:13-15); even the Ethiopians will be slain by His sword (2:12). The LORD is God of *all* the earth and He executes judgment in *all* the earth. The broad view of this prophet of Judah encompasses all the space of all the world.[3]

And the day of the LORD is near: the LORD has prepared a sacrifice, and has consecrated His guests (1:7).[4] Great and dreadful will that day be beyond anything that has gone before:

> > That day is a day of wrath,
> > A day of trouble and distress,
> > A day of wasteness and desolation,
> > A day of darkness and gloominess,
> > A day of clouds and thick darkness,
> > A day of the horn and alarm
> > Against the fortified cities,
> > And against the high towers (1:15-16).

But, in spite of all the frightfulness of "that day" and in spite of the general destruction which looks out from it to all the earth, special individuals will be saved in it. There is one possibility of being saved from it—by means of *repentance*. The prophet calls to the people

---

[3] Modern scholars consider as later verses 2:4-15, containing prophecies against foreign peoples, 3:9-10, containing universalism of the type of Second Isaiah, and also 3:14-20 (the end of the book), the aim of which is to conclude on a note of consolation, like the end of the books of Amos and Micah (Budde, *Geschichte der altheb. Litt.*, p. 89; C. Steuernagel, *Einleitung in das Alte Testament*, Tübingen, 1912, pp. 636-637; S. Bernfeld, *Introduction to the Holy Scriptures* [in Hebrew], II, 482-484). But all this is unproved and unnecessary.

[4] See on this H. Gressmann, *Eschatologie*, pp. 136-141.

Israel—this is the "shameless nation"—to mend its ways before "the day of the LORD's anger" comes (2:1-3). The prophet calls out:

> Seek ye the LORD, all ye humble of the earth,
> That have executed His ordinance;
> Seek righteousness, seek humility.
> It may be ye shall be hid in the day of the LORD's anger (2:3).

"The humble of the earth" will be saved, and they will be found a kingdom lowly in the political sense, but great and noble in the spiritual sense:

> For then I will take away out of the midst of thee
>   —says the LORD—
> Thy proudly exulting ones,
> *And thou shalt no more be haughty*
> *In My holy mountain.*
> *And I will leave in the midst of thee*
> *An afflicted and poor people,*
> And they shall take refuge in the name of the LORD (3:11-12).

And the "afflicted and poor people," this remnant of Israel, will be great and exalted in its spirit:

> The remnant of Israel shall not do iniquity,
> Nor speak lies,
> Neither shall a deceitful tongue be found in their mouth (3:13).

The LORD will bring back those of His people who are captives and make them "to be a name and a praise among all the peoples of the earth" [3:20]. They will be at peace and happy not with spiritual happiness alone: they will also have *material prosperity*. They will not be afraid of the heathen nations and their hands will not be slack, for the LORD will cast out their enemies; therefore, "they shall feed and lie down, and none shall make them afraid" (3:13, 15, 19). They will also have *political success:* without war or the spilling of blood, the house of Judah—when the LORD redeems them and brings back their captive ones—will take possession of the Philistine cities (2:7). Likewise, concerning the cities of Moab and Ammon, the LORD says: "The residue of My people shall spoil them, and the remnant of My nation shall inherit them" (2:9). The people of the LORD will not fear evil any more, for the LORD will be in their midst, and He, the Mighty One, will save them, while He rejoices over them with gladness and exults over them with singing (3:15, 17).

It is self-evident that there will be an *ingathering of exiles* at that time: even those widely dispersed and far removed from Israel will be gathered to their own land; and these ingathered ones will be "a name and a praise among all the peoples of the earth" (3:19–20). Then the LORD will become king over *all* the earth and over *all* nations: "For He will famish all the gods of the earth: then shall all the isles of the nations worship Him, every one from its place" (2:11). Even the peoples "from beyond the rivers of Ethiopia" will bring Him an offering (3:10; compare Isa. 18:1–3). The spread of the acknowledgment of the LORD throughout all the world, among all humanity, is described by Zephaniah in these forceful and exalted words:

> For then will I turn to the peoples
> A pure language,
> That they may all call upon the name of the LORD,
> To serve Him with one consent (3:9).

This is universalism unique in kind. It encompasses the whole human race and dreams of the moral purification of all peoples and of their uniting in belief in one God, whom all of them will worship together, standing side by side,[5] without one people having an advantage over another. Not even Isaiah reached this prophetic height. The seventy years from Isaiah to Zephaniah did not pass by the prophets of Israel without leaving an impression. The inmost nucleus of prophecy, its *positive* part, the Messianic idea, continued to grow and develop, until it included all the peoples in the world without any distinction whatever.

Alongside the development of the Messianic universalism which is discernible in large measure in the book of Zephaniah's prophecies, we do not find in this book any traces of the individual human Mes-

---

[5] The expression "To serve Him with one consent" is literally "to serve Him one shoulder," and its interpretation is "to carry the yoke on one shoulder." The meaning in Zephaniah is that all peoples will serve the LORD with one pure heart, just as all will have one pure language to call upon the name of the LORD.

siah. The LORD Himself is the king and also the redeemer. It is possible that the kings of Judah preceding Josiah (Manasseh and Amon) and even Josiah himself in his youth did not furnish sufficient food for the imagination of the prophet so that he could dream about a human Messiah. By contrast, Hezekiah, for example, furnished food for the imaginations of Isaiah and Micah, who spoke about an individual human Messiah with great enthusiasm.

As in Nahum's three chapters of prophecy, so also in the three prophetic chapters of Habakkuk it is difficult to find Messianism.[6] Therefore, Castelli, for example, considers the book of Habakkuk as lacking Messianic verses altogether.[7] Yet actually, it contains two or three Messianic verses. Habakkuk prophesies a day of punishment for the Assyrians (or the Chaldeans) and says of this day (and not of the day of redemption, as the Talmud interprets): "Though it tarry, wait for it; because it will surely come, it will not delay" (2:3). Along with this, Habakkuk promises that in the day of punishment all the upright and good will be saved: "But the righteous shall live by his faith" (2:4). Like Isaiah (11:9), he too is convinced that the day will come when "the earth shall be filled with the knowledge of the glory of the LORD, as the waters cover the sea" (2:14).

The reason for the scarcity of Messianic verses in the prophecies of Habakkuk is, in my opinion, that which we have already seen in the book of the prophecies of Nahum: Habakkuk also definitely does not prophesy against the people Israel. The point of agreement between them—that they did not speak concerning the fate of the people Israel, but directed all their hard words against the Assyrians or against the Chaldeans—was the result of their love for the people Israel, which both the Assyrians and the Chaldeans strove to swallow up.

[6] Chap. 3 of Habakkuk is considered by the great majority of Biblical scholars to be later.
[7] See his book *Il Messia*, p. 112.

CHAPTER VIII

Jeremiah

(625–586 B.C.E.)

LIKE ISAIAH, Jeremiah also prophesied over a very long period. His prophetic career began, according to the witness of the text, "in the days of Josiah the son of Amon, King of Judah, in the thirteenth year of his reign," and continued during the time of Jehoahaz, Jehoiakim, Jehoiachin, and Zedekiah "unto the carrying away of Jerusalem captive in the fifth month" (1:2–3). This is a span of about forty years. During this long period, many political changes and vicissitudes took place in all the ancient world.

When the prophetic career of Jeremiah began (625), Assyria was still the dominant power, and King Ashurbanipal (668–626) was sending out from Nineveh authoritative royal commands to almost the whole ancient world; but thirteen years later (612) Nineveh was destroyed down to its foundations and literally disappeared from history,[1] until its ruins were uncovered in the nineteenth century. At the same time the kingdom of Babylonia raised itself up and returned to its ancient greatness under the rule of Nabopolassar (625–605) and his son Nebuchadrezzar II (604–592); and from that time it became the dominant power. Likewise Egypt, which had been torn by internal dissension for a long period, with its petty rulers subservient

---

[1] According to the prophecy of Nahum (3:11): "Thou also shalt be drunken, thou shalt swoon" [or "vanish"]. On the date of the destruction of Nineveh, which has now been made certain by a new Assyrian inscription, see above, p. 79, Note 13.

JEREMIAH 89

and paying tribute to the kings of Assyria, roused itself in those days and became a powerful kingdom thanks to the long and prosperous reigns of Pharaoh Psamtik (Greek form, Psammetichus) I (663–610) and his son, Pharaoh Necho (609–595). The latter conquered Syria and Palestine, and slew Josiah at Migdol [2] near the Egyptian-Palestinian border. Also, a powerful new kingdom appeared in those days upon the stage of history—the kingdom of Media, which took part in the conquest of Assyria.[3] And in Elam there rose to power at that time the royal house of Anshan, from which came forth Cyrus, king of Persia. Besides all this, the peoples of the East came into contact at that time with the peoples of Asia Minor (for example, with the Lydians and "Gugu"—Gyges in Greek—their king, who is the prototype of Gog,[4] king of Magog), and (634) with the barbarian Scythians (Ashkuza, related, of course, to Ashkenaz in the Bible). All these widespread political changes occurred during the thirty years in which Jeremiah prophesied not only to Judah but also to all the rest of the peoples of the [Near] East: "I have appointed thee a prophet unto the nations" (1:5), says the LORD to him in his first vision.

In Judah also great changes took place. In the eighteenth year of Josiah (620 B.C.E.), five years after Jeremiah began to prophesy, the high priest Hilkiah found a book of the law, which, according to the accepted opinion among the majority of modern scholars, was the Book of Deuteronomy, Chapters 4–28.[5] Josiah made, according to the injunction of the book that was found, a fundamental reform in the land of Judah and in parts of the kingdom of Israel (which, apparently, were also subject to him), burning idols and enforcing the statutes of the book of the law in all the territory under his rule. In this reform, which was, like every true reform, in large measure a

[2] So, apparently, we must read instead of "Megiddo," since the location of events requires it. Herodotus called this place "Magdolos" (see F. Hommel, *Geschichte des alten Morgenlandes*, 2nd ed., p. 152, note). In Zechariah (12:11) there is a "valley of Megiddon," and this is more like "Migdol." But see J. Klausner, *History of the Second Temple* [in Hebrew], I, 25.
[3] This event is now known in abundant detail (see J. Klausner, "The Fall of Nineveh" [in Hebrew], *Ha-Shiloah*, XVIII, 337–345).
[4] See below, in the chapter on Ezekiel.
[5] Against this view new objectors have come forth in recent years. See, e.g., Th. Oestreicher, *Das deuteronomische Grundgesetz*, Gütersloh, 1923 (*Beiträge zur Förderung christlicher Theologie*, XXVII, pp. 352–466).

return to the good practice of earlier times, Jeremiah of course participated. Josiah was slain by Pharaoh Necho (609), as said above. His son Shallum-Jehoahaz (609) reigned only a few months, and his second son, Jehoiakim (608–598), whom Pharaoh Necho made king over Judah instead of his brother Jehoahaz, did not walk in the ways of his father and was one of the worst among the kings of Judah in everything having to do with religion and morals. Meanwhile, Nebuchadrezzar II defeated Pharaoh Necho near Carchemish (605) and conquered all of Necho's subject territories. Jehoiakim, king of Judah, was likewise forced to pay him tribute for three years. Afterward he ceased paying the tribute, and Nebuchadrezzar invaded Judah (598); but in that year Jehoiakim died and Jehoiachin his son ruled in his stead three months. However, this unfortunate king ruled in the time of the siege of Jerusalem, and he was forced to go out to the king of Babylon, he and his princes and many of his nobles; and along with many of the heads of the state, military leaders, and men of wealth, he went into exile to Babylon (597). Nebuchadrezzar made king in his stead his uncle, the third son of Josiah, Mattaniah-Zedekiah (597–587).

The land of Judah had become like a ball tossed back and forth between Egypt and Babylon, the royal crown of Judah being given by the kings of Egypt or the kings of Babylon to whomever they saw fit. The fearful destruction drew near and arrived. An important part of the people had already gone into exile from the land and were scattered to the four winds of heaven. Pharaoh Hophra, Apries in Greek (588–569), stirred up Judah, likewise Edom, Moab, Ammon, Tyre, and Sidon to rebel against the king of Babylon. The weak Zedekiah listened to his princes and rebelled. All this Jeremiah saw —and he opposed the revolt. He knew from the beginning the end of the matter. He saw the long and fearful siege of Jerusalem, the destruction of the city so perfect in beauty, and the burning of the Temple; and he felt that the people needed strong and severe chastisement in order that they might mend their ways, but, at the same time, they needed also the cup of comfort in order that they might not reach the point of despair and come to abhor their calamitous national life.

This is the background against which the Messianic prophecies of Jeremiah, his visions of the day of punishment and his hopes for the end of days, took form. It is no wonder that these visions and hopes are very much different from the Messianic visions and hopes of Isaiah and all the rest of the prophets preceding "the man who saw affliction by the rod of His wrath" (Lam. 3:1).

While in the books of all the rest of the prophets it is only hinted at more or less distinctly that it is sin that causes punishment, in Jeremiah this principle is expressed any number of times with unique clarity. Says the prophet.

> Thine own wickedness shall correct thee,
> And thy backslidings shall reprove thee:
> Know therefore and see that it is an evil and a bitter thing,
> That thou hast forsaken the LORD thy God (2:19).

And it shall come to pass, when ye shall say: "Wherefore hath the LORD our God done all these things unto us?" then shalt Thou say unto them: "Like as ye have forsaken Me, and served strange gods in your land, so shall ye serve strangers in a land that is not yours" (5:19).

Their sin is great and very dreadful: the people have forsaken the LORD and gone after the Baals, and especially after the Assyro-Babylonian deities Shamash and Ishtar (2:20–23; 7:18, and so on). "For according to the number of thy cities are thy gods, O Judah" (2:28), complains the prophet. The heads and leaders of the people are no better than the rest:

> The priests said not: 'Where is the LORD?'
> And they that handle the law knew Me not,
> And the rulers transgressed against Me;
> The prophets also prophesied by Baal (2:8).

Nor have their sins become manifold only in matters between man and God; also in matters between man and his fellowman have they committed great sin. The prophet does not make such a sharp distinction between the two, since indeed idolatry could not make good social ethics strike root in the hearts of the people. King Jehoiakim, who turned aside from following the LORD, "buildeth his house by unrighteousness, and his chambers by injustice:" and "useth his neighbor's service without wages, and giveth him not his hire" (22:13). The blood of the innocent poor can be found in Judah not in a hidden place, but out in the open in every street (2:34). The princes of Judah do not plead the cause of the orphan nor defend the rights of the needy (5:28). And the common people of Judah belie the LORD, saying: "It is not He, neither shall evil come upon us, neither shall we see sword nor famine" (5:12). Therefore, they refuse to receive discipline and are unwilling to turn about in complete repentance (5:3). "Shall the LORD not punish for these things, and shall not His soul be avenged on such a nation as this?" (5:9).

Dreadful and numerous sins like these necessarily bring after them *punishment:* "Your iniquities have turned away these things, and your sins have withholden good from you" (5:25), says the prophet. Therefore, great and fearful will be the day of punishment. The LORD will scatter the sons of His people among nations whom they and their fathers have not known, and He will send the sword after them till He has devoured them (9:15). Even the remnant of them He will hand over to the enemy (15:9). Death, sword, famine, and captivity—these are the plagues that will come upon them (15:2). Those who are besieged by the enemy will eat the flesh of their sons and daughters (19:9). Those who fight the enemy will fall by the sword, their corpses becoming food for the birds of heaven and the beasts of the earth (19:7). Those left alive will lose the land which they possessed and serve the enemy in a strange land (17:4). For their land will become so desolate that every one passing by will be amazed and shake his head (18:16; see also 19:8). And not only will the common people suffer on the day of punishment:

> And it shall come to pass at that day,
> Saith the LORD,
> That the heart of the king shall fail,
> And the heart of the princes;
> And the priests shall be astonished.
> And the prophets shall wonder (4:9).

The palace of the king of Judah will become a ruin (22:5). And in general, the LORD will cast out of His sight the sons of Judah, just as He cast out of His sight their brethren, all the seed of Ephraim (7:15).

But the sons of Judah will not be disciplined alone on that day: also Egypt, Philistia, Arabia, Canaan (Phoenicia), Elam, Media, and so on, will drink from the cup that causes staggering (25:15-28). Likewise Babylon and all the land of the Chaldeans will become everlasting desolations (25:12).[6] Along with men *nature* also will suffer: natural evil [catastrophe] comes on the heels of human evil and as the result of it, as we have seen already a number of times in the words of the prophets. In a lofty poetic description, Jeremiah pictures all the darkness and all the terror of the great and fearful day of the LORD:

> I beheld the earth,
> And, lo, it was waste and void;
> And the heavens, and they had no light.
> I beheld the mountains, and, lo, they trembled,
> And all the hills moved to and fro.
> I beheld, and, lo, there was no man,
> And all the birds of the heavens were fled.
> I beheld, and, lo, the fruitful field was a wilderness,
> And all the cities thereof were broken down
> At the presence of the LORD,
> And before His fierce anger.
> For thus saith the LORD:
> The whole land shall be desolate;
> Yet will I not make a full end (4:23-27).

In the last words are already embodied the idea that after the punishment will come the redemption—at least for individuals of special merit [the elect]. "Behold, a storm of the LORD is gone forth in fury, yea, a whirling storm; it shall whirl upon the head of the wicked," says the prophet (23:19). But whoever turns from his transgression will be saved. *Repentance* is as a shield before punish-

---

[6] "Seventy years" is not an exact number, but an approximate one, to be interpreted as a complete generation. So it is with regard to the Babylonian exile, which according to Jeremiah (25:12; 29:10) had to last seventy years, but actually was not longer than forty-nine years (586-537). Cf. also "Tyre shall be forgotten seventy years, according to the days of one king," etc. (Isa. 23:15 and 17).

ment. No other prophet emphasized the value of repentance for the whole nation as did Jeremiah:

> Return, thou backsliding Israel,
> Saith the LORD;
> I will not frown upon you;
> For I am merciful, saith the LORD,
> I will not bear grudge for ever (3:12).

> And if thou wilt put away thy detestable things
>   out of My sight,
> And wilt not waver (4:1).

> O Jerusalem, wash thy heart from wickedness,
> That thou mayest be saved (4:14).

All these verses show clearly that everything depends on repentance and good works. To be sure, the prophet says, "The anger of the LORD shall not turn back until He have executed, and till He have performed the purposes of His heart" (23:20). Nevertheless, the prophet was firmly convinced that in the end Israel would not be entirely destroyed even in the fearful day of punishment. Time after time, even while describing the plagues, afflictions, and disasters, the prophet is emboldened to conclude his threats with a note of comfort: with the firm assurance that the LORD will not completely destroy His people, that of the Israelite nation there will be a remnant. This attitude we have already seen above, in the most fearful description of the day of the LORD. In another place the prophet says: "Go ye up into her rows and destroy, *but make not a full end*" (5:10). Also after the fearful prophecy that "a nation from afar" will carry out slaughter, pillage, and destruction in Judah, the prophet concludes, "But even in those days, saith the LORD, *I will not make a full end with you*" (5:18). Twice the prophet repeats these forceful words: "For I will make a full end of all the nations whither I have scattered thee, *but I will not make a full end of thee*" (30:11; also 46:28). Jeremiah emphasized more than all the prophets who preceded him *the eternity of the people Israel:* just as it is impossible that the laws of nature should be changed, that the sun should cease to give light by day and the moon and stars by night, so is it impossible that

Israel should cease to be a nation before the LORD for all time (31:34–36).⁷ *A remnant* of Israel will always remain, and this remnant will be gathered and gleaned as the grapes fallen from the vine (6:9). And for this remnant redemption will spring forth from the punishment itself:

> Alas! for that day is great,
> So that none is like it;
> And it is a time of trouble unto Jacob,
> But out of it shall he be saved (30:7).

Jeremiah even specifies how long this time of trouble will last: "After seventy years are accomplished for Babylon, I will remember you, and perform My good work toward you, in causing you to return to this place" (29:10; see also 25:12). To be sure, we have already seen that these "seventy years" are not an exact number, but are to be interpreted as about one generation; ⁸ yet

the prophet thinks of so long a time that he himself and the greatest part by far of his contemporaries cannot expect to live to see the beginning of the new period. What no other prophet did, Jeremiah does: he prophesies the redemption in the "end of days" without himself being able to hope that he will take part in it; for the belief in the resurrection of the dead, and the hope of thereby retaining the possibility of participation in the joys of the redemption, the prophet did not know. Thus this prophecy bears witness of the greatest unselfishness. Great value was placed, not upon single individuals but upon the nation as a whole. The belief in individual immortality had not yet developed; the people Israel as a group was considered immortal.⁹

At the beginning of the redemption there will be an *ingathering of exiles*. I have already referred to the words of the prophet, that the LORD will gather the remnant of His people as the grape cutter gathers up the grapes fallen from the vine (6:9). The house of Judah will be brought out from among the nations to whose lands they were banished, and will be led back to Zion (12:14; 23:3; 29:14; 30:3; 32:37; 46:27). Ephraim also will be ransomed at that time:

---

⁷ In Chap. 33 (25–26) almost the very same expressions are used with regard to the everlastingness of "the seed of Jacob and of David." But Verses 14–26 in Chap. 33 are completely lacking in the Septuagint, and apparently are a later addition.

⁸ See Note 6 above.

⁹ See E. Hühn, *Die messian. Weissag.*, I, 38.

"Rachel, weeping for her children" (the Ephraimites), will receive answer from the LORD that her "children shall return to their own border" (31:15–17). The LORD will have compassion on His "darling son," Ephraim, and "become a father to Israel," since Ephraim is his first-born (31:9, 20). The sons of Ephraim will join with the sons of Judah:

> For there shall be a day,
> That the watchmen shall call upon the mount Ephraim:
> "Arise ye, and let us go up to Zion,
> Unto the LORD our God" (31:6).[10]

For at the time of redemption, the LORD will be "the God of *all* the families of Israel" (31:1).

In the Book of Jeremiah there are five verses, in which are expressed precisely and with complete clarity almost all the Messianic ideas of this prophet:

> Return, O backsliding children, saith the LORD: for I am a lord unto you, and I will take you one of a city, and two of a family, and I will bring you to Zion; and I will give you shepherds according to My heart, who shall feed you with knowledge and understanding. And it shall come to pass, when ye are multiplied and increased in the land, in those days, saith the LORD, they shall say no more: The ark of the covenant of the LORD; neither shall it come to mind; neither shall they make mention of it; neither shall they miss it; neither shall it be made any more. At that time they shall call Jerusalem The throne of the LORD; and all the nations shall be gathered unto it, to the name of the LORD, to Jerusalem; neither shall they walk any more after the stubbornness of their evil heart. In those days the house of Judah shall walk with the house of Israel, and they shall come together out of the land of the north to the land that I have given for an inheritance unto your fathers (3:14–18).

In these few verses are included: (1) the repentance; (2) the ingathering of the exiles and the concentration of the nation in Zion;

---

[10] There are in Jeremiah still other unmistakable verses concerning this union: "In those days, and in that time, saith the LORD, *the children of Israel shall come, they and the children of Judah together;* they shall go on their way weeping, and shall seek the LORD their God. They shall inquire concerning Zion with their faces hitherward: 'Come ye, and join yourselves to the LORD in an everlasting covenant that shall not be forgotten'" (50:4–5). But almost all modern Biblical scholars consider Chaps. 50 and 51 later, since the conquest of Babylon and the kings of Media are mentioned in these chapters (50:46; 51:11, 28).

(3) Jeremiah's collective Messiah, that is, many kings, every one of whom will be good and worthy in the eyes of the LORD (about his individual Messiah I shall speak below); (4) the covenant with the nation and its material prosperity; (5) abrogation of the commandments in the Age to Come (see below); (6) the expansion of the recognition of the One God into all the nations in the world; (7) the union of the sons of Judah with the sons of Israel.[11] Every one of these Messianic ideas is set forth in any number of places in Jeremiah at great length. We have already seen this with regard to repentance, the ingathering of exiles, and the union of Judah and Israel. Also with regard to the abrogation of the commandments in the Age to Come, which is hinted at in the abrogation of "the ark of the covenant of the LORD," he speaks in a number of places at length and with clarity. Twice Jeremiah emphasizes the similarity between the redemption to come and the first redemption, the deliverance from Egypt—a similarity which I emphasized in Chapter II of the present work, having found it a number of times in the words of almost all the prophets. Jeremiah also points out the superiorities and advantages which the coming redemption will have over the older deliverance:

Therefore, behold, the days come, saith the LORD, that it shall no more be said: "As the LORD liveth, that brought up the children of Israel out of the land of Egypt," but: "As the LORD liveth, that brought up the children of Israel from the land of the north, and from all the countries whither He had driven them"; and I will bring them back into their land that I gave unto their fathers (16:14–15; 23:7–8).

The deliverance from Egypt will be forgotten in the presence of the redemption to come, because this last redemption will bring with it a new spiritual life for the Israelite nation. Here we reach those chapters in Jeremiah which have no parallel in prophetic utterances before or after him. Jeremiah dreams of a *fundamental change*, a *complete* revolution in the spiritual life of Israel. The LORD will create *a new heart* for his people and will pour out *a new spirit* upon them. *Instead of the law that is written will come a law that is in the heart:*

---

[11] See Castelli, *Il Messia*, p. 114.

> Behold, the days come, saith the LORD, that I will make a new covenant with the house of Israel, and with the house of Judah; not according to the covenant that I made with their fathers in the day that I took them by the hand to bring them out of the land of Egypt; forasmuch as they broke My covenant, although I was a lord over them, saith the LORD. But this is the covenant that I will make with the house of Israel after those days, saith the LORD: I will put My law in their inward parts, and in their heart will I write it; and I will be their God, and they shall be My people; and they shall teach no more every man his neighbor, and every man his brother, saying: "Know the LORD"; for they shall all know Me, from the least of them unto the greatest of them, saith the LORD; for I will forgive their iniquity, and their sin will I remember no more (31:31–34).[12]

It is almost possible to say with certainty that this great Messianic promise is that which brought about a fundamental change in the hearts of the exiles in Babylonia and caused a complete revolution in the life of Israel after the exiles had returned to their own land. From this deep and pure fountain Israel drew the finest of its qualities: the power of concentration on the *deep inner meaning* of the Torah; and the power of revolt against deeds that do not come from the heart—what is included in the great Talmudic demand: "Religious acts require the [right] intention"; also immeasurable love for the Torah and the conviction bound up with this love, that the Torah must be disseminated through all ranks of the people.

Also from this pure and deep fountain Israel draws everlasting life even to this day. For the intense preoccupation with the inner meaning of the Torah made it possible for them, without conscious intention, to adapt the Torah to the demands of life, since this intense preoccupation accustomed them to find in the Torah their whole spiritual life. The Torah which the LORD put in their "inward parts" and wrote on their "hearts" is the great and enlightening teaching which has remained very old, yet always new. So, the Messianic expectation, that the LORD will make a new covenant with his people for the Age to Come, has become a strong faith, whose *complete* realization is always expected in the future, but whose partial realization has not ceased from the time of the Babylonian

---

[12] Cf. with all this also 32:37–42 and 50:20.

exile to the most recent period. In this sense, Jeremiah broadened the Messianic idea and gave it power to form new national values more than all the prophets who had gone before him.

But whoever thinks that Jeremiah forgot, because of much spirituality, the *political-earthly* side of the redemption is quite wrong.[13] Jeremiah makes assurances that along with the spiritual welfare the political-material prosperity will be great. He prophesies that the LORD will break the yoke of Babylon and Egypt from off the neck of Israel and will burst Israel's bands, "and strangers shall no more make him their bondman" (30:8). He emphasizes any number of times that Jacob (Judah) will live in peace and security, and will not be terrified for any reason (23:4; 30; 32:37; 33:9, and so on). For his oppressors will be cut off:

> Therefore all they that devour thee
> shall be devoured,
> And all thine adversaries, every one of them,
> shall go into captivity;
> And they that spoil thee shall be a spoil,
> And all that prey upon thee will I give for a prey (30:16).

As the LORD watched over Israel to pluck up and to break down and to destroy and to afflict, so will He watch over them to build and to plant (31:28). The city of Jerusalem will be rebuilt on its own hill, and the *royal palace* will again be there as before. All the cities of Judah will be densely populated, while husbandmen and those that go forth with the flock will be numerous in the land (31:24).[14] For the LORD will multiply Jacob and make him exceedingly fruitful

---

[13] The opinion of Hühn (*op. cit.*, I, p. 40) is that, according to the prophecies of Jeremiah, the physical side does not hold a significant place in the Messianic kingdom. Hühn explains this, *first*, by the claim that Jeremiah's imagination is not very rich; *second*, by the serious nature of this prophet, for whom the fundamental thing was to show the importance of the forgiveness of sins and purity of heart. But by the claim that Jeremiah's imagination is not very rich can be explained only the fact that material prosperity is not described in his prophecies in excessively bright and imaginative colors; and the serious nature of the prophet from the time when the people Israel was still living on its own soil need not have prevented him from pointing out and emphasizing the importance of political-material prosperity. And of course the importance of this is emphasized in Jeremiah a number of times, as I have shown herewith.

[14] See on this at more length 33:12-13; see also 32:42-44.

(30:19). The city of Jerusalem will be expanded and be spread out on all sides, and all the nearby places which were desolate and in ruins will be joined to its borders (31:38-40). Also the "virgin of Israel" will be rebuilt, and on the mountains of Samaria the sons of Ephraim will plant vineyards and will have the use of their wine (31:4-5). A great company will return from the northland (Babylonia and Media) to the land of Israel, among them "the blind, the lame, the woman with child and [she] that travaileth with child together" (31:8); in other words, even the sick and those confined to their beds will muster up courage and return to their own land. Samaria will be "adorned with . . . tabrets and . . . go forth in the dances of them that make merry" (31:4). Also in Judah will be heard "the voice of them that make merry" (30:19). Judah and Israel will join together on the height of Mount Zion and will take delight in the abundance of good things:

> And they shall come and sing in the height of Zion,
> And shall flow unto the goodness of the LORD,
> *To the corn, and to the wine, and to the oil,*
> *And to the young of the flock and of the herd:* [15]
> And their soul shall be as a watered garden,
> And they shall not pine any more at all (31:12).

Jeremiah is the great mourner and the fearful pessimist, but his predictions of good things are greater than his predictions of punishment. As though by an inner feeling, the great seer senses that by words of rebuke and bitterness *alone* it is impossible to raise and exalt a nation. An unfortunate and downtrodden people needs divine consolation, shining hope, an affirmative ideal. But we have already seen that the affirmative part in the teaching of the prophets restricted itself not to what *is*, but to what *ought* to be. And the "what ought and must be"—that is the Messianic expectation. Therefore the most mournful prophet of Israel was also a prophet of comfort to a very large extent. We have already seen the spiritual well-being which the LORD has in store for Israel in the Age to Come. But

---

[15] These words alone are enough to prove that the opinion that the material side holds no place in the Messianic idea of Jeremiah is not justified.

material prosperity also is described in bold and shining colors. A sort of festival enthusiasm is felt in the following verses:

> Thus saith the LORD: Yet again there shall be heard in this place, whereof ye say: It is waste, without man and without beast, even in the cities of Judah, and in the streets of Jerusalem, that are desolate, without man and without inhabitant and without beast, the voice of joy and the voice of gladness, the voice of the bridegroom and the voice of the bride, the voice of them that say: "Give thanks to the LORD of hosts, for the LORD is good, for His mercy endureth for ever," even of them that bring offerings of thanksgiving into the house of the LORD. For I will cause the captivity of the land to return as at the first, saith the LORD (33:10–11).

It is self-evident that in that blissful time a noble king, filled with the fear of the LORD, will rule over Judah and Israel:

> And their prince shall be of themselves,
> And their ruler shall proceed from the midst of them;
> And I will cause him to draw near,
> And he shall approach unto Me (30:21).

This king will be of the house of David:

> But they shall serve the LORD their God,
> And *David their king*,
> Whom I will raise up unto them (30:9).

There is no doubt that here, as in Hosea (3:5), "David their king" is used in the sense of a king of the house of David.[16] There is also no doubt that here, as in the verses quoted above, "and I will give you shepherds according to My heart," and so on (3:15), is still intended only a collective Messiah, that is, one king of the dynasty of the kings of the house of David, whom the LORD will raise up for Israel. But we also find in Jeremiah *the individual Messiah*. After the verse, "And I will set up *shepherds* over them, who shall feed them; and they shall fear no more," and so on (23:4), in which also is to be seen an expectation of a collective Messiah, come splendid verses like these:

[16] See above, p. 47.

> Behold, the days come, saith the LORD,
> That I will raise unto David *a righteous shoot*,[17]
> And he shall reign as king and prosper,
> And shall execute justice and righteousness in the land.
> In his days Judah shall be saved,
> And Israel shall dwell safely;
> *And this is his name whereby he shall be called,*
> *The LORD is our righteousness* (23:5-6).

These last words are changed in another passage into a different form of expression:

> Behold, the days come, saith the LORD that I will perform that good word which I have spoken concerning the house of Judah.
> In those days, and at that time
> Will I cause a shoot of righteousness to grow up unto David;
> And he shall execute justice and righteousness in the land.
> In those days shall Judah be saved,
> And Jerusalem shall dwell safely;
> *And this is the name whereby she shall be called,*
> *The LORD is our righteousness* (33:14-16).
> [or, And this is the name whereby the LORD will call her: Our righteousness.]

If we could translate these verses according to the latter form of expression [as given in the brackets], we should be forced to conclude that the words "the LORD" are to be separated from the words "our righteousness" and that "our righteousness" is the name by which the LORD will call Jerusalem.[18] But I have already remarked above [19] that Verses 14-26 in Chapter 33 are entirely lacking in the Septuagint, and therefore it is to be supposed that they are a later addition. This supposition is strengthened by the fact that in Verses 17-24 of this chapter is emphasized the great importance of the Levitical priests, who here stand on the same level as the royal offspring of the house of Judah; and this is not in accord with the spirit

---

[17] In one Canaanite inscription we find the title "shoot of righteousness" [Cooke translates "legitimate offspring"] applied, apparently, to the heir apparent of the king of Sidon. See N. Slouschz, *Thesaurus of Phoenician Inscriptions* [in Hebrew], Tel-Aviv, 1942, pp. 110-111; G. A. Cooke, *A Text-Book of North-Semitic Inscriptions*, Oxford, 1903, pp. 83, 86.

[18] Cf. "Afterward thou shalt be called *the city of righteousness*" (Isa. 1:26).

[19] P. 95, Note 7.

of Jeremiah. Therefore, it is nearly certain that this addition came into the Book of Jeremiah at a later time; namely, in the period when Ezekiel had begun to enlarge upon the praise and importance of the Levitical priests.

But the text in Chapter 23, Verse 6, is also understood by different scholars in different ways. Some of them read: "And this is his name whereby the LORD shall call him: Our righteousness"; others read: "And this is his name whereby he shall be called [or, "one shall call him"]: The LORD is our righteousness," in such a way that the word *yiqre'o* [a form of the verb meaning "to call"] is indefinite.[20] Apparently even our Masorah itself is in doubt about the matter. The accents under [the Hebrew words for] "the LORD [is] our righteousness" serve to join these two words ["the-LORD" and "our-righteousness" are single words in Hebrew], but between them is a *pesiq* [vertical line], which serves to divide them.

It is worth while to take into consideration that the Septuagint (which, of course, differs more from the Hebrew text in the Book of Jeremiah than in the rest of the prophetic books) reads in this place: "and this is his name which the LORD will call him: Jozedek ('Ιωσέδεκ) *among the prophets.*" From ancient interpretations [21] it is possible to see that the authors of Talmud and Midrash considered the two words "the-LORD [is] our-righteousness" *together* as the name of the Messiah. This compound name will not seem so strange if we take into consideration that it actually has the same meaning as "Zedekiah" [the name of the last king of Judah].[22] "Jozedek" (or "Jehozedek") of the Septuagint, "the LORD is our righteousness" of the Hebrew text, and the name "Zedekiah" are basically one name. "Jozedek" or "Jehozedek" and "Zedekiah" are like "Jehoiachin" (II

---

[20] Kautzsch translated, "Und dieses ist sein Name, mit dem man ihn benennt: Jahve ist unsere Gerechtigkeit"; by contrast Castelli translated "E questo è il nome, col quale l'Eterno lo chiamerà: *nostra giustizia*" (*Il Messia*, p. 115, Note 1). On the translation of the Septuagint, see in the body of this chapter. The Vulgate and many Hebrew texts read: "And this is his name which they (plural number) will call him: the LORD [is] our righteousness" [or "righteous one"].

[21] See Baba Bathra 75*b*, Lam. Rabba 1:16, on the phrase "Because the comforter is far from me" (ed. Buber, p. 88), etc.

[22] This likeness has been correctly observed by Hühn, *op. cit.*, I, p. 41, Note 3. But he did not draw the proper conclusions from his observation.

Kings 24:6) or Joiachin (Ezek. 1:2) and Coniah (Jer. 22:24, 28; 37:1) or Jeconiah (Jer. 24:1). On the basis of all this, it appears to me that in this verse [Jer. 23:6] Zedekiah himself is indicated, he and no other. This proposal may appear strange at first sight, but after careful examination all who reflect will recognize its correctness, or at least its possibility.

Zedekiah was the son of Josiah, the brother of Jehoiakim, and the uncle of Jehoiachin. During the reigns of Jehoiakim and Jehoiachin, Zedekiah was an heir to the throne, who had grounds for hoping he would become king. From all that is told of him in Jeremiah (see in particular 37:3, 17–21; 38:14–27), it seems clear that he was not a hardhearted or cruel man and that he had confidence in Jeremiah. Several times he took counsel with Jeremiah and tried to do good to him. He made a covenant with the princes and all the people in Jerusalem to set free the Hebrew slaves, male and female "that none should make bondmen of them, even of a Jew his brother" (see 34:8ff.). And in spite of the severe rebuke which Jeremiah gave him for his rebellion against the king of Babylon, the great prophet prophesied of him thus: "Thou shalt die in peace; and with the burnings [of incense] of thy fathers, the former kings that were before thee, so shall they make a burning for thee; and they shall lament thee" (34:5). Jeremiah did not hate him, therefore, as he hated, for example, Jehoiakim. Is it, then, not possible that, during the reigns of Jehoiakim and Jehoiachin, when this young son of Josiah was not yet king, but was the king's son eligible for the throne of the kingdom, he was much closer to the prophets than he was afterward, when he had become king? And since he was by nature tenderhearted and amenable to discipline, Jeremiah and his fellow prophets might have hoped that he would follow their lead and return to the ways of his father Josiah, and upon becoming king would turn aside from the abominations of his brother Jehoiakim.

When I spoke of the personal Messiah of Isaiah,[23] I pointed out that the prophecies concerning the expected Messiah, "For a child is born unto us," and so on (9:5), and "There shall come forth a shoot out of the stock of Jesse" (11:1), were spoken originally with

[23] See above, pp. 56–57 and pp. 64–65.

regard to Hezekiah son of Ahaz while he was still heir to the throne and not king. Isaiah and his contemporary prophets hoped that he would become that ideal personal Messiah which they envisioned in their powerful imaginations. But Hezekiah was such a King-Messiah only to a limited extent; hence the people—and perhaps also the prophet himself—postponed the fulfillment of the prophecies bearing upon a personal Messiah to a later time, the Age to Come. Thus it happened also to Jeremiah: he dreamed that the kindly and gentle son of the king (in contrast to his brother, who as king was a much harder man) would be that "righteous shoot" whom the LORD would raise up to David, and when he became king would "prosper and execute justice and righteousness in the land" (23:5). Therefore in the prophetic circle (this is the interpretation of the words "Jozedek among the prophets" in the Septuagint) they called Mattaniah son of Josiah by the name "the LORD is our righteousness" or "Jehozedek"; and Mattaniah, when he ascended the throne at the behest of Nebuchadrezzar, changed this name to "Zedekiah," which is so close to it.[24]

The hope of Jeremiah was not fulfilled. Zedekiah deferred more to the princes than he did to Jeremiah.[25] So Jeremiah's prophecy about "the LORD is our righteousness" or "Jozedek" (Jehozedek) or "Zedekiah" was postponed to a later time, since it was not fulfilled

[24] From II Kings (24:17) it would appear that Nebuchadrezzar himself changed the name "Mattaniah" to "Zedekiah." But this explanation does not appeal to reason. Would the Babylonian king have given the king of Judah such a Judean name, containing the name of the God of Judah? We are forced to say that Mattaniah named himself thus with the permission of Nebuchadrezzar, and perhaps that this name ("Zedekiah") was well known even before this as a by-name. We find another example of this in "Eliakim," who according to the Book of Kings could be thought to have had his name changed to "Jehoiakim" by Pharaoh Necho (II Kings 23:34); but actually it is impossible that a pagan king should have changed the name "Eliakim," which could have been borne by a pagan, to the name "Jehoiakim," which could have been borne only by a king believing in the God of Israel (against Kittel, *Geschichte des Volkes Israel*, 5th ed., II, 535, Note 3; Ed. Meyer, *Der Papyrus-Fund von Elephantine*, p. 38, Note 2; M. Noth, *Die israelitischen Personennamen*, etc., 1928, p. 99, Note 1). We are forced to say also in this case that Pharaoh did not give the new king the new name, but that the Judean king so named himself, or others so named him, with the permission of the king of Egypt. That Mattaniah called himself by the name "Zedekiah" was also recognized long ago by the Midrash (see Pesiqta Rabbathi, Chap. 26, ed. M. Friedmann, Vienna, 1880, folio 129*b*).

[25] Cf. Jeremiah (38:5) with II Chronicles (36:12).

even to the extent that Isaiah's prophecy about the "shoot out of the stock of Jesse" who "shall smite the land with the rod of his mouth and with the breath of his lips shall he slay the wicked" was fulfilled. Hezekiah, the successful and religiously proper king, was much nearer the Messianic ideal of the prophets than the weak and unfortunate Zedekiah; and so the personal Messiah of Jeremiah was put further away in time.

The presentation of the Messianic opinions of Jeremiah would not be complete if we did not mention his sublime portrayal of the condition of the non-Israelite nations in the period of redemption.

At the very beginning of the Book of Jeremiah, we hear that the LORD had made him "a prophet unto the nations" (1:5); and we have already seen that "in the day of the LORD's anger" also Egypt, Babylonia, Philistia, Canaan (Phoenicia), Arabia, Elam, Media, and others will suffer. But Jeremiah includes the Gentile nations not alone in punishment; he also gives them a part and a heritage in the expected redemption. He clearly promises in the name of the LORD that "in the end of days" the LORD "will bring back the captivity of Elam" (49:39). Even to the evil neighbors of Israel, the LORD says: "After that I have plucked them up, I will again have compassion on them; and I will bring them back, every man to his heritage, and every man to his land." And he adds:

And it shall come to pass, if they will diligently learn the ways of My people to swear by My name: "As the LORD liveth," even as they taught My people to swear by Baal; *then shall they be built up in the midst of My people* (12:15-16).

This is the only condition which the LORD lays upon the Gentiles. And the great prophet is convinced that all the peoples in the world will fulfill this condition and acknowledge the lordship of the God of Israel. He says to the LORD:

> Unto Thee shall the nations come
> From the ends of the earth, and shall say:
> "Our fathers have inherited nought but lies,
> Vanity and things wherein there is no profit" (16:19).

"Then shall they be built up in the midst of My people," "Unto Thee shall the nations come from the ends of the earth"—to such a high degree of revelation does the weeping prophet attain, even though he saw all the peoples of his time trampling and treading upon his own small and lowly people! In spite of the fact that Jeremiah lived in the time of the decline of the people Israel, in spite of the fact that he saw with his own eyes the overthrow of the kingdom, the ruin of the country, the grave moral and social deterioration, he believes in the eternity of the Jewish nation, and he hopes, he is convinced, that the spiritual power which is stored up in this nation will prevail over military might, and that the plundered and despoiled people will become the spiritual center of all humanity. And he is so pure of heart and broad of mind that he does not keep the expected material and spiritual well-being for his people alone. All those who will learn to swear by the name of the LORD, that is, who believe in the God of Israel, will be built up in the midst of His people and will receive an equal share of the expected inheritance which the LORD will cause His people to inherit in the end of days. Also the prophet hopes that *all* the peoples will come and receive an inheritance in the midst of the children of Israel. This is the unique dream dreamed by the prophet of a small and humble people in a tiny land in a corner of Asia 2,500 years ago in the period of the despotic dominion of Nebuchadrezzar and his fellows!

Truly, the spirit of the LORD spoke through this great prophet, and only a few have attained the ethical height and the sublime dreaming of the last of the prophets in the period of the First Temple!

CHAPTER IX

Ezekiel

(592–570 B.C.E.)

EZEKIEL IS, in a certain sense, actually "the prophet of the Exile"; he began to prophesy in the fifth year of the exile of Jehoiachin (that is, in 592 B.C.E.) "among the captives by the river Chebar" (Ezek. 1:1–2);[1] and even if we assume that the prophecy which he delivered in the twenty-seventh year of the captivity of Jehoiachin (29:17), that is, in 570, was not his last, in any case his prophesying ceased a long time before the decree of liberation by Cyrus. Twenty-two years at least (from the fifth to the twenty-seventh year of the captivity of Jehoiachin) this great prophet prophesied, and perhaps longer; and all these long years he prophesied in the Exile, in the land of Babylonia. In this sense he may be called "the prophet of the Exile."

But not all of this long prophetic activity occurred in a time of complete servitude. Part of it fell in a time of relative freedom. For when the prophetic career of Ezekiel began, Judah was still a kingdom, "a sinking kingdom" to be sure, subservient to the Babylonians or looking for the aid of the Egyptians, but a kingdom in the ordinary sense of this word: Jerusalem was still a royal city, and the Temple still stood on its hill. Between the exile of Jehoiachin and

---

[1] Now there are those who think (e.g., Bertholet in his second commentary on Ezekiel, and others) that the prophetic career of Ezekiel began while he was still in Jerusalem, before he went into exile. But the arguments for this are not convincing. Torrey's thesis of a "Pseudo-Ezekiel" has been rejected by the majority of modern scholars.

the exile of Zedekiah eleven years passed (597–586); thus Ezekiel prophesied, since he began at the latest in the fifth year of the exile of Jehoiachin, six years before the Temple was destroyed and royal authority ceased from Israel (592–586). A great part of his prophecies were delivered, therefore, during a time when the last spark of hope that a change for the better in the political life of the land of Israel would still come had not yet been extinguished. The people who remained in the country placed their hope in the political maneuvering of King Zedekiah and expected the yoke of the king of Babylon to be broken; and the first exiles—that important Jewish "colony," ten thousand men in number, most of them owners of large properties, "mighty men of valor," and "the chief men of the land," who had gone into exile to Babylon with King Jehoiachin, his mother, his wives, all his eunuchs, and his high officials (II Kings 24:14–16; Jer. 29:2)—these first exiles to Babylon lived the political life of the metropolis and cherished the same hopes with which those remaining in Judah blinded themselves. Thus they considered their domicile in Babylon a temporary one, and the false prophets so strengthened their minds in this conclusion that Jeremiah was forced to send them letters to warn them that they must build houses, plant gardens, take wives in Babylon, and make an effort to settle down comfortably there after the fashion of people coming to settle permanently in a country, and must not live as mere temporary sojourners (Jer. 29). The prophet of the Destruction felt that Israel must be refined in "the crucible of affliction" in order to come forth purified like silver. A few days after the exile of Jehoiachin, the prophet already sees the vision of the "two baskets of figs" and considers the exiles in Babylon as good figs and those left behind in Judah with Zedekiah as bad figs; then he prophesies that the future belongs to the exiles in Babylon and not to those left behind (Jer. 24). Seventy years, in the opinion of Jeremiah, must the Judahites be refined and purified in the crucible of exile, after which time they will return and renew the people and the land (29:10).

This was in general the opinion of Ezekiel also. In his opinion likewise the exile is necessary and has a refining function. However, it will last not seventy years, as in the prophecy of Jeremiah, but forty years (Ezek. 4:6). In this Ezekiel was nearer the truth than Jeremiah. For, from the time of the exile of Zedekiah to the decree of Cyrus forty-eight years passed (586–538), while to obtain seventy years one must reckon from the destruction of the First Temple to the completion of the Second Temple (586–516). But in his view of the exiles, Jeremiah was nearer the truth than Ezekiel. The latter, although sometimes also in his eyes the exiles had a great advantage over the inhabitants of Judah, who took a hostile attitude toward those who had been removed from their land (11:15–21), nevertheless for the most part complained against the exiles no less than against those left in Judah. Because he had gone into exile with them, and because he lived in their midst, he was not able to see as well as he should have the great change which had taken place in them since they had been exiled from their land. As a prophet with radical moral demands it was enough for him to see—what was so natural and so human!—that a considerable part of them were still doing what their fathers had done or that all of them were still indulging in *some* of the corrupt practices out of the *many* being carried on by those remaining in Judah—seeing these things was enough to make him complain and rage against them and to shower on them fire and brimstone. The essence of the effort of the prophet was to convince them early and thoroughly that there was no hope for Jerusalem to escape and that, therefore, they must draw the line on everything that had been up to now and begin *a new life;* for, as long as the Destruction had not been consummated, the exiles were more or less close in their acting and thinking to those remaining in the land. Only when the words of the prophets had been fulfilled, and Jerusalem lay in ruins, did a new life *really* begin for the exiles. The change in thinking and doing which began in a certain part of the nation in the times of Isaiah and Jeremiah was completed in the time of Ezekiel, and of course not without influence from the ethical demands of the prophet of the Exile.

This was brought about by the political events and the material environment, to which was joined the influence of the prophets as a contributing factor.

Both in the exile of Jehoiachin and in the exile of Zedekiah, the heads of the nation, political and spiritual, were deported to Babylonia, leaving only the common people in the land. As I have already indicated, there were among these leaders of the nation many upon whose minds the teaching of the prophets had made an impression. In the Book of Jeremiah we find that a number of princes and elders of the land, such as Ahikam son of Shaphan, Zephaniah son of Maaseiah the priest, and Ebed-melech the Ethiopian (Jer. 26:16, 24; 29:29; 38:7–12)—all these being officials of high rank—were among those who sided with the prophet. There is no doubt, therefore, that when these important persons were exiled to Babylonia and experienced with their people all the evil which Jeremiah had foreseen, they were more than ever convinced that the prophets had spoken in the name of the LORD and that all their teaching was true. Thus these heads of leading families influenced greatly the whole community of exiles in the spirit of the prophets.

These exiles, who were a group of the elite, lived in Babylonia in large, crowded settlements, of the nature of Jewish "quarters" or ghettos, where they had dealings for the most part with each other, there being no stranger among them, although as merchants and vinedressers they also came in contact with the inhabitants of Babylonia;[2] and of course they accumulated wealth in this fertile land, as we see from the possessions which those returning from the Exile brought with them (Ezra 2:65–69; Neh. 7:67–72). We have in the "Murashu documents" reliable witnesses of the respectable occupations, large possessions, and important appointive positions which the Jews of the Exile held in Babylonia in the time of Ezra and Nehemiah;[3] and of course it was true even before this. We hear of the exiled group at Tel-abib, dwelling by the River Chebar (Ezek. 3:15; compare 1:1), of the settlements in Tel-melah, Tel-harsha, Cherub, Addan [Immer] (Ezra 2:59; Neh. 7:61), and elsewhere. It is the irony of fate that the two devastators of Judea, Nebuchadrezzar and

[2] See E. Klamroth, *Die jüdischen Exulanten in Babylonien*, 1912; E. Ebeling, *Aus dem Leben der jüdischen Exulanten in Babylonien*, 1914; J. Wellhausen, *Israel. u. jüd. Geschichte*, 7th ed., 1914, p. 142.
[3] See on this, S. Daiches, *The Jews in Babylonia in the Times of Ezra and Nehemiah According to Babylonian Inscriptions*, London, 1910; J. Klausner, "The Exiles in Babylonia in the Times of Ezra and Nehemiah" [in Hebrew], *Ha-Shiloah*, XXIV, 408–415.

Titus, are considered merciful kings (perhaps not altogether justly), who avenged themselves only on the Jewish rebels with fearful cruelty, according to the custom of their times. Nebuchadrezzar is shown by his many extant inscriptions to have had a love for magnificent buildings.[4] He did not oppress the exiles unduly and he gave them a certain amount of autonomy, so that many of them did not wish afterward to return to their own land.

In the midst of this economic and social ease there was also a rich cultural and religious life. In the large settlements, which were called by the general name "Golah" [Exile], the Hebrew language was preserved in its purity. There, especially on Sabbath days, which became days of festive assembly and gathering together, were heard frequent discussions about the politico-national and religio-ethical questions which were current at that time in the world of Jewry. There prophesied true prophets, false prophets, and prophetesses (Jer. 29:8, 15; Ezek. 13), and the elders of Israel would come to the prophet to hear from his mouth the word of the LORD (Ezek. 8:1; 14:1; 20:1). There people would discuss the prophet and his abilities and demands, talking about him "by the walls and in the doors of the houses"; and they would examine the words of the prophet not only from the standpoint of their truthfulness, but also from the standpoint of their artistic skill, saying of him that he was a "maker of parables," or was as "one that hath a pleasant voice, and can play well on an instrument" (33:30–32; 21:5). There they would read on Sabbaths passages of the Torah from the Book of Deuteronomy and passages from the early prophets.[5] And there, in this full political and spiritual environment, were coined various proverbs and epigrams, the very existence of which bears witness to the spread of characteristic religio-ethical views within broad strata of cultured persons, and to the intensive study of important social questions. Of this sort is the popular proverb, "The fathers have eaten sour grapes and the children's teeth are set on edge" (18:1), or the epigram,

---

[4] See C. H. Cornill, *Der israelitische Prophetismus*, 2nd ed., Strassburg, 1896, pp. 129–130.

[5] See Wellhausen, *op. cit.*, pp. 142–144.

"Our bones are dried up, and our hope is lost" (37:11), against which Ezekiel fought as views widely current in the Babylonian "Exile."

In this Exilic environment, which was full of national life and nationalistic thought, there sprouted and grew up among other things *the idea of redemption*. Naturally, this idea developed in one way among the majority of cultured people among the exiles, led by the false prophets, and in another way among *the few*: the true prophets and their disciples, led by Ezekiel. But even in the Messianic prophecies of Ezekiel, one must distinguish between those spoken *before* the exile of Zedekiah and those spoken *after* it.

As long as Judah was not completely devastated, most of the exiles believed that the redemption was very near. One prophet from Gibeon, Hananiah son of Azzur, prophesied at the beginning of Zedekiah's reign that "within two full years" the yoke of the king of Babylon would be broken and that Jehoiachin king of Judah and all the Judean exiles would return to Judah bringing all the vessels of the LORD's house (Jer. 28:1–4). A redemption more or less near was also prophesied by the "false prophets," Ahab son of Kolaiah, Zedekiah son of Maaseiah, and Shemaiah the Nehelamite, the last of these prophesying without any doubt in Babylon itself (Jer. 29:21–32). But after these dreams of theirs failed to materialize, many of the ordinary exiles began to despair of any redemption whatever. These despairing words became a current epigram: "Our bones are dried up, and our hope is lost; we are clean cut off" (Ezek. 37:11). And those who did not despair entirely of the redemption put the day of deliverance far away and changed its character as much as possible (12:22, 27).

We find the exact opposite of this in the Messianic prophecies of Ezekiel. In those oracles which preceded the final destruction, he definitely follows after and continues the Messianic idea of the older prophets, Amos and Hosea, Isaiah and Micah, Zephaniah and Jeremiah,[6] and prophesies of a comparatively remote time. However,

[6] This view is contrary to the opinion of many scholars (see, e.g., K. Budde, *Geschichte der altheb. Litt.*, pp. 152-153) that up to 33:21, where begin the prophecies after the Destruction, there are no Messianic oracles of restoration,

for political reasons, about which I shall speak below, they do not contain that universalistic breadth to be found in many of the Messianic oracles of these earlier prophets. Not so the Messianic prophecies after the Destruction. The Messianic conceptions in them are so closely connected with the political hopes of the *near* "return to Zion," of the great change destined to come about quickly in the status of the exiles, as well as in the status of devastated Judah, that it is sometimes possible to doubt their *Messianic* character altogether, that is, that they are conceptions of a distant expectation, of "the end of days."

But I have already touched on this important question in the chapter on the Messianic ideas of Isaiah.[7] If we understand properly the character of the prophets, and recognize that they were not only preachers and reprovers, but also *practical politicians*, who strove to make real their religio-ethical ideals in the political, national, and social life of their land and their people; and if we at the same time remember that the Messianic idea was never an abstract idea, above time and place—then we shall be forced to recognize that in every generation the Messianic conceptions were influenced on the one hand by the political situation, and on the other hand by a desire to take over the controls of the machine of the national, political, and social life of Israel and to incline this machine toward the will of the prophets, the creators of the Messianic conceptions. And when the machine of actual life would not or could not incline toward the ideal, the Messianic yearning of the prophet, then the prophet was forced to transfer his Messianic ideal to a later time, even to "the end of days." Thus did Isaiah attempt to realize his Messianic ideal in and through Hezekiah; but when he saw that all this ideal could not be realized in the actual life of the reign of Hezekiah he postponed the realization of that Messianic ideal itself to "the end of days." Thus did Jeremiah attempt to realize his religio-ethical and politico-social ideal through Josiah. He succeeded to a considerable extent, but not completely. Hence he was forced to postpone what remained to a

and that whatever Messianic prophecies appear in the chapters preceding Chap. 33 are nothing but later additions. This opinion of modern scholars is not based upon sufficiently strong proofs.

[7] See above, pp. 56–57.

remote time. I have already attempted to prove in the chapter on Jeremiah [8] that this prophet believed for a short time that Zedekiah ("the LORD is our righteousness") would be that expected Messiah, who would turn his people to a better way and prepare his land for the reign of the Almighty (witness the freeing of the slaves, which took place in his time, Jer. 34:5–22). Only after it became clear that Zedekiah did not dare to carry out the words of the prophet out of fear of his princes—only then did the prophet despair of this "puppet-king," while his *imminent* Messianic hopes became *remote* expectations, which he assumed would be fulfilled only after a long moral refinement and purification.

And thus the matter also in everything touching the Messianic prophecies of Ezekiel in the period before the exile of Zedekiah, except that "the prophet of the Exile" did not have a royal ideal of the present. For when he began to prophesy, it was already clear that Zedekiah was not an ideal king in any way. Ezekiel saw the Destruction as inevitable. He saw that complete political overthrow *had* to come and that after it would follow a more or less lengthy exile. Thus his Messianic expectations could not be connected with a time *very* near. Nevertheless, all these expectations do relate to a period *relatively* near, the period after the Exile, the period of "the return to Zion," and not to "the end of days"; but what appears to us as a period near at hand did not appear very near to the prophet, who saw in his imagination preceding it a period of complete devastation, a period of national ruin and of total exile. A period of bliss, which would come after destruction and exile, was already in the view of the prophet something like "the end of days," since the cessation of political life in his eyes was necessarily a tremendous, fearful, extraordinary event, the like of which the nation had not known before (the Egyptian exile occurred before the nation had a land and a kingdom, hence there was nothing to destroy). Therefore, even the hopes which he put into the heart of the nation, that it would return to its land and to its former condition, and would become greater than before—such hopes in the midst of such circumstances were actually Messianic expectations, even though they were not

[8] See above, pp. 102–105.

visions of "the end of days." For in these hopes are seen the same flight of fancy and the same sublimity which distinguish all the Messianic expectations of all the ancient seers. Here we have no *concrete description*, with details of the new political structure and of the new life, but *generalizing* imaginative descriptions, which embrace a new national era.

In everything having to do with the Messianic prophecies which Ezekiel delivered before the exile of Zedekiah, it is impossible, therefore, to cast doubt on the fact that although they were intended for a period not so far away from our point of view, yet they are properly to be considered as truly Messianic. The doubt is possible only in connexion with the Messianic conceptions offered by the prophet of the Exile after the destruction of the Temple. Then the calamity had already come. The great and terrible event—the total destruction—had already happened, and it only remained, therefore, to describe the *near* redemption, the expected future, which in a little while (after forty years, according to Ezekiel) would be realized in all its fullness. Here we cannot speak of "the end of days" at all. Everything spoken in these prophecies is intended in relation to "the return to Zion." Since the prophet did not live to the time when he would be able to see and to be convinced that his politico-social ideal had not been realized in actuality, he therefore did not have any occasion to transfer the realization of his ideal to a later time, to "the end of days." Since the expected future of Ezekiel in the second period of his prophetic career was near, and since it was not a poetic-imaginative creation, but a realistic affair, which soon, very soon, must be actually accomplished, there are in the Messianic prophecies of this second period detailed, concrete Messianic conceptions; therefore Ezekiel concerns himself with many details of the situation about to be, and therefore it is possible to consider these Messianic expectations a kind of political "Utopia," but a "Utopia" which the author believed with all his heart could be realized in life *very soon;* he was even ready, if time had permitted, to try and bring it into being.

Here it is possible to ask the same question that I asked about those Messianic prophecies of Isaiah son of Amoz which were intended to apply to Hezekiah, and the realization of which had to be near: Can the prophecies from the second period of Ezekiel be considered as truly Messianic? Here again I do not hesitate to return *an affirmative answer*. In the last analysis, the essential thing is not the belief of the prophet about the *time* of the realization of the expectations, but *the expectations themselves*, which by their very nature cannot be realized in a short time, and which even against the will of their creators necessitate the postponement of their realization for a long time. The very fact that we have here before us the prophetic ideal, that is to say, the positive part of the prophet's work, is sufficient to make these expectations Messianic and to give them a place in this study.

However, one obligation is laid upon us: to distinguish between these *near* expectations and the *remote* expectations, to emphasize properly the difference in the Messianic prophecies of Ezekiel before the Destruction and after it, and not to confuse one with the other in any manner. This distinction between these two kinds of prophecies is of course difficult, because the time of composition is not recorded in every chapter of the Book of Ezekiel.[9] Yet this general rule must be kept in mind: in any place where the Messianic prophecies of Ezekiel are close in spirit and content to those of the prophets who preceded him, in any place where he speaks of political success and material prosperity in a general way, or in a specific way about the kingdom of the house of David—there we have prophecies which preceded the Destruction or which followed it after a very short time. In contrast to this, in any place where the prophet speaks in great detail of the restoration of the land, the revival of the nation, and the rebuilding of the Temple, while the king of the house of David is not mentioned at all, or in his place comes the "Prince"— there we are concerned with prophecies after the Destruction.

The Messianic prophecies of Ezekiel have one special characteristic: the *redemption* does not come in them as the result of *repent-*

[9] See the statements of Budde (*op. cit.*, p. 152, Note 2) about indications of the dates of prophecies in the Book of Ezekiel, which for the most part are more exact than in the rest of the prophetic books; but there are also later additions in Ezekiel, which were inserted by Ezekiel himself or by his immediate disciples into his earlier prophecies (*ibid.*, pp. 154-155). S. Bernfeld (*Introduction* [in Hebrew], II, 415-446) went further than this.

ance. The Messianic chain already known to us—sin, punishment, repentance, redemption—has been here pulled apart, therefore, and one of its links is missing, even in the oracles of Ezekiel which preceded the Destruction. Not as a reward because Israel had turned from its evil way would Israel be redeemed and return to its own land, but rather, the Holy One, Blessed is He, would do Israel an act of mercy "for His name's sake." The LORD cannot approve of His holy name's being profaned among the nations, "in that men said of them: These are the people of the LORD, and are gone forth out of his land" (Ezek. 36:20–21; see also 20:44; 28:25; 39:25, 27, and so on).[10] The prophet expressly says in the name of the LORD: "I do not this for your sake, O house of Israel, but for My holy name" (36:22–23); and farther on, with special emphasis and sharp rebuke: "Not for your sake do I this, saith the Lord God, *be it known unto you;* be ashamed and confounded for your ways, O house of Israel" (36:22). The idea of "the sanctification of the divine Name" and of "the profanation of the divine Name"—this religio-philosophical concept, the depth of whose meaning modern scholars have not yet plumbed to this day—receives in the prophecies of Ezekiel a content and value, before the profundity of which we stand trembling. The *glory of God* is here elevated to a kind of exalted ethical maxim like "the dignity of man" (*Menschenwürde*), which is the cornerstone in the structure of the ethical teaching of Kant. The LORD is *obligated* to redeem His people not because the people will turn in repentance, but because He made a covenant with them in the days of their youth (16:60–62) and through this they were called by His name; so how can He give them over to derision and reproach among the nations? Israel will return to its God not *before* the redemption, but *after it:* after it has returned to its own land. There and then, and only then, will it be ashamed of its iniquities, and cease to do its evil deeds. This idea is emphasized in almost all of the Messianic prophecies of Ezekiel (see particularly 11:18; 20:43; 36:31; 39:26, and so on).

How shall we explain this special characteristic of the Messianic expectations in Ezekiel?

---

[10] On Chap. 36 in particular see D. Castelli, *Il Messia*, p. 122.

In my opinion the explanation is to be sought in the personal character of the prophet, on the one hand, and in his relation to the events of his time, on the other hand.

Ezekiel was perhaps the most severe of the prophets. The rebukes in his prophecies are very fearful, piercing down to the depths of the soul and pitilessly laying bare the uncongealed wounds of the inmost life of the nation. Chapters 16 and 23 will remain as credible witnesses to his bitter feelings and severity of expression. He does not rebuke—he strikes with rods of iron. Sodom is virtuous in his eyes as compared with Jerusalem (16:48); Philistia is ashamed of the wicked way of Judah (16:27). This prophet is filled with a sort of flaming hatred against the nation, which he calls with suppressed fury "the rebellious house" (2:5; 3:9, and so on), and against Jerusalem, which he calls "the pot whose filth is therein" (24:6); and he prophesies for them a decisive end without mercy and without pity (9:10). If a few men of Judah survive, they will survive not from the compassion of the LORD for His people, but "that they may declare all their abominations among the nations whither they come" (12:16). At the same time, the victories and consolations, which he heralds like all the prophets of Israel, are not great in quantity nor even so splendid in quality. They are not portrayed in rich and glorious poetic descriptions like those in the prophecies of Isaiah and Jeremiah. This will surprise us all the more, if we remind ourselves of the fact that Ezekiel was possessed of an extraordinarily vivid imagination, and that his "visions of God" surpass in magical beauty anything seen by the rest of the prophets. Moreover, his idea of divine consolation does not contain softness and pleasure in that degree which we find in Hosea, Isaiah, and Jeremiah, preceding him, and in Deutero-Isaiah, following him. This fact can be explained partly by his naturally harsh disposition, which was hardened still more by his enforced exile from the land of his birth, and by his growing up in a strange environment, on foreign soil; also, the imminent hope of a change for the better did not soften the hardness of his lot of exile, as it did in the case of Deutero-Isaiah.

But besides this, the paucity of consolation and the abundance of rebuke are to be explained even more by *the circumstances of the time.* The Exile, that is, the uprooting from the national soil and the cessation of political life, whose prosperity or decline were a reward or punishment for the whole nation *collectively,* forced the prophet to stress the importance of the religio-ethical *personality* and to point out that "a man shall die for his own sin." In other words, from now on, private individual rewards and punishments had to take the place of collective national rewards and punishments. Therefore, the prophet of the Exile was forced to lay upon each man of Israel the moral responsibility for all his deeds, and consequently to enlarge and deepen the "ethical imperative"—that moral rigorism which has no place for softness and delicacy, its victory over sentiment and its subjection of all the sentiment to the postulates of moral obligation being its greatness and its high dignity.

The very strength of the religio-ethical imperative, this effort at religio-ethical rigorism, brought it about (as I have already indicated above) that Ezekiel did not clearly see at first the changes for the better that the exiles were gradually beginning to experience. Since they did not satisfy *all* his religio-ethical demands, he still saw in them a "rebellious house, that have eyes to see, and see not, that have ears to hear, and hear not" (12:2). He still saw in them evil and sinful men, who still persisted in their rebellion and by all the blows which they had received had not been roused to repentance. And indeed in Ezekiel's time, the fundamental revolution, which afterward changed the exiles beyond recognition, had not yet had sufficient time to take on final form or to be revealed in its strength; thus the prophet concluded that the redemption must come without any relation to the repentance which normally would precede it. With this we approach those splendid verses in Ezekiel, the grandeur of which amazes us no less than their severity, and both together make them one of the marvels of the entire literature of mankind.

Israel does not wish to turn to the ways of repentance. Indeed, it does not wish to be redeemed at all. It wishes to be as all the nations and be free of both afflictions and redemption. . . . Such a conception could not occur to the people before the Destruction. Then afflictions were not so great, and redemption was necessary only to strengthen the political and national power of a people still vital and healthy. But in the time of Ezekiel a conception like this was natural, and almost necessary. The afflictions were very great, and the exiles, when they contemplated the political and national power of the mighty and potent Babylonian nation, which had subjugated them and subdued half the world, were necessarily small and humble in their own eyes, truly "the worm Jacob" (Isa. 41:14). Why, therefore, should they remain *a peculiar people* in the midst of all the rest of the idolatrous and power-worshiping peoples, alone to serve only one God, and alone to satisfy a burdensome ethical requirement? Ezekiel, for whom *duty* became the fundamental of all fundamentals, once again cannot be satisfied with the ideas dear to the earlier prophets: that the acknowledgment of the LORD, which is peculiar to Israel, is its special privilege, that Israel's preservation and continued existence are matters of its own choice, that the redemption and the Days of the Messiah are great advantages for a specially favored people. With his usual ethical severity he raises his voice against his people and like thunder in the storm he roars his harsh word: No! An obligation is laid upon Israel to live by its faith! There is no choice, no privilege! The LORD will *compel* His people to preserve themselves and be redeemed, and *afterward*—also to return to Him! The words of the prophet truly are like fire and like a hammer breaking in pieces a rock:

and that which cometh into your mind shall not be at all; in that ye say: We will be as the nations, as the families of the countries, to serve wood and stone. As I live, saith the Lord God, surely with a mighty hand, and with an outstretched arm, and with fury poured out, will I be king over you; and I will bring you out from the peoples, and will gather you out of the countries wherein ye are scattered, with a mighty hand, and with an outstretched arm, and with fury poured out (20:32-34).

The matter is clear: not only preservation, but also the ingathering of exiles and the redemption themselves will be "with a mighty hand, and with an outstretched arm, and with fury poured out. . . ."

The elements in the Messianic chain in Ezekiel, therefore, exchange places and the chain receives this form: sin—punishment—redemption—repentance. How great the sin, we have already seen: Judah has sinned more than Sodom, and the Philistines are ashamed of the sins of the Judahites; they have not even done according to the ordinances of the nations round about them (5:7). And *the punishment* will not be less than the sin: the LORD will do in Israel what He has not done up to now and what He will never do again (5:9). Sword, pestilence, evil beasts, and famine—terrible famine, which will force sons to eat their fathers and fathers to eat their sons—and, the principal thing, exile and dispersion in the lands, where they will be made "a reproach and a taunt . . . and an astonishment unto the nations"—these are the kinds of punishment which will come as a penalty for their dreadful abominations (5:10–17). But not only as a penalty do these punishments come. With the penalty comes also *refining* and *purification*. There is now too much dross in the people of Judah. As silver is smelted in the midst of a furnace, so will the people be smelted in the midst of Jerusalem by the slayings, the distresses, and the destruction, in order that the few who emerge from the furnace safely may be refined silver (22:18–22). Before the redemption will come the great Day of Judgment, which we find in the Book of Joel, except that here it is called not "the valley of Jehoshaphat" but "the wilderness of the peoples" (20:35).

Here again we have the parallel between the exodus from Egypt and the coming redemption, a parallel which we found in most of the prophets and which is to us a sign and witness that the memory of the Egyptian exile and of the deliverance from it was the prime mover of the Messianic idea: "Like as I pleaded with your fathers in the wilderness of the land of Egypt, so will I plead with you, saith the Lord God" (20:36). In the time of the Egyptian exile Israel was subjected to only one people, but in the time of the new exile it will be scattered among many nations and submit to them. Thus "the wilderness of the land of Egypt" is parallel to "the wilderness of the peoples." In this "wilderness of the peoples" will die the rebels and transgressors among the sons of Israel: "I will bring them forth out of the land where they sojourn, but they shall not enter into the land of Israel" (20:38)—exactly as it was in the wilderness beyond the land of Egypt.[11] And as Israel in that wilderness was made into a people by the covenant which the LORD made with them at Mount Sinai, so it will be also in "the wilderness of the peoples": "And I will bring you into the bond of the covenant" (20:37).

When the LORD gathers the sons of His people from the lands where they were scattered and brings them "into the land of Israel, into the country which I [He] lifted up My [His] hand to give unto your [their] fathers," they will be ashamed of their deeds and confounded by their transgressions. To this idea—shame after the redemption because of [former] transgressions—found in definite relation to Ezekiel's special expression "stumbling block of iniquity," the prophet returns times without number (16:61, 63; 20:43; 36:31, and so on). Then all the sons of the house of Israel will serve Him, every one of them. Then they will become acceptable to God and then He will seek from them their sacrifices and heave-offerings (20:40–44). We see, therefore, that Ezekiel does not give up the sacrifices even in the Age to Come.

Christian scholars explain this by reference to Ezekiel's origin, since he belonged to the priestly class.[12] This reason is not sufficient. For Jeremiah also came from the priests, yet he is far from exaggerating the importance of the Temple and the sacrifices. We are forced to say that because Ezekiel prophesied far from the Temple and for a considerable time even after the Destruction, the Temple along with its sacrifices became for him more beloved. For, in principle, the prophets did not oppose the sacrifices, but only at the time when people and priests were offering them with impure hearts and unclean hands, and when the people believed that they could do any abomination and the sacrifices would atone for them. Even the prophets who were not priests did not oppose the sacrifices in themselves, nor the Temple—the religio-national center of Israel—in itself. Perhaps if Isaiah son of Amoz had been living at the time of the Destruction, even he would have yearned for the Temple and the sacrifices—albeit for sacrifices offered to the God of Israel

---

[11] See on this also E. Hühn, *Die messian. Weissag.*, I, 44.
[12] See what has been written on this by K. Budde, *op. cit.*, p. 151; J. Wellhausen, *op. cit.*, pp. 144–148.

with a pure heart and a right spirit, after the renunciation of evil deeds.[13]

The people will turn from their evil way, removing their detestable things and abominations from the entire land of Israel, and then the LORD will grant forgiveness of all their iniquities (11:18; 16:63). Like Jeremiah, Ezekiel also prophesies that the LORD will give to all those reassembled another heart, a new heart, a heart of flesh instead of a heart of stone such as they have had, and He will put a new spirit within them (11:19; 36:26). Then they will walk in His statutes, and keep and do His ordinances; and they will be His people and He will be their God in the land of their fathers (11:20; 36:27-28). He will sprinkle clean water upon them and purify them from all their uncleannesses and from all their idols, and from all their iniquities in general (36:25, 33; 37:23). The LORD will be sanctified in the midst of all the nations by the good which He does to His people, just as He was sanctified by the evil which He did to them.

To this idea—the idea of "the sanctification of the divine Name," closely connected with the idea of the "profanation of the divine Name," about which I spoke above—Ezekiel returns many times (20:41; 36:23; 37:28, and so on). There is already in the words of Ezekiel a certain special religious quality, of the sort possessed by Judaism and Christianity in later times—it is religion abstracted from nationalism, no longer closely connected with national and political life, and unlike anything in the prophets who preceded Ezekiel. Such a religious duality was essential to the prophet of the Exile, since he was the first to emphasize—for very understandable historical reasons!—*religious individualism:* personal faith, the sin and punishment of the individual. However, the spirit of ancient prophecy still lived in him, and his "sanctification of the divine Name" is a conception whereby religion abstracted from natural nationalism (of origin and race) is transformed into a nationalism of choice and peculiar value: the LORD will be sanctified among the nations not

---

[13] See in the important article "Ezekiel the Prophet" [in Hebrew] by I. N. Simhoni (*He-'Atid* of S. I. Horowitz, IV, 209-234; V, 47-74).

by individuals from Israel, but by the whole Israelite nation, regarded as a *collective* individual.

Political well-being is also emphasized by Ezekiel in a striking manner. Along with Judah, Samaria will be restored to life and will become subject to her younger sister in a subjection both spiritual and political: Samaria will be the daughter and Judah the mother, the metropolis (16:53, 54, 61). Ezekiel emphasizes this idea more than the rest of the prophets, and on it turns *the vision of the two sticks joined into one* (37:19-28). The sons of Israel, whom the sons of Judah had considered as dry bones, as a dead member in the body of the nation, will also be gathered from all the lands where they have been driven, and will be restored to national and religious life on their own soil. This is indicated by the sublime vision of "the Valley of Dry Bones" (37:1-14).[14] Not for nothing does "the vision of the two sticks joined together" follow immediately after the vision of "the resurrection of the dry bones." For the prophet goes on to say in the name of the LORD:

and I will make them one nation in the land, upon the mountains of Israel, and one king shall be king of them all; and they shall be no more two nations, neither shall they be divided into two kingdoms any more at all (37:22).

This one king will be David, that is—as we have seen in Hosea and in Jeremiah—*a king from the house of David*. This king will be "their prince for ever" (37:24-25). This Messianism of the rule of the house of David is emphasized by Ezekiel in still another passage (34:23-24), and we see here the prophet of the Exile following in the footsteps of the prophets of freedom who preceded him. There

---

[14] To conclude from this that Ezekiel already knows resurrection from the dead of individuals from Israel, as do certain modern scholars (see E. Hühn, *op. cit.*, I, pp. 46-47), and as did many Jewish interpreters before them, I do not find to be correct (see the commentary of Meir Lambert, ed. A. Kahana, on Daniel 12:2). The vision of the resuscitation of the dry bones is only symbolical, like the vision of the two sticks joined into one that follows it. The only question that can be raised is whether this symbolism signifies the revival of the Ten Tribes alone ("the whole house of Israel"), which had been considered as "dry bones," as completely lost, or also the resuscitation of many of the Judean exiles, who likewise had been close in Babylonia to a state of despair, as I have indicated above. The latter solution appeals to me more.

is no doubt in my mind that these prophecies were uttered a short time after the Destruction, during the lifetime of Zedekiah. Fourteen years after the Destruction, Ezekiel already speaks only of a "prince," and at that time there is no longer any mention in his words either of David or of a king. I shall return to this fact in the course of the discussion.

The king from the house of David is not described as a victorious warrior, nor even as the possessor of very high spiritual qualities of the kind attributed by Isaiah to the "shoot out of the stock of Jesse." This king will be a *shepherd*, a good shepherd, who will feed the flock and not himself, who will not allow the strong and fat sheep to thrust aside the sick and the lean.[15] But in one prophecy, which without any doubt was delivered before the Destruction, because in it the prophet complains against Zedekiah for violating his oath to Nebuchadrezzar, we still find the hope that the king from the house of David will achieve a great *political* success. From the top of the cedar the LORD will crop off a tender twig and will plant it "in the mountain of the height of Israel"; and "it shall bring forth boughs, and bear fruit, and be a stately cedar; and under it shall dwell all fowl of every wing, in the shadow of the branches thereof shall they dwell" (17:22-24). It is possible that by "fowl of every wing" is meant only all the dispersed tribes of Israel, and it is possible that the words "a stately cedar" are only an exaggeration for rhetorical effect. But it is also possible that before the complete Destruction the prophet had not yet given up the hope of seeing at a time more or less distant the house of David at the head of a great and powerful kingdom.[16]

But before the *final* political Golden Age comes to Israel, the people of the LORD will once more be in great distress—*though they are already dwelling upon their own soil.* This is a new conception, which we find only in the Book of Ezekiel. In the Messianic oracles of the rest of the prophets, the Day of Judgment always preceded the day of redemption and consolation; even in Ezekiel punishment comes before redemption, except that he is not satisfied with this. There

---

[15] See on this, C. H. Cornill, *op. cit.*, p. 121.
[16] See for details D. Castelli, *op. cit.*, p. 121.

is in his prophecies something like *a second day of judgment*, which, like repentance in his scheme, does not come before the redemption but after it.[17] This is the war with Gog and Magog. According to the opinion of most scholars, the two long prophecies in Ezekiel (38 and 39) concerning the war with Gog and Magog are only an echo of the prophecy of Jeremiah and Zephaniah concerning the onslaught of the Scythians at the approach to the land of Judah in the time of Josiah.[18] King Ashurbanipal (668-626), the Asenappar of the Bible (Ezra 4:10), had already fought against these "Ashkuzites" (Ashguzai); and he also mentions his war against "the sons of Gâg." The next Assyrian king before the last, Sin-shar-ishkun, the Sarakos of the Greeks (c. 620-612), also fought against them. These "sons of Gâg" are, according to Hommel, the "Gog of the land of Magog" of Ezekiel, who could not forget, even after forty years, the devastation (described in such vivid colors in the prophecy of Jeremiah from the year 625, Jer. 5:15-17) [19] which these barbarians made near the land of Judah (the prophecy of Ezekiel concerning the war with Gog is from about the year 585); and it seemed to Ezekiel that as long as these barbarians were not completely destroyed, there could be no true peace in the land of Israel.[20]

In my opinion, it is more probable that a distant report reached the prophet concerning the kingdom of Lydia, which at that time —before its king, Croesus son of Alyattes, had been decisively defeated by Cyrus—had grown very strong; and concerning the founder of the new dynasty of the Mermnads, Gyges. This is the powerful king who sent a force from the Carians and from the Ionian Islands to help Psamtik I, king of Egypt, and by means of this force Psamtik threw off the yoke of Assyria. This is the powerful King Gugu (thus his name in Assyrian), whom Ashurbanipal

---

[17] See on this, E. Hühn, *op. cit.*, I, 44-54.
[18] See for details J. Wellhausen, *op. cit.*, pp. 145-146.
[19] Of this prophecy of Jeremiah it is possible that Ezekiel hints when he says: "Art thou he of whom I spoke in old time by My servants the prophets of Israel . . . that I would bring thee against them?" (Ezek. 38:17). In the Talmud (Sanhedrin 17a) this verse is explained by reference to Eldad and Medad. See also Targum Yerushalmi, Numbers 11:26; Numbers Rabbah, Chap. 15; Tanhuma, Beha'alothekha, 12; Tanhuma, ed. Buber, *ibid.*, 22, Folio 29.
[20] See F. Hommel, *Geschichte des alten Morgenlandes*, pp. 149, 151.

commends for defeating the Cimmerians in the year 657, but whom he cannot forgive for extending help to Psamtik against Assyria, though he cannot do anything about it. Perhaps Ezekiel had already heard in his time about the valorous deeds of the Lydians; and since in his time the Persians and Medes had not yet arisen to rule over all the territories of the kingdom of Babylonia, it seemed to him that danger from the kingdom of Lydia was threatening all Asia to the east, and even Syria and Palestine. Therefore he did not see any possibility that political security and material prosperity could come to Israel until the Lydians and their king of the dynasty founded by "Gyges" or "Gog" should be vanquished. Both the kings ruling after "Gog" and the land over which they ruled were called after his name: "Gog of the land of Magog"—just as Jehu son of Nimshi was called by the Assyrians "Mar Ḥumri," that is, "of the house of Omri," although he was not of the family of Omri at all; but he was so called only because Omri was the founder of the kingdom of Samaria [really, the founder of Samaria as the capital of the kingdom].[21]

However that may be, the people Israel, even after it is gathered in to its own land, will not have quiet and rest until the crucial war against Gog and against many of the nations which are near his land and are submissive to him.[22] Gog will attack the land of Israel with excessive boldness, because it will then be a "land of unwalled villages . . . without walls, and having neither bars nor gates," and because its inhabitants will be "at quiet and all of them dwelling safely" (38:11). But the LORD will come to the aid of His people, and will shake the earth against Gog and his army until the mountains and all the walls fall down; and He will pour out upon them a torrential rain and hailstones and fire and brimstone, and then every man's sword will be against his brother (38:19-23). Gog and his army will be slain on the mountains of Israel; their bodies will be-

---

[21] The fact that the Lydians were not mentioned among the numerous peoples accompanying Gog (38:1-5) can only indicate that "the land of Magog" itself is the land of the Lydians. Gressmann (*Eschatologie*, 1905, pp. 174-192) sees here an ancient tradition mixed with mythological elements—and there is some justification for his contention. See also I. N. Simhoni, *op. cit.*, V, 67-70.

[22] The Carians and Ionians of Asia Minor were subject to Gog, king of Lydia, since he sent them to the aid of Psamtik I, king of Egypt, against the armies of Assyria.

come food for the beasts of the field and for the birds of the air; and with their weapons the children of Israel will be able to kindle fires for seven whole years (39:9–10). This will be the great second "day of judgment," in which all peoples will see the glory and the powerful hand of the LORD, and all the children of Israel will recognize that they were exiled only because of their iniquity, and that henceforth they will dwell on their own soil in safety, with none to make them afraid; and that none of them will be left in foreign lands, nor will they be exiled any more, nor be afflicted with suffering (39:17–29). Thus the ingathering of exiles will be complete and final.

The active participation of the people Israel in the war against Gog and Magog is not very apparent here, and the participation of the King-Messiah does not appear at all. Therefore it was still widely held at the beginning of the Tannaitic period that the LORD *alone* would fight against Gog and Magog; only at the *end* of that period did some Tannaim hold that Messiah son of David would fight against Gog and Magog; and at the latter time many thought that Messiah son of Joseph would undertake this last battle. The Tannaim also held that this battle would come after "the Days of the Messiah" had already begun, placing it midway between the beginning of this new period (with or without Messiah son of Joseph) and the coming of Messiah son of David.[23]

Ezekiel emphasizes in general that the LORD will "cause a horn to shoot up unto the house of Israel" (29:21). When He gathers in the sons of His people, He will execute "judgments upon all those that have them in disdain round about them" (28:26); then neither the people nor the land will any longer bear the shame and the reproaches of the nations (36:6–7, 13–15). A wave of pent-up love for the nation, such as the prophet is not at all accustomed to reveal openly, floods from the lips of Ezekiel when he comes to speak of the rejoicing at the misfortune of Israel in which the nearby nations indulged, and of the reproaches which they heaped upon his nation because of its downfall and destruction. Along with the zeal for the profaned name of the LORD, there is felt here also the zeal for the profaned honor of the nation, and it is recognized that the prophet

[23] See in detail below, Part III, Chap. IX, pp. 497ff.

suppressed his compassion for his people because he was *forced* to justify the overthrow of the people in order to justify thereby the acts of his God. But when he saw the shame of his people among the nations, he could not restrain himself any longer; all his wrath was aroused against his people's enemies, and he offered compensatory consolation to his people by prophesying for them honor and well-being, national, political, and spiritual, in the days to come.

He also prophesied *material prosperity* for them. The children of Israel will dwell safely in their land. They will build houses and plant vineyards (28:26). Like a flock they will lie down in a good fold and feed upon a rich pasture (34:13–14). The LORD will break the bars of their yoke, and deliver them out of the hand of their subjugators, and they will not be afraid any more of any people or tongue, and they will no longer be plunder for the nations (34:27–28). The LORD will also "cause evil beasts to cease out of the land," and the children of Israel will "dwell safely in the wilderness and sleep in the woods" (34:25). It is difficult to know whether a change in the order of nature is here intended or whether this is spoken figuratively, representing evil nations as beasts of prey. In favor of the second interpretation would be the words, "And they shall no more be a *prey to the nations,* neither shall *the beast of the earth* devour them" (34:28). In any case, there is no doubt that Ezekiel, like all the prophets who preceded him, prophesies of a productivity of the earth and an increase of human beings far beyond what is usual and natural. The LORD will not only give showers of blessing in their season, in such a manner that the tree of the field will yield its fruit and the earth yield its produce, so that the children of Israel will never again suffer the reproach of famine (34:26–27, 29; 36:29–30); but He will also multiply the population of the land, the fruit of the tree and the increase of the field to an unusual degree (36:5–12, 30, 37–38). The devastated cities will be rebuilt and the ruins will become fortified places, and all of them will be filled with men until there is no room (36:10, 33–38).

These are the fundamentals of the Messianic expectations of Ezekiel in the first period of his prophecy. It must be confessed that they do not excel either in soaring imagination or in poetical quality.

But all these Messianic ideas (except, perhaps, the idea of the war with Gog and Magog) were conceived by Ezekiel before the Destruction or shortly thereafter. When fourteen years of the exile of Zedekiah had passed, both prophet and people realized more and more the great significance of the fearful event, and also recognized that by it, so to speak, a break had been made in the continuity of the history of Israel. Then the people—who saw in the fulfillment of the visions of the prophets a sign and proof of the truth of their words and needed *religio-spiritual* aid and support to avoid intermixture with the Gentiles in the absence of *political* aid and support —turned more and more to their God. Moreover, the prophet felt more and more the need not to rebuke and chastise (since the transgressors were fewer and the people had received from the hand of the LORD double for all their sins, Isa. 40:2), but to give comfort and point out a new way of life; in clearer words: *to create a positive ideal of national regeneration, religious and political.*

So then, in the year 572, Ezekiel—who has now been made over from a prophet into a *scribe*, the father of all the scribes of the time of the Second Temple, chief among them being Ezra—writes his "political Utopia" (if a prophetic vision can be so called), which is included in the last nine chapters of the Book of Ezekiel (40-48). There is no doubt that Ezekiel considered his "kingdom of priests" or "theocracy" (Joseph Salvador calls it more correctly a "nomocracy"—rule by statutes) as an ideal that was close to realization; but we have already seen above that it is nevertheless possible to consider all these chapters as Messianic. *In its entirety* this ideal was never realized, but *in its essentials* it was realized in the period of the Second Temple, when the high priests ruled.

I am not able or obligated to enter into the minute details of this politico-religious ideal. This is the essential characteristic of the "Utopia"—that it portrays the future not only in a general way, but also in great detail, something that is not true of the usual Messianic prophecies, which are satisfied with general descriptions. Likewise, I cannot discuss here even briefly the many important differences between the laws of Ezekiel included in these chapters and the laws of the Pentateuch, particularly the Priestly Code.[24] Only in broad outline can I present this great vision of the future.

The center of everything here is the Temple and the worship of God therein. Ezekiel does not here conceal his origin from the priestly stock. After the Temple was destroyed, he yearned for it and for the sacrifices offered in it, and he speaks much of their renewal. Perhaps, as I have already indicated above, another prophet also would have yearned for them; but their minutest details could be described only by a prophet of priestly family—and a prophet of the Exilic period. Of a king of the house of David there is no mention. There is a *prince*, who apparently transmits his office to his sons (46:16), and it is his duty to look after the divine service, to enter the Temple first, to present burnt-offerings, meal-offerings, peace-offerings, sin-offerings, and drink-offerings (45:17, 22; 46:2–13), and to collect contributions from the people for all those things which are offered in the sanctuary (46:13–17). Indeed, what else is there for him to do? Then no one will commit willful transgressions, and for transgressions by error sacrifices will atone. Thus there will be no need for the prince to act as judge of the land. There will be no more war in the land, except if there should be the one against Gog and Magog, then the LORD will fight for his people. Thus there will be no need for the prince to set up and maintain an army. Nor will it be necessary to look after the economic needs of the country, since—as we shall see below—everything will be in abundance. It will remain for him, therefore, only to look after the needs of the Temple. Such a person will not be a king, nor even indeed a prince, but only an official of the LORD's house, and a sort of president of a religious republic, who represents the nation in festive processions. The high priest was actually such a person in Judah during those times when it was subject to the kings of Persia, Egypt, and Syria, and during those times the dream of Ezekiel was realized to a considerable degree.[25] It would be more correct to say that this politico-religious dream, born out of the

[24] See on this the important article of Samuel Krauss, "The Statutes of Ezekiel in Their Relation to the Law of Moses" [in Hebrew], *Ha-Shiloah*, VIII, 109–118 and 300–306.

[25] See J. Wellhausen, *op. cit.*, pp. 146–148; K. Budde, *op. cit.*, pp. 153–154.

bitter conditions of the time of the Babylonian exile, which allowed no place in the heart for shining hopes of the restoration of the kingdom of the house of David to its pristine glory, had its influence on the development of the rule of the priests, which extended in Judah *from the time of Jeshua son of Jozadak to the Hasmonean revolt*.[26]

The land will be divided for inheritance into equal portions (47:13–14); the prince also will receive a portion of land, which he can transmit by inheritance to his sons, but not to his servants (46:16–17). From the income from this property he will take out a certain portion as a contribution to the Temple. The prophet is concerned not for the prince, when he sets aside a portion for him, but for the people: "*and My princes shall no more wrong My people; but they shall give the land to the house of Israel according to their tribes*" (45:8). So says the prophet in one place. In another place, he emphasizes as follows:

Moreover the prince shall not take of *the people's inheritance, to thrust them wrongfully out of their possession;* he shall give inheritance to his sons out of his own possession; *that My people be not scattered every man from his possession* (46:18).

Political power is not indicated here at all. On the contrary, the name "The LORD is there," by which Jerusalem, the holy city, will be called, shows that the city will be entirely spiritual.

In spite of the abstractness and spirituality in this Messianic portrayal, it does not lack *material prosperity* or even *national pride*. From the Temple a stream will go forth, in which fish will be very abundant, and upon the banks of which, on both sides, will grow food-bearing trees, whose leaves will not wither nor the fruit thereof fail, for *they will bear new fruit every month*. Their leaves will serve as medicine and the fruit as food (47:1–12). Even when Ezekiel becomes entirely spiritual, he nevertheless cannot let his feet get off the ground and satisfy himself with celestial joy alone. This is the power of a true prophet of Israel!

And like a true prophet of Israel he cannot forget the importance of the *national traits* of the people Israel—traits that elevate them

---

[26] See what has been written on this by C. H. Cornill, *op cit.*, pp. 123–126; see also I. N. Simhoni, *op. cit.*, V, 70–74.

above foreign peoples. In his vision of the future no foreigner can enter the sanctuary (44:6–9). Truly he says: "No alien, uncircumcised in heart and uncircumcised in flesh, shall enter" (44:7, 9); thus the uncircumcised in heart, even if he is circumcised in the flesh, will not be acceptable to Him. In any case, in all the Book of Ezekiel we do not find that lofty universalism which we saw in all its majesty and splendor in Amos, Isaiah, Micah, and Zephaniah. When the political status of Israel was good, its heart was open to receive all the foreigners who would come to join themselves to the people of the LORD. But when its political status had suffered a severe decline and its very national existence was in danger, its heart shrank and became restricted, and it began to be fearful of the foreign elements which were striving to devour it. Then it was compelled to think of its own immediate problems. Its mind was not turned at all to its mission among the Gentiles. It was sufficient for it to consider well how it might preserve its existence under these unfortunate circumstances. And only Messianic portrayals of a *national* future, near at hand and brilliant, could preserve its existence in times of affliction and distress. This was also the purpose of the Messianic promises of Ezekiel, who in his "visions of God" strengthened the heart and restored the spirit of the exiles in Babylonia with fair hopes, and pointed out to them a new way of life, which the people Israel were to follow during almost the whole period of the Second Temple.

CHAPTER X

Obadiah

(C. 580 B.C.E.)

THE OPINIONS about the time of composition of the little book of one chapter, which has at its head the words "The Vision of Obadiah," are exceedingly various and remote from one another. Seventy years ago there were still Jewish and Gentile scholars who thought, with all ancient Jewish interpreters, that this book was composed about the year 850 by that Obadiah who lived at the time of Ahab (I Kings 18:3-16) and beyond, composing his prophecy during the reign of Jehoram son of Jehoshaphat, king of Judah (850-842), since at that time Edom rebelled against Judah and set up its own king; while more recent scholars (Cornill, Marti, *et al.*) push the time of composition down almost to the period of Nehemiah (*c.* 450).[1]

In my opinion, there is no foundation for the contentions of either the former or the latter. To put back Obadiah to the period before the Destruction is impossible, because Verses 11-14 show clearly that Obadiah knew of the conquest by Nebuchadrezzar ("In the day that thou didst stand aloof, in the day that strangers carried away his substance, and foreigners entered into his gates, and cast lots upon Jerusalem," and so on). But to think that near the time of Nehemiah the Jews were still filled with profound hatred against Edom because it stood aloof when Nebuchadrezzar destroyed Judah, and that this hatred was expressed by the prophet in words as full of

---

[1] Apparently it is put still later by Budde (in his book, *Geschichte der altheb. Litt.*, pp. 213-214); and so S. Bernfeld, *Introduction* [in Hebrew], II, 514-515.

vindictive fury as these—this is something which the mind cannot endure. At that time the Jews and their last prophets had other enemies and other anxieties. Therefore, I think that Obadiah wrote immediately after the Destruction, when the hatred of Edom for its evil deeds was freshest and most severe.[2]

For this opinion, I find support in the words of Ezekiel (35). He also was enraged, immediately after the Destruction, at the joy manifested by Edom over the calamity of Judah, and at the assistance given to Judah's enemies in pursuing and slaying the fugitives (see particularly 35:5, 10, 12, 14-15). In like manner, support is to be found in the harsh words against Edom and against its joy over Judah's downfall as recorded in Lamentations (4:21-22), which scholars also date later, incorrectly, in my opinion. But I am particularly well supported by the prophecy against Edom in Jeremiah (49:7-22). This is so similar in spirit and in much of its wording to the vision of Obadiah that Ewald among earlier scholars and Cornill among the later concluded that it and our Obadiah had a common source ("Urobadiah" in their language). And Marti even concluded that the prophecy of Jeremiah is much later, being only an imitation of our Obadiah.[3] Really, there is nothing to compel us to accept either the former hypothesis or the latter. I have already said [4] that the well known Messianic prophecy common to Isaiah and Micah was certainly composed by Isaiah, the older of the two prophets, and from him passed to Micah, his younger contemporary. So it appears to me also concerning the prophecy against Edom. It was composed by Jeremiah and passed, with important changes, omissions, and additions, to Obadiah, who in my opinion was a younger contemporary —and perhaps also a disciple of Jeremiah.

The fact that "the captivity of this host of the children of Israel that are [among the] Canaanites even unto Zarephath, and the

---

[2] See the introduction to Obadiah by J. J. B. Weinkoop in the Book of the Twelve Prophets, Part I, edited by Abraham Kahana (*The Bible with Scientific Commentary* [in Hebrew], Kiev, 1907, p. 54. Weinkoop rejects the opinion of those who date Obadiah late with evidence from Malachi 1:3, where it appears that in the time of Malachi Edom was already a desolate waste.

[3] See on the relation between Obadiah and Jeremiah in particular K. Budde, *op. cit.*, p. 214, Note 1.

[4] See above, pp. 69-70, Note 31.

captivity of Jerusalem that is in Sepharad," are mentioned in Obadiah need cause us no surprise with respect to the time following the Destruction. I have already had occasion to show [5] that even before the Destruction, the Israelites, like their Canaanite neighbors, and like their Greek contemporaries, had been dispersed both willingly and unwillingly among many lands and provinces; and the meaning of the words "that are [among the] Canaanites even unto Zarephath" is that the Israelites who had been exiled from their land, but had still not been swallowed up among the Gentiles at the time of the Babylonian exile, would take possession, when they returned, of the land of the Canaanites as far as Zarephath (Sarepta), a well known city in Canaan, a dependency of Sidon and near the border of the kingdom of Israel (I Kings 17:9); while "the captivity of Jerusalem that is in Sepharad" would possess "the cities of the South," that is, the land of Edom, which is near the border of the land of Judah. It is almost certain that "Sepharad" is the city of Sardis in the state of Lydia in Asia Minor ("Saparda" in Assyrian), to which Jews went into exile of their own free will. So why is it impossible that a prophet, who lived only a short time after the first Destruction, should mention these groups of exiles? [6]

The Messianic ideas in Obadiah are few, naturally, since we have only one prophecy consisting of twenty-one verses; but they are worthy of careful attention. Since Edom became very insolent when Judah's power was broken, and since Edom rejoiced at the misfortune of the children of Judah and aggravated their disaster in the day of distress (2–4, 10–14), therefore Edom's mighty men will be dismayed, the wisdom of its sages will come to nought, and no one will be left in the mountain of Seir (8–9, 18). Not only will Edom suffer on "the day of the LORD" soon to come, the day of punishment, but also all the nations with it (15–16). Both Israel ("the house of Joseph") and Judah ("the house of Jacob") have suffered much, but "in mount Zion there shall be those that escape"; this mount will be holy, and

[5] See above, p. 42, Note 8.
[6] On the dispersion of the Jews in various lands up to the time of the First Destruction, see an important study in the book of L. Herzfeld, *Handelsgeschichte der Juden des Altertums*, 2nd ed., Braunschweig, 1894, pp. 50–60. See also A. Causse, *Les Dispersés d'Israel*, Paris, 1929.

Judah will take over its own possessions (17). Israel also will become powerful and be avenged on its enemies: the house of Jacob will be a fire, and the house of Joseph a flame, while the house of Esau will be stubble, so that Judah and Israel will burn up Edom completely (18). Then Judah will return and take possession of the mount of Esau, as it was until the time of Jehoram son of Jehoshaphat; it will also take possession of the land of Philistia, as it was in the time of Ahaz; Benjamin will possess Gilead, but the Judahites will possess the field of Ephraim and the field of Samaria (18), which at that time were in the hands of Gentiles or half-Gentiles (the Samaritans). The exiles of Israel will return to their own land and possess the land of the Canaanites as far as Zarephath, which is near the border of the kingdom of Israel; but the exiles from Jerusalem, who will return to their own land, will possess the cities of the land of Edom, which is near the border of the kingdom of Judah (see above).

These are *political* Messianic expectations, which, it was thought, would soon come to pass, since there is in them nothing impossible of realization. The single prophecy of Obadiah which we have closes with a Messianic oracle that is political at its beginning and spiritual at its end:

> And saviors shall come up on Mount Zion
> To judge the mount of Esau;
> And the kingdom shall be the LORD's.

The "saviors" are certainly something like the ancient "judges": a collective name for the kings and warriors of Israel and Judah who were—as the end of the verse shows—of the nature of political and spiritual Messiahs.[7] A single personal Messiah, described in political and spiritual terms, is not recognized by Obadiah at all. We have already seen in Ezekiel's idea of "the end of days," that immediately after the Destruction the prophets were not able to dream dreams of an individual Messiah. The downfall of the kingdom of the house of David was still very near, and there was no possibility of hanging bright hopes upon the descendants of David, especially since in

---

[7] See the commentary by J. J. B. Weinkoop on Obadiah 21, Book of the Twelve, Part I, p. 112. There is no need to read "the saved" instead of "saviors," although the Septuagint inclines toward this correction.

general at that time no hope for the restoration of the Jewish kingdom could be seen. Moreover, there was not at that time much place for universalistic religious and ethical hopes, as explained at the end of the preceding chapter. Therefore the Messianic dreams became quite general and hazy. Likewise the dream of Obadiah. He dreams of the national hope, of political saviors, and even the rule of the God of Judah and Israel over the whole world; but all these Messianic expectations do not take on a clear and definite form, and they appear to us only through the mist.

CHAPTER XI

Hymns of the Exile in the Book of Psalms

THERE IS no book in Holy Scripture regarding which opinions on the date of its composition in general and the date of composition of its individual chapters in particular are so divided as the Book of Psalms. It is sufficient to mention that while the ancient interpreters attributed all or most of it to David, king of Israel, most modern scholars conclude that it contains no hymn earlier than the Babylonian exile, but it does contain hymns composed in Hasmonean times.

In a work on the Messianic idea there is no place for detailed researches on the date of composition of the various psalms; for if I should attempt an extended treatment of this subject I would need to dedicate a whole book to it.[1] Therefore, it must suffice for me to say that according to my opinion (for the correctness of which proofs cannot be offered in this place) the following psalms belong to the period before the Babylonian exile: 15 (24), 18, 20, 21, 28, 45, 47, 60 (108), and 89. But it is not worth while to expend words on these in a work on the Messianic idea, since in only three of them (18, 28, and 89) is to be found the assurance that the throne of David will be established forever (18:51; 28:8; 89:4-5, 29-38).

[1] Against the opinion of Ezekiel Kaufmann, *History of the Israelite Religion* [in Hebrew], Vol. 2, Book 2, pp. 631-727, see J. Klausner, *History of the Second Temple* [in Hebrew], II, 202.

More than this can be found in the hymns of the Exile, among which, in my opinion are to be numbered these psalms: 51, 69, 80, and 137. Out of all these psalms there are Messianic expectations, near or remote, only in Psalm 51. These Messianic expectations are here clothed—as is proper in psalms, which are not prophetic oracles but expressions of prayer and praise—in the form of supplications and entreaties that the LORD will bring back His captive people and from Zion give salvation to Israel, He alone being the redeemer and savior, without a human Messiah; and also that He will do good to Zion and build the walls of Jerusalem, and that then the Temple will be restored and the service of sacrifices be renewed (51:20–21). In Psalm 89, which was apparently composed on the occasion of the death of Josiah in his battle with Pharaoh Necho [2] and already has a sense of the spirit of the approaching Exile, there is a prayer and urgent entreaty that the LORD will remember His promise to David, that his seed would rule forever and his throne be established as the sun and as the days of the heavens; and also that if his descendants should commit sin the LORD would punish them with tribulations and plagues, but would not forsake them forever and would eventually restore their kingship (89:4–5, 21–38).

But, perhaps, an importance greater than that of these expectations and entreaties is to be attached to those profound yearnings for the return to Zion and for complete redemption, political and spiritual, which we find in Psalms 80 and 137. We hear here the groan of a captive, the cry for help of a sojourner in a foreign land, whose soul yearns to return to the dear native land and clings to the promises of the prophets, the Messianic promises which the LORD will not spurn forever, that He will relent and redeem His people, thus making great the honor of His name and the honor of His nation among the Gentiles.

> If I forget thee, O Jerusalem,
> Let my right hand fail;
> Let my tongue cleave to my palate,
> If I remember thee not,

---

[2] See the commentary of H. P. Chajes on the Psalms in *The Bible with Scientific Commentary* [in Hebrew], ed. A. Kahana, Zhitomir, 1903, on Psalm 89 (p. 97).

cries out this expatriate at the end of the period of the Babylonian exile in the abundance of his love for the native city of his fathers.[3] And the great outpouring of emotion, the outpouring of pent-up love for his people, which we saw in the Book of Ezekiel every time the prophet remembers the disgrace of Israel among the nations, is found in these psalms with even more depth and even more psychical inwardness. The reproach to the *nation* here takes on increased significance and becomes a reproach to the *God* of the nation, an act of blasphemy. The aspiration that the *people* Israel may be exalted and made great and restored to its own land becomes a strong aspiration that the name of the *God* of Israel may be exalted and made great and sanctified among all the nations. Thus the hope for the political redemption of Israel is here connected and joined with the aspiration for the spiritual redemption of the whole world *through* Israel. For the rule of God throughout the whole world is here the natural outgrowth of the rule of the house of David in Zion, the Holy City.

This is the great importance of the hymns of the Exile in the Book of Psalms for the history of the development of the Messianic idea, even though the actual Messianic references in them are very few: the fundamental thing in them is not the Messianic *idea*, but a Messianic *mood*, if one may so speak. Budde [4] rightly says, "In a broader sense the Psalter is Messianic from one end to the other, since throughout the salvation at the end of time is kept in view and everything moves in that direction."

[3] On the Exilic origin of this psalm, see H. Graetz, *Geschichte der Juden*, II, 2, p. 19, Note 6, and Chajes in his aforesaid commentary on the Psalms, Ps. 137 (p. 282).

[4] *Geschichte der altheb. Litt.*, p. 269.

CHAPTER XII

Deutero-Isaiah

(C. 545–518 B.C.E.)

THAT CHAPTERS 40–66 of the Book of Isaiah as we now have it do not belong to that Isaiah who prophesied in the days of Uzziah, Jotham, Ahaz, and Hezekiah, kings of Judah, was already recognized by R. Abraham Ibn Ezra;[1] and from him this knowledge spread among Christian and Jewish scholars in the eighteenth and nineteenth centuries. A prophet, out of his broad understanding of basic principles and out of his accurate observation of the events taking place in his time and of conditions as they actually existed, could, of course, have visions of the future; but these visions would always be of a *general* sort. To know the details of future events so well as to name the participants in them, as Isaiah apparently names Cyrus, king of Persia (Isa. 44:28 and 45:1)—this is something that is not only unnatural, but also beyond all reason. What possible impression could the prophet have made upon his contemporaries by mentioning to them the name of a man who was to appear in the world only after 150 years?

We inevitably conclude that the prophetic author of chapters 40–66, which were added to the prophecies of the Isaiah of Hezekiah's time, actually lived in the time of Cyrus. Moreover, the content, style, and purpose of his prophecies confirm us in this opinion. The prophet

[1] See Nachman Krochmal, *The Guide of the Perplexed of Our Time* [in Hebrew], Sect. 11, Par. 2 (writings of N. Krochmal, ed. Rawidowicz, Berlin, 1924, pp. 114–118).

who uttered these words of comfort urges a return to Zion; thus he lived toward the end of the Babylonian exile and helped to strengthen the movement that began immediately after Cyrus conquered Lydia —that movement the purpose of which was to bring back the Jews to their own land, to restore the ruins of Jerusalem, and to rebuild the Temple.² Since the name of this prophet is not known to us, and since the chapters of his prophecies were added to those of Isaiah son of Amoz, it is customary to call him Deutero-Isaiah (the Second Isaiah). E. Ben-Yehudah called him "the prophet of comfort to Zion," while Bernfeld called him "the prophet of salvation." These names are fitting, but I do not wish to depart from custom in this respect. The name "Isaiah" is more or less suitable to this prophet, since to him or to a prophet who lived in his time and was his disciple we must attribute Isaiah 13–14, in which is mentioned the fall of Babylon brought about by Media (13:17); while in the time of the first Isaiah Babylon had not yet fallen, nor even as yet become prominent. At the beginning of this prophecy, it is clearly written, "The burden of Babylon, which Isaiah the son of Amoz did see" (13:1). It is possible, therefore, that by chance the prophet (or prophets) of the time of the Exile also had the name Isaiah son of Amoz.³ At any rate, the word "Second," which we attach to the name "Isaiah" in order to distinguish this prophet from the one of the time of Hezekiah, serves to show the difference in personality and in time.⁴

² The weighty considerations which prevent us from attributing Chaps. 40–66 to the Isaiah of the time of Hezekiah are set forth in the introduction to Isaiah by S. Krauss, ed. Kahana, p. ix. See also the introduction to the commentary of Prof. M. Z. Segal on Isaiah, Jerusalem, 1941, pp. 20–24, and for more details his book *Introduction to the Bible* [in Hebrew], Book II, the Latter Prophets, pp. 322–340; J. Klausner, *History of the Second Temple* [in Hebrew], I, 1949, pp. 155–160.

³ In the "Murashu documents," mentioned above (p. 111), occurs a Jewish name, *Yasheyama*, equivalent to Isaiah (see J. Klausner, "The Exiles in Babylonia in the Time of Ezra and Nehemiah" [in Hebrew], *Ha-Shiloah*, XXIV, 411, Note 1).

⁴ The new attempt of A. Kaminka (see "Evolution of the Ideas of Isaiah and the Unity of His Book" [in Hebrew], *Ha-Tequphah*, XXII, 230–255; XXIII, 295–309; *Studies in the Bible and Talmud and in the Rabbinic Literature* [in Hebrew], Book I, Tel-Aviv, 5698 [1938], pp. 1–89; and in French, *Le Prophète Isaïe*, Paris, 1925 = *REJ*, LXXX, 42–59, 131–152; LXXXI, 27–45) to prove that all sixty-six chapters of the book of Isaiah have only *one* author— the Isaiah of the time of Hezekiah, except that there were added to it, in the

DEUTERO-ISAIAH

But modern scholars still have not been satisfied with this division of the chapters of the Book of Isaiah. They separate Chapters 40–55, which they assign to the Second Isaiah, from Chapters 56–66 (others even divide these into two parts: 56–62 and 63–66). These chapters (56–66) they assign to a still later prophet, Trito-Isaiah (the Third Isaiah), who lived in the time of Malachi, a time shortly before Ezra the Scribe, or in the time of Ezra himself;[5] or they even attribute these chapters to a number of prophets, some of whom lived near the time of Ezra.[6] They base these views on the differences in content and in style within these prophecies: while Chapters 40–55 are concerned almost entirely with preaching the return to Zion and with glowing assurances for the future, Chapters 56–66 are particularly concerned with the preaching of ethics, with warnings about the keeping of the Sabbath, and even with complaints about the wretched condition of the people; they also contain hints that there is no need of the Temple (56:1).

In my opinion, Christian scholars come to such conclusions only because they forget, when they begin to assess the prophet's words in a critical spirit, two fundamental things. *First*, they forget that the prophet is not a philosopher of systematic theories, but *a philosopher of life*. Since they themselves are rationalistic theologians from the soles of their feet to the tops of their heads, they cannot endure any contradiction whatsoever in the words of any prophet—as though the

---

time of Haggai and Zechariah and even later, single words and whole sentences, including the name "Cyrus" (*Ha-Tequphah*, XXIII, 296–297; *Studies*, p. 75). This attempt cannot succeed in the face of the totally different atmosphere of the chapters denied to the first Isaiah. See, e.g., Reuben Levy, *Deutero-Isaiah*, London, 1925, pp. 1–38.

[5] Duhm holds to this opinion in his well known commentary on Isaiah. He also considers the last sections on the Servant of the LORD (from 52:13 to the end of 53) to be later: they were written, in his opinion, in Palestine by one of the exiles who had returned thither about the year 450 B.C.E. Against the opinion of Duhm on "the Servant of Yahweh Songs," see K. Budde, *Die sogenannten Ebed-Jahve-Lieder*, Giessen, 1900; also his instructive discussion of the content of Isaiah 40–55 in the work previously cited, p. 166.

[6] This is also the opinion of Budde, *Geschichte der altheb. Litt.*, pp. 176–182, and of S. Bernfeld, *Introduction* [in Hebrew], II, 297–309. Marti, *Das Buch Jesajah*, Tübingen, 1900, pp. 361–362, and Steuernagel, *Einleitung*, Tübingen, 1912, pp. 525–532, assign all of Chaps. 56–66 basically (except for a few additions) to *one* author, whom they call the Third Isaiah [Trito-Isaiah].

prophet were a scientific scholar or a philosopher like Aristotle or Kant. Actually, the prophet, as a philosopher-poet, that is, a man of very sensitive nature, deeply moved by everything he experiences, cannot possibly avoid small, or even great, inconsistencies. For as a philosopher of life, of social life and national life, the prophet is influenced by events, not of course to such a degree that he would be hurled about by them from one opinion to another—the voice of God in his heart, *the fundamental tone* in him, always remains consistent and unaffected—but to such a degree that certain inconsistencies would *necessarily* be found in his words. Christian Biblical critics, who are rationalistic theologians, frequently forget this fact.

Secondly, they forget that the same prophet himself could and necessarily would undergo changes if he prophesied for a relatively long period of time. I have already pointed this out in the chapters on the Messianic ideas of the first Isaiah and of Ezekiel. It is quite impossible that all the prophecies of a prophet like Deutero-Isaiah, who prophesied for at least twenty-seven years, could have remained truly consistent. They had to change both as to form and content in many details and in many ways. Even between books of Kant which appeared forty years apart a great difference in both form and content is found; and the prophet is not a systematic philosopher like Kant. Only the *fundamental tone* must remain the same, since it never changes: it *cannot* change unless man is re-created as a new creature.

And the fundamental tone of all of Chapters 40–66 is one and the same. Even Duhm admits this, and by this fact he attempts to explain why Chapters 56–66 were joined to Chapters 40–55. Truly, only the blindness of an excessive hypercriticism could conclude that a prophet of the time of Malachi or of the time of Ezra could have such a strong likeness to the prophet of comfort to Zion. Those marvelous words of comfort in Chapter 60, with their fervid and extraordinary style, with their flow of vivid colors, with their poetic portrayals and their original metaphors, from which pour out abundance of life and exuberance and national pride—who could say these things except the same prophet offering the very same kind of comfort as in Chapter 54? In the time of Malachi or Ezra, when about eighty years had passed since the great promises of Deutero-Isaiah had been made, when a whole generation had passed since the exiles had returned, and after they had found time to rebuild the Temple, yet the great promises had not been fulfilled, yet the condition of the people was miserable, and in place of glowing expectations a long "period of insignificance" [literally "day of small things," Zeph. 4:10] was continuing—in this "period of insignificance" could a *great* prophet like this (or a number of great prophets like these) have arisen, a prophet of surpassing eloquence, with an imagination soaring heavenward and a great spirit embracing the whole world like the author of the prophecies in Isaiah 56–66? Could a prophet like this (or prophets like these) have arisen in the time of the epigones Haggai, Zechariah, and Malachi, the last of the prophets, who indeed hardly any longer merit the name "prophets"?

As far as I can see, all of Chapters 40–66 (and perhaps 13–14 along with them) belong to one prophet,[7] who is called Deutero-Isaiah, and whose prophetic career began at the end of the Babylonian exile, immediately after the sun of Cyrus rose in hither Asia after his great victory over Croesus king of Lydia in the year 546, continuing until after he succeeded in bringing about the first Return in 537 and after the first returners had laid the cornerstone of the Temple (though they neglected to complete the building until the time of Haggai). His *last* prophecy (Chapter 66, which mentions "a sound from the Temple" in Verse 6) was spoken at the time of the actual rebuilding (520–515) in the days of Haggai and Zechariah. However, when Haggai urged this rebuilding and rejoiced over it, Deutero-Isaiah stood in opposition ("What sort of house would you build for me, and what sort of place is My residence?"—66:1), because there still remained in him something of the spirit of the pre-Exilic prophets, who were suspicious of the sacrifices, lest the children of Israel by means of them should be kept from good deeds, and who feared the restriction of the Divine Presence to the Temple—that Divine Presence which the prophet of comfort to Zion longed to see ruling throughout the whole world.

All the last twenty-seven chapters of the Book of Isaiah were

---

[7] Such is also the opinion of Samuel Krauss in his aforementioned introduction to his commentary on Isaiah, ed. Kahana, pp. ix–xiii.

composed, therefore, in my opinion, by *one prophet*, but at different times. The first nine chapters, 40–48, were uttered partly during a few years preceding the conquest of Babylonia (542–539) and partly during the year that witnessed both the conquest and the proclamation of Cyrus. In this period the heart of the prophet was full of joy over the approaching redemption, and his imagination was aflame with the hope that soon all the glowing promises of the prophets who had preceded him would be fulfilled. For as soon as Cyrus had defeated Croesus king of Lydia, who had conspired against him with Ahmose (Amasis) king of Egypt and with Nabunaid (Nabonidus) king of Babylonia, it was possible for a man of penetrating intelligence like the prophet to see that soon Cyrus would bring an end to Babylonia also.

For this was inherent in the condition of the Babylonian kingdom after the death of Nebuchadrezzar. His son Evil-merodach (Amil-Marduk in Assyrian) ruled only two years (562–560), and then was killed by his brother-in-law Nergal-sharezer (perhaps it is he who is mentioned in Jeremiah 39:3 as one of the chief princes of Nebuchadrezzar; in Greek called Neriglissar), who himself ruled no more than four years (560–556). His son Labashi-Marduk succeeded him, but after a few months was slain by courtiers because of his wickedness and cruelty. He was followed by Nabonidus (556–539), the last king of Babylon. Nabonidus was a king who loved art and archaeological research, but was no warrior and also lacked the talent for leadership of the state. Apparently he turned over the latter function to his eldest son Belshazzar (in Assyrian Bel-shar-uṣur, "Bel will protect the king," or Belteshazzar = Balaṭ-shar-uṣur, "He will protect the life of the king"), who is mentioned in Daniel as the king of Chaldea who was defeated and slain by Cyrus.[8] The prophet saw, therefore, that the Babylonian kingdom was filled with disturbances and disorders and could not hold out very long. So when the sound of the wheels of Cyrus's victory chariot was heard from afar, it was a foregone conclusion that he would wreak vengeance on the Babylonians, since their king, Nabonidus, along with the king of Lydia and the

---

[8] See on this R. H. Dougherty, *Nabonidus and Belshazzar*, 1929.

king of Egypt, had conspired against Cyrus (547).[9] Thus it was natural that the prophet should see that the fall of Babylon was imminent. And the fall of the conqueror of his beloved land and the oppressor of his beloved people filled the heart of the prophet with vengeful joy and fair hope.

Likewise, the "Golah," that is, the large Jewish communities in Babylonia, was changed for the better. The words of Jeremiah concerning this "Golah" were fulfilled. The Babylonian exile was a crucible of affliction to the Jews, and in this crucible the dross was separated from the silver. A great part of the exiles became refined silver. Tribulations purified them, prophecy elevated them. The fact that they did not intermingle with the Babylonians, even though the Babylonians were numerous, strong, victorious, and filled with the joy of living while despising the Jews, "the worm Jacob"—by this very fact the Jews elevated themselves to the views of the prophets, who had no regard for brute force or for superficial physical pleasure, but recognized that the LORD God of Israel is not the God of a certain land alone and does not require sacrifices or a temple.

Moreover, the material condition of the Jews in Babylonia was not bad, as I have already indicated in the chapter on Ezekiel.[10] Nebuchadrezzar was not a very oppressive king; he was only irritated by the rebellion of Jehoiachin and Zedekiah. His son Evil-merodach, although he was not noted for kindness of heart, forgot the rebellion after a time and extended clemency to Jehoiachin, king of Judah (561). To be sure, the Jews in exile suffered many afflictions and hardships, like any conquered and captive people, like any sojourner in a foreign country (Isa. 52:5); but these afflictions were not beyond endurance. Therefore they did not crush the spirit of the Jews, but on the contrary revived in them their humiliated national pride, the hatred of their oppressors, their contempt for brute force, the love for their God and for the teaching of the prophets, and above all their yearning for the land of their fathers. So when the door of

---

[9] See J. Wellhausen, *Israel. u. jüd. Geschichte*, pp. 149-150.
[10] See above, pp. 111-113. See also J. Klausner, *History of the Second Temple* [in Hebrew], I, 65-99.

hope was opened, these considerations pushed everything else aside and filled the soul of the great prophet with only one desire: to instigate and to hasten the exodus from Babylonia, the return to Zion. Hence his vivid imagination pictured to him this return in most brilliant colors, since he saw therein the beginning of the realization of the Messianic promises offered by the prophets preceding him. His heart was captivated by these imperial dreams, and with this magic upon his lips he aroused the people to revival and exodus.

This is the historical milieu of Isaiah 40–48.

These chapters are Messianic almost from beginning to end: hopes of redemption fill them throughout. Of these hopes, some were near, grounded in the nature of the time and the environment, and therefore they were fulfilled; some were remote, such as only the imagination of the prophet could bring forth in a time of great expectation; these were not fulfilled during the whole course of time near the period of the prophet, but remained promises for *the distant future*, although the prophet himself, of course, saw in them promises for *the immediate future*. Between these two kinds of Messianic expectations we must distinguish as far as possible.

The Messianic chain in these chapters is of a special kind: it abandons most of its links. Only the elements "repentance—redemption" are present in it, and only the last element is completely preserved. These chapters contain no rebukes against sin: the "Golah" had actually mended its ways; and in general this solemn hour was not an opportune time for searching out sins. Even for *punishment* there was then no place: "her warfare (Jerusalem's time of servitude) is accomplished, *her iniquity is pardoned, for she hath received of the LORD's hand double for all her sins*," cries the prophet (Isa. 40:2). Now is not an hour of rebuke and punishment, but an hour of consolation. For repentance will come of its own accord: everybody now knows that "Jacob was given for a spoil and Israel to the robbers" because they sinned against the LORD (42:24). And as Ezekiel, so prophesied also Deutero-Isaiah that the LORD would blot out the transgressions of His people for His "own sake" (43:25). For repentance and atonement for transgression precede redemption. *The heralding of redemption* will also precede: the prophet speaks of "thou that tellest good tidings to Zion" and "thou that tellest good tidings to Jerusalem"; also of "a messenger of good tidings" whom He will give to Jerusalem, and of the first one who will point out to Zion her children, saying "Behold, behold them" (40:9–11; 41:27). Likewise the *ingathering of exiles* will precede it: as a shepherd gathers in his flock so will the LORD gather in His people; the weak and the faint He will carry in His arm and in His bosom as the shepherd carries the lambs and the ewes that give suck (40:11). What the expected shepherd from the house of David does in Ezekiel is done in the Second Isaiah directly by God himself. He brings the children of Zion from the east and from the west, from the north and from the south, and He gathers them from the end of the earth (43:5–6). All, "every one that is called by My name," without exception, will return to the land and glorify the name of the LORD (43:7). The prophet calls to the people in a loud voice:

> Go ye forth from Babylon,
> Flee ye from the Chaldeans,
> With a voice of singing!

and he gives a command to proclaim the good news of departure "even to the end of the earth" and to say to all, "The LORD hath redeemed His servant Jacob" (48:20).

The fear of stumbling-blocks on a road filled with horrors need not disturb those going back; the prophet does not grow weary of returning to this theme. Partly in literal language and partly in poetic metaphor, it is to be seen in all those numerous verses wherein the prophet emphasizes and re-emphasizes that the LORD will make smooth in the desert a highway for those returning, will lift up every valley and plain, will make low every mountain and hill, and will remove all rough and crooked places (40:3–4; 42:16). Not only will He make a road in the desert for those returning, but He will also change the order of nature for their sake: He will open up rivers on the mountains and fountains in the midst of the valleys, He will transform the barren places into pools and from the rock He will cause water to flow out for them as at the time of the exodus from Egypt (41:18; 43:19–20; 48:21). And not only this. In order to make things pleasant for the returners while they are passing through the desert, the LORD will cause to spring up in the desolate wilderness numerous kinds of trees to provide shade and sweet odors: cedar, acacia, myrtle, olive, cypress, plane, and larch (41:19). He will lead the blind in ways and paths which they never knew, and will make darkness light before them (42:16). All these wonders will the LORD perform for those returning to their own land!

We found in the first Isaiah and in the rest of the earlier prophets that changes in the lot of the people Israel are accompanied by comparable changes in inanimate nature. This should occasion no surprise. For according to the views of the prophet, nature and man are both in the hand of God, and evil in nature is only punishment for the evil deeds of man, just as good in nature is only a reward for the good deeds of man.[11] In this regard, Deutero-Isaiah is exactly like that great prophet by whose name his prophecies are called. *The redemption of Israel is the redemption of the world,* even the inanimate world. Therefore, the prophet-poet, with his strong imagination, cries out:

> Sing, O ye heavens, for the LORD hath done it;
> Shout, ye lowest parts of the earth;
> Break forth into singing, ye mountains,
> O forest, and every tree therein;
> For the LORD hath redeemed Jacob,
> And doth glorify Himself in Israel (44:23).

Jacob has a strong redeemer, like Whom there is none other, Who is the first and the last, and to Whose power there is no limit or end; therefore the "worm Jacob" need not fear anything:

> When thou passest through the waters,
>   I will be with thee,
> And through the rivers,
>   they shall not overflow thee;
> When thou walkest through the fire,
>   thou shalt not be burned,
> Neither shall the flame kindle upon thee (43:2).

---

[11] See an extended discussion of this idea in my essay *Our Spiritual Values,* sections on "The Idea of Monotheism," "Prophecy," and "The Messianic Idea" (J. Klausner, *Judaism and Humanity* [in Hebrew], 3rd ed., Jerusalem, 1941, pp. 143-148, 160-169).

The God of Jacob will lay hold of His people to strengthen and help them. All who rise up to fight against Him will perish and become as nothing (41:10–13). The "worm Jacob" will become "a new threshing-sledge having sharp teeth," which will thresh the mountains and beat them small and make the hills as chaff to be scattered by the wind (41:14–16). But not alone by physical strength will Jacob conquer his enemies; he will conquer them more by the spirit. He—the servant of the LORD, His chosen one in whom His soul delights—"will make justice go forth to the nations" without needing to cry out or to make his voice heard in the street; and without his breaking even a bruised reed or his quenching even a dimly burning wick, his truth will be spread throughout the world and "the isles shall wait for his teaching" (42:1–4). Finally the prophet describes the great *spiritual* promise of the people Israel in words that will remain eternal, as is the people Israel itself:

> I the LORD have called thee in righteousness,
> And have taken hold of thy hand,
> And kept thee, and set thee for a covenant of the people,
> For a light of the nations;
> To open the blind eyes,
> To bring out the prisoners from the dungeon,
> And them that sit in darkness out of the prison-house (42:6–7).

Then all the world will acknowledge that the LORD He is God and there is none other. Then will be brought to pass what had already come forth from the mouth of this God; namely, "unto Me every knee shall bow, every tongue shall swear" (45:22–23). All the Gentile nations will then be ashamed of their gods, and only Israel will not be ashamed and confounded forever and ever; for Israel will be saved by the LORD with an everlasting salvation (45:14–17). The salvation is near and will take place in Zion (46:13). The LORD will pour out his spirit upon the seed of Judah (Jacob) and Israel, and his blessing upon their offspring, so that every one of them will take pride in being called by the name Jacob and in being inscribed among the servants of the LORD (44:3–5).

This is the great *spiritual* expectation contained in the first nine chapters of Deutero-Isaiah.

Material and political expectation is not yet expressed here with such great clarity. Material expectation, produce of the soil, and the like, could not much influence the exiles, since their economic condition was relatively good; moreover, the prophet saw no necessity of using this expectation to arouse love of the fatherland, since it was certain that the flame of this love in their hearts had not been quenched. Nevertheless, material expectation is included within the spiritual expectation in plain words: the prophet promises that "the labour of Egypt and the merchandise of Ethiopia" and whatever the caravans of "Sabeans, men of stature," may bring with them will pass over to the land of Judah and belong to her; all the people of these nations will walk after her in chains like prisoners of war and bow down to her in recognition that only in her is God and that outside her there is no God (45:14).[12] The prophet also promises that Jerusalem will be repopulated, the cities of Judah rebuilt, and her ruined places raised up (44:26).

Greater political expectation the prophet could not voice so long as he was forced to live among the Babylonians and Persians, the overlords of Judah; for particularly until the decree of Cyrus these overlords would of course look upon political expectations with extreme suspicion; and Babylonian officials were obliged to transmit to the king anything which they might see or hear.[13] Besides, there was then no place for bright and immediate political hopes. There was no longer a king in Israel and it was not possible to hope that soon there would be; yet deliverance was near, as has been said.

For this reason there is almost no indication in Deutero-Isaiah of an individual human Messiah, who will deliver his people and stand at their head, such as we found in most of the prophets preceding. The LORD Himself will be the redeemer; the prophet emphasizes this numberless times. But as a means and instrument for His great work He will use Cyrus, king of Persia, the foreign king whom the prophet, speaking in the name of the LORD, calls "My shepherd," [14]

[12] For the exegesis of this verse, see Krauss in his commentary on Isaiah (Chap. 45). In his opinion, the meaning of the prophet is that Cyrus will give gifts to the Temple from the wealth of Egypt, Ethiopia, and the Sabeans.
[13] See on this B. Meissner, *Babylonien und Assyrien*, I (1920), 134.
[14] F. Hommel (*Geschichte des alten Morgenlandes*, p. 163, note) says that

and "My anointed" (44:28; 45:1), promising him that He will subdue nations before him, that He will open before him gates and bronze doors (of the fortified and enclosed city of Babylon), that He will even level off before him rugged places and give him treasures kept in darkness and hidden riches of secret places (45:1–3). All these things He will do not for the sake of the foreign king, but for the sake of Judah and Israel, in order that Cyrus may give permission to rebuild Jerusalem and to lay the foundations of the Temple (44:28; 45:4). Otherwise, what would the God of Israel have to do with the Persian king?—"I have surnamed thee, though thou hast not known Me," "I have girded thee, though thou hast not known Me," says the prophet with obvious emphasis (45:4–5).

Naturally, the word *Messiah* ("anointed one") is not used here in the later sense of this word, nor was the foreign king considered by the prophet as the redeemer in the same sense in which the "shoot out of the stock of Jesse," for example, was intended by the first Isaiah. Cyrus was in the prophet's eyes "the anointed of the LORD" in that sense intended by the prophets when they applied this title to the more prominent of the kings of Israel and Judah (I Sam. 24:7; and Lam. 4:20). Nevertheless, many of the exiles spoke ill of the prophet and even complained against the LORD Himself on the ground that He had handed over the carrying out of the promise to return and to re-establish Zion to a king who was not from Israel. The prophet, apparently, answered this with severe words: Can the clay tell the potter what to do? The Israelites have no authority to instruct the LORD as to what He shall do with His children, the work of His hands. Says the prophet, speaking of Cyrus in the name of the LORD:

> I have roused him up in victory,
> And I make level all his ways;
> He shall build My city,
> And he shall let Mine exiles go free,
> Not for price nor reward,
> Saith the LORD of hosts (45:9–13).[15]

---

in the Cassite language *kuras* means "shepherd," and this is indicated in Isaiah 44:28.

[15] See on this Cornill, *Der israel. Prophetismus*, pp. 135–136.

Political deliverance this time had to come not through a king of the house of David, but through a foreign king; thus had events turned out, and therefore, of course, the LORD so wished it. Earlier, Assyria had been the rod of His anger, but now Cyrus was the instrument with which He worked. Therefore the prophet refrained from speaking of a Jewish Messiah, and in general from saying overmuch about political expectation. Everything revolved for him about one pivot: about the nearness of redemption, about the urgency to depart, to flee from Babylon as quickly as possible, and about the abolishment of the stumbling blocks and hindrances to this departure, inasmuch as the LORD had put it into the mind of Cyrus to authorize the departure and the rebuilding of the city and Temple, and inasmuch as the whole rough and hazardous road would be converted at the word of the LORD into a broad highway lined with beautiful streams and fountains and trees. The main point was the return to Zion—then the rest would follow.

This is the first part of the prophecies of Deutero-Isaiah. This is the first period of his prophetic career, which fell in the last years before the fall of Babylon and in the first year of the victory of Cyrus over Babylon, until his decree came forth: "Whosoever there is among you of all His people—his God be with him—let him go up to Jerusalem!" (Ezra 1:3). From this point began a new period in his prophetic activity.

Until the decree of liberation came forth, the prophet did not doubt at all that the "Golah" which had been tested in "the furnace of affliction" (48:10), this "Golah" which had suffered so much and without doubt had thoroughly repented, would hasten "to flee from Chaldea with a voice of singing" (48:20). But when the first group of returners actually had to be organized, it immediately became apparent that the prophet had erred in his judgment: that many did not wish to return at all and many would not even support the returners with money. Even in the early period we hear the prophet speaking severely to his people: "Who swear by the name of the LORD, and make mention of the God of Israel, but not in truth nor in righteousness" (48:1); "because I knew that thou art obstinate, and thy neck is an iron sinew, and thy brow brass" (48:4); "for I knew that thou wouldest deal very treacherously, and wast called a transgressor from the womb" (48:8). And we also hear the prophet of comfort to Zion saying, like Ezekiel in his time, that the LORD will show mercy to His people only "for His own name's sake," in order that His name might not be profaned among the Gentiles (48:9, 11).

As the time of departure drew nearer and nearer, the number of persons who did not believe in the possibility of redemption, or perhaps did not even desire it, increased: "Wherefore, when I came, was there no man? when I called, was there none to answer?" sorrowfully cries the prophet; then he questions further in the name of the LORD: "Is My hand shortened at all, that it cannot redeem? or have I no power to deliver?" (50:2). And we feel that the wings of the prophet have been clipped, so to speak. He is no longer so certain of the speed and effectiveness of the redemption, and his joy is no longer complete. He is forced to make a distinction between the wicked ones who scorn the redemption and those "that know righteousness, the people in whose heart is My law"; and these latter he instructs not to pay heed to the reproaches and derision of their opponents (51:7). These "that know righteousness" are the servants of the LORD, the disciples of the prophets—the disciples of *the prophet*, who are like him because God's law is in their hearts. Therefore sometimes the prophet calls them by the collective name "the servant of the LORD," and sometimes they are in his eyes *the true Judah*, "the servants of Jacob." Even when he describes himself as the prophet suffering for the iniquity of others and persecuted by others for doing good to them, he does not intend thereby to describe himself alone, but all who are faithful to God's covenant, "the people in whose heart is His law." If we take this into consideration, we shall understand clearly all those passages in the Second Isaiah about which the interpreters have had difficulty in knowing whether the intention is to portray the entire people Israel or only the prophet, the servant of the LORD, alone. These are the "Songs of the Servant of Yahweh" so famous among Christian scholars, who have found them in 52:13–

15 and 53:1–12, to which must be added also 42:1–7, 40:1–9, and 50:4–9.[16]

In the second period of the work of Deutero-Isaiah, in which were spoken the prophecies included in Chapters 49–55—the short period extending from the decree to the departure—the prophet no longer urges on the departing ones so strongly. Instead of saying as formerly, "Go forth from Babylon, flee from Chaldea," he now says, "Ye shall not go out in haste, neither shall ye go by flight" (52:12). But the coldness which many of the exiles showed to the idea of the return to Zion, and the doubtfulness which was aroused in them after they saw that in the Persian deliverance there was almost no sign of the great and wonderful things promised by the prophets—this coldness and doubtfulness forced the prophet to emphasize much more *the political and material welfare* in store for Israel after its return to its own land; he even hints of "the sure mercies of David" (55:3). The friendly attitude of Cyrus toward the Jews, the permission which he gave to Zerubbabel, the branch from the stem of the kings of the house of David, to stand at the head of the movement of emigration, though not as governor (Sheshbazzar was governor at first), justified the prophet in at least hinting of the politico-Messianic expectations connected with the kingdom of the house of David, although of course he could not speak at length about them for fear of arousing suspicion and hostility. However, with regard to the rest of the political expectations, he did not curb his spirit but portrayed them in marvelously bright colors—something which he did not do in the first period of his prophetic activity.

So much for the historical background and general contents of Chapters 49–55.

Many of their Messianic descriptions closely resemble those which we found in the preceding prophecies; this clearly proves that the prophecies in these chapters came forth from the mouth of the very same prophet and were uttered at a time very near to that of the first prophecies of consolation. Here also the prophet speaks of "the messenger of good tidings" who will go upon the mountains and proclaim to Zion, "Thy God reigneth!" (52:7). Here also he speaks of the

[16] See on them in detail Steuernagel, *Einleitung*, pp. 516–522.

gathering of the exiles from the north, from the west, and from the distant lands (49:12). Here also he speaks of the removal of all impediments from the way, of the leveling of the mountains and the opening of fountains in the desert; and he promises the pilgrims that they will not be hungry or thirsty and that the blazing sun and the "Fata Morgana" (mirage) [17] will not hurt them (49:9-11). Here also the prophet calls upon nature to participate in the rejoicing of the people (compare 44:23, quoted above, with 49:13). In delightful figures he describes the joy that will lay hold upon all nature in the day of redemption: "The mountains and the hills shall break forth before you into singing, and all the trees of the field shall clap their hands" (55:12). The imagination of the prophet is so fired by the vision of salvation that he calls for exultation and singing even from the ruins of Jerusalem (52:9). They too must participate in the rejoicing of the pilgrims, because salvation will come to them also:

> For the LORD hath comforted Zion;
> He hath comforted all her waste places,
> And hath made her wilderness like Eden,
> And her desert like the garden of the LORD;
> Joy and gladness shall be found therein,
> Thanksgiving, and the voice of melody (51:3).

For "instead of the thorn shall come up the cypress, and instead of the brier shall come up the myrtle" (44:13). Thus will the productivity of the soil be changed for the better. Not less will be the increase of human beings. The population of the land of Israel will be so increased that the land will be "too cramped for the inhabitants" (49:19). For the peoples will bring her sons "in their bosom" and her daughters will be carried "upon their shoulders" (49:22). The prophet's excessive enthusiasm carries his imagination aloft to immeasurable heights, and he portrays the political and worldly future in glowing colors, the like of which cannot be found in the visions of any prophet preceding or following him:

[17] *Sharab* in Hebrew, in Arabic *sarâb*. According to other opinions, the word means the burning desert air, and perhaps also the dry, burning soil: "refreshed the parched ground" (Ben-Sira 43:22 [S.P.C.K. ed., p. 125]). See Gesenius-Buhl, *Handwörterbuch über das Alte Testament*, 17th ed., Leipzig, 1921, p. 863.

> And kings shall be thy foster-fathers,
> And queens thy nursing mothers;
> They shall bow down to thee
>   with their face to the earth,
> And lick the dust of thy feet (49:23).

For all the enemies of Judah will be cut off, and all who lift themselves up against her will not succeed (49:17–19, 25–26; 54:17)—just as the prophet had said in his prophecies of the first period. So great will be the *political success*. And *material prosperity* will not be less. "O thou afflicted one, storm-tossed, uncomforted!"—the prophet turns toward the beloved homeland in great compassion—

> Behold, I will set thy bases with beryl,[18]
> And lay thy foundations with sapphires.
> And I will make thy pinnacles of rubies,
> And thy gates of carbuncle stones,
> And all thy border of jewels (54:11–12).

At the same time spiritual blessings will multiply:

> And all thy children shall be taught of the LORD;
> And great shall be the peace of thy children (54:13).

For Zion will be established in righteousness (54:14), Jerusalem will be "the Holy City," and the uncircumcised and unclean will no more enter it (52:1)—just as Ezekiel had said. In spite of all the universalism of the prophet, which we shall soon see in all its glory, his nationalism is not diminished, just as in spite of all his spirituality his political and worldly hopes are not impaired. The Gentiles will exalt Israel as the Chosen People, as their kings bow down to the earth before him and lick the dust of his feet. The Gentiles, therefore, will not be equal to Israel in glory and honor,[19] although all of them will become sons of God because all of them will be called by the name of the LORD. Israel will remain the center, while the Gentiles will be only points on the circumference.

On what basis should Israel have an advantage over the rest of the

---

[18] So reads Wellhausen according to the Septuagint, instead of "thy stones in fair colours." "Thy bases with beryl" corresponds closely to "thy foundations with sapphires." But see S. Bernfeld, *op. cit.*, II, 301, Note 1.

[19] See Cornill, *op. cit.*, pp. 143-154.

nations? The answer could have been only this: because Israel will teach the knowledge of the LORD and ethical insight to all peoples. But this answer was the result of a long evolution of ideas and the cause of a new chain of profound ideas closely bound together by their own nature.

Not *all* the people of Israel have acknowledged the LORD; among this Chosen People are evil ones and sinners, who do not wish to know the LORD and to walk in His ways. Only the prophets and their disciples are the servants of the LORD, and only they have spread His teaching in Israel—and for this they have been persecuted by their own people, slain like Uriah the son of Shemaiah, or cast into cisterns and into prison like Jeremiah. Thus the one attempting to spread the knowledge of the LORD and the love of the good, that is, to *benefit* the people, is forced to endure many *evils* for the LORD's sake and to take comfort in the hope that finally the sinful people will acknowledge and understand that the servant of the LORD was in the right.

The people Israel is the only nation within which is the knowledge of the LORD and the recognition of the good; therefore it must disseminate these two things among the other peoples, as the prophets disseminate them within it. This ethical demand was already made by the pre-Exilic prophets from Amos to Zephaniah and Jeremiah. And if the Exilic and post-Exilic prophets saw that Israel was suffering greatly, that its land was laid waste and its Temple ruined, that it had gone into exile among the Gentiles and become in its political weakness an object of mockery and derision among them, verily— unless the prophet and his disciples were willing to conclude that the God of Israel had no power or ability to save His people and that the whole idea of the choice of the people Israel is only vanity and emptiness—there was left to them only the conclusion that just as the prophet suffers without having committed a fault, suffers from the transgressors among his own people whom he is seeking to benefit, that is to say, *takes upon himself the iniquity of others,* so suffers also the people Israel from other peoples more sinful than Israel, because Israel seeks to benefit them. In other words, *the people Israel takes upon itself the iniquity of all the rest of the peoples, the iniquity of the whole world.* What the prophet is to Israel, Israel becomes to all the world: the servant of the LORD, holding up the standard of the highest righteousness in the world and suffering for his pursuit of good.

This is the profound conception that lies hidden in 42:1–7; 49:1–9; 50:4–9; 52:13–15 plus 53:1–12. The ancient Jewish interpreters were divided as to whether these passages refer to the prophet alone or to the whole people Israel. The early Christians, from Paul the Apostle (Acts 8:32–35) onward, saw in them a reference to the sufferings and death of Jesus of Nazareth. (As a matter of fact, some of his career did resemble what is described in Chapter 53; and the rest of his career is *intentionally* portrayed in the Gospels in such a manner that the events appear to have happened in fulfillment of the words in this chapter.) Some modern Christian scholars wish to see in these passages a description of the fate of Zerubbabel or Jehoiachin (Sellin), or of some other great man of Israel who lived in the middle of the sixth century B.C.E. (Duhm).[20] After what I said above by way of explanation, it should now be clear that the prophet could not separate his own fate, as one persecuted for his pursuit of good, from the fate of his disciples and of all the servants of the LORD, whom he considered to be the real nucleus of the people Israel, the Israel in whom the LORD "will be glorified" (49:3). Thus everything said in these chapters can and must be related in one process both to the prophet and to the whole Jewish nation: the servants of the LORD are this nation's chosen remnant, to which alone belongs the future.[21]

[20] Against Duhm I have already called attention above (p. 145, Note 5) to the books of Budde. Sellin, in his book *Serubabel* (1898), expressed the opinion that "the Servant of Yahweh" is Zerubbabel; but later, in his books *Studien zur Entstehungsgeschichte der jüdischen Gemeinde* (1901), and *Heilandserwartung* (1909), pp. 51–60, he turned away from this opinion and said that "the Servant of Yahweh" is King Jehoiachin; and finally, in *Mose und seine Bedeutung für die israelitisch-jüdische Religionsgeschichte* (1922), pp. 77–113, he said that "the Servant of the LORD" is Moses. But see against him F. Giesebrecht, *Der Knecht Jahves des Deuterojesaia*, Königsberg, 1902. See also the commentary of Rabbi S. Krauss on Isaiah 45–49 and 52–53.

[21] In agreement with this opinion, which I expressed forty-five years ago, in 1907 (see *Ha-Shiloah*, XVI [1907], 352–353), is the eminent scholar W. F. Albright, *From the Stone Age to Christianity*, 1940, pp. 254–255. But see also M. Z. Segal, *op. cit.*, II, 330–332.

Nevertheless, there is a kernel of Messianism—not Christian, but completely Jewish Messianism—in these chapters.

I have already said in a number of places that the Jewish Messiah is composite in his nature: in him are some of the politico-worldly virtues of the king and some of the ethico-spiritual virtues of the prophet. In the period of the Second Isaiah there was no place for an individual political Jewish Messiah, as was said above; and apart from the reference to "the sure mercies of David" we do not find this subject mentioned at all by the prophet of consolation to Zion. But precisely because the ethico-spiritual virtues of the Messiah were exalted and became the shining symbols of Messianism, the bearer of Messianism came to be either the individual "servant of the LORD," the prophet, or the collective "servant of the LORD," the best of the people Israel. Thus the *whole* people Israel *in the form of the elect of the nation* gradually became *the Messiah of the world, the redeemer of mankind.* This Messiah must suffer just as the prophet suffers. Here also punishment precedes redemption; but this punishment is unique: it comes as a penalty *for the sin of others.* And it redeems the world; for if Israel had not been willing to suffer and to spread the knowledge of God and of pure morality in the earth, the world would have remained sunk in sin against religion and morality. And for this punishment, bringing good to all peoples except Israel, this people receives a worthy reward in "the end of days" [future age], in that it becomes "a light to the Gentiles," in that it is placed in the center of mankind.

This, *in its broadest aspects,* is the content of those chapters which treat of the servant of the LORD. In it are included the spiritual, the universalistic, Messianic expectations of the people Israel, expectations which serve to supplement the nationalistic, the worldly, and the political expectations of which I have already spoken above. Therefore it is impossible to pass over them in silence; they must be presented as completely as possible here, since the greatness of their value for the development of Messianism in the future is incalculable.

The servant of the LORD, "Israel in whom He will be glorified," suffers, and it seems that he has labored in vain and spent his strength for nothing; but actually his accomplishment is great and his reward is with the LORD, who says to him:

> It is too light a thing that thou shouldest be My servant
> To raise up the tribes of Jacob,
> And to restore the survivors of Israel (the nationalistic expectation);
> *I will also give thee for a light of the nations,*
> *That My salvation may be unto the end of the earth* (49:1-6).

And not only for "a light of the nations" but also for "a covenant of the people" (49:8)—as Deutero-Isaiah had said in his earlier prophecies (42:6). "The Redeemer and the Holy One of Israel" promises His servant, whom He has chosen and who was despised and abhorred and "a slave of rulers" (from this it seems clear that even here the meaning does not apply to the prophet alone),[22] that "kings shall see and arise (before him), princes, and they shall prostrate themselves" (49:7)—something which the prophet had already promised to the whole people Israel (49:23). In lifelike figures the prophet describes everything which the servant of the LORD must suffer—and this is particularly appropriate to the prophet himself—when he comes in the name of the LORD to preach His morality to the people:

> I gave my back to the smiters,
> And my cheeks to them that plucked off the hair;
> I hid not my face from shame and spitting (50:6).

But he sets his face like flint, knowing that in the end he will be vindicated, while all who rise against him will become as though they had never been (50:7-9).[23] For in the end the servant of the LORD will prosper, "he shall be exalted and lifted up, and shall be very high" (52:13). Just as many gazed upon him with shaking of the head because his visage was marred and his figure was frightening and unlike the figure of a man on account of the blows which the

[22] Gressmann, *Eschatologie*, Tübingen, 1905, pp. 301-333, considers the *basis* of "the Servant of Yahweh" to be mythological. This is possible. But the prophet utilized mythological material for lofty religious purposes, and hence the contradiction, at times, between the original pattern and the thing patterned after it.

[23] S. Krauss attempts to prove, in his commentary on Isaiah, 50:7-11, that even here the reference is to the Jewish community only. It is hard for me to agree with his opinion at this point.

enemies of the word of the LORD had struck him, so will he compel many nations to leap from their places (*yazzeh*) in great astonishment,[24] and kings will shut their mouths before him in great fear because of seeing a thing which had not been told them and of which they had never heard (52:14–15). For as a weak and tender sapling the servant of the LORD sprang up, and as a root out of dry ground, without form or comeliness or pleasing appearance. He was despised and of no esteem in the eyes of all (53:1–3). The prophet puts into the mouth of the enemies and persecutors of the servant of the LORD, who in the end of days will acknowledge their error and their guilt, the following words:

> Surely our diseases he did bear,
> And our pains he carried;
> Whereas we did esteem him stricken,
> Smitten of God, and afflicted.
> But he was wounded because of our transgressions,[25]
> He was crushed because of our iniquities:
> The chastisement of our welfare was upon him,[26]
> And with his stripes we were healed.
> All we like sheep did go astray,
> We turned every one to his own way;
> And the LORD hath made to light on him
> The iniquity of us all (53:4–6).

The description of the afflictions of the servant of the LORD continues at length: "He was oppressed," yet he remained silent and suffered in humility ("he humbled himself"), "and he opened not his mouth, as a lamb that is led to the slaughter, and as a sheep that be-

---

[24] Since it is difficult to conceive that many nations will leap from their places, Cheyne reads "many nations shall bow down," and S. Krauss reads, according to the Septuagint, "shall be amazed." But, in my opinion, there is no need for emendations, since the prophet could have spoken about the leaping of whole nations in amazement by way of hyperbole.

[25] "Wounded" = stabbed, the same word as in "pierced the dragon" (Isa. 51:9). In parallelism to this, various scholars read "pierced because of our iniquities" instead of "crushed."

[26] That is, the afflictions that we should have borne in order to have peace (welfare) later were cast upon him; perhaps it is necessary to read *shillumenu* ["our requital" instead of "our welfare"], i.e., our recompense and our punishment.

fore her shearers is dumb." [27] Dominion [28] and judgment were plucked away from him; and who could tell his generation [29] that he was cut off from the land of the living because he had been smitten for the transgression of his people? [30] His generation, which did not know this (or the servant of the LORD himself), made his grave with the wicked and with the evildoers [31] at his death,[32] "although he had done no violence, neither was any deceit in his mouth." But the LORD saw fit to cleanse him of affliction.[33] So the prophet, as it were, turns to some individual persecutor, saying to him: "If you make his life a guilt-offering, he shall see his offspring, he shall prolong his days, and the purpose of the LORD (to retrieve many from iniquity) shall prosper in his hand." He will see the good that will spring forth from the travail of his soul, and will be satisfied by this good.[34] The

[27] The *second* occurrence of "he opened not his mouth" at the end of Verse 7 is, of course, superfluous, as Kautzsch has said, being merely an erroneous duplication ("dittography").

[28] Thus, in my opinion, is the interpretation of the word '*otser* [usually translated "oppression"]. Cf. "possessing authority" (Judges 18:7), and also "there was none shut up [or "under authority"] nor left at large, neither was there any helper for Israel" (II Kings 14:26), which I have already explained above, p. 37, Note 2.

[29] One Christian scholar has proposed to read, in place of *doro*, "his generation," *de·wayo*, and to translate "His *pains*, who can express them?" (see Hühn, *Die messian. Weissag.*, I, p. 147, Note 1); perhaps the interpretation of the word *dor* here is similar to Isa. 38:12, where it means "life."

[30] The Septuagint reads, instead of "For the transgression of my people a blow, to them," "For the transgression of my people he was smitten to death" (ἤχθη εἰς θάνατον). Perhaps "my people" now stands [in error] for "the peoples" (S. D. Luzzatto).

[31] So reads Böttcher instead of "the rich" (sing.). Duhm proposes to read, instead of this word, '*ashîq*, "the deceitful" (sing.); but this is a later Aramaic word. The medieval grammarian R. Jonah Ibn-Janah, author of *Ha-Riqmah*, read "the wicked" (sing.) instead of "the rich" (sing.).

[32] So reads Kautzsch with the Septuagint (ἀντὶ τοῦ θανάτου αὐτοῦ) instead of "in his deaths." Others read "his tomb" [without the preposition, parallel with "his grave"], in the sense of an ornamental structure over the grave (*bamato*).

[33] According to the Septuagint: καθαρίσαι αὐτὸν τῆς πληγῆς. It is to be supposed that in the Hebrew original which was before the Seventy there stood, instead of *dakke'o heheli, zakke'o* (or *zakkotho*) *meholi*; perhaps these words should be understood in the sense of to cleanse or purify *by means of* affliction and not only to cleanse *from* affliction.

[34] According to the Septuagint we should read here: "From the travail of his soul He will deliver (him), He will show (him) light and satisfy (him)"; obviously the Seventy in this instance are interpreters rather than translators. The word "deliver" (יציל) was probably in the Hebrew text, and was later omitted

righteous one, the servant of the LORD, will turn many [35] to righteousness by his knowledge (that is, by his knowledge of God), "and he shall bear their iniquities." Therefore the LORD will assign him the portion of the great, and with the strong he will divide plunder, because he exposed himself to death for the LORD's sake "and was numbered with the transgressors" while truly "he bore the sin of many" and chastened [36] the transgressors (53:7–12).[37]

It is clear that here "the servant of the LORD" is both the prophet, along with his disciples, and also all the righteous and upright of Israel, who in the eyes of the prophet are the whole people Israel. The lofty idea that a people or a whole group should suffer for the iniquity of others precisely because that group has been exalted above others was natural to the Jewish prophet who himself suffered without sin, saying: "I have not lent, neither have men lent to me, yet every one of them doth curse me" (Jeremiah 15:10). But the consolation that the people Israel could and had to find in its tribulations by means of this view—that it suffers more than others because it is better than others, that others attain to their meritorious condition because it bears their iniquity and their afflictions, that it does good to all the world while all the world repays it evil for good—how necessary was this consolation to revive Israel's spirit and to fill it with pride and self-esteem! And how necessary was such a view to lift the people above all its trials and afflictions and to silence the argument that "evil befalls the righteous, good befalls the wicked!"

Just as every great man feels and recognizes that by his greatness he provides atonement for his people or even for all humanity, hav-

---

because of its similarity to the word "prosper" (ויצלח) at the end of the preceding verse.

[35] Cf. "they that turn the many to righteousness" in Daniel (12:3) following "they that are wise"; note that this passage begins [52:13], "Behold, My servant shall *deal prudently* (be wise)." The word "righteous one" (צדיק) is perhaps to be stricken out as a duplication of "justify" (יצרוק).

[36] Thus should *yafgia'* be translated, with the idea of "evil occurrences" [I Kings 5:18, Eng. 5:4], and not with the idea of prayer ["intercession"]; thus also the interpretation of *hifgia'* above (Verse 6) ["*laid on him* the iniquity of us all"].

[37] On the versions and more recent interpretations of this passage, see R. Levy, *op. cit.*, pp. 258–269.

ing as a highly ethical person not many privileges but many obligations, so also was the people Israel forced to recognize, particularly in its time of exile, that it is a great people, a supreme people, whose obligations are manifold, and that this is the cause of its afflictions; yet that there will come a day when all will acknowledge its righteousness, and that what it preached, alone and persecuted, will become the faith of the whole world. The great idea of the prophet of necessity implanted eternal life within the people Israel. And perhaps this view was the basic reason for the great change which took place among those exiles, disciples and friends of the Second Isaiah, who returned to Palestine and became there completely different persons.

As though the prophet sensed the great importance of his new viewpoint for the continued existence of the nation, he emphasized many times the eternity of the redeemed nation, placing its preservation above even the preservation of nature. "The grass withereth, the flower fadeth, but the word of our God shall stand forever," said the prophet in his prophecies of the first period (40:8).

> For the heavens shall vanish away like smoke,
> And the earth shall wax old like a garment,
> And they that dwell therein shall die in like manner;
> But My salvation shall be for ever,
> And My favour shall not be abolished (51:6).

This idea is repeated, thus:

> For the mountains may depart,
> And the hills be removed;
> But My kindness shall not depart from thee,
> Neither shall My covenant of peace be removed,
> Saith the LORD that hath compassion on thee (54:10).

We pass to the third period in the prophetic activity of the Second Isaiah. In it were composed the last eleven chapters of the Book of Isaiah (56–66). To separate Chapters 56–62 from Chapters 63–66 and to attribute them to various prophets (or even to two widely separated periods), as do a number of recent scholars—of this I see no necessity. On the contrary, the great similarity between Chapter 57,

Verses 3-11, and Chapter 65, Verses 1-7, on the one hand, and between 65:12-13, 17 and 66:4-5, 17, 22, on the other hand, forces us to consider all these prophecies as the creation of one prophet in one period, though a certain number of years passed between the beginning and the end of them (about fifteen to twenty years, but not more). Nevertheless, it is possible to separate from these prophecies Chapter 66, which contains a hint of the existence of the Temple, as mentioned above,[38] and to attribute it to a slightly later time, about the year 518, at the end of the time of Zechariah (the first), especially since Verses 19-21 of this chapter call to mind the end of the Book of Zechariah (Deutero-Zechariah, which in any case is not to be dated so late as 280 B.C.E. with Stade, as we shall see in its place).

But I have already said that, since the style and content of this section are completely Deutero-Isaianic, and since there is an evident relationship between 65:12-13, 17 and 66:4-5, 17, 22, it is reasonable to suppose that Deutero-Isaiah lived until the Temple was nearly complete, so that his prophetic career extended over twenty-two to twenty-seven years, nearly the length of time of the prophetic career of Ezekiel; and that the prophecy in Chapter 66 is of course his last. The rest of the prophecies of the third period were delivered after the first Return. From the phrase "When thou criest, let them that thou hast gathered deliver thee" (57:13), and from the whole of Chapter 62, particularly the verses "I have set watchmen upon thy walls, O Jerusalem," [39] and so on (62:6-9), it seems evident that when these prophecies were spoken Jerusalem was no longer completely desolate and many of the exiles had already returned thither; but that the condition of affairs was so low and wretched in contrast to what the prophets had dreamed that the prophet laments bitterly about this in 63:7-19 and 64:5-11, which in their style remind us of

---

[38] S. Krauss in his commentary opposes even this, and concludes that the prophet was able to use language like this even at a time when the Temple was not standing. See his commentary on 66:6.

[39] From Nehemiah (1:3) it appears that Jerusalem had walls before he came, but that they were broken down, and thus there was all the more need of watchmen; it is to this that the prophet refers, and not to the wall that Nehemiah built. S. Krauss thinks that the reference here is merely to some elevated place. On the wall from the time of Zerubbabel, see H. Graetz, *Geschichte der Juden*, II.2, p. 106.

the psalms composed soon after the Return, with their sorrowful complaints about the wretched state of affairs in the fatherland and their manifold yearnings for the fulfillment of the prophetic promises, political, material, and spiritual. The prophet sees that the Persians, with their many burdensome taxes, are eating the grain and drinking the new wine of the LORD's people, so he says:

> The LORD hath sworn by His right hand,
> And by the arm of His strength:
> Surely I will no more give thy corn
> To be food for thine enemies;
> And strangers shall not drink thy wine,
> For which thou hast laboured (62:8).

Most of the cities of Judah were in ruins, and Jerusalem itself was so thinly populated that Nehemiah later had to *force* part of the inhabitants of the small towns roundabout to settle in Jerusalem (Nehemiah 11). The prophet sees this and makes "the LORD's remembrancers" swear that they will "give Him no rest till He establish, and till He make Jerusalem a praise in the earth" (Isaiah 62:6–7).

Concerning the religious situation, Ezra and Nehemiah have left us clear impressions of the disordered conditions that prevailed even before their arrival. Those who had remained in the land and even those returning had intermarried with Gentiles, learning the Gentiles' language and customs, and of course not obeying many of the precepts of the prophets. Likewise in Babylonia some of the exiles apparently had fallen into idolatry, completely forgetting their native land ("ye that forsake the LORD, *that forget My holy mountain*, that prepare a table for Fortune, and that offer mingled wine in full measure unto Destiny," (65:11).[40] Also among those returning were many who would "sacrifice in gardens and burn incense upon bricks," who would practice soothsaying and divination, and eat "swine's flesh and the detestable thing and the mouse" (65:1–6, 11; 66:17). Therefore the prophet now becomes a chastiser and reprover, and

---

[40] See for details H. Graetz, *op. cit.*, II.2, pp. 22ff. On the aping of Persian practices, referred to in Isa. 66:17, see J. Scheftelowitz, *Die altpersische Religion und das Judentum*, Giessen, 1920, p. 5. But see also J. Klausner, *History of the Second Temple* [in Hebrew], I (1949), 85.

we almost hear in his severe rebukes the voice of the first Isaiah or of Jeremiah, especially in Chapter 59.

The Messianic chain is now complete in all its elements. The prophet speaks this time of *sin and punishment*, and therefore he speaks also of *repentance* with even more emphasis. Sin causes punishment, and repentance brings *the redemption*. The LORD was angry with His people because they walked rebelliously in the way of their own desires, but when they mended their ways He was ready to ransom them from all their afflictions and to comfort the mourners in Zion (57:16–18). But a redeemer will come only "unto them that turn from transgression in Jacob" (59:20). The LORD will not redeem "every one that is called by His name," as Deutero-Isaiah promised in the period of his first enthusiasm as to the possibility of the return to Zion, but only every one who achieves repentance. The rest will be delivered over to the sword and brought down to slaughter (65:12; 66:4, 14–17). But this is not all. The righteous will "look upon the carcasses of the men that have rebelled" against the LORD, whose "worm shall not die, neither shall their fire be quenched,[41] and they shall be an abhorring to all flesh" (66:24). Only a limited number will be saved by virtue of the fact that they observed justice and did righteousness; by this they will have brought redemption and salvation nearer. But those who are saved will be "all of them righteous" and "they shall inherit the land forever" (60:21).

In the third period the prophet is no longer urging the departure from Babylon nor describing the miracles which will attend the returners on the way, since the first Return has already been completed; and yet disillusionment has come from many sides—hence there is no more place for exaggerated portrayals. Faced with this situation, the prophet with unwearied diligence does not fail "to bring good tidings of comfort," that is, to strengthen the spirits of those returning and those remaining in Babylon, that they may not compromise with the idea that the materially and spiritually weak

[41] The reference here is not to hell-fire, which is a later conception, but to the LORD's wrath, which will unceasingly burn against the wicked. And this is the meaning of the words "their worm shall not die," viz., their punishments will have no end.

and lowly community in Palestine is the embodiment of the shining promises of redemption given by the prophets both earlier and later. And in order that all these people may not give up hope of consolation, the prophet repeatedly holds before them magic visions of expected well-being, material and political no less than spiritual.

It is not now enough for the prophet that the LORD should gather in the dispersed of Israel: he adds to the ingathered many foreigners, who will join themselves to the LORD to serve Him and to love Him. These will be "every one that keepeth the Sabbath from profaning it, and holdeth fast by My covenant," that is, those who submit to circumcision (56:6-9). Apparently, by this is meant the peoples round about Judah who joined the returning Jews, and perhaps also "they that went up from Tel-melah, Tel-harsha, Cherub-addon, and Immer" in the time of Zerubbabel, who "could not tell their fathers' houses, and their seed, *whether they were of Israel*" (Ezra 2:59; Neh. 7:61). But it is also possible that proselytes from among the Babylonians came and joined themselves to the people Israel.[42] The prophet promises these in the name of the LORD as follows:

> Even them will I bring to My holy mountain,
> And make them joyful in My house of prayer;
> Their burnt-offerings and their sacrifices
> Shall be acceptable upon Mine altar;
> *For My house shall be called*
> *A house of prayer for all peoples* (56:7).

Here we see before us the *reception of proselytes* as one of the signs of the redemption, a feature that in later times had such an important place in Messianic expectations. Apparently the words of the Second Isaiah in one of the earlier prophecies, "there shall no more come into thee the uncircumcised and the unclean" (52:1), were intended for those who would not join the LORD to observe the Sabbath and

---

[42] This is the opinion of Graetz (*op. cit.*, II.2, pp. 20-22). From the Elephantine Papyri it is evident that in the time of Ezra there were Gentiles who became proselytes (see S. Daiches, "Aramaic Documents from the Time of Ezra" [in Hebrew], *Ha-Shiloah*, XVII, 511); and of course, such was also the case some time before this.

circumcision.[43] For nations will walk by Israel's light and kings by the brightness of his shining forth (60:3). And that will not be strange:

> For, behold, darkness shall cover the earth,
> And gross darkness the peoples;
> But upon thee the LORD will shine forth,
> And His glory shall be seen upon thee (60:2).

Therefore all nations will consider themselves blest by Israel and by Israel's God, the God of truth, by Whom also they will swear (61:9; 65:16, 23). All peoples will be gathered to Jerusalem to see the glory of the LORD; and the Jews will go abroad among distant nations—even Lydia and Greece [44] are mentioned among these—to spread the knowledge of the LORD in the world. And the Gentiles will bring all the Jews on horses and in chariots to Jerusalem as an offering to the LORD, like the offering which the Jews will bring in a clean vessel into the house of the LORD. Moreover, from these Gentiles (or from the Jews brought from the isles afar off) the LORD will take some to be priests and Levites (66:18-21). For from one new moon to another, and from one Sabbath to another, all flesh will come to worship before the LORD (66:23).

From these verses it seems clear that the prophet was *not* opposed to sacrifices and the Temple even for the Age to Come (this is shown also by 56:7 and 60:7). And when it is said at the beginning of this very chapter, "The heaven is My throne, and the earth is My foot-

[43] The importance of the Sabbath must have been especially great in the eyes of a prophet living in the Exile, even though he may have been very universalistic and spiritually-minded, because the Sabbath commandment does not depend upon the country and it can be observed in exile. The importance of circumcision as a covenant-symbol and a sign of separation was also increased in Babylonia for the same and other reasons. See David Neumark's *'Iqqarim* [Dogmas] ("Hoveret le-Dogma" of *Otsar ha-Yahadut*, ed. *Ahiasaf*, Warsaw, 1906, pp. 23-25; *History of Dogmas in Israel* [in Hebrew], Odessa, 1913, I, 107-115).

[44] Undoubtedly the reference is to the Ionian islands in Asia Minor (as is attested by the words "the isles afar off" following immediately after the word "Javan" [Greece]), which could have been known to the Jews immediately after the Exile, since the Assyrians from the time of Ashurbanipal on, and also the first kings of Persia, came into conflict with them time after time. See the commentary of Krauss on this verse; he also opposes the opinion of those who date this passage late because of the mention of these peoples.

stool; what sort of house is it that ye build unto Me?" the meaning was only that one cannot deem sacrifices sufficient and thereby be exempt from doing good deeds ("He that killeth an ox is as if he slew a man; ... he that maketh a memorial-offering of frankincense, as if he blessed an idol."); and not, as was the opinion of Castelli, that Deutero-Isaiah opposed sacrifices and the rebuilding of the Temple *on general principles.*[45]

In order to conclude the presentation of Deutero-Isaiah's promises of spiritual benefit with the choicest promise of all, I call to mind that, just as he prophesied in his second period that all the sons of Zion would be "taught of the LORD" (54:13), so he again prophesied in his last period, that the LORD would make with His people a covenant of this nature:

My spirit that is upon thee, and My words which I have put in thy mouth, shall not depart out of thy mouth, nor out of the mouth of thy seed, nor out of the mouth of thy seed's seed, saith the LORD, from henceforth and for ever (59:21).

This, perhaps, is the most sublime Messianic promise of spiritual import: the eternity of the Torah in the eternal nation!

As the loftiness of the spiritual expectations, so is the greatness of the political and material expectation. The choicest of the political and material promises of the prophecies from the first and second periods are found in even broader and brighter form in the third period. Outstanding in this respect is Chapter 60. In his prophecies of the second period the prophet said: "And they shall bring thy sons in their bosom, and thy daughters shall be carried upon their shoulders" (49:22), but now he says: "And thy daughters shall be nursed on the hip" (60:4); also, "Ye shall be borne upon the side, and shall be dandled upon the knees" (66:12). In his prophecies of the first period he said:

> The labour of Egypt, and the merchandise of Ethiopia,
> And of the Sabeans, men of stature,
> Shall come over unto thee, and they shall be thine (45:14).

But now he says:

[45] See his book *Il Messia,* pp. 141–142.

DEUTERO-ISAIAH 175

Thy heart shall throb and be enlarged,
Because the abundance of the sea shall be turned unto thee,
The wealth of the nations shall come unto thee.
The caravan of camels shall cover thee,
And of the young camels of Midian and Ephah,
All coming from Sheba;
They shall bring gold and frankincense,
And shall proclaim the praises of the LORD (60:5-6; see also 60:12, 16; 61:6; 66:12).

And the prophet adds, as he continues, that all the flocks of Kedar and the rams of Nebaioth will be gathered unto Zion in order to provide acceptable sacrifices on the altar of the LORD; also cedars of Lebanon, cypresses, and all other kinds of fine woods will be brought in order to beautify thereby the Sanctuary (60:7, 13). The Gentile kings will not only bring the Jews to their own land, but they will also minister unto them and serve them together with the nations which they represent (60:9-10): "For that nation and kingdom that will not serve thee shall perish; yea, those nations shall be utterly wasted" (60:12). And as the prophet said in his earlier prophecies, "They shall bow down to thee with their face to the earth, and lick the dust of thy feet" (49:23), so now he says:

> And the sons of them that afflicted thee
> Shall come bending unto thee,
> And all they that despised thee
> Shall bow down at the soles of thy feet (60:14).

Instead of Zion's being forsaken and despised and desolate as formerly, now she will be "an eternal excellency, a joy of many generations" (60:15). Peace and righteousness will lodge within her, while violence, desolation, and destruction will no more be seen within her borders; her walls will be called Salvation, and her gates Praise. She will no longer need the sun by day or the moon by night, for God will be to her an everlasting light, hence her sun will not set nor her moon wane (60:17-20). The Jewish state will be rich, since those returning will bring with them their silver and their gold (60:5). Besides, the LORD will bring it gold instead of bronze, silver instead of iron, bronze instead of wood, and iron instead of stone

(60:17). And it will be prosperous: the former waste places and the cities long in ruins will be rebuilt and revived (61:4). Judah will inherit its ancestral hills; Sharon will become a fold of flocks and the valley of Achor a place for herds to lie down in for the elect of Israel (65:9–10; see also 62:8–9 and 65:21–22). All this great material prosperity will come to the Chosen People without toil or trouble: aliens will build the walls of Jerusalem (60:10), strangers will tend the flocks of the Jews, and foreigners will be their plowmen and vinedressers, while they themselves will be called the priests of the LORD, the ministers of the God of Israel (61:5–6). For all the Gentiles will call Zion "the city of the LORD, Zion of Israel's Holy One," or—as the prophet says in another place—she will be called by a new name "which the mouth of the LORD shall mark out" (62:2), while her sons will be called "The Holy People, the redeemed of the LORD" (62:12). For the LORD will make an *everlasting covenant* with His people, a covenant which will stand forever, like the new heavens and the new earth which the LORD will make in the millennial age (61:8; 66:22).

Here the prophet has reached that extreme spirituality, which on the one hand made the people Israel a supreme people in the full sense of the word, and on the other hand accustomed this people to think that it itself had no need to undertake the authoritative conduct of a state; for "it was privileged to have its work done by others" —first by the kings of Persia and afterward by Alexander the Great and the kings of Egypt and Syria. There can be no doubt that the depressed condition of Palestine during most of the period of the Second Temple, from the time of Zerubbabel to the days of the Hasmoneans, brought it about that Jewish statecraft, although very strongly emphasized by the prophet, assumed mostly a form of supernatural authority, in such a manner that all the nations and kingdoms would serve Israel only because they might wish to serve Israel's God and Torah. Thus it came about that the prophets dreamed of a political situation in which there would be no need for the Jews to build walls, or even to tend flock and herd or to cultivate field and vineyard; for all these things would be done for them by the Gentiles—those Gentiles who in the period of the Second Temple took from the hands of the Jews all political authority and left in their hands only internal and hence relatively unimportant affairs. The prophets, who had always fought against the spirit of conquest and the secularistic politics of the kings of Israel, became now, after their principles had been vindicated, the "ideologists" of the new life, which they justified *ex post facto* and according to which they portrayed also the future, except that they adorned it with imaginative colors and exalted it to the point where it became almost supernatural. Nevertheless, as prophets of Israel—the people which never let its feet be pulled *completely* off the ground—they did not altogether forget wealth, possessions, temporal authority, and worldly success, even though in many places they exceeded the bounds of the natural and the possible, so that even their political and material ideal appeared as if "not of this world."

Supernatural in particular are the promises about *the increase in population and the length of life:* "The smallest shall become a thousand, and the least a mighty nation" (60:22). Children will not die while they are small (65:23), nor will the infant die then, nor the "old man that hath not filled his days." For whoever dies a hundred years old will be considered still a youth; even the sinner, though cursed with a shortened span of life, will live to be a hundred (65:20). The voice of weeping and the sound of crying will no more be heard in the land of Israel, which will be filled with peace as a river is filled with water (65:19; 66:12).

Along with man, *nature* also will be changed for the better; for man and nature are closely bound together in the vision of the prophet, so that apart from man nature has no significance at all, as I demonstrated above several times.

The LORD will create new heavens and a new earth (65:17; 66:22), and then—

> The wolf and the lamb shall feed together,
> The lion shall eat straw like the ox;
> And dust shall be the serpent's food.
> They shall not hurt nor destroy
> In all My holy mountain,
> Saith the LORD (65:25).

The climactic expectations of the prophet of comfort to Zion are entirely equal to those of the great prophet of the time of Hezekiah, to whose book were added the twenty-seven chapters of the prophet of the Return. Truly, these two prophets are fittingly joined together! At least, with respect to Messianic expectations, it is difficult to decide which is greater: that prophet who saw in his vivid imagination "a shoot out of the stock of Jesse" filled with the spirit of the LORD and slaying the wicked with the breath of his lips, or that prophet who wished to make *the whole people Israel* such a superb and exalted Messiah!

There still remain Chapter 13 and Chapter 14, Verses 1–23, of the Book of Isaiah, which seem to me also to have been composed by Deutero-Isaiah, but are out of their proper place for the following reason: Deutero-Isaiah, is—and in this he differs from almost all the rest of the prophets—the only prophet all of whose prophecies (and they are many) either were spoken against Israel exclusively or else have a direct relation to Israel, while the prophets preceding him, especially Amos, Jeremiah, and Ezekiel, delivered special prophecies against the nations round about Israel; but the prophecy included in Chapters 13 and 14 is a *special* prophecy against a foreign nation: "the burden of Babylon." Therefore it was transferred into the prophecies of the first Isaiah, who prophesied a relatively large amount against the other nations. In any case, this prophecy was spoken at the time of the fall of Babylon. Or perhaps even at the time of the fall of Assyria, since in it Media, but not Persia, is mentioned as a factor in the downfall of the kingdom of Assyria or Babylon (13:17). Thus it cannot belong to Isaiah.

The "day of the LORD," the day of judgment, the day of punishment, is described in this "burden" in brilliant colors, unique in kind. The "day of the LORD" will come suddenly "as destruction from the Almighty" (13:6). Therefore all hands will be slack and every heart will melt (13:7). All will be frightened and the pains of childbirth will seize them (13:8). From this came at a later time the term "the birth pangs of the Messiah." Cruel will be the day of the LORD: it will come to make the earth a desolation in order to visit upon the wicked their iniquity, in order *to destroy sinners out of the earth* (13:9, 11). Punishment comes, therefore, as a penalty for sin. And when man suffers, *nature will suffer with him:* the stars of heaven will not shine, the sun will be dark at its rising, and the moon will not shed its light (13:10); the heavens will tremble and the earth be shaken "for the wrath of the LORD of hosts, and for the day of His fierce anger" (13:13). Men will suffer exceedingly: every one that is found will be thrust through, and every one that joins the enemy will fall by the sword; houses will be plundered, babies will be torn to pieces, and women will be ravished. Then the pride of the arrogant will cease, and the haughtiness of the tyrants will be brought low (13:11, 15-16).

Following close upon the punishment, although in this instance it falls particularly upon Babylon, comes *the redemption of Israel.* Here in three short verses are presented almost all the basic Messianic expectations, conforming to those which we saw above in the prophecies of Deutero-Isaiah. The LORD will have compassion on His people, and once again will choose Israel and set them on their own soil (the return to Zion); then the stranger will join himself with them to be added to the house of Jacob (the reception of proselytes, as we have already seen in Deutero-Isaiah); the peoples will then take the Jews and bring them to their own land (this is also stressed by Deutero-Isaiah), and the Jews will acquire the Gentiles in the LORD's land as servants and handmaids (to do all the work for the Jews: to tend their flocks and be husbandmen and vinedressers for them, as we found in Deutero-Isaiah); then the Jews will take captive their former captors and subdue those who had oppressed them (as mentioned above). Then Israel will have rest from his afflictions and hard servitude, while peace will prevail in his land (14:1-3).

These are all the Messianic expectations that we find in these two chapters. These expectations are not found in greater detail here because this "burden" is essentially and primarily against Babylon, while the redemption of Israel is mentioned only incidentally, as being bound up with the fall of Babylon.

Here is the place also for Chapters 24–27 and 34–35. They do *not* belong to the first Isaiah either in content or in language.[46] We have in Chapters 24–27 a time full of tumult and confusion, the whole earth being in terror to its very borders (24:1–3, 17–20). "The kings of the earth" are in great distress: they are gathered together as "prisoners in a dungeon" (24:22), and God is preparing "for all the peoples," on a mountain unknown to us, "a feast of fat things, a feast of wine on the lees" (25:6). Here we also have strange apocalyptic conceptions (24:21, 23; 27:1), and there are hints of the cessation of death and the resurrection of the dead in the Age to Come (25:8; 26:19), and the like.[47] In Chapters 34–35 is to be recognized that hatred of Edom resulting from the participation of this brother-people in the conquest by Nebuchadrezzar. Therefore, many scholars incline to date these chapters in the time of the destruction of Sidon by Artaxerxes III (348 B.C.E.), or in the time of the attack of the Nabateans on Edom (in 560/1); many scholars also assign these chapters to the time of Alexander the Great's conquest (332), or even (Duhm, Marti, and following them, Bernfeld) to the time of the Hasmoneans, John Hyrcanus and Janneus Alexander![48] But to date so late whole chapters like these *in the Prophets* (not in the Hagiographa!) is to make the whole cultural history of the Jewish nation unintelligible. Since Ben-Sira (48:24–25) already considered in his day First Isaiah and Second Isaiah as one book, as is well known, who would have dared in still later times to insert into this sacred and revered book chapters written only a short time before? We necessarily conclude that even these later chapters are relatively early.

[46] See on this Steuernagel, *Einleitung*, pp. 496-498, 504. A. Kaminka (*Studies* [see above, Note 4], pp. 8–18); *Le Prophète Isaïe*, Paris, 1925, pp. 60–65 = *REJ*, LXXXI, 27–42) assigns all these passages to the first Isaiah, and so I also believed twenty-five years ago in the first edition of the present book; but further intensive examination into the *spirit and language* of these passages made me turn away from this opinion.

[47] That here we have certain remnants of popular beliefs possibly originating in Babylonia, Egypt, or Persia—this has been rightly claimed by Gressmann (*Eschatologie*, pp. 190–192); but he exaggerates the importance of these beliefs in comparison with the fundamental changes which the prophets made in them for their high ethical purpose.

[48] See Marti, *Das Buch Jesaja*, 1900, pp. 182–183, 201–202, 248; Bernfeld, *op. cit.*, II, 272, 280.

In my opinion, they were written by the Second Isaiah in the last period of his life. In the next chapter will be described in detail the rebellion of Gaumata, who disguised himself as the slain brother of Cambyses, king of Persia, in the year 522; then Elam, Babylonia, Egypt, Media, Armenia, and Assyria revolted against Darius, so that practically the whole world was in terror. To such a time corresponds very well the mood described in Chapters 24–27 of Isaiah, and there is no need at all to search for such a mood at a later time. And as for Chapters 34–35, we know so little of the history of Edom that it is very possible that some attack upon this land followed that of the Nabateans in 561–560, during the last years of Deutero-Isaiah.

The Messianic expectations in these chapters (24–27, 34–35) are original in content and in form, but their general purport is not so far from that in the rest of the prophets.

Sin brings in its wake *punishment:*

> Because they have transgressed the laws, violated the statute,
> Broken the everlasting covenant,
> Therefore hath a curse devoured the earth,
> And they that dwell therein are found guilty (24:5–6).

The LORD will make the earth empty and waste, and will scatter its inhabitants abroad. The earth will be despoiled and plundered (24:1, 3). Tribulation will be great, with no way of escape: "He who fleeth from the noise of the terror shall fall into the pit, and he that cometh up out of the midst of the pit shall be taken in the trap" (24:18). The kings of the earth will be gathered together like prisoners in a dungeon and will be shut up in prison (24:22). Not only will the inhabitants and kings of the earth suffer on the day of punishment, but also the earth itself: it will be broken and split and shaken. It will reel like a drunkard and sway like a reed hut; "and the transgression thereof is heavy upon it, and it shall fall, and not rise again" (24:19–20). A cosmic catastrophe. Not only upon the earth will the LORD visit punishment on that day, but also upon "the host of the high heaven on high" (24:21). The moon will be confounded and the sun ashamed from fear of the LORD and because of the splendor of His majesty, when He comes to rule on

Mount Zion (24:23). Here we have a kind of echo of popular mythological beliefs.

If the LORD is to exact punishment on the Day of Judgment from both the earth and the heavenly bodies, of course the nations other than Judah and Israel will not be exempt. The LORD will make "*unto all peoples* a feast of fat things, a feast of wines on the lees, of fat things full of marrow, of wines on the lees well refined" (25:6); which is to say: the good things which He will confer upon the good people will be the best of the good; and the evil things which He will apportion to the evil people will be the worst of the evil. For "the LORD hath indignation against all the nations"; "He hath utterly destroyed them, He hath delivered them to the slaughter" (34:2).

> Their slain also shall be cast out,
> And the stench of their carcasses shall come up,
> And the mountains shall be melted with their blood (34:3).

God will visit punishment upon Assyria and Egypt:

In that day the LORD with His sore and great and strong sword will punish Leviathan the slant serpent, and Leviathan the tortuous serpent; and He will slay the dragon that is in the sea (27:1).

It is not to be forgotten that the rebellion of Gaumata came about after the conquest and devastation of Egypt by Cambyses.

Nor will Edom be exempt (34:5–6). The land of Edom will lie waste forever: its streams will be turned into pitch and its dust into brimstone, thorns will come up in its palaces and thistles in its fortresses, while jackals and ostriches will dwell there (34:9–17). This will be a day of vengeance for the LORD, "a year of requital for the hostility against Zion" (34:8)—in the time of Nebuchadrezzar's destruction.

And again in this day of vengeance, not only will Edom suffer, but also *nature:*

> And all the host of heaven shall moulder away,
> And the heavens shall be rolled together as a scroll;
> And all their host shall fall down
> As the leaf falleth off from the vine (34:4).

This is the sin and this its fearful punishment!

But punishment arouses people to *repentance*. To be sure, not all will repent; but a part will repent—the righteous, "the elders," and the best in the nation: they will praise the LORD and sing joyfully of His majesty (24:13-14). The LORD will rule on Mount Zion and give honor to His elders (24:23). He will remove the reproach of His people from off the earth, He will swallow up death forever—the slaughter and destruction of war between nations [49]—and He will wipe tears from every face (25:8).

The *ingathering of exiles* will take place at the time of redemption. The children of Israel will be gathered one by one from all the lands in which they were then scattered: from the Euphrates to the river of Egypt (27:12).

> And it shall come to pass in that day,
> That a great horn shall be blown;
> And they shall come that were lost
>   in the land of Assyria,
> And they that were dispersed
>   in the land of Egypt;
> And they shall worship the LORD
>   In the holy mountain at Jerusalem (27:13).

The parts of the nation that were accounted as dead bodies will arise to new life, for the earth will give up these shades from within it (26:19).[50] The redeemed will walk on a clean highway,[51] which will be called "the Holy Way" because no unclean person will pass over it, nor will lions and wild beasts be found upon it (35:8-9). Material prosperity will also be great: waters will break out in the wilderness and streams will appear even in the desert (35:6); the

---

[49] So must this expression be understood: it is difficult to believe that at this early date the prophet could conceive that in the end of days the decree of death which had been laid upon humanity would be abrogated.

[50] So must be understood the verse "Thy dead shall live, my dead bodies shall arise" (26:19). It is difficult to believe that at this early date the prophet could refer to the resurrection of the dead for *individuals*. This, like Ezekiel's "Vision of the Valley of Dry Bones," is a vision of the immortality of the Jewish nation.

[51] So we must read instead of "a highway and a way" in this verse (35:8), since the Seventy translated ὁδὸς καθαρά ["a clean road"] and the word *wāderekh* is the repetition of *wederekh* in the next clause through a scribal error. "A clean highway" agrees with the phrase "The way of *holiness*," and also with "The *unclean* shall not pass over it" in this verse.

mirage [52] will become a pool and the thirsty ground springs of water (35:7).

Thus is finished the presentation of the *Messianic* ideas of the Second Isaiah in the different periods of his prophetic activity—perhaps also the Messianic ideas of his disciples who followed in his footsteps, and so had their prophecies called by his name.

[52] See above, p. 159, Note 17.

CHAPTER XIII

Haggai (520 B.C.E.), Zechariah 1–8 (520–518 B.C.E.) and 9–14 (*c.* 500–485 B.C.E.)

BY PERMISSION of Cyrus, and under the leadership of Zerubbabel son of Shealtiel and grandson of King Jehoiachin, Jeshua son of Jozadak and grandson of the last chief priest Seraiah, and ten other heads of families, about fifty thousand Jews (together with male and female slaves) set out from Babylonia in the spring of the year 537 to return to the land of Judah.[1] The comforting words of Deutero-Isaiah accompanied them on their way. They were dreaming his glorious dreams of the plain which the mountains and hills would become, of the pools of water that would break forth in the wilderness, of the beautiful trees that would spring up in the desert. The return to Zion was pictured in their imaginations as a festive procession, and the restoration of the Jewish nation as a great *world* event,

[1] The French scholar M. Vernes, the Dutch scholar W. H. Kosters, and the American scholar C. C. Torrey have concluded that there were not two returns (one in the time of Zerubbabel and Jeshua and the other in the time of Ezra and Nehemiah), but only one—in the time of Ezra and Nehemiah; and that the Second Temple was built not by returned exiles, but by those left in Judah after the Destruction and the slaying of Gedaliah. For, in their opinion, the data at the end of Chronicles and the beginning of the Book of Ezra (which are actually the same) and in Ezra 5:13–6:5 are not to be believed at all. But see against this opinion Ed. Meyer, *Die Entstehung des Judentums*, 1896; S. Jampel, *Die Wiederherstellung Israels unter den Achaemeniden*, Breslau, 1904 (*Monatsschrift für Geschichte u. Wissenschaft des Judentums*, 46. u. 47. Jahrgg. 1902-1903); W. F. Albright, *From the Stone Age to Christianity*, 1940, pp. 246-248.

at which all the Gentiles would be amazed. They imagined, they believed, that the political power of the people returning to its own land would be very great: "And kings shall be your male nurses" (Isa. 49:23); and material prosperity would be almost supernatural: "I will lay your foundations with sapphires" (Isa. 54:11).

These wonderful promises were *not* fulfilled. The journey was long and wearisome, extending over all the spring and summer of the year 537. Not until the month of Tishri [September–October] in that year did those returning set up an altar and offer sacrifices upon it. And not until Marheshvan [October–November] of the following year (536) was the foundation of the Temple laid by Sheshbazzar the governor, with the assistance of Zerubbabel, Jeshua, and the rest of the returned exiles (Ezra 3:8; 5:15); but no more than the foundation was completed, "for fear was upon them because of the peoples of the countries" (Ezra 3:3; compare 4:4–5).[2] The condition in which the returned exiles found the land of Judah, and their own condition in this land at the beginning of their settlement, did not even slightly resemble the magical imaginings which they had constructed for themselves after the fashion of the visions of Deutero-Isaiah, or even those of Ezekiel. To take over all Palestine, according to the promises of the prophets—this the returned exiles could not even consider. For Cyrus had given them permission to return only to Judah, which the Babylonians had conquered, and not at all to Samaria and Galilee, which the Assyrians had conquered earlier.

And the little province of Judah was surrounded by various alien peoples. On the north of Judah, extending as far south as Bethel, lived the Samaritans. To be sure, most of them were descended from Ephraimites who had intermingled more or less with Assyrian colonists. But because they had not had an Israelite government for more than two hundred years, and even their religious center at Bethel had

---

[2] Many scholars, following Wellhausen (*Israel. u. jud. Geschichte*, p. 155, Note 4), deny the fact of the laying of the foundation of the Temple immediately after the return from Babylonia, since Haggai and Zechariah do not mention this matter with even one word. But here is not the place to discuss this at length, since this matter is not important to the theme of the present book. I have treated this in detail in *History of the Second Temple* [in Hebrew], Part I, Jerusalem, 1949, pp. 192–220.

been destroyed by Josiah; and because they had not been refined in the crucible of exile, they had become more and more alien to the people of Judah. On the west lived Ashdodites—Philistines mixed with other peoples ("And a bastard shall dwell in Ashdod," Zech. 9:6), since in the year 711 Philistia had become an Assyrian province with the name "Ashdudu." [3] In the course of time these people influenced the Jews to such an extent that many Jewish children spoke the language of Ashdod (Neh. 13:24). On the east lived the Ammonites, whose king, Baalis, had meddled in the affairs of Judah in the time of Gedaliah (Jer. 40:14). On the south were settled the Edomites, who had even taken over the ancient capital city of Judah, Hebron. Apparently there had already begun at that time the movement of the Nabatean Arabs, who drove out the Ammonites and Edomites and forced them into the territory of Judah and Israel.[4] Gibeon in the north and Hebron in the south were already lost to Judah. Thus the whole Jewish settlement was confined to an area of about seventy kilometers from south to north, between Hebron and Bethel, and about eighty kilometers from east to west, between Jericho and Lydda. Within these narrow and restricted boundaries lived "the remnant of Judah" which was left after the destruction of the First Temple and the murder of Gedaliah, without a political or religious center and without any orderly existence. Thus this "poorest sort of the people" [II Kgs. 24:14] became mixed with neighboring peoples; it began to speak their languages and to imitate their idolatrous practices (see Isa. 46 and 65–66).

The land too was poor and forsaken. There was no way to make a living, and "he who earned wages earned to put them into a bag with a hole in it"(Haggai 1:6). Taxes were numerous and bore particularly upon the poor: the Jews paid "the king's tribute" (*middah* or *mindah*, *mandattu* in Assyrian), apparently a poll tax, "impost" (*belô*, apparently a consumer tax—*baru* in Persian), and "toll" (perhaps a highway tax). They were also forced to give "the bread of the

---

[3] See A. Alt, *Palästina-Jahrbuch*, XXVII (1931), 72.
[4] See on this in detail H. Graetz, *Geschichte der Juden*, II.2, pp. 118–119, and not according to the opinion of Wellhausen (*op. cit.*, pp. 154–155), that it only began afterward. See G. Hölscher, *Palästina in der persischen und hellenistischen Zeit*, Berlin, 1903, pp. 21–25.

governor" (Neh. 5:14-15); and of course they also set aside contributions and tithes for the multitude of priests, who were a fourth part of all who had returned. The streets of Jerusalem were deserted: neither children nor old persons were seen in them.[5] Safety of life and of property was not to be expected (Zech. 8:10). The old aristocratic "Golah" (only the more eminent people of the nation had been exiled in the time of Jehoiachin), which had separated itself from those remaining in Judah and had become like a state within a state, had settled almost entirely in Jerusalem and its environs. And as though to make the tribulations even worse, there came years of drought one after another. All these are normal and almost inevitable things in any new colonization. So when we turn our attention to the beginning of the settlement in Palestine in our own times, it is hard to refrain from crying out, "Everything hath been already!" [Ecclesiastes 1:9–10].

But the exiles looked for deliverance and consolation. They brought with them glowing Messianic expectations—yet the actuality was the exact opposite of these expectations. Hence many began to cast doubt upon the entire Messianic idea, actually questioning whether there would be any redemption at all. We learn this from the fact that the Jews continued to observe the fasts commemorating the Destruction (Zech. 7:3; 8:19), as though the Destruction continued in effect, as though the Exile had not yet come to an end. The situation was very bad—more correctly, it was very humiliating. Zechariah points this out in an incisive, well chosen, and unique phrase: "For who hath despised the day of small things?" (4:10). Precisely so! This period was a "day of small things," a period of minor doings and minor personalities. There were no great events and no creative personalities. Zerubbabel son of Shealtiel, a scion of the house of David, could not do great things lest he arouse suspicion against himself on the part of the king of Persia. At first he was not even governor of Judah, but that post was held by Sheshbazzar, hardly to be considered as another name for Zerubbabel, as is indicated in one passage in the Apocryphal I Esdras (6:18), and as Graetz thinks.[6] And Jeshua son of Jozadak was

---

[5] This we learn from the promises of Zechariah (8:4-5).
[6] In his book, *op. cit.*, II.2, p. 74, Note 2. In opposition to this, Wellhausen, *op. cit.*, p. 154, and B. Stade, *Biblische Theologie des Alten Testaments*, Vol. I, Tübingen, 1905, p. 311, think rightly that Sheshbazzar was governor and Zerubbabel leader.

apparently a man of many limitations, since Zechariah (3:1-5) describes him as "clothed with filthy garments," with "Satan standing at his right hand to accuse him."

In a condition of inferiority and humiliation like this there was no place for a great undertaking like the building of the Second Temple. The people became more and more immersed in secular life and despaired of the hope for political power and spiritual greatness.

But suddenly "the day of small things" was brought to an end by *great events*, which took place, to be sure, not in Judah, but in the territory to which it was subject—the kingdom of Persia. After Cyrus (559-529), there came to the throne his son Kambujiya, Kanbuzi in Aramaic,[7] Cambyses in Greek (529-522). In the year 525 he went to war against Egypt and conquered it. Of course, he passed through the land of Judah—and this poor land suffered greatly thereby. In the year 522, while Cambyses had still not returned from his campaign, the Magian Gaumata, impersonating the slain brother of Cambyses, Bardiya in Persian, Smerdis in Greek, conspired against him. Apparently this Magian had plans to cut off sovereignty from Persia and restore it to Media. And in order to make this plan agreeable to the peoples subject to Persia, he lightened the yoke of all these peoples and remitted their taxes. This brought the result that almost all the provinces attempted to throw off the yoke of Persia. Meanwhile, Cambyses died on the way to Persia and the great empire was filled with riots and disorders on the one hand, and hopes of speedy deliverance and political freedom on the other hand. Elam, Babylonia, Egypt, Media, and Armenia (the last two under the leadership of Fravartish, or Phraortes in Greek), and even Persia (under the leadership of Vahyazdata), revolted; Babylonia finally revolted a second and a third time. It was as though the whole world was filled with upheaval and shook to its uttermost limits.

Then arose like a lion Darius I (522-485). During the years 522-521 he destroyed the Pseudo-Smerdis, and during 521-519 he put an end to the Babylonian rebellion of Nidintu-Bel ("gift of Baal," compare Mattaniah and Mattathias, "gift of Yah"), who was shut

---

[7] This is his name in the new Aramaic documents of the period after Ezra from the city of Elephantine on the border of Egypt (see S. Daiches, "Aramaic Documents from the Time of Ezra" [in Hebrew], *Ha-Shiloah*, VII, 507).

up in Babylon and besieged by Darius for twenty months. The rebellions continued until the year 516, and Darius says of himself in the Behistun Inscription that he was forced to fight against nine rivals and to conquer them in nineteen great battles before the kingdom was safely in his hands.

A time of rebellion against ruling authority is always a time of the awakening of hope in subject states. So even little Judah laid plans for becoming an independent kingdom as of old. A king was ready to hand: Zerubbabel was of the house of David, and even at that time he already stood at the head of the people as governor of Judah (Haggai 1:14). Meanwhile Jeshua, son of Jozadak and grandson of the last chief priest, had already become high priest. There was lacking only *the religious center*, which had to take precedence over the political center in a state like the new Judah, which had been created by a religio-national, a priestly-prophetic awakening.[8] It was necessary, therefore, to make use of the opportunity to arouse the people to build the Temple, without which the prophetic promises could not be fulfilled, and also to strengthen the Messianic hope for a king of the house of David and direct it toward Zerubbabel. These things were done by the first two prophets of the Second Temple, Haggai and Zechariah.

Haggai prophesied in the second year of Darius (520), from the beginning of the month of Elul until the twenty-fourth of Kislev, about seventy years after the Destruction and about seventeen years after the first Return. That was the opportune time to build the Temple, since the Persian government was then occupied with other matters and had granted the subject peoples all they requested—provided only that they did not rebel. But the people of Judah argued stubbornly that a time of perplexity is precisely not "the time that the LORD's house should be built" (Hag. 1:2). Against this argument the prophet rises up in great indignation: "Is it a time for you yourselves to dwell in your ceiled houses, while this house lieth waste?" (Hag. 1:4). The drought and deprivation then in evidence are in the eyes of the prophet nothing more than a punishment

[8] See what I have written about the political "Utopia" of Ezekiel, above, pp. 131-134.

for the great sin that the LORD's house has not yet been built.

His words bore fruit: on the twenty-fourth of Elul, twenty-three days after his first prophecy, construction began. But what is related in Ezra (3:12-13) about the painful impression made by the laying of the foundation in the time of Sheshbazzar upon those elders of Judah who had seen the First Temple is also noted by Haggai on the twenty-first of Marheshvan, about a month after construction began. In Ezra we read:

But many of the priests and Levites and heads of fathers' houses, the old men that had seen the first house standing on its foundation, wept with a loud voice, when this house was before their eyes; and many shouted aloud for joy: so that the people could not discern the noise of the shout of joy from the noise of the weeping of the people,—

a highly tragic picture, with few like it in world history, which still awaits a great artist to portray it on canvas as an everlasting memorial. Then here, in Haggai (2:3), we find this:

Who is left among you that saw this house in its former glory? and how do ye see it now? is not such a one as nothing in your eyes?

But the prophet takes his stand against this pessimistic view, crying out "Be strong!" to Zerubbabel, to Jeshua, and to all the people of the land engaged in the work of building. Then Messianic promises come forth from his tongue: the building of the Temple is only the beginning. Behold, great events are now being brought forth in the world—the end of which is to bring all nations to this Temple, which seems to you now so small and insignificant:

Yet once, it is a little while, and I will shake the heavens, and the earth, and the sea, and the dry land; and I will shake all nations, and the choicest things of all nations shall come,[9] and I will fill this house with glory, saith the LORD of hosts. Mine is the silver, and Mine the gold, saith the LORD of hosts.[10] *The glory of this latter house shall be greater than that of the former*, saith the LORD of hosts; *and in this place will I give peace*, saith the LORD of hosts (2:6-9).

[9] Cf. Isa. 50:11.
[10] Thus the new Temple is not to be despised on account of its poverty: the desirable things of the Gentiles—their silver and their gold—will enrich it in the Age to Come.

Here we have most of the Messianic promises that are already familiar to us, except that they now come with striking brevity, without the help of imaginative colors: the time of punishment, in which the LORD will exact retribution from the Gentiles (the Jews had already "received of the LORD's hand double for all their sins," Isa. 40:2), and in which all nature will also suffer; the fear of the LORD, filling the hearts of all peoples and causing them to support the LORD's house with gold and silver; the high repute of the religious center of Israel; and finally, the peace that will come to the beloved nation.

Immediately following the punishment which the LORD will exact from the Gentiles will come the Messiah, who is none other than Zerubbabel, the "shoot out of the stock of Jesse," the grandson of Jehoiachin king of Judah:

Speak to Zerubbabel, governor of Judah, saying: I will shake the heavens and the earth; and I will overthrow the throne of kingdoms, and I will destroy the strength of the kingdoms of the nations; and I will overthrow the chariots, and those that ride in them; and the horses and their riders shall come down, every one by the sword of his brother. In that day, saith the LORD of hosts, will I take thee, O Zerubbabel, My servant, the son of Shealtiel, saith the LORD, and will make thee as a signet; for I have chosen thee, saith the Lord of hosts (2:21–23).

In view of the disturbances in the Persian Empire, which at that time were numerous, as related above, it might have been possible for Zerubbabel to be what Jehoiachin, his grandfather, had failed to be, as related by Jeremiah (22:24): "As I live, saith the LORD, though Coniah the son of Jehoiakim king of Judah were the signet upon my right hand, yet would I pluck thee thence." [11]

Here we find a new stage in the development of the Messianic idea. Haggai does not prophesy of remote times. The Messiah is not across the sea, but is already present in the midst of the people. The Messianic expectations will be fulfilled not "in the end of days," but immediately after the Temple is rebuilt. Nor is this to be wondered at. The "Golah" had not yet let itself sink into new sin, while tribulations had purged away its former iniquities. Hence the prophet was

---

[11] The last point has already been made by B. Stade, *op. cit.*, p. 315.

forced to point out that redemption was *near*, lest the people conclude that their "exile" was not finished, and consequently that the whole idea of the return to Zion and all the work of rebuilding the Temple were entirely in error. Not so! The time of exile is already past, and soon will come "the day of the LORD"—for the idolaters. But if only the Temple be rebuilt, everlasting welfare will come to the people Israel, with Zerubbabel governor of Judah standing at their head as a king of the house of David.

We find the very same ideas, only amplified and clarified, in the first eight chapters of Zechariah, who began prophesying two months after Haggai, in Marheshvan 520 (Zech. 1:1); and we have from him a prophecy dated "in the fourth year of Darius" (7:1), that is, in 518. He began to prophesy, therefore, after the construction of the Temple had already started, thanks to the preaching of Haggai. But he had to urge that the building not cease because of the interference of Tattenai, governor of Syria,[12] who apparently suspected Zerubbabel and his followers of rebellious designs. Although Tattenai allowed the construction to continue until a directive could be received from Darius, while the Jews relied upon the authorization of Cyrus, which of course was confirmed by Darius (Ezra 5:3–6:14), nevertheless the effect of this incident was to slacken the work. Zechariah fought against this slackness by means of various visions, which he brought forth after the fashion of Ezekiel. All these visions have only one purpose: to comfort the people and to strengthen their resolution. He comforts and strengthens them with the promise that upon "the nations that are at ease" while oppressing and plundering Israel will come great punishment (Zech. 1:15; 2:12–13); but the LORD will return to Jerusalem with compassion, His house will be built in it, and the boundaries of the city will be extended ("and a line shall be stretched forth over Jerusalem"); she "shall be inhabited without walls, for the multitude of men and cattle therein"—and the LORD Himself will be unto her a wall of fire round about, and will be the glory in the midst of her (1:16; 2:8–9). And not only Jeru-

---

[12] Actually, he was the satrap of "Transpotamia" [Greater Syria], but he was also called "governor" by the Babylonians and Persians.

salem; the rest of the cities of Judah will also be filled with people and all good things (1:17). And from the four winds of heaven will come the sons of Zion to the land of their fathers (2:10-11). Many nations will join themselves to the LORD and become His people, while Judah will inherit its portion in the Holy Land (2:15-17).

There will be great *spiritual welfare* in Jerusalem. She will be called "the city of truth" and Mount Zion will be called "the holy mountain" (8:3). Many peoples and strong nations and the inhabitants of numerous cities will come with one accord to entreat the favor of the LORD and to seek the LORD of hosts in Jerusalem, and "ten men out of all the languages of the nations shall take hold of the skirt of him that is a Jew, saying: 'We will go with you, for we have heard that God is with you'" (8:20-23). Here we have the marvelous promise of Isaiah, "And all nations shall flow unto it" (Isa. 2:2), only expressed in more concrete form and assured for a nearer time.

Material prosperity will also be great. Before the rebuilding of the Temple the inhabitants of Jerusalem were few, with almost no children and old people at all; security of life and property was very slight and the economic condition was exceedingly bad. But when the Temple is rebuilt, old men and old women will sit in the broad places of Jerusalem, while boys and girls play in them (8:4-5). Peace will reign in the land, "the vine shall give her fruit, and the ground shall give her increase, and the heavens shall give their dew"; the children of Israel will be a blessing among the nations, instead of being, as formerly, a curse—if they will only speak truth, execute righteousness, and love peace (8:9-17). The Exile and the Destruction will be completely forgotten, so that the fasts will cease and be turned into "joy and gladness and cheerful seasons" (8:19).

Such a complete redemption naturally is not possible without a King-Messiah; also in the opinion of Zechariah this king is Zerubbabel, son of Shealtiel and grandson of Jehoiachin, king of Judah. In Jerusalem at that time there were apparently two parties, one religio-nationalistic following Jeshua the high priest, the other politico-nationalistic following Zerubbabel the governor. The latter party, to which the prophet Zechariah was more closely related, was talking against Jeshua, as mentioned above. The prophet tries to persuade this party not to demand too much of "a brand plucked out of the fire" (3:2), and he absolves Jeshua of the faults (in prophetic-figurative language: "Take the filthy garments from off him") which the partisans of Zerubbabel found in him. But at the same time he says to Jeshua and his friends: "Behold, I will bring forth My servant the Shoot" (3:8). We already find "Shoot" as an appellative of the Messiah in Jeremiah (23:5; compare 33:15, which is lacking in the Septuagint): "I will raise up unto David a righteous shoot." I have already shown in the chapter on Jeremiah [13] that Jeremiah intended these words to apply to Zedekiah but that his prophecy was not fulfilled. Zechariah, who sought to verify the prophecy of Jeremiah concerning the seventy years of destruction (compare Jer. 25:11-12 and 29:10 with Zech. 1:12), sought also to verify the prophecy concerning the "Shoot" that would spring forth unto David; and such a "Shoot" he saw in Zerubbabel: he is not only the "seed of Babylon" (*zeru* in Akkadian is *zera'*, "seed," in Hebrew) but also the Shoot which the LORD has brought forth for His people. For "the hands of Zerubbabel have laid the foundation of this house; his hands shall also finish it"; even the one "who hath despised the day of small things" must rejoice to see the builders' plummet in the hand of Zerubbabel, who is "the Shoot of David" (4:5-10).

The prophet crowns Zerubbabel as King-Messiah with a royal crown. The "Golah" remaining in Babylonia had sent silver and gold, from which the prophet makes "crowns" (presumably two) and places them on the heads of Zerubbabel and Jeshua. To be sure, in Zechariah (6:11), where the text reads "crowns" in the plural number, it is said only, "And set upon the head of Joshua the son of Jehozadak, the high priest"; but why should the prophet crown Jeshua with *two crowns?* It could be imagined that this is a reference to the two crowns of the high priesthood and the political leadership, which in the period of the Second Temple were combined in the hands of the high priest; but if so the following verses do not harmonize well:

and speak unto him (Jeshua the high priest), saying: Thus speaketh the LORD of hosts, saying: Behold a man whose name is the Shoot, and who

---

[13] See above, pp. 103-106.

shall shoot up out of his place and build the temple of the LORD; even he shall build the temple of the LORD; and he shall bear the glory, and shall sit and rule upon his throne; and there shall be a priest *upon his right hand* (so it must be read instead of "upon his throne," which occurs here a second time through dittography, since in the Septuagint we find ἱερεὺς ἐκ δεξιῶν αὐτοῦ, "a priest upon his right hand"); *and the counsel of peace shall be between them both* (6:12-13).

Therefore the reference here is to *two* leaders, both of whom will be fitted with "crowns." Since Zechariah could say only of Zerubbabel, "he shall build the temple of the LORD," having already said, "the hands of Zerubbabel have laid the foundation of this house and his hands shall finish it"; and since the "Shoot" in Zechariah 3:8 can be only Zerubbabel, the prophet having said *to Jeshua* that the LORD "will bring forth His servant the Shoot"; and finally, since the "priest shall be upon the right hand" of the "Shoot," who "shall build the Temple" and "shall bear the glory, and shall sit and rule upon his throne"—we necessarily conclude that one of the "crowns" is for Zerubbabel as King-Messiah. And only after this prophecy was not fulfilled, and Zerubbabel did *not* become Messiah, was his name obliterated, leaving only the name of Jeshua, who afterward became in fact both religious and political leader.[14]

A great change in the Messianic idea took place, therefore, at the beginning of the period of the Second Temple. The remote expectations became near at hand—and their magnitude was reduced. The Messiah was brought nearer in time and was made less exalted: he was a contemporary of those holding the expectations and he did not engage in large undertakings; hence his chief virtue was his descent from the house of David.[15] And the hopes for political power were

---

[14] See on this in detail the book of E. Hühn (*Die messian. Weissag.*, I, particularly Note 5 on pp. 63-64). Stade (*op. cit.*, I, 316), Marti (*Dodekapropheton*, Tübingen, 1904, pp. 420-421), Steuernagel (*Einleitung*, 1912, pp. 642-643), and Bernfeld (*Introduction* [in Hebrew], II, 498) think that the name of Zerubbabel should not be *added* to the name of Jeshua, but that we must put Zerubbabel *in place of* Jeshua and read only "crown" and not "crowns" (or that we must translate the plural as "elements of a crown"), and that the prophet made only *one* crown for Zerubbabel alone, and afterward, when Zerubbabel failed to become Messiah, the name of Jeshua was substituted in this verse. But this does not appear probable to me: the omission is more likely than intentional changes.

[15] To be sure, I have already shown that Isaiah and Jeremiah also saw at first their Messiahs in their contemporaries Hezekiah and Zedekiah; but the virtues

small, as though their wings had been clipped: the flight of imagination of Haggai and Zechariah did not lift itself above a humble kingdom in the little land of Judah, to which would be added the Shephelah and the Negeb (Zech. 7:7). Even *the material prosperity* was pictured without especially glowing colors. Only *the spiritual promise* was great: the prophecy of Zechariah about the many powerful peoples that will come to seek the LORD, and the "ten men out of all the languages of the nations" who "shall take hold of the skirt of him that is a Jew," *in its content* hardly falls below the glorious vision of Isaiah and Micah, although its colors are not so brilliant.

Everything that I have said up to now applies only to Zechariah 1–8. From Zechariah 9 to the end of the book we find prophecies ("Deutero-Zechariah") that are to a large extent different in their content and in their style from the prophecies in the first eight chapters. On the one hand, we find here mention of "the sons of Greece" (9:13) and the placing of Jerusalem in *opposition* to Judah (12:2, also 6–7, and so on); sharp opposition to the prophets in general, placing them in the same category as "the spirit of uncleanness" (13:2–6); also a very late ideal that the Gentiles would come up to Jerusalem to celebrate the Feast of Tabernacles and every pot in Jerusalem and Judah would be holy to the LORD for offering sacrifices in them and there would no longer be a trader in the house of the LORD (14:16–21). All this shows that these are much later prophecies.

On the other hand, these chapters speak much of Tyre, Sidon, and Assyria, and of Ephraim and the house of Joseph (see all of Chapters 9–10). And to make the confusion greater, the verse Zechariah 11:13 is quoted in Matthew (27:9–10) as the words of Jeremiah. Therefore the English savant Joseph Mede, as early as the year 1653, made a distinction between Zechariah 1–8 and 9–14.[16] Many have thought, on the basis of Matthew, that the latter chapters were composed by Jeremiah; and others—since "Assyria" and "Ephraim" are

---

which these two prophets attributed to the two kings went beyond the bounds of the ordinary.

[16] Also, Nachman Krochmal, in *The Guide* [in Hebrew], Sect. 11 (writings of N. Krochmal, ed. Rawidowicz, p. 131), already distinguished between the two parts of Zechariah, and assigned Zech. 9–14 to the time of Antiochus the Great.

mentioned in 9–10—that they were written even before the fall of the kingdom of Ephraim, at the time of Assyrian dominance, and hence near the beginning of the prophetic activity of the *first* Isaiah, who mentions "Zechariah the son of Jeberechiah" (Isa. 8:2). According to this, the *first* Zechariah, he of the time of Isaiah, would be the author of the *last* chapters of the Book of Zechariah, while the *second* Zechariah, he of the time of Haggai, would be the author of the *first* chapters of the book!

But the mention of the name "Greece," the strong opposition to prophecy in general (which would have been possible only when prophecy had run its course and come to an end), the veneration of the Feast of Tabernacles, and the like, prevent us from accepting this opinion. Here we have, without any doubt, a prophet who prophesied after the Destruction. But when?

Sellin and Steuernagel [17] think that this is an old prophecy from the years 740–730 B.C.E., which had alterations made in it during the time of the return to Zion or during the time of the Diadochi. Budde [18] thinks that we must expunge the words "Against thy sons, O Greece" (Zech. 9:13), and that Deutero-Zechariah prophesied in the fourth century B.C.E. Stade [19] puts him still later: in his opinion, Chapters 9–14 reflect the wars of the "Diadochi," the successors of Alexander the Great, who after the battle of Ipsus (301) attacked Syria in general and Jerusalem in particular a number of times. "Assyria" and "Egypt" are here nothing but Syria (this name is the same as "Assyria," which was confused by the Greeks and became "Syria") of the Seleucids and Egypt of the Ptolemies; and in Chapter 12 there are even to be found indications of the bloody conflicts between the people of Judah and the inhabitants of Jerusalem that arose at this time. On this basis, Stade and many scholars with him conclude that

---

[17] See Steuernagel, *Einleitung*, pp. 644–646.
[18] *Geschichte der altheb. Litt.*, pp. 207–210.
[19] See his penetrating articles on this subject in the periodical *Zeitschrift für die Alttestamentliche Wissenschaft*, 1881, pp. 1–96; 1882, pp. 151–172, 275–309. With this opinion C. H. Cornill also agrees, in *Der israel. Prophetismus*, pp. 166–168. In accord with this opinion S. Bernfeld wrote his article "War in the Midst of Peace" [in Hebrew] (*Luah Ahiasaf*, 5662 [1902], pp. 31–32; see now his *Introduction*, II, 507–512). See my refutation of his position in *Ha-Shiloah*, Vol. 9, pp. 244–245.

Chapters 9–14 were written in the year 280. But some have gone even farther than Stade. Marti,[20] for example, relates these chapters to the time of Jonathan the Hasmonean, about the year 160, and Chapter 12 for the most part he relates to the time of Janneus Alexander, while Verses 7–8 of this chapter were composed "only at the beginning of the first century B.C."! Wellhausen[21] is not satisfied even with this, and attributes them to the time of John Hyrcanus, who ruled in the years 135–104 B.C.E.!

There is no need to do battle here with those scholars who can imagine that chapters from the books of the Latter Prophets—not from the Writings!—could have been received into the Prophetic collection as late as the times of John Hyrcanus or Janneus Alexander. Even the Book of Daniel, which is earlier than the time of John Hyrcanus, was not received into the Prophetic collection, but found a place in the Writings. Yet even the proposal of Stade is unnecessary. I have already pointed out in the chapter on Deutero-Isaiah,[22] that the Greeks [literally "Ionians," *Yavan* in Hebrew] could have been known to the prophets of Judah as inhabitants of the Ionian islands as early as the time of Darius (whence the borrowing of the word *Yavan*, which was afterward extended to cover the Hellenes).[23] This is particularly true, since from the year 500 onward the Ionian cities, incited by Histiaeus of Miletus and his son-in-law Aristagoras, were in revolt against Persia, conquering and burning Sardis (Sepharad) with the help of the Athenians, but being defeated by the Persians in 494. And from 492 onward, Darius and his successors were fighting against the Greeks in the Greeks' own land in order to be avenged on them for having supported their brethren living on the islands. If we remember that this rebellion was preceded by the rebellions in Babylonia, in Persia, and elsewhere, as described above, and by the wars with the Thracians and the Scythians (from 513 on-

---

[20] See his book (an elaboration of August Kayser's book) *Geschichte der israelitischen Religion*, 5th ed., Strassburg, 1907, pp. 87, 218, 296, 299, and his commentary *Dodekapropheton*, pp. 445–446.
[21] See *op. cit.*, p. 262, Note 1.
[22] See above, p. 173, Note 44.
[23] Ezekiel (27:13) already knew "Javan" as "a trafficker in the persons of men" and in vessels of brass with Tyre.

ward), it will be easy for us to suppose that Chapters 9–14 of Zechariah were composed somewhere during the years 500–485, and perhaps, *in his old age*, by the very same Zechariah who composed Chapters 1–8 *in his youth*.

This is the whole error of the Biblical scholars—that the prophets who wrote these little books are in the minds of the scholars like the angels created for their moment, who utter one poem and then sink down into the river of fire [Genesis Rabbah Chap. 78; Exodus Rabbah Chap. 15]. These scholars cannot imagine that some prophet might have lived a long time, with the content and even the style of his prophecies changing in the course of time. However, if we suppose that Zechariah prophesied not merely two years (520–518), but thirty or forty (though many of his relatively unimportant prophecies were not preserved), or that his prophetic activity ceased for a time while no very important events were taking place, and afterward began again about the years 500–485, at the time of the great wars of the end of the reign of Darius—then Chapters 9–14 will be intelligible to us without any difficulty.[24]

For in those times, before the coming of Ezra and Nehemiah, the Samaritans (the house of Joseph, Ephraim) had not yet separated completely from Judah, and it is possible that some Israelites also were returning from the Assyrian exile, that is, from the captivity of the Ten Tribes;[25] so Zechariah, of whom Budde[26] has already remarked that he followed in the footsteps of Ezekiel, dreamed for a time of the union of Joseph and Judah, exactly as did Ezekiel in his "Vision of the Two Sticks" (Ezek. 37:15–28). The evidence for this is the Vision of the Two Staves, Graciousness [or Delight] and Binders [or Union] (Zech. 11:7–14), which reminds us exactly of the vision of the two sticks joined together, except that Ezekiel could still dream of unity between Ephraim and Judah, while Zechariah,

---

[24] If we did not know for certain that Shalom Jacob Abramowitz and "Mendele Mokher Sefarim" (Mendele the Bookseller) were one man, would we agree that the same man who wrote *Fathers and Sons* and *Natural History* in his youth wrote in his old age *In the Vale of Weeping* and *The Life of Solomon*, which are so different from the early works in content and style alike?

[25] See on this the Russian article of J. L. Katzenelson, "The Babylonian Exile" (*Voskhod*, March 1902, pp. 129-139).

[26] *Op. cit.*, p. 171.

especially in the last period of his life, already sensed that the conflict between the Samaritans and the Jews would inevitably lead to that complete separation that afterward came to pass in the time of Ezra and Nehemiah; therefore he said: "Then I cut asunder mine other staff, even Binders, that the brotherhood between Judah and Israel might be broken" (11:14). So likewise, in describing the wars which the Gentiles will wage against Jerusalem, in Chapters 12 and 14, Zechariah modeled his description after the wars of "Gog and all his hosts" in Ezekiel 38–39,[27] without indicating thereby any historical event.

The name "Assyria" remained in use, signifying Babylonia and Persia, of which Assyria became a part, as we find in Ezra (6:22) concerning the returned exiles: "and had turned the heart of *the king of Assyria* unto them," instead of "the king of Persia"; and at that time many Jews lived in Egypt, as we now know from the Aramaic papyri found at Elephantine; therefore the prophet could say, "I will bring them back also out of the land of Egypt, and gather them out of Assyria" (Zech. 10:10).

Jerusalem and Judah still took an attitude of hostility to each other, since the upper-class "Golah," concentrated mostly in Jerusalem, did not deign to mingle with those left in the land at the time of Nebuchadrezzar, who were now living in the other towns of Judah.

Prophecy at that time had already fallen to a low estate (as Haggai, and Zechariah himself, demonstrate), and we see from Nehemiah (6:7–18) that in his day hireling prophets and prophetesses had become numerous in Jerusalem; and of course there were many like them in preceding decades: never is a flame extinguished suddenly, but it burns low for a long time, and when it finally goes out, it sends up smoke and a foul odor. It is not to be wondered at, therefore, that the aged (or the Second) Zechariah took a completely negative view of the prophets in general: *true* prophets of the type of Ezekiel and Deutero-Isaiah no longer exist, and the present ones have made of prophecy an artful trade: "They wear a hairy mantle to deceive" (Zech. 13:4).

[27] This was perceived also by Budde, *op. cit.*, p. 208.

The Feast of Tabernacles, which has great importance in Zechariah (14:16–19), has special significance in the time of Nehemiah (8:13–18); but of course it had already become important in the eyes of those returning from exile with Zerubbabel, since they had made their long journey from Babylonia to Judah during the spring and summer, and had undoubtedly made at that time booths to shade them from the burning heat of the sun.

Thus everything is settled satisfactorily, if we conclude that Zechariah 9–14 was written by the same Zechariah in his old age, or by another prophet called Deutero-Zechariah, who prophesied not before the year 500, or at any rate not after 460, by which time the author of the Book of Malachi had already prophesied and Ezra was soon to come (458).

The Messianic ideas in Zechariah 9–14 fit perfectly the *widespread* turbulence of the age, on the one hand, and "the day of small things" which continued *in Judah* even after the rebuilding of the Temple was completed (3rd of Adar, 515), on the other hand.

The rebellions and wars that took place at that time throughout the Persian Empire put hope into the heart of the prophet that "the day of the LORD" was near, when retribution would be exacted of Damascus, Tyre, and Sidon, Gaza, Ashkelon, and Ekron (9:1–7). Judah and Ephraim will return from Assyria and from Egypt; the pride of these two nations will be brought low and their scepter will be removed from other peoples, while the sons of Judah and Ephraim will be strengthened and all of them will become mighty men (10:6–12). The sons of Zion will be stirred up to wage war with the sons of Greece (9:13); that is, the sons of Zion will arise to go forth to battle against Persia in company with the sons of Greece [Ionians], who fought the Persians from the year 500 onward. And the sons of Zion will be saved in that day. For

> . . . the LORD shall be seen over them,
> And his arrow shall go forth as the lightning;
> And the LORD God will blow the horn,
> And will go with whirlwinds of the south (9:14).

Then there will be no more a foreign army in the city of the house of God, and no oppressor will pass through her any more (9:8). For the house of Judah will be as a majestic horse drawn up for battle, and their own princes and commanders and king ("cornerstone," "tent-pin," "master") will rule over them and not strangers (10:3–4). Also, *material prosperity* will be great: grain and new wine will be plentiful in the land (9:17), for the rain will come in its season (10:1) and living waters will go forth from Jerusalem in summer and in winter (14:8). The prophet continues in his exaltation of spirit:

> Rejoice greatly, O daughter of Zion!
> Shout, O daughter of Jerusalem!
> Behold, thy king cometh unto thee,
> He is triumphant and victorious,
> Lowly and riding upon an ass,
> Even upon a colt, the foal of an ass.
> He shall cut off [28] the chariot from Ephraim,
> And the horse from Jerusalem;
> The battle bow shall be cut off,
> And he shall speak peace unto the nations;
> His dominion shall be from sea to sea,
> And from the River to the ends of the earth [land] (9:9–10).

Zechariah prophesies of a kingdom as extensive as was the kingdom of David in his time: it will reach from the Mediterranean to the Red Sea and from the River Euphrates to the limits of the land of Canaan.[29] But the king who will stand at the head of this kingdom will be a meek ("lowly") king, who will abolish war and speak peace to the nations. We do not know if this king will be of the house of David; but from what appears farther on it is to be supposed that he will be: the offspring of Zerubbabel yearned for the throne of David as did their father.

It is not superfluous to point out here that these Messianic verses were of great importance for the development of the Messianic idea among both Jews and Christians: the Jews wait for one "lowly and riding upon an ass" *who is to come*, and the Christians affirm that

---

[28] Thus we must read instead of "I will cut off," because "he shall speak" in the second half agrees with this, and the Septuagint also agrees: ἐξολεθρεύσει.

[29] And so of no value is the contention of Gressmann (*Eschatologie*, 1905, p. 254) that the expression "from the River (Euphrates) to the ends of the earth (bounds of the world)" can have been formulated only in Babylonia. "Earth" [or "land"] is the land of Canaan, and the northern Hamath is the boundary of the Messianic kingdom according to Zech. 9:2 also.

the Messiah *has already come* as one "lowly and riding upon an ass." [30]

However, along with Ezekiel, Deutero-Zechariah envisions the war of the Gentiles against Jerusalem, which will come after Israel is settled peacefully in its own land. This war is described by Zechariah in Chapters 12 and 14. All the peoples will be gathered together against Jerusalem and Judah,[31] but the LORD will destroy them by means of the chiefs of Judah, who trust in the LORD that dwells in Jerusalem (12:5-6, 9).

> And I will pour upon the house of David,
> And upon the inhabitants of Jerusalem,
> The spirit of grace and of supplication;
> And they shall look *unto the one* [32]
>   whom they have pierced;
> And they shall mourn for him,
>   as one mourneth for his only son,
> And shall be in bitterness for him,
>   as one that is in bitterness for his first-born (12:10).

This vision, apparently, was born in the imagination of the prophet because of some unknown historical event, in which one of the leaders of the people was slain by the group venerating the house of David; but the Talmud [33] and the New Testament [34] saw in these words a reference to the Messiah—the former to Messiah son of Joseph who was slain and the latter to Jesus of Nazareth who was crucified. The idea of the "suffering Messiah" has its source in this verse of Zechariah together with Isaiah 53.

[30] Matt. 21:4-5 and parallels.
[31] Stade and his followers read: "And also the people of Judah (instead of "against Judah") will be in the siege against Jerusalem" (12:2); with this support and the support of the phrase "and Judah shall also fight against [instead of "at" or "in"] Jerusalem" (14:14), they have built a great structure, to the effect that the inhabitants of Judah at some time or other fought against the inhabitants of Jerusalem. But, apparently, the meaning of the prophet is that "in the siege against Jerusalem" the peoples will be also against Judah, that is, they will also attack the rest of the cities of Judah; then Judah will fight in the midst of Jerusalem against the peoples, and the LORD will save the tents of Judah first, in order that the inhabitants of Jerusalem with the descendants of the house of David among them may not be exalted above the common people inhabiting Judah (12:7). See what I have written on this in *Ha-Shiloah*, Vol. 9, pp. 244-245.
[32] So we must read instead of "unto me"; other texts have "unto him."
[33] Sukkah 52a.
[34] Matt. 24:30; John 19:37; Rev. 1:7.

More Messianic because it is more imaginative is the war described in Chapter 14. The nations go to war against Jerusalem, capturing the city, plundering the houses, and ravishing the women; but only "half of the city shall go forth into captivity and the residue of the people shall not be cut off from the city" (14:1–2).[35] And as in the wars with Gog, so also this time the LORD will fight in person for His people: He will stand upon the Mount of Olives, He will hurl half of the mountain against the Gentiles and put them to flight (14:3–5); He will smite them with a great plague, He will set them one against the other in fearful confusion, He will also smite their domestic animals, and Jerusalem will collect great booty: gold, silver, and clothing in abundance (14:12–15). Jerusalem will become very large and dwell in safety (14:10–11). Every pot in her and every bell on a horse in her will be a holy object, and there will be no more traders (or Canaanites) in the house of the LORD (14:20–21). Every one that is left of all the nations that besieged Jerusalem will go up from year to year to celebrate the Feast of Tabernacles, and those that do not go up will receive their punishment (14:16–19).

> And the LORD shall be King over all the earth;
> In that day shall the LORD be One,
>   and His name one (14:9).

These are the Messianic expectations of this later prophet. He prophesies of material welfare and political power, but without political grandeur, without dazzling triumphs. He prophesies of spiritual welfare, of the spread of the rule of Israel's God in all the world; but limitation reveals itself by the proviso that first the Gentiles besieging Jerusalem shall fall slain in heaps, while those that remain will be *forced* to celebrate the Feast of Tabernacles (see above); and also by the provisos that every pot and bell in Jerusalem must be holy to the LORD, and no trader (or Canaanite) is ever again to be found in His house!

How far are we here from the sublime expectations of Isaiah and Jeremiah!

---

[35] According to 13:8–9 only a third will be left, but even the third will be refined like silver and tested like gold.

CHAPTER XIV

Joel (c. 490–475 B.C.E.) and Malachi (c. 475 B.C.E.)

JUST AS opinions about Zechariah 9–14 are divided, so are they divided about Joel son of Pethuel. His beautiful style and his position in the Scriptures between Hosea and Amos caused the ancient interpreters to think that he was one of the earlier prophets; the fact that he mentions no king at all, but on the contrary that the priests and the "ministers of the altar" are mentioned three times (1:9, 13; 2:17), gave rise to the idea that Joel was the earliest of the prophets, prophesying in the time of Jehoash son of Ahaziah, king of Judah (836–796), who became king at seven years of age, Jehoiada the priest ruling the land until the king came of age (II Kings 12:1–4).[1] But this is not possible. *First*, the kingdom of Israel is not mentioned at all in Joel;[2] *second*, Joel stresses repeatedly not only the importance of the priests, but also the fact that there is no meal-offering or drink-

[1] This opinion is still held by the liberal scholar Castelli (in his book *Il Messia*, p. 83, Note 1) along with Rashi and Abravanel.
[2] In order to get out of this difficulty, J. J. Weinkoop, author of the commentary on Joel in *The Bible with Scientific Commentary* [in Hebrew], ed. A. Kahana (Kiev, 1907), holds to the opinion of the author of *Seder 'Olam*, that Joel prophesied in the time of Manasseh, after the exile of the Ten Tribes; other scholars think that Joel prophesied during the minority of Josiah and afterward, when the Scythians passed near the land of Judah in the year 627 (see E. Koenig, *Die messianischen Weissagungen des Alten Testaments*, Stuttgart, 1923, pp. 205–213), and that the Scythians are the locusts which Joel describes metaphorically. But—apart from the fact that the locusts are described as real locusts—it is possible thus to solve only one difficulty: the fact that the kingdom of Israel is not mentioned in the book of Joel—and the rest of the difficulties mentioned in the text are still present.

offering in the house of the LORD (1:9, 13, 16) as though this were the essence of calamity; *third*, we find this in Joel:

> Spare Thy people, O LORD,
> And give not Thy heritage to reproach,
> That the nations should make them a byword:
> Wherefore should they say among the peoples:
> Where is their God? (2:17)

—which is exactly what we find in psalms dated after the Destruction; *fourth*, Judah and Jerusalem in Joel also (4:1 [Eng. 3:1], and so on), as in Deutero-Zechariah (see above), are regarded as two separate parts of the nation; *fifth*, in Joel are mentioned (4:6; Eng. 3:6) "the sons of the Greeks," to whom the Tyrians, the Sidonians, and the Philistines are selling Jews; *sixth*, it says in Joel, "Then shall Jerusalem be holy, and there shall no strangers pass through her any more" (4:17; Eng. 3:17), implying that once already strangers had passed through her, something which happened in the time of Nebuchadrezzar.

On the basis of all this and of the words, "They leap upon the city, they run upon the wall" (2:9), most modern scholars conclude that Joel was written after the rebuilding of the wall by Nehemiah, about the year 400.[3] But in my opinion it should not be put so late: fifty years after Ezra and Nehemiah it would have been difficult to write in such excellent style, although we must agree with the opinion of those who say that Joel imitates the older prophets and makes use of their ancient metaphors, just as the poets in our day make use of "archaisms" (see below). It seems to me that Joel is an earlier prophet, standing between Deutero-Isaiah—that master of rich and brilliant language—and Ezra and Nehemiah, so that his prophecies fall near the time of the prophecies of Malachi.

I have three reasons for this. *First*, the words about the Day of Judgment in the valley of Jehoshaphat (4:9-17, Eng. 3:9-17) have

---

[3] See Budde, *Geschichte der altheb. Litt.*, pp. 211-213; Marti, *Dodekapropheton*, 1904, pp. 112-113. But Steuernagel (*Einleitung*, 1912, pp. 613-615) thinks it impossible to find a fixed time for the composition of this book because we do not have any point to get hold of for this. Prof. M. Z. Segal (*Introduction to the Bible*, II [1946], 455-456) dates it still later, "to the last generations of Persian rule in Palestine, about 450 years before the destruction of the Second Temple."

a similarity to Zechariah 14—a prophecy which I have already shown, to my own satisfaction at least, to have been delivered at the end of the reign of Darius.[4] *Second*, the years of privation about which Joel speaks are mentioned in Haggai and Zechariah; and concerning the locust plague Malachi speaks plainly:

> And I will rebuke *the devourer* for your good,
> And he shall not destroy the fruits of your land;
> Neither shall your vine cast its fruit before the
> time in the field (Mal. 3:11).

Likewise, Joel, with his words, "And He causeth to come down for you the rain, the former rain and the latter rain" (2:23), recalls the words of Zechariah (10:1), which according to the Septuagint (καθ' ὥραν πρώϊμον καὶ ὄψιμον) are to be read, "in the time of the former rain and the latter rain." *Third*, we found in Zechariah (9:13) "the sons of Greece," exactly as in Joel; moreover, we find in Nehemiah (5:8) these clear words concerning the selling of Jews to Gentiles: "We after our ability have redeemed our brethren the Jews *that have been sold unto the heathen*"—which agree perfectly with the words of Joel (4:6, Eng. 3:6): "The children also of Judah and the children of Jerusalem *have ye sold unto the sons of the Greeks*, that ye might remove them far from their border."

All this together gives me a right to think that Joel stands midway between Deutero-Isaiah and Zechariah on the one hand and Malachi and Ezra-Nehemiah on the other. That the word "wall" in Joel does not prove that he prophesied after Nehemiah I have already explained in the chapter on Deutero-Isaiah.[5] Perhaps the reference here is to a temporary wall that was in existence before Nehemiah, or perhaps the meaning is the walls of the houses.

And like the style of Joel, which is a mixture of imitations of the older prophets and of very original figures, so are his Messianic expectations: they also resemble in many ways those of the preceding prophets and in many ways they tend to go beyond them and to differ from the pattern which they formulated.

Like Zephaniah, Joel also speaks of "the great and terrible day of

---

[4] See above, pp. 199-200.
[5] See above, p. 169, Note 39.

JOEL AND MALACHI 209

the LORD," which will be "a day of darkness and gloominess, a day of clouds and thick darkness" (2:2, 11; 3:4, Eng. 2:31), and which has now come in the form of locusts to destroy the earth. But the day of the LORD will come a second time:

> And I will show wonders in the heavens
>   and in the earth,
> Blood, and fire, and pillars of smoke.
> The sun shall be turned into darkness,
> And the moon into blood,
> Before the great and terrible day of the LORD
>   come (3:3-4, Eng. 2:30-31).

Hereby was laid the foundation of the alarming descriptions of the great changes for the worse that will take place in nature in the time of "the birth pangs of the Messiah," as they are set forth in detail in the Pseudepigrapha, in the Talmudic and Midrashic Aggadah, and in the New Testament.

The prophet urges *repentance:* he presses the people to turn to the LORD with all their hearts, and with fasting, weeping, and lamentation, and to rend their hearts and not their garments (2:12-13); then the LORD will have pity on His people, giving them rains in season and increasing the grain and the fruit of the trees (2:18-27). This is *the material prosperity.* Concerning *political success* there is nothing here at all. What more than this could there have been in "the day of small things" between the building of the Second Temple and the coming of Ezra and Nehemiah?

But by way of contrast, the description of the *spiritual blessedness* is very lofty:

And it shall come to pass afterward,
That I will pour out My spirit upon *all flesh;*
And your sons and your daughters shall prophesy,
Your old men shall dream dreams,
Your young men shall see visions;
And also upon the servants and upon the handmaids
In those days will I pour out My spirit (3:1-2, Eng. 2:28-29).

And it shall come to pass,
  that whosoever shall call on the name of the LORD shall be delivered;

For in Mount Zion and in Jerusalem
  there shall be those that escape,
As the LORD hath said,
And among *the remnant* those whom the LORD shall call (3:5, Eng. 2:32).

We have here not the redemption of the Jews alone, as many Christian scholars would see it,[6] but a universal redemption, a redemption of "all flesh." Obviously, redemption will come only to the good and upright among all the nations, the "remnant" to be saved from "the day of the LORD" and from the judgment upon the peoples,[7] as we have already seen in Ezekiel 39 and Zechariah 14, and as described by Joel in even stronger colors.

In clear contrast to Isaiah (2:4), who says, "And they shall beat their swords into plowshares, and their spears into pruning-hooks," Joel says, "Beat your plowshares into swords, and your pruning-hooks into spears" (4:10, Eng. 3:10). Let all the peoples be gathered to the valley of Jehoshaphat, for there the LORD will sit to judge all the nations round about. "Put in the sickle, for the harvest is ripe," says the prophet, and he himself explains this incisive metaphor: "For their wickedness is great" (4:13, Eng. 3:13). The sickle will reap on the right hand and on the left, and multitudes upon multitudes will fall in the valley of decision, the valley of Jehoshaphat.[8] At the time of judgment the sun and the moon will be darkened and the stars will withhold their brightness (4:14-15, Eng. 3:14-15). Like Amos, Joel says: "And the LORD shall roar from Zion, and utter His voice from Jerusalem" (4:16, Eng. 3:16; compare Amos 1:2), and the heavens and the earth will shake; Egypt will become a desolation and Edom a wilderness, because they shed innocent blood in the land of the children of Judah (4:19, Eng. 3:19). This is the magnificent portrayal of "the day of judgment" which remained engraved in the memory of succeeding generations, and was described, along with "the birth pangs of the Messiah," in brilliant colors both in Jewish and in Christian legend.

But the prophet also *comforts* his people. The children of Judah

[6] See Hühn, *Die messian. Weissag.*, p. 68.
[7] See Castelli, *op. cit.*, pp. 84-85.
[8] Perhaps here we actually have remnants of popular beliefs and traces of mythology, as Gressmann says (*Eschatologie*, 1905, pp. 187-188).

will return from the place to which they have been sold (4:7, Eng. 3:7); "Judah shall be inhabited for ever, and Jerusalem from generation to generation" (4:20, Eng. 3:20). For "the LORD will be a refuge unto His people and a stronghold to the children of Israel"; He will dwell in Zion, Jerusalem will be holy, and strangers will not pass through her any more (4:16–17, 21, Eng. 3:16–17, 21). In the words of Amos (9:13) and also of Ezekiel (47:1–12), Joel here describes the *material prosperity:*

> And it shall come to pass in that day,
> That the mountains shall drop down sweet wine,
> And the hills shall flow with milk,
> And all the brooks of Judah shall flow with waters;
> And a fountain shall come forth from the house of the LORD
> And shall water the valley of Shittim[9] (4:18, Eng. 3:18).

The light of prophecy had not yet gone out. The Messianic expectations of Joel with their portrayals of "the birth pangs of Messiah" and of "the day of judgment" bore fruit in the Jewish apocalypticism of the Pseudepigrapha (in which was laid the foundation of all Christology) and of the Talmud and Midrash to the highest degree.

But the light of prophecy did go out a short time after Joel. The last prophet that can properly be so designated is the one called by us "Malachi" because we do not know his real name. That Malachi ("My messenger") is not a proper name and that it is derived from the verse "Behold I send *My messenger*" (Mal. 3:1) is apparent from the fact that in the Septuagint we find at the beginning of the Book of Malachi (1:1) "by the hand of *His* messenger" instead of "by the hand of *My* messenger." In the Talmud[10] we read that "Malachi is the same as Ezra," and this proposition is true in relation to the expression "My messenger" in Malachi 3:1, since the messenger, "the messenger of the covenant," for whom the prophet known to us as "Malachi" waited, was in fact Ezra the Scribe—whether the author of the Book of Malachi actually had in mind Ezra himself or another emissary who would come to Palestine on a mission for the LORD.

[9] On "the valley of Shittim" see Gressmann, *loc. cit.*
[10] Megillah 15a.

But we do not know for certain the *actual name* of the author of the Book of Malachi.

In contrast to this uncertainty, the time in which the prophet prophesied and the material and spiritual condition of Israel at that time are clearly reflected in the book.

The Temple had been completed in the year 515—yet the Messianic expectations of Ezekiel, of Deutero-Isaiah, or even of Haggai and Zechariah were still not fulfilled. The subjection continued. Zerubbabel not only did not become Messiah, but was forced to yield place to Jeshua and disappeared completely from the stage of Jewish history. "The day of small things" did not cease. The years of privation continued, and the locust was a familiar visitor in the land (Mal. 3:9, 11). Along with this, the governors oppressed the people with heavy taxes, until the Jews felt themselves slaves in their own land, which was yielding "much increase unto the kings" (Neh. 5:15; 9:36-37). Also, the great capitalists and landowners among the Jews themselves were oppressing the common people and seizing for debt the property and even the sons and daughters of the poor (Neh. 5:1-8).[11] Such was *the material condition*.

The spiritual condition was no better. The priests were "despising" the LORD (Mal. 1:6), they were misleading the common people, they did not follow the ways of the LORD, and they failed to show favor to the Law. Therefore they were contemptible and base in the eyes of the people (2:8-9). The rich had increased their power by marriages with the powerful neighboring peoples, so that the Hebrew women were thrust out in favor of "the daughters of a strange god" and were coming "to cover the altar of the LORD with tears"—to weep in the Sanctuary because they were thrust out in favor of the foreign women (2:11-15).[12] And the people, seeing that the violators

[11] This distressing situation, which reached the height of extremity in the time of Nehemiah, had of course been developing for a number of years previously. See S. Jampel, *Die Wiederherstellung Israels unter den Achaemeniden*, Breslau, 1904, pp. 111-112 (*MGWJ*, XLVII, 1903, p. 8).

[12] Some think that in these verses Malachi is opposing Ezra and Nehemiah because they expelled the foreign wives, and hence is to be dated in their time or later; but the words "Judah hath profaned the holiness of the LORD which he loved, and hath married the daughter of a strange god" (2:11) show that *the Jewish women were thrust out in favor of foreign women*. It is also doubtful if

of the covenant were rich, powerful, and prosperous, were wont to despise the obligations between man and God, such as the sacrifices (1:7-8), and the heave-offerings and tithes (3:8-10). Likewise with the obligations between man and his fellow man: there were among them "sorcerers, . . . adulterers, . . . false swearers, . . . those oppressing the hireling in his wages, the widow, and the fatherless, and those turning aside the stranger from his right" (3:5). These evil deeds were not chance occurrences or things done under stress of desire, but had become almost habitual, so as to cause justifiable anger:

> In that ye say: "Every one that doeth evil
> Is good in the sight of the LORD,
> And He delighteth in them";
> Or "Where is the God of justice?" (2:17)

> Ye have said: "It is vain to serve God;
> And what profit is it that we have kept His charge,
> And that we have walked mournfully
> Because of the LORD of hosts?
> And now we call the proud happy;
> Yea, they that work wickedness are built up;
> Yea, they try God, and are delivered" (3:14-15).

Heretical ideas like these, the result of the non-fulfillment of the promises of the prophets, apparently had struck deep root among the people, and the prophet is forced to argue with the authors of such words. To be sure, there were also God-fearing persons, of whom the prophet says that they will be written in "a book of remembrance . . . before Him" (3:16); but they were the minority. The small and insignificant state was exposed to a great danger: it was gradually disintegrating.

To meet this dreadful situation, there arises the prophet who wrote the Book of Malachi, prophesying after the completion of the Temple but before the coming of Ezra and Nehemiah, about the year 475. He does not distinguish between man's obligations to God and to his

---

foreign women would have come "to cover the altar of the LORD with tears." Incidentally, the fact that the foreign women were filling the places of the divorced Jewish women takes away from the hard task of Ezra and Nehemiah—to expel the foreign wives—all its cruelty and "barbarity." See J. Klausner, *History of the Second Temple*, I, 237-238.

fellow man. He cries out violently against the dishonoring of the consecrated objects (sacrifices and tithes), reaching such a pitch that he says:

> Oh that there were even one among you
>   that would shut the doors (of the Temple),
> That ye might not kindle fire
>   on Mine altar in vain!
> I have no pleasure in you,
> Saith the LORD of hosts,
> Neither will I accept
>   an offering at your hand.
> For from the rising of the sun
>   even unto the going down of the same
> My name is great among the nations;
> And in every place offerings
>   are presented unto My name,
> Even pure oblations;
> For My name is great among the nations (1:10-11);

and further:

> For I am a great King,
> Saith the LORD of hosts,
> And My name is feared among the nations (1:14).

Most scholars interpret these latter verses thus: the prophet thinks that since the LORD, the God of Judah, is actually the King of the whole world, therefore whatever the peoples offer to their own gods they really offer to the God of Judah.[13] But it seems to me that the reference is to the various lands in which the Jews were scattered and in which they offered sacrifices to the LORD upon altars set up outside Palestine, and in which they probably made *converts to Judaism*, as appears from the Aramaic papyri of the time of Malachi, found at Elephantine near the southern border of Egypt.[14]

In order that the sons of Judah may return to their God, there must come a great man, a messenger sent from the LORD, who will

---

[13] See, e.g., B. Stade, *Biblische Theologie*, p. 333.

[14] See the article of S. Daiches, "Aramaic Documents of the Time of Ezra" [in Hebrew] (*Ha-Shiloah*, XIII, 11, 506–608, 511). Of this sort is now the view of Bernfeld, *Introduction*, II, 517. For details on this see J. Klausner, *op. cit.*, II, 70–75.

separate the good from the bad, the numerous sinners from the few fearers of the LORD. This messenger, whose coming the fearers of the LORD are awaiting, will be "the messenger of the covenant" (that is, he will disseminate the law of the LORD, as it already existed among the best of the priests in Babylonia); he will come suddenly to the temple of the LORD and clear the way before the LORD. For he will be "like a refiner's fire" (what a striking expression this is!) "and like fullers' soap," he will refine and purify the priests ("sons of Levi") and choose out the worthy among them; then the offering of Judah and Jerusalem will be pleasing to the LORD (3:1–4).

Then will come the judgment—"the day of judgment" which we have already seen in Ezekiel, Zechariah, and Joel. This time, however, it will not be a judgment upon the Gentiles, but *a judgment upon the Jews:* God will discern "between the righteous and the wicked, between him that serveth God and him that serveth Him not" (3:18). In advance of "the great and terrible day of the LORD" (exactly as in Joel), the LORD will send *the prophet Elijah,* who "shall turn the heart of the fathers to the children, and the heart of the children to their fathers," since otherwise it would be impossible to distinguish between the bad and the good and the land would be smitten "with utter destruction" (see below). Then those who fear the LORD will be the LORD's "own treasure," and He will spare them as a father spares his son; the sun of righteousness will arise for them with healing in its wings, and they will become healthy and fat like calves in the stall. But "the day that cometh" will consume the proud and those that do wickedness as a furnace burns stubble, while the righteous will trample them with their feet, because the wicked will be ashes under the soles of their feet (3:17–21, Eng. 3:17–4:3).

The spirit of the later psalms already hovers over these words, which complete the picture of "the day of judgment" upon the transgressors in Israel.

The end of Malachi is the conclusion of all prophecy. However, I cannot accept the opinion of a number of modern scholars, that the last three verses (3:22–24, Eng. 4:4–6) of Malachi, "Remember ye the law of Moses My servant," and so on, "Behold I will send you Elijah the prophet," and so on, do not belong to Malachi at all but are a general conclusion to *all* prophetic books.[15] For the whole purpose of the judgment is to separate the good from the bad, in order that the LORD may not "come and smite the land with utter destruction"; hence it is necessary for a prophet to come to "turn the heart of the fathers to the children and the heart of the children to their fathers," in order to save what can be saved. And let us not forget that Ben-Sira (in his Hebrew original, 48:10) already knows that Elijah is

> . . . written, ready for the time,
> To still wrath before the fierce anger [of God],
> To turn the heart of the fathers unto the children,
> And to restore the tribes of Israel.

These lines were already considered very ancient in the time of Ben-Sira (*c.* 200 B.C.E.).[16] And the prophet who waited for "the messenger of the covenant," prepared the people for the proclamation of the Law in the time of Ezra, and esteemed so highly unblemished sacrifices and the setting aside of heave-offerings and tithes, could and must have put into the conclusion of his prophecies the lines:

> Remember ye *the law of Moses* My servant,
> Which I commanded unto him in Horeb for all Israel,
> Even *statutes and ordinances.*

Hence not even this verse is a later addition for the purpose of forming a conclusion to the prophetic collection.

But this verse is the conclusion of *prophecy:* the hour of reproof and instruction by the prophets to meet a specific historical and social situation had passed, and there had come the hour of the Law of Moses, which was proclaimed by Ezra and accepted as the constitution of the land and people of Judah, that is, as a book regulating every detail of the life of the entire nation and guiding it in the fear of the LORD and in the ways of uprightness by means of firmly fixed ceremonial laws and ethical demands laid down in the form of definite statutes.

---

[15] See Budde, *op. cit.*, pp. 175-178; Stade, *op. cit.*, pp. 334-335.
[16] See what has been written *in favor of* these verses' belonging to Malachi by A. Kuenen, *Historisch-kritisch Onderzoek*, II², 428; and *against* their belonging to Malachi, see Steuernagel, *op. cit.*, p. 650.

CHAPTER XV

Psalms from the Period of the Second Temple

(C. 538–104 B.C.E.)

I HAVE SPOKEN above [1] of "Hymns of the Exile in the Book of Psalms" and of the Messianic ideas embodied in them. But the Hymns of the Exile are few, as are also the hymns from before the Exile. Most psalms were written in the Persian period (538–333); it is hard for anyone who takes a scientific attitude toward the Book of Psalms to cast doubt on this, even if he is not a disciple of Wellhausen. Some of them were written in the Greek period (333–175), down to the Hasmonean period.[2]

Whether we should say "inclusive" or "not inclusive," that is, whether we also have psalms from the period of the first Hasmoneans, before they became kings (167–104) or not, is a question that still awaits solution. The reformer Calvin concluded centuries ago that Psalm 44 should be ascribed to the time of Antiochus Epiphanes. During the past century the following Gentile scholars have declared their opinion *in favor of* psalms from the time of the Hasmoneans: Hitzig, Olshausen, Reuss, Cornill, Wellhausen, Delitzsch, Marti, Smend, Schürer, and others; and among Jewish scholars, Nachman

[1] See pp. 140–142.
[2] The opinion of Ezekiel Kaufmann, *History of the Israelite Religion* [in Hebrew], II.2 (1946), 506–532 and also 646–727, that there is not in the Book of Psalms even one hymn that can show proof from its plain meaning that it is later than Psalm 137 (*ibid.*, p. 508) depends upon his peculiar view about the origin of monotheism, which can be controverted from many sides. See J. Klausner, *History of the Second Temple*, II, 212–213.

Krochmal,³ Graetz,⁴ Z. P. Chajes,⁵ and S. Bernfeld.⁶ *Against* the existence of hymns from Hasmonean times in the Book of Psalms, the following among the best scholars have declared their opinion: Gesenius, Ewald, Dillmann, Robertson Smith, Cheyne (in spite of his radicalism in the rest of his source analysis), and others.

The possibility that psalms from Hasmonean times could have been *received* into the Hagiographa is proved by the reception therein of the Book of Daniel, of which at least a considerable part was composed in the time of Antiochus Epiphanes (see the next chapter); and the possibility that hymns like those in our Book of Psalms could have been *written* in Hasmonean times is shown by the "Psalms of Solomon," which were composed at the end of the Hasmonean period (63–37 B.C.E.), but were not received into the Hagiographa because of their very late date.⁷

However, most of the arguments that such psalms must necessarily be from Hasmonean times are not convincing. Most scholars consider Psalms 44, 74, 79, and 83 as Hasmonean; but these psalms are ascribed by others to the time of the Babylonian exile or to the persecutions in the time of Artaxerxes Ochus.⁸ The argument from the occurrence of the word *Ḥasidim* ["saints" or "the pious," supposedly a technical term not used before Hasmonean times]—"the flesh of *Thy saints*" (79:2), "the death of *His saints*" (116:15), "His praise in the assembly of *the saints*" and "the glory of all *His saints*" (149:1, 9)—according to which were considered Hasmonean not only the four psalms mentioned above, but also Psalms 113–119 (the Great Hallel) and 145–150—this argument was considered convincing as long as we did not have Ben-Sira *in his Hebrew original,* in which one hymn (in Chapter

---

³ See *The Guide* [in Hebrew], ed. Lvov, 1851, pp. 130–136; writings of N. Krochmal, ed. Rawidowicz, pp. 152–161.

⁴ See *The History of the Jews* in the [Hebrew] translation of S. P. Rabinowitz, I, 349–350, and his book *Kritischer Kommentar zu den Psalmen*, Breslau, 1883.

⁵ See his commentary on the Book of Psalms (*The Bible with Scientific Commentary*, ed. A. Kahana), Zhitomir, 1903, *passim*.

⁶ See S. Bernfeld, *Introduction*, III, pp. 91, 96–97, 99, 113–114, etc. Bernfeld is inclined to date a number of psalms late, "even to the time of Herod"!

⁷ See the introduction to the Psalms of Solomon in the Hebrew translation of A. S. Kaminetzky (*Ha-Shiloah*, XIII, 44–45); M. Stein "The Psalms of Solomon" (*Pseudepigrapha* [in Hebrew], ed. A. Kahana, I.2, pp. 432–433).

⁸ See on this Schürer, *Geschichte des jüdischen Volkes*, III⁴, 203–205.

PSALMS FROM THE PERIOD OF THE SECOND TEMPLE 219

51), very similar in its form to Psalm 136 and in its content to the *Shemoneh Esreh* prayer, concludes exactly as does Psalm 148, with the verse:

> And He hath lifted up a horn for His people,
> A praise for all *His saints*,
> Even for the children of Israel,
>   a people near unto Him.
> Hallelujah! [9]

On the basis of this and various other arguments from the Book of Ben-Sira, S. Schechter concludes that the dating of canonical psalms as late as Hasmonean times is in any case a very doubtful procedure.[10] As the reader can see, the problem is a most complicated one, and it is not the obligation of the present book to solve it. For our undertaking it is more important to know about the Messianic ideas expressed in those psalms which are in any case from the period of the Second Temple.

It must be admitted that these psalms do not add much to what we have already found in the psalms from the time of the Babylonian exile.[11] As in Psalm 89, we find also in Psalm 132 (11–18) that the LORD swore to David that his descendants would sit on his throne forever, and from this oath He will not turn back, if only they will keep His commandments. David and his descendants are the Anointed Ones of the LORD, and in Zion, which He has chosen as His habitation, He will cause a horn to spring forth for them and will place the diadem upon them after He has clothed their enemies with shame (see also 18:51). For the most part, the LORD alone is here the redeemer, without a human Messiah: in the Persian and Greek periods there was no king in Israel, and it was as though the house of David

---

[9] It is proper to note that Z. P. Chajes in his Hebrew commentary on Psalm 148 thinks that this verse in the Psalms (148:14) was added at a later time, without any reference to its presence in Ben-Sira 51.

[10] See S. Schechter, *Studies in Judaism*, 2nd series, Philadelphia, 1908, pp. 42–54, and the article of David Kahana, "The Book of Ben-Sira in Its Hebrew Original" [in Hebrew] (*Ha-Shiloah*, III, 134); see also Kahana's book, *The Wisdom of Simeon Ben-Sira* [in Hebrew], Warsaw, 1912, Introduction, p. xii.

[11] On the Messianic idea in the Book of Psalms, see in detail B. Stade, "Die messianische Hoffnung in Psalter" (*Zeitschrift für Theologie und Kirche*, 1892, pp. 369–413); D. Castelli, *Il Messia*, pp. 50–76 ("Il Messia nei Salmi").

had passed away and disappeared from the world. Therefore, in the Messianic thinking of these periods and in the Psalms—the characteristic literary creations of these periods—an individual Messiah had no great importance. By contrast, much is said in the Psalms about *the Consolation of Zion and the ingathering of exiles:*

> Thou wilt arise, and have compassion upon Zion;
> For it is time to be gracious unto her,
>   for the appointed time is come.
> For Thy servants take pleasure in her stones,
> And love her dust.
> So the nations will fear the name of the LORD,
> And all the kings of the earth Thy glory;
> When the LORD hath built up Zion,
> When He hath appeared in His glory (102:14-17).[12]

Thus says the psalmist, "The LORD loveth the gates of Zion more than all the dwellings of Jacob" (87:2). And he prays, "Save us, O LORD our God, and gather us from among the nations, that we may give thanks unto Thy holy name, that we may glory in Thy praise" (106:47). *The ingathering of exiles* is here, as in Ezekiel, a sanctification of the Name.

The Psalms also know of *punishment and the Day of Judgment* upon the peoples: the LORD will judge the world with righteousness and the peoples with equity; then the peoples will tremble and the earth quake, the mountains will melt like wax at the presence of the LORD, all worshipers of graven images, who take pride in idols, will be put to shame and all the gods will bow down to Him (Psalms 96-99). Then "all the ends of the earth shall remember and turn unto the LORD, and all the clans of the nations shall worship before Him. For the kingdom belongs to the LORD, and He rules over the nations" (22:28-29). Then the peoples and the kingdoms will be gathered together to serve the LORD (102-23). This is the great *spiritual expectation*, which is also present, generally speaking, in Psalms 12, 46, 66, 68, 117, and others.[13]

By contrast, *material expectation* is mentioned with striking brevity and infrequency, and it is dependent—exactly as in the expectations

---

[12] See also 14:7; 51:20-21; 53:7; 69:36-37, etc.
[13] See D. Castelli, *op. cit.*, p. 76, Note 1.

of the prophets—upon the righteousness and justice that must prevail in the world: when the LORD comes "that glory may dwell in our land," mercy and truth will meet together; righteousness and peace will kiss each other, truth will spring out of the earth, and righteousness will look down from heaven—then "the LORD will give that which is good, and our land shall yield her produce" (85:10–13).

The Psalms were composed by consecrated poets who poured into them their bitter complaints and recounted the private miseries of their hearts. But, as David Castelli has already said: [14]

... his (the psalmist's) private misfortunes did not prevent him from rising up to consider that evil with which his people *as a whole* were afflicted and to hope for a better future for them. And filled with faith in a just and omnipotent God, he prophesies of a time in which all the peoples will be called to this faith and will flock to it. Then will ensue the true reign of the LORD, in which the powerful will be humbled, all those who were about to lose their life will return to the true God, and from one generation to another these redemptive beliefs will be maintained.

(These are) the noble expectations of the ancient poets of the people Israel—expectations that must not be sought for before its [Israel's] political decline and its not very distant collapse as an independent state. For it is natural that precisely then should arise such a (more spiritual and universalistic) attitude, very different from the close exclusiveness of the preceding centuries. Misfortune always gives to great souls delicacy and generosity of feeling.

This characterization of the Messianic expectations in the Psalms is close to the truth.

[14] *Ibid.*, pp. 67–68.

CHAPTER XVI

Daniel

(C. 167-164 B.C.E.) [1]

AFTER "THE day of small things," lasting from the time of Ezra and Nehemiah almost to the middle of the Seleucid period, "the day of big things" came back. For "the small things"—as they appeared to the eye—prepared for and made possible the larger things. At the end of the Persian period (424-333) Judah gradually bestirred herself out of her depressed condition; during the rule of Alexander the Great and his successors (333-301) and the rule of the Ptolemies in Judah (301-198), Judah began to flourish; and during the rule of the first Seleucids (198-175) she achieved prosperity and wealth (the Tobiads).

This material success brought in its wake a vigorous cultural development: at that time were composed many of the Psalms, the Song of Songs, Koheleth, Esther, Ben-Sira. Jewish "Wisdom," having become at that time a kind of world-view mediating between theology, philosophy, and the practical understanding of life, was deepened and rounded out by the Greek thought which had penetrated into Palestine. The life of the individual became richer and fuller, a spirit of ease was felt in the land, and the space within the

---

[1] Actually, it would be proper to give here the Messianic expectations in the Book of Ben-Sira, which in any case cannot be later than the years 200-180, and so is prior to the Book of Daniel; but I do not wish to mix the Apocryphal and Pseudepigraphical books with those that were received within the canon of Holy Scripture.

walls with which Ezra and Nehemiah had surrounded their people became too restricted for the Jewish aristocracy.

Hellenism, which brought with it the beautified and broadened life, also brought much licentiousness: the acceptance of a foreign culture is always accompanied by a certain superficiality and frivolousness, inasmuch as it is hard to penetrate to the *heart* of the foreign culture, which is the fruit of the historical development, the racial characteristics, and the peculiar life-circumstances of the foreign people; but it is very easy to adopt the *external* symbols of the foreign culture.

So it has been always and everywhere, and so it was also in Judah in Ptolemaic and Seleucid times. In the time of Seleucus IV Philopator (187–175), the overseer of the Temple, Simon [or Simeon], "Prince of the Sanctuary," incited Heliodorus against the Temple treasury and against Onias III; and in the time of Antiochus IV Epiphanes (175–164), Yeshua-Jason bought the high-priesthood for money and established a gymnasium in Jerusalem (174–171); then Menelaus paid a higher price for the high-priesthood and received it from the king (171–170).

Antiochus came to Jerusalem during his first campaign against Egypt (170) and plundered the Temple. In the year 168 he sent to Jerusalem Apollonius, who conducted massacres in the cities of Judah, forced people to violate the religious laws (after greater Hellenization they violated them willingly), stopped the continual burnt-offerings, and on the 15th of Kislev (168) set up "the detestable thing that causeth appalment" [Dan. 11:31, 12:11] beside the altar, upon which on the 25th of Kislev was offered as a sacrifice—a swine. The whole land, which had been fairly quiet for three hundred years, was filled with the moans of the tortured. The betrayers increased, but along with them the "pious" (Hasidim) and the holy, who actually died the death of martyrs; also "they that turn the many to righteousness" [Dan. 12:3], that is, those who aroused others to stand by their convictions and to die for the sanctity of Judaism, which at that time was already a complete and lofty world-view. Mattithiah [Mattathias] son of Yohanan Hashmonai [John Hasmoneus] arose as one that would "turn the many to righteousness" with sword in hand (167–166). He was followed by his son Judah the Maccabee [Judas Maccabeus], who even during the first two years of his political activity (166–164) was able to accomplish such great things as to amaze with his prowess Jews and Syrians alike. It was apparent that with a little more effort he would succeed in gaining control of the city and the sanctuary and in restoring Judaism to its former dignity.

And in the natal hour of great things like this, as in every hour of great men and extraordinary events, there appeared a great new book —great in its value for the time and for future generations. This book is the one we now have bearing the name "the Book of Daniel."

Ezekiel (14:14, 20) speaks of three righteous men, "Noah, Daniel, and Job"; and in another place (28:3) he says to the prince of Tyre, "Behold, thou art wiser than Daniel!" From these passages it appears clear that this Daniel was famous in the nation in Ezekiel's time as a righteous man and a great sage; could this be the Daniel of whom it is related in the Book of Daniel (1:1–6) that he was brought to Babylon *as a youth* "in the third year of the reign of Jehoiakim"? Ezekiel went into exile with the exile of *Jehoiachin* and began to prophesy in the fifth year of this exile, being then, apparently, thirty years of age (Ezek. 1:1–2); and if he had previously prophesied in Jerusalem he was then all the more not a youth. Thus he was not in any case younger than Daniel. So how could he speak of Daniel as being a righteous and wise man famous in his own time, and mention him immediately after Noah? Now most scholars have concluded that the reference is to "Danel," the righteous judge in the Ugaritic texts.

Moreover, the author of the Book of Daniel could not have been a prophet of the time of the Babylonian exile and the return to Zion —for various reasons. *First*, the historical data in Daniel in everything having to do with the time of the Babylonian exile and the Persian empire are full of startling errors: the conquest of Jehoiakim by Nebuchadrezzar is not mentioned in Kings at all, and from II Chronicles (36:3, 10) it appears that Nebuchadrezzar came up against him not in the third year of his reign but at the end of it; Belshazzar is here the son of Nebuchadrezzar, ruling after him (5:2, 11), while in fact the king after Nebuchadrezzar was Evil-Merodach his son, and

Belshazzar was the first-born son of Nabunaid; Darius is called "the Mede" (6:1, Eng. 5:31, and 11:1) and "Darius the son of Ahasuerus of the seed of the Medes" (9:1), while actually he was a Persian and not the son of Ahasuerus at all; only four kings arise in Persia after Darius the Mede or including him (11:2), while in fact seven kings ruled after him.

In contrast to this we find in Daniel 8 and 11 almost exact details of the events that took place from the time of Alexander the Great to Antiochus Epiphanes. We find here "the king of Greece," who conquers the kings of Persia and Media, and at his death "his kingdom . . . shall be divided toward the four winds of heaven" (the four kingdoms that were founded after the death of Alexander the Great, particularly after the battle of Ipsus in the year 301); the wars of "the kings of the south" (the Ptolemies) with "the kings of the north" (the Seleucids) in the time of Ptolemy II Philadelphus (285–247) and Antiochus II Theos (261–247) and following; the doings of Antiochus IV Epiphanes in all his relations with Egypt and Judah, the stoppage of the continual burnt-offering, the setting-up of "the detestable thing that causeth appalment," those who "do wickedly against the covenant," and the "wise among the people" who "cause the many to understand"; and even the "little help" with which these "wise" ones have been helped by Mattathias and Judas (11:7–42). Only the end of Antiochus is not known clearly by the author of the Book of Daniel,[2] and he also does not yet know exactly the time of the dedication of the Temple by Judas Maccabeus.[3] All these things demonstrate that we have before us not a prophet of the time of the

---

[2] According to 11:45, Antiochus should have died approaching Palestine, but he actually died at the end of the year 164 in a distant Persian city. See on this Budde, *Geschichte der althebr. Litt.*, pp. 328–330; Steuernagel, *Einleitung*, pp. 560–661; Bernfeld, *Introduction*, II, 201–222; J. Klausner, *History of the Second Temple*, III, 36, Note 1. Bernfeld goes so far as to agree with Lagarde that Daniel 7 was written at the time of the siege of Jerusalem by the Emperor Vespasian (*op. cit.*, II, 215–220). See in detail H. H. Rowley, *Darius the Mede and the Four World Empires in the Book of Daniel*, Cardiff, 1935.

[3] See Schürer, *Geschichte*, III⁴, 264–265. And not according to the opinion of Hühn, *Die messian. Weissag.*, I, 77, Note 7, that in Daniel 8:14 the Dedication is already indicated, since actually the words "then shall the sanctuary be victorious" [or "cleansed"] are only *a hope for the future*, like the rest of the verses containing computations, and not an account of an established fact (see on this Marti, *Daniel*, 1901, p. 60).

Babylonian exile, but an apocalyptist of the time of Antiochus Epiphanes, who composed his book near the year 164 B.C.E. (approximately 167–166 B.C.E.).

Second, it is said in the Book of Daniel that the time has come "to seal [finish] vision and prophet" (9:24)—something that could not have been said in the days of Ezekiel and Deutero-Isaiah. In the Book of Daniel the angels are called by personal names: "the man Gabriel" (9:21) and "Michael, the great prince who standeth for the children of thy people" (12:1; 10:21). Also in it are "the prince of the kingdom of Persia" and "the prince of Greece" (10:13, 20). In it (12:2) comes for the first time *the belief in the resurrection of the dead* in a clear and decisive form. And finally, in it Daniel is praised because he did not defile himself with the king's food and wine, but was nourished only by vegetables and water (1:8–16); and because "his windows were open in his upper chamber toward Jerusalem, and he kneeled upon his knees three times a day and prayed and gave thanks before his God" (6:11).

Third, in its Hebrew language occur late words such as *miqtsath* (part, 1:2), *hayyeb* (endanger, 1:10); *hathakh* in the sense of "determine" or "decree" (9:24), *rasham* (inscribe, 10:21), *hattamid* in the sense of "the continual burnt-offering" (8:11), and so on. Its Aramaic language is later than that of Ezra. And finally, there are in it *Greek words,* such as *kaitheros* [lyre], *sumponeyah* [bagpipe or dulcimer] and *pesanterin* [psaltery] (3:5).[4]

Fourth, the Book of Daniel stands in the collection of the Prophets after Ezekiel only in the Septuagint, while in the *Hebrew,* the original Holy Scriptures, it stands not among the Prophets but among the Writings—which clearly proves that it was written at a late date, when the collection of the Prophets was already finished and closed. Only the Gospels [5] call the author of the book "Daniel the prophet," while in ancient Jewish literature he is not considered as a prophet, or at least he is not called by that name. Finally, Ben-Sira, who speaks much of Noah (44:17–18) and mentions Job (49:9) along with

---

[4] See the brief introduction to the commentary on the Book of Daniel by Meir Lambert (*The Bible with Scientific Commentary,* ed. A. Kahana), Kiev, 1906.

[5] Matt. 24:15; Mark 13:14.

Ezekiel,[6] does not notice Daniel (who comes in Ezekiel along with Noah and Job, as mentioned above) with even one word.

If we take these facts into consideration, we must confess that the Daniel mentioned in Ezekiel, or the Daniel mentioned in Ezra (8:2) as one of those returning from exile and in Nehemiah (10:7) as one of those making the covenant and setting their seal upon it, could not have been the author of the book before us. The actual author of this book lived in the time of the persecution by Antiochus Epiphanes, as was already recognized by Porphyry (233–305 C.E.) almost seventeen centuries ago;[7] and in order to strengthen the people in their faith, he felt the urge to tell them, in a series of scrolls, about Daniel, who also suffered persecution for his religion, and in whose time also certain kings (Nebuchadrezzar, Belshazzar, and Darius) forbade the observance of the ceremonial laws, showed impudence toward God, and plundered the vessels of the Temple, just as Antiochus had done in their own time. This author perceived from the beginning the troubles that would come upon Israel, but he also foresaw by the Holy Spirit that the troubles would not be prolonged and that salvation was soon to come.[8] Thus Daniel became the progenitor of two new types of literature that flourished like mushrooms from Hasmonean times until the rebellion of Bar-Cochba: (1) the "outside books" in general, which are called the "Pseudepigrapha" because they are attributed to ancient worthies (the Book of Enoch, the Book of Baruch, IV Ezra, and so on); and (2) the special kind of these books called by the name "revelation" or "apocalypse" because they contain prophecy of the future in the form of "revelations," "visions," and "appearances" filled with enigmatic figures of

[6] See what has been written on this by David Kahana in his article, "The Hebrew Ben-Sira and Its Texts" [in Hebrew] (*Ha-Shiloah*, XVIII, 366).

[7] This fact has been transmitted to us by one of the Church Fathers, Jerome (*Prologus in Danielem*); also in his commentary on Daniel 7:7 (Ed. Migne, Col. 530).

[8] There is, to be sure, an opinion that Daniel 1–6 was written at the time of the Babylonian exile and afterward by the earlier Daniel, while only Daniel 7–12 was composed in the time of Antiochus. But it is difficult to agree with this, since there is already found in Daniel 2 "the Vision of the Four Kingdoms," of which the fourth is undoubtedly the kingdom of Greece (Schürer, *op. cit.*, III[4], 265), and this vision is completely parallel with Daniel 7 (Budde, *op. cit.*, pp. 332–333). See also Rowley, *op. cit.*, pp. 2–5, 176–178.

speech, which are actually a review of what is past, but purport to be *a look into the future,* a glimpse of things to come.[9]

From what we have said, it follows as a matter of course that almost all of Daniel is Messianic in spirit; but Chapters 2, 6–9, and 12 are Messianic in essence.

In Chapter 2 there comes as the interpretation of the dream of Nebuchadrezzar by Daniel "the vision of the four kingdoms." The first kingdom is that of Nebuchadrezzar (kingdom of Babylonia), the second is the kingdom of Media (the author of the Book of Daniel thought that Darius *the Mede* preceded Cyrus *the Persian*), the third is the kingdom of Persia, and the fourth is the kingdom of Greece, which will be "a divided kingdom" (2:41): the kingdom of Greece will be divided into the kingdom of the Ptolemies and the kingdom of the Seleucids.

And in the days of those kings shall the God of heaven set up a kingdom, which shall never be destroyed; nor shall the kingdom be left to another people; it shall break in pieces and consume all these kingdoms, but it shall stand for ever (2:44).

This kingdom is *the world-wide Messianic kingdom.* It is described in more brilliant colors in the dream of Daniel in Chapter 7, which is known as "the vision of the four beasts."

Four beasts come up from the sea. The first beast is a lion—the kingdom of Babylonia, the strongest of the kingdoms; the second is a bear—the kingdom of Media; the third is a leopard—the kingdom of Persia; and the fourth beast, "diverse from all the beasts that were before it," "dreadful and terrible and strong exceedingly, having great iron teeth, devouring and breaking in pieces and stamping the remains with its feet," and equipped with "ten horns" (7:7), is the kingdom of Greece. Its ten horns are the ten kings (as known to the author of the Book of Daniel) that ruled from Alexander the Great to Antiochus Epiphanes. In the opinion of most interpreters they are: Alexander the Great, Seleucus I (Nicator), Antiochus I (Soter), Antiochus II (Theos), Seleucus II (Callinicus), Seleucus III (Cer-

---

[9] See for details on this J. Klausner, "Outside Books" [in Hebrew] (*Otsar ha-Yahadut, Hoveret le-Dogma*, Warsaw, 1906, pp. 97ff.).

aunus), Antiochus III (the Great), Heliodorus, Seleucus IV (Philopator), and Demetrius I (Soter).[10]

From the midst of these ten horns comes forth "another horn, a little one" (7:8), or, as it is said farther on in Hebrew, "a little horn" (8:9), in which are "eyes like the eyes of a man, and a mouth speaking great things" (7:8). However, the LORD, the "ancient of days," sits upon His throne for judgment *and books are opened*, the horn speaks "great words," but "because of the voice" of these words (that is, as a punishment for them) the beast is slain, its body is destroyed, and it is given to be completely burned with fire; as for the rest of the beasts, only their dominion is taken away, while their lives are "prolonged for a season and a time" (7:9–12). Then the scene continues thus:

> I saw in visions of the night,
> And behold there came *with the clouds of heaven*
> *One like unto a son of man,*
> And he came even to the Ancient of days,
> And he was brought near before Him.
> And there was given him dominion,
> And glory, and a kingdom,
> That all the peoples, nations, and languages
> Should serve him;
> His dominion is an everlasting dominion,
>   which shall not pass away,
> And his kingdom that which shall not be destroyed (7:13–14).

Daniel asks one of those standing before the LORD to tell him the interpretation of the matter, and this one explains to him that the four beasts are four kings (in the sense of kingdoms), and that after them *"the saints of the Most High* shall receive the kingdom, and possess the kingdom for ever, even for ever and ever" (7:18).

It is clear that the "son of man" [meaning "human being"] coming "with the clouds of heaven," whose kingdom is an everlasting kingdom, is the same as these "saints of the Most High," for Verse 18 is only an explanation of Verse 14. Since the rest of the peoples possessing kingdoms (the Babylonians, the Medes, the Persians, and the

---

[10] See the aforesaid commentary of R. Meir Lambert on Daniel 7:7 (p. 14); Marti, *op. cit.*, pp. 49–51; Rowley, *op. cit.*, pp. 98–124.

Greeks) were portrayed as devouring *beasts* coming up from the sea, the righteous but oppressed people Israel was portrayed as a *human being* coming from heaven with the clouds. This conclusion will not be denied by anyone who takes the plain meaning of Scripture.[11]

But in a comparatively short time after the composition of the Book of Daniel it was thought among the Jews that this "son of man" was the Messiah. This is not surprising: a "human being" that could approach the throne of God and that could be given "dominion, and glory, and a kingdom" and whom all the peoples would serve and whose dominion would be an everlasting dominion could not possibly be other than the King-Messiah.[12] So thinks the author of the Ethiopic book of Enoch (Chapters 37–71, which are among the earlier ones), and of this Jesus *hints* in his use of "the son of man" in the Gospels;[13] according to the Gospel writers, he said that in the Messianic age "they will see the son of man coming on the clouds of heaven with power and great glory."[14] Actually, there is no *individual Messiah* in Daniel: the entire people Israel is the Messiah that will exercise everlasting dominion throughout the whole world. This is to be seen again in the details about the little horn with the "mouth speaking great things," which is nothing else, according to the explanation in Daniel itself, than a cruel and impudent king. Of him it is said:

And he shall speak words against the Most High, and shall wear out the saints of the Most High; and he shall think *to change the seasons and the law;* and they shall be given into his hand until *a time and times and half a time.* But the judgment shall sit, and his dominion shall be taken away, to

---

[11] This is opposed by Gressmann, *Eschatologie*, pp. 334–365, who of course was right about the mythological elements in the "son of man with the clouds of heaven," but was not right in his conclusion that the meaning of "son of man" here was *the Messiah from the very beginning.* This is also the answer to the argument of W. Bousset, *Die Religion des Judentums im späthellenistischen Zeitalter*, 3rd ed., ed. Gressmann, Tübingen, 1926, pp. 265–268; 352–355.

[12] This is the natural cause of the ancient and widespread error which Gressmann (*op. cit.*, pp. 337–339) and Bousset (*loc. cit.*) cannot understand.

[13] I have emphasized the word "hints" because complete clarity could not have been present, since in Ezekiel the term "son of man" is on no account used in this sense (see J. Klausner, *Jesus of Nazareth*, 5th [Hebrew] ed., Jerusalem, 1945, pp. 266–268 [Eng. ed., pp. 256–257], and the additions at the end of the book, pp. 500–501 [not in Eng. ed.]).

[14] See Matt. 24:30; Mark 13:26; Luke 21:27, etc.

be consumed and to be destroyed unto the end. And the kingdom and the dominion, and the greatness of the kingdoms under the whole heaven, shall be given to *the people of the saints of the Most High;* their kingdom is an everlasting kingdom, and all dominions shall serve and obey them (7:25-27).

It is clear that the one spoken of here is Antiochus Epiphanes, the only Greek king who thought "to change the seasons and the law"; and that in the "son of man" coming "with the clouds of heaven" Daniel sees "the people of the saints of the Most High," that is to say, the entire people Israel, which at first will be delivered over to Antiochus "until a time and times and half a time" (see below), but afterward will be given world-wide Messianic dominion.

The same ideas are set forth in the Hebrew language in Chapter 8, where are mentioned "the king of Greece" (8:21)—Alexander the Great—and "a king of fierce countenance and understanding stratagems" (8:23)—Antiochus the man of "culture," who destroyed "them that are mighty and the people of *the saints,*" who relied upon "his cunning" and destroyed many "in time of security" (8:24-25), and by whom "the continual burnt-offering was taken away, and the place of [the] sanctuary was cast down" (8:11). There is also in this chapter something like an explanation of "a time and times and half a time": the continual burnt-offering will be taken away and Baal-Shamayim ("the detestable thing"—or "transgression"—"that causeth appalment") [15] will be set up upon [or beside] the altar "unto two thousand and three hundred evenings and mornings; then shall the sanctuary be victorious" (8:13-14). This means 1,150 days, amounting to a little less than three and a half (lunar) years, the equivalent of "a time and times and half a time," or "a time, times, and a half," as it is in the Hebrew part of Daniel (12:7). But at the end of Daniel we find:

And from the time that the continual burnt-offering shall be taken away, and the detestable thing that causeth appalment [16] set up, there shall be *a*

---

[15] See on all this many important details in E. Bickermann, *Der Gott der Makkabäer,* Berlin, 1937, pp. 90-139; 169-183. But one must beware of the extreme conclusions that come forth under the influence of the great number of Jew-hating scholars in Germany; these men have even influenced important Jewish scholars without the latter realizing it.

[16] The profanation of the Temple by Antiochus Epiphanes is called exactly

thousand two hundred and ninety days. Happy is he that waiteth, and cometh to *the thousand three hundred and thirty-five days* (12:11-12).

These numbers amount to more than three and a half years or the 1,150 days that we found above. The numbers could not be made exact, because the author did not know *exactly* when Judas Maccabeus would win such a decisive victory over the Syrians that he could come to Jerusalem and restore the suspended continual burnt-offering to its former condition. Therefore the Book of Daniel was written before the dedication of the Temple by Judas Maccabeus, as has already been said above.

This idea stands forth in Chapter 9 also. Daniel relates that in the first year of Darius the son of Ahasuerus he was meditating "in the books, over the number of the years, whereof the word of the LORD came to Jeremiah the prophet, that He would accomplish for the desolations of Jerusalem seventy years" (9:2).[17] Then he prayed to the LORD that He would turn away His anger from His people and His city. After that came "the man Gabriel" to make him "skilful of understanding" with these words:

Seventy weeks are decreed upon thy people and upon thy holy city, to finish the transgression, and to make an end of sin, and to forgive iniquity, and to bring in everlasting righteousness, and to seal vision and prophet, and to anoint the most holy place. Know therefore and discern, that from the going forth of the word to restore and to build Jerusalem unto one anointed, a prince, shall be seven weeks; and for threescore and two weeks, it shall be built again, with broad place and moat, but in troublous times. And after the threescore and two weeks shall an anointed one be cut off, and be no more; and the people of a prince that shall come shall destroy the city and the sanctuary; but his end shall be with a flood; and unto the end of the war desolations are determined. And he shall make a firm covenant with many for one week; and for half of the week he shall cause the sacrifice and the offering to cease; and upon the wing of detestable things shall be that which causeth appalment; and that until the

---

the same thing [usual translation "abomination of desolation"] in I Maccabees (1:54). Nestle explains these words thus: *shiqquts* is a term of opprobrium for Baal and *shomem* is Shamayim; thus we have here Baal-Shamayim, which is the name given to Zeus-Jupiter in the Phoenician and Palmyrene inscriptions (see the commentary of M. Lambert on Dan. 8:13; 11:31). See Bickermann, *loc. cit.*

[17] Cf. Jer. 25:11-12; 29:10.

extermination wholly determined be poured out upon that which causeth appalment (9:24-27).

We have arrived at "the matter of the seventy weeks," about which heaps upon heaps of books have been written. Most modern scholars interpret these verses thus: Daniel wishes to vindicate the prophecies of Jeremiah about the seventy years after which Judah will be restored to its previous condition—a prophecy which was not completely fulfilled, since during the Persian and Greek periods Judah was an insignificant and subject state, while in the time of Antiochus misfortunes and ruin had overtaken it; therefore Daniel considers the seventy years of Jeremiah to be seventy sabbatical years, something already intimated at the end of II Chronicles (36:21): "to fulfil the word of the LORD by the mouth of Jeremiah, until the land had been paid her sabbaths; for as long as she lay desolate she kept sabbath, *to fulfil threescore and ten years.*" Seventy weeks (sabbatical years) are, therefore, 490 years. Of this total, "seven weeks," that is, forty-nine years, had passed down to the time of Cyrus ("one anointed, a prince," as we found in Isa. 45:1—"to His anointed, to Cyrus"), when Jerusalem was "restored and built" (586–537). "Threescore and two weeks" are 434 years, and these are the years that passed, in the opinion of the author of the Book of Daniel, from the Edict of Cyrus until "an anointed one" was "cut off," that is, until Onias III was removed from his high-priestly office at the beginning of the reign of Antiochus Epiphanes.[18] These years were "troublous times" for Judah, for she did not then grow great and strong according to the promises of the prophets; indeed, she did not even have independence.

As a matter of fact, from the Edict of Cyrus to the beginning of the reign of Antiochus there passed not 434, but 362 years (537–175). The author of the Book of Daniel erred, therefore, by about seventy years. But this is not to be wondered at, since Josephus made errors like this in his *Antiquities* and *Wars*, and the Alexandrian Jew

---

[18] Wellhausen (*Israel. u. jüd. Geschichte,* 7th ed., 1914, p. 234, Note 1) remarks that in Hebrew the interpretation of "an anointed one shall be cut off" is not that the anointed priest will be slain, but that the high-priestly office will cease to exist.

Demetrius[19] (*c.* 200 B.C.E.) erred in the Jewish chronology of the period of the Second Temple by seventy years, *exactly as did the author of the Book of Daniel.*[20]

"For one week" [according to the author of Daniel], that is, for seven years, the first deeds of Antiochus will continue (175-168). He will "destroy the city and the sanctuary" together "with" (according to the reading of the Septuagint) the "prince that shall come" (Jason), and will force many to transgress the holy covenant (or will "make a firm covenant with many" of the Hellenizers). And "for half of the week," that is, for three and a half years ("a time and times and half a time"—"a time, times, and a half"), he will stop sacrifices and offerings and place upon the altar "detestable things that cause appalment" (168-165).[21]

Actually, the service in the Temple was suspended less than three and a half years, since according to I Maccabees the continual burnt-offering was stopped on the 15th of Kislev 145 (Seleucid era) and restored on the 25th of Kislev 148; and in the opinion of Kautzsch,[22] this offering was not stopped until the 25th of Kislev, as would appear from I Maccabees 4:42 and 54. However, as I have already said, the author of the Book of Daniel did not yet know exactly when the dedication of the Temple would take place; but on the basis of the first victories of Judas Maccabeus he expected an early deliverance, to be manifested first of all by the restoration of the divine service in its proper place; and along with this he expected the Jews, "the people of the saints of the Most High," to attain to an everlasting kingdom, while the kingdom of the wicked Antiochus would come to an end and pass away together with the rest of the kingdoms of the Gentiles.

This is the Messianic ideal of the author of the Book of Daniel. It does not contain *material prosperity*, but it does contain a strong

---

[19] Cited by Clement of Alexandria (*Stromata*, I, 21, 141).

[20] See in detail Schürer, *op. cit.*, III⁴, 265-266.

[21] [According to an emended text in 9:26-27.] See the lucid interpretation of Castelli, *Il Messia*, pp. 152-156.

[22] See Note *p* on p. 36 of his translation of I Maccabees in his edition of *Apokryphen und Pseudepigraphen des Alten Testaments*, Vol. I. According to the reckoning of Marti (*op. cit.*, p. 60), the author of the Book of Daniel erred by the short time of forty-five days.

hope for political power and for political and religious authority over all the Gentiles. Nor can it be said that this hope was entirely disappointed. The Hasmoneans were inflamed by a strong faith that the hour had come for the "kingdom of heaven," that is, the kingdom of the God of heaven, to be revealed to the world and for the kingdom of Greece to fall. They established, after severe struggles, a Jewish kingdom, which, to be sure, did not spread over the whole world and did not destroy all the kingdoms of the Gentiles, but did achieve independence, became measurably powerful, and had much to do with the spread of the knowledge of the God of Israel in the pagan world.

However, these Messianic expectations are expectations only for the people Israel as one collective entity. But in the time of Daniel most of the Jews were already far from the old national life, in which the individual was completely swallowed up in the community; therefore, those who went forth to a death of martyrdom and could no longer see with their own eyes the felicity of their nation needed *personal reward and punishment*. So the author of the Book of Daniel supplies this need by the belief in *the resurrection of the dead:* after the downfall of Antiochus there will be a time of trouble for Israel such as never was since they became a nation, and Michael, "the great prince," will fight for them:

And at that time thy people shall be delivered, *every one that shall be found written in the book*.[23] And many of them that sleep in the dust of the earth shall awake, some to everlasting life, and some to reproaches and everlasting abhorrence. And they that are wise shall shine as the brightness of the firmament; and they that turn the many to righteousness [24] as the stars for ever and ever (12:1–3).

The resurrection of the dead, which is mentioned here in such a clear manner for the first time in the Bible, is, therefore, shared by both the good and the bad; but the former rise to everlasting life and

---

[23] Cf. Mal. 3:16: "And *a book of remembrance* was written before Him, *for them that feared the LORD*, and that thought upon His name" (see above, p. 215). From here came "the book of heaven" in the Ethiopic book of Enoch, and "the heavenly tablets" in the Book of Jubilees, etc.

[24] I.e., those who arouse others also to hold fast to their faith like the righteous. Cf. Isa. 53:11: "by his knowledge shall my righteous servant justify many" (see above, p. 167, Note 35).

the latter to everlasting reproaches. However, it is to be concluded from the word "many" that the clear conception that *all* would rise from the dead had not yet penetrated into the nation.[25] In any case, Judaism was already near the idea of reward and punishment for *each individual* in the nation. The collective national system of rewards and punishments of the ancient prophets was no longer sufficient. Daniel thus served as a progenitor of the Apocrypha and Pseudepigrapha: his Messianic idea eventuates in "the Age to Come" and "the World to Come," in which the dead rise and "the righteous sit enthroned, their crowns on their heads, and enjoy the lustre of the Shekhinah" [Ber. 17a]. The latter idea is already embodied in the words "they that are wise shall shine as the brightness of the firmament." Thus the Messianic idea became bound up with and attached to "eschatology" (not in the sense of "the end of this age" but in the sense of the life after death) something that we find not only in the Pseudepigrapha, but also in Talmud and Midrash from the Mishnah onward.

The age of prophecy had passed and the age of Talmudic Aggadah had come.

[25] Against the opinion of Hühn, *op. cit.*, I, 79, who thinks that the word *rabbim* ("many") is not restrictive, and that the resurrection of the dead in the Book of Daniel is general. See Marti, *op. cit.*, p. 90.

CHAPTER XVII

General Survey

NOW THAT I have gone through *all* the sacred writings and have laid before the reader all the Messianic expectations in every one of them, it is fitting to look at these Messianic expectations in a general survey, in order that we may observe them according to their internal, logical order, and not only according to the external, historical order of their creators.

Sin brings after it punishment—this is said *expressly* in most of the prophetic books or it follows *by implication* from their words: without sin there is no place for the idea of redemption. And punishment means *the day of the LORD* or (in the later Hebrew language) *the Day of Judgment*, which comes, according to some of the prophets (Amos, Hosea, Second Isaiah, and Malachi) upon Israel alone, according to other prophets (Nahum, Habbakuk, Obadiah, Haggai, First and Second Zechariah, the later Psalms, and Daniel) upon the pagan peoples alone, and according to the rest of the prophets upon Israel and the Gentiles alike; according to some it comes also upon nature (Amos, First Isaiah, Zephaniah, Jeremiah, Isaiah 13, Joel, and the later Psalms). Ezekiel and Joel describe the Day of Judgment as a public tribunal, and Daniel even says that "books were opened."

The events of the Day of Judgment are: frightful wars, destruction, exile, humiliation, and changes for the worse in the order of nature; Amos adds also a forgetting of the word of the LORD, or, in the later Hebrew language, *cessation of Torah*. All these elements were afterward included in the term "the birth pangs of Messiah."

The punishment is for some prophets (Amos, Micah, Nahum,

Habbakuk, and others) a righteous judgment upon sinners. But for most of the prophets it is only a means to moral improvement (Hosea, Zephaniah, Jeremiah, Ezekiel, Second Isaiah, and others).

Malachi adds that before the day of the LORD *the prophet Elijah* will come and turn the heart of the fathers to the children and the heart of the children to their fathers.

The Day of Judgment brings after it *repentance*. Of this speak Amos, Hosea, Isaiah, Jeremiah, and Joel. Ezekiel speaks of a repentance that will come *after* the redemption; the redemption itself is but an act of *mercy*, which the LORD will do for His people for the purpose of *sanctifying His name*. This view of the redemption was also held by all those prophets who did not speak of repentance at all, but emphasized the concepts of "the sanctification of the Name" and "the profanation of the Name."

The repentance will bring after it *the redemption*, according to most of the prophets. Nahum and Deutero-Isaiah also speak of a *herald* (or "messenger of good news to Zion"), who in later times was confused with *Elijah*, although the herald comes before *the redemption*, while Elijah comes, according to the words of Malachi, before *the Day of Judgment*. Some of the prophets speak also of *the blowing of a horn* (Isa. 27:13; Zech. 9:14)—something that gives place afterward to the idea of "the trumpet of Messiah." Many of the prophets (Amos, Micah, Zephaniah, Obadiah, Haggai, First and Second Zechariah, Joel, and Daniel) prophesy of *a victory over the Gentiles* at the time of the redemption; but most of these prophets (from Zephaniah onward) also hope that the victory will come without war on the part of Israel, but that the LORD will apportion to His people the inheritance of the Gentiles; and the rest of the prophets (Hosea, First and Second Isaiah, Jeremiah, Ezekiel, and others) hardly know of such a victory at all.

At the time of redemption there will remain, according to most of the prophets, only "the remnant of Israel" (Amos, who speaks of "the remnant of Joseph," First and Second Isaiah, Zephaniah, Jeremiah, Obadiah, Ezekiel, Joel, Malachi; it is also mentioned in Micah 2:12). This "remnant" is described particularly in Isaiah and Zephaniah as a small group of the upright, the blameless, and the humble

GENERAL SURVEY 239

among the sons of Israel. This "remnant of Israel" will be left from the sons of Judah and the sons of Ephraim alike: *the union of Judah and Ephraim* is something that is prophesied by almost all the prophets from Amos to Ezekiel (Amos, Hosea, First Isaiah, Micah, Jeremiah, and Ezekiel; and it is alluded to in Deutero-Isaiah), while Deutero-Zechariah expects the redemption and the strengthening of Judah and Ephraim (10:6–12) and the rule of one king over both (9:9–10), but does not expect their union (11:14). Besides this union there will be in the time of redemption an *ingathering of exiles,* which is already alluded to in the Book of Deuteronomy, and which is expected by almost all the prophets (Amos, Hosea, First and Second Isaiah, Micah, Zephaniah, Jeremiah, Obadiah, Ezekiel, First and Second Zechariah, Joel, and Psalms).

The *political power* of Israel after the redemption is portrayed by almost all the prophets (see what was said above about "victory over the Gentiles"); but some of them emphasize it very strongly as the superiority of Israel in the Age to Come over all the rest of the peoples (Amos, Micah, Obadiah, Haggai, and Joel), while most of them see in it not a superiority over other peoples, but an equality of strong peoples, that is, a condition of peace and prosperity in which Israel will not be subservient to any other people nor in fear of any foreign king, and all the peoples will lift up and exalt Israel only because they recognize its spiritual superiority and its ethical qualities (First and especially Second Isaiah, Nahum, Zephaniah, Jeremiah, Ezekiel, First and Second Zechariah, Psalms, and Daniel). Hosea does not know of even a voluntary subservience of the nations to Israel.

The *material prosperity* after the redemption is portrayed in glowing colors by most of the prophets (Amos, Hosea, First and Second Isaiah, Jeremiah, Ezekiel, Haggai, First and Second Zechariah, Joel, and Psalms). But, it must be pointed out, of the more spiritual among them (that is, those prophets with whom the spiritual Messianic expectations take a greater place, see below), only First and Second Isaiah speak extensively of material prosperity, while Hosea, Jeremiah, Joel, and Psalms speak little of it, and Zephaniah, Habbakuk, and Daniel do not speak of it at all.

The elements of the material prosperity are: peace among nations and individuals (abolition of wars) and in nature (wild animals harm neither man nor each other), unusual productivity of the soil, extraordinary increase of human beings, resettlement of ruined cities, extension of the borders of the land of Judah in general and of the cities of Judah—above all Jerusalem—in particular, the healing of the sick and the handicapped, the lengthening of human life, and so on.

The spiritual welfare which will accompany the redemption is also found in almost all the books of the prophets, but only from Isaiah onward (First and Second Isaiah, Micah, Zephaniah, Habbakuk, Jeremiah, Ezekiel, Obadiah, First and Second Zechariah, Joel, Malachi, Psalms, and Daniel). In Amos it is still lacking and in Hosea it is only hinted at.[1]

The elements of the spiritual welfare are: (1) The knowledge of God, for the spread of which at the end of the present age among *all* peoples (and not just in Israel alone) hope most of the prophets from Isaiah onward (First and Second Isaiah, Micah, Zephaniah, Habbakuk, Jeremiah, First and Second Zechariah, Joel, and Psalms); apparently Obadiah also alludes to this in the last verse of his prophecy, and Malachi (1:10–11 and 2:14) already sees this spreading in his own time. The rest of the prophets expect this within Israel alone (on Daniel see below). (2) The doing of the good and the right, the love of justice and mercy (in almost all the prophets, expressly or by implication). (3) A new heart, a heart of flesh, and a new spirit and a new covenant (Torah in the heart). This was stressed especially by Jeremiah and Ezekiel. Hence they emphasized: (4) The perpetuity of the nation, which is already alluded to in the Book of Numbers. And Deutero-Isaiah emphasized: (5) The perpetuity of the Torah, in contrast to Amos, who foresaw the forgetting of the Torah on the Day of Judgment. Thus the Messianic expectation of spiritual welfare includes the idea of *human perfection and the perfection of humanity* in the Age to Come (especially in Zephaniah), and thus also the idea of *improvement and progress,* which are incorporated in the idea of repentance, and which also involve a definite material prosperity for society and for nations.

Ezekiel added to the cycle of Messianic expectations *the war against*

[1] See above, pp. 49–51.

Gog, king of Magog ("the war of Gog and Magog" in the later language), which will take place *after* the redemption and in which the LORD will fight for His people and win a great victory. Deutero-Zechariah also prophesied of a war like this. Daniel added to the national reward and punishment—retribution and redemption—personal reward and punishment: *the general resurrection of the dead*, in which the good and upright dead will awake to everlasting life and the evil and impious to reproaches and everlasting abhorrence.

In many of the books of Holy Scripture there is *no human Messiah at all:* the LORD alone is the redeemer and no other (Nahum, Zephaniah, Habbakuk, Malachi, Joel, and Daniel). In many other books there is *no individual Messiah but only a collective Messiah: the kingdom of the house of David* (Amos, Ezekiel, Obadiah and his "saviours," Deutero-Isaiah and "the sure mercies of David," and Psalms). In two of them there is an individual Messiah, though he is not an ideal man but an actual person, Zerubbabel of the house of David (Haggai and First Zechariah). In the rest of the prophetic books there is *an ideal human Messiah* (Hosea, First Isaiah, Micah, Jeremiah, and Second Zechariah). All these prophets describe this human Messiah as replete with lofty spiritual and ethical qualities. He is filled with wisdom and understanding, knowledge and the fear of the LORD. He slays the wicked with the breath of his lips, and executes justice and righteousness in the earth. In general he is righteous and humble; but along with this he is a king of the house of David, a noble ruler, filled with a spirit of heroism, to whom Israel and all the Gentiles submit. He is not a redeemer per se, as the Messiah became in later times: the LORD is the redeemer, and the King-Messiah is only the head of the redeemed people, its political and spiritual king; and since he is righteous and free from transgression he is also king of the world, for all the nations submit to Israel because they long to hear the word of the LORD and to learn of His ways.

Deutero-Isaiah and Daniel made a great change in the conception of the Messiah: the Messiah is not *one man* from the house of David or any other royal line, but *the whole people Israel*. But, while Israel is portrayed in Deutero-Isaiah as "a light of the Gentiles" and "the servant of the LORD," that is, as *a spiritual and a suffering Messiah*, this people is portrayed in Daniel as "a son of man coming with the clouds of heaven," to whom rulership of the Gentiles is handed over forever and ever, that is, as *a politically and materially successful Messiah*.

This is the sum total of the Messianic expectations from the period of the prophets.

After this survey it is not difficult to answer the question that naturally arises: Is there in the Messianic expectations of the prophets *a gradual evolution*, that is, a development from a lower stage to a higher stage? The answer is: There is an evolution here, but—like history in general—it is not in a straight line, but zigzag. And it is so for a very good reason: because the Messianic idea depends both upon the historical life of the Israelite nation, in which there are ascents and descents, and upon the spiritual elevation of each and every prophet as an individual. There is no doubt that Isaiah and Micah, in comparison with Amos and Hosea, who preceded them, represent a more comprehensive development of Messianism; but there is also no doubt that Ezekiel is less spiritual in his Messianic expectations than Hosea, who preceded him by a considerable time; and the later Haggai is less spiritual than any of them. Historical conditions brought this about, and perhaps also the personal character of Ezekiel or of Haggai.

Nevertheless, it can be said with confidence that only a long development could have brought Jeremiah to the idea of the eternity of the nation and the new covenant, Ezekiel to the conception of the profanation of the Name and the sanctification of the Name, Deutero-Isaiah to the conception of "a light to the Gentiles" and "the servant of the LORD" who "bears the sin of many," and Daniel to the idea of the kingdom of the saints of the Most High and the idea of the resurrection of the dead. The reciprocal relationship between the influence of historical conditions and the manifestations of personality in the Messianic idea is thus apparently as follows: the prophets who fathered the great Messianic expectations are very much superior to the people of their own time, but their expectations have rootage in their own time. That is to say, their own time is for them the point of departure from which they rise to the skies—*to the kingdom of heaven*—or penetrate into the mists of the distant future—*to the end of the present age.*

PART II

THE MESSIANIC IDEA IN THE BOOKS OF THE APOCRYPHA AND PSEUDEPIGRAPHA

General Note

LIKE THE Apocrypha and Pseudepigrapha, with which this part of our book is concerned, so also is this part of our book itself a link joining the Messianic expectations of the Holy Scriptures with the expectations of this kind in the Mishnah, the Baraithas, and the early Midrashim. The sources and the literature which I have utilized for the present book have been mentioned briefly in the text. The framework of historical events has not been given here in full, as in the preceding part, because the connexion between the Apocrypha and Pseudepigrapha and political events and cultural phenomena has been much emphasized in the three volumes of my work *Historia Yisreelit* [Israelite History] (II–III, Jerusalem-Tel-Aviv 5684 [1924], IV, *ibid.* 5685).[1]

Because of the difficulty of setting up Ethiopic and Syriac type, I have been forced to transcribe Ethiopic and Syriac words in Hebrew letters. I have not used notes excessively at the bottom of the pages, but have included the greater part of the references in the text of the book, in order not to make the reading burdensome. On the other hand, I have tried as hard as possible not to present the Messianic ideas in the Apocryphal and Pseudepigraphal books in my own language, but to render them as they are, in a translation as exact as possible, from the Ethiopic, Syriac, Greek, and Latin texts themselves. Thus, as it seems to me, I have accomplished two objects at the same time: I have made it possible for the Hebrew reader to become acquainted with the ancient *Hebrew* books which were translated into other languages two thousand years ago and only recently have

---

[1] Now see also my *Historia shel ha-Bayit ha-Sheni* [History of the Second Temple], Vols. III–V, Jerusalem, 5710–5711 [1950–1951].

been rendered again into Hebrew (*"Outside Books,"* edited by A. Kahana, four parts in two volumes, Tel-Aviv, 5679 [1937]); and also, I have enabled the reader to make his own judgment about the Messianic expectations in these books, and to accept or reject my opinion about these expectations.

It was a strong reproach to us that only Christian scholars would concern themselves with our ancestral heritage from the end of the period of the Second Temple and the beginning of the time after the Second Destruction. By this book the reproach is partially removed. For in this time of the Jewish people's revival, they must return to their ancient possessions and build a new life upon the national-humanitarian ideals which the former generations have left them. In this part of the book the reader will find a portion of the ancient national heritage which the best spirits of the nation set forth and elaborated in the period between the Bible and the Talmud. He will inevitably, therefore, give heed to everything presented in this book from the ancient writings if he wishes to be worthy of being called a son of his great fathers, and to achieve complete regeneration—which means a firm connexion between the past and the present, but also between Judaism and humanity.

Jerusalem, 2nd of First Adar, 5681 [February, 1921]—Kislev 5687 [December, 1926.]

A. THE MESSIANIC IDEA IN THE APOCRYPHA

NOT WITHOUT justification did the first Hebrew translator of the entire corpus of the Apocryphal books, Isaac S. Fränkel, call these books the "Later Hagiographa." For indeed, they are the continuation of the Hagiographa and not of the Prophets. They contain not even a trace of the great spiritual force of the prophets, whose books are full of fiery rebukes of those wielding worldly power in their time, and who, like volcanoes with their lava, poured out their holy wrath upon the oppressors of their people.

But even in relation to the Hagiographa they are "later": later in time—*almost* without exception (Ben-Sira is the one that precedes a canonical book—Daniel), and inferior in quality—without exception. The authors of the Apocrypha were under the influence of the Scriptural books. A considerable part of the Apocryphal books is in imitation of the Hagiographa, but only a small part imitates the Prophets. Many of them (Epistle of Jeremiah, Dream of Mordecai, Prayer of Manasseh) are additions to canonical books. Many of them are historical legends or even pure legends (Judith, Tobit, Susanna, and so on). Only a few of them are actual historical compositions (I and II Maccabees, especially I), or literary compositions bearing the name of the author (Wisdom of Ben-Sira), or are attributed to an ancient author (Book of Baruch, Wisdom of Solomon). This characteristic itself brings it about that there could not be much in them concerning the Messianic idea. In this they are like the Hagiographa. For, in contrast to the Prophets, the greater part of the Hagiographa contains nothing—or only very little—concerning the Messianic idea. Only the Book of Psalms is thoroughly suffused with the *spirit* of the Messianic idea; but even in it explicit and detailed Messianic ideas are lacking. The one book of the Hagiographa in which the Messianic idea takes a large place is the Book of Daniel. But only the Christians have placed this book among the Prophets (in the Septuagint translation it comes immediately after Ezekiel); actually, in its whole character and spirit it belongs to the non-canonical books, and even its language is for the most part not Hebrew.

The Apocrypha—like the Hagiographa—are different from the Pseudepigrapha in that "apocalyptic" (revelations—visionary descriptions) and "eschatology" (descriptions of the life after death: the World to Come, the resurrection of the dead, retribution, and so on) occupy no important place in them. They contain no imaginative "revelations" or "prophecies after the event" (*vaticinia post eventum*), with which the Pseudepigraphical books are filled to overflowing. *Even the Messianic idea occupies no great place in the Apocrypha.* The Apocrypha antedate the Pseudepigrapha almost entirely, nearly all of them having been written before the destruction of the Second Temple, and a good part of them in the more prosperous period of the Hasmonean dynasty; hence they do not show evidence of the despair which the Second Destruction put into the hearts of the nation's leaders, nor of the Messianic hope and the hope for a life after death, of which the nation had such need following the frightful catastrophe.

But even in the best times for Israel during the period of the Second Temple the Messianic idea was not *completely* forgotten. It was not enlarged and developed, nor was it embroidered with strong imaginative colors. Yet it was preserved and it endured, even though its scope was restricted, and the sages of Israel did not deal with it often or in an elaborate fashion, because the time was not ripe for doing so. Their main effort was to teach Torah to the people, to train them in the ceremonial laws, to preach moral precepts and good manners to them, and to establish their life in their own land on sound principles, national, religious, and secular; for there was great danger from overwrought imaginations and from delusive forms of the Messianic idea, which actually caused most of the rebellions at the end of the Second

Temple and brought about the final destruction.[1] In a great part of the Apocryphal books, the main features of the Messianic idea are mentioned. But they are mentioned in an offhand manner, as an important yet well known matter, which needs no elaboration; they are mentioned in a general way and in broad outline, without discussion and without details.

It is proper to pay attention to one important item: *the personality of the Messiah is not mentioned in any book of the Apocrypha.* The *house* of David is mentioned, but not the *son* of David. Also in this the Apocrypha resembles the Hagiographa and differs from the Prophets. By this, and not only by the fact that he was not of the house of David can we explain, in my opinion, why Judas Maccabeus was not proclaimed as the Messiah.[2] It has not been proved that Bar-Cochba was of the house of David, nevertheless Rabbi Akiba recognized his Messiahship. But neither Judas Maccabeus nor any other member of the Hasmonean house could have been considered in their time as the Messiah, because the first generations could not have conceived of a man not of the house of David sitting on the royal throne of Israel. The Messianic idea was not a dominant idea (what the French call an *idée-maîtresse*) in Israel at that time, although it was not denied, but continued to live a hidden and secret life; and the personality of the Messiah did not occupy an essential place in this form of the idea.

Only after the three chief parties in Israel—the Pharisees, the Sadducees, and the Essenes—had split off from the moderate Hasidim and Hellenists—and particularly after the rift that came about between the Pharisees and John Hyrcanus, who apparently sought to be Messiah; and after the severe struggle that the Pharisees carried on with Janneus Alexander, which likewise had its beginning in the opposition to the title of "King" assumed by this Hasmonean—then and only then did the popular imagination of the Pharisees and particularly of the Essenes—these being the extreme Pharisees, the Pharisaic ascetics—begin to weave legends around the personality

---

[1] See on this the discerning remarks of R. T. Herford in *The Pharisees*, London, 1924, pp. 186-193. For a summary, see *idem, Talmud and Apocrypha*, London, 1933, pp. 171-269.

[2] Cf. Conder, *Judas Maccabaeus*, London, 1894, pp. 68-70, and Greenstone, *The Messiah Idea in Jewish History*, Philadelphia, 1906, pp. 64-65.

of the Messiah and to spin out farther the marvelous Messianic thread of the prophets. Those books of the Apocrypha that antedate the time of the break with John Hyrcanus, or that are concerned with historical stories, with legends, or with ethical precepts, and are in their essential content remote from the ideas entering into the complex ideological web which we call "the expectations of the Days of the Messiah," add nothing to the Messianic portrayals set forth in the canonical Scriptures; but neither do they subtract anything from them (except the Isaianic portrayal of the "shoot out of the stock of Jesse"), and they mention them when there is occasion to do so.

In seven books of the Apocrypha there are Messianic ideas: in the Wisdom of Ben-Sira (*c.* 190–170 B.C.E.), in I Maccabees (*c.* 130–110 B.C.E.), in II Maccabees (an epitome of the book of Jason of Cyrene, which was written *c.* 130 B.C.E., while the epitome itself was made *c.* 70 B.C.E.), in Judith (*c.* 130–110 B.C.E.), in Tobit (same date as Judith), in Baruch (the first part 130 B.C.E., the latter part 90 C.E.), and in the Wisdom of Solomon (*c.* 70–50 B.C.E.).[3] Of these, Ben-Sira, I Maccabees, Judith, Tobit, and Baruch were written in Hebrew and in Palestine; II Maccabees and the Wisdom of Solomon were written in Greek and in Egypt.

[3] On the date and historical background of Ben-Sira, Judith Tobit, Baruch, and the Wisdom of Solomon, see J. Klausner, *History of the Second Temple* [Heb.], II, 233-242; III, 182-193; IV, 54-65.

CHAPTER I

Ben-Sira

(C. 190–170 B.C.E.)

A STRONG SPIRIT of love for the nation breathes forth from a few chapters of Ben-Sira. Most of his book is still filled with the same universalistic, broadly humanitarian spirit that we find in Proverbs, Job, and Ecclesiastes to such a degree that the Jews as a separate nationality hold almost no place in them. But sometimes there is suddenly aroused in Ben-Sira—while he is setting forth broad ethical precepts or good advice for living such as would not be relevant to one nation alone—a consciousness of the peculiar status of Israel among the nations; and a zeal for his nation flames up like fire in his heart. Thus, for example, in Chapter 35, while he is speaking of "the cry of the poor," that is, of the oppressed individual, which rends the clouds and "resteth not till it reach" to God, and "shall not remove till God doth visit and the righteous Judge execute judgment," he suddenly turns to *the oppressed nation*, which also cries out from the intensity of its woes and seeks justice:

> Yea, God will not delay,
> And like a warrior will not refrain Himself,
> Till He smite the loins of the merciless,
> And on the nations requite vengeance;
> Till He dispossess the sceptre of pride,
> And the staff of the wicked wholly cut off;
> . . .

> Till He plead the cause of His people,
> And make them glad with His salvation (35:22-25).

Whether the reference is to a time near at hand or far distant it is hard to decide. But there is here a Messianic stamp. This is again shown by the verse that follows:

> Salvation (is fitting) in the time of affliction,
> As rain-clouds in the season of drought (35:26).

This solemn verse (in Syriac it begins, "Their enemies shall be put to shame") shows that also in the preceding verses there is to be seen not a description of the present, but a vision of the Age to Come. And following this verse comes Chapter 36, half of which is Ben-Sira's famous prayer of hope, completely filled with Messianic expectations:

> Save us, O God of all,
> And (cast) Thy fear upon all the nations.
> Shake (Thy hand) against strange people,
> That they may see Thy power.
> As Thou hast sanctified Thyself in us before their eyes,
> So glorify Thyself in them before our eyes;
> That they may know, even as we know,
> That there is none other God but Thee.
> Renew the signs and repeat the wonders,
> Make glorious Thy hand and strengthen Thine arm.
> Awaken wrath and pour out anger,
> Subdue (the foe) and drive out the enemy.
> Hasten the end and ordain the appointed time,
> For who can say to Thee: "What doest Thou?"
> In raging fire let the survivor be consumed,
> And let the wrongers of Thy people find destruction.
> Make an end of the head of the enemy's princes,
> That saith, "There is none beside me."
> Gather all the tribes of Jacob,
> To receive a heritage as in days of old.
> Have mercy on the people called by Thy name,
> Israel whom Thou didst surname Firstborn.
> Have mercy on Thy holy city,
> Jerusalem, the place of Thy dwelling.
> Fill Zion with Thy majesty,
> And Thy temple with Thy glory.

> Give testimony to the first of Thy works,
> And establish the vision spoken in Thy name.
> Give reward to them that wait for Thee,
> That Thy prophets may be proved trustworthy.
> Thou wilt hear the prayer of Thy servants,
> According to Thy favor towards Thy people.
> That all the ends of the earth may know
> That Thou art the (Eternal) God (36:1-22).

Here we have in bold outline all the Messianic expectations of the books of the prophets and of the Psalms: the humiliation or even the destruction of the oppressors of Israel, the sanctification of the divine name by the raising of the lowly condition of the nation, the performance of signs and miracles, which is an inseparable part of the works of the Messiah ("the signs of the Messiah"), the ingathering of exiles, the glorification of Jerusalem and the Temple (not merely their rebuilding, since they were already re-established in the time of Ben-Sira), reward ("recompense" in the sense of "Behold, His reward is with Him, and His recompense before Him," Isa. 40:10) for the righteous together with punishment for the wicked, and the fulfillment of the vision of the prophets. Only about *the rule of the house of David* is there nothing here, and there is no need to speak of *the individual Messiah*. The latter idea is lacking in Ben-Sira, as it is lacking in the rest of Apocryphal books, as said above. But about *the house of David* and its preservation, Ben-Sira speaks a number of times. When he relates David's great political accomplishments, and also his religious reforms (according to Ben-Sira, as according to the author of Chronicles, David put in order the music in the Temple and also "the festivals in the course of the year"), he says that as a reward for this, God gave him "the decree of the kingdom and established his throne over Jerusalem" (47:11); and after he speaks of Solomon and his sins with an excess of women, and of the division of the kingdom into two, he adds:

> (Nevertheless,) God will not forsake his mercy,
> Nor suffer any of His words to fall to the ground;
> He will not (cut off) the posterity of His (chosen),
> And the (offspring of them that love) Him He will
>   not destroy:

But He will give to (Jacob a remnant),
And to (David a root from him) [1] (47:22).

And as the rule of the house of David is an everlasting rule, so also is the priesthood of Aaron, according to Ben-Sira, an everlasting priesthood:

And He exalted a holy one,
Even Aaron of the tribe of Levi,
And made him an eternal ordinance (45:6–7).

And he adds later:

Before (him) there were never (such things),
(Never) would a stranger (put them on).
Thus He trusted (him and) his sons,
And so his offspring throughout their generations (45:13).

And when he speaks of Simeon son of Johanan, the high priest, he concludes his eulogy with these words:

May His mercy be established with Simeon,
And may He raise up for him the covenant of Phinehas;
May there not one be cut off from him,
And as to his seed, may it be as the days of heaven (50:24).

Ben-Sira believes, therefore, in the perpetuity of the priesthood delivered to the seed of Aaron and to the house of Zadok, as he believes in the perpetuity of the kingdom delivered to the house of David. This is all the more surprising, inasmuch as Ben-Sira is a believer in a theocratic republic, as was the prophet Hosea earlier, and his views on kingship are similar to those which the Former Prophets attribute to the prophet Samuel: "Over all the nations He hath appointed rulers" (or, according to the Greek text: "For every nation He appointed a ruler"), *"but the portion of God is Israel"* (Ben-Sira, Syriac and Greek, 17:17). Yet the belief in the throne of David and the priesthood of Aaron had at that time taken root in the nation, and Ben-Sira believed in both of them equally and in their preservation to the Age to Come. So of course, both of them appear together in his book a number of times. When he speaks of Phinehas the zealous, he says:

[1] In the Syriac: "He will give to Jacob salvation, and to David a great kingdom."

> Therefore for him too, He established an ordinance,
> An eternal covenant to maintain the sanctuary;
> That to him and to his seed should appertain
> The high-priesthood forever.
> Also His covenant was with David,
> The son of Jesse, of the tribe of Judah;
> An inheritance of fire before His glory,
> While the inheritance of Aaron belongs to all his seed (45:24–25).

The last verse [two lines] is, according to the Syriac version: "The heritage of a king he alone inherited, while the inheritance of Aaron belongs to all his seed." And according to the Greek version: "The inheritance of the king's son is from the son alone" (perhaps a Christian alteration), or, according to the reading of Israel Lévi in his Hebrew text on the basis of the Greek: "The inheritance of the king is his son's alone." There are some who read "the heritage of a man (*ish*)" instead of "an inheritance of fire (*ēsh*)." However that may be, the meaning here is not that the kingship of the house of David belongs to David alone or to his son alone, but that *as a general principle* the kingship is a thing which the one son receives by the authority of his father (and all the descendants of David by the authority of David), while the priesthood was delivered to Aaron and all his sons—"all his seed"—as an inheritance directly from God.[2] We have already seen that Ben-Sira pronounces an invocation on Simeon son of Johanan that God will "raise up for him the covenant of Phinehas."

In still another passage David and Aaron appear side by side: in the "Thanksgivings," which come after the prayer of Ben-Sira in Chapter 51, and which are in neither the Greek nor the Syriac versions. After "Give thanks unto Him that causeth a horn to sprout for *the house of David*, for His mercy endureth forever," comes: "Give thanks unto Him that chooseth *the sons of Zadok* to be priests, for His mercy endureth forever" (51:12, supplementary verses viii and ix). That after the political and religious downfall of the Zadokites in the time of the decrees of Antiochus, when Hasmoneans displaced them both as high priests and as temporal rulers, it would have been

---

[2] For another, a historical interpretation, see R. H. Charles, *The Apocrypha and Pseudepigrapha of the Old Testament in English*, Oxford, 1913, I, 489–490.

impossible to find someone who would have added a verse about the preferential status of the sons of Zadok to the Hebrew text—this much is clear. Hence it is necessary to suppose that all these "Thanksgivings" were omitted by the translators, Greek and Syriac, because this verse about the sons of Zadok appeared strange to them; especially since all the rest of these "Thanksgivings" were also not in accord with the spirit of the Greek translator (from whom the Syriac translator derived his translation), a spirit close to that of the later Hellenists or of the conservative Sadducees.

Here, in these Thanksgivings, there is much of the Eighteen Benedictions (*Shemoneh Esreh*)˙ and of benedictions preceding them (there is no benediction of Him "who quickenest the dead"), including most of the Messianic expectations: "Give thanks unto Him that gathereth the outcasts of His people Israel"—the ingathering of exiles; "Give thanks unto Him that buildeth His city and His sanctuary"—the rebuilding of Jerusalem and the Temple after the First Destruction; "Give thanks unto Him that causeth a horn to sprout for the house of David"—Messiah son of David; "Give thanks unto the Redeemer of Israel"—the idea of the redemption in its totality; "Give thanks unto Him that chooseth the sons of Zadok to be priests" —the eternity of the service in the Temple and of the priesthood of Aaron; "Give thanks unto Him that chooseth Zion"—the restoration of Zion (51:12, supplementary verses v-ix, xiii). Here we have the substance and the greater part of the most important Messianic expectations (except the personality of the Messiah).

But there is in Ben-Sira still another important Messianic expectation: the coming of Elijah in the Messianic age. After a marvelous and lofty poetic description of the life, character, and mighty deeds of Elijah, Ben-Sira says, in allusion to the end of the Book of Malachi (3:23-24—Eng. 4:5-6):

> Who art written as ready for the time,
> To still wrath before (fierce anger),
> To turn the hearts of the fathers unto the children,
> And to restore the tribes (of Israel) (48:10).

Here we have the Talmudic-Midrashic belief in the prophet Elijah, who comes as the herald of the Messiah, as a maker of peace among families, and as the gatherer of the tribes of Israel from the four corners of the earth.

And along with the belief in the eternity of the priesthood and of the kingdom of the house of David, we find here a strong faith in the eternity of the entire people Israel:

> The life of a man is few in days,
> But the life of the people Israel is days without number (37:25).

Ben-Sira recognizes not only the eternity of the people Israel, but also its status as the Chosen People, in his spiritual expectation that it will be a light of the Gentiles, and also in his political expectation that it will be spread throughout the world, either literally or by the influence of its teaching. When he speaks about Abraham and the test (Ben-Sira calls it "trial") which Abraham withstood, he joins the Pentateuch with the Prophets,[3] and the people Israel with the Messiah, saying:

> Therefore with an oath He promised him,
> To bless nations in his seed;
> To cause them to inherit from sea to sea,
> And from the River to the ends of the earth (44:21).

Likewise Wisdom [personified], which is portrayed in the Book of Ben-Sira with even greater fervor than in Proverbs, shall have "a dwelling-place in Jacob and establish herself in Israel." "In the holy tabernacle" she ministers before Him, she is "established in Zion, in the city beloved of her fathers," and Jerusalem is "the city of her authority." She "took root among an honored people, in the portion of the LORD, and of his inheritance, Israel"; and she is present in "the book of the covenant of God Most High," in "the Law which Moses commanded as an heritage for the assemblies of Jacob" (24:8, 10–12, 23, according to the Syriac and Greek versions).

This is the prophetic view along with all its expansions in the Hagiographa. Nothing new is to be found here, but the little which is found testifies to the vitality of the Messianic idea in the storm-heralding time that preceded the Hasmonean uprising.

---

[3] Gen. 12:2–3, 26:4, and 28:14 with Zech. 9:10.

CHAPTER II

I Maccabees

(130–110 B.C.E.)

TO AN even less extent than in the Book of Ben-Sira can new Messianic ideas be found in the Book of I Maccabees. This fact is to be explained by its content. It is an excellent historical book, in which the narration of events is the main purpose; and along with the piety of which it is full, the political spirit of the time of John Hyrcanus fills it even more. Moreover, it is closely related to the opinions of the Sadducees—although not in the narrowly partisan sense of this word. There can be no doubt of the fact that even though John Hyrcanus and Janneus Alexander did not actually consider themselves as Messiahs, they were not content with the belief that the Messiah would come from the house of David; thus they—especially Judas Aristobulus and Janneus Alexander, both of whom assumed royal authority—were nothing less than usurpers of the crown which properly belonged to the house of David. I have no doubt that the ambition on the part of the Hasmonean kings to be considered Messiahs is what brought about their inclination toward the Sadducees, and also the severe struggle which the Pharisees waged against them—even to the point of treachery and alliance with the alien king of Syria. Therefore, the Book of I Maccabees has no place for elaborating on Messianic expectations, and exhibits no strong desire for so doing. With the life after death it is not concerned. It chooses worldly fame rather than eternal life.

Nevertheless, even from this book one can recognize that the Messianic idea was not dead, even in the most prosperous days of the Hasmonean dynasty—at least in the time preceding the *kings* of the Hasmonean dynasty. In the last words of Mattathias before his departure from this world, he recalls that all those who did great things for their people inherited great things. And he says among other things: "David for his righteousness inherited the throne of a kingdom for ever and ever" (I Macc. 2:57).[1] Here we have the eternity of the rule of the house of David. And when Judas Maccabeus had defeated Lysias, and he and his forces entered Jerusalem and cleansed the Temple, he pulled down the altar which had been defiled by the Gentiles, and "put away the stones in the Temple mount, in a suitable place, *until a prophet should come to decide concerning them*" (I Macc. 4:46). This corresponds exactly to the well known Talmudic expression: "It must be left until Elijah comes."[2]

At still another time, on an important occasion, there is a reference to Elijah: at the time of the "great assembly (συναγωγὴ μεγάλη) of priests and people and leaders of the nation and elders of the country" that decided to appoint Simon son of Mattathias as prince over them, him and his posterity. On that occasion "the Jews and the priests" decided "that Simon should be their leader and high-priest *for ever, until a true prophet should arise*" (I Macc. 14:41). Since the Hasmonean dynasty was not of the house of David, this dynasty could not rule in Israel without a limitation; namely, that when a true prophet should arise and say, "He who is of the descendants of David is worthy to be king over Israel, as was promised by the prophets," then the Hasmonean house would have to give way to the house of David.

It seems clear to me that if it had not been for this strong belief in the rule of the house of David, there would have been a different attitude on the part of the Pharisees and their supporters toward John Hyrcanus and Janneus Alexander. The nation would have been able to accept these men as the venerated extenders of its territory, if the "shoot out of the stock of Jesse," with all the lofty virtues with which

---

[1] I translate and quote passages from the Apocrypha according to the edition of O. Fr. Fritzsche, *Libri Apocryphi Veteris Testamenti, Graece,* Lipsiae, 1871.

[2] Mishnah, Baba Metsia 1:8 (end of the chapter); *ibid.* 3:4; Baraitha, Menahoth 3*a*, etc.

the prophets had endowed him, had not stood before it like a magic dream. If such acceptance had taken place, perhaps all Jewish history, and with it the whole history of mankind, would have been completely different. This will be seen below, when we come to the book of the Psalms of Solomon, which was written in the very days of the downfall of the Hasmonean dynasty.

CHAPTER III

II Maccabees

(The Epitome of C. 70 B.C.E.) [1]

IN THIS book, which in spirit and intention is the exact opposite of I Maccabees (being filled with signs and wonders, and lacking chronological order and close-knit pragmatic connexion), beliefs concerning the life of the World to Come are more in evidence than purely Messianic expectations. Eternal life, the life after death (the World to Come and the resurrection of the dead) are found here in contrast to ephemeral life, the life of this world (II Macc. 7:9, 36). The author believes in rewards and punishments after death as in life (10:26). The idea of *the resurrection of the dead* fills the whole book (7:14, 23). Famous is the passage which seems to contain a polemic against the Book of I Maccabees or against the Sadducees in general. In this passage it is said that Judas Maccabeus was "bearing in mind the resurrection—for if he had not expected the fallen [in battle] to rise again, it would have been superfluous and silly to pray for the dead" (12:43–44). Here the resurrection of the dead is much materialized: it is a bodily resurrection, in which the righteous person has restored to him the parts which he allowed to be cut off or afflicted for the sake of God (7:11; 14:46). But only the righteous will be restored to life: for reprobates like Antiochus Epiphanes there is no resurrection (7:14).

[1] See on this and its relation to I Maccabees, W. Kolbe, *Beiträge zur syrischen und jüdischen Geschichte* (*Beitr. z. Wissensch. vom Alten Testament*, ed. R. Kittel, N.F., Heft 10), Stuttgart, 1926, pp. 74–150. See also the original book of A. Momigliano, *Prime Linee di Storia della Tradizione Maccabaica*, Torino, 1931, pp. 69–170.

However, there are also actual Messianic expectations scattered here and there in this Pharisaic-Hellenistic book. The God of Israel redeems His people and gathers in His dispersed "from under heaven (ἐκ τῆς ὑπὸ τῶν οὐρανῶν) to the holy place" (2:17–18). The people Israel is eternal (14:15) and to it God has given "the heritage (the land of Israel or even the heritage of the Gentiles), and the kingdom (the house of David), and the priesthood (the line of Aaron), and the sanctity (the Temple)" (2:17).

Here we see before us in rapid summary most of the Messianic expectations in the books of Scripture and in Ben-Sira.

CHAPTER IV

Judith

(C. 130–110 B.C.E.)

IN ACCORDANCE with its nature—a historical tale—there is no place in this delightful little book for Messianic expectations. Only in the song which Judith sings in the last chapter of the book are there hard words against the Gentiles and those oppressing Israel; and mention is made of *the Day of Judgment:*

> Woe to the nations that rise up against My people!
> The Lord Almighty will take vengeance on them
>   in the Day of Judgment,
> To put fire and worms in their flesh,[1]
> And they shall wail in misery forever (16:17).

[1] Cf. the end of Isaiah (66:24):
> For their *worm* shall not die,
> Neither shall their *fire* be quenched.

CHAPTER V

Tobit

(C. 130–110 B.C.E.)

ALSO IN this book, which is a moralistic tale, there is no large place for Messianic expectations. Nevertheless, it has more expectations than the Book of Judith, its companion work in time, place, and language,[1] because Tobit is a *moralistic* and not a historical tale.

In Tobit's song of thanksgiving it is said that God will chastise Jerusalem, the holy city, but will also have mercy upon her, "and will again build His tabernacle in the midst of her with joy, and make glad in her all that are captives . . . from generation to generation unto eternity." Many peoples will come for the sake of the LORD our God, with gifts in their hands, gifts for the King of heaven; and they will praise Him and give Him thanks from generation to generation. Those who bless her (Jerusalem) will be blessed, and those who curse her will be accursed. The sons of the righteous will be gathered together unto Jerusalem; peace and security will be in the midst of her, while joy will abide in her forever (13:9–14). Jerusalem will be built of sapphire, emerald, and precious stones, her walls and towers will be pure gold, and her streets will be paved with beryl and carbuncle and stones of Ophir. And all her streets will say, "Hallelujah!" and they will utter praise, saying, "Blessed be God, who has raised you up forever and ever" (13:15–16). The house of God will be destroyed and the children of Israel will go into exile, but they will

---

[1] I have explained all this in my *History of the Second Temple* [Heb.], III, 188–193.

return and rebuild the house of God "gloriously, for all generations forever, as the prophets said of it." All the heathen will turn to truth and the fear of the Lord God, hiding their idols in the dust [2] and praising the Lord. "God will raise up His people, and all who love the Lord God in truth and righteousness will show mercy to our brethren" (14:5–7).

Here we have the return to Zion, the rebuilding of Jerusalem, the ingathering of the exiles, and the conversion of the Gentiles. And everything is in the spirit of Second Isaiah.

[2] See Isa. 2:18–20.

CHAPTER VI

The Apocryphal Baruch

(Earlier Part *c*. 130 B.C.E.; Later Part *c*. 90 B.C.E.)

THIS BOOK, *all* of which I consider, with W. Rothstein [1] and A. Kahana,[2] to have been translated from Hebrew, has two parts: an earlier (from the beginning of the book to 3:8) and a later (from 3:9 to the end—in disagreement with Rothstein, who separates 3:9-4:4 from 4:5-5:9).[3] The earlier part is an echo of the siege of Jerusalem by Antiochus VII Sidetes in the years 135-134 B.C.E., and the later part an echo of the struggle of the Pharisees against Janneus Alexander (90-85 B.C.E.).

In the earlier part, Messianic expectations do not have much place: this part is more or less prosaic, and was written in a time of political tranquillity; this is not the case with the second part, which is filled with lofty poetry, and was written in a time of troubles and distress. In the earlier part we find only this idea: that after God exiles His people, the people will turn from their evil way, and then God will restore them to the land of their fathers (2:24-35). Much more than this is contained in the later part. The poet turns to Jerusalem, saying:

---

[1] See Kautzsch, *Apocryphen und Pseudepigraphen*, Tübingen, 1900, I, 215.
[2] *Outside Books* [Heb.], I.2, p. 353.
[3] Whitehouse (Charles, *Apocrypha and Pseudepigrapha*, I, 570-577) divides this book into three parts like Rothstein, except that he considers the first two parts to have been written originally in Hebrew, but the third part as written originally in Greek. The date of the first is 48 B.C.E., the date of the second and third, 78 C.E. But this does not seem right to me. See my *History of the Second Temple* [Heb.], III, 182-184; A. Kahana, *The Outside Books* [Heb.], loc. cit.

O Jerusalem, look about thee toward the east,
And behold the joy that cometh unto thee from God.
Lo, thy sons come, whom thou sentest away,
They come gathered from the east to the west
At the command of the Holy One,
Rejoicing in the glory of God.

Put off, O Jerusalem, the garment of thy mourning and affliction,
And put on the comeliness of the glory from God forever.
Cast about thee the robe of the righteousness from God
Set a diadem on thine head of the glory of the Everlasting.
For God will show thy splendor unto all under heaven,
And thy name shall be called of God forever:
"The Peace of Righteousness" and "the Glory of Godliness" (4:36–5:4).

In this spirit he continues to describe the return of the exiles; and in so doing he imitates Deutero-Isaiah even more than does Tobit:

Arise, O Jerusalem, and stand upon the height,
. . .
And behold thy children
Gathered from the rising of the sun unto the going down thereof,
Rejoicing that God hath remembered them.

For they went away from thee on foot,
Being led away of their enemies;
But God bringeth them in unto thee
Borne on high with glory, like a royal throne,
For God hath appointed that every high mountain,
And the everlasting hills, shall be made low,
And the valleys filled up, to make level the ground,
That Israel may go safely in the glory of God.[4]

And the woods and every sweet-smelling tree
Will give shade to Israel,
By the commandment of God.
For God shall lead Israel with joy in the light of His glory,
With the mercy and righteousness that cometh from Him (5:5 to the end).

Here there is much enthusiasm and high-flown figurative language, but everything follows in the footsteps of Deutero-Isaiah. There is not even variety here: only the ingathering of the exiles and the

[4] Cf. Isa. 40:4–5.

rebuilding of Jerusalem in glory and splendor are described in borrowed, but glorious, colors. The author passes over the rest of the Messianic expectations in silence. After all, the Temple was still standing on its foundation and Israel had not again gone into exile.

CHAPTER VII

The Wisdom of Solomon

(C. 70–50 B.C.E.)

IN THIS Hellenistic book [1] there are many Messianic expectations; but, as would be natural for a Hellenistic Jewish philosopher, they are more spiritual than political. As in the other Hellenistic book of the Apocrypha, II Maccabees, so in this book the "World to Come" [the life after death] takes a larger place than the "Days of the Messiah" [the Messianic age]. Faith in the life of the World to Come, eternal life, and in retribution after death is very strong (3:1–4; 5:15–16).

But the author also knows the destruction of the wicked in this world, and he describes the instruments of God's wrath—the destructive powers in nature—with very strong figures and eloquent expressions (5:17–23). We have here a description of the prophets' "day of the LORD" in this world, wherein He will judge the peoples. But not only God will judge evildoers and those who despise righteousness, trusting in their own strength and saying in their hearts that there is no God; the righteous also will judge the heathen and burn them as sparks of fire burn reeds and rushes (3:7–8). Then will the wicked see their perversity and repent of their misdeeds—but too late! (5:12–14). But the righteous will receive in the World to Come from the hand of God a "diadem of beauty" (in Greek these words are translated from the Hebrew thus: τὸ διάδημα τοῦ κάλλους) and a

---

[1] See on its contents, language, date, and origin in full detail J. Klausner, *History of the Second Temple* [Heb.], V, 54–65.

glorious kingdom "because with His right hand shall He cover them, and with His arm shall He shield them" (5:16).

Here we have the Day of Judgment, the life of the World to Come, retribution for the righteous and the wicked. The picture of the life of the righteous in the World to Come in the Wisdom of Solomon is very similar to that in the Talmud: there also the righteous in the World to Come sit at the right hand of God, "with their crowns on their heads, basking in the brightness of the Divine Presence." [2] But beyond this the Hellenistic "Wisdom of Solomon" knows nothing at all: neither the return to Zion, nor the rebuilding of Jerusalem, nor Elijah, nor the Messiah.

With this we have finished gleaning the scattered Messianic kernels in the Apocryphal books. We have not gleaned much; but we have become convinced that nearly all of the Messianic hopes of the period of the Prophets and Hagiographa were still living in the hearts of the people in the time of the Apocrypha; but on account of the nature of the books and the circumstances of the time, these hopes did not attain full and complete expression.

We pass now to the books of the Pseudepigrapha, in which we shall find, instead of kernels, full ears, and sometimes whole sheaves.

[2] See, e.g., Kallah Rabbathi, Chap. 2.

B. THE MESSIANIC IDEA IN THE PSEUDEPIGRAPHA

THE BOOKS of the Pseudepigrapha, like those of the Apocrypha, were not included in the sacred collection of the Holy Scriptures of Judaism; but in contrast to the Apocrypha, which were received into the Bible of Christianity, most of the Pseudepigraphical books are also not sacred to the majority of Christian churches (only the Book of IV Ezra is found in most of the Latin editions of the "Canon"). But the Abyssinian Church, which received Christianity from the Graeco-Byzantine Church, included in its canon of Scriptures the Book of Enoch, the Book of Jubilees, and so on (and hence certain of the Pseudepigrapha were preserved only in the Ge'ez language).

But greater than this *external* difference—the difference in degree of canonicity in the various Christian churches—is the *internal* difference between the Apocrypha and the Pseudepigrapha. If the Apocrypha are, as I said above, the continuation of the Hagiographa, and for good reason were well known among Jews as the "Later Hagiographa," then the Pseudepigrapha signify a transition to the Talmudic Aggadah, on the one hand, and to Christianity in its earliest Jewish form, on the other hand. The Book of Jubilees, for example, is an Aggadic Midrash to the Book of Genesis, and not without reason was called "the Little Genesis" (*Leptogenesis*). "Visions" and "revelations" ("apocalyptic" in the broad sense), elaborate descriptions of the Days of the Messiah (the Messianic expectations, that is, "Messianology" in the strict sense); also descriptions of the "end of days" (the World to Come, reward and punishment after death, Paradise and Gehenna, the resurrection of the dead, and so on, that is, "eschatology"; also "prophecies," in which is reflected not so much what is to come as *what has been* (what is called "prophecy after the event")—all these things fill the books of the Pseudepigrapha everywhere.

Because of this, the Pseudepigrapha are inferior to the Apocrypha in one way and superior in another. They are quite inferior to the Apocrypha as regards simplicity, clarity, and naturalness. Not one of them has the simple beauty and artless splendor of Judith or Tobit, or the instructive clarity of the Book of Ben-Sira. Most of the Pseudepigrapha are completely filled with complicated imaginings and mysterious obscurities, and strange legendary portrayals appear in them, mixed with visions of the future, with almost prophetic rebukes, and with words of wisdom as it was understood at that time. Because of such characteristics, the Tannaim feared that these books would inflame overmuch the imagination of the masses and incite them to revolt, or alienate them from practical life and from the ceremonial requirements.[1]

But for the same reasons, the Pseudepigrapha are also superior to the Apocrypha. They are richer, more varied, more full of content. Within them it is possible to observe much better the spirit of the time, the people's conceptions of past and future, the spiritual condition of representative persons of that time, popular views current in the second half of the period of the Second Temple, the knowledge of nature and the world possessed by the "popular prophets" (as the apocalyptists were rightly called by M. Friedlaender)[2]; also their beliefs, opinions, and hopes for the future, which first found a way into the hearts of the common people in Israel in the period from the time of the Hasmoneans to the destruction of the Temple, and later influenced primitive Christianity. Here we truly have the "great Semiramis's garden" of the Aggadah, as Heinrich Heine expressed it; * but it is a "garden" of the *early* Aggadah, which is still not so

---

* See Israel Tabak, *Judaic Lore in Heine*, Baltimore, 1948, pp. 130, 183, 301, 310.—TRANS.

[1] See R. T. Herford, *The Pharisees*, 1924, pp. 186–193; idem, *Talmud and Apocrypha*, 1933, pp. 171–197.

[2] See his *Die religiosen Bewegungen innerhalb des Judentums im Zeitalter Jesu*, Berlin, 1905, pp. 78, 289.

subservient to the Biblical text, but weaves and embroiders marvelous pictures of the imagination with a certain freedom, like folklore of any vital nation that is rooted in its own soil.

The Pseudepigraphical books are especially rich in *Messianic portrayals*. The Day of Judgment and the "birth pangs of the Messiah" are portrayed here in terms that come in their essence from the description of the day of the LORD in the Scriptures, but are expanded and enriched with new colors. The personality of the Messiah takes here, for the most part, a more important place, with marvelous legends woven round about him. The Days of the Messiah here are treated with detailed descriptions, the like of which our Scriptures do not know. And legends about the angels and Satan and the evil spirits, the World to Come, Paradise and Gehenna, Leviathan and the wild ox [Behemoth], the resurrection of the dead, and the like—these are new conceptions and phantasies, which the canonical books hardly know at all; but the Talmudic Aggadah—in spite of the opposition of the Tannaim to these "apocalypses"—wove its embroidery of fine gold about them and made them an essential part of the popular Jewish faith.

Whence came this difference of content in different Jewish books, all of which in their own time were written in consecration, and all of which undoubtedly had a lofty religio-ethical purpose?

The persecutions in the time of Antiochus Epiphanes deepened the conceptions of the Day of Judgment and the Messianic birth pangs. The fearful afflictions that came upon the whole nation demanded a vindication of Divine Justice, on the one hand, and aroused a desire for vengeance, on the other. Subsequently, these two needs were met by more developed portrayals of the Day of Judgment— "the day of the LORD" of the prophets, which was converted into "the birth pangs of the Messiah." And the great victories of the Hasmoneans, victories of the spirit, all of them a great marvel—"the weak triumphed over the strong, the few over the many, the clean over the unclean, the righteous over the wicked" [3]—these victories lifted spirits with high and marvelous hopes, and gave a new bright-

[3] The prayer ʻAl ha-Nissim [on account of the miracles] for Hanukkah. [See *The Union Prayerbook for Jewish Worship*, Cincinnati, 1944, Part I, p. 90.—TRANS.]

ness of color to the descriptions of the vengeance which the LORD was going to wreak upon His enemies and the enemies of His people, and to the description of the Days of the Messiah in the Age to Come.

Possibly, in the times of Judas Maccabeus, Jonathan, and Simon, and even in the early days of John Hyrcanus, when the struggle for the existence of the nation and its religion was absorbing all energies, the best of the people did not turn to Messianic expectations "because of impatience of spirit, and cruel bondage" [Ex. 6:9]: *inter arma silent musae*. Possibly, in the time of Simon son of Mattathias, and in the first half of the rule of his son, John Hyrcanus, even the "popular prophets" were satisfied with the leadership of the Hasmonean dynasty, and did not concern themselves much with the Messiah and the Messianic age. But there came the rift between the "Pious" and Judas Maccabeus, and thereafter the separation into Pharisees, Sadducees, and Essenes (in the time of Jonathan); there came the quarrel between John Hyrcanus and the Pharisees, there came the wars between the Pharisees and Janneus Alexander, there came the withdrawal of the Essenes from political life; then the Messianic idea welled up like a mighty stream, and the people, through their leading representatives, the Pharisees or those near them in spirit, wove imaginative dreams of the Age to Come, finding consolation therein, since the Hasmonean dynasty did not fulfill all their hopes. At the same time, the exceptional individuals among them, the solitary and ascetic ones—the Essenes—steeped themselves in a multiplicity of dreams and visions, and thus were created the Pseudepigraphical books, with their multiplicity of visions and "revelations" (apocalypses). The best of these books—the Book of Enoch, the Book of Jubilees, the Psalms of Solomon, the Testaments of the Twelve Tribes [Patriarchs], and even the Sibylline Oracles—are from the Hasmonean period.

And when tribulations followed in rapid succession, when the house of Herod ruled over Israel with the help of the mailed fist of the Romans, and afterward, when the Roman procurators, those blood-sucking leeches, came and brought about the Revolt, and there came to pass that fearful catastrophe—the destruction of the Second Temple, with all its horrors—then the people found consolation and hope in the Messianic expectations and in descriptions of the life after death as found in the later Pseudepigrapha: the Assumption of Moses is from the time of the Herodian dynasty; the Syriac Apocalypse of Baruch and the Book of IV Ezra—the choicest among the books of the Pseudepigrapha—are from the first years after the Second Destruction.

The Pseudepigraphical books may be divided into the Palestinian and the Hellenistic. The Palestinian were composed for the most part in Jerusalem and in the Hebrew language (this is more probable, in my opinion, than the hypothesis that they were written in Aramaic such as that of the Book of Daniel); the Hellenistic were composed for the most part in Alexandria and in the Greek language. The Palestinian Pseudepigrapha containing important Messianic expectations are: the Book of Enoch, the Book of Jubilees, the Psalms of Solomon, the Assumption of Moses, the Syriac Book of Baruch, and IV Ezra; the Hellenistic Pseudepigrapha in which Messianic expectations take an important place are: the Sibylline Books.

We shall begin with the Book of Enoch, even though one of the books of the Sibylline Oracles is earlier than Enoch, for the reason that the Pseudepigrapha which were created in Hebrew and in Palestine are much more valuable for an understanding of the spirit of the Jewish nation than those which were created in Greek and in Alexandria of Egypt, under foreign influence; also for the reason that this book is, with the exception of IV Ezra, the most Messianic in its content.[4]

[4] See, for details on the opinions expressed here, J. Klausner, *Sepharim Hitsonim* (Pseudepigrapha) in "Hoveret le-Dogma" of *Otsar ha-Yahadut*, ed. Ahiasaf, Warsaw, 1906, pp. 95-120. Back in the year 1919, I began to prepare for publication in Odessa, in the "Moriah" edition, new translations of most of the Pseudepigrapha, together with full introductions and notes, in one large collection; but the Bolshevik Revolution delayed the project. From this I am taking the quotations in Hebrew translation. The fixing of dates is discussed in my *History of the Second Temple* [in Heb.], III, 194-213. Fifteen years ago there came out *The Outside Books*, including the Apocrypha, in Hebrew translation with brief introductions and notes, under the editorship of Abraham Kahana, in four parts, Tel-Aviv, 1937. Ben-Zion Katz, in his book *Pharisees, Sadducees, Zealots, Christians* [in Heb.], pp. 78-104, considers all the "Outside Books," except Ben-Sira, the Letter of Aristeas, I Maccabees, and the Book of Jubilees, to be entirely Christian forgeries, because they contain Christian additions. No one who carefully studies these books in the Greek and Ethiopic translations which we have could possibly agree with this opinion.

CHAPTER I

The "Ethiopic" Book of Enoch

(Its Earlier Parts, 110 B.C.E.; Its Later Parts, 68 B.C.E.)

WITH RESPECT to the Messianic conceptions in the Book of Enoch, it is necessary to distinguish between those in the earlier parts of the book (Chaps. 1-36 and 72-108) from the time of John Hyrcanus (after he broke with the Pharisees) or from the time of Janneus Alexander (*c.* 110-80), and those in the later parts of the book, which are taken together as a separate work called the "Parables" (German scholars call them *Bilderreden*) or the "Messianic Book" (Chaps. 37-71). This, in my opinion, is from the time of Queen Salome Alexandra (*c.* 70-68), when Tigranes, king of Armenia, had invaded Judea (*Antiquities of the Jews* 13:16:4; *Wars of the Jews* 1:5:3); for here (Enoch 56:5) the Parthians and the Medes are mentioned, the Medes being a Hebrew surrogate for the Armenians (see below), while the Romans are not mentioned at all.[1] With respect to the Messianic expectations in general and the portrayals of the Messiah in particular, there is a discernible difference between the different parts of the book, and I shall endeavor to give herein the Messianic conceptions of each part—and first of all the Messianic conceptions of the earlier parts. But even in them there must be a distinction between the "basic document" (*Grundschrift*) and the "historical section."

[1] See J. Klausner, *History of the Second Temple* [Heb.], III, 194-202.

1. *The Day of Judgment ("Birth Pangs of Messiah") in the "Basic Document"*

"The day of the LORD" of the prophets is "the Day of Judgment" of the Tannaitic period, more often called "the birth pangs of Messiah." The meaning of these words is not the pangs and suffering of the Messiah himself, but the pangs and tribulations of the Messianic *age;* likewise "the trumpet of Messiah" is not the trumpet of the Messiah himself but the trumpet of the Messianic *age*. In the later period "the Day of Judgment" serves to designate the day on which the *individual Jew* is judged for his deeds in this world [2] and the next,[3] but this does not apply to the nation as a whole nor to all humanity. In Hasmonean times and in the Pseudepigrapha, "the Day of Judgment" is a synonym for "the day of the LORD," "judgment of the peoples," and "the birth pangs of Messiah."

"The birth pangs of Messiah" are portrayed in the Book of Enoch in vivid colors. These descriptions are based upon the descriptions of the day of the LORD in the prophetic books, but they add much to them. The "Holy and Great One" (or, according to the Greek text, the "Holy Great One") will come forth from His dwelling, and the Eternal God will tread thence on Mount Sinai, having appeared with His hosts from the highest of the heavens. Then men will be smitten with fear and the "Watchers" [4] will quake, while anguish and quaking will seize all unto the ends of the earth. The lofty mountains will be shaken, and the high hills be made low; and all of them will be melted like wax before fire. The whole earth will sink and all who are upon it will perish. Everybody will undergo judgment: not only the wicked, but "also all the righteous." [5] God will come with holy myriads to destroy the wicked; He will enter into judgment with all flesh concerning all the evil deeds which the wicked have perpetrated, and concerning the arrogant words which sinners have spoken against

---

[2] Rosh ha-Shanah 16*b*.

[3] Abodah Zarah 18*a;* Gen. Rabbah, end of Sect. 93.

[4] The angels, from "a watcher and a holy one from heaven" (Dan. 4:10, 14, 20).

[5] These words are lacking in the Greek text; however, they were certainly not added in the Ethiopic translation, but were omitted in the Greek translation.

THE "ETHIOPIC" BOOK OF ENOCH 279

Him. But upon the righteous He will bestow peace, His elect He will guard, and show them kindness. They will receive His own blessing, and the light of God will shine upon them (1:3–9).

Not only will the wicked be severely judged in the great Day of Judgment. God will also judge Satan. Azazel will first be handed over to the angel Raphael, who will bind him hand and foot and place him in the darkness "in the desert which is in Dudael"—apparently Beth Hadudu or, more correctly, Beth Herodu.[6] According to the Targum Pseudo-Jonathan (on Lev. 16:10), the goat sent to Azazel will be cast into this place from the precipice of the mountain (Geiger). Raphael will place upon him stones that are heavy and sharp (*haddot* in Hebrew, a pun on Hadudu),[7] covering his face, and Azazel will dwell thus in darkness and see no light; then "on the day of the Great Judgment he shall be cast into the fire." Only then will Raphael "heal the earth which the angels have corrupted" (10:4–7). These angels who have corrupted the earth are the "Nephilim" of the Bible, also known in Talmud and Midrash by the names Shamhazzai and Azael.

These names in almost this very form are found in our Book of Enoch, in which the "Nephilim" occupy an important place. These "Nephilim," who coveted the daughters of men and thus brought lust into the world, also did evil in that they, together with Azazel, taught the sons of men all kinds of arts and crafts—*including the art of writing*. For the knowledge of digging metal from mines and casting it brought about the making of weapons, and through these men learned to wage war and spill the blood of their brethren. Knowledge of art and artifice brought about *the self-adornment of women* and the manufacture and pursuit of pleasing ornaments, which corrupted the morals of men. Even the knowledge of writing books resulted in the "making of books without end," containing false prophecies, illusory visions, and incitement to evil deeds. There-

---

[6] Mishnah, Yoma 6:8 (see Kohut, *Arukh ha-Shalem*, II, 70, article "Beth Herodu"); see also Graetz, *Geschichte der Juden*, III, 1, 219, Note 2.

[7] But the true reading is, in the opinion of Klein, "Herodi"—and thus the pun disappears (see S. Klein, *Erets Yisrael* [Land of Israel], Vienna, 1922, pp. 13, 37–38, 118; *Zeitschrift des Deutschen Palaestina-Vereins*, 1910, p. 33). But "Dudael" does not really resemble either "Hadudu" or "Herodi."

fore the LORD will judge the "Nephilim" harshly on the Day of Judgment (16:1; compare also 6:1, 4; 65:7-8; 69:9-11). This is the opposition to an external culture on behalf of an inward culture or morality—an idea which we find in our time in Rousseau and Tolstoy.

Along with the "Nephilim" there will also be judged on "the day of the Great Judgment" the evil spirits, the demons, and the devils; actually, these are only the various guises assumed by the "Nephilim" who mingled with the daughters of men. Complete destruction will come upon them in the Day of Judgment, and the women who enticed the "Nephilim" will become jackals and ostriches ["sirens" in the Greek] (19:1-2). God will sit upon his throne of judgment, which rests upon the seventh of the marvelous mountains seen by Enoch; round about the throne are trees giving forth fragrance, one fragrant tree in particular being beyond comparison. This tree and its fruit will be given to the righteous, who will be declared guiltless in the judgment. They will eat of its fruit in Jerusalem the Holy, they will live longer than their fathers, and they will not know trouble or sorrow, toil or hardship (25:3-6).

By contrast, the years of sinners will be shortened, the produce in their fields will be retarded, and because of their sin nothing will come forth in its proper time from the earth. The rains will be held back in the heavens, and the fruit of the tree will not ripen in its time on the earth. The moon will change its functioning and not appear at its regular time; the sun will not set at evening, but will make light beyond the ordinary "on the extremity of the great chariots in the west." Likewise, "many chiefs of the stars" will go astray, changing their courses and not appearing in their fixed positions, so that men will sin and go astray in taking them to be gods. Then many evils will come upon these men, and a sentence of destruction will be rendered against them (80:2-8).

Chapters 92-105 are filled with strong and vivid rebukes, rising to the very height of prophecy:

> Woe to those who build unrighteousness and oppression,
> And lay deceit as a foundation;
> For they shall be suddenly overthrown!

> Woe to those who build their houses with sin,
> For from all their foundations shall they be overthrown,
> And by the sword shall they fall!
>
> Woe to you, ye rich, who have trusted in your riches,
> And have not remembered the Most High;
> For ye shall be forced to leave your treasures!
>
> Ye have committed blasphemy and unrighteousness,
> And thus are destined for the day of slaughter,
> The day of darkness and the day of the great judgment.
>
> Thus I speak and declare unto you:
> He who created you will overthrow you,
> For your fall there shall be no compassion,
> And your Creator will rejoice at your destruction.
> And your righteous ones in those days shall be
> A reproach to the sinners and the godless (94:6–11).

And in the last chapter of the book (108), which is also filled with severe rebukes, it is said of the sinners that their names will be blotted out of the books of the holy ones and their offspring will be destroyed forever. Moreover, their spirits will also be punished; they will cry out and wail in a desolate place, and will burn in a flaming fire, the fire of Gehenna. There all the blaspheming sinners, the evildoers, and the perverters of prophetic words about the future will be tormented. Deliverance will be had only by the humble, those who have subdued their flesh, who have been reviled by evil men, who love God, not silver and gold and all the good things of the world—who love Heaven (God) more than their own lives, who blessed God while evil men trampled them underfoot and abused and reviled them. These, who have loved His holy name, will go forth from darkness to great light, and will shine for untold ages, while the sinners will cry aloud at the sight of the brightness of the righteous, who are "the generation of light," for "righteousness is the judgment of God" (108:3 to the end).

These ideas, which are reflected in many passages of the Gospels, are more pertinent to retribution and the World to Come than to expectations of the Days of the Messiah; yet "the judgment of God" is inseparably connected with the Day of Judgment. But in other chapters come actual portrayals of "the birth pangs of Messiah," recalling both the descriptions of Amos, Isaiah, Jeremiah, and Zephaniah, and the descriptions in the Talmudic Baraithas of "the week in which the Son of David will come." Severe affliction will come upon the whole world: upon peoples and kingdoms and individual human beings. In those days the nations will be aroused; generations of the peoples will raise themselves up on the day of destruction. In those days the destitute will abandon their children, pregnant women will miscarry, and mothers will thrust their sucklings from the breast, showing no pity on their loved ones (99:4–5). In those days fathers and sons will be slain in one place, and brothers will fall together as their blood is poured out like a river. For a man will not withhold his hand from slaying his son or his son's son, and the sinner will not withhold his hand from slaying his most honored brother; from sunrise to sunset they will slay one another. The horse will wade in the blood of sinners up to the breast, and the chariot will be submerged up to its height. In those days the angels will descend into the hiding places and gather into one place all those who assist in transgression (the "Nephilim," Satan, and the evil spirits?), and the Most High will arise on that day to execute great judgment among sinners. Only over the righteous will God appoint the "watchers" (the guardian angels), who will guard them as the apple of an eye until He blots out evil from the world. Even if the righteous do sleep "a long sleep" (compare "them that sleep in the dust," Dan. 12:2), let them have no fear (100:1–5): they will rise from the dust to everlasting life, while the wicked will be afflicted forever.

This is the picture of "the birth pangs of Messiah" in the earlier parts of the Book of Enoch. The world after death and the period before the Messianic age occur in it in confusion. And it contains still another confusion: within it the prophetic expectations are joined with and attached to the imaginative descriptions which we find at a somewhat later time in the Talmudic-Midrashic Aggadah. These Aggadic descriptions sprang from the imaginations of the people or of the "popular prophets" (the apocalyptists) on the basis of Holy Writ; and the Book of Enoch is a receiving vessel for these popular imaginings.

2. The Messianic Age in the "Basic Document"

Only the "elect," the chosen ones of God, are worthy of the Messianic age. After all the wicked and sinners are destroyed on the day of the Great Judgment, wisdom will be given to the elect, and they will live and never sin again, either through presumptuousness or through error; and there will be light for the enlightened and knowledge for the persons of understanding. They will not die by the divine wrath descending upon them before their time; only when the days of their life have been completed will they pass away in peace; and their years, which will pass in eternal gladness and in peaceful joy, will be many (5:8–9). We do not have here, therefore, a supernatural eternal life in the World to Come, but a long life of peace and joy in *this* world, of the kind that is promised for the Messianic age by Deutero-Isaiah (65:19–23).[8]

The following Messianic expectations are also completely *terrestrial*: In the end of days all the righteous will be delivered, they will beget a thousand children,[9] and will complete all the days of their youth and their old age [10] in peace. In those days the whole earth will be filled with righteousness, and all of it will be planted with trees (the ideal of a people tilling the soil!) and be full of blessing. They will plant all kinds of delightful trees in it; vines will be planted in it that will yield fruit in abundance; and from all the seed that is planted in it one measure will yield a thousand (or, according to the Ethiopic text, ten thousand) measures, and one measure of olives will produce ten baths of oil (10:17–19). These materialistic descriptions agree not alone with what we find in the "apocalypse" of the Syriac Baruch (29:5–8), and in the tradition of one of the oldest of the Fathers of the Christian Church, Papias, as preserved in Irenaeus [11]—which gave a place to the Christian belief in "the thou-

---

[8] See above, Part I, pp. 174–177.
[9] The author of the Book of Enoch understood the verse, "The smallest shall become a thousand" (Isa. 60:22) literally and according to its plain meaning.
[10] So it is necessary to translate instead of "their Sabbath," which the Greek translation wrongly reads, followed by the Ethiopic.
[11] See Irenaeus, *Adversus Haereses*, V, 33.

sand-year kingdom" (*chiliasmus*);[12] these descriptions also occur almost word for word in the Talmudic Baraithas and in the early Tannaitic Midrashim.[13] And I have already cited above the likewise physical expectation that the righteous will enjoy the fruit of a tree that gives forth a marvelous fragrance (25:3–5).

But along with the *material prosperity*, there is described in the very same Chapter 10, also in Chapter 11 following, the great *spiritual blessedness* of the Days of the Messiah: The earth will be purged of all violence, all unrighteousness, all sin, all wickedness, and all uncleanness. All men will be righteous, all nations will glorify and praise the LORD, and all of them will serve Him. The earth will be purged of all transgression and sinfulness, of all toil and tribulation (10:20–22). In those days the LORD will open the storehouses of heavenly blessing to empty them upon the earth—upon the deeds and labor of men; there will be peace and justice among men for all eternity and for all future generations (11:1–2). Sin will be blotted out in darkness forever and will no more appear from that day for evermore (92:5).

We pass now to the Messianic portrayal in the "Historical Section" which is also included in the Book of Enoch (83–90).

3. *The Messianic Descriptions of the "Historical Section"* (83–90)

Following in the footsteps of the Book of Daniel, the author of the "Historical Section" in the Book of Enoch brings before us all history, the history of the world and the history of Israel down to his time, as a prelude to the Days of the Messiah. And like the author of the Book of Daniel, he presents historical characters in the form of beasts, animals, and winged creatures. The sons of Israel are likened to "pure" and peaceful creatures: "the forefathers" (in the sense of Ben-Sira 44) to bulls, and their descendants to sheep. But the Gentiles,

---

[12] See on this below, Chap. VI, 2, p. 344, for details.
[13] Kethubboth 111a, and with minor differences, Kallah Rabbathi, Chap. 2; Siphre, Deut., 315, ed. Friedmann, f. 138a and b. See for details on this below Part III, Chap. 10.

who crushed the sons of the sheep, are likened to wild beasts and birds of prey. The angels are also divided into two classes: the angels who fell and descended from their high estate are represented as stars; [14] the angels who remained on high are likened to men (just as the Book of Daniel likens the people Israel to a "son of man," while likening the nations of the world to beasts).[15]

By means of such symbols, which are very transparent, the author of the "Historical Section" reviews all the history in Holy Writ from the original Adam down to his own time—the time of the victorious Hasmoneans. When he reaches the destruction of the kingdom of Samaria, he says that God appointed seventy shepherds over His people, the sheep, and permitted them to destroy a part of the sheep, which He delivered over, duly numbered, to the shepherds; but he commanded "another" to watch the shepherds carefully, lest they destroy more of the sheep than they were permitted (89:59–65). According to the hypothesis accepted by scholars, the seventy shepherds are the seventy nations, or the seventy guardian angels of these nations, and the "other" is another angel, Michael, the guardian angel of Israel.[16]

It appears to me that the reference is to the seventy elders (the prototype of "the council of the Jews" and the Great Sanhedrin that followed it), who were the leaders of the nation until Hasmonean times, and whom the author of the "Historical Section" sees as existing even from the time of the destruction of the kingdom of Samaria. The evidence is that farther on (90:5) the author speaks of *twenty-three* shepherds—the number of the members of a Little Sanhedrin, which also, in the opinion of the author, existed before Hasmonean times.[17]

[14] Well known is the homily on "Meroz" in the Song of Deborah, Judges 5:23; it is interpreted as a *star* (Moed Katan 16a; Shebuoth 36a). And a cursed star is a *fallen* star; therefore the "Nephilim" [fallen ones] are compared with it.
[15] See above, Part I, pp. 229–230.
[16] See Charles, *Apocrypha and Pseudepigrapha*, II, 255. See also H. Gressmann, *Eschatologie*, 1905, pp. 165–166; Bousset-Gressmann, *Die Religion des Judentums*, 3rd ed., Tübingen, 1926, pp. 246, Note 1, and 247 (over the "seventy weeks" of Daniel are set seventy angels).
[17] The interpreters of these verses are forced to explain the number 23 as the result of the division of the number 70 by the author of the "Historical Section"

However that may be, the evil shepherds handed over the sheep to lions (Assyrians), tigers (Chaldeans-Babylonians), and wild boars (Edomites), and later to eagles (Greeks), vultures (the Diadochi following Alexander the Great), kites (the Ptolemaic Egyptians), and ravens (the Seleucid Syrians)—all of whom devoured the humble of the sheep and picked out their eyes. But there came rams (the Hasidim in the time of the Hasmoneans), upon which grew horns (the sons of Mattathias), and from among these there came forth one great horn (Judas Maccabeus or John Hyrcanus); this horn the ravens wished to cut down, but they could not.

Here (90:17) begins the description of the Day of Judgment. "The Lord of the sheep" was filled with wrath against the ravens, and also against the eagles, the vultures, and the kites. He summoned the one who had written down in a book the number of the sheep destroyed by "the twelve last shepherds" (in the opinion of most scholars, the kings from Alexander of Macedon to Antiochus Sidetes; in my opinion the high priests from Jeshua son of Jozadak to Onias III, the exact number of whom we do not know even yet). He grasped "the staff of His wrath" and smote the earth until it was cleft asunder and swallowed up all the wild beasts and birds of prey. Then He handed a great sword to the sheep, and the sheep went forth against the beasts of the field to slay them, and the beasts fled before them. A throne was set up in "the pleasant land" (Palestine), "the Lord of the sheep" sat upon it, and the "other," [18] that is, Michael, guardian angel of Israel, opened the books before Him. Then God commanded to be brought before Him the seven first "Nephilim" who had lusted after the daughters of men,[19] and He commanded to be bound the seventy shepherds who had slain more of the sheep than was permitted to them. Then judgment was executed upon the "stars" (that is, the fallen angels), who were found guilty and cast

---

into two times 23 and two times 12 (23 + 12 + 23 + 12). See G. Beer in the edition of Kautzsch, *Apocryphen und Pseudepigraphen*, 1900, II, 294, Note c; 295, Note 1; 296, Note c.

[18] We must read in Ethiopic thus: *kal'e*—"the second," "the other," instead of *koella*—"all."

[19] "Whose privy members were like those of horses"—this coarse expression is repeated a number of times in this story. But see Jer. 5:8: "They are become as well-fed horses, lusty stallions; every one neigheth after his neighbour's wife."

into "the place of condemnation": into an abyss full of flames and pillars of fire. The seventy shepherds also were judged, found guilty, and cast into "the fiery chasm"—Gehenna; and there, "to the right of that house" (the Temple, which was not far from the Valley of Hinnom), were also cast the "blinded sheep" (apostate Jews).

This is the day of the Great Judgment. After it begin the Days of the Messiah. First of all, the "old house" is torn down, and all its pillars, beams, and ornaments are carried off to a place in the south of the land; in its place "the Lord of the sheep" brings a *new house*, greater and loftier than the former one, and establishes it in place of the former; its pillars and ornaments are new, and larger than the old ones; and "the Lord of the sheep" takes up His abode within it.

The "house" in all the present narrative is Jerusalem (the Temple is the tower which is in the house); thus we have here before us "the heavenly Jerusalem" which comes in the Messianic age in place of "the earthly Jerusalem." It is already alluded to in the prophetic books (for example, Ezek. 40ff.); it is found yet more in the Pseudepigraphical books,[20] and from there the Christians took it over.[21] But the Talmud and the Midrashim also speak of this "heavenly Jerusalem"; moreover, in the Talmud "the Jerusalem of this world" and "the Jerusalem of the world to come" are set in contrast one against the other.[22]

Then, after the heavenly Jerusalem has been built,[23] all the sheep that were left bend the knee, and all the beasts of the earth and all the birds of heaven worship those sheep, making petition before them and obeying them. In other words, all the sinners of Israel, and all the Gentiles who did not oppress Israel turn about and repent. All those sheep are white. That is to say, all who are worthy for the Messianic age are righteous. And they flourish: the wool of the sheep is abundant and clean. All who were lost and scattered are reassembled (the ingathering of the exiles), together with all the beasts and birds—the converted Gentiles—in the new house (Jerusalem), and "the Lord of the sheep" rejoices over this exceedingly. Then

[20] E.g., IV Ezra 7:26; 13:36.
[21] Gal. 4:25-26; Heb. 11:10; 12:22; Rev. 21:2, 10.
[22] E.g., Taanith 5a; Baba Bathra 75b.
[23] See on this, Bousset-Gressmann, *op. cit.*, p. 285.

the sheep return the sword that had been given them to kill the beasts of the field, they lay it down before the LORD in His house, and seal it with a seal—the beating of the swords into plowshares. The Jews do not avenge themselves upon their enemies in the Age to Come. All the sheep assemble themselves in the house of the LORD (Jerusalem), which, although large and spacious, cannot hold all of them.

At this point there appears before us for the first time the figure of the Messiah. Then is born "a white bull with large horns." All the beasts of the field and all the birds of the air fear him and make petition to him all the time. Finally, "all the families" are changed, *all of them* becoming white bulls; the first among them becomes a buffalo [24] with great black horns, and "the Lord of the sheep" rejoices over it and over all the bulls (90:17-38).

The Messiah, as an individual, takes here only a minor place. He is born as are all men. He is "a white bull," that is, completely righteous, and all the Gentiles fear him and seek his favor all the time; but that is all. "All the families," that is, all the families of the earth which are worthy of the Messianic age, are also changed into white bulls; thus the Messiah is only the first among equals (*primus inter pares*). In the time of the victorious Hasmoneans, before the struggle of the Pharisees against Janneus Alexander, the nation did not need the Messiah so much. Therefore, the compass of his deeds had not yet been extended, and such numerous legends had still not been woven around him.[25] The situation changes in the times immediately pre-

---

[24] In Ethiopic the reading is *nagar*, "a word," and some think that we have here a Christian alteration in reference to the Logos. But "word" in the sense of "logos" is in Ethiopic *qal* and not *nagar*. Therefore, Beer (Kautzsch, *op. cit.*, II, 298, Note q) conjectured that in Hebrew *re'ēm* ["buffalo"] stood here, and the Greek translator copied this word in Greek letters as ρημ [rēm]; but ῥῆμα [rēma] is Greek for "word," "utterance," and therefore the Ethiopic translator used *nagar*. And Lazarus (Eleazer) Goldschmidt (*Das Buch Henoch*, Berlin, 1892, pp. 90-91) conjectures that the translator from Hebrew became confused and read MLH ["word"] instead of TLH ["lamb"]. But this is not convincing to me. How can you have a lamb "with great black horns"? This word (*taleh*) denotes a lamb that is young and weak (as "a sucking lamb," I Sam. 7:9)

[25] See Beer, *loc. cit.*, Note a, and also E. Hühn, *Die messian. Weissag.*, 1899, p. 87.

ceding Pompey's conquest, as appears in the later parts of the Book of Enoch—in the "Book of Parables," almost all of which is Messianic.

4. *The Messianic Conceptions of the "Book of Parables" (the "Messianic Book," 37-71)*

Between the earlier parts of the Book of Enoch and the "Book of Parables" there have intervened the stormy years of the separation of John Hyrcanus from the Pharisees, and of the wars of the Pharisees against Janneus Alexander. The people by and large reasoned that the Hasmoneans, who had brought them *freedom*, had not brought them *redemption*. The grievous afflictions—all the more grievous because they suffered them not from foreign hands but from the hands of a Jewish king and high priest—intensified the longings for complete redemption and for a redeemer-Messiah. And these longings begot within the "popular prophets," who were not Pharisees, but were close to the Pharisees (even if they were Essenes) because they were close to the mass of the people,[26] dreams and visions. These dreams and visions were incorporated in the Messianic expectations of the "Book of Parables," which is *an essentially Messianic document*. It is all filled with supernatural mysteries and speculations, and approximates the Messianic views of the later Midrashim and of early Christianity. In it the personal Messiah stands in the center of the Messianic age.

When the congregation of the righteous shall appear, and when "*the* Righteous One" (with the definite article, that is, the Messiah) shall appear before the "elect righteous," whose deeds are stored up with "the God of spirits" (or "the Lord of spirits"—*egzie manafest*—a regularly recurring appellative in the "Book of Parables"),[27] and

[26] Travers Herford (*Talmud and Apocrypha*, 1933, pp. 87-88, 177-178, 190-194) is right when he thinks that there were not just three or four sects among the Jews in the time of the Second Temple, and that the authors of the Pseudepigraphical books could have belonged to other sects, which are not known to us [note now the sect of the recently discovered Dead Sea Scrolls.— TRANS.]. But that the authors of works like the Book of Jubilees and similar works were close to the Pharisees in spirit there is no doubt.

[27] Cf. "the LORD, the God of the spirit of all flesh" (Num. 27:16); "who makest winds [spirits] His messengers" (Ps. 104:4); "but the LORD weigheth

when light shall be shed upon them, then shall the sinners be punished for their sins and be driven from the face of the earth. It would have been better for them if they had never been born! The rulers that possess the earth shall no longer be powerful and exalted, and shall not be deemed worthy to see the light of the presence of the LORD, which shall shine forth upon His righteous elect. Then shall the kings and the mighty (or, according to Dillmann,[28] the "mighty kings") be destroyed and handed over to the righteous and holy; they shall not even seek mercy from the Lord of Spirits, for the end of their lives shall have come (38:1-6).

The Messiah existed before the creation of the world—as in the later Baraithas of the Talmud (Derekh Erets Zuta, end of Chap. 1) and in the Midrashim.[29] "At the end of the heavens" (or, according to Dillmann, "in those days") Enoch sees "the Elect One of righteousness and of faith." [30] Righteousness shall prevail in his days (or in their days), and the righteous elect without number shall be before him forever; and his dwelling-place (or their dwelling-place) shall be under the wings of "the God of Spirits." All the elect righteous shall shine before him like the brightness of fire; their mouths shall be full of blessings and their lips shall be praising the name of "the God of Spirits," from before whom righteousness and uprightness shall not pass away (39:6-7).

This is the first "parable." In the second "parable" comes the sequel: on that day "the Elect One" will sit on the throne of glory and choose the occupations of men and their dwelling-places without number (that is, in whatever place it is suitable for each man to live). Their spirits will grow strong within them when they see the Messiah and

---

the spirits" (Prov. 16:2). *Egzie* in Ethiopic means "Lord" and "God" (the LORD), and so the Lord of Spirits and the God of Spirits are the same thing. See also II Cor. 3:18 (end), in the text of the "Apostolikon" of Marcion (see P. L. Couchoud, "La première édition de Saint Paul," *Revue de l'Histoire des Religions*, 1926, p. 261).

[28] See also J. Flemming, *Das Buch Henoch, aethiopischer Text*, Leipzig, 1902, p. 41, whose text also reads *wanagast 'azizan* without the "and."

[29] See on this in detail below, Part III, Chap. VII (to be sure, there only the *name* of Messiah preceded the creation of the world). But see farther on in this chapter.

[30] I.e. the Messiah, who is called "Mine elect" according to Isa. 42:1; but Dillmann reads "the place of the elect ones and of righteousness and of faith."

the righteous ones, who have called upon the name of the LORD: "the Elect One" will sit in the midst of the righteous. Heaven and earth will be transformed, becoming a blessing and an eternal light. The elect will dwell in the new and blessed earth, upon which sinners and evildoers will never again set foot; for the righteous will be filled with peace and dwell in the presence of the LORD. As to the wicked, judgment will have been rendered before Him to destroy them from upon the face of the earth (45:3-6).

The chapter following this (46) begins with the imagery of Daniel:

I saw there the Ancient of Days (*r'esa mawa'el*—"the head of days"), and His head was like pure wool, and with Him was another, whose countenance was like the visage of *a son of man* ("one like unto a son of man" in Daniel), and whose face was full of graciousness like one of the holy angels. And I asked one of the angels who went with me, and he showed me all the hidden things concerning the Son of Man: who he was, whence he came, and why he went with the Ancient of Days. And he answered me and said unto me: This is the Son of Man who hath righteousness, with whom dwelleth righteousness, and who revealeth all the treasures of hidden things; for the God of spirits hath chosen him, and his lot hath surpassed everything before the God of spirits in uprightness forever. This Son of Man, whom you have seen, will raise up the kings and the mighty from their seats, and the strong from their thrones. He will loosen the bands [loins] of the strong and break the teeth of sinners. He will expel kings from their thrones and their kingdoms, because they do not extol and praise (God), and do not acknowledge whence the kingdom was bestowed upon them. He will make vain the arrogance of tyrants and shame will fill them. Darkness will be their dwelling, and worms will be their bed (46:1-6).

The personality of the Messiah here stands out strongly. He is not only the Chosen One of the LORD, but he is also the "son of man" of Daniel.[31] In the "Book of Parables," in the Ethiopic text, he is given these names: (1) *walda sab'e* (46:2-4; 48:2)—the son of man [*filius hominis*]; (2) *walda eguela ema heya'u* (62:7, 9, 14; 63:11; 69:26; 70:1; 71:17—the son of the sons of man (more exactly, "the son of the offspring of the mother of the living"); (3) *walda b'esi*

---

[31] Actually, the reference both of "Mine elect" in Isaiah and of the "son of man" in Daniel is to the people Israel, which is in these books a collective, not an individual, Messiah. See above, Part 1, pp. 229-230, against Gressmann.

(69:29; 71:14)—the son of a male [*filius viri*] (in the sense of the Son of Man, to be sure); and (4) *walda b'esit*—the son of a woman. The last name occurs only once (62:5). Even though "born of a woman," the exact equivalent of *walda b'esit*, occurs in Job (14:1; 15:14; 25:4), it is nevertheless to be supposed that this is a Christian alteration of *walda b'esi* (the son of a male) [32] to make a reference to Jesus, who had a mother but not a father. The rest of the names are completely Hebraic, and derive from the "son of man" in Daniel, who took on broader interpretation in the mind of the author of the Parables. To consider *all* these chapters as a Christian interpolation is not reasonable: a Christian interpolator would have found here ample opportunity to refer to the sufferings of the crucified Christ—but there is no mention of them. These are popular Jewish notions about the personality of the Messiah, as revealed also at a later time in the Midrashim—the popular collections of legends, stories, and national hopes, both early and late.[33]

There will be judges who will execute judgment upon the stars of heaven in their pride, and upon those who raise their hands against God Most High, the inhabitants of the earth who manifest unrighteousness, whose wealth is their strength, and who serve idols made by their own hands and deny the God of Spirits. All these will be driven out from "the houses of His congregations" [34] and from among the faithful, over whom the God of Spirits keeps watch or who are watched over for His sake (46:7-8). The prayer of the righteous and "the blood of the righteous"—the blood of the martyred Pharisees who were slain in the time of the wars with Janneus Alexander [35]—will go up before the God of Spirits, who will not turn away unanswered this prayer and this blood nor delay in rendering justice to the righteous. Then the Ancient of Days will seat Himself on the

---

[32] See Lazarus Goldschmidt, *op. cit.*, p. 84.

[33] On the mythological elements in these popular conceptions, see H. Gressmann, *op. cit.*, 1905, pp. 355-365; Bousset-Gressmann, *op. cit.*, pp. 259-268. See also N. Messel, *Der Menschensohn in den Bilderreden des Henoch*, Giessen, 1922.

[34] In my opinion, from the synagogues, which were called "meeting-places of God" (Ps. 74:8).

[35] *Antiquities* 13:13:5 to 13:14:2; *Wars* 1:4:5-6.

throne of His glory and "the books of the living" [36] will be opened before Him; and all the host of heaven and His counsellors ("those who are round about Him") will be standing before Him; and the hearts of the righteous will be filled with joy, because "the number of righteousness" (that is, the number of the days designated for the vindication of righteousness) will have drawn near, the prayer of the righteous will have been heard, and the blood of the righteous will have been avenged (47:1-4). Thus, while in Chapter 45 (and also in Chapters 51, 55, 62, and 69) the judge is the Messiah, in the chapter before us (47), the LORD is the judge and not the Messiah. Likewise, in Bible and Talmud we find a similar variation in views on everything concerning the Day of Judgment. Only Christianity conceives its Messiah as sitting at the right hand of God on the Day of Judgment, so that the Day of Judgment cannot take place without Jesus.

In the sections that follow, the importance of the Messiah becomes greater and greater. The Son of Man and his *name* are named before the Ancient of Days. "Before the sun and the planets were created, before the stars in the heavens were made, his name was named before the God of Spirits" (48:2-3). Likewise in the Talmud—even in the earlier Baraithas—Messiah's *name* existed before the sun and stars: it is one of the seven things that preceded the creation of the world.[37] According to the opinion of Meir Friedmann[38] and Maurice Vernes,[39] by the "name of Messiah" is undoubtedly meant the conception and idea of the Messiah.

The Messiah will be a staff to the righteous and holy, whereon they may lean and not fall; he will be a light to the Gentiles and a hope to the broken-hearted.[40] All who dwell on earth will fall down before him to worship and bless him—and to praise the name of the

---

[36] See Ps. 69:28; "Let them be blotted out of *the book of the living*, and not be written with the righteous." See also Rosh ha-Shanah 16b (this verse in Psalms is also found in *Birkath ha-Minim* [the malediction on the heretics], in the Yerushalmi text which was found in the Genizah in Fostat).

[37] Pesahim 54a; Nedarim 39b; Targum Pseudo-Johathan, on Zech. 4:7.

[38] See his introduction to Seder Eliyahu Rabbah, Vienna, 1902, p. 114.

[39] See M. Vernes, *Histoire des idées messianiques depuis Alexandre jusqu'à l'empereur Hadrien*, Paris, 1874, pp. 268-269, 281, Note a.

[40] In accordance with Isa. 61:1.

God of Spirits (48:4-5). After all, in Judaism the Messiah does not come in place of God. For the very purpose that all who dwell on earth may praise the name of the LORD the Messiah was chosen and hidden before God "before the creation of the world and for evermore" (48:6). The wisdom of God has revealed the Messiah to the righteous and holy. For God preserves the lot of the righteous because they have hated and despised, in the name of the God of Spirits, this world so full of wrong, and all its deeds and ways. Therefore they will be saved in His name, and He is the avenger of their life. In this there is much of the views found in the Gospels, which of course were popular Jewish views of an earlier time.

In those days, the countenances of the kings of the earth and of the tyrants who rule the land will be downcast because of the deeds of their hands; for they will not save themselves in the day of anguish and affliction. God will give them over into the hands of His elect ones; as straw in the fire so will they burn before the face of the righteous, and as lead in water will they sink before the face of the holy, and no trace of them will be found. Then will peace come in the earth. They will fall and not rise again, and there will be no one to take them by the hand and raise them up, for they denied the God of Spirits and His *Anointed One* (48:7-10). In this instance the Messiah is called by his customary name: "Anointed One"—*Masîḥ* in Ethiopic (see also 52:4).

Then will come the blessed Days of the Messiah. "Wisdom" will be "as the waters cover the sea" [Isa. 11:9], the "glory" (the glory of the LORD) will never again be hidden, secret things will be revealed, unrighteousness will disappear as a shadow, and the Elect Messiah will stand before the God of Spirits, his glory being forever and ever and his might unto all generations. On him will rest the spirit of wisdom, the spirit that gives insight, the spirit of understanding and of might, and the spirit of those who have fallen asleep in righteousness—the seven characteristics of the holy spirit in Isaiah (11:2), with mysterious alterations. He "will judge the secret things," and none will be able to utter a lying word before him, for he was chosen before the God of Spirits according to His good pleasure (49:1-4).

Drastic changes will then take place in *nature:* the light of (the seven) days (of Creation) will shine upon the holy and elect ones, and glory and honor will surround them. Affliction and misery will come upon sinners; but they have a way out: *repentance*. Only those who do not repent will perish (50:1-4). But as to the kings and tyrants who in those days will become conscious of all their depravity and all their mistaken reliance upon "unrighteous gain," and will seek to serve the LORD and to make supplication before "the angels of punishment"—their repentance will avail them nothing: their faces will be filled with darkness and shame before the Son of Man, they will be driven from his presence, and the sword will pursue them (63, the whole chapter). Then the earth will bring to life the shades,[41] and Sheol will give back those it held. The Messiah will choose from among those who have risen the righteous and holy, he will sit upon his throne (or "upon *the* throne," that is, the throne of God), and will reveal all the secrets of wisdom. From excess of joy "the mountains will skip like rams, and the hills like young sheep satisfied with milk," [42] and all will become angels. The faces of all will be lighted up with joy, and the earth will also rejoice, because the righteous will dwell in it and the elect will walk upon it (51:1-5).

Here *the resurrection of the dead* is mentioned. But it is not clear whether the resurrection will be general and the wicked also will rise, but without enjoying all the benefits that the righteous will enjoy, or whether the wicked will not rise at all, since it is only said that the "righteous" and "elect" will walk and dwell on the earth. Apparently, however, the first alternative is the stronger, since the righteous and holy will be chosen from among those who rise.

In any case, the righteous become like ministering angels. The distinction between heaven and earth, between angels and men, disappears: saints and angels dwell together. The Messiah dwells in the midst of the righteous as one of them. They depend upon him (lean upon his righteousness), they bask in his light, they are close to him. All of them shine like the brightness of the firmament, their appearance is like lambent fire, and their mouths are full of song and praise

---

[41] Isa. 26:19.
[42] In accordance with Ps. 114:4, 6, with the addition of "satisfied with milk."

of the God of Spirits. Iron and copper, gold and silver, tin and lead, will melt like wax before the Messiah. There will be no need of all these things which civilization uses for moral corruption. Silver and gold will save no one. "There shall be no iron for war, and no material for a coat of mail; metal shall be of no value, tin shall be of no service or esteem and lead shall not be desired. All these things shall perish and be destroyed from the face of the earth, when the Elect One (Messiah) shall appear before the face of the God of Spirits" (52:6–9).

After the kings and tyrants are destroyed, the Righteous and Elect One (the Messiah) will cause to appear "the house of his congregation"—undoubtedly the synagogues of the Pharisees, which had been closed in the time of Janneus Alexander (note that Judah ben Tabbai, chief of the Pharisees, was forced, according to the Jerusalem Talmud, Hagigah 2:2, to flee to Alexandria,[43] and undoubtedly their synagogues were also molested); and Enoch promises that the congregation of worshipers in the places of assembly will no more be disturbed (53:6). Of course, the Baraithas on "the footsteps of the Messiah" also speak of "the place of assembly."[44]

The Messiah will judge Azazel and all his host. For they are the ones who enticed men to make life beautiful and luxurious, and by this means to turn aside from following the Torah and to corrupt morals. Michael, Gabriel, Raphael, and Phanuel (in place of "Uriel" of the Midrashic literature), the four "angels of the Presence," will seize them on the Day of Judgment, bind them with chains, cast them into a blazing furnace, the abyss of complete destruction, and cover their jaws with sharp stones, because they became subject to Satan and led astray those who dwell on the earth (54:5–6; 55:4). Also, those who went astray after the "Nephilim," like the "Nephilim" themselves, will be bound with chains of iron and lead [bronze?], and smitten with scourges, by the "angels of punishment," and finally will be cast into Gehenna (56:1–4).

---

[43] See on this J. Klausner, *Yeshu ha-Notsri* [Jesus of Nazareth], 5th ed. (1945), pp. 15–18 [Eng. ed., p. 25]; S. Stourdzè, *REJ*, LXXXII, 133–156.

[44] Sotah 49*b*; Sanhedrin 97*a*, and elsewhere.

But before the perfect rest and peace of the Messianic age can come, Israel must experience the very severe trouble of "the birth pangs of Messiah." The "Nephilim"-angels, from whom comes all evil, and wars in particular, will stir up the kings of the Persians [Charles reads "Parthians"] and Medes, and these "will arise like lions from their lairs, and like hungry wolves among flocks of sheep"; they will fall upon "the land of His elect ones," that is, Palestine, and will make the land "a threshing-floor and a highway" before them, that is, they will tread upon and march over everything. But "the city of my righteous ones," that is, Jerusalem, will be a hindrance to their horses—and the sword of each one will be against his fellow. Their slain will be numberless, and Sheol will open its mouth and swallow them (56:5-8). This is the same Day of Judgment of these peoples as was seen by Deutero-Zechariah (Chaps. 12 and 14) and Ezekiel (Chaps. 38-39). The Medes and Parthians are Gog and Magog for the author of the Parables, since "Magog" occurs in the Bible (Gen. 10:2; I Chron. 1:5) by the side of "Madai." In my opinion, the reference is to the Armenians, who threatened Judah in the time of Queen Salome Alexandra,[45] since in the time of the author the territory of Magog was thought to be on the north of the Sea of Me'at (or Mi'ot)—the Maeotis of the ancients, the Sea of Azov in our time (the Book of Jubilees 9:8);[46] thus Magog dwelt, in the opinion of the ancients, in the midst of the Armenians at that time.

After the war against Gog and Magog, there will be *the ingathering of exiles*—exactly as in the Talmud and the Midrashim. Enoch sees a great number of wagons, "and men riding thereon, and coming on the winds from the east, and from the west to the north [Charles reads "south"] (the south is lacking here, perhaps by chance, or perhaps because "from the east and from the west" balance one another, while "north" is not balanced here with "the south": the exiles come *to* the south and not *from* the south). The noise of the wagons will be heard, and when "the holy ones from heaven" (the angels)

---

[45] *Antiquities* 13:15:4, Secs. 419-421.
[46] See the notes of Dillmann to his translation of the Book of Jubilees (from which Dr. S. Rubin translated into Hebrew), 8:12-13, and 9:8; Abraham Epstein, *Eldad ha-Dani*, Presburg, 1891, Introduction, pp. xxix-xxxi.

perceive it, the pillars of the earth will be moved from their place. Then all those journeying will fall down before the God of Spirits and worship Him (57:1–3). Thus ends the second "Parable."

The third "Parable" (58–69) also begins with the day of the Great Judgment. Thereafter, the elect will live forever and the days of the holy will be without number. They will obtain righteousness and peace from the God of Spirits, who is also the Eternal God. There will come an end of darkness, "the secrets of righteousness" will be no more, and the light of the sun will illumine the earth (58:2–6). The meaning, of course, is this: Now, the good and upright in the nation are struggling with the problem: "He is wicked and prospers, he is righteous and suffers." This is a divine mystery, one of "the secrets of righteousness." Then, when there will be no more sin and wrong in the world, and the righteous along with the wicked will reap the fruit of their deeds on the Day of Judgment and afterward —then will come the end of this question of justice, the answer to which in our time is, "The ways of the LORD are hidden."

After a description (in Chap. 59) of the function of the lightning and thunder, there comes in the next chapter (60) a description of the judgment by means of *the Flood*. First, Enoch (or Noah, who is really the interlocutor in the third Parable) existed before the Flood and he prophesies it; second, a verse, "The LORD sat enthroned at the flood; yea, the LORD sitteth as King forever" (Ps. 29:10), is interpreted to mean that there will also be a flood *in the final days*. And of course, in the description of the flood in the time of Noah, we find Leviathan and the wild ox (Behemoth), who in the Messianic portrayals of the Talmud and Midrashim serve as a reward [food] for the righteous in the Age to Come. According to the "Book of Parables" (60:7–10), Leviathan is the female and Behemoth (the wild ox) is the male. They will be separated from each other. Leviathan will "dwell in the abysses of the sea over the fountains of the waters," while Behemoth will fill with his breast (his body?) "a waste wilderness" named Dendain,[47] on the east of the Garden of Eden, where the elect and righteous dwell. What this place is we do not

---

[47] Other readings are Dunedain, Dunaudain, Doyedain, Yendain, Dedain (see Flemming, *op. cit.*, p. 64).

know. The name is corrupt beyond recognition.[48] But the fact is clear that the two strange creatures are prepared for the benefit of the righteous (60:24).[49] Leviathan and Behemoth are likewise mentioned in IV Ezra (6:49–53). Also there it is said that they were separated from one another; but there Leviathan was given a portion of the dry land, and Behemoth a portion of the moist places. On the contrary, the Syriac Apocalypse of Baruch (29:4) knows that in the final days Leviathan will come from the sea and Behemoth from the dry land (as in Talmud and Midrash), and then they will be food for all who survive "the birth pangs of Messiah." This agrees exactly with the Talmudic legends,[50] and almost exactly with the words of the "Book of Parables."

Chapters 61–71 add new features to the spiritual aspect of the Messiah and of the relation of the righteous to him. All the heavenly powers praise the "Elect One" by command from on high. The God of Spirits seats him on "the throne of glory" (apparently at His right hand), and he judges all the deeds of the holy "above in the heavens," and weighs them in the balance (61:7–8). Then God also commands the mighty kings and the exalted rulers to acknowledge the Elect One, and they see him sitting on the throne of His glory, with the spirit of righteousness poured out upon him, while with the breath of his lips he slays the wicked,[51] and no lying word comes upon his lips. Then will pangs like the pangs of a woman in travail seize the mighty: they will be dismayed before "the Son of Man,"[52] they will fall down before him with their faces to the ground, they will praise and glorify and exalt him above all rulers, and seek mercy at his hands. For the Son of Man was hidden and the Most High preserved him by His might, and revealed him to the elect, that they might stand before him on that day. Then God will demand of the powerful that they remove themselves from the presence of the Messiah, and

---

[48] Perhaps it is corrupted from "the land of Nod" (Gen. 4:16), which is also "on the east of Eden" (same verse), and in the Septuagint is called "Naid"; or perhaps it is "Dudael" (see above, p. 279).
[49] See Beer's note on this verse (Kautzsch, *op. cit.*, II, 270, Note f).
[50] Baba Bathra 74*b* and 75*a*.
[51] In accordance with Isa. 11:2–4.
[52] Or "the son of a woman" (see above, p. 292).

their countenances will be abashed and darkness will cover them. "The angels of punishment," which Talmud and Midrash mention frequently,[53] will execute vengeance on them because they oppressed the children of the God of Spirits (the children of Israel) and His elect ones; the righteous will see and rejoice, how the wrath of the LORD rests upon them and His sword is drunk with their blood.

The righteous and elect will be saved on that day, and never again will they see the face of the sinners and unrighteous. The God of Spirits "will abide over them" [or "sit by them"],[54] "and with the Son of Man shall they eat and lie down and rise up forever and ever." They will shake off the dust and put on their glorious garments, which will be "the garments of life" from the God of Spirits; their garments will not wear out, as it was with the wanderers in the wilderness,[55] and their glory will not pass away from before the God of Spirits (62:1–16; 63:1, 11). The Days of the Messiah are prolonged forever, and eternal life ("the garments of life") is appointed for the righteous in the company of the Messiah and in proximity to divinity itself ("basking in the brightness of the Shekhinah").

And after the Son of Man has judged from the throne of his glory the sinners and the misleaders (those who led the world astray by means of arts and crafts and deceitful books), he will bind them with chains and imprison them in the place of destruction, and all *their works will be annihilated from the face of the earth*—there will no longer be in the world anything that causes hurt. For all evil will pass away from the presence of the Son of Man, and his word will be strong (enduring) before the God of Spirits (69:26–29).

Thus ends the third "Parable" and thus ends the "Book of Parables." Chapters 70–71 are an addition. In the latter chapter (71:14, 17) Enoch himself becomes the embodiment of the Messiah (he is the "son of a male"), who is born in righteousness, and righteousness abides with him, and the righteousness of the Ancient of Days forsakes him not. And finally the Days of the Messiah pass over into "the Days of the World to Come," in which there will be peace for the

[53] E.g., Shabb. 55a; Kidd. 72a; Ex. R., Par. 9.
[54] Of Abraham, when he ministers to *the angels*, it is written, "and he stood by [or "over"] them" (Gen. 18:8).
[55] Deut. 8:4 and 29:4.

righteous, and they will walk in the upright way of the Messiah forever and ever.

These are all the Messianic expectations in the Book of Enoch in all its parts both early and late. All the expectations of Holy Scripture here have been expanded and have become more detailed and more deeply felt; sometimes they are worldly and materialistic, sometimes sublime and spiritual. The Pseudepigraphical books that follow, likewise the Talmud and Midrash, altered considerably the arrangement and the characteristics of the expectations, but they did not add much to what is in this unique book, which is perhaps the Messianic book par excellence of Judaism in the period of the Second Temple.

CHAPTER II

The Book of Jubilees

(C. 100–90 B.C.E.)

THIS BOOK, which was called *Sepher-ha-Yobeloth* [Book of the Forty-nine-Year Periods] [1]—not *Sepher-ha-Yobelim*—and also went by the name of Λεπτὴ Γένεσις (Little Genesis), is actually a Midrash-Aggadah. It contains homiletical and legendary expositions on all chapters of the Pentateuch from Genesis 1 to Exodus 13 (the institution of Passover). But it is not only a Midrash-Aggadah, it is also a Midrash-Halakhah, like the Tannaitic Midrashim Siphra, Siphre, and Mekhilta. This is *the most ancient Midrash that we have*. It was written in the time of Janneus Alexander (or even in the time of John Hyrcanus), and at the latest in the time of Queen Salome-Alexandra (between 135 and 67 B.C.E.), in Palestine and in the Hebrew language (from which it was translated into Greek, and from that language into Ethiopic, and also into Latin).[2] But only the Ethiopic translation

---

[1] So it is called in the commentary on Chronicles attributed to a pupil of R. Saadia Gaon, which was published by Raphael Kirchheim (Frankfort on the Main, 1874, p. 36): "The Book of *Yobeloth*, which al-Fayyumi, Rav Saadia Gaon, brought from the books of the Yeshivah."

[2] On all this, see in detail J. Klausner, *History of the Second Temple* [in Heb.], III, 202–208. A. Büchler has published a part of a large work on the Book of Jubilees, in which he attempted to prove that the Book of Jubilees was written in Greek on the basis of the Greek translation of the Pentateuch ("Studies in the Book of Jubilees," *REJ*, LXXXII [1926], 253–274). In spite of all his arguments, which seem as though they have no refutation, it is enough to translate *one* chapter of the Book of Jubilees from Ethiopic into Hebrew to be convinced that this is an originally Hebrew and Palestinian book. (A fragment of this book in Hebrew was recently discovered among the Dead Sea Scrolls.) On the other hand, it is also difficult to accept the opinion of S. Zeitlin

has been completely preserved; from the Latin translation we have only about a third.

The Book of Jubilees is *in general* a Pharisaic work. But it comes from that time when the teaching of the Pharisees had not yet crystallized and become completely separate from the teaching of the Sadducees; therefore it contains rules contrary to the rules and opinions of the Pharisees. For example, the Feast of Weeks (Pentecost) is to be celebrated "in the middle" of the third month (Book of Jubilees 15:1; 16:13; 44:4-5), like all three festivals of pilgrimage;[3] sexual intercourse on the Sabbath is forbidden (50:8)—something also forbidden by Anan, the founder of Karaism on the basis of the passage "in plowing time and in harvest thou shalt rest" [Ex. 34:21],[4] it being well known that the Karaites accepted many ideas from ancient Jewish sects opposed to the Pharisees; the author believed in the survival of the soul, but without bodily resurrection (23:31), and so on.

That the book was written after John Hyrcanus had subjugated the Samaritans (the Cuthites) and the Edomites and had imposed harsh terms upon them, or after the bitter battles which Janneus Alexander fought with the Samaritans—this much is clear from the verse, "And the sons of Edom have not got quit of the yoke of servitude which the twelve sons of Jacob had imposed on them *until this day*" (38:14). Likewise from the verse, "And on the day when the sons of Jacob slew Shechem a writing was recorded in their favour in heaven that

(*JQR*, XXX [1939], 1-13), to which W. F. Albright agrees (*From the Stone Age to Christianity*, 1946, pp. 266-267); it is difficult to suppose that the Book of Jubilees antedates Ecclesiastes, Ben-Sira, and Daniel. The verse quoted below: "And the sons of Edom have not got quit of the yoke of servitude which the twelve sons of Jacob had imposed on them *until this day*" (Book of Jubilees 38:14), is weighted against all the arguments of Zeitlin.

[3] The Falashas celebrate the Feast of Weeks (Pentecost) on the 12th day of Sivan, since they count the seven weeks not from the second day of Passover, according to the opinion of the Pharisees, and as we, the rest of the Jews, are accustomed to do to this day, and not from "the morrow after the Sabbath," according to the opinion of the Sadducees, and as the Karaites are accustomed to do, but from the last day of the Feast of Passover (see J. Faitlovitch, *Quer durch Abessinien*, Berlin, 1910, p. 70, note).

[4] See Ibn Ezra in his commentary on the Pentateuch, Ex. 34:21: "Anan, may his name be blotted out like a cloud, said that this refers to lying with a woman." Perhaps the reference is to first intercourse, which was also forbidden in the Talmud "because of making a wound" (Kethubboth, 3*b* and 4*b* end).

they had executed righteousness and uprightness and vengeance on the sinners, and it was written for them as a blessing" (30:23; so also 30:17). This dating is also demonstrated by these harsh words of vengeance against *the Egyptians:*

... even as the people of Egypt had cast their (the Israelites') children into the river, He (God) took vengeance on 1,000,000 of them; and one thousand strong and energetic men were destroyed on account of one suckling of the children of thy people which they had thrown into the river (48:14).

Now it is well known that at the beginning of his reign, Janneus Alexander fought a long and bitter war with Ptolemy Lathyrus, son of Cleopatra, queen of Egypt; and in a battle by the Jordan the Egyptians defeated the forces of Janneus, pursued them, and slew them until "their weapons of iron were blunted, and their hands quite tired with the slaughter."[5]

Because the traditional law (Halakhah), the reckoning of the years (according to the number of jubilee-periods [forty-nine-year periods] that passed after the creation of the world—hence the name of the book), and the legends connected with the establishment of legal requirements and ordinances are the main interest in the Book of Jubilees, it is not much concerned with the Messianic idea. This is the first reason. The second reason is the victories of the Hasmonean dynasty, which reached their peak in the time of Janneus Alexander. The hopes for a distant future were in part thrust away because of the success of the present; the King-Messiah *from the house of David* was in part thrust away because of the kings of the Hasmonean dynasty *from the house of Levi.* Documents contemporary with the Book of Jubilees, the Testaments of the Twelve Tribes [Patriarchs] (see the next chapter) and the "Book of the Damascus Covenant" (as M. Z. Segal called the "Zadokite Work," fragments of which were found by S. Schechter in the Genizah), which mentions the Book of Jubilees and the Testaments of the Twelve Tribes,[6]—these

---

[5] *Antiquities* 13:12:4–5. On the general contents of the Book of Jubilees, see also R. T. Herford, *Talmud and Apocrypha*, 1933, pp. 223–231.

[6] See "The Book of the Covenant of Damascus" [Heb.] by M. Z. Segal, *Ha-Shiloah*, XXVI, 390–406, 483–506.

documents teach that the Messiah will come not from the house of David, but *from the house of Levi*. The Book of Jubilees does not mention the personality of the Messiah at all; either because the redeemer is the LORD Himself, as in many passages of Scripture; or because it is not proper to speak about the King-Messiah of the Age to Come while there exists in the present an anointed and victorious king and priest of the house of Levi—of the Hasmonean dynasty. The author of the Book of Jubilees sees "princes and judges and chiefs" coming forth from *Levi;* but *Judah* will also be "a prince . . . over the sons of Jacob." [7]

Yet there are Messianic ideas in the Book of Jubilees, although in restricted measure, as in the Apocryphal books. The great vision of Moses in the very first chapter of the Book of Jubilees is based entirely on the Messianic chain which we saw in the Scriptures, its four links being: sin—punishment—repentance—redemption. First of all comes the *sin:* the children of Israel will turn away from the covenant which the LORD made with them at Mount Sinai, they will serve other gods, they will profane the Sabbaths and the festivals, they will slay the prophets, the "witnesses" for God, and they will persecute the keepers of the Law. Then will come the *punishment:* God will deliver them into the hands of the Gentiles, who will have dominion over them and despoil them, even driving them out from their land and scattering them among the nations. Then will come the *repentance:* the children of Israel will return unto the LORD, turning to him from all the lands of the Gentiles with all their hearts and with all their souls and with all their strength. Only then will come the *redemption:* God will be found by them, He will not despise or abhor them, He will circumcise the foreskin of their hearts and will create in them clean hearts. Then it will be known to all (to "every angel and every spirit") that He is their Father and they His children, and they will be called "children of the living God." Then the LORD will change them into "a shoot of righteousness" (Jer. 33:15), and they will be a blessing and not a curse, a head and not a tail. God will build His sanctuary in their midst

---

[7] See the blessing of Jacob *upon Levi and Judah jointly* (Book of Jubilees 31:13-20; see also 30:18-19; 32:9, etc.).

and dwell among them, He will be to them a God, and they will be to Him a people in truth and righteousness. God will be revealed to the eyes of all, and all will know that He is the God of Israel, the Father of all the children of Jacob, and King on Mount Zion forever and ever. And Zion and Jerusalem will be holy. A *new world* ("new creation") [8] will be made, heaven and earth and all their creatures will be renewed, likewise the host of heaven and all the creatures of earth; and the sanctuary of the LORD (the heavenly sanctuary?) will be manifested in Jerusalem on Mount Zion, and all the events [Charles reads "luminaries"] will be renewed for healing, for peace, and for blessing on all the elect of Israel (the righteous) all the time of heaven on earth (1:8-18, 22, 26, 28-29).

Chapter 23 in particular is completely Messianic. And here also we have the Messianic chain with its four elements. After it is related in this chapter that after *the Flood* the years of the lives of men began to be shortened and men began to grow old before their time because of the wickedness of their ways and of manifold tribulations following upon evil deeds, then it is said that "all the generations which will arise from this time until *the day of the Great Judgment* will grow old quickly before they complete two jubilees"; and when they grow old, their knowledge will also vanish away. And if a man then lives a jubilee and a half (seventy-five years), they will say regarding him that his days were long; and the greater part of his days are pain and sorrow and tribulation, and there is no peace! [9] For upon an evil generation, which transgresses on the earth, whose works are uncleanness and fornication and pollution and abomination, will come calamity on calamity, wound on wound, tribulation on tribulation, evil tidings on evil tidings, illness on illness, and all kinds of punish-

---

[8] Cf. Num. 16:30 with Isa. 65:17 and 66:22.

[9] This verse (23:13) is after the manner of the Biblical passage, "The days of our years are threescore years and ten, or even by reason of strength fourscore years; yet is their pride but travail and vanity" (Ps. 90:10). In place of "their pride" the author of the Book of Jubilees read "the greater part of them" as in the Septuagint (τὸ πλεῖον αὐτῶν) and likewise in the Vulgate and the Syriac versions. So three verses later in the Book of Jubilees it is said, ". . . the days of our life, if a man hath lived many, are threescore years and ten, and, if he is strong, fourscore years, *and all of them evil*" (23:15).

ments at once: disease, pain in the belly (intestinal illness), frost, hail, snow, fever, ice, torpor, blight, death, captivity, and every misery and distress. In that generation sons will curse their fathers and their elders because of sin and unrighteousness, because of the words of their mouths, because of the great wickednesses which they perpetrate, and because they forsake the covenant which the LORD made between Himself and them, that they should observe and keep *all His commandments, all His ordinances, and all His laws, without turning aside either to the right or to the left*. For all of them have done evil, every mouth speaks iniquity, all their works are an uncleanness and an abomination, and all their ways are pollution, uncleanness, and destruction (23:11-17).

Following upon this great *sinfulness* will come severe *punishment*: the earth will be destroyed, there will be no "seed of the vine" and no oil, also beasts, cattle, birds, and all the fish of the sea will perish on account of the children of men and together with them. Men will strive with one another, the young with the old and the old with the young, the poor with the rich, the lowly with the great, and the beggar with the prince—on account of the Law and the covenant. For they have forgotten commandment, covenant, feast, new moon, Sabbath, jubilee, and every ordinance. And men will stand with bows and swords and war to turn them back into *the right way;* [10] *but* they will not turn back until much blood has been shed on the earth (23:18-20).

Repentance comes only as a result of the punishment. But even after the first punishment, most of the transgressors will not repent: after all that the first Hasmoneans had done, there arose new violators of the covenant—the Sadducees, or more exactly, the "antinomians." The people must have a second punishment, more severe than the first. For those who have been delivered will not turn from their wickedness to the way of truth, but all of them will be eager for deceit and wealth,[11] that they may take all that is their neighbors'

[10] An echo from the time of the sons of Mattathias, who used physical force on the Hellenizers.

[11] Cf. "As for the trafficker, the balances of *deceit* are in his hand, he loveth to oppress; and Ephraim said: Surely I am become rich, I have found me *wealth*" (Hos. 12:8-9).

and make for themselves a great name (or, according to the Latin version, "name the great name"—of God), but not in righteousness and in fidelity; and they will defile the holy of holies with their uncleanness and their corruption.

But *a great punishment* will come forth from the LORD upon the deeds of this generation, and He will give them over to the sword and to judgment and to captivity, and to be plundered and devoured. God will rouse up against them the sinners of the Gentiles, who have neither mercy nor compassion, and who respect neither old nor young, for they are more wicked and strong to do evil than all the children of men. They will use violence against Israel and transgression against Jacob; much blood will be shed upon the earth, and there will be none to gather (those fallen in battle) and none to bury. In those days they will cry aloud and implore to be saved from the hands of the Gentile sinners—but none will be saved (or "there shall be none to deliver" [Isa. 5:29]). The heads of the children will be white with gray hair, and a child of three weeks will appear old like a man of a hundred years; and their appearance will be ruined by tribulation and misery (23:21–25).

Only after this fearful punishment will come *complete repentance*, followed by the *redemption* and its blessings:

> And in those days the children will begin
> to seek the laws and the commandments,
> *and to return to the path of righteousness.*
> Then the days will begin to grow many
> and increase among those children of men
> from generation to generation and from day to day,
> till their days approach a thousand years,
> and their years are greater than (formerly) their days.
> And there will be no old man,
> nor one whose days are fulfilled,
> but all of them will be children and youths.[12]
> They will spend all their days in peace and joy,
> and live without Satan and without a destroyer,
> for all their days will be days of blessing and safety.
> At that time the LORD will heal His servants,
> and they will rise up and see true peace,

[12] Everlasting youth.

and drive out their adversaries.
And the righteous will see and be thankful,
and rejoice greatly forever and ever,
and see upon their enemies all their judgments and curses.
Their bones will rest in the earth,
and their spirits will rejoice exceedingly.[13]
And they will know that it is the LORD
who executes judgment and shows mercy
to hundreds and to thousands and to all who love Him (23:26-31).

These are the Messianic ideas in the Book of Jubilees. The colors here are pale and thin in comparison with what we find in the Book of Enoch. This is explained, in my opinion, by the fact that this book came forth from the circle of *the early Pharisees* (preceding the Tannaim), who, even before all their doctrines diverged from those of the Sadducees, considered in the last analysis *the Halakhah* [14] as the great essential; and they were careful not to emphasize *the Aggadah* too much, lest the people should on the one hand become immersed in mysteries and delusions and try to force the coming of the Messiah, and lest they should on the other hand neglect the ceremonial laws. But the Book of Enoch came forth largely from the circle of *the early Essenes,* who, even before they separated completely from the Pharisees, already had an inclination toward "the secrets of the Law"; and Messianic ideas are an important part of these "secrets," being the mystery of the future which is "shut up and sealed" (Dan. 8:26; 12:4, 9). The *date* of these two books is almost the same, but the circles from which they came are different. By this difference is explained the dissimilar attitude of the two toward the Messianic idea in general and the personality of the Messiah in particular.

[13] Hence we infer the survival of the soul, but not the bodily resurrection, as in the belief of the Samaritans (see above, p. 303).

[14] This is *the early Halakhah,* the nature of which Abraham Geiger was the first to discover and explain (see A. Geiger, *The Bible and Its Translations in Their Dependence upon the Inner Development of Judaism* [Hebrew translation of *Urschrift und Übersetzungen der Bibel, etc.*], Jerusalem, 1949, pp. 113-127, and the addenda, pp. 280-289, 343-348; see especially pp. 314-315).

CHAPTER III

The Testament of the Twelve Tribes

(In Its Early Hebrew Parts—110–70 B.C.E.)

THIS BOOK, which is called in Greek "the Testaments of the Twelve *Patriarchs*," has been completely preserved in Greek, from which we have old versions in Armenian and Slavonic, and more recent translations in Latin, German, French, English, Dutch, Danish, Icelandic, and Czech. But something more important than this is that in the Genizah of Fostat (near Cairo in Egypt) was found the Testament of Naphtali in *Hebrew*. It was published by Dr. Moses Gaster.[1] Fragments of the Testament of Levi in *Aramaic* were also found. They were published by Pass-Arendzen and Cowley.

These remnants, and the legends and moralistic injunctions in them that are also found in Talmud and Midrash and in the Book of Jubilees, the frequent reminiscences of the Book of Enoch (Simeon 5; Levi 10, 14, 16; Zebulun 3; Dan 5; Naphtali 4), and especially the Hebrew figures of speech along with a thoroughly Hebraic type of play on words—all these show plainly that the book is basically from a purely Jewish (and not Nazarene) source and was originally written in Hebrew; but afterward the Christians utilized it for their needs and interpolated in it much about Jesus and his crucifixion, and about baptism and the like.[2] Its whole spirit in its Jewish parts testifies that

---

[1] Printed at the end of *Pirqe Hekhalot* (Jerusalem, 1889), and from there at the end of *Sepher ha-Qaneh*, ed. Samuel Diamant, Cracow, 1894, pp. 315–319, and later also in the *Otsar Midrashim* of J. D. Eisenstein (I, 236–238).

[2] See on this in detail, J. Klausner, "Outside Books" (*Otsar ha-Yahadut, Hoveret le-Dogma*, Warsaw, 1906), pp. 113–114; *History of the Second Temple*,

it was written in the time of the last Hasmoneans and had two authors: [3] the one was from the "first Hasidim," to whom the fundamental thing was morality and established custom and whose spirit was uneasy over the secular kingdom of the later Hasmoneans; the other was from the admirers of this kingdom with its wars and great victories. The latter is the one who stresses the view, found also in the "Book of the Covenant of Damascus" mentioned above, *that the Messiah is from the house of Levi* (Reuben 6; Levi 8 and 18; Dan 5. Compare the Book of the Covenant of Damascus 15:4; 18:7; Text B, 9:10, 29. The Damascus Covenant alludes to the testament of "Levi the son of Jacob" in 6:10, but the words quoted there are *not* in the Testament which we now have).[4] On the basis of all this, it is to be concluded that this book in its early parts (before it was interpolated by the Nazarenes) was written in the time of the kings *from the house of Levi:* that is, in the time of John Hyrcanus or Janneus Alexander, or at the latest in the time of Queen Salome-Alexandra, since the Romans are not yet mentioned in it;[5] and the passages alluding to the destruction of the Temple and of Jerusalem (Levi 15; Dan, end of 5) are only later additions, like the Christian interpolations.[6]

The essence of the "Testaments" consists in ethical injunctions: praise for good conduct and warning against bad conduct (Reuben—against impure thoughts; Simeon—against envy; Levi—in censure of pride and in praise of the priesthood; Judah—in censure of unjust

---

III, 208-213. See also K. Kohler, "The Pre-Talmudic Haggadah" (*JQR*, V, 400-414); "Testaments of the Twelve Patriarchs" (*Jew. Encycl.* XII, 113-118); Charles, *Apocrypha and Pseudepigrapha*, II, 288-290; Herford, *Talmud and Apocrypha*, pp. 233-243.

[3] Thus the opinion of Kohler in his article last mentioned. Thus also the opinion of Charles, who assigns the first author to the years 109-106, before John Hyrcanus became a Sadducee (*loc. cit.*). But it seems to me that in the time of the victorious Hasmoneans the two views were still being held confused together and it is possible that they belong to *one* man. See also the introduction to the Hebrew translation of the Testaments of the Tribes by Israel Ostersetzer, *The Outside Books* (ed. Kahana), I.1, pp. 142-150.

[4] Cf. M. Z. Segal in *Ha-Shiloah*, XXVI, 400, and his notes on the verses from the "Damascus Covenant" cited in the text and on 1:6. But the kingdom belongs also to *Judah* (Issachar 8, etc.).

[5] See the article of Kohler mentioned above (*Jew. Encycl.* XII, 114a).

[6] See Klausner, *op. cit.*, p. 113b.

gain and fornication and in praise of valor, and so on). But preceding the ethical injunctions, by way of introduction, are appropriate stories about the lives of the tribal patriarchs. Most of these stories are also found in the Book of Jubilees or in the Aggadic Midrashim. In most of the Testaments occur also prophecies about the Age to Come, in which the Patriarch about to die reveals to his sons what will happen to his descendants in "the End of Days"; and here we have *Messianic* ideas. We even find a complete "revelation" (apocalypse) in the Testament of Levi.

In the last section of the Testament of Simeon there is a Messianic oracle written in a lofty, figurative style and in the form of an ancient Hebrew poem, with "parallelism of members."

"If ye remove from you," says Simeon to his sons, "your envy and all stiff-neckedness,"

As a rose shall my bones flourish in Israel,
And as a lily my flesh in Jacob,
And my odor shall be as the odor of Lebanon;
And (offspring) shall be multiplied from me forever
   like the holy cedars,[7]
And their branches shall stretch afar off.

Then shall perish the seed of Canaan,
And a remnant shall not be unto Amalek;
All the Cappadocians shall perish,
And all the Hittites shall be destroyed.
Then shall fail the land of Ham,[8]
And every nation [9] shall utterly perish.

Then shall all the earth rest from trouble,
And all the world under heaven from war.
Then shall Shem be glorified,
For the great LORD God of Israel shall appear on earth.[10]

---

[7] Cf. "R. Jose said: I cohabited five times and planted five *cedars* in Israel" (Shabb. 118b). Charles translates thus: "And as cedars shall holy ones be multiplied from me forever" (*op. cit.*, II, 302).

[8] Egypt.

[9] Charles (*op. cit.*, II, 303) translates, "And all the people."

[10] Charles (*ibid.*) restores the text and translates: "Then the Mighty One of Israel shall glorify Shem, for the Lord God shall appear on earth, and Himself save men." In this version we have before us a Christian addition.

Then shall all the spirits of deceit be given to be trodden under foot.
And men shall rule over wicked spirits.
Then shall I arise [11] in joy,
And will bless the Most High for His marvellous works (Simeon 6).

In the Testament of Levi we find a certain parallel to "the week [seven-year period] at the end of which the son of David will come." [12] The author of the Testament of Levi also enumerates seven weeks (with him also "weeks" are seven-year periods, but he sometimes confuses them with jubilees). By the first four weeks are indicated the events that occurred from the time of Aaron the Priest until the Hasmoneans. By the seventh high priest "shall be such pollution as I cannot express before men (in other texts, "before God or men"), for they shall know it who do these things; therefore shall they be taken captive and become a prey, and their land and their substance shall be destroyed" (Levi 17:7–9). Here are indicated, no doubt, the evil deeds of Janneus Alexander, which the author would have feared to publish during the lifetime of Janneus or in the time of his wife and his sons, who ruled after him; or there is indicated here the slander that was directed at John Hyrcanus to the effect that "his mother had been taken captive in Modi'im." [13] In the mention of captivity, plunder, and loss of land and possessions there is an allusion to the civil war and its consequences. Then the author adds: "And in the fifth week they shall return to their desolate country, and shall renew the house of the LORD. And in the seventh week shall become priests those who are idolators, contentious, lovers of money, proud, lawless, lascivious, abusers of children and beasts" (Levi 17:10–11).

After *punishment* has come from the LORD upon all these, "then shall the LORD raise up to the priestly office a new priest, to whom all the words of God shall be revealed; and he shall execute a righteous judgment upon the earth for a multitude of days" (here follow Christian additions).

> He shall shine forth as the sun on the earth,
> And shall remove all darkness from it,

---

[11] I.e., Simeon shall rise from the dead.
[12] Levi 17—Sanhedrin 97a; Derekh Erets Zuta, beginning of Chap. 10; Song of Songs R., on the verse "The fig-tree" [2:13]; Pesikta Rabbathi, Chap. 15.
[13] Kiddushin 66a; Antiquities 13:10:5.

> And there shall be peace in all the earth.
> The heavens shall exult in his days,
> And the earth shall be glad,
> And the peoples shall rejoice;
> And the knowledge of the LORD shall be poured forth upon the earth, as the water of the seas.
> Also the angels of the presence of the LORD shall be glad in him.
> The heavens shall be opened,
> And from the temple of glory shall come upon him sanctification (Levi 18:2-6).

Then comes a Nazarene allusion to the voice from heaven which Jesus heard at the time of his baptism by John. After this allusion come obvious references to the water of baptism; and on to the end of Chapter 18 continues the Christian interpolation of this Jewish oracle, which can still be recognized by the Hebrew expressions "tree of life" and "clothe themselves with joy." [14]

Messianic ideas are more numerous in the Testament of Judah, especially in the text of the Armenian version. In Chapters 21-24 there are first set forth the two crowns: the crown of the priesthood given to Levi and the crown of the kingship given to Judah. Light and darkness wait upon Judah in mixed fashion: good and bad rulers. There will be rulers from Judah who will swallow men like fishes; who will enslave the sons and daughters of freemen; who will plunder houses, fields, flocks, and money. And there will come forth from him "false prophets like tempests," who will persecute all the righteous. There will be divisions and controversies in Israel, which will bring about continual wars; and finally the kingdom of Judah will be destroyed by foreign peoples—"until the salvation of Israel shall come, until the appearing of the God of righteousness, that Jacob *and all the Gentiles* may rest in peace. And He Himself shall guard the might of my [15] kingdom forever, for the LORD swore to me an

---

[14] The interpolation is less obvious in the Greek text, on which is based the translation of Charles (*op. cit.*, II, 314-315). And it is hard to believe that "the voice from heaven" (Levi 18:6-7) is that heard by John Hyrcanus (Sotah 33*a*; Yer. Sotah 9:14, f. 24*b*; Tosephta, Sotah 13:5), as conjectured by Israel Ostersetzer (*op. cit.*, I.1, pp. 144-169).

[15] So says Judah.

oath that He would not cut off the kingdom from my seed ever in all time to come" [21 and 22].

In Chapter 23, which comes after this, are revealed the many fearful *sins* to be committed by the descendants of Judah: they will serve other gods and follow the practices of sorcery, witchcraft, and necromancy; their daughters will become dancing girls and actresses (or harlots), and they "shall mingle in the abominations of the Gentiles." For this will come severe punishment: famine and pestilence, death and the sword, rejoicing of their enemies over their misfortune, blighting of the eyes, the slaughter of children, the rape of wives, the plundering of possessions, the laying waste of the land, and enslavement among the Gentiles.[16] Then will come *the repentance*. The children of Judah will repent of their iniquities, they will return to God with perfect heart, and fulfill all the commandments. After the repentance will come *the redemption:* God will visit them with mercy and bring them back from captivity among their enemies.

Here [Chapter 24] begin shining pictures of the redemption, especially according to the text of the Armenian version: the star of peace will arise and walk in meekness among men. The heavens will be opened and will pour out blessings; the spirit of truth will be shed upon the children of Judah, and they will walk in the ways of their Father in heaven. A shoot will come forth from the stock of Judah, and the rod of righteousness will be in his hand to judge and to save all who call upon him, *including the Gentiles*. Jacob will return to life and Israel will awake [Chapter 25], and all the sons of Jacob will rise and be chiefs of their tribes. Each of the tribes will be blessed individually by another power: Judah by the Angel of the Presence, Simeon by the Angel of Glory, Reuben by the heavens, Issachar by the earth, Zebulun by the sea, Dan by the luminaries (sun, moon, and stars), Naphtali by the pleasures,[17] Gad by the supports and pillars (of the world), Asher by the olive trees; only Levi will be blessed by

---

[16] In the Greek text there is also "the burning of the temple of God"—which is lacking in the Armenian text; hence this is merely a later addition.

[17] Apparently the translation should be "by the [divine] favor" on the basis of the Biblical verse "O Naphtali, satisfied with *favor*" (Deut. 33:23). But according to Charles (*op. cit.*, II, 324), the translation should be "the *Garden of Eden*" instead of "the pleasures" (*'eden* in Hebrew).

the LORD Himself.[18] All the tribes will become one people, and all will have one language—*the Hebrew language*.[19] The spirit of deceit (the Greek text adds "of Beliar") will not be in them any more, for all the spirits of uncleanness will be cast into the fire of Gehenna ("for an everlasting judgment"). All who died in grief will arise, and all those who suffered martyrdom will awake to everlasting life. The hungry will be satisfied, the poor will be made rich, and the weak will become strong.[20] And "the harts of Jacob shall run in joyfulness, and the eagles of Israel shall fly in gladness; but the ungodly shall lament and the sinners shall weep, and all the peoples shall glorify the LORD forever."

These are the Messianic conceptions of the Testaments of the Twelve Tribes. Their author (or authors) had a connexion with the Hasmoneans, with the rulers from the house of Levi; therefore he no longer has detailed descriptions of the *personality* of the Messiah, and therefore neither does he enlarge upon the marvels of the Messianic *age*. But there is in the "Testaments" a certain noble spirituality which lifts their meager Messianic expectations to a great ethical height. There is also in them a certain solemnity which refreshes the spirit and restores the soul oppressed by grief for the nation and despair of the world (*Weltschmerz*). And this is their importance for humanity and this their special value for Israel.

[18] In the text of the Greek version there are differences in who or what does the blessing: Simeon is blessed by the powers of glory, Joseph (lacking in the Armenian text) by the mountains, Benjamin (also omitted in the Armenian) by the Tabernacle (the "tent of meeting," the prototype of the Temple, which was in the territory of Benjamin), Dan by the stars, and Gad by the sun. The rest agree in the two versions.

[19] See Charles, *op. cit.*, II, 324, Note 3. The Testaments of the Twelve Tribes is the only ancient book that prophesies the revival of the Hebrew language.

[20] The references to the hungry, the poor, and the rich are found only in the Greek text.

CHAPTER IV

The Psalms of Solomon

(C. 45 B.C.E.)

THIS MARVELOUS Pharisaic book clearly was written after Pompey had conquered Jerusalem and had sent captives from Judea to "the lands of the West" (something that had not occurred before his time), and after he had forced Aristobulus II to march behind his victory-chariot in Rome "to derision" (εἰς ἐμπαιγμόν, 17:14), and even after Pompey had died an unnatural death (48 B.C.E.).[1] This Pharisaic book deals harshly with the Hasmonean dynasty, and enlarges upon *the personality of the Messiah*—as though it wished to emphasize thereby, "after the event," that it was a mistake to regard the Hasmonean kings as Messiahs. For they did evil, acted corruptly, turned aside from the commandments of the LORD (the tenets of the Pharisees), and poured out innocent blood in civil wars: "They left no sin undone, wherein they surpassed not the heathen" (8:9–13). So the author turns to the LORD in a prayer for *redemption*, which he connects with *the ingathering of exiles:*

> Turn, O God, Thy mercy upon us,
>   and have pity upon us!
> *Gather together the dispersed of Israel,*
>   with mercy and goodness;
> For Thy faithfulness is with us.
> And though we have stiffened our neck,
>   yet Thou art our chastener.

[1] See on this in detail J. Klausner, *History of the Second Temple*, III, 229–234.

> Overlook us not, O our God,
> lest the nations swallow us,
> with none to deliver ² (8:27–30).

Thoroughly Messianic is Psalm 11. And it is surprising how much this psalm resembles Chapters 4–5 of the Apocryphal Book of Baruch, the Messianic expectations of which I have already treated.³ Since even the latest part of the Apocryphal Book of Baruch, as I have said, could not be later than the time of Janneus Alexander (*c.* 90 B.C.E.), it is therefore very possible that the book of the Psalms of Solomon took material from the Book of Baruch (contrary to the opinion of Perles); ⁴ but it is also possible that both of them drew from a common and older source.⁵ Indeed, I have already said, in the chapter on the Apocryphal Baruch, that we have here an imitation of Deutero-Isaiah, whose Messianic portrayals had become well known in the nation before the end of the period of the Second Temple:

> Blow ye in Zion on the trumpet a holy blast,
> Cause ye to be heard in Jerusalem
>   the voice of him that bringeth good tidings;
> For God hath had pity on Israel in remembering them.
>
> Stand on the height, O Jerusalem, and behold thy children,
> From the East and the West, gathered together by the LORD;
> From the North they come in the gladness of their God,
> From the isles afar off God hath gathered them.
> High mountains hath He abased into a plain for them;
> The hills fled at their entrance.
> The woods gave them shelter as they passed by;

---

² I quote the lines from the Psalms of Solomon according to the Hebrew translation of A. S. Kaminetzky (*Ha-Shiloah*, XI, 43–55, 149–159). See also S. Bernfeld, "The Creative Period in Our Ancient Literature" [Heb.] (the collective work *Ha-'Omer* [The Sheaf], ed. S. Ben-Zion, Vol. II, Jaffa, 1909, pp. 27–31). But I also had before me the Greek text in Fritzsche's edition, and I translated a number of lines according to that where Kaminetzky's translation seemed to me inadequate. See also the introduction to and translation of the Psalms of Solomon by Menahem Stein, *The Outside Books* [Heb.], I.2, pp. 431–462.

³ See above, pp. 267–269.

⁴ See F. Perles, "Zur Erklärung der Psalmen Solomo's" (*Orientalistiche Litteraturzeitung*, 1902, Nos. 7–10).

⁵ See A. S. Kaminetzky, "Psalms of Solomon" [Heb.], *Ha-Shiloah*, XI, 152, Note 5.

Every sweet-smelling tree [6] God caused to spring up for them,
That Israel might pass by in the visitation
   of the glory of their God.[7]

Put on, O Jerusalem, thy glorious garments;
Make ready thy holy robe;
For God hath spoken good concerning Israel,
   forever and ever.
Let the LORD do what He hath spoken
   concerning Israel and Jerusalem;
Let the LORD raise up Israel by His glorious name.
The mercy of the LORD be upon Israel forever and ever.

But even more Messianic is Psalm 17. First in it comes a strong accusation against the Hasmonean dynasty:

Thou, O LORD, didst choose David
   to be king over Israel,
And swaredst to him touching his seed
   that never should his kingdom fail before Thee.
But, for our sins, sinners rose up against us

—the Hasmoneans from the end of the reign of John Hyrcanus onward: "they took away with violence" royal authority, "they put on a crown in their pride," and "they laid waste the throne of David in tumultuous arrogance" (17:4–6). But God cast them down through "a man alien to our race" (Pompey), who slew their offspring, "sent them away even unto the west," exposed them "to derision" (in his triumph), laid waste their land, and destroyed young and old, while "the congregation of the pious" was scattered throughout the world. "For there was none among them that wrought righteousness and justice: from the chief of them to the least of them all were sinful: the king was a transgressor, the judge rapacious, and the people sinful" (17:6–20). And as a result of all these things comes the prayer of the author of the psalm:

Behold, O LORD, and raise up unto them
   their king, the son of David,

---

[6] Perles (*op. cit.*, p. 339) reads "trees of frankincense" (in accordance with Song of Songs 4:14).
[7] Singular [verb] and plural [pronominal adjective] in reference to Israel in a single verse, as in the Scriptures.

At the time in which Thou seest, O God,
    that he may reign over Israel Thy servant.
Gird him with strength to shatter unrighteous rulers,
And to purge Jerusalem from the nations
    that trample her down to destruction.
Wisely, righteously he shall thrust out
    sinners from the inheritance,
He shall destroy the pride of the sinner
    as a potter's vessel.
With a rod of iron he shall break in pieces
    all their substance,
He shall destroy the godless nations
    with the word of his mouth;
At his rebuke nations shall flee before him,
And he shall reprove sinners
    for the thoughts of their heart.

He shall gather together a holy people,
    whom he shall lead in righteousness,
And he shall judge the tribes of the people
    that has been sanctified by the LORD his God.
And he shall not suffer unrighteousness
    to lodge any more in their midst
Nor shall there dwell with them any man
    that knoweth wickedness,
For he shall know them, that they are all
    sons of their God.
And he shall divide them according to their tribes
    upon the land,
And neither sojourner nor alien shall sojourn
    with them any more.
He shall judge peoples and nations
    in the wisdom of his righteousness. *Selah*.[8]

The peoples of the nations [9] shall serve him
    under his yoke;
He shall glorify the LORD openly in all the earth;
And he shall purge Jerusalem,
    making it holy as of old,

---

[8] In Greek *diapsalma*, meaning "interlude"; this is the Septuagint's translation of the word *Selah*.

[9] I.e., the heathen peoples.

So that nations shall come from the ends of the earth
  to see his glory,
Bringing as gifts her sons who had fainted,
And to see the glory of the LORD,
  wherewith God hath glorified her.
And he shall be a righteous king,
  taught of God, over them,
And there shall be no unrighteousness
  in his days in their midst,
For all shall be holy and their king—
  the anointed of the LORD.[10]
For he shall not put his trust
  in horse and rider and bow,
Nor shall he multiply for himself
  gold and silver for war,
Nor shall he have confidence in a multitude [11]
  in the day of battle.

The LORD is his king, the hope of him
  that is mighty through hope in God;
And he shall have mercy upon all the nations
  (that stand) before him in fear.[12]
For he will smite the earth
  with the word of his mouth forever.[13]
He will bless the people of the LORD
  with wisdom and gladness,
And he himself will be pure from sin,
  so that he may rule a great people,
So that he may rebuke rulers,
  and remove sinners by the might of his word.

[10] In Greek here the reading is χριστὸς κύριος ("Messiah who is God") in place of χριστὸς κυρίου ("the anointed of the LORD," construct state); we find the latter reading in our book, Psalm 18:5 and 8, also in the superscription of Psalm 18. Obviously we have here a Christian alteration, as also in the Septuagint at Lamentations 4:20.

[11] Menahem Stein (*op. cit.*, I.2, p. 459) brings forward the emendation of Franz Delitzsch: *robim* [archers] in place of *rabbim* [multitude], from *robeh qashshath* (Gen. 21:20).

[12] I hold to the reading of the Greek manuscript, ἐλεήσει, except that the words "which will stand" or "that stand" are lacking here. This would agree with the whole spirit of the Psalms of Solomon: the Gentiles stand *in fear* before the King-Messiah, but he shows them favor in the Messianic age, after they have taken upon themselves the yoke of his kingdom.

[13] Cf. Isa. 11:4: "And he shall smite the land with the rod of his mouth."

> Throughout his days he will not stumble,
> (as he stands) before his God;
> For God will make him mighty
> by means of (His) holy spirit,
> And wise in the counsel of understanding,
> with strength and righteousness.
> And the blessing of the LORD (will be) with him
> in strength, and he will stumble not;
> His hope (will be) in the LORD: who then
> can prevail against him?
> Mighty in his works, and strong
> in the fear of God,
> He will be shepherding the flock of the LORD
> faithfully and righteously,
> And will suffer none among them
> to stumble in their pasture.
>
> He will lead them all aright,
> And there will be no pride in them
> in doing violence in their midst.
> This (will be) the majesty of the king of Israel,
> whom God knoweth
> To raise him up over the house of Israel,
> to correct him [or "to instruct them"].
> His words (shall be) more refined
> than choicest gold;
> In the assemblies he will judge the peoples,
> the tribes of the sanctified.
> His words (shall be) like the words of the holy ones
> in the midst of sanctified peoples.[14]
> Blessed be they that shall be in those days,
> To see the good fortune of Israel,
> which God shall bring to pass
> in the gathering together of the tribes! (17:21-44).

Likewise in the last psalm (18), which bears the superscription "A PSALM OF SOLOMON: CONCERNING THE ANOINTED OF THE LORD," there are significant Messianic expectations:

> Thy judgments are upon the whole earth in mercy,
> And Thy love toward the seed of Abraham,
> the children of Israel

[14] Here the meaning of "peoples" is the Tribes (cf. the preceding verse).

> Thy chastisement is upon us
>> as upon a first-born, only-begotten son,
> To turn back the afflicted [15] soul
>> from folly in ignorance.
> May God cleanse Israel with blessing
>> in the day of mercy,
> In the day of choice,
>> when He bringeth in His anointed.
>
> Blessed be they that shall be in those days,
> To see the goodness of the LORD,
>> which He shall perform for the generation to come,
> Under the rod of chastening of the LORD's anointed
>> in the fear of his God,
> In the wisdom of spirit [16]
>> and of righteousness and strength;
> To direct every man in the works of righteousness
>> by the fear of God,
> To establish them all before the LORD,
> A good generation in the fear of God
>> in the days of mercy. *Selah* (18:3-9).

It is hard to find a Messianic view more exalted and more noble. The Messiah is righteous and holy and "pure from sin"; to be sure, not after the manner of Christianity, since he is a human being and a king and even his "subjects" are all holy and sanctified and "sons of their God." There is no suggestion of wars and bloodshed in his time; but he expels the Gentiles (Romans) from Jerusalem and sets up a great and mighty kingdom, which is the center of the world, with Jerusalem the center of the kingdom. The Gentiles serve God and the King-Messiah; but in the end Palestine is apportioned only to the tribes of Israel, "and neither sojourner nor alien shall sojourn with them any more" (17:28), and the heathen peoples will be "under his yoke" (17:30). Like the "shoot out of the stem of Jesse" of the first Isaiah, he also "will smite the earth with the word of his mouth," and horse and bow and hosts and gold and silver for war he will not have (17:33-35). Nevertheless, "with a rod of iron he shall break in pieces" the wicked, he will destroy the godless nations, and will purge

---

[15] So translates M. Stein (*op. cit.*, p. 461), instead of "obedient."

[16] Another and more correct reading is "In the spirit of wisdom" (Charles, *Apocrypha and Pseudepigrapha* II, 651).

Jerusalem from the Romans who are oppressing it (17:22-24). And *the ingathering of the exiles* (the union of the tribes of Israel) is the prerequisite for the Days of the Messiah (17:28, 44; compare 8:28; 11:2-5).

Note that here there is indeed *a political and national side* to the Messianic kingdom; but *the spiritual side* is emphasized more. Of the *material prosperity* of which the Messianic visions in most of the Apocryphal books and in Talmud and Midrash are so full there is here hardly a trace (except for the apportionment of the land to the tribes, and "the woods" and the "sweet-smelling trees" for the returning exiles).

The Messiah is the judge of his land and of his people and their tribes, as in Isaiah 11; but he is more than this: he reproves and acts to "instruct" ($\pi\alpha\iota\delta\epsilon\hat{\upsilon}\sigma\alpha\iota$) in the popular "assemblies" ($\dot{\epsilon}\nu\ \sigma\upsilon\nu\alpha\gamma\omega\gamma\alpha\hat{\iota}\varsigma$), accomplishing this purpose by means of "words more refined than choicest gold," words which are "like the words of the holy ones" in the midst of the sanctified tribes of Israel (17:42-43). But in turn "God will make him mighty by means of the holy spirit, and wise in the counsel of understanding," giving him "strength and righteousness" (17:37); thus the Messiah is himself instructed by God. He is "a righteous king, taught of God" (17:32). Therefore peace and justice, understanding and wisdom and power (the power of the spirit, not the power of the mailed fist) will belong to the Days of the Messiah, for with all these will the LORD bless His people—and the Messiah all the more. Therefore, "blessed be they that shall be born in those days to see the good fortune of Israel which God shall bring to pass," and "to see the goodness of the LORD which He shall perform" for Israel (17:44; 18:7). All this will be done by the LORD through the mediation of the Messiah, but not by the Messiah *alone*. For the Jewish Messiah, no matter how noble and how spiritual, is nevertheless a human being, a king of flesh and blood of the house of David, and is only an instrument for the great work of the God of Israel, the God of the universe.

CHAPTER V

The Assumption of Moses

(4–6 C.E.)

THIS BOOK, which we have in an incomplete Latin translation, was composed, in my opinion, by one of the survivors of *the sect of the Hasidim* ("the first Hasidim"), from which the Essenes branched off; or by a member of that sect of the Essenes from which came the "Dead Sea Scrolls" (compare Note 3, below). It was written in the Hebrew language and in Palestine in the time of confusion and rebellion after the death of Herod, while his son Archelaus was in exile (*c.* 4–6 C.E.). It is intended to prove that the woes which have come upon Judea in the time of the author are in reality "the birth pangs of Messiah," the prelude to the Messianic age.[1]

In form, it is a visionary "revelation" like the Book of Enoch: *what has already happened* Moses relates before his death to his disciple Joshua *as things that are going to happen in the future*. Thus there passes before us in the "vision" the whole history of Israel down to the destruction of the First Temple, down to Hasmonean times, and down to the time of Herod and his sons and the campaign of Varus, when a part of the Temple was burned.[2] After this (4–6 C.E.) will come the "end" ("the times shall be ended," Assumption of Moses 7:1). Over the people of Judea will rule evil and sinful men, gluttons and drunkards, who will be, besides all this, flatterers and hypocrites.

---

[1] For details on the time of composition, the author, and the content of the Assumption of Moses, see Joseph Klausner, "Outside Books" (*Otsar ha-Yahadut, Hoveret le-Dogma*, pp. 115–118); *History of the Second Temple*, IV, 181–187; Abraham Kahana, *The Outside Books*, I, pp. 314–325.

[2] Assumption of Moses 6:9; *Antiquities* 17:10:1; *Wars* 2:3:3.

They will be "removers of the landmark,[3] provokers of strife, men of deceit," and "devourers of the inheritance of the poor" (or "of widows")—yet they will boast about their deeds of mercy: "Their hands and their minds are busy with unclean things, and their mouth speaks arrogance, while they furthermore say, 'Do not touch me, lest you pollute me!'" (7:9–10).

And in the time of persecutions (according to all indications, the reference is to the time of the decrees of Antiochus Epiphanes, except that they should have been described *preceding* the Hasmoneans and Herod and his sons, *and not following;* so perhaps Chapters 8 and 9 are not in place) "there shall arise a man of the tribe of Levi, whose name shall be Taxo and who shall have seven sons"; he will say to his sons that they must fast for three days and on the fourth day hide themselves in a cave which is in the field, and that it is better that they should die than that they should transgress the commandments of the LORD; for if they should die under these conditions, their sacrifice would be pleasing to the LORD (9:1–7).

On "Taxo" there is a whole literature. Charles conjectures that this is a corruption of *haqanna'* [the zealot], or that it must be "Taxoc" [תכסוק], which has the same numerical value as the letters of the name Eleazar [אלעזר]![4] Others say that this is a Greek word, "the orderer," from *taxis,* "order," or that it is a corruption of the Hebrew word *tekhasseh.* According to the latter suggestion, in the Hebrew original the reading was "whose name shall be *tekhasseh*" (that is, "you shall conceal"), and the reference is to Mattathias the Hasmonean.[5] In my opinion *taksa* is an error of the translator or copyist for *Matteya* [Matthew, short form of Mattathias]. But in any case,

---

[3] On "removers of the landmark" see the "Book of the Damascus Covenant" 1:11; 8:1 (*Ha-Shiloah,* XXVI, pp. 484, 490. See also the introduction of M. Z. Segal, *ibid.,* p. 403, Note 2). The "Damascus Covenant" is closely connected with the "Dead Sea Scrolls." On the activists among the Essenes, see the Supplement to the third edition of the fifth volume of my *History of the Second Temple* (1952), pp. 324–332.

[4] See Charles, *The Assumption of Moses,* London, 1897, p. 36; *Apocrypha and Pseudepigrapha,* II, 421. (The latter conjecture is that of Burkitt, *Hastings's Dictionary of the Bible,* III, 440.) See what I have written on this in *Israelite History,* III, 154–155.

[5] See "The Assumption of Moses," Hebrew translation, with brief introduction and notes, by A. S. Kaminetzky, *Ha-Shiloah,* XXV, 38–50. From this I took the

THE ASSUMPTION OF MOSES 327

Taxo is not the Messiah, but one of the leaders of the above-mentioned "first Hasidim" or sectarian Essenes, who with his sons suffered martyrdom.

The personality of the Messiah is lacking in this book, as in many other ancient Hebrew books. Messianic ideas occur only in Chapter 10, which follows the chapter on Taxo. Preceding this chapter there is only a single Messianic passage, in which, if it is not corrupt, Moses says to Joshua that the latter should preserve the books which he is delivering to him "in earthen vessels in the place which He [God] made from the beginning of the creation of the world, that His name should be called upon until the day of *repentance* in the visitation wherewith the LORD will visit them in the consummation of *the end of the days*" (1:17-18). But F. Rosenthal [6] proposes that "the day of repentance means here the day of the complete return to Zion [since the same Hebrew word may mean "repentance" or "return"], and that this is the meaning of "the end of the days" in this passage.

In Chapter 10 we have a little "revelation" (apocalypse), containing a marvelous description of "the day of the LORD" in the spirit of Zephaniah, and also a promise of bliss and freedom in the Age to Come:

> And then His kingdom shall appear
>   throughout all His creation,
> And then Satan shall be no more,
> And sorrow shall depart with him.
> Then shall be filled the hands of the angel
>   who stands on high,[7]
> And he shall forthwith avenge them
>   of their enemies.
> For the Heavenly One will arise
>   from His royal throne,
> And He will go forth

---

translation of Chap. 10 given below, except that I have introduced changes in accordance with the Latin text in the edition of Fritzsche.

[6] In his book *Vier apocryphische Bücher aus der Zeit und Schule Akiba's*, Leipzig, 1884, p. 36.

[7] In the Latin version which we have, the reading is "*in summo*"—*beramah* or *ba-meromim* in Hebrew. Could this not be a punning allusion to Rome?—the angel *who stands at the gates of Rome* will exact vengeance for Israel from its Roman enemies. But see also below.

> from His holy habitation
> With indignation and wrath
>   on account of His sons.
>
> And the earth shall tremble,
>   to its ends shall it be shaken;
> And the high mountains shall be made low and shaken,
> And the valleys shall fall.
> The sun shall not give light
>   and shall be turned into darkness,
> The horns of the moon shall be broken
>   and it shall be turned wholly into blood,
> And the circle of the stars shall be disturbed
> And the sea shall go back into the abyss,
> And the fountains of waters shall fail,
> And the rivers shall dry up.
>
> For the Most High will arise,
>   the Eternal God alone,
> And He will appear to punish the Gentiles,
> And He will destroy all their idols.
> Then thou, O Israel, shalt be happy!
> And thou shalt mount
>   upon the necks and wings of the eagle,
> And (his days) [8] shall be ended.
> And God will exalt thee,
> And He will cause thee to reach
>   to the heaven of the stars,
>   to the place of their habitation.
> And thou shalt look from on high
>   and see thy enemies in the dust
> And thou shalt recognize them and rejoice,
> And thou shalt give thanks and confess thy Creator (10:1-10).

After this, Moses again gives an oracle to Joshua, saying that from the time of his [Moses'] death until the coming of the kingdom of God there will be "250 times" (*tempora*) (10:12). If, as has been conjectured, the "times" are seven-year periods, this number corresponds closely to the time which passed, according to Josephus, from Moses until the reign of Archelaus. As regards the "eagle" upon

---

[8] The eagle's? Or, perhaps, after *implebuntur* the words *verba Domini* are missing ("the words of the LORD"—through the prophets—"shall be fulfilled").

the "necks and wings" of which the people Israel will mount, most scholars think that the reference is to Rome.[9] But there are opponents of this explanation, and they say that the meaning is exaltation or self-exaltation in general, as in the following Biblical verses: "I bore you on *eagles' wings*" (Ex. 19:4); or, "As an *eagle* stirs up its nestlings . . . spreading its *wings* to take them, lifting them up on its pinions" (Deut. 32:11); note that in the next verse (10:9) the people Israel is also exalted to the heaven of the stars.[10] However that may be, we have before us an enthusiastic, patriotic picture of the greatness of Israel in the future.

The appearance of the kingdom of heaven is here exceedingly splendid, almost grandiose. Not only are the enemies of Israel vanquished, but also "Satan" (*Zabulus*—Baal-Zebul or Diabolos). The "angel who stands on high" is, perhaps, Michael, guardian angel of Israel (Dan. 10:21), and he is the one who exacts vengeance for Israel from its enemies.[11] The description of "the Day of Judgment" recalls "the day of the LORD" of Zephaniah (1:14-18) and of Joel (3:3-5). This is the most marvelous portrayal, both in its brevity and in its rapidity, that is to be found in the Pseudepigraphical literature of this type.

More detailed Messianic expectations are not present here. Perhaps this is because not all the Book of the Assumption of Moses is in our hands. But it is also possible that in the time of confusion and desolation after the death of Herod, a time in which the Destruction had actually already begun, the essential part of the Messianic expectation was victory over the enemy and vengeance on the Roman leeches. So perhaps it is for this reason alone that we have this splendid picture of the Day of Judgment, in which the enemies of Israel are destroyed along with their idols, and the afflicted and oppressed people Israel mount up "on eagles' wings" to "the heaven of the stars"—to the height of national, political, and spiritual success alike.

[9] Cf. "By the Roman *eagle!*" (Pesahim 87*b*) [another interpretation, "By the Capitol of Rome," see Soncino Talmud, *ad loc.*]; "A couple [of scholars] have arrived from Rakkath who had been captured by *an eagle*" (Sanhedrin 12*a*); see also the "Eagle Vision" in IV Ezra 11-12 (see below p. 359).
[10] See Eugen Hühn, *Die messian. Weissag.*, p. 98, Note 3.
[11] See Note 7, above.

CHAPTER VI

The Syriac Book of Baruch

(70–80 C.E.)

THE *SYRIAC* Book of Baruch (so called to distinguish this Pseudepigraphical book from the *Apocryphal* Book of Baruch and from the *Greek* Apocalypse of Baruch) is an apocalypse which was composed, in the opinion of most scholars, immediately after the Second Destruction (it is said in it that Jerusalem was laid waste *two times;* see 32:2–3). It was written in the Hebrew language, which is still reflected in the Syriac version, in spite of the fact that this version is also in a Semitic language; moreover, this Syriac version is a translation of a translation (the Greek). The Hebrew original is reflected even more in the Latin version (which has been preserved, while the Greek version has been lost).

From the statement that Baruch left Jerusalem "at the time of the evening" and went and stood by the "oak"—undoubtedly *the one in Hebron* (compare 6:1 with 47:1–2)—scholars wish to draw the conclusion that the author of the book did not know the distance between Jerusalem and Hebron, and thus was not an inhabitant of Judah, or at least not of Jerusalem. But they forget that the whole Syriac Book of Baruch is only a *vision*—and in a vision anything is possible. In any case, the devotion to Pharisaic Judaism, which we feel in every verse of the "revelation" before us, proves that the author was a *Palestinian* Jew, and not an Alexandrian or Roman Jew. It may be that he was one of the exiles from Jerusalem, and far from his native city he no longer was exact about the distance between it and Hebron.

This book, written a short time after the Destruction, is full of national grief throughout. In this it is like the second Pseudepigraphical book after the Destruction—IV Ezra (the apocalyptic Ezra). The fearful catastrophe which came upon the land and the nation, the destruction of the religious and political center, along with the exile of the people and their dispersion among the Gentiles, who raised a shout of triumph over their downfall and celebrated a festival of victory over their God—all this induced minds to delve deeply into the causes of the severe punishment and to reveal "the end." Those spirits who were strongly attached to God and to their people alike *could not* see in the punishment afflictions leading to ruin, but they did see in it "the birth pangs of Messiah." It was clear to them that "the end" was near: "For truly My redemption has drawn nigh, and is not far distant as aforetime" (23:7); and Baruch himself (that is, the author of the book) will be privileged to see it (26:1; see also 13:3).

It is worthy of consideration that there is no Pseudepigraphical book in which are found so many detailed Messianic expectations as in the Syriac Book of Baruch; and there is no other Pseudepigraphical book the Messianic expectations of which are so like *those in the earliest parts of the Talmud and Midrash*. (For the most part they resemble those uttered by the Tannaim before the war of Bar-Cochba, and they resemble all the more those uttered at the time of the completion of the Mishnah and during the last stage of the Baraitha.) The great difference between "the Days of the Messiah" and "the World to Come," which I have tried to determine for the earliest parts of Talmud and Midrash,[1] is very strongly emphasized in this Book of Baruch. The personality of the Messiah stands out here more than in the rest of the Pseudepigrapha, in a certain sense even more than in the Book of Enoch, where the Son of Man is only a subject of mystery and his actual work is hardly recognizable; and only the Psalms of Solomon and the apocalyptic Ezra can compete with it in this. Moreover, the legends about material prosperity in the Messianic age, which we have already found alluded to in the Book of Enoch

[1] See below, Part III, Chap. II, pp. 408–419.

(10:17–19), were developed and expanded in the Syriac Book of Baruch until they have here an exact likeness to the early Talmudic and Midrashic Baraithas,[2] and to the traditions of the Church Father Papias, which Irenaeus attributes to Jesus himself in accordance with the witness of the "elders" who still knew John, Jesus' disciple.[3]

And even the Baraithas on "the birth pangs of Messiah"—the Baraithas about "the week [seven-year period] at the end of which the son of David will come," and the Baraithas beginning with the words "the son of David will not come until . . ."—even most of these are found almost verbatim in the Syriac Book of Baruch. This fact is of great importance. It shows that the Messianic portrayals in the Talmud, and those in the Pseudepigrapha, are not the fruit of imagination alone, but are *the product of outstanding historical events* which fructified the imagination of all perceptive persons in Israel and influenced them in a very similar manner. (Note that the imagination of the authors of the Aggadah was much different from that of the authors of the apocalypses, from whom the Talmudic authors had removed themselves.)

Since the Messianic portrayals in the Book of Baruch are numerous, it is possible to divide them into their natural divisions, as I did in regard to the Book of Enoch.

1. *The Birth Pangs of Messiah*

The prerequisites of the coming of the Messiah in the Syriac Book of Baruch resemble amazingly those in the Talmudic Baraithas which begin with the phrase "the son of David will not come until . . ."[4] When "the end" approaches, the number of souls destined to be born and to die will be completed—a number that was determined after the sin of Adam; these souls have been kept in "treasuries" ("treasuries of souls" in Syriac), which will give back in the Age to Come all the souls kept in them (Syriac Baruch 21:23; 4–7; 30:2). This agrees exactly with the Talmudic saying, "The son of David will not come before all the souls in *Guf* [the region inhabited by the souls of the

---

[2] Kethubboth 111b; Siphre, Deut., 315.
[3] Irenaeus, *Against Heresies*, V, 33.
[4] Sanhedrin 97a and 98a; Abodah Zarah 5a, etc.

unborn] will have been disposed of." [5] It is also to be seen in the Ezra Apocalypse (7:29–32). These treasuries of souls are called *promptuaria* in Latin.[6] And a statement confirming the commentary of Rashi and in complete agreement with the words of the Syriac Baruch on the origin of these "treasuries" in the time of Adam is found in the Midrash: "The King-Messiah will not come until all the souls which it was originally the divine intention to create shall have come to an end, namely, those spoken of in the book of Adam, the first man." [7]

We find here another sign of the Days of the Messiah, or, more correctly, of the days which will precede the advent of the Messiah (a similar item is found in the Talmudic Baraitha): "This shall be the sign," which "the Most High will work for the inhabitants of the earth in the end of days": great terror will fall upon the inhabitants of the earth, and many tribulations and fearful torments will come upon them, and because of these torments they will say: "The Mighty One doth no longer remember the earth." "Yea, it will come to pass *when they abandon hope*, that the time ('the end of days') will then awake" (Syriac Baruch 25:1–4). This statement agrees perfectly with the words of the Talmudic Baraitha: the son of David will not come "until the redemption *is despaired of*." [8]

Likewise, Baruch's portrayals of the years preceding the Messiah's coming correspond closely to the Talmudic portrayals of "the week at the end of which the son of David will come." [9] Here, in the Syriac Baruch, we have not a "week" (seven-year cycle), but "twelve parts" (periods) into which "that time" (the Messianic age) is divided. In the first part—the beginning of commotions; in the second part—the slaying of the great ones; in the third part—the death of many; in the

---

[5] Abod. Zar., *ibid.*; Yebamoth 62a and 63b; Niddah 13b. "There is a *treasury* named *Guf*, and at the beginning all the souls destined to be born were created, and He put them there" (Rashi on Abod. Zar. 5a).

[6] They are also mentioned in the interesting book "The Biblical Antiquities," attributed to Philo, Chaps. 21 and 32 (see M. R. James, *The Biblical Antiquities of Philo*, London, 1917, pp. 137, 177).

[7] Lev. R., beginning of Chap. 15. See on all this below, Part III, Chap. IV; see also Schürer, *Geschichte*, II⁴, 639–641.

[8] Sanhedrin 97a.

[9] Sanhedrin, *ibid.*; Derekh Erets Zuta, beginning of Chap. 10; Song of Songs Rabbah 2:13, on the verse "The fig-tree"; Pesiqta Rabbathi, Chap. 15.

fourth part—the sending of the sword; in the fifth part—famine and the withholding of rain; in the sixth part—earthquakes and terrors; in the seventh part—(what will happen is lacking); in the eighth part—a multitude of specters and attacks of the Shedim (demons); in the ninth part—the fall of fire (from heaven); in the tenth part—much rapine and oppression; in the eleventh part—wickedness and prodigality; and finally, in the twelfth part—confusion and the mingling together of everything that came before. These divisions of time will not be completely separate, but the events will be mixed together in such a fashion that those living on the earth at that time will not perceive the fact that this is "the consummation of the times" (27:1-15).

In the Talmud, in the previously mentioned Baraitha concerning "the seven-year cycle at the end of which the son of David will come," we find: first year—rain in one place and drought in another (compare "the withholding of rain" in the fifth part, above); second year—"the arrows of hunger will be sent forth" (compare "the sending of the sword" in the fourth part, above);[10] third year—a great famine and the death of men, women, and children, and the forgetting of the Torah (compare "famine" in the fifth part, "the slaying of the great ones" in the second part, and "the death of many" in the third part); fourth year—both plenty and no plenty (no parallel); fifth year—great plenty and the return of the Torah; sixth year—sounds (compare "the beginning of commotions" in the first part); seventh year—wars (compare "terrors" in the sixth part and "much rapine and oppression" in the tenth part); "and at the conclusion of the septennate the son of David will come."

Most of the events of "the week at the end of which the son of David will come" are, accordingly, to be found in the Syriac Baruch also.[11] It also contains the division into "weeks" in the sense of seven-year periods. "The birth pangs of Messiah" will continue "two parts (of) weeks out of seven weeks" (28:2) [Charles' ed., translates "two

[10] Cf. also Ezek. 5:16.
[11] It may be conjectured that the missing item in the "seventh part" of the Syriac Baruch is *the forgetting of the Torah*—an item that was suppressed at a later time from fear of the various ideas of the antinomians, the Gnostics, and the Nazarenes.

parts a week of seven weeks"]; and the Latin translation of Fritzsche [12] has "duae partes hebdomades septem hebdomadorum," that is, two parts, in each of which will be seven weeks (periods) of seven years.[13]

Just as according to the Talmud books are opened on the Day of Judgment of the individual,[14] so will be opened on the day of General Judgment the books in which sins are recorded; also the treasuries of the virtues of the righteous will then be opened (Syriac Baruch 24:1).[15] Likewise, the controversy of the later sages as to whether it would be desirable to attain the Days of the Messiah or would be better not to attain them, so as to avoid "the birth pangs of the Messiah" [16]—this controversy also found expression in the Syriac Book of Baruch: "It is good for a man to come and behold, but it is better that he should not come lest he fall" (28:3).

A broad portrait of "the birth pangs of Messiah" is given us by Chapter 48 (Verses 31–41). The appointed time is coming. The *time of affliction* ("birth pangs of Messiah") will arise. All the inhabitants of the world will be at rest in those days, because they will not know that the Day of Judgment is coming. For there will not be many wise at that time, and the intelligent will be few; moreover, those who know will be silent (agreeing with the saying in the Baraitha on "the footprints of the Messiah": "The wisdom of the scribes shall become insipid," [17] with the saying "Pious men and saints will be diminished" in "the seven-year cycle at the end of which the son of David will come," and with the further saying "Until scholars are few" in the Baraitha on "The son of David will not come," which I cited above).

Many "rumors" and "tidings not a few" will arise, and "doings of phantasmata" will appear (compare in "the seven-year cycle at the

---

[12] In his book *Libri apocryphi Veteris Testamenti, graece*, Lipsiae, 1871, p. 606.
[13] So I understand the phraseology, both Syriac and Greek. See V. Ryssel in Kautzsch's German edition of the Apocrypha and Pseudepigrapha, II, 422, Note e.
[14] Rosh ha-Shanah 16b.
[15] Cf. Rev. 20:12.
[16] "Let him come, but let me not see him"; "Let him come, and may I be worthy of sitting in the shadow of his ass's saddle (excrement?)" (Sanhedrin 98b).
[17] Mishnah, Sotah 9:15.

end of which the son of David will come": in the sixth year—"sounds" [or "voices"]); and it is related of "promises not a few" that some of them will prove idle, and some will be confirmed. Honor will be turned into shame and strength into weakness; might will fail, and beauty (*yophi*) will become blemish (*dophi;* it appears that we have here a play on words).[18]

Many will be amazed that intelligence has hidden itself and that wisdom has been obscured. Vengeance will be aroused in those in whom one would not expect to find it, and passion will seize those who were quiet; many will become wrathful and injure many, and will rouse up armies to shed blood (compare in the seventh year—"wars"); and in the end they will all perish together with them. And at that time every man will recognize the change of times, because in all those times men have been polluting themselves and doing evil, each one walking according to his own deeds and not remembering the law of the LORD. Therefore a fire will consume their purposes, and in a flame will the counsels of their hearts be tested, for the Judge will surely come and not tarry. Verily, every one of the inhabitants of the earth could have known that he was doing iniquity; but they did not recognize the law of the LORD because of their pride. At that time, indeed, many will weep, but more over the living than over the dead.

This is a splendid, almost prophetic, vision, having in it a practical wisdom drawn from the untoward historical experiences through which Israel passed at the time of the First Destruction, at the time of the decrees of Antiochus, and perhaps also at the time of the internal conflicts between Janneus Alexander and the Pharisees and the time of troubles before Herod, and also after him at the time of the Second Destruction. To this splendid vision is to be added a beautiful "parable" (allegorical vision): *the Vision of the Black and the Bright*

---

[18] Even more word play is found by Louis Ginzberg in 21:14: "Of what avail is power (*ḥayil*) turned to pain (*ḥil*), fullness of food (*mazon*) to leanness (*razon*), beauty (*yophi*) to blemish (*dophi*)?" (*Jew. Enc.*, II, 555*b*). According to Charles (*Apocrypha and Pseudepigrapha*, II, 494), the first line goes, "For of what profit is strength (*ḥayil*) that turns to sickness (*ḥoli*)?" And farther on, 48:35, Charles found that in the Hebrew text there was this paronomasia: "Honor shall be turned into shame, strength ('*oz*) humiliated (?) into contempt (*buz*), . . . beauty (*yophi*) shall become blemish (*dophi*)" (*ibid.*, p. 506).

Waters (53–54). The *last* black waters are "the birth pangs of Messiah":

> Behold! the days come,
> And it shall be when the time of the age has ripened,
> And the harvest of the seed of the good and the evil has come,
> That the Mighty One will bring upon the earth,
> And upon its inhabitants and its rulers,
> Perturbation of spirit and anxiety of mind.
>
> And they shall hate one another,
> And provoke one another to fight;
> And the mean shall rule over the honorable,
> And those of low degree shall be extolled above the famous.
>
> And the many shall be delivered into the hands of few,
> And those who were nothing shall rule over the strong;
> And the poor shall have control over the rich,
> And the impious shall exalt themselves above the heroic.
> And the wise shall be silent,
> And the foolish shall speak.

The hopes neither of the people nor of their rulers will be confirmed. Then confusion will come upon all men; some of them will fall in battle, some of them will perish in anguish, and some of them will be imprisoned by their own people.[19]

But the Most High will reveal Himself to the peoples whom He had appointed from the beginning, and they shall come and make war with the leaders that shall then be left. And it shall come to pass that whoever gets safe out of the war shall die in the earthquake, and whoever gets safe out of the earthquake shall be burned by the fire, and whoever gets safe out of the fire shall be destroyed by famine. And it shall come to pass that whoever of the victors and the vanquished gets safe out of and escapes all these things aforesaid will be delivered into the hands of *My servant, the Messiah.* For all the earth shall devour its inhabitants. But the Holy Land shall have mercy on its own, and it shall protect its inhabitants at that time (70:2–71:1).

This parabolic vision has numerous points of contact with the very ancient Baraitha which has been added to the Mishnah [20] and which

---

[19] Perhaps this is a reference to the acts of Janneus Alexander in relation to the Pharisees, among whom was his kinsman, Simeon ben Shetah. Or it is possible that this refers to certain deeds at the time of the Second Destruction.

[20] Sotah 9:15.

338   THE MESSIANIC IDEA IN ISRAEL

begins with the words "With the footprints of the Messiah presumption shall increase" (in Aramaic; another text says the same thing in Hebrew);[21] "presumption shall increase," "the wisdom of the Scribes shall become insipid and they that shun sin shall be deemed contemptible, and truth shall nowhere be found; children shall shame their elders, the elders shall rise up before the children"; and "the face of this generation is as the face of a dog." Only material poverty, which the Baraitha emphasizes ("dearth shall reach its height," and so on) is lacking in Baruch's version.[22] Apart from this it is full of understanding of the severe crisis that always comes in times of great decision in world history.

To the Vision of the Black and the Bright Waters is to be added, furthermore, "the Vision of the Forest, the Vine, the Fountain, and the Cedar," with its interpretation, *the Vision of the Four Kingdoms* (35-40). After Baruch laments over the fearful destruction and complains against heaven, he falls asleep and sees in his dream a great and broad *forest* of trees in a plain, surrounded by rugged mountains. Over against it arose a *vine*, from under which welled forth a clear *fountain*. The fountain grew strong and became great waves, which submerged the forest, uprooting its trees, overthrowing the mountains round about it, and leaving nothing but one *cedar*. Finally, they cast down the cedar also; thus there was left of the whole forest not a trace, and even the place where it had been was unknown. Then the vine together with the fountain approached the cedar that had been cast down to the earth, and the vine spoke harshly to it and rebuked it for the wrongs and the violence which it had committed. And the vine laid upon the cedar its punishment, that it should become dust and ashes like the rest of the forest. Then Baruch sees the cedar burning in the fire, while the vine flourishes and round about it the plain is full of unfading flowers (35-37).[23]

The interpretation (not agreeing very well with the parable) is:

---

[21] On the different texts and the interpretation of this Baraitha, see below, Part III, Chap. V, pp. 442-445.

[22] See on this S. Krauss, *Zeitschrift für die Neutestamentliche Wissenschaft*, X (1909), pp. 81-89.

[23] On the popular and legendary element in this parable, see Gressmann, *Eschatologie*, p. 106.

The *first* kingdom that destroyed Zion (Babylon) will itself be destroyed and become subject to the kingdom that will come after it. This *second* kingdom (Persia) will also be destroyed after a certain time. Thus it will happen to the *third* kingdom (Greece) also. Then will come the *fourth* kingdom (Rome), which will be harsher and more evil than all those before it. It will rule for a long time and be strong like *the forest* of the plain, and will exalt itself more than *the cedars* of Lebanon:

And by it the truth will be hidden, and all those who are polluted with iniquity will flee to it, as evil beasts flee and creep into the forest. And it will come to pass when the time of its consummation that it should fall has approached, then the principate (or beginning) of My Messiah will be revealed, which is like the fountain and the vine; and when it is revealed it will root out the multitude of its (Rome's) host. And as touching that which thou hast seen, the lofty cedar, which was left of that forest, and with which the vine spoke those words which thou didst hear, this is the word:—The last leader of that time will be left alive, when the multitude of his hosts will be put to the sword, and he will be bound, and they will take him up to Mount Zion, and My Messiah will convict him of all his impieties, and they will gather and set before him all the works of his hosts. And afterwards he will put him to death, and protect the rest of My people which shall be found in the place which I have chosen. And his principate will stand forever, *until the world of corruption is at an end*, and until the times aforesaid are fulfilled. This is thy vision, and this is its interpretation (39:3–40:4).

And with this the descriptions of the Day of Judgment and "the birth pangs of Messiah" in the Book of Baruch are finished. With the last items which I have just quoted we enter into

2. *The Days of the Messiah*

From the verses which I quoted last, it appears that the Messianic age is not an endless span of time (the word "forever" here, 40:3, and the word "eternally" in 73:1 are not used in their usual meaning), but a temporary period, a period of transition, "until the world of corruption is at an end, and until the times aforesaid are fulfilled," that is, until the "New World" shall arise, and until the years of the "World to Come" and the resurrection of the dead, about which I shall speak below, shall come. This is actually the case also in IV Ezra (7:28 and 12:34), and in the Talmudic Baraithas, which likewise distinguish between the Days of the Messiah and the World to Come.[24] The Messiah comes only to put an end to the Roman armies and their emperor. The Messiah's personality and influence are emphasized at the end of the Vision of the Black and the Bright Waters. He is likened to the "bright lightning" which Baruch saw in his vision: "After the signs have come, of which thou wast told before, when the nations become turbulent, and the time of My Messiah is come, he shall summon all the nations, and some of them he shall spare, and some of them he shall slay." "Every nation which knows (or knew) not Israel and has not trodden down the seed of Jacob," and which "shall be subjected to thy people," "shall indeed be spared"; "but those who have ruled over you, or have known you (and have persecuted you), shall be given up to the sword" (72:2-6).

With this view of the Syriac Baruch is to be compared a Talmudic Baraitha,[25] in which it is said that the King-Messiah will accept a *doron* (a gift as a sign of allegiance) from the Egyptians, in spite of the fact that they enslaved the children of Israel, because in the last analysis "they furnished hospitality to My (God's) children in Egypt"; and that he will accept a *doron* from the Ethiopians, because they did not know the children of Israel at all; and that he will reject only the Edomites (Romans), because they knew Israel but did the greatest evil to it.

After the Messiah "has brought low everything that is in the world, and has sat down *in peace* for the age (or "eternally"; see above) on the throne of his kingdom, joy (*busma, jucunditas*) shall then be revealed, and *rest* shall appear."

> And then healing shall descend in dew,
> And disease shall withdraw,
> And anxiety and anguish and lamentation
> pass from amongst men,

[24] Cf. what I have written below, Part III, Chap. II, pp. 408-419, with Hühn, *Die messian. Weissag.*, pp. 105, 107.
[25] Pesahim 118b.

And gladness proceed through the whole earth;
And no one shall again die untimely,
Nor shall any adversity suddenly befall.

And judgments and revilings and contentions and revenges,
And blood and passions and envy and hatred,
And whatsoever things are like these
Shall go into condemnation and be removed;
For it is these very things
  which have filled this world with evils,
And on account of these
  the life of man has been greatly troubled.

And wild beasts shall come from the forest
  and minister unto men,
And asps and vipers shall come forth from their holes
  to submit themselves to a little child;
And women shall no longer then
  have pain when they bear,
Nor shall they suffer torment
  when they yield the fruit of the womb.

And it shall come to pass in those days
That the reapers shall not grow weary,
Nor those that build be toilworn;
For the works shall of themselves speedily advance
Together with (for the sake of?) those who do them
  in much tranquillity,
For that time is the end of that which is corruptible,
And the beginning of that which is not corruptible.
Therefore those things which were predicted
  shall belong to it;
Therefore it is far away from evildoers,
And near to those who do not die (73:1–74:3).

For the purpose of comparison with other expectations in regard to the cessation of judgments, contentions, passions, bloodshed, hatred, and envy, there is need to quote from the Talmud but one well known Baraitha,[26] which, to be sure, is speaking not of the Messianic age, but of the World to Come, and therefore contains ideas

---

[26] Kallah Rabbathi, Chap. 2, as a Baraitha; and in Berakhoth 17*a* it comes as "a favorite saying of Rab."

not found in the Syriac Book of Baruch: "In the world to come there is no eating or drinking or procreation of children (all these, of course, are still present in the Messianic age) or *business transactions* or *envy* or *hatred* or *rivalry;* but the righteous sit enthroned, their crowns on their heads, and enjoy the lustre of the Shekhinah." The last idea we find also in the Syriac Baruch, which compares the World to Come to *"a crown with great glory"* (15:8). And as regards wild beasts, asps, and vipers, apart from the great vision of Isaiah (11:6–9), there are also to be cited the detailed words on this subject in the early Tannaitic Midrash, Siphra.[27] Finally, in regard to the elimination of the pains of childbirth, there is to be mentioned this Baraitha: "Woman is destined to bear every day," on the analogy of the hen.[28] But it must be confessed that expectations set in orderly arrangement and embracing *all* the life of man in all his occupations—even that of *tillers of the soil and laborers*—such as we have here before us, is not to be found in the early parts of the Talmud and Midrash.

On the other hand, all the exaggerated *material* expectations in the Syriac Book of Baruch agree perfectly with the ancient Talmudic Baraithas:

Whatever happens in the period of "the birth pangs of Messiah" will happen in "the whole earth," and so "all who live will experience it; but at that time I will protect only those who are found in those self-same days in this land" (Palestine). And after what has been said about "the seven-year cycle at the end of which the son of David will come" shall have been fulfilled, "the Messiah shall then begin to be revealed."

And Behemoth (the hippopotamus) shall be revealed from his place (the dry land) and Leviathan shall ascend from the sea, those two great monsters which I created on the fifth day of creation, and shall have kept until that time; and then they shall be food for all that are left. The earth also shall yield its fruit ten-thousandfold.[29] And on each vine there shall be a thousand branches. And each branch shall produce a thousand clus-

---

[27] Siphra, Behuqqothai, beginning of Chap. 2, edition of I. H. Weiss, 111a.
[28] Shabbath, 30b.
[29] According to R. Harris, the author interpreted the word *robh* in the expression "plenty (*robh*) of corn and wine" (Gen. 27:28) as meaning *ribbo'* ("ten thousand"; see *Expositor*, III, 448–449; V, 261).

ters. And each cluster shall produce a thousand grapes. And each grape shall produce a cor (more than 360 litres) of wine. And those who have hungered shall rejoice: moreover, also, they shall behold marvels every day. For winds shall go forth from before Me to bring every morning the fragrance of aromatic fruits, and at the close of the day clouds distilling the dew of health. And it shall come to pass at that self-same time that *the treasury of manna* shall again descend from on high; and they will eat of it in those years, because these are they who have come to the end of time.—And it shall come to pass after these things, when the time of *the advent of the Messiah* is fulfilled, that he shall return in glory (to heaven?). Then all who have fallen asleep ("those who sleep in the dust," Dan. 12:2) in hope of Him shall rise again (29:1–30:1).

Again we see that the Messianic age is only a transition to the World to Come. The Messiah, to be sure, does not die; neither does he remain on earth forever: he will return, apparently, to heaven, *like the prophet Elijah*. This view is different from that found in the Book of IV Ezra: there the Messiah dies along with all in whom there is human breath after four hundred years of the Messianic age.[30] The Talmud, like the Syriac Book of Baruch, does not know the death of Messiah *ben David;* only Messiah *ben Joseph* dies in the war with Gog and Magog. However, everything found here about "Behemoth" and "Leviathan" and about the fruitfulness of the earth we have already seen in the Book of Enoch [31] and in the Talmud and Midrash.[32] Especially striking is the strong likeness between the description of the productivity of soil and vine in the Book of Baruch and that in the Talmud and Midrash. It is as though one had copied from the other, or both had drawn from an earlier source common to them. For example, "There will be no grape that will not contain thirty kegs of wine," and so on.[33] But there is a still greater similarity between the Syriac Book of Baruch and the tradition handed down by Irenaeus in the name of one of the earliest of the Christian Church Fathers, one who is reckoned among the "Apostolic Fathers," Papias of Hierapolis in Phrygia (died *c.* 165 C.E.); Irenaeus testifies that the "elders" (eld-

---

[30] IV Ezra 7:28–29; see below, p. 354.
[31] Book of Enoch 60:7–10, 24; 10:17–19. See above, pp. 298–299.
[32] Baba Bathra 74*b* and 75*a;* Kethubboth 111*b;* Kallah Rabbathi, Chap. 2; Siphre, Deut., 315.
[33] Kethubboth, *ibid.*

ers of the Christian Church) who knew John, the disciple of Jesus, received this materialistic oracle from John as a saying of Jesus: [34]

The days will come, in which vines shall grow, each having ten thousand branches, and in each branch ten thousand twigs, and in each twig ten thousand shoots, and in each one of the shoots ten thousand clusters, and on every one of the clusters ten thousand grapes, and every grape when pressed will give twenty-five measures of wine (each measure being 36 litres). And when any one of the saints shall lay hold of a cluster, another shall cry out, "I am a better cluster, take me; bless the LORD through me!" In like manner a grain of wheat shall produce ten thousand ears, and every ear shall have ten thousand grains, and every grain shall yield ten pounds of fine flour; and all other fruit-bearing trees, and seeds and grass shall produce in similar proportions. And all animals feeding on these products of the earth shall become peaceful and harmonious among each other, and be in perfect subjection to man.

This is the tradition of Papias received from Jesus. And in spite of the fact that Christian scholars refuse to attribute "crude" and fanciful materialistic descriptions like these to Jesus,[35] I incline to believe that the *Jewish* Jesus, who lived a century after the composition of the Book of Enoch and forty years before the composition of the Syriac Book of Baruch, must have spoken to the hearts of the simple and pious multitude that followed him with mundane portrayals like these, since they were already widely current in the nation in his time; and that the authors of the Book of Enoch and the Syriac Book of Baruch, the Talmud and Midrash, and Jesus all drew from a single early popular source.[36]

It is proper to point out that the "winds" which "shall go forth from before Me (God)" are also mentioned in the Talmudic Baraitha about the fruitfulness of the earth: "Its fruit shall rustle like Lebanon [Ps. 72:16]; the Holy One, blessed be He, *will bring a wind* from His treasure houses which He will cause to blow upon it."[37] However,

---

[34] Quoted in Irenaeus, *Against Heresies*, V, 33, 3–4.

[35] See A. Resch, *Agrapha*, 2nd ed., Leipzig, 1906, pp. 166–167; in contrast to this, see A. Holtzmann, *Leben Jesu*, Tübingen, 1901, pp. 41–42.

[36] J. Klausner, *Jesus of Nazareth*, 5th Hebrew ed., 1945, pp. 62, 435–436, also 474 [English ed., pp. 65–66, 401–402].

[37] Kethubboth, *ibid.*

here the wind comes to make the flour drop down from the wheat (which does not agree with the verse "Its *fruit* shall rustle like Lebanon"). With regard to the "aromatic fruits," we have already found in the Book of Enoch (25:3-6) that the righteous will enjoy the fruit of a fragrant tree; that *the manna* will come again to Israel in the Days of the Messiah is also known to the early Tannaitic Midrash.[38]

In the Days of the Messiah the LORD will execute *vengeance on the enemies of Israel*. This fact, which was already indicated in the body of the book, is particularly emphasized, and even glorified and exalted to the height of poetic beauty, in *a letter* which Baruch sent *to the ten tribes* (or, to be precise, nine and a half tribes) across the River Euphrates, and which is appended to the Syriac Baruch at the end (Chaps. 78-87). It is full of hope for the *ingathering of the exiles* (78:7), which will come about after repentance on the part of the exiles (84:10). The end is near, and along with it the Day of Judgment, the day of vengeance, the day of consolation, the day of redemption are also near:

> For lo! we see now the magnitude
>   of the prosperity of the Gentiles,
> Though they act impiously,
> But they shall be like a vapor.
>
> And we behold the magnitude of their power,
> Though they do wickedly,
> But they shall be made like unto a drop (from a bucket).[39]
>
> And we see the firmness of their might,
> Though they resist the Mighty One every hour,
> But they shall be accounted as spittle.
>
> And we consider the glory of their greatness,
> Though they do not keep the statutes of the Most High,
> But as smoke shall they pass away.
>
> And we meditate on the beauty of their gracefulness,
> Though they have to do with pollutions,
> But as grass that withers shall they fade away.

---

[38] Mekhilta, Wayyassa, Chap. 5 (ed. Friedmann, 51*b*).

[39] Cf. Isa. 40:15 (see also the Septuagint at this verse). And with all these descriptions cf. IV Ezra 6:56; 7:61.

> And we consider the strength of their cruelty,
> Though they remember not the end (thereof),
> But as a wave that passes [40] shall they be broken.
>
> And we remark the boastfulness of their might,
> Though they deny the beneficence of God,
> who gave (it) to them,
> But they shall pass away as a passing cloud (82:2–9).

How the people's seer dropped the dew of consolation upon fainting hearts that could find no satisfaction in the success and power of the Romans, the destroyers of the land and the people!

The repentance will precede the redemption, since in the Messianic age there is no more place for repentance (85:12). For "that which exists now or which has passed away, or which is to come—in all these things, neither is the evil fully evil, nor again the good fully good" (83:9). This agrees in part with the saying of R. Johanan, "The son of David will come only in a generation that is altogether righteous or altogether wicked." [41]

In the Messianic age, *the heavenly Jerusalem* will come down to earth. It is already *revealed before the LORD, being preserved with Him in heaven since the day when He created Paradise;* He showed it to Adam before he was expelled from the Garden of Eden; He showed it to Abraham at the Covenant of the Pieces [Gen. 15]; He showed it to Moses "when I (He) showed to him the likeness of the Tabernacle and all its vessels" (agreeing with the Baraitha: [42] "An ark of fire and a table of fire and a candlestick of fire came down from heaven; and these Moses saw and reproduced"). This is Baruch's consolation for the destruction of the earthly Jerusalem (4:2–6). We have already found "the heavenly Jerusalem" in the Book of Enoch,[43] and we saw there that it is also found in IV Ezra [44] and the Talmud.[45] But the vessels of the Temple are entrusted to the earth by the angel

---

[40] Possibly a translation error for "as a shadow that passes away" (Ps. 144:4).
[41] Sanhedrin 98a.
[42] Menahoth 29a; and see there the words that follow concerning the tabernacle. See also Gen. R., Chaps. 16 and 44; and Siphre, Deut., 37, ed. Friedmann, f. 76.
[43] Book of Enoch 90:28–29.
[44] IV Ezra 10:26; 13:36.
[45] Taanith 5a; Baba Bathra 75b.

in order that foreigners may not get possession of them, and that they may be preserved within it until the end of days, when Jerusalem will be built again to last forever and ever (6:8–9).

Greater than "the birth pangs of Messiah" will be "the birth pangs of the Age to Come," when "the Mighty One will renew His creation" (32:6). This is *the New World*, with which the Talmud and Midrash are so much concerned.[46] The "new world" is *explicitly* mentioned in the Syriac Book of Baruch, and its nature is explained thus:

> And the hour comes which abides forever,
> And *the new world*, which does not turn to corruption
>   those who enter into its blessedness,[47]
> And has no mercy on those who depart to torment,
> And leads not to perdition those who live in it (44:12).

And such a world is near:

> For the youth of the world is past,
> And the strength of the creation already exhausted,
> And the advent of the times is very short,
> Yea, they have passed by;
> And the pitcher is near to the cistern,
> And the ship to the port,
> And the course of the journey to the city,
> And life to (its) consummation (85:10).

It is hard to describe in lovelier sad-bright colors the belief in "the end of the world" that always comes after a national or world catastrophe. And do we not find here the same kind of bitter feelings that followed the two World Wars in our own time?

The New World opens a new world-period and one that is different from the Messianic age. Before us is the World to Come—that "world to which there is no end," in which the righteous will receive "great light" (48:50). In it *the resurrection of the dead* occupies a large place, after which death will be swallowed up forever and Sheol will "restore those which are enclosed" in it (21:23; 42:7; 50:2). Resurrection will be attained both by those who were originally

---

[46] Sanhedrin 92*b*, beginning; Mekhilta, Wayyassa, Chap. 4, ed. Friedmann, 50*b*.
[47] So reads Charles in place of "in its beginning." According to him, *bero'sho* was read here by mistake for *be'oshro* (*op. cit.*, II, 503).

righteous but later "mingled themselves with the seed of mingled peoples," and by those who were originally wicked but later joined with the people Israel, that is to say, *the Ten Tribes and the righteous proselytes* (42:1–5).

At the time of their resurrection, the appearance of those rising will not be changed, and it will be possible for all of them to recognize one another (50:2–4). But after the Day of Judgment, the faces of both the wicked and the righteous will be changed. The faces of the wicked, who did not keep the law of the LORD, will be altered, and they will become estranged spirits and will depart to the place of torment (Gehenna); but the faces of the righteous will be bright with the brightness of angels, and they will become like the stars; time will no longer age them, and they will dwell in the heights; "the extents of Paradise" will be opened before them, and they will see "the beauty of the majesty of the living creatures which are beneath the throne of glory, and all the armies of the angels"; "moreover, there shall then be excellency in the righteous surpassing that in the angels." The angels will receive the righteous, whom they, the angels, have been expecting for some time; and the righteous will never again know toil or sorrow or tribulation (51:1–14).

Again, this description recalls, in its general aspect and in its details, the descriptions of the World to Come in the Talmud. Undoubtedly, in the time of the Syriac Book of Baruch these Messianic expectations and these pictures of the World to Come were already widely current in the nation; and in due course of time they penetrated into the great treasury of the nation's wisdom, poetry, and hopes, which we call the Talmudic-Midrashic Aggadah.

CHAPTER VII

The Pseudepigraphic (Fourth) Book of Ezra

(C. 90–100 C.E.)

THE PSEUDEPIGRAPHIC book which is called "Fourth Ezra" to distinguish it from the Book of Ezra in the Bible (*First* Ezra), from the Book of Nehemiah, which the Septuagint (and the Christian versions following it) calls "Second Ezra," and from the *Apocryphal Book of Ezra* (*Third* Ezra), is the profoundest and the most exalted in its lofty spirituality of all the books of the "Pseudepigrapha." Its author excels in the purity of his idealism, in the loftiness of his visions, in his penetrating and deeply probing doubts about divine Providence, in his profound questions about worldly justice, and particularly in his lofty conceptions of the Messiah, the Day of Judgment, retribution, and the like.[1]

The Pseudepigraphic Ezra was written, almost certainly, a short time *after* the Syriac Baruch, about 90–100 C.E., in Hebrew and in Palestine, or by an exile from Palestine. The Syriac Baruch, of which

[1] See the splendid characterization given by H. Gunkel to IV Ezra in his excellent introduction to the translation of this book (Kautzsch, *Apocryphen und Pseudepigraphen*, II, 335–350). See also C. G. Montefiore, *IV Ezra*, London, 1929. Abraham Kahana (*The Outside Books* [Heb.], I.2, pp. 576–653) calls the Apocryphal Ezra (III Esdras) "the Outside [Pseudepigraphic] Ezra," and the Pseudepigraphic Ezra (IV Ezra) he calls "the Vision of Ezra." A. Kaminka called his Hebrew translation of IV Ezra "Visions of the Captive Shealtiel" (Tel-Aviv, 1936) on the basis of a weak hypothesis. In Kahana's translation there is a variation in the numbering of verses in two chapters.

I spoke in the preceding chapter, and the Pseudepigraphic Ezra together constitute another "Book of Lamentations" over the destruction of the Second Temple.[2] And in both of them the numerous Messianic expectations, for which alone, apparently, all such books came into being—divine consolation after such severe affliction—in both of them the numerous Messianic expectations are amazingly like the Messianic portrayals in the earlier parts of the Talmud and Midrash. In spite of the fact that the Tridentine [Roman Catholic] Christian Church decided to exclude this book from the canon of Christian Scripture, and that Luther also did not reckon it among the Sacred Writings, "Fourth Ezra" is still to be found in the Vulgate (the officially accepted Latin [Roman Catholic] version of the Bible), and until this day it continues to be printed in the "Zürich Bible"; and it was even admitted to the Lutheran Bible as late as the eighteenth century. To such an extent did this Pseudepigraphical book appeal to people's hearts.

I give herewith the essence of its Messianic ideas:

1. *The Birth Pangs of Messiah*

"The signs of the Messiah," that is, the signs that will precede the coming of the Messiah, are these: great confusion will seize the inhabitants of the earth, the way of truth will be hidden, and the land of faith will be desolate. Iniquity will be increased above what it is now or what it was before. The land that now rules (Rome) will become "a desert way,"[3] and be forsaken. "After three" (days, in the sense of periods of time) will come "confusion" (compare "After two days will He revive us, on the third day He will raise us up, that we may live in His presence,"[4] from which also stemmed the belief of Christians in the resurrection of Jesus on the third day after his crucifixion):

> Then shall the sun suddenly shine forth by night,
> and the moon by day;

[2] See on this theme J. Klausner, *History of the Second Temple* [Heb.], V, 294-295.
[3] Ps. 107:4.
[4] Hosea 6:2.

And blood shall trickle forth from wood,
    and the stone utter its voice; [5]
The peoples shall be in commotion,
    the courses (of the stars) [6] shall change.

And one whom the dwellers upon earth do not look for (the tyrant) shall wield sovereignty, and the birds shall fly away, and the sea of Sodom (the Dead Sea, in which fish cannot live) shall cast forth its fish.[7] And a voice that many do not understand will come forth by night; but all shall hear its sound. The interior of the earth shall be opened up in many places, and fire shall burst forth at frequent intervals.[8] Wild beasts shall wander from their haunts, and women shall bear monsters. Salt (*salsae*) shall be found in sweet waters; and friends shall attack one another suddenly.

Then shall intelligence hide itself,
And wisdom withdraw to its chamber,
By many shall they be sought and not found.

And unrighteousness and presumptuousness shall be multiplied upon the earth. One land shall also ask another and say: "Has righteousness—which doeth the right—passed through thee?" And it shall answer, "No." And it shall be
    In that time men shall hope and not obtain,
        shall labor and not prosper (5:1–13).

These "signs" are already known to us in large part from the Book of Enoch and the Syriac Book of Baruch, and from the Talmudic Baraithas about "the footprints of the Messiah" and "the seven-year cycle at the end of which the son of David will come," which I discussed at length in the preceding chapters. But the "Fourth Ezra" presents many more "signs of Messiah." On the basis of the passage "And his hand had hold on Esau's heel" (Gen. 25:26), he brings out, like a thoroughly Talmudic expounder, that "the heel of the first age" is Esau-Edom-Rome (exactly as in the Talmud in many places),

---

[5] Cf. Habakkuk 2:11: "For the stone shall cry out of the wall, and the beam out of the timber shall answer it."

[6] In Latin *gressūs* ("course," in the plural number); "of the stars" is to be added in accord with the Ethiopic text. But Gunkel (*op. cit.*, p. 359, Note o) takes the reading *egressus*, and conjectures that it is a translation of the word "outgoings" (Ps. 65:9), in the sense of the heavenly portals through which the stars and the winds go out.

[7] See Ezek. 47:8–10.

[8] See Rev. 9:2.

and that "the hand of the second (age) is Jacob"; for "the beginning of a man is his hand, and the end of a man is his heel." That is to say, this age comes to an end with the rule of Rome (Esau-Edom), and the coming age begins with the rule of Israel (Jacob). And there is no interval between them, since the hand of Jacob had hold of the heel of Esau. This interpretation was given to Ezra by God Himself (6:5–10). It is precisely what we find in the Midrash: to the question of the Roman prefect, "Who will enjoy power after us?" Rabbi Eliezer (or Rabban Gamaliel) "brought a blank piece of paper, took a quill, and wrote upon it, 'And after that came forth his brother, and his hand had hold on Esau's heel.' " [9]

Afterward Ezra asks God to show him "the end of the wonders" (Dan. 12:6). Then a majestic voice is heard to say:

Behold the days come, and it shall be, when I am about to draw nigh to visit the dwellers upon the earth, and when I require from the doers of iniquity the penalty of their iniquity, and when the humiliation of Zion shall be complete, and when the age *which is about to pass away* shall be sealed—then will I show these signs: the books shall be opened before the face of the firmament, and all shall see (them) together. And one-year-old children shall speak with their voices; pregnant women shall bring forth untimely births at three or four months, and these shall live and run about. And suddenly shall the sown places appear unsown, and the full storehouses shall suddenly be found empty. And *the trumpet* [10] shall sound aloud, at which all men, when they hear it, shall be struck with sudden fear. And at that time friends shall war against friends like enemies,[11] the earth shall be stricken with fear together with the dwellers thereon, and the springs of the fountains shall stand still so that for three hours [12] they shall not run.

And it shall be, whosoever shall have survived all these things that I have foretold unto thee, he shall be saved and shall see my salvation (*salutare meum*) and *the end of my world* (this world). And the men who have been taken up,[13] who have not tasted death from their birth,

---

[9] Gen. R., Chap. 63.
[10] "The trumpet of Messiah" in the Talmud, which comes from Isa. 27:13 and Zech. 9:14, and is mentioned in the *Shemoneh Esreh*: "Sound the great trumpet for our freedom."
[11] See above, p. 351.
[12] No doubt three periods of time, as mentioned above.
[13] To heaven, such as Enoch and Elijah.

shall appear.¹⁴ Then shall the heart of the inhabitants of the world be changed, and be converted to a different spirit.¹⁵

> For evil shall be blotted out,
>   and deceit extinguished;
> Faithfulness shall flourish,
>   and corruption be vanquished;
> And truth, which for so long a time
>   has been without fruit,
>   shall be made manifest (6:11-28).

Among these "signs" there are a number which we have not hitherto met anywhere, while some of them can be found here and there only in the later Midrashim. But most of them are based on passages in the prophetic books, being, however, much expanded and embellished with the products of the popular Oriental imagination that was so prevalent in the very difficult period following the Second Destruction.

Here are more "Messianic signs." In answer to Ezra's question as to when all these signs will occur, he receives *new signs*, which will be clear indications that the "end" is near:

> When in the world (*in saeculo*) there shall appear
>   quakings of lands,
>   tumult of peoples,
>   schemings of nations,
>   confusion of leaders,
>   disquietude of princes,

then shalt thou understand that it is of these things the Most High has spoken since the days that were aforetime from the beginning.¹⁶ For just as with respect to all that has happened in the world, it has a beginning in the word (of God at creation) and a manifest end,¹⁷ so also are the times of the Most High: the beginnings are revealed in portents and powers (*prodigiis et virtutibus*), and the end in deed and in signs (8:62–9:6).

---

[14] So reads Gunkel (*op. cit.*, p. 366, Note h) instead of "shall see" (the Latin text has *et videbunt*).

[15] Ezek. 36:26-27.

[16] Apparently the reference is to the time of Gog and Magog, according to Ezek. 38:17, 19-23.

[17] So Gunkel translates (*op. cit.*, p. 383, Note q), approximately, according to the Ethiopic version.

Here again, we have before us much of what we found in the Talmudic Baraitha on "the seven-year cycle at the end of which the son of David will come"; wars and tumults and confusions are clear indications of the nearness of the end; of similar import are the signs and portents and wonders and disruption of the order of the heavenly bodies.

2. *The Messianic Age and the Day of Judgment*

After the "signs of Messiah" have come, the city that is now invisible (the heavenly Jerusalem) will appear in the likeness of a bride,[18] and "the land which is now concealed (Paradise, from which Adam was expelled) shall be seen; and whosoever shall be delivered from the predicted evils, the same shall see my wonders."

For My son the Messiah [19] shall be revealed, together with those who are with him (the righteous), and the survivors shall rejoice for *four hundred years*. And it shall be, after these years, that *My son the Messiah shall die, and all in whom there is human breath*. Then shall the world be turned into *the primeval silence seven days*, like as at the first beginnings (*in prioribus iniciis*), so that no man is left.

And it shall be after seven days that the age which is now asleep shall be roused, and that which is corruptible (the age of corruption) shall perish. And the earth shall restore those that sleep in her (those "that sleep in the dust of the earth," Dan. 12:2), and the dust those that are at rest therein (those "that dwell in the dust," Isa. 26:19); and the chambers (*promptuaria*) shall restore those that were committed unto them (7:26–32).

We have already seen "the heavenly Jerusalem" (which appears again as "Zion . . . prepared and builded" in 13:36) in the Book of Enoch, in the Syriac Baruch, and in the Talmudic Baraithas; likewise

[18] So it is according to the Syriac and the Latin; but Gunkel translates according to the Armenian and the Ethiopic: "Then shall the city that is now invisible appear"; in his opinion the Greek words νῦν μή (not now) were misread and became νύμφη (bride). See *op. cit.*, p. 370, Note d. See also Charles, *Apocrypha and Pseudepigrapha*, II, 582.

[19] "Jesus," which comes here only in the Latin text, and is lacking in the Syriac, the Ethiopic, and the Armenian, is a Christian addition. The Syriac has here "My son the Messiah," the Ethiopic has "My Messiah," the Armenian has "the Anointed of the LORD," and other texts have only "Messiah." Calling the Messiah "My son" is something commonly found in ancient Jewish literature, and is here not due to Christian influence at all.

Paradise, which will be revealed in the Messianic age. We have also seen previously the replacement of the old world, the world of corruption in the Book of Baruch (40:3). Those "that sleep in the dust of the earth" are mentioned in Daniel (12:2) and those "that dwell in the dust" in Isaiah (26:19), where comes also the assurance that "the earth shall bring to life the shades." Likewise "the treasuries of souls," mentioned here, and also farther on (7:100–101), where seven days like the days of creation are given to the souls to see the agonies of the wicked, after which they return to their chambers—these "treasuries" we have seen previously in the Syriac Book of Baruch (21:23; 23:4–7; 30:2) and in the Talmud, where they are called "Guf" (Abodah Zarah *5a* and parallels).[20] That the Messianic age is only a period of transition to the World to Come—this is also known by the Syriac Baruch (40:3, see the preceding chapter); and in the Talmud this belief is held with such complete certainty that there are differences of opinion among the Sages as to how long the Messianic age will continue. R. Dosa said that it would continue *four hundred years*—exactly the number of years in IV Ezra.[21]

Only the notion that between the Old World (the world of corruption) and the New World (this latter being mentioned more explicitly farther on, 7:75) there will be seven days of silence—only this we do not find in any other book, unless we compare with this "primeval silence" the two thousand years of "desolation" (*tohu*) in the Talmudic Baraitha.[22] This notion comes from the view of IV Ezra that the "end" is like the "beginning"; and that since at the time of the old creation there was a "primeval silence" for six days, until man was formed, it must be so again in the "new creation" before the New World can arise. (The "new creation" is well known also in the Christian Greek literature under the names *kainē ktisis* and *palingenesia*). In any case, this is a lofty and wonderfully majestic

---

[20] Hence the whole matter of the "bird nest" in which the souls dwell and from which the Messiah will come according to the *Zohar* (II, *7b;* III, *196b*). See V. Aptowitzer, "Die Seele als Vogel," *MGWJ*, LXIX (1925), 150–169; K. Kohler, *Jew. Encycl.*, III, 219.
[21] Sanhedrin 99*a*. See for details below, Part III, all of Chap. II and the beginning of Chap. III; Hühn, *Die messian. Weissag.*, p. 109, Note 3.
[22] Sanhedrin 97*a*, end.

view. Between the old and the new a decided hush prevails. Silence, all the earth! An incomparably new and an immeasurably great creation is being made ready to come forth into the world's atmosphere.

For this world is only a period of transition to the Messianic age, and the Messianic age is only a period of transition to the World to Come (7:11-14, 18, 112). The end of this world and the beginning of the World to Come is the Day of Judgment, which will come after the advent of Messiah (7:113). The Day of Judgment was prepared before the creation of the world and before Adam and his descendants (7:70). On the Day of Judgment

> the Most High shall be revealed
> upon the throne of judgment,
> and then cometh the End.
> And compassion shall pass away,
> and long suffering be withdrawn;
> But judgment alone shall remain,
> truth shall stand,
> and faithfulness triumph.
> And recompense [23] shall follow,
> and reward be made manifest;
> Deeds of righteousness shall awake,
> and deeds of iniquity shall not be repeated.
> Then shall the pit of torment appear,
> and over against it the place of refreshment;
> The furnace of Gehenna shall be made manifest,
> and over against it the Paradise of delight.

And then shall the Most High say to the nations that have been raised (from the dead): Look now and consider Whom ye have denied, Whom ye have not served, Whose commandments ye have despised.

> Look, now, before you:
> here delight and refreshment,
> there fire and torments!

Thus shall He speak unto them in the Day of Judgment, for thus shall the Day of Judgment be:

---

[23] Payment (for work), Lat. *opus*, from "May this be the *reward* of my accusers from the LORD" (Ps. 109:20); likewise "And giveth him not his *hire*," i.e., wages (Jer. 22:13). Cf. also "Behold, His *reward* is with Him, and His *recompense* before Him" (Isa. 40:10); "there is a *reward* for your *labor*" (Jer. 31:16). See also above, p. 92, and p. 253.

> In it neither sun, nor moon, nor stars;
> neither clouds, nor lightning, nor thunder;
> neither wind, nor rain-storm, nor cloud-rack;
> neither darkness, nor evening, nor morning;
> neither summer, nor autumn, nor winter;
> neither heat, nor frost, nor cold;
> neither hail, nor rain, nor dew;
> neither noon, nor night, nor day;
> neither shining, nor brightness, nor light,

save only the splendor of the brightness of the Most High, whereby all shall be destined to see what has been determined (for them).[24]

And that day, the Day of Judgment, will last "a week of years," that is, a period of seven years.

Once more we have before us the "chaos" which is transferred from the time of creation to the period of emptiness before the new creation—the New World, although in place of *seven days* of "primeval silence" we have here *seven years* of emptiness.

As for the Syriac Baruch (85:10), so also for Ezra this world grows senile; and the weaker it becomes from old age, the more troubles increase in it, truth is farther removed from it, and falsehood comes nearer (14:15–17). Because of the terror of the Day of Judgment, the World to Come will bring delight to only a few and torments to many (7:47). The torments of the World to Come will be so severe that IV Ezra says: ". . . woe unto them that shall survive in those days! but much more woe unto them that do not survive!" Those who do not survive will know about the bliss reserved for the future, but will not enjoy it. "But woe unto them also that survive, for . . . they must see great perils and many distresses" (13:16–17) —exactly what we heard in the Syriac Baruch (28:3), and something like what we found in the Talmud: "Let him [the Messiah] come, but let me not see him."[25] IV Ezra, however, like the Talmud,[26] concludes that it is nevertheless better to reach this new era, even through perils, than "to pass away as a cloud out of the world and

---

[24] 7:33–43 according to Gunkel; 7:33–35 and 6:1–16 according to Fritzsche; 5:33–43 according to Kahana.
[25] Sanhedrin 98b.
[26] *Ibid.*

not to see what shall happen in the New Age (*in novissimo*)" [13:20].

We see, therefore, that the Messianic age and the World to Come are only for the few. This is emphasized many times (8:1-3, 41; 9:7-17, 22): "Many have been created, but few shall be saved!" Only the righteous will escape "on account of their works or their faith by which they believed in God." Nor can the righteous be sureties for the wicked—not even a father for his son, or a son for his father (7:102-105)—exactly as in the Book of Ezekiel (18:20).

The "End" will come about *through God alone and through no other* (6:6). That is to say, *not even through the Messiah*—something that we find in many books of Holy Scripture, of the Apocrypha, and even of the Pseudepigrapha. This is the thoroughly Jewish view, in complete opposition to Christianity, in which the Messiah takes the place of God in the Day of Judgment and what follows. *Perfect righteousness* will prevail in "the eternal age that is to come; wherein corruption is passed away, hardness of heart is abolished, infidelity is cut off; while righteousness is grown, and faithfulness is sprung up. So shall no man then be able to save that which is lost,[27] or cast down [28] that which is victorious" (7:113-115).

The personality and work of the Messiah are described specifically in two marvelous visions: *the Vision of the Eagle Ascending out of the Sea* (11-12); and *the Vision of the Son of Man Ascending out of the Sea* (13). We have already heard God calling the Messiah "My son" (7:28-29). This designation, based upon the verse "Thou art *My son*, this day have I begotten thee" (Ps. 2:7), occurs again in these visions (13:32, 37, 52; 14:9); but the Messiah is here also called the "son of man [who flew] with the clouds of heaven" (13:3), in imitation of Daniel (7:13), and also simply "man" (*homo*, 13:12) and "male person" (*vir*, 13:25, 32). And he is likened to a lion (11:37; 12:31), either in reference to his strength or because he is from the tribe of Judah, "a *lion's* whelp," that "stooped down, he couched *as a lion*, and as a lioness; who shall rouse him up?" [29] He existed before the creation of the world and is being kept with God until

---

[27] I.e., is found guilty in the judgment.
[28] More exactly, to submerge (*demergere*).
[29] Gen. 49:9.

the time for him to be revealed (12:32; 13:26, 52; 14:9), as in the Ethiopic Enoch (39:6–7), and in the later Baraithas of the Talmud,[30] and so also in the Targum attributed to Jonathan ben Uzziel (on Zechariah 4:7) and in the later Midrashim.[31] The Eagle Vision moves about within the limits of the visions of Daniel and of the Syriac Baruch. The eagle rising from the sea is *Rome*, which is also called "eagle" in the Talmud,[32] and is perhaps the "eagle" of the Assumption of Moses (10:8).[33] In the interpretation of the vision we read: "The eagle which thou sawest come up out of the sea is *the fourth kingdom* which appeared in vision *to thy brother Daniel;*[34] *but it was not interpreted unto him as I now interpret it*" (12:11–12). That is to say, Daniel saw the interpretation of the fourth kingdom in the kingdom of *Greece*, but IV Ezra in the kingdom of *Rome*.

And as for the lion whom thou didst see roused from the wood and roaring, and speaking to the eagle and reproving him for his unrighteousness and all his evil deeds, as thou hast heard: This is the *Messiah (Unctus)* whom the Most High hath kept unto the end of the days, who shall spring from the seed of David, and shall come and speak unto them;[35] he shall reprove them for their ungodliness and rebuke them for their unrighteousness. . . . For he shall set them alive for judgment; and after he hath rebuked them [36] he shall destroy them. But my people who survive he shall deliver with mercy, even those who have been saved throughout my borders,[37] and he shall make them joyful until the End come, even the Day of Judgment, of which I have spoken unto thee from the beginning (12:31–34).

This vision, which sets forth the victory of the lion-Messiah over the eagle-Rome, is entirely *spiritual*. The Vision of the Man Coming Up from the Sea [38] is more *political*. Ezra sees in the vision a great

---

[30] Derekh Erets Zuta, end of Chap. 1. On the name of Messiah, which preceded the creation of the world, see Pesahim 54a and Nedarim 39b.
[31] See Schürer, *Geschichte*, II⁴, 615–620; see also below, Part III, Chap. VII.
[32] Sanhedrin 12a.
[33] See above, pp. 328–329.
[34] Dan. 7:7.
[35] According to the Syriac, Ethiopic, and Armenian versions—meaning "to the Gentiles."
[36] I.e., rebuked their iniquities.
[37] In Palestine.
[38] On the popular-mythological element in the earliest source of this vision, see H. Gressmann, *Eschatologie*, pp. 337–339, 349–357.

wind on the sea (Dan. 7:2-3: "... the four *winds* of the heaven broke forth *upon the great sea;* and four great beasts *came up from the sea*"). And the wind caused to come up out of the heart of the sea *one like a man* ("one like unto a son of man"), who flew with *the clouds of heaven* (Dan. 7:13). Wherever he turned, everyone that the Man looked at trembled; and wherever his voice was heard from his mouth, everyone who heard it melted as wax melts before fire. Then an innumerable multitude of men came from the four winds of heaven to make war against the Man that came up out of the sea (Gog and Magog). He, the Man, cut out for himself a mountain ("a stone was cut out of the mountain," Dan. 2:45) and flew up upon it. All who were gathered together to wage war with him were seized with great fear, yet they dared to fight. But he, the Man, when he saw the onslaught,

neither lifted his hand, nor held spear nor any warlike weapon; but I saw only how he sent out of his mouth as it were a fiery stream (*flatus ignis*), and out of his lips a flaming breath, and out of his tongue he shot forth a storm of sparks.[39] And these were all mingled together—the fiery stream, the flaming breath, and the great storm [of sparks]—and fell mightily upon the multitude which was prepared to fight, and burned them all up; so that suddenly nothing more was to be seen of the innumerable multitude save only dust of ashes and smell of smoke.

Afterward the same Man came down from the mountain and called unto him "another multitude which was peaceable" (*multitudo alia pacifica*). Then drew nigh unto him the faces of many men, some of whom were glad, some sorrowful; while some were in bonds, some brought others who should be offered" (13:2-13). Apparently, both the "glad" and the "sorrowful" are Gentiles; but the "glad" are the Gentiles who did not oppress Israel, while the "sorrowful" are those who did, just as we have seen in the Syriac Baruch (72:2-6) and in the Talmud.[40] Those "in bonds" are, no doubt, *the exiled Jews* whom

---

[39] About Bar-Cochba a Christian source relates that he made himself appear as though breathing forth a flame of fire from his mouth (Jerome, *Against Rufinus*, III, 31). Do we not have proof from this that IV Ezra was written after Bar-Cochba's war? However, it is possible, of course, that the Christian legend was influenced by IV Ezra.

[40] Pesahim 118*b*.

the Gentiles are bringing back as ones "who should be offered" (*qui offerebatur*), to fulfill the prophecy of Deutero-Isaiah: "And they shall bring all your brethren *out of all the nations for an offering unto the LORD*," and so on (Isa. 66:20–21).[41]

Farther on (13:25–52) comes the interpretation of the vision: the "Man coming up from the heart of the sea" is "he whom the Most High is keeping many ages and through whom [42] He will deliver His creation; and he shall determine who are to be the survivors." The Messiah is, therefore, *the savior of the world*. This is an ancient Jewish idea and there is no need to find here a Christian interpolation. Christianity only altered this idea in the matter of the redemption of the world by means of the voluntarily shed blood of the Son of God; this latter thing was unknown to the *oldest* Judaism (in the *later* Midrashim this idea of a suffering Messiah appears; Messiah *ben Joseph* is indeed slain, but *in battle*, fighting as king and commander). As for the destruction of the army of the peoples without spear or any warlike weapon, but only by means of "fire, flame, and storm" coming as it were out of the mouth of the Messiah—this is its interpretation:

Behold, the days come when the Most High is about to deliver them that are upon the earth (thus "the Most High" is the true redeemer, the Messiah being only an instrument for His work). And there shall come confusion of mind (*excessus mentis*) upon the dwellers on earth. And they shall plan to war one against another, city against city, place against place, people against people, and kingdom against kingdom.

Then, when the signs of the Messiah mentioned above shall appear,

My son shall be revealed whom thou didst see as a Man ascending. It shall be, when all the nations hear his voice, every man shall leave his own land and the warfare which they have one against another; and an innumerable multitude shall be gathered together, as thou didst see, desiring to come and to fight against him.[43] But he shall stand upon the summit of Mount Zion. *And Zion shall come and shall be made manifest to all men, set in order and builded*, even as thou didst see the mountain cut

---

[41] See also Isa. 18:7; Psalms of Solomon 17:34.
[42] See for the correct reading Wellhausen, *Skizzen und Vorarbeiten*, Berlin, 1899, VI, 236, Note 1.
[43] I.e., a multitude like the multitude of Gog and Magog, which came to fight against the Messiah.

out without hands ("a stone was cut out of the mountain without hands").[44]

Thus we again have before us *the heavenly Jerusalem*, in addition to having seen it before (7:26–27). And God adds:

But he, My son (the Messiah), shall reprove the nations that are come for their ungodliness—which things (that is, the rebukes) are like unto a storm—and he shall reproach them to their face with their evil thoughts and with the tortures with which they are destined to be tortured—which are comparable unto a flame; and then shall he destroy them without effort by his command, which is comparable unto fire (13:37–38).

This interpretation deviates in part from the parable in which was presented the manner of the destruction of the host coming to make war on the Messiah.

The "multitude which was peaceable" is *the Ten Tribes*, which were exiled from their land in the time of Hoshea,[45]

which Shalmaneser the king of the Assyrians led away captive; he carried them *across the River*, and they were transported *to another land*. But they took this counsel among themselves, that they would leave the multitude of the heathen, and go forth to a land further distant, where the human race had never dwelt, there at least to keep their statutes which they had not kept in their own land. And they crossed by the narrow passages of the river Euphrates. For the Most High then wrought wonders for them, and stopped the flow of the River until they were passed over.[46] And to that country there was a great way to go, a journey [47] of a year and a half; and that region was called *Another Land*.[48] There they have

---

[44] Dan. 2:45.

[45] The Latin, Syriac, and other versions read erroneously *Josiae* instead of *Oseae*.

[46] Therefore it is now impossible to reach them; an allusion to the legend about the river Sambation (Sanhedrin 65*b*; Yerushalmi, *ibid*. 10:6, f. 29*c*; Gen. R., Chaps. 11 and 73; Targum Pseudo-Jonathan on Exodus 34:10; Josephus, *Wars* 7:5:1; Pliny, XXXI, 2).

[47] Thus is *via multa itineris* to be translated.

[48] In Latin *Arzareth, Arsareth*, in Syriac and Ethiopic *Arzaph, Azaph*, in Armenian *Acsarari, Araawin*. To judge by the Syriac and Ethiopic, it might be thought the translators of these versions saw here the words *erets soph* ["land of the end," "remotest land," in Hebrew], (see also A. Epstein, *Eldad ha-Dani*, Vienna, 1891, Introduction, p. xii, Note 1). But Schiller-Szinessy (*Journal of Philology*, III, 113) proposed that the Latin name is corrupted from *erets ahereth* ["another land" in Hebrew] ("and the LORD rooted them out of their land . . . and cast them into *another land*," Deut. 29:27); this is what occurs previously, in

dwelt until the last times; and now, when they are about to come again the Most High will again stop the flow of the River, that they may be able to pass over (13:39-47).

This is the multitude that was gathered together in peace; but included in it are also the survivors of the people Israel found within God's Holy Land. For when the LORD destroys the multitude of the Gentiles that are gathered together, He will protect all that remain of the people Israel, and will show them "many great wonders" (13:46-50).

We find here time after time that God will destroy "the multitude of the nations" and will save Israel alone (compare also 9:22: "Perish, then, the multitude which has been born in vain; but let my grape be preserved, and my plant"); and from Israel He will save only the righteous. About "the righteous among the nations" [righteous Gentiles], who according to R. Joshua (contrary to the opinion of R. Eliezer, who was excommunicated) "have a share in the World to Come," [49] nothing is said here. But *in general* the nations that did not oppress Israel will enjoy the Days of the Messiah, as we saw above.

IV Ezra emphasizes with all force the expectation of *the attack of the nations* (the war of Gog and Magog) in the Days of the Messiah, and in connexion with this *the ingathering of the exiles* and *the return of the Ten Tribes*. In regard to the Ten Tribes there is already a difference of opinion in the Mishnah and in the Tosephta. And it

---

Verse 40. See also below. But for this very reason, that this supposed transliteration occurs only a few verses after a correct translation of *erets ahereth*, F. Perles (*REJ*, LXXIII [1921], 185) opposes the suggestion of Szinessy, and offers the opinion that the name of the land is *Arzaph*, as in the Ethiopic version; this was corrupted in Latin to *Arzar et* (the word *et* belonging to the following verse, as in the Syriac version). But what is the land of "Arzaph"? Perles found such a land in Armenia, and even an adjective derived from it: "Arzaphi" (*Archiv für Orientforschung*, III [1926], 121-122). But it is hard to imagine that in an apocalyptic book an actual land would be mentioned by its own proper name.

[49] Tosephta, Sanhedrin 13:2. In the Tosephta it is not said, "The pious (*Hasidim*) of the nations of the world have a share in the World to Come," but rather it is "*the righteous among the nations*" who have a share in the World to Come." However, the Babylonian Talmud (Baba Bathra 15b) says, "There was a certain *pious* man among the heathen named Job, who came into this world only to receive his reward"; and from this comes the expression, "The pious of the nations of the world [Gentiles] have a share in the World to Come." But the idea of "the righteous among the nations" and "the pious of the nations of the world" is the same.

is a surprising thing that the disagreeing Tannaim lean upon the very same verse from which the author of the Pseudepigraphic Ezra derives support, and according to which these tribes are to be found in "another land":

> The Ten Tribes shall not return again, for it is written (Deut. 29:27), *And he cast them into another land like as this day*. Like as this day goes and returns not, so do they go and return not. So R. Akiba. But R. Eliezer says: Like as the day grows dark and then grows light, so also after darkness is fallen upon the Ten Tribes shall light hereafter shine upon them.[50]

In the Tosephta [51] the same verse is interpreted thus: "He will pluck them up from upon their own land in anger and wrath and great indignation—in this world; and He will cast them into *another land*—for the World to Come." But R. Simeon ben Judah of Kefar Ikkos [52] makes this contingent upon their deeds; [53] and R. Judah the Patriarch says: "All these have a share in the World to Come, as it is said (Isa. 27:13), *And it shall come to pass in that day, . . . and they shall come that were lost in the land of Assyria*," and so on,[54] in substantial agreement with the Book of IV Ezra.[55] And in one other place (14:33), the Pseudepigraphic Ezra mentions the Ten Tribes as being in a distant land.

The *spiritual bliss* of the Days of the Messiah is very strongly emphasized by the Pseudepigraphic Ezra, as we have seen. *Political success* is emphasized in the claim that all the righteous who live in Palestine will be delivered and all the tribes that went into exile will return to Palestine. But the *material prosperity* which occupied such a large place in the Ethiopic Enoch and in the Syriac Baruch is *hardly mentioned* in the Pseudepigraphic Ezra at all. Only when it speaks of the creation of the world and mentions the formation of Leviathan and Behemoth (the wild ox) on the sixth day of creation, does it say:

---

[50] Mishnah, Sanhedrin 10:3.

[51] *Ibid.*, 13:12.

[52] And not "Kefar Acco" (see W. Bacher, *Agada der Tannaiten*, I, 95, Note 3, and the translation [of Bacher's work] by A. Z. Rabinowitz entitled *Aggadat ha-Tannaim*, Vol. I, Part I, Jaffa, 1920, p. 70, Note 5, and p. 101, Note 5 from the preceding page).

[53] See also Babli, Sanhedrin 110b.

[54] Tosephta, Sanhedrin 13:12, end.

[55] See on this in detail below, Part III, Chap. VIII.

And Thou didst separate the one from the other; for the seventh part (of the world), where the water was gathered together, was unable to hold them (both). And Thou didst give Behemoth [56] one of the parts (of the world) which had been dried up on the third day, to dwell in, where are a thousand hills; [57] but unto Leviathan Thou gavest the seventh part, namely *the moist; and Thou hast reserved them to be devoured by whom Thou wilt and when* (6:49-52).

If we compare these modest words, almost mere hints, with the strongly colored presentations of this subject in the Syriac Baruch (29:4), in the Talmud,[58] and even in the Ethiopic Enoch (60:7-10, 24), then we shall see how "spiritual" is the author of the Pseudepigraphic Ezra, and how far he is from "stories as coarse as sackcloth" and from *excessive* "materialism," although as in any thoroughly *Jewish* book he does not nullify the political expectations, and his book is filled with a spirit of territorial nationalism, like all the Jewish Pseudepigraphical books, but not to the same degree.

This is why I said that the Pseudepigraphic Book of Ezra is the profoundest and the most exalted in its lofty spirituality of all the books of the Pseudepigrapha.

[56] The Latin reads erroneously "Enoch."
[57] "The cattle [Heb. *behemoth*] upon a thousand hills" (Ps. 50:10).
[58] Baba Bathra 74*b* and 75*a*.

CHAPTER VIII

The Biblical Antiquities

(C. 110–130 C.E.)

THIS BOOK, which is attributed—without any basis whatever—to Philo, is a Midrash-Aggadah on Bible stories, similar to the Book of Jubilees (in which, however, the ceremonial laws are basic); and there is no doubt that it originated in the same circle from which came the Syriac Baruch and IV Ezra.[1] It was written originally in Hebrew, but we have preserved to us only an incomplete Latin version, which was translated from Greek. The book was composed not earlier than the Second Destruction,[2] and in my opinion, *after* the Syriac Baruch and IV Ezra,[3] since grief over the Destruction and the difficult problems which that event raised among the thinkers in the nation do not disturb the author of the Biblical Antiquities as they do "Baruch" and "Ezra." And the extreme cruelty manifested in this

---

[1] This interesting book, to which sufficient attention has not been given, appeared thirty-five years ago in English translation with introduction and excellent notes (M. R. James, *The Biblical Antiquities of Philo*, London, 1917). See on it also L. Cohn, "An Apocryphal Work Ascribed to Philo of Alexandria" (*JQR*, X [1898], 277–332); Schürer, *Geschichte*, II⁴, 384–386. See now also Guido Kisch, *Pseudo-Philo's Liber Antiquitatum Biblicarum*, Notre Dame, Ind., 1949.

[2] To the proofs presented by James (*op. cit.*, pp. 29-33, I can add another interesting one: of the army of Sisera there were slain, according to the Biblical Antiquities (21:2, James, p. 172) 90 times 97,000 men. But 97,000 (*sic!*) are exactly the number of those carried captive at the time of the war leading to the Destruction (*Wars* 6:9:3). From this it seems to me that the author of the Biblical Antiquities was acquainted with the works of Josephus.

[3] Contrary to the opinion of James, that the Biblical Antiquities was already known to the author of the Syriac Baruch (James, *op. cit.*, p. 58).

366

book toward transgressors in Israel and toward Gentiles [4] attests the period of revolts in the time of Trajan and Hadrian (*c.* 110–130).

The Messianic ideas in this book are not numerous, perhaps because it is a collection of stories and legends. The King-Messiah is not directly mentioned here even once, except in the prayer of Hannah (51:5, p. 218), wherein it is said, "And so shall all judgment endure until he be revealed which holdeth (*qui tenet*)." James [5] likens this expression to the phrase ὁ κατέχων [he who restrains] in the Second Epistle of Paul to the Thessalonians (2:6–7). But it seems to me that the words *qui tenet* refer to the passage "Until Shiloh come" (Gen. 49:10), "Shiloh" being taken as *shello*, "the one to whom (shall be the obedience of the peoples)," in accordance with the Septuagint; [6] and that the words *qui tenet* must be translated not "he who restrains" but "he who grasps," that is, he who takes over the rulership ("the one to whom shall be the obedience of the peoples").

We find often mentioned in the Biblical Antiquities the treasuries of souls (*promptuaria*), the retribution in store for the righteous and the wicked in the World to Come (Paradise and Gehenna), the resurrection of the dead, the "End"—the end of the world—and *the New World*, the light reserved for the righteous in the Age to Come, and the like.[7] Political success and material prosperity are only hinted at here—apparently the time of the composition of the book was not an appropriate time for political and worldly expectations (the revolts did not succeed).

What this book does emphasize with all force is *the eternity of the people Israel and its Law*. Amram, the father of Moses, says, "It will sooner come to pass that the age shall be utterly [8] abolished and the

---

[4] See, e.g., 26:2–3, 5 (pp. 153–154); 27:15 (p. 163); 32:11 (p. 177); 47:8 (p. 209); 58:1 (p. 230); 61:7–9 (p. 235); etc.

[5] *Op. cit.*, p. 42.

[6] See above, Part I, pp. 29–30.

[7] All this is collected and arranged by James (*op. cit.*, pp. 34–37); but to it are to be added 15:5 (p. 119); 16:3 (p. 121); 18:10 (p. 125); 19:13 (pp. 130–131); 23:6 (p. 142); 25:7 (p. 149); 44:4 (p. 200, ironical); 60:3 (p. 233—at the end of this there is probably a Christian interpolation, and there may be something of the sort also at the end of 21:6, p. 137).

[8] The words *in victoria*, which come here in the Latin version, are a sure sign of the Hebrew language in the original book. The word *lanetsaḥ* [utterly, for-

immeasurable world fall, or the heart of the depths touch the stars, than that the race of the children of Israel should be diminished" (9:3, p. 100). And Balaam the Sorcerer says, "It is easier to take away the foundations and all the topmost part of them [9] and to quench the light of the sun and darken the shining of the moon, than for him who will to root up the planting of the Most Mighty or spoil his vineyard" (18:10, p. 125). For before Israel was created, God had already spoken concerning it (9:4, p. 100). Israel was created from the rib of Adam, like Eve (32:15, p. 178), and the habitable earth was created only for Israel (39:7, p. 190); and if the LORD should destroy Israel, there would be no one to praise Him (12:9, p. 113). Therefore Israel will live forever. Likewise will the Law endure for all time (11:2, 5, pp. 106, 107), for the Law was created with the birth of the world (32:7, p. 176). And days will come when Israel will forsake its evil deeds and return to its God and to its Law, as a dove returns to its nest and to its young; then will its salvation come (21:6, p. 137).

The essence of the Messianic ideas of the Biblical Antiquities is contained in one passage, which I find it proper to quote here, because it is characteristic of the whole composition:

But when the years of the world shall be fulfilled, then shall the light cease and the darkness vanish; and I (the LORD) will quicken the dead and raise up from the earth them that sleep ("them that sleep in the dust," Dan. 12:2); and Sheol shall pay its debt and Abaddon give back that which was committed unto it, that I may render unto every man according to his works and according to the fruit of their imaginations, until I judge between the soul and the flesh. And the world shall rest, and death shall be quenched, and Sheol shall shut its mouth. And the earth shall not be without birth, neither barren for them that dwell therein; and none shall be polluted that hath been justified in Me. And there shall be another earth and another heaven, even an everlasting habitation (3:10, pp. 81–82).

The whole spirit of this ancient book and its thoroughly Hebraic language are revealed in this Messianic passage, in which the basic

---

ever] was confused by the Greek translator with *lammenatseaḥ* [to the victor], and he translated it εἰς νῖκος [to victory]; from this the Latin translated *in victoria* (James, *op. cit.*, pp. 28, 100).

[9] I.e., "the foundations of heaven" (II Sam. 22:8).

element is not the nationalistic-worldly expectation, but the End of Days and the Age to Come.

And with this is concluded my presentation of the Messianic idea in the Hebrew and Palestinian Pseudepigraphical books, and I pass on to the Hellenistic Pseudepigraphical books.

CHAPTER IX

The Sibylline Oracles

III 97-829—140 B.C.E.; III 1-92—27 B.C.E.; IV—80 C.E.;
V—120-130 C.E., with a Few Fragments from 70-80 C.E.

THE SIBYLS were the quasi-prophetesses of the Gentile nations. The Romans had oracles of the Sibyls from early times, and the Jews in Alexandria or Asia Minor took advantage of this and wrote *Jewish oracles*, attributing them to the Sibyls. Of such a kind are the *third, fourth, and fifth* Sibylline books. Of fifteen Sibylline books mentioned in various ancient works, we have only twelve; the ninth, tenth, and fifteenth books are missing. Almost all of them have a Jewish substratum, but they contain many Christian interpolations; and sometimes the Jewish literary creation is built upon the foundation of a pagan oracle. Besides the three books already mentioned (III, IV, and V), Book XI is also Jewish; but the Messianic ideas in it do not have great importance, and therefore I shall not discuss it here.

The Jewish Sibylline books are, according to Schürer's well conceived expression, "Jewish propaganda under a pagan mask" (*jüdische Propaganda unter heidnischer Maske*), like the Letter of Aristeas, for example.[1] In these oracles the Sibyl who calls herself "Babylonian" [III 809] and represents herself as the daughter-in-law of Noah [III 827] rebukes the Gentiles for their idolatry and moral corruption (particularly pederasty), and prophesies of "the birth

---

[1] In opposition to this view of Schürer is A. Tscherikower, Hans Levy Memorial Volume, Jerusalem, 1949, pp. 139-160 (Jewish propaganda among Jews).

pangs of Messiah" and the terrible Day of Judgment on the Gentiles; and along with this she proclaims good tidings to the land of *Judah*. This last idea is of much importance for our task in the present work.

The *third* book divides itself into two unequal parts: III 1–92 and III 97–829. The latter part is older than the former. In spite of the hypotheses of Bousset, Jülicher, and Schürer that the "holy ruler" mentioned in the former part is Jesus, and that "Beliar," also mentioned there, is Simon Magus,[2] it seems to me necessary to suppose— because of the "woman who shall reign," the "three who with piteous fate shall bring ruin on Rome," and the "Sebastenes"—that this part refers to the [Second] Triumvirate, to Cleopatra, and to Herod, who built Sebaste (in 27 B.C.E., four years after the fall of Antony and Cleopatra, to be sure; but the Sibyl is not so exact in historical details). The latter part, in which is mentioned the seventh king of Egypt of Greek birth, that is, Ptolemy Physcon, could have been composed only about 140 B.C.E.

The *fourth* book, in which is mentioned the destruction of the Temple, the eruption of Mount Vesuvius, and the belief that the Emperor Nero had fled across the River Euphrates and would return to his kingdom, is, without doubt, from the year 80 C.E. (here again the Sibyl is not exact in historical details).

And finally, the *fifth* book, which contains pagan elements and Christian interpolations, cannot be later, *in its original form,* than the period preceding Bar-Cochba, since in it the Emperor Hadrian is praised; thus the original form of this book was composed in the years 120–130 C.E. But it contains isolated verses in which are expressed the hope of the return of the Emperor Nero and a recollection of the temple of Onias in Egypt; thus these were composed in the years 70–80 C.E.[3] I shall present herewith the Messianic ideas by books as

[2] See on this in detail E. Schürer, *Geschichte*, III[4], 579. Charles supposes that the reference is to Nero (*Apocrypha and Pseudepigrapha*, II, 380).

[3] I have explained all this in detail in the introduction to the Sibylline Oracles appearing in my book *Sepharim Ḥitsonim* [The Pseudepigrapha], the printing of which was interrupted at the beginning of the year 5680 [end of 1919]. In this book I have added to the poetical translation of Joshua Steinberg ("The Sibylline Oracles," in the *Measseph* [Collection] of the Society for the Promotion of Haskalah, Warsaw, 1887, also published in Vilna as a separate book) a prose translation of 382 lines omitted by Steinberg in his poetical translation; but I have

a whole, so as not to break them into bits. And in order not to weaken the poetry in them, I shall not separate the Messianic ideas into their earlier and later parts.

1. *Book III*

After fiery denunciations, actual prophecies, against the idolatry, the moral corruption, the greed, and the pursuit after the carnal pleasures of the pagans, and particularly of the Greeks, the Sibyl says:

> But when Rome shall rule over Egypt as well, as she still hesitates to do—then shall *the mistress of the kingdoms of the Lord of all* appear among men. And a *holy ruler* shall come who shall have rule over the whole earth for all ages of the course of time. Then shall implacable wrath fall upon Latin men: *three men shall ravage Rome with pitiable affliction;* and all its people shall perish in their own dwellings, when a torrent of fire shall flow down from heaven. O wretched me! When shall that day come, even the judgment of the eternal God, the mighty King? Yet for the present be ye founded, O ye cities, and adorned all of you with temples and race-courses, with markets and images of gold and silver and stone, that ye may come to the day of bitterness. For it shall come, when the smell of brimstone shall pass upon all men.

"The mistress of the kingdoms of the Lord of all" (more exactly, "the greatest kingdom of the Immortal King"—βασιλεία μεγίστη ἀθανάτου βασιλῆος) is, without any doubt, "the kingdom of the saints of the Most High" of Daniel, "the kingdom of heaven" of the Talmud and the Gospels; and the "holy ruler" (ἁγνὸς ἄναξ) is the King-Messiah. The great civil wars between Roman leaders from the time of the assassination of Julius Caesar until Augustus was made emperor, wars which shook the world in general and that part of Africa nearest to Palestine in particular—these wars are for the Sibyl the Day of Judgment ("the judgment of the eternal God"), the "birth pangs of Messiah" which will precede the advent of the Messiah.

However, the Alexandrian Jewish imagination connected the "birth

---

made use of Steinberg's translation in my book and also here, in spite of its inaccuracy, because of its Biblical beauty. [In the present English rendering the prose translations of Bate and Lanchester are utilized, but with modifications to suit Klausner's meaning and arguments.—TRANS.] A new and complete translation into Hebrew by Joseph Reider has been published in *The Outside Books* [Heb.], II.2, pp. 377-434.

pangs of Messiah" not only with events and peoples, as did the apocalyptists in Palestine, but also—after the manner of the Greeks— with an evil *personality:* just as there were ruler and rival ruler in Rome (Pompey and Julius Caesar, Antony and Octavian), so there are also a Messiah and an anti-Messiah (called "Antichrist" by the Christians). In the later Midrashim he becomes "the evil Armilus"; but in the last analysis even he is a collective personality, since "Armilus" is "Romulus," founder and symbol of Rome and thus is not an individual personality as with the Sibyl, who is under Greek influence, but is a symbol of the evil *nation. The early Talmudic and Midrashic Aggadah, like all the Palestinian Messianic literature, knows nothing at all of an anti-Messiah.* But it is worth while to call attention to the rôle of "Satan" and the "Nephilim" in the Book of Enoch with respect to the Messianic age, and also to the rôle of the former (Satan) in the Assumption of Moses: from them the "anti-Messiah" could have developed.

The description of "Beliar"-Belial (Satan, the anti-Messiah) and his marvelous deeds in the Sibylline Oracles is very impressive:

Now from the Sebastenes [4] shall Beliar [5] come, and he shall move the high mountains, still the sea, make the great blazing sun and the bright moon stand still, raise the dead, and do many signs among men; but his signs shall not be effective in him. Yet he leads many astray, and shall deceive many faithful and elect of the Hebrews, and lawless men besides, who never have hearkened to God's word.

But when the threatened vengeance of the Almighty God draws near, and a fiery power comes through the deep to land and burns up Beliar and all men of pride, even all that put their trust in him—*then shall the world be ruled beneath a woman's hand and obey her in all things.* And when a *widow* rules over *the whole world,* and casts gold and silver into the deep sea with the bronze and iron of short-lived mortals, then shall all the elements of the world be as one widowed, when God that dwelleth in the heavens shall roll up the sky as a book is rolled up. And the whole firmament with its many signs shall fall upon the earth and the sea; and then shall flow a ceaseless torrent of liquid fire, and shall burn up the earth and burn up the sea; and the firmament of heaven and the stars and creation it shall melt into one molten mass and clean dissolve.

[4] Steinberg erroneously has "from Sebaste" (in Greek ἐκ δὲ Σεβαστηνῶν).
[5] Almost certainly *Belial,* and he is Satan.

374   THE MESSIANIC IDEA IN ISRAEL

Then no more shall there be the luminaries' twinkling orbs, no night, no dawn, no constant days of care, no spring, no summer, no winter nor autumn. And then shall come forth the judgment of the great God, in the great age, when all these things shall come to pass (63–92).

The prophetic descriptions of "the day of the LORD" in Amos, Isaiah, Jeremiah, Zephaniah, Joel, and others have here taken on brighter and more imaginative colors. "Beliar" is possibly Satan, as in the Book of Enoch, in the Assumption of Moses, in the later Midrashim, in the Gospels, and in the books of the Kabbalah; but it is also possible that the reference is to Herod, who built Sebaste on the ruins of Samaria (to be sure, not until the year 27, as already noted), and made it one of his royal cities—this Herod, who almost came into sharp conflict with Cleopatra (the "woman ruler"), who cast longing eyes on his territory, no doubt because Palestine had been subject to Egypt in earlier times. So she denounced Herod before Antony, going so far as to request Antony to slay Herod and give her his territory (in 34 B.C.E.).[6]

A convincing argument for this is afforded by the lines preceding those just quoted (56–59), in which is mentioned the building of new cities, with temples, race-courses, market-places, and statues—the sort of thing with which Herod busied himself most, as is well known. To be sure, it is strange that Herod should appear here as a miracle worker. But we have evidence that Herod regarded himself as Messiah,[7] whereas the Jews hated him so much (as appears from the works of Josephus and from the stories of the Talmud) that they considered him to be Satan the Destroyer (Beliar-Belial), the complete antithesis of the Messiah. Along with his *external* success—his wealth, his splendid building projects, his popularity with the Roman rulers and with foreign peoples, his secret longings to rule the whole world—they saw miraculous deeds, which Satan also, and not only the Messiah, knows how to perform. And the fire, the flame, and the storm, and the cessation of day and night and the seasons of the year

---

[6] *Antiquities* 15:3:4–5.
[7] *Ibid.*, 17:2:4, end; Epiphanius, *Haereses*, I, 20, ed. Dindorf, II, 330–331. See on this in detail Joseph Klausner, *Jesus of Nazareth*, 5th Heb. ed. (1945), pp. 167–168, 485 [Eng. ed., pp. 170–171].

we have already seen in IV Ezra also.[8] Perhaps IV Ezra borrowed them from the Sibylline Oracles, or perhaps we have before us popular portrayals which influenced the Sibyl and IV Ezra alike.

In spite of the fact that the Jewish Sibyl knows an *individual anti-Messiah*, she also knows the *collective anti-Messiah—Gog and Magog* (and in exactly this form [of wording, Gog *and* Magog, and not Gog *of* Magog] as in the post-Biblical Palestinian literature, while in Ezekiel 38-39 Gog is prince of the *land* of Magog):

> Woe to thee, land of Gog and Magog,[9] in the midst of the rivers of Ethiopia! What a stream of blood shall flow out upon thee! And thou shalt be called among men the house of judgment, and thy land shall drink and be drenched with red blood (319-322).

As in the Book of Ezekiel, and in a certain sense in the early Talmudic Aggadah also,[10] likewise in the Sibylline Oracles the war with Gog and Magog comes *after* the Messianic age has begun, when the children of Israel are already living on their own soil and the King-Messiah (in the Talmud, Messiah ben Joseph) is ruling over them:

> (But do thou beware of the wrath of the mighty God), whenever the consummation of pestilence comes upon all mortals, and, overthrown, they meet with a terrible retribution, and king captures king and takes his land, and nations ravage nations and potentates people, and rulers all flee to another land, and the world of men shall be changed, and a barbarian empire ravages Hellas, and drains the rich land of its wealth, and men come face to face in strife for the sake of gold and silver—love of gain shall be the evil shepherd of the cities—in a foreign land. And all shall be unburied, and vultures and savage beasts of the earth shall devour the flesh of some. And when all these things are fulfilled, the giant earth shall devour the remnants of the dead. And it all shall be unsown and unploughed, proclaiming in its misery the corruption of myriads of men. And then for many spaces of time in circling years [men shall gather and

---

[8] See above, pp. 356-357.
[9] Steinberg translated "Gog of the land of Magog," in order not to vary from the passage in Ezekiel, without taking into consideration the fact that the post-Biblical Palestinian literature says "the war of Gog *and* Magog." It is exceedingly important to us, therefore, to know that the *Alexandrian* Sibyl also says the same thing.
[10] See above, Part I, pp. 126-129, and below, Part III, Chap. IX.

burn in their houses] spears and shields and javelins and divers kinds of weapons; nor shall wood be cut from the thicket to kindle fire (633–651).

Here we have the thought of Ezekiel concerning the war with Gog: "... they shall take no wood out of the field, neither cut down any out of the forests, for they shall make fires of the weapons."[11] The Sibyl adds:

And then from the sunrise God shall send a king who shall give every land relief from the bane of war; some he shall slay and to others he shall make faithful vows. Nor shall he do these things by his own counsel, but in obedience to the good ordinances of the Mighty God.

And again the people of the Mighty God shall be laden with excellent wealth, with gold and silver and purple adornment. The land shall bear her increase, and the sea shall be full of good things (652–659).

The "king from the sunrise" (in Greek ἀπ' ἠελίοιο) is, without any doubt, *the King-Messiah.*[12] He will put an end to wars on the earth. With the righteous he will make a covenant, and the wicked he will slay; he will do all this not "by his own counsel," but in accordance with "the good ordinances of the Mighty God." Then will the people of the Mighty God be rich and happy, and their land flourishing and fruitful. Only then will "the kings of the nations again throw themselves against this land," they will penetrate into it and set up each his throne in the city.[13] But God Himself will fight against them, in accordance with the prophecy of Ezekiel (38:18–23). The description of the warfare of God (669–697) is one of the most sublime in world literature; and in Steinberg's *Hebrew* translation the language of Scripture imparts to the description some of its own lofty grandeur.

After the war, "all the sons of the Great God shall live quietly around the temple," rejoicing in the salvation of their God who will protect them "as it were, with a wall of flaming fire." "Free from war shall they be in city and country." Not "evil war," but "the Immortal" (God) will be their protection. God's heaven, His sun, the brightness of the moon—all of these will be to them a refuge and a salvation.

[11] Ezek. 39:10.
[12] On the source of this expression, see Bousset-Gressmann, *Die Religion des Judentums*, 3rd ed., Tübingen, 1926, pp. 225–226.
[13] In Jerusalem. Cf. Jer. 1:15.

THE SIBYLLINE ORACLES 377

Then all the peoples will see the mercies of the LORD and will turn to Him alone:

And earth, the universal mother, shall shake in those days, and a sweet strain shall they utter from their mouths in hymns: "O come, let us all bow to the ground and supplicate the Eternal King, the mighty, everlasting God, . . . for He is the sole Potentate" (714–717).

All will acknowledge the rightness of the commandments of the only God and will forsake their idols. Finally, it is described, substantially as in Ezekiel, how they will collect the weapons of the enemy and make fire with them; and a preceding verse [651] is repeated: "For even wood shall not be cut from the thicket for kindling fire" (727–731).

But the description of the Messianic age is full of pleasantness and tenderness. After Rome falls and the Greek islands are desolated,

. . . tranquil peace shall make its way to the land of Asia. And Europe shall then be happy, the heavens (that is the God of Heaven [other versions say "the air"]) shall be favorable year after year, giving long life and health, without storms and hail, producing everything, birds and creeping things of the earth. Happy the man or woman who shall live in that time!—as though they were dwelling in the isles of the blest. For good law shall come in its fullness from the starry heaven upon men, and good justice, and with it sober concord, best of all gifts for mortals, and love and faith and hospitable ways; but lawlessness, blame, envy, jealousy, anger, and folly shall depart. Poverty too shall flee from men; and penury, murder, destructive strife, shameful wrangling, theft by night, and every evil shall pass away in those days (356–380).[14]

Here we have before us both *material* prosperity and *spiritual* felicity. The material prosperity is portrayed in two other places in Book III in exceedingly bright colors. When there shall arise over Egypt a new king (βασιλεὺς νέος), "the seventh" (Ptolemy VII Physcon, who ruled first jointly with his brother and later alone as a "new king," 146–117 B.C.E.), and he devastates and crushes everything—then men will cast away their idols and bow down to the Great God, "the Immortal King":

[14] All this is lacking in Steinberg's translation.

And then shall God give great joy to men; for the earth, the trees, and the full flocks of sheep shall give their proper fruit to mankind: wine and honey and white milk and corn, which is the best of all gifts to mortals (619–623).

Signs of the Messiah are also found in the Sibylline Oracles:

When by night in the starry heaven swords are seen westward and eastward, then shall a dust fall from heaven over all the earth, and the light of the sun shall fail from heaven at midday, and suddenly the moon-rays shall shine out and come upon the earth; there shall be a sign of dripping of blood from the rocks; and in a cloud ye shall see a warring of footmen and horse, like a hunting of beasts, in the likeness of a mist; this is the end of war (or of all things) which God, who dwells in heaven, is bringing to pass; but all must do sacrifice to the Great King (796–808).

These signs follow the portrayal of "the wolf dwelling with the lamb," [15] which is rendered by the Sibyl almost word for word as in the Book of Isaiah (Sibylline Oracles III 788–795). But the most wonderful description of material prosperity, closely bound up with *social felicity*—the brotherhood of man—is this:

But when this destined day is fully come, . . . the fertile earth shall yield her best fruit of corn and wine and oil and sweet honey from heaven for drink, trees bearing fruit after their kind, flocks of sheep, oxen, lambs, and kids of the goats; it shall gush out in sweet fountains of white milk. The cities shall be full of good things, and the fields with fatness; no sword shall come against the land, nor shout of war; nor shall the earth again be shaken, deeply groaning. No war nor drought shall afflict the land, no dearth nor hail to spoil the crops, but deep peace over all the earth. *King shall live as friend to king to the end of the age,* and the Immortal shall establish in the starry heaven one law for men over all the face of the earth for all the doings of hapless mortals. For He alone is God, and there is no other; He too will burn up with fire the race of stubborn men (741–761).

All the earth will be filled with knowledge of God; famine will be ended, wars will cease, and one system of law will prevail for all men. All nations will belong to one kingdom, even as God is one. Every people will have its own king, nations will not be abolished nor kingdoms cease, but "king shall live as friend to king to the end of the age"

---
[15] Isa. 11:6–9.

(or "forever"). We have before us, therefore, the "League of Nations" or the "United Nations," which will bring about *everlasting peace*, and war will never again be known.[16] This is substantially the ideal of our own time, but with one addition: the center of the worldwide kingdom will be Jerusalem. And even this idea has been urged by some of the supporters of the League of Nations or the United Nations.

No other Jewish apocalyptist rose to this high plane of Isaianic universalism. Because the Jewish Sibyl is a prophetess also to the Gentiles, she recognizes more than all the rest of those from Israel who saw visions the value of the universal faith and the universal social ethics of Israel within the world empire of Rome and the world culture of Greece. She wishes thereby to influence the Gentiles. And to a certain extent she succeeded. For the greatest pagan Roman poet, Vergil, describes in his Fourth Eclogue (40 B.C.E.) "the Age of Gold" in marvelous colors, taken almost without doubt from the descriptions of the Jewish Sibyl which are before us. "The Age of Gold" is called by Vergil "the last age of Cumaeic verse" (*ultima Cumaei carminis aetas*)—and indeed, in the city of Cumae in Italy there was a famous sibyl, to whom perhaps were attributed the oracles of the Jewish Sibyl. Thus Isaiah became "a light to the Gentiles" through an Alexandrian Jew, who styled himself "Babylonian Sibyl." [17]

2. *Book IV*

In contrast to the third book, the fourth is poor in Messianic expectations. It contains "signs of the Messiah": a fire will come upon the world, also swords and trumpets. All the world will hear a roar and a fearful blast. The whole earth will be burned to ashes—the *Ekpyrosis* of Greek literature and the "Flood of Fire" of our Jewish literature.[18] Only then will *the resurrection of the dead come*, and after that *the Day of Judgment*. The wicked will go down to Sheol,

[16] See also on this, Eugen Hühn, *Die messian. Weissag.*, p. 85.
[17] For the recent literature on this Eclogue of Vergil, see Bousset-Gressmann, *op. cit.*, p. 225.
[18] See Levi Ginzberg, "Flood of Fire" [Heb.] (*Ha-Goren*, ed. S. A. Horodetzky, VIII, 35–51). See also R. Eisler, Ἰησοῦς βασιλεύς, II (1929), 106–114.

the earth will cover them, and they will dwell in Gehenna; but the righteous will live again on earth, they will look at one another, and behold the lovely and pleasing sunlight. Happy the one who lives in that time! (172–192).

3. Book V

Its Messianic expectations are also scant. The "signs of the Messiah" in it are the rotating constellations: when the arched Axis, Capricorn, and Taurus among the Twins revolve in mid-heaven, and Virgo comes up, and the sun rules, fastening "the girdle" around his forehead, then "there shall be a great *celestial conflagration* on the earth, and from the battle of the stars *a new creation* shall come forth" (207–212).[19] Here we have the same "flood of fire" which we saw in Book IV; but there is also that "new creation" which is the "new world" of the Syriac Baruch, IV Ezra, and the Talmud and Midrash, also the καινὴ κτίσις [20] of Paul.

And the Jewish Sibyl has divine consolation for "the fair and lovely Judean city":

Vex no more thy soul in thy breast, thou blessed one, thou seed of God, full of riches, thou only-beloved flower, thou good light, noble offshoot, . . . Judaea, land of grace, fair city of inspired song. The unclean foot of the Greek shall no more walk wantonly in thy land, for he shall have in his heart a mind to share thy laws.[21] But thy noble sons shall encircle thee with honour, and with holy music they shall attend thy table, with divers kinds of sacrifices and prayers to the honour of God. The righteous who in a little oppression endured hardness shall have prosperity greater and fairer than before; but the wicked who raised their voice to heaven in lawlessness shall cease from speaking one to another, and shall hide themselves, until *the world be made new* (260–273).

Again we have *the renewal of the world*. Next (274–285) comes a severe oracle, that the earth shall be waste and desolate because of

---

[19] All this is lacking in Steinberg. And indeed, the words can be understood only poorly (see Charles, *Apocrypha and Pseudepigrapha*, II, 401).

[20] II Cor. 5:7; Gal. 6:15. [The older English versions render "a new creature," since the reference is to the individual: but RSV has "a new creation."—TRANS.]

[21] Here Steinberg has been led astray by his obsolete German source [the clause "for he . . . thy laws" being omitted]. Reider, *op. cit.*, p. 426, translates: "for their (the Greeks') hearts in their bosoms will meditate on thy laws; but thy noble sons will crown thee with honor."

idolatry. But "the holy land" alone shall produce everything, the mountains shall drop down sweet wine [22] and milk shall flow for all the upright. The Sibyl prays for "the fertile and fruitful land, great Judaea" (325–331). She prophesies a new war, which will be "world-convulsing" and "deceitful in guilefulness," a war that will be brought about by "a man who slew his mother" (Nero?). But finally:

. . . war's piteous ruin shall be stopped, and no man shall fight any more with swords or steel, nor with javelins either, for these things shall no more be permitted. But the wise people that are left shall have peace, having had trial of evil that later they might rejoice (381–385).

There is nothing new here. Everything is based on the Messianic expectations of the prophets.[23]

[22] Amos 9:13; Joel 4:18.
[23] On the Messianic expectations in the Sibylline books, see also the article of Zechariah Frankel, "Alexandrinische Messiashoffnungen" (*Monatsschrift für die Geschichte und Wissenschaft des Judentums*, VIII [1859], 241–261, 285–308).

CHAPTER X

The Greek Book of Baruch

(C. 150 C.E.)

THE SCANTY Messianic expectations in this book are deeply tinged with Christian coloring, and therefore this is not the place to concern ourselves with them.[1]

[1] See for details on this apocalypse Joseph Klausner, "Outside Books" [Heb.] (*Otsar ha-Yahadut, Hoveret le-Dogma*), pp. 118–119.

CHAPTER XI

The Slavonic Book of Enoch

(C. 30–40 C.E.)

THIS SECOND Book of Enoch, which is extant only in the Slavonic language, is a mixture of parts written originally in Hebrew and parts written originally in Greek.

This book contains ancient Messianic ideas which were current in Alexandrian Judaism, and in its earlier parts Palestinian Messianic expectations have also been preserved. Although it is an independent work, it has points of contact with the Ethiopic Book of Enoch. But it contains many *Christian additions*, and it is difficult to distinguish between the Jewish and the Christian expectations in it. Therefore it also has no place in the present work.[1]

[1] On the Messianic expectations in the Slavonic Book of Enoch, see E. Hühn, *Die messian. Weissag.*, pp. 101–102. On the book in general, see *Die Bücher der Geheimnisse Henochs*, ed. D. Bonwetsch, Leipzig, 1922.

C. GENERAL SURVEY

WITH THIS the presentation of the Messianic ideas in the Apocrypha and Pseudepigrapha is concluded. The basic expectations therein have been reduced to three groups: the Birth Pangs of Messiah, the Days of the Messiah, and the New World (including the resurrection of the dead). The later Messianic expectations have two main sources: *decisive historical events* and *Holy Scripture*. The replacement of Persian rule by Macedonian rule, and of this by the rule of the Ptolemies, and of the latter by the rule of the Seleucids, the decrees of Antiochus and the amazing victories of the Hasmoneans—all these things aroused great designs and wonderful expectations in the hearts of the noblest spirits of the nation, the "popular prophets," so that they had sublime visions for their people and for all humanity.

These "prophets" had already found a path which they could enter upon and broaden: the glorious prophecies of Holy Scripture. The "birth pangs of Messiah" of the Pseudepigrapha followed the lead of the Day of the LORD in Amos, Zephaniah, Ezekiel (the war with Gog and Magog) and Joel. The material prosperity and spiritual felicity of the Days of the Messiah were found portrayed in First Isaiah. The New World was found in Second Isaiah ("the new heavens and the new earth," 66:22). And all these expectations, overlaid with a mysterious, captivating coloration, were found in Daniel. Upon this splendid fabric these new dreamers embroidered the designs of their imaginations. They broadened, even if they did not deepen, the Messianic ideas of the prophets. They adorned them with the flowers of an imagination for which political events and spiritual development (perhaps occasioned even by Persian and Greek influences) served as stimulus and incentive. And thus was forged that *complete* Messianic chain whose separate links are: *the signs of the Messiah, the birth pangs of Messiah, the coming of Elijah, the trumpet of Messiah, the ingathering of the exiles, the reception of proselytes, the war with Gog and Magog, the Days of the Messiah, the renovation of the world, the Day of Judgment, the resurrection of the dead, the World to Come.* Not all the links of this chain are found in every book of the Apocrypha and Pseudepigrapha, or in this order; but *in general* you find it with these links and in the order mentioned. These links are also found in the Talmudic-Midrashic literature, to which the Apocryphal and Pseudepigraphical books serve as a transition from the Bible. The Apocrypha and Pseudepigrapha are only a link connecting Holy Scripture with the Talmud in its broad sense.

These Messianic expectations played a great part in the life of the Jewish nation. *First*, they furnished an outlet for the inclination to poetry and creative storytelling which was natural to the Jewish nation, as to any gifted nation. The Scribes, the Pharisees, and the first Tannaim did not make sufficient allowance for this inclination, since they were more concerned with Halakhah and the exegesis of Scripture than with a free and original Aggadah based upon whole books or sections of the Bible, and not upon *separate* verses and *single* words. *Second*, great numbers of people found in the Pseudepigraphical apocalyptic literature divine consolation in their severe tribulations. The marvelous expectations and the glorious hopes, filled with the flowers of imagination, were as dew to the souls of the majority of the cultured persons in the nation who were not inclined toward Halakhah even though they observed strictly the ceremonial laws. These wonderful promises were balm to the broken hearts of the educated in the nation and food for the marvel-seeking imagination of the common people. Not without reason did the Pseudepigraphical books influence the first Christians, and perhaps also Jesus himself. For from the common people (*amme ha-arets*) came most of the believers in the new Messianism. Perhaps it was for this very reason that the "apocalypses" were thrust out from the midst of Israel and likened to "books of the Minim (heretics)." This was a reason in addition to the fact that they were late in date and the fact that they contained many Messianic delusions and were well adapted to fan the dangerous flames of rebellion.[1] And indeed they do not have the supreme originality and the decided freshness of the Sacred Writings, and they might have unsettled a people's faith by their excessive fantasies.

Now, in our own time, they are not only an important source for understanding the beliefs and opinions of the best of the Jewish populace in the period of the Second Temple, and not only national Hebrew literary creations, which to our great sorrow have not been preserved in the national language, but also an inspiring source of national and social ideals. There are no documents (except a few ancient Baraithas) in which are revealed love of the homeland, love of the nation, and everlasting hatred for the oppressors of Israel and the devastators of its homeland as in the Apocryphal and Pseudepigraphical books. And at the same time there are no documents (except the Prophets, a few Hebrew prayers, and the works of Philo) in which is revealed Jewish universalism—the hope for the acknowledgment of the God of Israel by all peoples, the longing for worldwide righteousness, for social justice, for the transformation of nature for the better, for the return of the world to its pristine condition, *for the union of nations and everlasting peace*—as in the best of the Apocryphal and Pseudepigraphical books. We even found in them a Messianic expectation relating to the revival of the Hebrew language in the mouths of the whole nation.[2]

Even now the time for many of these social ideals has not passed. Even in our days we feel "the senility of the world" and long for a "renewal of its youth"; also in our days the longing for everlasting peace has created the League of Nations and its successor, the United Nations. Consequently, the Messianic expectations in the Apocrypha and Pseudepigrapha are precious jewels in the crown of Judaism from the period of the Second Temple; and an important place has been set apart for them in ancient Hebrew literature—between the expectations in the Holy Scriptures and those in the Talmud and Midrash.

---

[1] This last fact has already been observed by R. T. Herford, *The Pharisees*, London, 1924, pp. 186–193. The discovery of the Dead Sea Scrolls sheds new light on these important documents from the time of the Jewish-Roman wars (66–70 C.E.). Many of the Apocrypha and Pseudepigrapha are products of the spirit of the Zealots and Sicarii in those warlike times. Cf. my *History of the Second Temple*, V (3rd ed., 1951), 324–332.

[2] Testament of the Twelve Tribes (Judah 25:3). See above, p. 316.

PART III

*THE MESSIANIC IDEA IN THE
PERIOD OF THE TANNAIM*

General Note

WHAT FOLLOWS is the third part of a work embracing "the Messianic Idea in Israel" in ancient times. The work first appeared in separate parts. The *first* part (*The Messianic Idea in Israel from Its Beginning to the Present Day—Part I: The Messianic Idea in the Period of the Prophets*, Cracow, 5669 [1909]) was primarily concerned with the period of the First Temple. The *second* part (*The Messianic Idea in Israel, etc.—Part II: The Messianic Idea in the Apocrypha and Pseudepigrapha*, Jerusalem, 5681 [1921]) dealt with the period of the Second Temple. The present part, the *third*, deals with the period of the Tannaim; namely, the period beginning with Hillel and Shammai and ending with the final redaction of the Mishnah. With these three parts the treatment of the creative period of the people Israel on its own soil is complete.

This third part was first written more than fifty years ago as a dissertation for the doctorate at the University of Heidelberg, and published under the title *Die messianischen Vorstellungen des jüdischen Volkes im Zeitalter der Tannaiten* (Berlin, 1903–1904). This book in German caused Emil Schürer, in the *fourth* edition of his great work *Geschichte des jüdischen Volkes im Zeitalter Jesu Christi* (Leipzig, 1907), to make considerable changes in the interpretation which in the *third* edition he had put upon the Messianic idea in the time of the Second Temple and later. These changes were in accord with the material and the observations in my book, which he expressly mentions a number of times.[1] Since then, almost all who have dealt with the Jewish Messianic idea have made use of this German

---

[1] See Schürer, *Geschichte*, II[4], 609–636.

book of mine.[2] I myself during the intervening half-century have added to it all that I could from researches on the subject; consequently it has become virtually a new book.

I spoke above of "the *creative* period of the people Israel on its own soil." What could be more Hebraically original than the Messianic idea, which absorbed into itself the most splendid national-humanitarian ideals of Israel! And what is more closely linked with the land of Israel than this idea, in which even Hugo Gressmann detected "the odor of the soil of Palestine"?[3] Indeed, in the Tannaitic period the Messianic idea had not yet become *solely imaginative and spiritualized*. It still had a definite *political side* along with its exalted *spiritual side*; and the exuberant Oriental imagination had not yet made it merely a religious delusion embroidered with a spate of colors. It still remains in this period an exalted outlook upon its own future and the future of the human race—the outlook of a people closely linked with its own land and looking forward to both political and spiritual rulership—an outlook still retaining the remnant of a nation's strength and the remnant of the freshness of its soil.

This is the great and unchanging value of the Tannaitic Messianic views for the Jews who look forward to redemption. And Christians can see from them what there is in "Christology" (the Christian doctrine of the Messiah) that comes from Judaism; and so what there is in it of the original views of Jesus and the earliest Christians, and what there is of pagan ideas adopted by Paul and his successors from the pagan religious beliefs of Babylon, Persia, Greece, and Rome. To further this understanding, I have appended to this book the short article on "The Jewish and the Christian Messiah," which is a summary of researches covering more than forty years.

May this Hebrew version receive such a welcome as did the German book! For, to tell the truth, the Hebrew is not a translation, but the original; even if the German book was first in print, the Hebrew

---

[2] See, e.g., Bousset-Gressmann, *Die Religion des Judentums*, 3rd ed., Tübingen, 1926, pp. 48, 202, 220, 224, Note 2; 227, 230, 231, 232, Note 1; 235, 237, 248, Note 2; 250, Note 2; 261, Note 3; 277, 289. See also F. J. Foakes-Jackson and Kirsopp Lake, *The Beginnings of Christianity*, Part I, Vol. I, p. 277, Note 3.

[3] I refer to his excellent little book *Palaestinas Erdgeruch in der israelitischen Religion*, Berlin, 1909.

book is first in importance, since in it appears all the old material, with new scholarly material added.

Jerusalem, 9th of Tebeth, 5683 [end of 1922]—the day after the Feast of Tabernacles, 5710 [autumn, 1949]—April 24, 1953.

CHAPTER I

The Messianic Idea in the Tannaitic and Post-Tannaitic Periods

(Introduction)

THE SPAN of more than a thousand years which saw the rise, growth, and completion of the Talmudic and Midrashic literature falls into two unequal parts. The first part is the period of the Tannaim, the second is the period of the Amoraim and Geonim. The dividing line between these two periods is *the completion of the Mishnah*, about 200 C.E. These two periods are of course not absolutely separate from each other. There is a period of transition lying between the two and binding them together. There are no skips in history. Certain of the contemporaries of R. Judah the Patriarch, the redactor of the Mishnah—for example, R. Hiyya, Bar-Kappara, and others—are reckoned as only "semi-Tannaim," since they already engaged in controversies on Halakhah and Aggadah with Amoraim.

Nevertheless, the boundary between Tannaim and Amoraim remains fixed and unchanging. No Amora had the authority to disagree with a Tanna unless his opinion had the support of that of another Tanna. In general, an Amora was forbidden to disagree with an "anonymous Mishnah." A great part of the Talmudic controversies consists of attempts to harmonize the opinions of the Amoraim with those of the Tannaim. Thus the line of distinction between Tannaim and Amoraim was carefully preserved and never transgressed.

It is obvious, therefore, that in describing the Messianic idea we must distinguish between the Messianic sayings of the Tannaim and those of the Amoraim; for the Tannaim are earlier, *more original,* and rightly regarded as greater authorities. This is the case also, of course, from the purely historical point of view; for if we put before ourselves the Tannaitic period and observe the course of Jewish history during that period, we see immediately that the historical events of that period *must* have influenced, *and in fact did influence in a very special way,* the nature and form of the Messianic ideas of the Jewish people.

In the course of the long evolution of the Jewish Messianic idea, two different conceptions were inseparably woven together: *politico-national salvation* and *religio-spiritual redemption.* These two elements walked arm in arm. The Messiah must be both *king* and *redeemer.* He must overthrow the enemies of Israel, establish the kingdom of Israel, and rebuild the Temple; and at the same time he must reform the world through the Kingdom of God, root out idolatry from the world, proclaim the one and only God to all, put an end to sin, and be wise, pious, and just as no man had been before him or ever would be after him. In short, he is the great political and spiritual hero at one and the same time. "My kingdom is not of this world"—this saying, attributed to Jesus by the Gospel of John (18:36), cannot be imagined in the mouth of a *Jewish* Messiah, not even a Messiah of the more spiritual type portrayed in the Psalms of Solomon.[1]

This idea of the twofold nature of the Messiah was current in the best Pharisaic circles, led by the Tannaim, even *before* the destruction of the Second Temple. This is very evident from the Psalms of Solomon, written about 45 B.C.E., after the Tannaitic period had already begun. Jose ben Joezer and Jose ben Johanan, Joshua ben Perahiah and Nittai the Arbelite, Judah ben Tabbai and Simeon ben Shetah, Shemaiah and Abtalion, Hillel and Shammai—all these lived and worked in Hasmonean and Herodian times and died *before* the Destruction. This was the first generation of Tannaim. But from all these Tannaim not a single Messianic saying remains. To be sure, most of them have left us only a few even of Halakhic sayings; but

---

[1] See in this thoroughly Pharisaic work 7:9; 11 entire; 17:4-6, 23-51; 18:6-10. See on this above, Part II, pp. 317-324; Schürer, *Geschichte,* II[4], 597-598; III[4], 205-212.

from Simeon ben Shetah, and especially from Hillel and Shammai, we have a considerable number of aphorisms and Halakhahs.

Why has not a single *Messianic* saying of these great Sages been preserved? Certainly it is not because these earliest Tannaim rejected the Messianic idea. It is for an entirely different reason: as long as Judea retained a remnant of political autonomy, and the Temple still stood in all its glory, the leaders of the popular party, the foremost Pharisees, did not see the necessity of elaborating further the Messianic ideas of the prophets. In the circles of the nation from which came the "popular prophets," the creators of the Book of Enoch, the Psalms of Solomon, the Assumption of Moses, IV Ezra, the Syriac Baruch, and the like, Messianic expectations were very much alive. But the "Scribes," the precursors of the Tannaim, immersed themselves in the exposition of the Law, adapting it to everyday life and to the understanding of the people (for example, Simeon ben Shetah and Hillel the Elder); they indulged very little in Messianic expectations, which sought "to hasten the end," [2] and so could have destroyed such semblance of Jewish political power and autonomy as still remained in the days of the Herods and the Roman procurators. And in Hasmonean times this was all the more true.

Then came the fearful Destruction. The uprising of the Jewish national party (the "Zealots") was not approved by the disciples of Hillel.[3] What could they gain by the battle for freedom? Complete national independence? This the nation had in Hasmonean times; nevertheless, the leading Pharisees had found themselves in opposition to the most valiant of the Hasmonean kings because the latter were not sufficiently observant of the Law.[4] The disciples of Hillel, of course, had no love for Rome. But they were so convinced of the great importance of the study of the Law that by comparison all political ambitions seemed to them of small significance—especially since these could not possibly be achieved to the extent pictured by the bold Messianic imagination. During the siege of Jerusalem by the

---

[2] See I. M. Elbogen, *Perushim* [Pharisees] (*Otsar ha-Yahadut, Hoveret le-Dogma*, Warsaw, 1906, pp. 93–94); Herford, *Pharisees*, 1924, pp. 186–193.

[3] I. H. Weiss, *Dor Dor we-Doreshav* [Each Generation and Its Interpreters], I³, 175–176, 225–226; II², 2.

[4] *Kiddushin* 66a; *Antiquities* 13:8–10, 12–15; *Wars* 1:2, 4; Ps. Sol. 17:6–8, 21–22.

Emperor Vespasian, Rabban Johanan ben Zakkai (the youngest disciple, or the disciple of a disciple, of Hillel) left the beleaguered city in order to find a refuge for the Law while there was still time.[5] He did not leave Jerusalem because of lack of love for freedom. Indeed, he gave this splendid saying:

> This ear (of the Hebrew slave who did not wish to go free in the seventh year), which heard My voice on Mount Sinai when I proclaimed, "For unto Me the children of Israel are servants, they are *My* servants" (Lev. 25:55), and not servants of servants, and yet this man went and acquired a master for himself—let this ear be pierced.[6]

He left the doomed city because he well knew that the Jewish people could recover from its defeat only through the Law.

When the long and hopeless war was over, leaving Judea ruined and the Temple a heap of ashes, Rabban Johanan ben Zakkai felt the full force of the blow, and gave expression to his profound grief by means of various enactments having one clear purpose: to keep alive in the hearts of the people the memory of Jerusalem and the Temple.[7]

Through this great misfortune, which fell so heavily upon the Jewish people, the Messianic hopes, and particularly the politico-national part of them, were revived in full force. "Out of grief over the overthrow of the Sanctuary," says Emil Schürer,[8] "the Messianic hope drew new nourishment, new strength. This was significant and portentous also for *political* relations." It was quite natural that people should have started looking for that Messiah who would take vengeance on the Romans for the blood they had shed and restore Israel's former glory.

The political element in Jewish Messianism certainly came to the fore at that time. Otherwise we could not explain at all how about sixty years later, and only a few years after the death of Rabban Johanan ben Zakkai, the great revolt of Bar-Cochba could break out; or how the aged Rabbi Akiba, who reached his prime about 110 C.E.

---

[5] Gittin 56 ab.
[6] Kiddushin 22b; Tosephta, Baba Kama 7:5; Mekhilta, Mishpatim 2 (ed. Friedmann, 77a).
[7] All are brought together in Weiss, *op. cit.*, II², 37, especially Note 1.
[8] *Op. cit.*, I⁴, 660.

and so must surely have witnessed the destruction of the Temple,[9] could have participated in this revolt, even going so far as to take his stand beside Bar-Cochba as the spiritual leader of the revolutionary movement. R. Akiba proclaimed Bar-Cochba as Messiah,[10] even though he was not of the house of David, had done no miracles,[11] and was not even distinguished for great piety. Bar-Cochba's great spirit of heroism was sufficient *in itself* to make him Messiah in the eyes of one of the greatest of the Tannaim, R. Akiba.[12] Yet we know that before the time of Bar-Cochba descent from the house of David ("son of David") was considered so essential a qualification of the Messiah that the emperors Vespasian, Domitian, and Trajan ordered that any Jew claiming to be of the house of David should be sought out and executed.[13] If, therefore, R. Akiba and the greater part of the Jewish people saw in Bar-Cochba, who is nowhere said to be of the house of David, the King-Messiah, it must be assumed that between the Destruction and the revolt of Bar-Cochba (70–132 C.E.) the political element in the Messianic idea was dominant. Graetz [14] rightly remarks that in this period "people expected of the Messiah that above all he should bring freedom and the restoration of the national life."

To this period belongs the rise of the very noteworthy group called the "Mourners for Zion," which is mentioned a number of times in the Talmudic and Midrashic literature,[15] and to which I

---

[9] Siphre, Deut., 357 (ed. Friedmann, 150a). Cf. Z. Frankel, *Darkhe ha-Mishnah* [Introduction to the Mishnah], 2nd ed., Warsaw, 1923, pp. 127–129.

[10] Yerushalmi Taanith 4:5 (68d); Lam. R. on 2:2 ("The LORD hath swallowed up").

[11] Only a single *Christian* source [Jerome, *Against Rufinus*, III, 31; see above p. 360, Note 39] attributes miracles to Bar-Cochba; the Jewish sources know nothing of this. Cf. Schürer, *op. cit.*, I⁴, 685.

[12] This fact has always caught the attention of Jewish scholars. Maimonides (*Mishneh Torah*, Hilkhot-Melakhim XI 3) concludes from this that the Messiah is under no obligation to perform miracles. I. H. Weiss (*op. cit.*, I³, 216) infers that in Akiba's time Davidic descent was not yet an absolute requirement for the Messiah. Thus also the opinion of Maurice Vernes, *Histoire des idées messianiques depuis Alexandre jusqu'à l'empereur Hadrien*, Paris, 1874, p. 136, Note 1. See also J. Klausner, *Jesus of Nazareth*, 5th Heb. ed. (1945), pp. 344–345, 509 [Eng. ed., pp. 310, 320].

[13] See Schürer, *op. cit.*, I⁴, 660–661.

[14] *Geschichte der Juden*, IV, 516.

[15] Tosephta, Sotah 15:11 end; Baba Bathra 60b; and especially Pesiqta Rabbathi, Chap. 36. See Klausner, "Palestine and Jewish Revolutionary Movements"

shall return at the end of Chapter IV of the present part of this book. During this same period Rabban Gamaliel II, the younger contemporary of Rabban Johanan ben Zakkai, prescribed those benedictions (in the Shemoneh Esreh) relating to the rebuilding of Jerusalem, the re-establishment of the throne of David, and the restoration of the Temple.[16] Likewise the most Messianic books among the Pseudepigrapha, IV Ezra and the Syriac Baruch, are from the first years after the Destruction. The idea of redemption was strengthened and given new life, especially in its purely political aspect, by the catastrophe of 70 C.E.

Thus is explained the very interesting fact that, while we have no Messianic sayings from the time *before* the Destruction, from the first years *after* the Destruction we have a whole series of such sayings. From Rabban Johanan ben Zakkai himself we have reliable testimony of his strong belief that the Messiah was not far away. Before his death he said to his disciples, "Prepare a throne for Hezekiah, king of Judah, who is coming." [17] This saying can only be explained on the assumption that the great Rabban of Jamnia wished to indicate to his disciples the near approach of the King-Messiah.[18] For below (Chapter VII) we shall see clearly that in the time of the later Tannaim Hezekiah was still considered almost identical with the Messiah.[19]

(*When a Nation Fights for Its Freedom*, 5th ed. [Heb.], 1947, pp. 233–235, 237–245).

[16] Weiss, *op. cit.*, II², 67; Bacher, *Agada der Tannaiten*, I, 94, Heb. trans., Vol. I, Part I, Jaffa, 1920, pp. 67–68.

[17] So in Berakhoth 28*b;* in Aboth de R. Nathan, Chap. 25 (Recension A, ed. Schechter, p. 80), the words "who is coming" are lacking (see *loc. cit.*, Note 16). See also Yer. Sotah 9:16, and Abodah Zarah 3:1, where it says, "and prepare (or place) a throne for Hezekiah, king of Judah."

[18] This saying was so understood by Ferdinand Weber, *System der altsynagogalen palästinischen Theologie*, Leipzig, 1880, p. 341 ("Hold yourselves ready to receive the Messiah"); it was also understood in this way by M. Friedmann in the introduction to his edition of Seder Eliahu Rabba and Zuta, Vienna, 1902, p. 21.

[19] I call attention here to a most splendid saying of Rabban Johanan ben Zakkai, which has a bearing on his Messianic belief, and also has great importance for our own times: "If you have a seedling in your hand, and they say to you, 'Look, here comes the Messiah!'—go on and plant the seedling first, and then come out to meet him" (Aboth de R. Nathan, ed. Schechter, Recension B, Chap. 31, p. 34). In our whole literature there is hardly a saying as fine as this in praise of the tilling of the soil.

THE TANNAITIC AND POST-TANNAITIC PERIODS 397

From the contemporaries and disciples of R. Johanan ben Zakkai we have numerous Messianic sayings; for example, Rabban Gamaliel II,[20] R. Eliezer ben Hyrcanus, R. Joshua ben Hananiah,[21] R. Eleazar of Modiim, and many other Tannaim of that period. There is a particularly strong political coloring in the Messianic sayings of R. Jose ben Kisma, a Galilean Tanna, whose great work as rabbi and teacher preceded the Hadrianic war.[22] It is clear that the Messianic hopes awoke to a new and fuller life in the first decades after the Destruction.[23] This new stage of development is most important for us because it is *explained* by the outstanding historical event that preceded it—the Second Destruction; and it in turn *explains* the almost as outstanding historical event that followed it—the revolt of Bar-Cochba and R. Akiba's participation therein.

From R. Akiba himself we have—and this is characteristic of him —only a few specifically Messianic sayings. His confidence that the restoration of the Jewish kingdom was near can be seen from the delightful Talmudic story that R. Akiba could laugh at hearing the merriment of the crowds at Rome, and also at the sight of a jackal coming forth from the Holy of Holies of the ruined Temple, while the rest of the Sages who were accompanying him began to weep.[24] His faith, strong as a rock, in the redemption soon to come and in the rebuilding of the Temple can also be seen from the following Benediction, which R. Akiba prescribed for the first night of Passover, the night of the "Seder":

Therefore, O Lord our God and the God of our fathers, bring us in peace to the other set feasts and festivals which are coming to meet us, while we rejoice in the building-up of Thy city and are joyful in Thy worship; and may we eat there of the sacrifices and of the Passover-offerings. . . . Blessed art Thou, O Lord, *Who hast redeemed Israel.*[25]

This Benediction was deemed worthy to be received into the Mishnah. Likewise found in the Mishnah is another saying of R.

[20] Shabbath 30b.
[21] Sanhedrin 97b, 98a, 99a; Rosh ha-Shanah 11b, etc.
[22] See Bacher, *op. cit.*, I, 401–402, Heb. trans., Vol. I, Part II, pp. 118–120.
[23] This is also emphasized by M. Friedmann, introduction to *op. cit.*, p. 21.
[24] Makkoth 24ab (near end); Siphre, Deut., 43 (ed. Friedmann, 81ab; Lam. R. on 5:18 (ed. Buber, f. 80).
[25] Mishnah, Pesahim 10:6.

Akiba's which can only be interpreted in the light of his political views. In his opinion, as opposed to that of R. Eliezer, "the Ten Tribes shall not return again, for it is written, 'And he cast them into another land like as this day' (Deut. 29:28). Like as this day goes and returns not, so do they go and return not." [26] Many years ago [27] it was suggested that R. Akiba brought forth this harsh judgment against the Ten Tribes only after his long journeys for the purpose of arousing enthusiasm among Jews in distant lands for the national war against Rome.[28] As a result of these journeys, so it was said, he decided that the remnants of the Northern Kingdom no longer had the requisite national feeling. But in the opinion of Bacher,[29] he was trying to strengthen the hope of the Jews for an early redemption by interpreting the Scriptural passage "And ye shall perish among the nations" (Lev. 26:38) as applying to the Ten Tribes *only*.

The Mishnah has another Messianic saying of R. Akiba: "The judgment of Gog and Magog *in the Age to Come* (or, *which is to come*) shall endure twelve months." [30] This saying may possibly have reference to the war with Hadrian, since a full year elapsed from the outbreak of the revolt in 132 C.E.[31] to the minting of Jewish coins with the inscription "Of the Redemption of Israel." The whole war covered the years 132–135, but we have coins of Bar-Cochba from only two years.[32] In any case, this saying of R. Akiba has a political coloring, since it speaks of a long war against the enemies of Israel lasting an entire year (twelve months).[33]

[26] Mishnah, Sanhedrin 10:3 (11:3 in some editions). Somewhat different is the interesting version in Siphra, Behuqqothai 8 (ed. Weiss, 112a). See in more detail below, Chap. VIII.

[27] David Castelli, *Il Messia*, Florence, 1874, p. 253 (top).

[28] See Z. Frankel, *op. cit.*, 2nd ed., p. 128; Graetz, *op. cit.*, IV, 157-158; in opposition is R. Isaac Halevy, *Dorot ha-Rishonim* [The Early Generations], Part I, Vol. V, pp. 620-629. See also L. Finkelstein, *Akiba*, p. 130.

[29] *Op. cit.*, I, 292, Heb. trans., Vol. I, Part II, pp. 38-39.

[30] Mishnah, Eduyoth 2:10.

[31] See Schürer, *op. cit.*, I^4, 682.

[32] *Ibid.*, 760-770. See also M. Narkiss, *Coins of Palestine* [Heb.], Jerusalem, 1936, pp. 40-41, 120-128; A. Reifenberg, *Coins of the Jews* [Heb.], Jerusalem, 1947, pp. 29-32, 56-61; [Eng. ed., pp. 33-38, 61-64]; S. Yeivin, *The War of Bar-Cochba* [Heb.], Jerusalem, 1946, pp. 74-80.

[33] Details on this below, Chap. IX.

Besides these Mishnaic sayings, we have in a Baraitha [34] the tradition of R. Nathan that R. Akiba found a hint of the beginning of the Messianic age in the verse "Yet once, it is a little while, and I will shake the heavens and the earth" (Haggai 2:6). R. Akiba saw in this, naturally, the approaching desperate struggle with Rome, but R. Nathan disagreed. In none of R. Akiba's sayings do we find a trace of supernatural hopes or mystical interpretations concerning the Messiah and his functions, such as we find among his older contemporaries. This need cause no surprise if we remember that this great Tanna was the trusted supporter of a simple and completely human military leader of unknown origin. His Messiah was already in the world, and his kingdom was wholly "of this world."

But R. Akiba was mistaken. Bar-Cochba was not the redeemer of Israel. For this mistake R. Akiba himself and his companions had to atone by violent death and manifold humiliations—and with them a great part of the nation. The harsh decrees of Hadrian followed.[35] This was the first persecution of Judaism *as a religion* since the time of Antiochus Epiphanes. One reason for this was that the greatest religious authority in Judaism at that time had participated actively in the revolt. A reign of terror began. Teaching of the Law was made punishable by death, it was strictly forbidden to observe the more important of the ceremonial laws, and other great calamities came upon the people. The land was laid waste once more, the site of the Temple was plowed up, Jerusalem was given the pagan name Aelia Capitolina, and the Jews were forbidden to enter the Holy City on pain of death.

In such a time of grief and distress, the Messianic hopes perforce were again revived, in spite of the dreadful disillusionment through which the people had just passed.[36] For the Messianic idea is a product of the *afflictions* experienced by the Jewish people in the course of

[34] Sanhedrin 97b.
[35] Described in detail by Weiss, *op. cit.*, II², 118-121; Graetz, *op. cit.*, IV, 157-197; Schürer, *op. cit.*, I⁴, 695-704; S. Krauss, "Ten Martyrs of the Roman Government" [Heb.], *Ha-Shiloah*, XLII (5685 [1925]), 10-22, 106-117, 221-233 (an important article from a number of standpoints).
[36] This fact has already been recognized and emphasized by G. H. Dalman, *Der leidende und sterbende Messias*, Berlin, 1888, p. 22.

their *history*, a history which at the very beginning involves the story of bondage in Egypt, and which was and is unique in its record of alternating affliction and salvation. The afflictions gave birth to intense longings for deliverance and these longings brought forth the exalted figure of the Messiah. Moses, the great deliverer from the Egyptian bondage, functioning in the dual rôle of military leader and prophet-lawgiver, is the prototype of the conception that was to develop and achieve splendid embodiment in the form of a Messiah who is both king and redeemer.[37]

The time of misery following the fall of Bethar [38] inevitably caused the revival of Messianic hopes; but—and this point deserves emphasis—this time of misery necessarily imparted a new coloring to these hopes. The political orientation of the Messianic idea had not succeeded. It had brought disaster upon the whole nation, because Bar-Cochba had not been sufficiently God-fearing—at least this is the later Talmudic explanation of the tragedy.[39] Now, after the disaster, it became necessary to emphasize the spiritual side of the Messiah. Moreover, the dreadful calamities through which the nation had passed as a result of the work of *the slain Messiah* cast their gloomy shadows over the Messianic conceptions of the depressed and suffering people. Inevitably but unconsciously the Days of the Messiah became associated with the idea of pain and sorrow in the minds of all those who survived the execution of R. Akiba.

The "birth pangs of Messiah," that is, the sufferings that must precede Messiah's advent, is an idea which had always been connected with this advent, since punishment is a prerequisite of the redemption (the day of the LORD followed by "the end of days"); but hitherto the imagery connected with it had not been very clear or concrete (the day of the LORD was a day of punishment for man and nature *in general*). Now this conception receives a fixed form, and is depicted in the darkest colors.[40] A *second* Messiah, who is *solely a warrior*, and who of course could not have been imagined

[37] See for details on this above, Part I, pp. 15–19.
[38] I write "Bethar" according to the usual transcription. "Beth-ter" would be more correct according to the best Hebrew and Greek manuscripts.
[39] Sanhedrin 93*b*; Yerushalmi Taanith 4:7.
[40] For details on the "birth pangs of Messiah" see below, Chap. V, pp. 440–450.

earlier by Jewish sages, could now play a rôle in the saddened Messianism of the post-Hadrianic generation.

So *Messiah ben Joseph* became a *Messiah who dies:* he is fated to fall in the war with Gog and Magog, as Bar-Cochba had fallen in his war against Rome.[41] This by no means implies that Messiah ben Joseph was at any time identified with Bar-Cochba in the thinking of the people—something which, according to Dalman,[42] has no foundation in fact. Bar-Cochba is *not* Messiah ben Joseph; but his fate was, so to speak, the *historical cause* which poured the idea of a second Messiah into a new mold, giving it the form we are now considering, even though the idea itself may already have been in existence. For the fashioning of the Jewish Messianic idea is inevitably influenced by the outstanding historical events of the time.[43]

And in fact all the detailed descriptions of the "birth pangs of Messiah" come from Tannaim who flourished *after* the fall of Bethar. What is even more noteworthy is that the four consecutive Baraithas [44] which actually give the only description of the "birth pangs of Messiah" (though afterward they were combined with a Mishnah) [45] all come from the younger disciples of R. Akiba. These younger disciples (to be distinguished from his older disciples, who flourished before the revolt of Bar-Cochba) were six in number: R. Meir, R. Judah ben Ilai, R. Jose ben Halaphta, R. Simeon ben Yohai, R. Nehemiah, and R. Eleazar ben Shammua.[46] All of these except the last [47] were spiritual leaders of Israel after Palestine had recovered from the tragic results of the revolt and after the Hadrianic persecution had slackened. None of them received ordination at the hands of their own teacher, R. Akiba, whom the Romans had executed after the fall of Bethar. They were ordained by R. Judah ben Baba while the decrees forbidding ordination were still in force; and as a result R. Judah ben Baba was put to death.[48]

---

[41] For details on this see below, Chap. IX.
[42] See his book, *op. cit.*, p. 21.
[43] Friedmann, introduction to Seder Eliahu, p. 22, Note 3.
[44] Sanhedrin 97*ab*.
[45] Mishnah, Sotah 9 (near end), same as the Baraitha, Sotah 49*b*.
[46] Abodah Zarah 8*b;* Sanhedrin 13*b* and 14*a*.
[47] See Bacher, *op. cit.*, II, 275, Heb. trans., Vol. II, Part II, pp. 1–8.
[48] Abodah Zarah 8*b;* Sanhedrin 13*b* and 14*a*.

Thus all of these men lived through the years of decrees, persecutions, and oppressions. Therefore it is not surprising that the four Baraithas mentioned above were delivered by four of these six disciples of R. Akiba. Two Baraithas occur in the tractate Sanhedrin itself [49] in the names of R. Judah and R. Nehemiah.[50] The third appears in Sanhedrin [51] anonymously, but a later Talmudic source [52] has preserved the name of the author: it is R. Simeon ben Yohai, the fourth of R. Akiba's disciples mentioned above. The fourth Baraitha comes in the name of R. Nehorai.[53] But in an early Talmudic tradition we find: "His name was not R. Meir but R. Nehorai. Then why was he called R. Meir [enlightener]? Because he enlightened the Sages in the Halakhah." [54] However, there was also a Tanna by the name of R. Nehorai, who disagrees with R. Meir in two Talmudic passages.[55] And there is another Talmudic tradition as follows: "A Tanna taught: His name was not R. Nehorai but R. Nehemiah.[56] In any case, R. Nehorai could be here either one of two younger disciples of R. Akiba (R. Meir, since R. Nehemiah teaches in another Baraitha), or he was a Tanna of the time of R. Meir who disagreed with the latter twice, and thus was also from the period after the fall of Bethar. Hence all four of the Baraithas dealing with the "birth pangs of Messiah" come from the period after Bar-Cochba—after the Jews had experienced severe persecutions connected with the appearance of a Messiah.[57]

Thus it can be shown that *the dying Messiah* is a product of the time of Hadrian.[58] At that time the dual nature of the Messiah had to be given up. The warrior Messiah had to be separated and distinguished from the spiritual Messiah. While the belligerent Messiah

---

[49] Sanhedrin 97a.
[50] In the tractate Derekh Erets Zuta, Chap. 10, "Rabban Gamaliel" occurs; but this is an error.
[51] Sanhedrin 97a.
[52] Derekh Erets Zuta, beginning of Chap. 10.
[53] Sanhedrin 97a; Derekh Erets Zuta, Chap. 10.
[54] Erubin 13b. To be sure, some raise objections to this identification, perhaps rightly.
[55] Mishnah, Kiddushin 4:14 (the last Mishnah); Sanhedrin 99b.
[56] Shabbath 147. See also Bacher, *op. cit.*, Heb. trans., Vol. II, Part I, p. 160; Vol. II, Part II, p. 75.
[57] The text of these Baraithas will be found below, pp. 442-448.
[58] The detailed evidence for this will be given below, Chap. IX.

ben Joseph must die in battle, Messiah ben David, by virtue of his spiritual excellence alone, will rule over both Israel and all those Gentiles who voluntarily submit to him. In the time after Hadrian the political element is more and more suppressed, and the farther we go in this period, the more mystical and supernatural the Messianic idea becomes. Already R. Jose ben Halaphta, a disciple of R. Akiba, forbids the practice of "calculating the end." [59] From this time come those noteworthy Baraithas according to which the Messiah will appear "when the mind is diverted" and one must not calculate the beginning of the Messianic age.[60] R. Nathan, the older contemporary of R. Judah the Patriarch, criticized severely R. Akiba's proclamation of speedy redemption, and also opposed the calculations of "our teachers" (that is, the pre-Hadrianic Tannaim). He himself applied to the "Messianic end" the words of the prophet Habakkuk (2:3):

> For the vision is yet for the appointed time,
> And it declareth of the end, and doth not lie;
> Though it tarry, wait for it;
> Because it will surely come and not delay.[61]

And R. Judah the Patriarch, the most outstanding personality of the last generation of Tannaim, had so little understanding of the *political* element in the life of his people, or was so afraid of the Roman emperor's power, that he sought to abolish the fast of the Ninth of Ab, the day of mourning for the Jews' loss of political freedom, although this would have eliminated the last remembrance of their political independence.[62]

This brings us to the end of the Tannaitic period. Political Messianic expectations were still in existence, though they had lost much of their earlier character. The Tannaitic period came to an end about 220 C.E., only eighty-five years after the destruction of Bethar. In so short a time it would have been impossible for the glorious political hopes to be completely forgotten. From R. Meir, R. Simeon ben Yohai, R. Jose ben Halaphta, R. Eleazar ben Simeon, and even R.

---

[59] Derekh Erets Rabbah, near end of Chap. 11.
[60] Sanhedrin 97a; Pesahim 54b (beginning); Mekhilta, Wayyassa 5 (ed. Friedmann, 51a).
[61] Sanhedrin 97b. See above, p. 399.
[62] Megillah 5ab. See Weiss, *op. cit.*, II², 161.

Judah the Patriarch we possess a considerable number of Messianic sayings, the tone of which is still thoroughly Tannaitic, and which have not yet lost completely the *political* Messianic tendency.

With the completion of the Mishnah and the beginning of the period of the Amoraim, an important change in the Messianic idea took place. The leadership in Judaism passed gradually from Palestinian to Babylonian Jewry, so that the Jews became more and more remote from their native soil and from the source of their political life. Consequently, the clear and more or less realistic desires for political and moral redemption inevitably gave way to new, mystical-religious fantasies. These fanciful conceptions are at times highly poetic and appealingly beautiful; but they deviate more and more from the earlier and more original conceptions. Even one of the earliest Amoraim, Samuel, the opponent of Rab (of whom it was said, "Rab is a Tanna, and so can disagree"),[63] says this of the Days of the Messiah: "There is no difference between this world and the Days of the Messiah, except our bondage to the heathen kingdoms." [64] Thus all the Messianic hopes, all the shining expectations of the prophets, are blotted out in an instant; Samuel apparently relegated them all to the World to Come. And his contemporary, the Palestinian Amora R. Johanan, teaches: "The son of David will come only in a generation that is altogether righteous or altogether wicked." [65] By this he means to say that to bring the "End" by natural means is almost impossible!

Some fifty years later the Amora Rab Hillel [66] permits himself to say, "There shall be no Messiah for Israel, because they have already enjoyed him in the days of Hezekiah." [67] To be sure, this view of Rab Hillel provoked a strong dissent ("God forgive R. Hillel") from the Amora Rab Joseph; but the very fact that an Amora could

---

[63] Kethubboth 8a; Erubin 50b; Gittin 38b; Baba Bathra 42a; Sanhedrin 83b; Hullin 122b.

[64] Berakhoth 34b; Shabbath 63a, 151a; Pesahim 68a; Sanhedrin 91b, 99a. Sanhedrin 91b has "bondage of exile" instead of "bondage to the heathen nations" (perhaps a change from fear of the censor).

[65] Sanhedrin 98a.

[66] Not to be confused with Hillel the Elder, who is never called "Rabbi" or "Rab."

[67] Sanhedrin 98b and 99a.

express such a sentiment shows plainly that a deep gulf lies between the Messianic conceptions of the Tannaim and those of the Amoraim, even though the Amoraim do occasionally manifest a decidedly political tendency in their sayings. The decline of the political side of the Messianic idea is also shown by the frequently quoted saying of the Amoraim that the Holy One, blessed be He, adjured Israel "that they should not rebel against the Gentiles" and "should not go up against a wall," that is, that they should not try to bring the Messianic age by violence, rebellion, or war.[68] This is certainly in clear opposition to any *political* interpretation of the Messianic idea.

But there are even more significant things to be considered. *In the whole Jewish Messianic literature of the Tannaitic period there is no trace of the "suffering Messiah."* All the references to the suffering Messiah in Rabbinic literature that were so diligently collected by Dalman[69] belong *without exception* to the post-Tannaitic period, when Christian influences cannot be wholly discounted.[70] August Wünsche, who attempted to discover the suffering Messiah in the oldest Jewish literature, could find only two passages in the Targum attributed to Jonathan ben Uzziel (Isa. 52:13–15 and 53:11–12) and one passage from "Siphre" as reported by Raymundus Martini.[71] But the passage in Siphre cannot now be found in any ancient or modern edition, nor did Castelli[72] or Dalman[73] find it in their time. Apparently, Raymundus Martini had before him an interpolated text of Siphre, or he himself invented some "Midrashic" material.[74]

As to the two passages from the Targum-Jonathan, Wünsche himself is forced to confess of the first that what is said by the translator about undergoing suffering "had reference to the people" (*auf das Volk bezogen worden*);[75] this is the exact opposite of what Wünsche

[68] Kethubboth 111a.
[69] *Op. cit.*, pp. 35–84.
[70] See the very interesting arguments of Castelli, *op. cit.*, pp. 222–224.
[71] See A. Wünsche, *Die Leiden des Messias*, Leipzig, 1870, pp. 40–42, 65–66.
[72] *Op. cit.*, p. 219, Note 1.
[73] *Op. cit.*, p. 43.
[74] See also below, p. 407, Note 88. In *Sheqi'in*, Jerusalem, 1939, Prof. Saul Lieberman says there is much truth in this general view; cf. J. Baer, "The Forged Midrashim of Raymundus Martini" [Heb.] (memorial volume to A. Gulak and S. Klein, Jerusalem, 1942, pp. 28–49).
[75] Wünsche, *op. cit.*, p. 41.

wished to prove. And of the second passage from Targum-Jonathan cited by Wünsche,[76] Dalman [77] says: "The giving up of life to death (Isa. 53:12) can only be understood of the life-risking zeal of one who, as it says immediately following, makes refractory Israelites amenable to the Law." Eugen Hühn [78] says plainly: "It is never said (in the Targums) that he (the Messiah) must suffer." It must furthermore be remarked here that the Messianic title "the leper of the house of Rabbi," [79] to which Wünsche attaches so much importance,[80] cannot belong to the Tannaitic period, since those spoken of as "of the house of Rabbi" lived many years *after* R. Judah the Patriarch, and hence must be reckoned among the Amoraim.[81] Again, in the story dealing with the sufferings of the Messiah which is cited by Castelli,[82] R. Simeon ben Yohai himself does not figure, but only the cave in which he hid from the Romans. For the story is in a setting that comes a century after the death of this Tanna; otherwise, the Amora R. Joshua ben Levi could not have been the main character in the story.

As with the "suffering Messiah," so with the anti-Messiah (Antichrist), whom Dalman, Wünsche, M. Friedländer, and Bousset found in Rabbinic literature. To be sure, this figure is mentioned frequently in certain Midrashim; but these Aggadic works are of very late date, none being earlier than the eighth century C.E.[83] In some of these Midrashim the victorious *Arabs* are mentioned, and in others there are even allusions to the *Crusades*.[84]

[76] *Ibid.*, p. 42.
[77] *Op. cit.*, pp. 48–49, also note.
[78] *Die messian. Weissag.* I, 114.
[79] Sanhedrin 98*b*.
[80] *Op. cit.*, pp. 62–63, 121–123.
[81] Z. Frankel, *op. cit.*, 2nd ed., p. 228, Note 6; Weiss, *op. cit.*, II², 159, Note 1. Dalman (*op. cit.*, p. 37), on the contrary, interprets this expression to mean the contemporaries of R. Judah the Patriarch.
[82] *Op. cit.*, p. 227.
[83] See Wilhelm Bousset, *Der Antichrist*, pp. 67, 70. Contrariwise, Bousset, p. 74, and M. Friedländer, *Der Antichrist*, pp. 126–129, conclude that the idea of Antichrist is of Jewish origin. But in my opinion they have not adduced sufficient evidence for this from *early* Rabbinic literature.
[84] See M. Buttenwieser, *Outline of the Neo-Hebraic Apocalyptic Literature*, Cincinnati, 1901 (an expansion of his article in *Jew. Encycl.*, I, 675–685); Castelli, *op. cit.*, p. 243; Judah ibn-Shemuel (Kaufman), *Midreshe-Geullah* [Midrashim of Redemption], Tel-Aviv, 1943, pp. 50–55.

THE TANNAITIC AND POST-TANNAITIC PERIODS 407

When, therefore, we are dealing with the earlier, more original Jewish traditions about the Messiah, we should leave out of account the suffering Messiah and the "evil Armilus," who is identical with the Antichrist. Nevertheless, even so careful a scholar as Schürer has introduced into his excellent presentation of the fundamentals of the Jewish Messianic idea [85] a saying of R. Alexandri, an Amora of the second half of the fourth century C.E., also the story about R. Joshua ben Levi, as proof that the notion of the suffering Messiah is original to Judaism,[86] though he considers it only a "scholastic opinion" (*Schulmeinung*), which was foreign to Judaism in general.[87] The truth is that this conception cannot even be considered as an isolated opinion of one early Tanna; for not a single Tannaitic saying that can be interpreted in this way is to be found in early Rabbinic literature.[88]

All this is the inevitable result of the confusion of different stages in the development of the Jewish Messianic idea after the Destruction. I shall attempt, therefore, to deal *only* with the earlier and more original Messianic ideas of the Jewish people; and to that end I shall confine myself here to the Tannaitic period. It is already clear from the foregoing that this period, with regard to the Messianic idea, falls into two parts: the generation *before* Bar-Cochba and the generation *after* Bar-Cochba. Therefore, wherever it is possible (in anonymous Baraithas it is not always possible), I shall indicate to which of the two generations any particular Messianic saying belongs. Thus all the Messianic sayings will appear before us within the framework of Jewish history; for Jewish history alone is the true key to the Jewish Messianic idea.

[85] *Op. cit.*, II⁴, 579–651.
[86] *Ibid.*, pp. 648–651.
[87] *Ibid.*, pp. 650–651.
[88] Schürer's argument (*ibid.*, p. 650, Note 98; see also pp. 444–445) that the saying of R. Jose the Galilean cited by Wünsche could have been found in an old and unforged text of Siphre still extant in the time of Raymundus Martini, on the ground that R. Jose engaged in controversy with R. Tarphon, who is identical with Justin Martyr's "Trypho the Jew"—this argument can hardly stand in the face of the objections of Z. Frankel (*op. cit.*, p. 112; *Monatsschrift für die Geschichte und Wissenschaft des Judentums*, IV, 211) against the identification of Tarphon with Trypho. And even if they were one and the same, the *style* of the saying quoted by Martini is not completely Tannaitic. See also above, p. 405, Note 74.

CHAPTER II

The Messianic Age and the World to Come

ONE OF the most difficult problems in connexion with the Jewish Messianic idea is this: In what manner and to what extent can we distinguish the Messianic age from the World to Come in its broader sense?

As I see the matter, "the World to Come in its broader sense" is, on the one hand, the life after death with its rewards and punishments (Paradise and Gehenna), and on the other hand, the ideas about the judgment of the righteous and the wicked after death, the resurrection of the dead, and the renewal of the world. Until the tenth century C.E., the Jewish religion had no fixed and rigid dogmas. Even its most devout teachers used the greatest freedom in dealing with Messianic ideas, as well as with ideas of the life after death. It is no cause for surprise, therefore, that throughout the post-Biblical literature the Messianic age, the life after death, and the New World that is to follow the resurrection of the dead are constantly interchanged.[1] For the two latter conceptions (the life after death and the New World) the Talmudic and Rabbinic literature has only one phrase, "the World to Come" (*'Olam ha-Ba*), corresponding to the Gospel expressions "the world to come" [KJV] or "the age to come"

---
[1] See Castelli, *Il Messia*, pp. 248–251; I. H. Weiss in his commentary on Mekhilta (in his edition of Mekhilta, Vienna, 1865), pp. 38 (Note 4) and 39.

[RSV].[2] Both the Hebrew and the Greek phrases express merely a contrast to "this world."[3]

A few examples will suffice to show how "the World to Come" is frequently interchanged or confused with "the Days of the Messiah."

In a Baraitha describing how Palestine in the future will be divided into thirteen parts,[4] we read as follows:

> And the division in *the World to Come* will not be like the division in *this world*. In this world, should a man possess a cornfield he does not possess an orchard; should he possess an orchard he does not possess a cornfield. But in the World to Come, there will be no single individual who will not possess land in mountain, lowland, and valley (that is, every man will have different kinds of land, on which he can grow cereals, grapes, or fruit trees, as he likes); for it is said (Ezek. 48:31), "the gate of Reuben, one; the gate of Judah, one; the gate of Levi, one" (that is, all these tribes will have equal possessions).[5]

Here, "the World to Come" certainly does not mean the life after death or after the resurrection of the dead, but the Messianic age only. The division of Palestine, the bestowing of fields and orchards, and the appeal to Ezekiel 48—all these point to the Messianic age. In fact, the Amoraim themselves interpreted the phrase as referring to the Messianic age; for in answer to the question, "For whom is that (thirteenth portion)?" R. Hisda answers "For the prince";[6] and R. Samuel ben Meir (Rashbam) interpreted this as meaning "For the King-Messiah."

There is another interesting Tannaitic tradition based upon Deuteronomy 32:14 ("And of the blood of the grape thou drankest foaming wine"):[7]

---

[2] Matt. 12:32; Mark 10:30; Luke 18:30; Heb. 11:5. The Greek reads ὁ αἰὼν ὁ μέλλων or ὁ αἰὼν ὁ ἐρχόμενος.

[3] In Greek ὁ νῦν αἰών or ὁ αἰὼν οὗτος.

[4] "It was taught: The land of Israel will in time to come be divided between thirteen tribes" (Baba Bathra 122*a*, beginning).

[5] Baba Bathra 122*a*.

[6] *Loc. cit.*

[7] It begins with the words "They (i.e., the men of old) said" in Kethubboth 111*b*. But we find this same passage, though in abbreviated form, in the Tannaitic Midrash, Siphre, Deut. 317, end (ed. Friedmann, 136*a*, beginning).

The World to Come is not like this world. In this world there is the trouble of harvesting and treading (the grapes); but in the World to Come a man will bring one grape on a wagon or in a ship, put it in a corner of his house, and use its contents as if it had been a large wine cask. . . . There will be no grape that will not contain thirty kegs of wine.

There can be no doubt about it: all these exaggerated pictures of the fruitfulness of Palestine are irrelevant to the life after death or after resurrection, but they are thoroughly Messianic. We shall have the opportunity below [8] to cite a number of parallel passages containing similar exaggerations—passages referring without any doubt to the Messianic age. It can be concluded with certainty, therefore, that the expression "the World to Come" is used here in the sense of the Messianic age.

A good example to show how "the World to Come" could be interchanged with "the Days of the Messiah," even in the earliest times, is to be found in the Mishnah text of the Palestinian Talmud. The last Mishnah of the first chapter of the Tractate Berakhoth [9] includes a controversy between Ben Zoma (an older disciple of R. Akiba) and other Sages on the question whether the Section on Fringes (Numbers 15:37-41), which contains a reference to the Exodus from Egypt, should also be recited at night (in the evening prayer). From the word "all" in the verse "that thou mayest remember the day when thou camest forth out of the land of Egypt *all* the days of thy life" [Deut. 16:3], Ben Zoma deduces that the passage on the Exodus is to be recited at night also. "But the Sages say, 'The days of thy life' would mean this world only, but '*all* the days of thy life' is to include the Days of the Messiah." [10] Such is the text of this argument not only in the separate editions of the Mishnah, but also in Mekhilta and even in the Mishnah of the Babylonian Talmud. However, in the Mishnah of the Palestinian Talmud the words of the Sages opposing Ben Zoma are given thus: "But the Sages say, 'The days of thy life' would mean this world only, but '*all* the days of

---

[8] See below, Chap. X.
[9] Mishnah, Berakhoth 1:5; Babli Ber. 12b.
[10] These words are found, with slight variations, in Mekhilta, Pisha 16 (ed. Friedmann, 19a).

thy life' means the World to Come, including the Days of the Messiah."[11] According to this passage in the Palestinian Talmud, therefore, "the World to Come" and "the Days of the Messiah" cannot be separated.

But in the Talmudic literature there are also many passages in which "the Days of the Messiah" stand in contrast to "the World to Come." In commenting on the verse "He covereth him all the day, and He dwelleth between his shoulders" (Deut. 33:12), one Baraitha[12] relates the words "He covereth him" to the period of the First Temple, the words "all the day" to the period of the Second Temple, and the words "and He dwelleth between his shoulders" to the Messianic age. On this, Rabbi (Judah the Patriarch) says: " 'He covereth him' alludes to this world; 'all the day' to the Days of the Messiah; 'and He dwelleth between his shoulders' to the World to Come."[13]

In another Baraitha we read:

R. Judah (ben Ilai, one of the younger disciples of R. Akiba) said: The harp in the Temple had seven strings, as it is written (Ps. 16:11), "In Thy presence is fulness [*soba'*] of joy"; do not read "fulness" [*soba'*] but "seven" [*sheba'*]. The harp of the Days of the Messiah will have eight strings, as it is written (Ps. 12:1), "For the Leader,[14] on the Sheminith" [that is, the eighth (string)]. The harp of the World to Come will have ten strings,[15] as it is written (Ps. 92:4), "With an instrument of ten strings, and with the psaltery; with a solemn sound upon the harp." Furthermore, it is said (Ps. 33:2-3), "Give thanks unto the LORD with harp, sing praises unto Him with the psaltery of ten strings, sing unto Him a new song."[16]

[11] Z. Frankel has already observed this: *Darkhe ha-Mishnah*, 2nd ed., 1923, p. 237. The conclusion which Schürer (*Geschichte*, II⁴, 637) drew from this Mishnah appears to me unfounded.
[12] Zebahim 118b.
[13] See also below, pp. 417-418.
[14] The "Leader" is for the Tanna not a musical director, but a military leader —the King-Messiah.
[15] According to Josephus (*Antiquities* 7:12:3), the harp (κινύρα) of the Temple had ten strings; thus the tradition based upon the exposition of R. Judah, which assumes that the Temple harp had seven strings, is unhistorical.
[16] Arakhin 13b (near the end of Chap. II); Pesiqta Rabbathi, beginning of Chap. 21 (ed. Friedmann, Vienna, 1880, 98b and 99a). In Friedmann's commentary on this passage, the texts of the later Midrashim are quoted.

Here there is a clear distinction between the Days of the Messiah and the World to Come; the "new song" is taken as a reference to the New World.

We have another Baraitha which makes clear the true nature of the World to Come:

> In the World to Come there is neither eating nor drinking nor begetting of children; but the righteous sit with crowns on their heads, basking in the brightness of the Shekhinah, as it is written (Ex. 24:11): "And they beheld God, and did eat and drink" (that is, for them the vision of God took the place of eating and drinking).[17]

To be sure, it might be supposed that the meaning of "the World to Come" here is the life after death, beyond the grave; but the discussion of the Amoraim which immediately follows this Baraitha makes it completely certain that the reference is to the World to Come in the form which it is to take after the Days of the Messiah:

> It was objected (by the Amoraim): "There shall be an abundance of corn in the land on the top of the mountains" (Ps. 72:16). They (the Tannaim) have said: "Not like this world is the World to Come. In this world there is hard labor in treading and gathering (the grapes); but in the World to Come the Holy One, blessed be He, will bring forth the

---

[17] Kallah Rabbathi, Chap. 2. In the Babylonian Talmud (Ber. 17a), this definition of the World to Come is repeated almost verbatim; it is cited, however, not as a Baraitha but as "a favorite saying in the mouth of Rab." But I have already cited in the preceding chapter (p. 404, Note 63) a whole series of Talmudic passages in which it is said, "Rab is a Tanna, and so can disagree." Moreover, the men of the Talmud were accustomed to quote sayings of others that were in accord with their views. Samuel the Little, e.g., chose as his saying (Aboth 4:19) a verse from Proverbs (24:17), and R. Levitas of Jabneh (Aboth 4:4) chose a saying from Ben-Sira (7:17). See for other examples V. Aptowitzer, *A. Schwarz-Festschrift,* Vienna, 1917, p. 125.

In Berakhoth (17a) these are added to the signs of the World to Come: "no business transactions, no envy, no hatred, no rivalry." This saying recurs in Aboth de R. Nathan (Chap. 1, Recension A, ed. Schechter, end of f. 3) as characteristic of "the day which is all Sabbath," i.e. of the World to Come (see Mishnah, Tamid 7:4; Babli, Tamid 33b). After quoting the aforesaid verse (Ex. 24:11), Aboth de R. Nathan adds "like the ministering angels"; this supports my explanation in the text above. But the strongest confirmation of the view that in the earliest Tannaitic period there was a distinction between the Days of the Messiah and the World to Come is to be found in the fact that in IV Ezra (6:51-74) the "new world" which is to follow the Messianic age is described in terms very similar to the "world to come" of our Baraitha. This Baraitha, therefore, may be very old; for IV Ezra in its general spirit is a Pharisaic work (see above, Part II, pp. 352-357).

wind from His treasuries,[18] and it will blow upon them (the vines) and make them (the grapes) fall to the ground; then a man can go out to the field and bring in the fullness of its fruits [19] as sustenance for himself and his household." [20] And if it should occur to you to ask, in accordance with the Baraitha, "Why do they need sustenance?"—again it is written, "The woman conceives and bears at once" (Jer. 31:8); woman is destined to bear every day, by inference from the hen.[21] (Thus, at that time, there will be begetting of children.) But what we have taught *here* relates to the time *before the resurrection of the dead*,[22] whereas what we taught *there* relates to *the Days of the Messiah*.[23]

Manifestly, then, the Days of the Messiah should not be confused with the World to Come. Emil Schürer was wrong when he said: "With the appearance of the Messianic Age a new 'world' (*'Olam*) begins. This future course of the world ('the World to Come') is however in all respects the complete antithesis of the present course of the world ('this world')." [24] Schürer considers this view to be the older; but it is actually supported only by Christian traditions.[25] He asserts rightly, of course, that the hope of the resurrection and the idea of the Messianic age were closely bound up together at a much earlier time (according to Dan. 12:2).[26] But in the Mishnah and the earlier Baraithas these two conceptions are, more or less consciously, kept distinct. To be sure, this distinction cannot be completely ob-

---

[18] According to Jer. 10:13 and 51:16; Ps. 135:7.
[19] So in Kallah Rabbathi, Chap. 2, which does not correspond with what precedes. Kethubboth 111b reads more correctly "his abundant handful" (*melo' pissat yado*), which would depend on the Scriptural words "abundance of corn" (*pissat bar*) above, and would make understandable the words "from it" (*mimmennah*) which follow.
[20] Baraitha, Kethubboth 111b. Thus also in the Tractate Kallah, edition of Nahman Nathan Coronel (*Hamishshah Konteresim*, Vienna, 1864), 4a.
[21] Shabbath 30b (Rabban Gamaliel).
[22] Perhaps instead of "before" we should read "after," since the New World and the World to Come can come only after the resurrection of the dead. But also "the time before the resurrection of the dead" can only be the time *after* the Messianic age, since even the time "before the resurrection of the dead" stands in antithesis to the Messianic age.
[23] Kallah Rabbathi, Chap. 2. Sayings of Amoraim showing a clear contrast between the World to Come and the Days of the Messiah are found in Berakhoth 34b, Shabbath 63a, Pesahim 68a, Sanhedrin 91b, and many other passages.
[24] See *Geschichte*, II⁴, 586.
[25] *Ibid.*, pp. 619, 636–638.
[26] *Ibid.*, pp. 633–634, Note 60. For a contrary view, see Staehlin, *Jahrbücher für deutsche Theologie*, 1874, pp. 199ff.

served; for in the last analysis the Messianic age also is a world of the future, a world that has not yet come, in comparison with the present world; hence the occasional confusion in the sayings of the Tannaim.[27]

There is but one criterion for keeping these two conceptions distinct: where we find in a saying about "the World to Come" materialistic and political expectations, where we find in visions of "the World to Come" features that recall the exaggerations of the Book of Enoch, IV Ezra, the Syriac Baruch, Papias, and other dreamers about the millennium (the "chiliasts")—with respect to these passages we can confidently say that "the World to Come" is another name for the Messianic age. On the other hand, we must exclude from the area of the Messianic idea all sayings dealing with the resurrection of the dead, Paradise and Gehenna, and the New World; [28] for all this comes *after* the Messianic age, and is related not to the Messianic idea, but to eschatology.[29] Therefore I have excluded all these things from the present work. For the same reason I can ignore all studies relating to the influence of the Persians on the Messianic idea, since most of these works are concerned only with eschatology.[30]

---

[27] This accounts for the many contradictions concerning the World to Come collected from the Talmudic and Rabbinic literature by Ferdinand Weber, *System der altsyn. palästin. Theologie*, ed. Franz Delitzsch and Georg Schnedermann, Leipzig, 1880, pp. 354-356. Some of the sayings referring to the future pertain to the "new world," but others are concerned with the Messianic age.

[28] See Castelli, *op. cit.*, p. 250.

[29] In Mekhilta, Wayyassa, Chap. 4 (ed. Friedmann, 50b), R. Eleazar of Modiim, who according to the Aggadah (Jer. Taanith 4:5-68d-69a) was killed by Bar-Cochba, puts "the New World" immediately after the "World to Come." On this, Bacher says, "The New World is the new order of the world that follows the advent of the Messiah" (*Agada der Tannaiten*, I, 202, Note 3; Hebrew translation by A. Z. Rabinowitz, I, 147, Note 2). And according to I. H. Weiss (I³, 217), the New World comes after the resurrection of the dead (cf. Tanhuma, Eqeb 7). See also James Drummond, *The Jewish Messiah*, pp. 380f., 388.

[30] In the important book of Bousset, in the third edition, ed. Gressmann (Bousset-Gressmann, *Die Religion des Judentums*, Tübingen, 1926, pp. 202-301), "the national hope" (pp. 213-242) is separated from "apocalyptic" (pp. 242-289) and from "eschatology and religious individualism" (pp. 289-301). But all this is done, unfortunately, with the more or less clear intention of emphasizing the superiority of the later apocalyptic over the Talmudic literature and over the earlier Pseudepigrapha, and thus the superiority of Christianity over Judaism—a proceeding lacking in scholarly objectivity.

THE MESSIANIC AGE AND THE WORLD TO COME   415

This distinction between the Messianic age and the World to Come was recognized by Maimonides and pointed out by him three times: *firstly*,

The final reward and the ultimate good, endless and perfect, is the life of the World to Come; but the Days of the Messiah belong to *this* world, and will be as the world customarily is, except that sovereignty will be restored to Israel.[31]

Secondly:

Think not that in the Days of the Messiah any terrestrial custom will be nullified, or that there will be a new creation; but the world will pursue its ordinary course. . . . The desire of the Sages and the prophets was not for the Days of the Messiah, . . . but that they might be accounted worthy of life in the World to Come.[32]

And *thirdly*, in a letter concerning the Yemenite Jews, he wrote: "They interchange the World to Come and the Days of the Messiah."[33] The philosophic, religious, and social significance of this distinction in Maimonides is well set forth even for our present undertaking by the philosopher Hermann Cohen.[34]

As with the idea of "the world to come," so with the expression *Le'Atid Labo'* [literally "(for) the future to come," frequently translated "the Age to Come"]. Since it indicates a general contrast to

[31] *Mishneh-Torah* (*Ha-Yad ha-Hazaqah*), Sepher ha-Madda', Hilkhot-Teshuvah 9:2.
[32] *Ibid.*, Hilkhot-Melakhim 12:1-4 (end of *Mishneh-Torah*).
[33] *Letters of Maimonides* [Heb.], ed. D. Z. Baneth, Fascicle I, Jerusalem, 1946, p. 66. And in the prayer "All Shall Thank Thee," for the Sabbath, we say: "There is none to be compared unto thee, O Lord our God, in *this world*, neither is there any beside thee, O our King, for the life of *the World to Come;* there is none but thee, O our Redeemer, for *the Days of the Messiah*, neither is there any like unto thee, O our Saviour, for *the resurrection of the dead*" [Singer, *The Standard Prayer Book*, New York, 1944, p. 187]. Here again "the Days of the Messiah" are parallel to "this world," while "the resurrection of the dead" is parallel to "the World to Come." And my diligent pupil Mr. Sternberg has called my attention to a noteworthy passage in "Questions of R. Eleazar" (A. Jellinek, *Bet ha-Midrash*, VI, 149): "Just as the one who acts righteously *in this world* has his reward stored up *for the Days of the Messiah*, so the one who acts righteously or according to precept *in the Days of the Messiah* has his reward stored up and preserved *for the World to Come*."
[34] Hermann Cohen, *Charakteristik der Ethik Maimunis* (Moses ben Maimon, Leipzig, 1908, I, 125-131); *Das Gottesreich* (*Soziale Ethik im Judentum*, 5th ed., Frankfurt am Main, 1918, pp. 120-127).

the present, this expression can denote the life after death as well as the Messianic age and the New World. When R. Tarphon says in the Mishnah: "And know that the bestowal of reward upon the righteous is *for the future to come*" [35] undoubtedly the meaning is the reward in Paradise. And when we read in another Mishnaic passage: "But *for the future to come* it says (Isa. 25:8): 'He hath swallowed up death forever, and the Lord God will wipe away tears from off all faces,'" [36] certainly the reference is to the life of the World to Come, in which the resurrection of the dead will take place and death itself will be abolished. This time *after* the advent of Messiah is expressly designated as "the future (age) to come" in a Baraitha telling of twelve questions which the men of Alexandria propounded to the early Tanna, R. Joshua ben Hananiah. One of these questions was:

Will the dead *in the future to come* be required to be sprinkled [for uncleanness, according to Num. 19:19] on the third and seventh days, or not? He said to them: "Once the dead have actually come to life we shall know these things" (Rashi's commentary: "we can reconsider the matter").[37]

Here the resurrection of the dead and "the future to come" belong together.

But we have a long series of passages in which the expression "the future to come" [the Age to Come] is equivalent to the Days of the Messiah [the Messianic age]. I have already referred [38] to the discussion in the Mishnah (Ber. 1:5) between Ben Zoma and other Sages about the recitation of the verse on the Exodus [Num. 15:41] at evening prayer. We have also seen that this discussion is repeated almost word for word in Mekhilta [39] with emphasis on the Messianic age. A Baraitha in the Babylonian Talmud bearing on this discussion says:

---

[35] Aboth 2:16 (near the end of the chapter).
[36] Moed Katan 3:9.
[37] Niddah 69b and 70b. In the first reference various editions have "Joshua ben Hinena," but the last name must of course be corrected to "Hananiah."
[38] See above, p. 410.
[39] Mekhilta, Pisha, Chap. 16 (ed. Friedmann, 19a).

There is a teaching: Ben Zoma said to the Sages: Will the exodus from Egypt be mentioned in the Days of the Messiah? Has it not long ago been declared (Jer. 23:7-8): "Therefore behold, the days come, saith the LORD, that they shall no more say, As the LORD liveth that brought up the children of Israel out of the land of Egypt; but, As the LORD liveth that brought up and that led the seed of the house of Israel out of the north country, and from all the countries whither I had driven them"? [40]

This same objection of Ben Zoma and the same proof-text from Jeremiah (23:7-8) are also found in Mekhilta;[41] but there the discussion begins with the words, "Israel is not to recite the exodus from Egypt in the future to come." Thus the words "in the future to come" stand precisely in place of "in the Days of the Messiah."

It is likewise with another discussion already cited,[42] that between R. Judah the Patriarch and other Sages concerning the interpretation of Deuteronomy 33:12. In the Babylonian Talmud[43] the Sages say: "'He covereth him'—this alludes to the First Temple; 'all the day'—to the Second Temple; 'and He dwelleth between his shoulders'—to the Days of the Messiah." But in Siphre, in place of the last sentence, we read: "'And He dwelleth between his shoulders'—built up and perfected *for the future to come*."[44]

But we have another Baraitha in which "the future to come" stands in clear contrast to the Messianic age. This Baraitha relates to the verse "And she did eat and was satisfied and left therof" (Ruth 2:14). This verse is thus expounded: "And she did eat—in this world; and was satisfied—in the Days of the Messiah; and left thereof—for the future to come."[45] Here "the future to come" is the direct antithesis of the Messianic age; and this "future to come" cannot be other than the New World or the World to Come.

As in the case of "the World to Come," these inconsistencies are readily explained by the broad connotation of the term "the future to come" [or "the Age to Come"], as I have already insisted above.

[40] Berakhoth 12b (near end).
[41] Mekhilta, *loc. cit.* (Note 38).
[42] See above, p. 411.
[43] Zebahim 118b.
[44] Siphre, Deut. 352 (ed. Friedmann, 145b).
[45] Shabbath 113b.

For the life after death and the World to Come, as well as the Messianic age, are in contrast to the present world order; all of them denote *what must be, what is destined to come*—the antithesis of this world. Those passages in which we find this expression must be treated exactly as those containing the expression "the World to Come": we must exclude everything referring to the life after death, the resurrection of the dead, the last judgment, and the New World. What is left belongs to the Messianic idea; and only this can we fairly include in work on the Jewish Messianic idea. The rest belongs to Jewish eschatology, which of course has many points of contact with the Messianic idea, and may even be derived from it;[46] but the two should not be confused.

Jewish eschatology, to be sure, has its beginning in the prophecies of the first Isaiah, and it also contains Persian influences, as is well known; hence its main principles took shape before the Hasmonean period. But it acquired popularity and sanctity in the nation only when, during the martyrdoms which marked the first stages of the Hasmonean revolt, the need was felt for spiritual solace for the *individual souls* of the martyred, a solace which Messianic hopes, whether political or spiritual, failed to provide. For the Messianic idea is primarily the hope for the fulfillment of the political expectations of the Jewish people; and these expectations remained by nature more or less mundane. Yet, because of afflictions and persecutions, there was to come a time when the Jews perforce would dream of a "kingdom of heaven" and "a kingdom not of this world."

But this kingdom is *not* the kingdom of the Messiah. For where earthly life does not cease completely, there sin cannot pass away or be abolished, and the complete perfection of human nature remains impossible. Pure spirituality and near approach to divinity ("basking in the brightness of the Shekhinah") belong only to the World to Come of Jewish eschatology. Therefore the Messianic idea and eschatology must not be confused, in spite of their common origin. Most of the contradictions which we find in presentations of Jewish Messianic ideas are the result of this confusion and of the practice of

[46] See Schürer, *op. cit.*, II⁴, 633–634, Note 60.

bringing eschatology into the discussion of the Messianic idea.⁴⁷ In the older Rabbinic literature, to be sure, the same *words* are frequently used for different ideas; but the *ideas* themselves are interchanged only infrequently. Hence in discussing the Messianic ideas of the Tannaim, I shall endeavor to the best of my ability to avoid confusing these ideas with eschatology.

⁴⁷ This is particularly obvious in the work of M. Rabinsohn, *Le Messianisme dans le Talmud et les Midraschim*, Paris, 1907. Although he emphasizes "the national and temporal (this-worldly) character of the Rabbinic Messianic idea" (see especially pp. 27–28), and separates it from "the World to Come" (pp. 45–46)—the three basic principles of my German book, which he does not mention although it preceded his French book by three years—nevertheless his book exhibits confusion in the discussion of the Messianic idea along with eschatology, in emphasis on Persian influences, and in indiscriminate use of early and late sources.

CHAPTER III

The "End" and the Messianic Age

WE HAVE already seen that the Messianic age is not the end of all human life on earth: it is a period of transition to the last judgment, the resurrection of the dead, and the New World. It is not strange, therefore, that the Aggadists attempted to calculate not only the *beginning* of the Messianic age, but also its *duration*.[1] As in all Messianic studies, we must here again distinguish between sayings which belong to a time earlier than the Hadrianic persecution and those which come from a later time. Here again the earlier sayings are fewer in number, but more definite, more assured, and more mundane, still less remote from the primary source of popular belief. On the contrary, the later sayings are more numerous, but also more abstract, more mystical, and more academic.

A pre-Hadrianic Baraitha runs as follows:

R. Eliezer (ben Hyrcanus) said: The Days of the Messiah will last forty years, as it is written (Ps. 95:10), "For *forty years* shall I be wearied with that generation." R. Eleazar ben Azariah said: Seventy years, as it is written (Isa. 23:15), "And it shall come to pass in that day that Tyre shall be forgotten *seventy years*, according to the days of one king." What particular king is this? The Messiah, of course. R. Jose (the Galilean) [2]

---

[1] See Bacher, *Agada der Tannaiten*, I, 145, Heb. trans. by A. Z. Rabinowitz, I, 102.

[2] The reading here is "Rabbi," meaning R. Judah the Patriarch; but in Midrash Tehillim (Shoḥer Tob) 90:17 (ed. Buber, 197) the reading is "Rabbi Jose." This is more plausible, since R. Jose the Galilean was the contemporary of R. Eliezer ben Hyrcanus, R. Eleazar ben Azariah, and R. Dosa the Elder. See Bacher, *op. cit.*, I, 145-147 (Heb. trans., I, 102-103), and Buber's notes to Midrash Tehillim, *ad loc.*

said: Three generations, as it is written (Ps. 72:5), "They shall fear Thee while the sun endureth, and so long as the moon (endureth), *a generation and generations.*" [3]

Another Baraitha reads:

R. Eliezer said: The Days of the Messiah will be forty years; for it is written in one place (Deut. 8:3), "And He afflicted thee, and suffered thee to hunger, and fed thee with manna"; and in another place it is written (Ps. 90:15), "Make us glad according to the days wherein Thou hast afflicted us, according to the years wherein we have seen evil" (Israel was forty years in the wilderness). R. Dosa said: Four hundred years; for it is written in one place (Gen. 15:13), "And they shall serve them, and they shall afflict them four hundred years"; and in another place it is written (Ps. 90:15), "Make us glad according to the days wherein Thou hast afflicted us." R. Jose (the Galilean) [4] said: Three hundred and sixty-five years, according to the number of days in the solar year, as it is written (Isa. 63:4), "For the day of vengeance that was in My heart, and My year of redemption are come." [5]

The most interesting points in these Baraithas are *first*, that according to most of the Tannaim the duration of the time of redemption corresponds to the duration of the tribulations; [6] and *second*, that one of the figures, the four hundred years of R. Dosa, agrees with the duration of the Messianic age in IV Ezra,[7] where likewise this figure is obtained by joining Gen. 15:13 with Ps. 90:15.[8]

A much later Baraitha, belonging to the post-Hadrianic period,[9] offers a quite different calculation:

It was taught in the school of Elijah: The world will endure six thousand years: two thousand in chaos,[10] two thousand under the Law, and two thousand during the Messianic age; but because of our many iniquities time

---

[3] Sanhedrin 99a; also without the names of the Tannaim in Siphre, Deut., 310 (ed. Friedmann, 134 a).
[4] See Note 2 above.
[5] Sanhedrin 99a.
[6] See above, Part I, pp. 15-19.
[7] IV Ezra 7:28; see also 12:34.
[8] See above, Part II, p. 355, E. Hühn, *Die messian. Weissag.*, Freiburg im Breisgau, 1899, I, 109, Note 3.
[9] See M. Friedmann, Introduction to Seder Eliyahu Rabba and Zuta, pp. 46, 83.
[10] This is the time of ignorance, like the Moslem *Jahiliyyah*: the time between Adam and Abraham (Rashi) or Moses, when the Torah was unknown.

has been lost from the last period (that is, four thousand years have already passed, yet the Messiah has not come).[11]

Here is fixed not only the duration of the Messianic age, but also its predestined time of beginning (*c.* 240 C.E.), although that has been delayed "because of our many iniquities." This view is very similar to that of R. Eliezer (to be discussed in the next chapter), according to whom the redemption is dependent upon repentance, that is, upon the elimination of "our many iniquities." But it is not said here that if the iniquities continue without repentance, redemption will not come at all.

Another late Baraitha deals only with *the beginning* of the Messianic age:

In a Baraitha it is taught: If, four thousand two hundred and thirty-one years (how exact!) after the Creation of the World, a man should say to you, "Take this field, worth a thousand denars, for one denar," do not take it;[12]

for in that year Messiah will come and all fields will be redistributed without price.[13]

Parallel to this Baraitha is a saying, which admittedly is from the Amoraim, yet in style and manner of expression appears to belong to an earlier time:

Rab Hanan bar Tahlifa sent this word to Rab Joseph: I met a man who had a scroll written in the Assyrian character and in the holy language. I said to him, "Where did you get this?" He said to me, "I hired myself as a mercenary in the Persian [Roman] army, and I found it among the secret archives of Persia [Rome]. In it it is written: 'Four thousand two hundred and ninety-one years after its creation, the world will be orphaned. As to the years which follow, some of them will witness the wars of the dragons, some the wars of Gog and Magog, and the rest will be the Messianic age; and the Holy One, blessed be He, will not renew His world until after seven thousand years.' "[14]

[11] Sanhedrin 97*ab;* with a few differences in Abodah Zorah 9*a*. The number of elapsed years is in Seder Eliyahu Rabba "more than seven hundred"; but this is a later addition (see Friedmann, *op. cit.*, p. 83).
[12] Abodah Zarah 9*b*.
[13] See Rashi *ad loc.*
[14] Sanhedrin 97*b*.

Apparently the numbers in the two Baraithas should be regarded as the same, and we should read 4231 in both places. According to this reckoning, the Messianic age would begin in the year 471 C.E. [4231–3760 = 471].* It is worthy of note that this year is one of those in which the downfall of the Roman Empire in the West (476) was rapidly approaching. Anthemius, Olybrius, Glycerius, Julius Nepos, Romulus Augustulus (the last Roman emperor)—these five ruled in the decade 467–476. But I have already mentioned that this whole tradition gives an impression of much greater antiquity. It is also possible that the date of the Creation of the World held at the time of this tradition was different from that which we now hold [3761–3760].

But such "reckoning of the End,"[15] in which R. Akiba and his contemporaries were occupied, proved to be mistaken. And how great must have been the disappointment when even R. Akiba, at the time of the Bar-Cochba rebellion, was found in error! Quickly the view spread that the "End" was something hidden from men, something that could not be known. In a Baraitha we read thus:

Seven things are hidden from men. These are the day of death, the day of consolation,[16] the depth of judgment;[17] no man knows what is in the mind of his friend; no man knows which of his business ventures will be profitable, or *when the kingdom of the house of David will be restored, or when the sinful kingdom will fall*.[18]

---

* The traditional Jewish year of Creation began in the autumn of 3761 B.C.E., and hence is approximately coterminous with 3760 B.C.E.—TRANS.

[15] Cf. "the end" (Hab. 2:3), "the end of the days" (Dan. 12:13); hence in the Talmud "the End" or "the Messianic end" (Meg. 3a). See for details A. H. Silver, *Messianic Speculation in Israel*, New York, 1927, pp. 13–29.

[16] In the sense of "the resurrection of the dead," for *nuḥama* in Syriac means "resurrection"; see Levy, *Neuhebr. Wörterbuch*, II, 346a; III, 370b (article KSY, to "cover," "hide"; and article *Neḥamah*, "consolation," etc.). Rashi's explanation (Pes. 54b, beginning), "The day of consolation: when every man shall be relieved of his cares," is too literal.

[17] According to Levy, *op. cit.*, II, 364a; III, 664b (see article *'Omeq*), this means retribution.

[18] Pesahim 54b, beginning; Mekhilta, Wayyassa, Chap. 6 (ed. Friedmann, 51a [Lauterbach, II, 125]). The last clause in the ordinary editions of the Talmud reads thus: "or when the kingdom of Persia will fall"; but the Munich manuscript, which was not damaged by Christian censorship, reads, "or when the sinful kingdom will come to an end." This agrees with the established text in the Mekhilta editions of Friedmann (51a) and Weiss (p. 60), which reads, "or

The circumstance that the restoration of the Davidic kingdom is here connected with the fall of "the sinful kingdom" (Rome) can serve as an argument (if not positive proof) that this Baraitha is early.

Somewhat later is the following Tannaitic [19] tradition: "Three things come unexpectedly: the Messiah, a lucky find, and a scorpion." [20] This tradition means to say, without doubt, that no calculations of the "End" are trustworthy: just as the sting of a scorpion or a piece of luck like the finding of a treasure cannot be foreseen, so it is impossible to predict the beginning of the Messianic redemption.

The same view is expressed in another interesting Baraitha:

It has been taught: R. Nathan (a post-Hadrianic Tanna, an older contemporary of R. Judah the Patriarch) said: This verse pierces and descends to the very abyss (Hab. 2:3): "For the vision is yet for the appointed time, and it declareth of the end, and doth not lie; though it tarry, wait for it; because it will surely come, it will not delay." It is not according to our teachers, who expounded it by (Dan. 7:25) "Until a time, times, and half a time"; and not according to R. Ishmael,[21] who expounded it by (Ps. 80:6) "Thou hast fed them with the bread of tears and hast made them to drink tears *a third time*" (that is, the coming of Messiah will only take place after three generations have suffered and wept over the destruction of the Temple); and not according to R. Akiba, who expounded it by (Hag. 2:6) "Yet but a little while and I will shake the heavens and the earth." But (all these verses refer to) the first kingdom (the Hasmoneans, according to Rashi), lasting seventy years; the second kingdom (the Herodian dynasty), lasting fifty-two years; and the reign of Bar-Koziba, lasting two and a half years.[22]

---

when the wicked kingdom will be uprooted." Other editions of the Mekhilta, which have passed under the rod of censorship, read, "the kingdom of Macedonia."

[19] It is introduced by the formula "We have been taught (in the Mishnah)"; hence this is not a saying of the Amora R. Zera, as James Drummond (*The Jewish Messiah*, p. 220) thinks. R. Zera merely reported this older saying.

[20] Sanhedrin 97*a*.

[21] So we must read instead of "R. Simlai"; for R. Simlai was an Amora (see on him in Graetz, *Geschichte der Juden*, Hebrew trans. by S. P. Rabbinowitz, II, 338–340). How could the Tanna, R. Nathan, have mentioned his interpretation in a Baraitha, even putting his words before the words of R. Akiba? Therefore, we conjecture that "Ishmael" is to be read in place of "Simlai," since R. Ishmael had disputes with R. Akiba, and his name is sufficiently like "Simlai" to make confusion possible.

[22] Sanhedrin 97*b*.

What all this amounts to is that the advent of Messiah and the establishment of his kingdom cannot be discovered or determined by exegesis of Scripture.

But many went further than R. Nathan: "R. Jose (post-Hadrianic) says, He that attempts to give the End [23] has no share in the World to Come." [24] And an Aggadah which is relatively early, though reported by Amoraim, relates that when Jonathan ben Uzziel, the oldest disciple of Hillel the Elder, sought to make a translation of the Hagiographa "a heavenly voice came forth and said, 'Stop!' Why? Because the date of the Messiah is foretold in it [in the Book of Daniel]." [25] The Tannaim did not wish to arouse vain hopes among the people, lest a second Bar-Cochba bring another calamity upon them. The ardent faith in imminent redemption characteristic of the pre-Hadrianic period grew considerably weaker after the fall of Bethar.[26]

But in the pre-Hadrianic period there were still Tannaim who believed that they could calculate not only the year, but even the month, of the End. R. Eliezer and R. Joshua differed in general about the redemption, and specifically about the month. According to R. Joshua, the children of Israel would be redeemed for the Age to Come in the month of Nisan, on the same day on which they were delivered from the Egyptian bondage, on the basis of Exodus 12:42:

"It was a night of watching unto the LORD for bringing them out from the land of Egypt; this same night (14th of Nisan) is a night of watching unto the LORD for all the children of Israel *throughout their generations.*"

But according to R. Eliezer, the children of Israel could be redeemed for the Age to Come only in the month of Tishri, on the basis of Psalm 81:4–5:

"Blow the horn at the new moon, at the full moon for our feast-day" (this is Rosh ha-Shanah, which is celebrated in Tishri). Why (are we to blow the horn at the new moon)? "For it is a statute for Israel, an ordinance of the God of Jacob." [27]

[23] An expression equivalent in meaning to "those who calculate the End" (San. 97b). See Bacher, *op. cit.*, II, 159, Note 7 (Heb. trans., Vol. II, Part I, p. 107, also p. 108, Note 20).
[24] Derekh Erets Rabbah, Chap. 11 (near the end of the tractate).
[25] Megillah 3a.
[26] See below, Chap. IV, pp. 431–439.
[27] Mekhilta, Bo', Pisha, near the end of Chap. 14 (ed. Friedmann, 16b); Rosh

The opinion of R. Joshua was more acceptable than that of R. Eliezer, *first*, because the general rule was: "Where R. Eliezer and R. Joshua disagree, the Halakhah is according to R. Joshua"; *second*, because R. Jose agreed with the opinion that the day of the *last* redemption will be the same as that of the *first* redemption, saying: "Good things are brought about on a good day, and bad things on a bad day." [28] The 14th of Nisan, once already chosen to be the day of redemption, was also to be the first day of redemption in the Messianic age.

---

ha-Shanah 11b, with minor variations. From the latter passage it can be seen that this dispute depends upon the opinions of R. Eliezer and R. Joshua with regard to the month in which the world was created. According to R. Eliezer, the Scriptural words "an ordinance (*mishpat*) of the God of Jacob" [Ps. 81:5] point to the judgment (*mishpat*) of God upon the Gentiles in the Messianic age.

[28] Arakhin 11b (see Rashi *ad loc.*). See also Taanith 29a, where this saying occurs as an anonymous Baraitha.

CHAPTER IV

The Prerequisites of Messiah's Coming

THE SUFFERINGS of the Jewish nation were, as I have already pointed out many times, both the source of the Messianic hopes, and the stimulus which caused their revival within the nation time after time. Yet the Jewish nation saw in these sufferings a fitting punishment for its misdeeds. Therefore, redemption from sufferings, the Messianic age, had to come through redemption from sin. Hence repentance and the keeping of the commandments were the prerequisites of redemption, since they would bring about the great changes that must precede the Messiah's coming.

There is hardly any need to mention here the early and common Talmudic saying, "He that tells a thing in the name of him that said it brings redemption to the world, as it is written (Esther 2:22): 'And Esther told the king thereof in Mordecai's name.' "[1] As the verse from Esther shows, this saying refers to redemption from trouble in general, and not specifically to Messianic redemption. A much more important saying is that of R. Simeon ben Yohai (post-Hadrianic):

If Israel were to keep two Sabbaths according to the laws thereof, they would be redeemed immediately, for it is said (Isa. 56:4), "Thus saith the LORD concerning the eunuchs that keep My Sabbaths"; and following that it is written (Verse 7), "Even them will I bring to My holy mountain," and so on.[2]

[1] Mishnah, Aboth 6:6; Megillah 15a; Hullin 104a; Niddah 19b; Tractate Kallah, near end; Kallah Rabbathi, Chap. 8.
[2] Shabbath 118b.

But Messianic redemption is brought about by charity and repentance, as well as by observance of the ceremonial laws. R. Jose says, in a Baraitha:

Great is *charity*, in that it brings the redemption nearer, as it is said (Isa. 56:1), "Thus saith the LORD, Keep ye justice and do *charity* [the word may also be translated "righteousness"]; for My salvation is near to come, and My favor to be revealed." [3]

Repentance is particularly emphasized:

R. Jose the Galilean (pre-Hadrianic) [4] said: Great is repentance, because it brings near [5] redemption, as it is said (Isa. 59:20), "And a redeemer will come to Zion, and unto them that turn from transgression in Jacob." Why will a redeemer come to Zion? Because of those that turn from transgression in Jacob.[6]

This same emphasis on repentance as a prerequisite of redemption is also found in the sayings of the greatest of the pre-Hadrianic Tannaim. And of course, the preaching of John the Baptist "in the fifteenth year of the reign of Tiberius Caesar" (29-30 C.E.) sprang from the same thoroughly Jewish conception: "Repent, for the kingdom of heaven is at hand." [7] Every word of this is completely Talmudic.

There is recorded a very interesting controversy, in the form of a dialogue, between two disciples of Rabban Johanan ben Zakkai, R. Eliezer ben Hyrcanus and R. Joshua ben Hananiah, both of whom began their careers before the destruction of the Temple. The point at issue between them was whether repentance is an indispensable prerequisite of redemption or not:

R. Eliezer said: If Israel repent, they will be redeemed; if not, they will not be redeemed. R. Joshua said to him: If they do not repent, will they

---

[3] Baba Bathra 10a.

[4] Yoma 86b reads "R. Jonathan" instead of "R. Jose the Galilean," an error due possibly to confusion arising from the use of the initials "R. J." See Bacher, *Agada der Tannaiten*, I, 369, Note 3; *ibid.*, Heb. trans., Vol. I, Part II, p. 94, Note 4 (the reference herein should be Yoma 86b instead of 86a).

[5] So in Yoma 86b; in Yalkut on Isaiah 59 (Sect. 358) the reading is "brings."

[6] Yoma 86b; Yalkut on Isa. 59 (Sect. 358).

[7] Mark 1:4; Matt. 3:2; Luke 3:3. See J. Klausner, *Jesus of Nazareth*, 5th Heb. ed., pp. 255-256 [Eng. ed., pp. 245-247].

not be redeemed? R. Eliezer replied: [8] The Holy One, blessed be He, will set up over them a king, whose decrees shall be as cruel as Haman's; then Israel will repent, and He will bring them back to their own land.[9]— Another (Baraitha) taught: R. Eliezer said: If Israel repent, they will be redeemed, as it is written (Jer. 3:22), "Return, ye backsliding children, I will heal your backslidings." R. Joshua said to him: But is it not written (Isa. 52:3):—"Ye have sold yourselves for nought, and ye shall be redeemed without money"—"Ye have sold yourselves for nought," i.e. for idolatry; "And ye shall be redeemed without money," i.e. without repentance and good deeds? R. Eliezer retorted to R. Joshua: But is it not written (3:7), "Return unto Me, and I will return unto you"? R. Joshua rejoined: But is it not written (Jer. 3:14), "For I am master over you,[10] and I will take you one from a city, and two from a family, and I will bring you to Zion"? R. Eliezer replied: But is it not written (Isa. 30:15), "In returning (that is, repentance) and rest shall ye be saved"? R. Joshua replied: But is it not written (Isa. 49:7), "Thus saith the LORD, the Redeemer and Holy One of Israel, to him who is abhorred of nations (that is, even when the Israelites are abominably sinful), to a servant of rulers: Kings shall see and arise, princes, and they shall prostrate themselves"? R. Eliezer countered: But is it not written (Jer. 4:1), "If thou wilt return [repent], O Israel, saith the LORD, unto Me thou shalt return" (that is you will be worthy of the Messiah's coming)? R. Joshua answered: But is it not written (Dan. 12:7), "And I heard the man clothed in linen, who was above the waters of the river, when he lifted up his right hand and his left hand unto heaven, and swore by Him that liveth forever, that it shall be for a time, times, and a half; and when they have made an end of breaking in pieces the power of the holy people, all these things shall be consummated" (hence there is a determined end, even if Israel does not repent)? At this R. Eliezer remained silent.[11]

Thus R. Eliezer was refuted, and the opinion of R. Joshua, that the redemption of Israel must *inevitably* come in any case, prevailed.[12]

[8] In the Babylonian Talmud (San. 97b) we have the word "but" instead of "R. Eliezer replied," and R. Joshua's answer seems to continue; but in the Palestinian Talmud (Taanith 1:1, 63d) we have the reading followed here, and this is more logical. The erroneous reading seems to have arisen through the practice of abbreviation.
[9] So I read instead of "to the right path," which is only a repetition of the idea of repentance.
[10] According to Rashi, "This means against their own wills, and without their repentance."
[11] Sanhedrin 97b and 98a; and with variations, Pal. Talmud, Taanith 1:1, 63d.
[12] See Castelli, *Il Messia*, p. 185, note.

Sins cannot completely frustrate the redemption; but they can delay it. This is the prevalent view in the Talmud. This has already been pointed out in the preceding chapter in the Baraitha from "the school of Elijah." An anonymous and very strange Baraitha says: "Our rabbis have taught: Proselytes and those that play with children delay the Messiah." [13] The puzzling expression "those that play with children" is explained by the Gemara thus: "What does 'those that play with children' mean? . . . They that marry girls too young to bear children." [14] This interpretation, which seems so odd to us, gives the true sense of the saying. For we have another version of this Baraitha, which says: "It has been taught: Proselytes and those that emit semen to no purpose delay the Messiah." [15] In two Talmudic passages, this severe comment on proselytes is explained on the ground that they are not scrupulous in keeping the commandments because they still hold to their ancestral customs.[16]

As regards "those that play with children" (or "those that emit semen to no purpose"), the opinion that they delay the Messiah is explained by another strange saying. This saying is found in *five* Talmudic passages. Two of these passages stand almost side by side in the same tractate,[17] and therefore can be considered as one. In this passage the saying is attributed to the later Amora Rab Assi. In two other passages, R. Jose is named as the author of the saying.[18] And finally, in a late Talmudic tractate,[19] the name is given as Rab Johanan (the well known early Amora, the teacher of Rab Assi). It seems to me that we can conclude with certainty that the post-Hadrianic Tanna R. Jose, one of the disciples of R. Akiba, is the author of the saying. R. Jose is often referred to by the initials R. J.; these initials could be wrongly read as "R. Johanan" instead of "R. Jose." But the name of Rab Assi is almost never abbreviated; besides, it would be difficult to misinterpret the initials R. A. as "R. Johanan." Also, the

---

[13] Niddah 13*b*.
[14] *Loc. cit.*
[15] Kallah Rabbathi, Chap. 2.
[16] For more details on this, see below, Chap. VIII.
[17] Yebamoth 62*a* and 63*b*.
[18] Abodah Zarah 5*a;* Niddah 13*b*.
[19] Kallah Rabbathi, Chap. 2 ("Five Tractates" [Heb.] by N. N. Coronel, 4*a*).

THE PREREQUISITES OF MESSIAH'S COMING 431

fact that this saying serves as an explanation of an early and somewhat ambiguous Baraitha is a further proof that it is Tannaitic. Here is the short form of the saying (Nid. 13*b*):

R. Jose stated: The Son of David will not come until all the souls in *Guf* [20] are disposed of, since it is said (Isa. 57:16): "For the spirit shall fail [21] before Me, and the souls which I have made."

Clearer and more understandable is the form in the Midrash Rabbah:

R. Tanhum son of R. Hiyya (an Amora) said, and some say it in the name of the Rabbis (Amoraim): The King-Messiah will not come until all the souls which it was originally the divine intention to create shall have come to an end.[22]

The correct explanation of this curious saying of the post-Hadrianic period is to be sought, in my opinion, in the circumstances of the time. After the Destruction, and especially after the Hadrianic persecutions, there were Jews who did not wish to marry and beget children, because the Roman government had forbidden circumcision, and because in general they could expect to see their children slain in wars or in persecutions.[23] R. Ishmael ben Elisha, a contemporary and opponent of R. Akiba, and one of the first to suffer martyrdom during the Hadrianic persecutions (or Rabban Simeon II ben Gamaliel II, who survived the persecutions almost by a miracle),[24] said:

And since the wicked kingdom (Rome) has come into power which issues cruel decrees against us and forbids to us the observance of the Torah and the precepts and does not allow us "to enter into the week of the son" (that is, to circumcise a son after seven days), we ought by rights to

---

[20] According to Rashi's commentary (on Ab. Zar. 5*a*), *Guf* is "the treasury of souls" established at the creation of the world. The Syriac Baruch (30:2) and IV Ezra (7:29–32, etc.) also speak of "treasuries" (*promptuaria*) in which souls were deposited (see above, Part II, p. 355); thus the source of this conception cannot be late Persian, as supposed by Kohut, *Aruch Completum*, II, 335. On these "treasuries" see also Schürer, *Geschichte*, II⁴, 641 (the souls are found in these after death). [See also Moore, *Judaism*, II, 353, Note 3; 390.]

[21] According to Rashi, "shall fail" (*ya'atoph*) here means "shall delay," and is to be connected with "the feebler" or "the slower" (*ha'atuphim*) in Gen. 30:42.

[22] Lev. R. beginning of Chap. 15.

[23] See I. H. Weiss, *Each Generation and Its Interpreters* [Heb.], II², 118, Note 1.

[24] Sotah 49*b*; Baba Kamma 83*a*.

bind ourselves not to marry and beget children; thus the seed of Abraham our father would come to an end of its own accord.[25]

Others, however, who could not control their impulses, practiced onanism or married immature girls who could not bear children. There was thus great danger that the nation would perish from wars, rebellions, and persecutions, on the one hand, and from scarcity of births, on the other. Therefore R. Jose ben Halafta, one of the last disciples of R. Akiba, taught that the redemption would come only after all the souls in the celestial *Guf* (treasury of souls) had been clothed with bodies by birth. And therefore the Baraitha [in Niddah 13*b* and Kallah Rabbathi, Chap. 2] from the time of the Hadrianic persecution taught that those who avoided begetting children—by unnatural practices or by "playing with children"—were delaying the coming of the Messiah.[26]

The saying of R. Jose begins with the words, "The Son of David will not come until . . ." Many sayings which attempt to determine the prerequisites of the Messiah's coming begin with these words. But first of all we should notice the sayings of R. Jose ben Kisma, a Galilean Tanna from the last years before the Hadrianic persecution. It was he who urged his colleague, R. Hanina ben Teradion, to obey the Roman edict forbidding the public teaching of the Law. These are his words:

Brother Hanina, knowest thou not that it is Heaven that has ordained this nation [Rome] to reign? For though she laid waste His House (Palestine), burnt His Temple, slew His pious ones and caused His best ones to perish, still is she firmly established! [27]

Nevertheless, in spite of the fact that R. Jose ben Kisma recognized Rome's power and greatness, he looked forward to its overthrow by the kingdom of the Parthians, the only kingdom which was making

---

[25] Baba Bathra 60*b* (end of Chap. 3); Tosephta, Sotah 15:10. See Graetz, *Geschichte der Juden*, IV, 186 (Heb. trans. by S. P. Rabbinowitz, II, 255–256). It is interesting that we find the same advice in the Biblical Antiquities attributed to Philo (discussed above, Part II, pp. 366–369), 9:2 (James's ed., p. 100).

[26] In Bousset-Gressmann, *Die Religion des Judentums*, 1926, p. 248, Note 2, this explanation is considered incorrect. But these passages can hardly be explained in any other way.

[27] Abodah Zarah 18*a*.

THE PREREQUISITES OF MESSIAH'S COMING 433

a strong stand against Rome at that time; and the fall of the Roman world-empire would make possible the appearance of the Messianic world-empire. The following ancient tradition has preserved for us the opinion of this Tanna, who died a short time before the Hadrianic persecution:

> The disciples of R. Jose ben Kisma asked him: "When will the Son of David come?" He answered: "I fear lest ye demand a sign of me." They said to him: "We will demand no sign of you." So he answered them: "When this gate [of Caesarea Philippi] falls down, is rebuilt, falls again, and is again rebuilt, and again falls—they will not have time to rebuild it (a third time) [28] before the Son of David come." They said to him: "Master, give us a sign." He protested: "Did ye not assure me that ye would not demand a sign?" They replied: "Nevertheless, we desire one." He said to them: "Very well, let the waters of the cave of Pamias be turned into blood." And they were turned into blood. When he was about to die, he said to them: "Put my coffin deep down in the earth; for there is not one palm-tree in Babylonia to which a Persian horse will not be tethered, nor one coffin in Palestine out of which a Median horse will not eat straw." [29]

The cave of Pamias (or Paneas, modern Banias) from which the Jordan flows out,[30] is near Caesarea Philippi. This city was in ancient times the most northerly point in Palestine. Its gate was, therefore, the gateway through which invaders would enter the country. Thus R. Jose ben Kisma wished to indicate that the gate of Caesarea Philippi would fall several times; in other words, that the Parthians would penetrate this gate several times and defeat the Romans; but the Romans would recover each time and defeat the Parthians. (This would be like the case of Mattathias Antigonus, the Jewish king sup-

---

[28] So according to Rashi (on San. 98a). In *Dikduke Sopherim* ("Variae Lectiones in Mischnam et in Talmud Babylonicum") by Raphael Rabbinovicz, IX, 292, Note 7, there is another reading, according to which the words "falls and is rebuilt" are added once more; but this is apparently only a simple dittography. Rashi did not so read, and "a third time" is a more customary number than "a fourth time." This is contrary to Bacher, *op. cit.*, I, 402, Note 1 (Heb. trans., Vol. I, Part II, p. 119, Note 1).

[29] Sanhedrin 98ab. The last passage is also found with some modification, as a saying of R. Simeon ben Yohai: "If you see a Persian horse tethered (to a grave) in the land of Israel, look for the footsteps of Messiah" (Lam. R. 1:13, ed. Buber, 39a; Song of Songs R., 8:10).

[30] Bekhoroth 55a.

ported by the Parthians, who was finally defeated by Herod I, supported by the Romans). Finally, however, according to R. Jose ben Kisma, the Parthians would completely overwhelm the Romans and thus prepare the way for the King-Messiah.[31]

This solitary saying from the pre-Hadrianic period concerning the conditions leading to the Messiah's coming has a purely political character. The post-Hadrianic sayings concerning the prerequisites of redemption are naturally more numerous, but all of them are permeated with a spirit of sadness and pessimism, since they bear the stamp of religious persecution. An anonymous Baraitha says:

> Our Rabbis taught: "For the LORD will vindicate His people . . . when He sees that their power is gone, and that there is none remaining, shut up or left at large" (Deut. 32:36)—meaning that the Son of David will not come until traitors are many. Another interpretation: until disciples are few. Another interpretation: until the last farthing is gone from the purse. Still another interpretation: until the redemption is despaired of, for it is written, "there is none remaining, shut up or left at large"—as though Israel had neither helper nor supporter.[32]

The reference to the increase of traitors is convincing proof that this Baraitha was composed during the Hadrianic persecutions; for never was the number of informers in Palestine so great as in those days. To carry out the harsh decrees was impossible without a host of spies and traitors. The Romans had forbidden the various religious customs which concerned the most intimate relations of Jewish family life, such as circumcision, separation during menstruation, and the like. So from where could the Romans have known about these customs or how could they have prevented their observance, except with the aid of certain Jewish, Samaritan, and to some extent even Christian, informers,[33] who betrayed all the "secrets" of the Jews, their kinsmen in religion and national origin? According to one Tannaitic tradition,

---

[31] Bacher, *op. cit.*, I, 402 (Heb. trans., Vol. I, Part II, pp. 118–119).
[32] Sanhedrin 97a.
[33] See J. Klausner, "Simon Bar-Cochba" (*When a Nation Fights for Its Freedom* [Heb.], 8th ed., 1952, pp. 244–245). According to M. Friedländer (*Der Antichrist, passim*), the culprits were especially the Jewish antinomians, including the Jewish Gnostics, who rejected the ceremonial laws; these "traitors" did not hesitate to denounce loyal Jews who were keeping the religious requirements.

it was a Samaritan betrayer who brought about the fall of Bethar—a tradition supported in part by a Samaritan source.[34] Graetz has already called attention to the large part played by traitors and informers during this fearful time.[35] It was perfectly natural, therefore, that Jewish ideas about the conditions leading to redemption should have this feature (increase of traitors) added to them.[36]

The same applies to the falling away of disciples; for during the period of persecution, instruction in the Rabbinical schools and the ordination of disciples were suppressed by the Romans with particular harshness. R. Hananiah [Hanina] ben Teradion, who persisted in public teaching, was burned together with the scroll of the Law from which he taught.[37] And of R. Judah ben Baba, who ordained the last disciples of R. Akiba, it is related that the Romans "pierced him through with three hundred spears of iron and made him like a sieve." [38]

The widespread poverty resulting from these persecutions found expression in the opinion, "until the last farthing is gone from the purse." And the ensuing despair about the redemption is plainly revealed in the desperate cry of R. Ishmael ben Elisha (or Rabban Simeon II ben Gamaliel II) that it would be better if "the seed of Abraham our father would come to an end of its own accord."

Much later is a saying of R. Eleazar, son of R. Simeon, as handed down by R. Simlai:

The Son of David will not come until all judges and officers are gone from Israel, as it is written (Isa. 1:25-26): "And I will turn My hand upon

---

[34] Graetz, *op. cit.*, IV, 174–176 (Heb. trans., II, 246–247).

[35] *Ibid.*, IV, 187–189, 526 (Heb. trans., II, 256–267); see also Isaac Halevy, *Dorot ha-Rishonim* (The Early Generations), Part I, Vol. V, Frankfurt am Main, 1918, pp. 665, 669.

[36] Since the necessary conditions for the Messiah's coming and the Messianic "birth pangs" have points in common, material in the next chapter must be regarded as supplementary to what is said here.

[37] Abodah Zarah 18a.

[38] Sanhedrin 13b and 14a; Abodah Zarah 8b. See above, Chap. I, p. 401. T. Colani finds a connexion between the ordination of the six disciples by R. Judah ben Baba and the seven sons of Taxo who suffered martyrdom for the Law, as related in the Assumption of Moses, Chap. 9. See M. Vernes, *Histoire des idées messianiques*, pp. 288–290. See also above, in the chapter on the Assumption of Moses, pp. 326–327.

thee, and purge away thy dross as with lye, . . . and (afterward) I will restore thy judges as at the first." [39]

The author of this saying was a fellow student of R. Judah the Patriarch.[40] At the time of the rule of this patriarch of the school of Hillel (c. 190–220 C.E.), the Palestinian patriarchate had reached a dignity never before attained. The patriarch lived as richly and luxuriously as a king.[41] The judges and officials appointed by him possessed almost unlimited authority. Various important functions, such as the determination of leap years and the ordination of teachers, were entirely in his hands. And he was wont to administer his office in a highhanded manner. Thus is to be explained the hostility manifested toward him even by his closest friends. R. Hiyya and Bar Kappara became highly incensed against him; [42] likewise R. Eleazar son of R. Simeon, who had become jealous of him while the two of them were attending school together.[43] This disapproval of the conduct of the patriarch found expression in the saying of R. Eleazar quoted above. The same attitude is apparent in another saying of his, also handed down by R. Simlai and directed against tyrannical judges and officials.[44]

There is an interesting parallel to the Messianic saying which we have been discussing. The Talmud relates that the two sons of the aforesaid R. Hiyya, Judah and Hezekiah, while attending a banquet of R. Judah the Patriarch, sat silent. So the patriarch said:

"Give the young men plenty of wine, so that they may say something." When the wine took effect, they began by saying: "The Son of David cannot appear until the two ruling houses in Israel shall have come to an end, namely, the exilarchate in Babylonia and the patriarchate in Palestine, as it is written (Isa. 8:14), 'And He (the Messiah—Rashi) shall be a sanctuary (to Israel—Rashi), but a stone of stumbling and a rock of offense to both houses of Israel.'" He said to them: "My boys, you are

[39] Sanhedrin 98a.
[40] Baba Metzia 84b. Cf. Frankel, *Darkhe ha-Mishnah*, 2nd ed., 1923, pp. 203-204; Weiss, *op. cit.*, II², 165; Bacher, *op. cit.*, II, 400-401 (Heb. trans., Vol. II, Part II, p. 92).
[41] See on this Weiss, *op. cit.*, II², 159; cf. Schürer, *op. cit.* I⁴, 659
[42] Weiss, *op. cit.*, II², 169-170.
[43] Baba Metzia 84b.
[44] Shabbath 139a; cf. Weiss, *op. cit.*, II², 165.

throwing thorns in my eyes." Then R. Hiyya said to him: "Rabbi, do not be disturbed; for the numerical value of the letters in the word *yayin* (wine) is seventy, likewise the letters in the word *sod* (secret). When wine goes in a secret comes out." [45]

It is clear that R. Hiyya thought the boys had spoken the truth, although a truth that should have been left unsaid (secret).

These Messianic sayings by R. Eleazar son of R. Simeon and the sons of R. Hiyya are no longer inspired by the nation's great yearning for redemption; they no longer flow forth from the people's rich creative imagination; nor are they expressed through the nation's popular conceptions and daring dreams. They merely express the personal viewpoint of a few dissatisfied individuals, who felt themselves humiliated by the tyranny of their spiritual leader, a tyranny which was perhaps only imaginary.[46]

For we now stand at the end of the Tannaitic period. The great grief over the loss of political freedom had gradually subsided, and even the memory of the fearful agonies following the fall of Bethar had begun to fade. R. Judah the Patriarch himself went so far as to seek to abolish the fast on the Ninth of Ab.[47] So little did the national leader see the crucial significance of the destruction of the Jewish state, although he opposed the Aramaic language out of love for the national tongue, and in his home even his maidservants spoke Hebrew! This was the direct antithesis of what pious Jews had felt immediately after the Destruction.

We come now to a matter that is very important, although we can devote only a few words to it here. An ancient Baraitha says:

[45] Sanhedrin 38*a*.
[46] From a much later (actually Amoraic) time comes this story:

Elijah used to frequent Rabbi's academy. One day—it was New Moon—he was delayed and did not arrive at the expected time. When he arrived, Rabbi said to him: "Why was my lord delayed?" He replied: "I had to wait until I awoke Abraham, washed his hands, and he prayed and I put him to sleep again; likewise with Isaac and Jacob."—"But why not awake them all together."—"I feared that they would make such a powerful prayer (all together) that they would bring the Messiah before his time" (Baba Metzia 85*b*).

Both the Aramaic language of this passage and the idea that the Messiah's advent can be hastened by vehement prayer are very late.
[47] Megillah 5*ab*; Pal. Tal., Meg. 1:6 (70*c*).

When the Temple was destroyed for the second time, large numbers in Israel became ascetics, binding themselves neither to eat meat nor to drink wine.[48]

R. Joshua opposed this extreme asceticism, and advised these "Mourners for Zion" to express their deep sorrow over the Destruction by less rigorous tokens of mourning. The Baraitha goes on to say:

Whoever mourns for Jerusalem will be privileged to behold her joy, as it is written (Isa. 66:10): "Rejoice ye with Jerusalem, and be glad for her, all ye that love her; rejoice for joy with her, all ye that mourn for her." [49]

R. Joshua himself asserted:

Since the day that the Temple was destroyed there has been no day without its curse; and the dew has not fallen in blessing and the fruits have lost their savour.[50]

R. Ishmael ben Elisha (mentioned above), who was carried captive to Rome in childhood, after having seen the Temple where his father served in the priesthood,[51] said:

Since the day of the destruction of the Temple we should by rights bind ourselves not to eat meat nor drink wine.[52]

Immediately after the Second Destruction, apparently, there came into being a large group of "Mourners for Zion." Of them a late Midrash speaks in detail;[53] they still existed in the early times of the Karaites, at the end of the Geonic period, and even as late as the time of Benjamin of Tudela [c. 1170].[54] But even those early Tannaim (R. Joshua, R. Akiba, Rabban Simeon II ben Gamaliel II) who opposed this extreme and ascetic "mourning for Zion" were very strict about the observance of the Ninth of Ab. Thus a Baraitha taught:

---

[48] Baba Bathra 60b; Tosephta, Sotah 15:11 (near end of tractate).
[49] In Taanith 30b occurs the negative form of this saying ("Whoever does *not* mourn," etc.).
[50] Mishnah, Sotah 9:12.
[51] Frankel, *op. cit.*, p. 112, Note 9.
[52] Baba Bathra 60b.
[53] Pesiqta Rabbathi, Chap. 34 (ed. Friedmann, 159).
[54] See, on all this, J. Klausner, *When a Nation Fights for Its Freedom* [Heb.], 8th ed., 1952, pp. 301-306.

R. Simeon ben Gamaliel says: "Anyone who eats or drinks on the Ninth of Ab is as if he ate and drank on the Day of Atonement." R. Akiba says: "Anyone who does work on the Ninth of Ab will never see in his work any sign of blessing." And the Sages say: "Anyone who does work on the Ninth of Ab and does not mourn for Jerusalem will not share in her joy." [55]

This view is in sharp contrast to that of R. Judah the Patriarch about this national day of mourning. Mourning over the Destruction is here an essential condition for personal participation in the redemption of the Messianic age.

As signs of the Messiah's approach, a Baraitha of uncertain date gives the following:

> If a man see an ass in his dream, let him expect salvation, as it is written (Zech. 9:9), "Behold, thy king cometh unto thee; he is triumphant, and victorious, lowly, and riding upon an ass." [56] . . . (And if a man see in his dream) a choice vine, let him expect the Messiah, as it is written (Gen. 49:11), "Binding his foal unto the vine, and his ass's colt unto the choice vine." [57]

It would appear from these examples that as early as the Tannaitic period not only Zechariah 9 but also Genesis 49 were interpreted as referring to the King-Messiah.

[55] Taanith 30b.
[56] Berakhoth 56b.
[57] Ibid. 57a. These words are the continuation of the Baraitha which begins in 56b and is interrupted several times by Amoraic discussions in Aramaic. For the ass as a sign of the Messiah's coming in connexion with the verse in Zechariah, see Matt. 21:2-5; for the "choice vine," compare the branches which the admirers of Jesus cut off and spread on the road (Matt. 21:8-10; Mark 11:8-10). See J. Klausner, *Jesus of Nazareth*, 5th Heb. ed., pp. 330-331 [Eng. ed., pp. 309-310].

CHAPTER V

The Birth Pangs of Messiah

BEFORE I DISCUSS the woes that are to precede the Messiah's coming, I must emphasize, *first*, that the expression "the birth pangs of Messiah" or "the Messianic travail" [1] does not mean "sufferings endured by the Messiah." Thus August Wünsche was mistaken when he asserted that this technical term denotes "partly the woeful time that supposedly will precede the Messiah's coming, *and partly the sufferings and woes of the Messiah himself.*" [2] The latter statement is without foundation. Only because Wünsche understood the Hebrew expression too literally could he reach this erroneous conclusion.[3]

Secondly, it must be pointed out here that although a number of the prerequisites of the Messiah's coming which were detailed in the preceding chapter are related to "the Messianic travail" (such as increase of traitors, dearth of disciples, extreme poverty, and so on) nevertheless, it is on the whole possible to distinguish between the severe preliminary conditions and the "birth pangs" themselves. Castelli admits this, although he discusses both matters in a single chapter.[4]

---

[1] The plural form occurs only once in the Talmud (Ket. 111*a*), and there it may be corrupted by Aramaic influence. See Dalman, *Der leidende und sterbende Messias*, p. 47, Note **.

[2] See *Die Leiden des Messias*, p. 74, bottom.

[3] This has already been pointed out by Castelli, *Il Messia*, p. 191, and Dalman, *op. cit.*, pp. 42-43.

[4] *Op. cit.*, p. 190. James Drummond, who also treats them in a single chapter entitled "Signs of the Last Times" (*The Jewish Messiah*, pp. 209-221), apparently

THE BIRTH PANGS OF MESSIAH 441

These "birth pangs" or "travails" of the time preceding the Messiah's advent, the "sorrows" or "sufferings" of the Gospels,[5] are an essential part of the very idea of the redemption. I have already mentioned several times that the whole Messianic idea was the inevitable outcome of *the history of afflictions* which beset Israel from the beginning of its national existence until the time after the persecutions of Hadrian. *When suffering is severest, the redeemer is nearest.*

Thus we find, during the tyranny of Herod and his sons, and especially during the rule of the procurators in Judea, a whole series of false Messiahs, who suddenly appear and quickly disappear. But it seems to me that the gloomiest delineations of "the birth pangs of Messiah" came out of Bar-Cochba's unsuccessful attempt at rebellion, and are patterned after the cruel persecutions that followed the fall of Bethar. To this idea I have already alluded in Chapter I of this part of the book. There we saw that the outstanding Baraithas giving the most complete description of these "birth pangs" *all* belong to the younger disciples of R. Akiba; namely, those disciples who taught and worked in the period immediately after the Hadrianic persecutions.

This hypothesis is strengthened if we notice two basic points which constantly recur in descriptions of "the Messianic travail" and which have special significance: *forgetting of the Law* and *scarcity of disciples*. At no other time before the close of the Tannaitic period could it be said that there was an attempt to compel neglect of the Law and to abolish the Rabbinical schools. The Roman procurators in autonomous Judea before the Destruction never ventured to attack the Rabbinical schools; moreover, they took very little interest in the spiritual activity of the tiny state. In the time of Antiochus Epiphanes the observance of the ritual requirements was forbidden with severe penalties; and there is no doubt that a number of the descriptions of "the Messianic travail" in Daniel 9:24–26 and 12:1, 7 and especially in the Pseudepigrapha came from that time. But it is not mentioned anywhere that the schools for teaching Torah were the special target

---

does not think they can be distinguished, for at the end of the chapter (p. 221) he almost identifies them completely.

[5] See Matt. 24:8; Mark 13:8.

of the "enlightened" tyrant's persecutions; in fact, such schools in pre-Hasmonean times had only begun their development.

Harsh persecutions directed against the Law and the schools did not occur until the time of Hadrian.[6] Hence we can assert with considerable confidence that it was at this particular time that the portrayals of "the Messianic travail" took on their final and most distinctive form. Graetz[7] conjectured that the "sufferings" (ὠδῖνες) decribed in the Gospels[8] owe their origin to the rule of Bar-Cochba and the persecutions that followed his failure. But he is wrong in his conclusion that the various descriptions in the Gospels of "the beginning of the sufferings" (ἀρχὴ ὠδίνων) corresponding to the descriptions in the Talmud, such as famines, children rising up against their parents, and the like (with no mention, naturally, of the suppression of the schools of the Law), "are borrowed partly from the literary style of the canonical prophets, and partly from the popular belief about 'the birth pangs of Messiah.' "[9] Similar historical events put similar expressions into the mouths of both Talmudic Sages and Christian Church Fathers. It is also possible to suppose that they borrowed from each other.

I now pass to the descriptions themselves.

First to be considered is a notable Talmudic passage, thought by some interpreters to be a Mishnah, by others a Baraitha; it is actually a combination of three Messianic Baraithas. It reads:

With the footprints of the Messiah,[10] insolence will increase [11] and dearth reach its height;[12] the vine will yield its fruit but the wine will be

---

[6] Thus M. Friedländer (*Der Antichrist*, pp. 26-30) is wrong in supposing that the Baraithas concerning "the Messianic travail" are pre-Christian traditions emanating from Jewish antinomian circles.

[7] See Graetz, *Geschichte der Juden*, IV, 165-167, 196-197, 515-518. In the Hebrew translation by S. P. Rabbinowitz all this is abbreviated because of censorship.

[8] Mark 13:5-27; Matt. 24:4-31; Luke 21:8-28.

[9] Graetz, *op cit.*, IV, 516.

[10] Rashi changes this phrase from Aramaic to Hebrew, with no change of meaning.

[11] Sanhedrin 97a has this phrase in Hebrew instead of Aramaic, with no change of meaning.

[12] The Hebrew verb ('MR) used here is related to the expressions "the top of the uttermost bough" and "lofty forests" in Isa. 17:6, 9. San. 97a says "*hywqr y'wt*," "dearth will be prolonged" (connecting the verb with '*t*, "time") [but the

THE BIRTH PANGS OF MESSIAH 443

costly.[13] There will be none to offer reproof, and the whole empire will be converted to heresy.[14] The meeting-place [15] of scholars will be laid waste and Gablan [16] be made desolate; and the people of the frontier [17] will go about from city to city with none to take pity on them. The wisdom of the Scribes will become foolish,[18] and they that shun sin will be despised. The young will insult their elders, and the great [19] will wait upon the insignificant.

>   For the son dishonoreth the father,
>   The daughter riseth up against her mother,
>   The daughter-in-law against her mother-in-law;
>   A man's enemies are the men of his own house.[20]

The face of this generation is as the face of a dog; and a son does not feel ashamed before his father. On whom, then, can we rely?—On our Father who is in heaven.[21]

The concluding words indicate clearly that this whole noteworthy passage alludes to events that actually happened. But events such as these occurred only at the time of the Hadrianic persecutions. At the

---

Soncino Talmud translates "esteem be perverted" at this point]; see Levy, *Neuhebr. Wörterbuch*, I, 48b; Kohut, *Aruch Completum*, I, 330; VI, 181; cf. *wywqr hwwh*, Song of Songs R. 2:13.

[13] In Derekh Erets Zuta, Chap. 10, we have "the vine will not yield its fruit and the wine will be costly." This is a smoother reading, and therefore a later one.

[14] San. 97a has a different spelling of the word for "reproof"; and in the ordinary editions the next clause is entirely lacking because of censorship, or else "to the opinion of the Sadducees" stands instead of "to heresy." ["Heresy" could be considered a reference to Christianity, hence the censorship.]

[15] On "the place of meeting," see above, p. 296.

[16] Bacher (*Agada der Tannaiten*, II, 222) thinks that "Gablan" is Golan [Gaulanitis, modern Jaulan, northeast of Palestine]; Krauss (*ZATW*, XXVIII, 246, 260–261) agrees. Neubauer (*Géographie du Talmud*, Paris, 1868, p. 66) and Castelli (*op. cit.*, p. 298, Note 3) think, rightly, that this is the province of Gabalena in the southwest of Palestine. The words "and Gablan (will) be made desolate" are lacking in Derekh Erets Zuta.

[17] Castelli (*loc. cit.*) translates "the people of Gebul" and sees in "Gebul" the city of Gebal in Edom (Ps. 83:8). In Derekh Erets Zuta, Chap. 10, and Pesiqta Rabbathi, Chap. 15 (ed. Friedmann, 75b), we have "and the people of Galilee," which Bacher considers a better reading. But it seems to me that "Galilee" is a late correction owing to the fact that it was not understood in later times who "the people of the frontier" were; moreover, it has already been said just before that "Galilee will be laid waste." Clearly the reference here is to the residents along the border, who are the first to suffer in times of tumult and war.

[18] See Jer. 49:7 [8:8–9].

[19] So reads '*En Ya'akob* [The Fountain of Jacob, a popular collection of Talmudic Aggadah] instead of "the elders," as in our ordinary texts.

[20] These words are from Micah 7:6. See also Matt. 10:35–36; Luke 12:53.

[21] Sotah 49b (Mishnah, Sotah 9:15).

time of the persecutions by Antiochus matters never reached such a state; and at the time of the Destruction all the conflicts had a more political tinge. References to "the meeting-place of scholars" and "the wisdom of the Scribes" are not relevant to an essentially political catastrophe.

Having seen the combined version, with all its variants, we can now examine the three separate Baraithas on "the Messianic travail" from the school of R. Akiba:

(1) R. Nehemiah said: In the generation when the son of David comes, impudence will increase and esteem will be perverted; the vine will yield its fruit but the wine will be costly; and the whole empire will be converted to heresy, with none to offer rebuke.[22]

(2) R. Judah [23] said: In the generation when the son of David comes, the meeting-place of scholars will be given over to harlotry. Galilee will be laid waste and Gablan be made desolate; and the people of the frontier will go about from city to city with none to take pity on them. The wisdom of the Scribes will become foolish, and they that shun sin will be despised. The face of this generation is as the face of a dog, and truth is lacking, as it is written (Isa. 59:15): "And truth shall be lacking, and he that departeth from evil maketh himself a prey." [24]

(3) R. Nehorai [25] said: In the generation when the son of David comes, the young will insult their elders, and the elders will wait upon the young; "the daughter riseth up against her mother, the daughter-in-law against her mother-in-law"; and the face of this generation is as the face of a dog; and a son does not feel ashamed before his father.[26]

In these three Baraithas, "the Messianic travail" is depicted at more length than in Sotah 49b. In a fourth Baraitha, also from the school of R. Akiba, we find new features:

---

[22] Sanhedrin 97a; Derekh Erets Zuta, Chap. 10; Song of Songs R. 2:13.

[23] Derekh Erets Zuta here reads, incorrectly, "Rabban Gamaliel" instead of "Rabbi Judah."

[24] San. 97a. In Derekh Erets Zuta the verse from Isaiah is lacking. In Song of Songs Rabbah this whole Baraitha is wrongly attributed to the Amora R. Simeon ben Lakish.

[25] See on "Rabbi Nehorai" above, p. 402.

[26] Sanhedrin 97a; Pesiqta Rabbathi, Chap. 15 (ed. Friedmann, 75b). On the variant readings in Pesiqta Rabbathi see Bacher, *op. cit.*, II, 382, Note 6 (Hebrew trans., Vol. II, Part II, p. 79).

THE BIRTH PANGS OF MESSIAH   445

Rabbi Simeon ben Yohai [27] said: In the week [28] when the son of David comes, in the first year this verse will be fulfilled: [29] "I will cause it to rain upon one city, and cause it not to rain upon another city" (Amos 4:7). In the second year the arrows of hunger will be sent forth.[30] In the third a great famine; men, women, and children will die; pious men and saints (will be few),[31] and the Law will be forgotten by its students.[32] In the fourth, partial plenty.[33] In the fifth, great plenty, when men will eat, drink, and be merry, and the Law will return to its students. In the sixth, voices.[34] In the seventh, wars; and at the end of the seventh year, the son of David will come.[35]

The most interesting items in these four Baraithas from the time after Bar-Cochba are those that speak of the whole empire's being converted to heresy and the forgetting of the Law by its students (more correctly, by Israel). The first item may be explained by the fact that Bar-Cochba's persecution of Christians and Hadrian's decrees against Jews caused the "heretics" [36] to separate themselves completely from the Jews. It was only then that they agreed to make the Gentile bishop Mark head of the Christian church in Jerusalem.[37] To keen observers like the disciples of R. Akiba, it was no longer a secret that Christianity was on the way to becoming a world religion,

---

[27] So in Derekh Erets Zuta, beginning of Chap. 10. In Sanhedrin 97a this passage occurs as an anonymous Baraitha. In Pesiqta Rabbathi, Chap. 15, the source is given as "our teachers" (*Rabbanan*). In Song of Songs R. 2:13, the passage is wrongly attributed to the Amora R. Yohanan.

[28] In the sense of a seven-year period, as in Dan. 9:27. Cf. the use of the word "sabbath" in Lev. 25:8.

[29] Instead of the words "this verse will be fulfilled," which are completely lacking in Pesiqta Rabbathi, Derekh Erets Zuta has only "it will be fulfilled."

[30] See Ezekiel 5:16.

[31] The words "will be few," lacking in Sanhedrin, are to be supplied from Derekh Erets Zuta and Song of Songs Rabbah; in Pesiqta Rabbathi all this last section is omitted.

[32] Pesiqta Rabbathi has "by Israel" instead of "by its students." See below.

[33] Pesiqta Rabbathi adds "and partial famine."

[34] These are no doubt the "rumors of wars" of the Gospels (Mark 13:7; Matt. 24:6). See Joseph Klausner, *Jesus of Nazareth*, 5th Heb. ed. (1945), p. 347 [Eng. ed., p. 322].

[35] Sanhedrin 97a; Pesiqta Rabbathi, Chap. 15; Derekh Erets Zuta, Chap. 10; Song of Songs R. 2:13. Cf. Syriac Baruch 70:2–71:1; IV Ezra 8:62–9:6 (see above, Part II, pp. 333–335); Mark 13:3–8; Matt. 24:3–8; Luke 21:7–11.

[36] M. Friedländer is partly right in his conclusion that the term "heretics" (*Minim*) does not *always* mean early Christians; but for the most part it does. See T. Herford, *Christianity in Talmud and Midrash*, London, 1903, pp. 361–397.

[37] Eusebius, *Historia Ecclesiastica*, IV, 6.

that is to say, the religion of the world empire of Rome.[38] R. Simeon ben Yoḥai, who journeyed to Rome in an attempt to have repealed certain harsh decrees of the Roman government against the Jews, and so came into contact with the imperial court,[39] could recognize this better than any other man. The continuing conquests of this Jewish "heresy," which from the time of Paul onward took a wholly negative attitude toward the Law, fostered the idea that in the period preceding the Messiah's advent the Law would be forgotten.

But the faith of the Tannaim that the Law would be restored to Israel was strong as a rock. At a later time, perhaps under Christian influence—one can learn even from one's adversaries—a belief became current that the Law would return to Israel in a new form. Only then, and not earlier, as I. H. Weiss [40] supposes, was the sentence "And the Law will return to its students" (or "to Israel") changed to "And the Law will return *to its new form*." [41] For this variant, which contains an unnatural expression (one may say that something returns to its *old* form, but it cannot *return* to its *new* form), is found in a very late Midrash; the same is true of the additional words, "And it will be made new for Israel," in Song of Songs Rabbah, and likewise of the saying cited by I. H. Weiss [42] that "The Holy One, blessed be He, sits (in Paradise) and expounds for Israel a new Law, which is to be given by the Messiah." [43] Also from a later time is the saying, "The ceremonial laws will be abolished in the Time to Come"; [44] for it was handed down by the Amora Rab Joseph. Moreover, judging by the immediate context, "the Time to Come" here

---

[38] Friedländer thinks this insight impossible by the end of the second century C.E., and he therefore takes "heresy" to mean Jewish antinomianism (*Der Antichrist*, pp. 26–30); but his reasoning is hard to follow.

[39] Me'ilah 17b. On this journey to Rome, see Z. Frankel, *Darkhe ha-Mishnah*, pp. 178–179; Bacher, *op. cit.*, II, 76 (Hebrew ed., Vol. II, Part I, pp. 47 and 99–100).

[40] *Each Generation and Its Interpreters*, I³, 215, Note 4.

[41] Pesiqta Rabbathi, Chap. 15 (ed. Friedmann, 75a). Song of Songs R. 2:13 adds the words "and it will be made new for Israel."

[42] *Loc. cit.*

[43] Yalquṭ Isaiah 26, Sect. 296. Also from a later time is everything presented by Castelli (*op. cit.*, pp. 277–281) as proof that the Torah will be abolished in the Messianic age.

[44] Niddah 61b.

signifies the time after death.⁴⁵ Besides all this, the expression "will return to its new form" does not convey the idea of complete newness in the sense of the abolition of the old; it only means that the Law will return anew to its former glory and importance. To be sure, it may suffer partial modification (the Law "which will hereafter be changed");⁴⁶ but it cannot be abolished and replaced by something else.

The notion of a completely new Law is, therefore, of late date. On the other hand, the belief that the Law will be temporarily forgotten preceding the advent of Messiah, during "the Messianic travail," is undoubtedly much earlier. However, the following very early Baraitha certainly does not refer to the Messianic age:

> When our teachers entered the vineyard [school] at Yabneh, they said: The Torah is destined to be forgotten in Israel,⁴⁷ as it is written (Amos 8:11): "Behold, the days come, saith the Lord God, that I will send a famine in the land, not a famine of bread, nor a thirst for water, but of hearing the words of the LORD." It is further written (Amos 8:12): "And they shall wander from sea to sea, and from the north even to the east; they shall run to and fro to seek the word of the LORD, and shall not find it."—"The word of the LORD" means Halakhah; "the word of the LORD" means The End; "the word of the LORD" means prophecy.⁴⁸

This early Baraitha cannot refer to the Messianic age, since it is followed in the Talmud ⁴⁹ by another Baraitha, which reads:

⁴⁵ To be sure, it is possible that R. Joseph was handing down an earlier view, according to which abolition of the ceremonial laws was to take place in the Messianic age (Klausner, *Jesus*, p. 289 [Eng. ed., p. 275]); clear proof of this is lacking, but see S. Lieberman, *Sheqi'in*, 1939, pp. 80–81. Incidentally, the late Michael Guttmann attributed to me an opinion on this matter which is the opposite of what I have written here and in *Jesus of Nazareth* (*loc. cit.*); he did this on the basis of the German translation, without taking the trouble to examine the Hebrew original. See, on this, *Jesus of Nazareth*, additions and corrections to the fifth Hebrew edition, p. 470, and in the second edition of the German translation (Berlin, 1934), pp. 588–589.

⁴⁶ Siphre, Deut., 160 (Friedmann ed., 105b). And Tosephta (San. 4:7) also says "the Law is destined to be changed," but only in the sense of a change in the script.

⁴⁷ Tosephta, beginning of Eduyyoth, says more explicitly: "The time will come when a man will seek a single word of the words of the Law and not find it, and a single word of the words of the Scribes and not find it."

⁴⁸ Shabbath 138b; Tosephta, Eduyyoth 1:1 (beginning of the tractate).

⁴⁹ Shabbath 138b and 139a.

R. Simeon ben Yohai said: Heaven forfend [50] that the Torah be forgotten in Israel, as it is said (Deut. 31:31): "For it shall not be forgotten out of the mouths of their descendants." Then how do I interpret "They shall run to and fro to seek the word of the LORD, and shall not find it"? That they will not find a clear Halakhah or a clear Mishnah in any place.

Nevertheless, it is this same R. Simeon ben Yohai who said that in the third year of the "week" [seven-year period] wherein the son of David will come "the Torah will be forgotten by its students" (or "by Israel"). Therefore, the Baraitha quoted in the preceding paragraph has no reference to the forgetting of the Law in the period just before the advent of the Messiah. Indeed, in the Tosephta this Baraitha opens the tractate Eduyyoth, which according to Talmudic tradition [51] was taught on the day when the patriarchate was taken from Rabban Gamaliel II (of Yabneh) and bestowed upon R. Eleazar ben Azariah.[52]

In the Tosephta (Eduy. 1:1), the third explanation of the phrase "The word of the LORD" is this: "that not one of the words of the Law shall be like another word. They (the teachers at Yabneh) said, 'Let us begin from Hillel and Shammai.'" Obviously, the reference here is to the great controversies first between the schools of Shammai and Hillel, afterward between R. Eliezer ben Hyrcanus and R. Joshua ben Hananiah, and finally the differences of opinion between this same R. Joshua and the Patriarch Rabban Gamaliel of Yabneh, leading to the latter's deposition and the appointment of R. Eleazar ben Azariah. All these religious controversies had the effect, as the Talmud expresses it, of making the Law into two Laws, so that actually "not one of the words of the Law" was "like another word." [53]

It is to this that our early Baraitha refers. In its original form (that of the Tosephta) it knows nothing of the Law's being wholly for-

---

[50] Heb. *ḥas* (*ve-shalom*). It is interesting that a similar word, *ḥasa*, is used in Ethiopic to express *absit*, "God forbid," etc. See A. Dillmann, *Chrestomathia Aethiopica*, Leipzig, 1866, p. 169.
[51] Berakhoth 27b, 28a.
[52] Weiss, *op. cit.*, II², 86–101.
[53] *Ibid.*, II², 71–72, 84–88; Graetz., *op. cit.*, Hebrew translation by S. P. Rabbinowitz, II, 172–176; Halevy, *The Early Generations* [Heb.], I⁵, 302–332 (an attack upon Graetz, Weiss, and Frankel, of a sort characteristic of this author, yet with almost the same conclusions as those of the men he attacks).

THE BIRTH PANGS OF MESSIAH 449

gotten. Only later, *after its form had been altered*, was this Baraitha explained by R. Simeon ben Yohai in a general sense.[54] For the Baraitha of R. Simeon ben Yohai quoted above is not found in the Tosephta at all.[55]

But we have sufficient proof that the idea of a *temporary* oblivion of the Law preceding the Messianic age was not strange to the Tannaim of the period *after* Hadrian's decrees. Very characteristic in this regard is the way "the school of Elijah" contrasts the "two thousand years under the Law" with the "two thousand of the Messianic age."[56] A later Baraitha of the Babylonian Talmud reads:

R. Simeon ben Eleazar (a contemporary of R. Judah the Patriarch) said: "And the years draw nigh, when thou shalt say, I have no pleasure in them" (Eccles. 12:1). This refers to *the Messianic era*, wherein there is neither innocence nor guilt.[57]

The meaning of this is, of course, that the Law and the ceremonial regulations will no longer be in force in the Messianic age.[58] And in the Tannaitic Midrash, Mekhilta, we find also "that ultimately the Torah is destined to be forgotten."[59] These sayings refer, apparently, to "the week [seven-year period] in which the son of David will come." If we remember the boundless love felt by the Tannaim for the study of the Law, we shall understand that forgetting the Law would be a most unnatural idea for them unless it was reckoned among the fearful "birth pangs" that must precede the Messianic age. But that this conception, like all the more extreme portrayals of "the Messianic travail," did *not* antedate Hadrian's decrees—of this we have convincing proof in two early and very interesting sayings, which may be considered decisive in this regard.

[54] See also Siphre, Deut., 48 (ed. Friedmann, 84b), which reads: "R. Simeon ben Yohai says, 'The Law is destined to be forgotten by Israel.'" But what follows shows that the reference is to explicit Halakhah [not to the Law in general].
[55] See on this C. Albeck, *Untersuchungen über die Redaktion der Mischna* (Veröffentlichungen der Akademie für die Wissenschaft des Judentums, Talmudische Sektion, B. II), Berlin, 1923, pp. 108–121.
[56] Sanhedrin 97ab; Abodah Zarah 9a; see above, Chap. III, pp. 421–422.
[57] Shabbath 151b.
[58] Ferdinand Weber's interpretation of this saying (*System der altsyn. palästin. Theologie*, p. 362) appears to me too artificial.
[59] Mekhilta, Pisḥa, Chap. 12 (ed. Friedmann, 13a, beginning).

At an early time the question was asked, How can one escape the Messianic travail? The first answer came in this Baraitha:

> The disciples of R. Eliezer (ben Hyrcanus, pre-Hadrianic) asked: "What must a man do to be spared the pangs of the Messiah?" (To this R. Eliezer replied): "Let him busy himself with *the Law* and with the practice of good works." [60]

And in the Tannaitic Midrash, Mekhilta, we read:

> R. Eliezer says, If you will keep this Sabbath, you will be saved from three visitations: the Messianic birth pangs, the day of Gog and Magog, and the great day of judgment.[61]

If the keeping of the Sabbath still has such marvelous power a short time before the Messiah's advent, it is not possible that this commandment could ever be annulled. And there is an express statement that the Temple and the sacrifices will be "standing for ever and ever." [62]

Thus it is clear that the pre-Hadrianic Tannaim did not see in "the birth pangs of Messiah" either the cessation of study of the Law or the forgetting of the Law. Only the fearful persecutions of the students of the Law after the fall of Bethar, which dismayed even such a man as R. Jose ben Kisma, could have added this despairing note, the temporary disappearance of the Law from Israel, to the already dark picture of "the Messianic travail," so as thereby to make it even more gloomy and depressing.

---

[60] Sanhedrin 98*a*.

[61] This saying of R. Eliezer occurs in two parallel versions: in Mekhilta, Wayyassa, near the end of Chap. 5 (ed. Friedmann, 50*b*), it begins, "R. Eleazar says, If you succeed in keeping the Sabbath," but in *ibid.*, Chap. 6 (ed. Friedmann, 51*a*), it begins, "R. Eliezer says, If you will keep this Sabbath." Otherwise the two versions agree. From this early Talmudic saying is derived the later saying of Bar Kappara: "He who observes the practice of three meals on the Sabbath will be saved from three evils: the travails of the Messiah, the retribution of Gehinnom, and the wars of Gog and Magog" (Shabb. 118*a*).

[62] Siphre, Num., 92 (ed. Friedmann, 25*b*).

CHAPTER VI

Elijah, the Forerunner of the Messiah

WE HAVE already seen, in the last chapter, that disputes among the Tannaim and their various "schools" brought about a fear that a time would come when there would no longer be a "clear Halakhah." This fear was expressed in the first Baraitha of the Tosephta to the tractate Eduyyoth, composed in the time of the Patriarch Rabban Gamaliel II. But *the last Mishnah* of this tractate, redacted by this Gamaliel's grandson, is more optimistic concerning the future. On the basis of the passage at the end of Malachi (3:23-24 [Eng. 4:5-6]), there had arisen in the nation at an earlier time [1] a widespread belief that the prophet Elijah—the great zealot and wonder-worker who ascended to heaven in a chariot of fire drawn by horses of fire, without having to taste death—would [return and] solve all sorts of problems and difficulties in the fields of both religion and jurisprudence; that he would clarify all doubtful matters and make plain every obscurity.

One result of this was that in the Talmud the Aramaic word *tēqū*, which occurs when a religious question cannot readily be decided (and almost certainly means "let it stand undecided," from *qūm*), is re-interpreted as the abbreviation of a phrase meaning "the Tishbite will resolve difficulties and problems." [2] Hence already in the Mish-

[1] Cf. Ben-Sira 48:10-11; Mark 9:11-13.
[2] Everything in Jewish literature pertaining to Elijah has been diligently and expertly collected by M. Friedmann in his lengthy introduction to Seder Eliyahu, Vienna, 1902, pp. 2-44. See also Y. M. Guttmann, "Elijah the Prophet in the Legends of Israel" [Heb.] (*He-Atid*, ed. S. I. Horowitz, V, 14-46); *idem, Key to the Talmud* [Heb.], III, 17-56, item "Eliyahu."

nah, if a question arises that cannot readily be decided, the Tannaim say, "Let it be left until Elijah comes"[3] (in cases of property of disputed ownership, for example), or, "Let one not touch them until Elijah comes"[4] (referring to vessels of gold or glass when they are found but no owner can be discovered). Hence also a Baraitha reports: "R. Judah (the younger disciple of R. Akiba) said, 'This chapter (Ezekiel 45) is to be interpreted by Elijah.' "[5] An interesting old Baraitha of Halakhic type shows how deeply rooted among the Jewish people was the belief in Elijah's return and his mission to resolve religious doubts:

If the fourteenth (of Nisan) falls on the Sabbath, everything (that is leavened) must be removed before the Sabbath; and heave-offerings, whether unclean, or doubtful, or clean, must be burnt. . . . This is the ruling of R. Judah ben Eliezer of Bartotha, which he stated in the name of R. Joshua (pre-Hadrianic). But they said to him: "Clean heave-offerings should not be burnt, lest persons be found who need to eat them (before the Passover)." . . . He retorted: "Then on your reasoning even those in doubt should not be burnt, *lest Elijah come and declare them clean.*" They said to him: "It has long been assured to Israel that Elijah will come neither on the eve of the Sabbath nor on the eve of festivals on account of the trouble" (so as not to disturb the Jews in their preparations for Sabbath or festival).[6]

Likewise, R. Jose (a young disciple of R. Akiba) asks:

But how can we burn even that which is doubtful together with that which is unclean? Perhaps Elijah will come and declare it clean![7]

Here we have not merely Aggadic homily, which for the most part is very lax, and in which the Tannaim do not exercise exactness, but *Halakhic decisions*, which according to the Talmudic view are of great importance. Therefore we should not fail to recognize the significance of the belief in Elijah's return and in his function as arbiter of questions of religious law, as set forth in these Baraithas.[8]

[3] Mishnah, Baba Metsia 1:8 (end of the chapter); *ibid.*, 3:4; Baraitha, Menahoth 63*a*.
[4] Mishnah, Baba Metsia 2:8.
[5] Menahoth 45*a*.
[6] Pesahim 13*a*. The last saying is also found in Erubin 43*b*.
[7] Pesahim 20*b*.
[8] See F. Weber, *System der altsyn. palästin. Theologie*, pp. 337ff.

ELIJAH, THE FORERUNNER OF THE MESSIAH 453

The principle passage concerning the mission of Elijah in the Messianic age is this Mishnah in the tractate Eduyyoth:

R. Joshua said: I have received as a tradition from Rabban Johanan ben Zakkai, who heard from his teacher (Hillel), and his teacher from his teacher, as a Halakhah given to Moses from Sinai, that Elijah will not come to declare unclean or clean (families in general), to remove afar or bring nigh (in general), but to remove afar those (families) that were brought nigh by force and to bring nigh those (families) that were removed afar by force. The family of Beth-Zerepha was in the land beyond Jordan, and the sons of Zion removed it afar by force. And yet another (family) was there, and the sons of Zion brought it nigh by force.[9] The like of these Elijah will come to declare unclean or clean, to remove afar or to bring

[9] The last saying is also found in Kiddushin 71a. Some editions of the Mishnah have "son of Zion" (*ben-Zion*, singular) instead of "sons of Zion" (*bene-Zion*, plural); the reading is also singular in Tosephta, Eduyyoth 3:4 (with an important addition), and in Yerushalmi, Yebamoth 8:3 (near end). See A. Büchler, "Familienreinheit und Familienmakel in Jerusalem vor dem Jahre 70" (*A. Schwarz-Festschrift*, Vienna, 1917, pp. 137-138). On the place-name Beth-Zerepha see J. N. Epstein, *MGWJ*, LXV (1921), 89; S. Klein, *MGWJ*, LXIV (1920), 181; LXV (1921), 371-372. Who could this "son of Zion" or these "sons of Zion" have been, vested with the power to remove and to bring in families— even in Transjordania? According to Joseph Derenbourg, *Massa Erets Yisrael* (Hebrew translation from French, 1896), p. 102, Note 5, it was the high priest Hanan (Annas or Ananus) son of Seth or Siah. In my opinion, both "son of Zion" and "sons of Zion" are corruptions of the name Shelom-Zion—the name of the queen called by Josephus (*Antiquities* 13:12:1) Salome (Salma, Salina) Alexandra. The Hebrew name of this Jewish queen was much corrupted in Talmud and Midrash: "Shelamtu" (Eccl. R. on 7:12), "Shelamzah" (Lev. R., Chap. 35), "Shelamzu" (Siphra, Behuqqothai, Chap. 1, ed. Weiss 110b), "Shelzion" (Shabb. 16b), and "Shalminon" (Scholion to Megillath Taanith, Chap. 10, Tebeth). We find this name on ancient tombstones of women of the priestly class; see S. Klein, *Jüdisch-Palästinisches Corpus Inscriptionum*, Vienna, 1920, pp. 9, 12-13, 27, 30, especially No. 66, where the Hebrew and Greek forms occur together. See *Massa Erets Yisrael* by Derenbourg, p. 26, Note 1; D. Chwolsohn, *Das letzte Passamahl Christi*, 2nd ed., Leipzig, 1907, p. 14, Note 3; E. Schürer, *Geschichte*, I⁴, 287, Note 2; Klausner, *History of the Second Temple* [Heb.], III, 165-166. Undoubtedly Queen Shelom-Zion, as a devout Pharisee, was concerned about the purity of family stocks and had the authority to remove and bring in families even in Transjordania, where many towns had been conquered by her husband, Janneus Alexander (*Antiquities* 13:15:3-4). To the objection of S. Klein (*Palestinian Researches* [Hebrew], II, 6, Note 9), see my answer in a note to the article "Men of Jerusalem . . . Sons of Zion" of S. Klein [Heb.] (*Madda'e ha-Yahadut*, Jerusalem, 5686 [1926], Vol. I, p. 77, Note 22). That we have here a *fact* and not a legend is to be seen from the addition in Tosephta (Eduy. 3:4): "And the Sages did not wish to reveal concerning them (the disgrace of the families removed), but they communicate them [the names of these families] to their sons and disciples once every seven

nigh. R. Judah (ben Bathyra) [10] says: To bring nigh but not to remove afar.[11] R. Ishmael [12] says: To bring agreement where there is matter for dispute. And the Sages say: Neither to remove afar nor to bring nigh, but to make peace in the world, as it is written (Mal. 3:23-24), "Behold, I will send you Elijah the prophet. . . . And he shall turn the heart of the fathers to the children, and the heart of the children to their fathers." [13]

In order to clarify further the above references to the ritual cleanness of families, I quote here another Baraitha:

Bastards and Nethinim (temple slaves) will become clean in the Age to Come, according to R. Jose (post-Hadrianic). R. Meir (also post-Hadrianic) says they will not become clean. R. Jose said to him, Has it not been written (Ezek. 36:25): "And I will sprinkle clean water upon you, and ye shall be clean"? R. Meir replied, Since it adds "from all your uncleannesses and from all your idols," bastardy is not included. R. Jose rejoined, Since it further adds "I will make you clean," one must conclude, Also from bastardy.[14]

That it would be part of Elijah's duty as the Messiah's forerunner to certify the ritual cleanness of families that had suffered at one time or another from mixed marriages or even forbidden unions, and to grant permission to hitherto excluded peoples to intermarry with the Jews—this is made clear from a saying of the Amora Rab Judah in the name of the very early Amora Samuel—a saying that follows immediately after the above Baraitha.[15]

---

years." And Yerushalmi, which quotes these words with slight changes, adds: "Said R. Johanan 'I swear I know them [these families], and very prominent men are intermixed with them.' "

[10] This is to be added according to Friedmann's introduction to Seder Eliyahu, pp. 23-24.

[11] Tosephta has: "Rabbi Meir says, To bring nigh but not to remove afar; R. Judah says, Reverse the terms."

[12] So reads R. Abraham ben David (RABaD) instead of "R. Simeon."

[13] Eduyyoth 8:7 (end of the tractate).

[14] Kiddushin 72b; with slight differences in Tosephta, Kidd. 5:4. In Yerushalmi we have: "Said R. Yassa (Jose) in the name of R. Johanan: Also in the Age to Come God will give attention only to the tribe of Levi. Why? Because, as it is written (Mal. 3:3), 'He shall sit as a refiner and purifier of silver, and he shall purify the sons of Levi and purge them' " (Yeb. 8:3, near end, f. 9d). See on this L. Freund, "Ueber Genealogien und Familienreinheit in biblischer und talmudischer Zeit" (A. Schwarz-Festschrift, pp. 183-190).

[15] Kiddushin, ibid.

Indeed, as early as the time of Ben-Sira, it was the function of Elijah "to make ready the tribes of Israel" (or in the Greek version, "to restore the tribes of Jacob").[16] And if we add this function of Elijah to his task of resolving all religious and judicial controversies, the Mishnah passage at the end of Eduyyoth takes on a plainer meaning. Elijah will come to bring back to their people all those who have been wrongfully excluded from the Jewish community (the opinion of R. Judah ben Bathyra), or to expel those actually unfit (the opinion of R. Joshua),[17] or "to bring agreement where there is matter for dispute" (the opinion of R. Ishmael), or even (according to the opinion of other Sages) to make peace in the world in general. All these functions belong to the great forerunner of the Messiah. The dreaded zealot, the avenging prophet, who commanded 450 priests of Baal to be slaughtered, is in the Messianic age transformed into an angel of peace for the whole nation, or even a "refining fire" coming to burn out of the world all unrighteousness and all doubt.

But Elijah has still other functions. He will, in the Messianic age, restore three things to Israel: "The flask of manna,[18] the flask of water for purification, and the flask of oil for anointing. And some say, Also Aaron's rod, with its ripe almonds and blossoms,[19] as it is written (Num. 17:25), 'Bring back the rod of Aaron.' "[20]

"The flask of oil for anointing" is of a very special kind. It dated back to the time of the wilderness wanderings. At that time it contained only twelve logs (a comparatively small amount), yet with this amount of oil it was possible to anoint the Tabernacle and its vessels, Aaron and his sons, and a long line of high priests and kings throughout the period of the First Temple. Nevertheless, the oil in this flask remained undiminished, for with it the King-Messiah will

---

[16] Ben-Sira 48:10.
[17] See Friedmann's Introduction to Seder Eliyahu, p. 23, Note 2.
[18] That the manna will again come down from heaven in the Messianic age to serve as food for Israel—this we find also in the Syriac Baruch 29:8.
[19] See Num. 17:23. This miraculous rod will serve as a royal scepter for the King-Messiah (Num. R., end of Chap. 18).
[20] Mekhilta, Wayyassa, Chap. 6 (ed. Friedmann, 51b). See also Seder Eliyahu Rabbah, Chap. 25 (ed. Friedmann, Chap. 23, p. 129); M. Friedmann, *Addenda to Seder Eliyahu Zuta* [Heb.], Vienna, 1904, p. 34 (Pirqe R. Eliezer, Chap. 3—Seder Eliyahu Zuta, Chap. 21).

be anointed in the future.[21] And this same Elijah, who will restore this marvelous flask to Israel, will of course himself anoint the Messiah with its oil. This we know from a source that is non-Talmudic, but ancient and trustworthy.[22] For, according to several Talmudic traditions, Elijah is not only a prophet, but also a high priest. Thus the Talmudic literature identifies him with Phinehas, the son of Eleazar and grandson of Aaron [Ex. 6:25], and calls him "Righteous Priest" (*Kohen-Zedek*) or even "Melchizedek."[23] It was the custom for the high priests and prophets to anoint the kings. The political and spiritual king, the King-Messiah, will be anointed by Elijah, who is both prophet and high priest.

It is said in certain Baraithas that Elijah will play a part in the resurrection of the dead.[24] But the resurrection of the dead belongs to the sphere of Jewish eschatology, and we are concerned here only with the Jewish Messianic idea.

The Tannaitic literature has little to say with respect to the activity of Elijah in his rôle as the Messiah's forerunner. It is only said specifically that Elijah must come one day before the Son of David.[25] Apparently, he will announce the Messiah's coming from the top of Mount Carmel, the site which had such an important place in his earthly life.[26] We have already seen that in Tannaitic circles the belief

---

[21] Kerithoth 5*ab*; Horayyoth 11*b*; Siphra, Tsav, Chap. 1, Sect. 9 (ed. Weiss, 41*a*). My great and never-to-be-forgotten teacher, Prof. C. Bezold, called to my attention that these wonders are mentioned, although in a slightly different form, in the Ethiopic book *Kebra Nagast* (Glory of Kings), Chap. 98.

[22] We find this function of Elijah for the first time in Justin Martyr (*Dialogue with Trypho the Jew*, Chap. 8 near end; Chap. 49 beginning). Trypho represents the anointing of the Messiah by Elijah as a well established view in Jewish circles, and he uses it as an argument against the messiahship of Jesus. This has already been pointed out by James Drummond (*The Jewish Messiah*, p. 222). See also E. Hühn, *Die messian. Weissag.*, I, 115 (especially Note 3).

[23] For details on this problem, see M. Friedmann, Introduction, pp. 6–11; Dalman, *Der leidende und sterbende Messias*, pp. 7–11; V. Aptowitzer, "Malkizedek" (*MGWJ*, LXX [1926], 93–113); G. Wuttke, *Melchisedech, der Priesterkoenig von Salem* (Beihefte zur ZNW, 5), Giessen, 1927.

[24] Sotah 49*b* (in some editions of Mishnah and Talmud also found at Mishnah, Sotah 9:15); cf. Drummond, *The Jewish Messiah*, p. 224. This matter is presented in greater detail in Yerushalmi, Shekalim 3:3 end.

[25] Erubin 43*ab*.

[26] Yerushalmi, Pesahim 3:6. See Justin Martyr, *Dialogue with Trypho*, Chap. 8 near end.

was current that he would not come on a Sabbath or a festival day, or even on the eve of a Sabbath or festival day.[27]

In the generations following the Tannaitic age, Elijah's coming and his proclamation of the Messiah were embellished with a whole series of legends and miracle stories.[28] These stories are sometimes very charming. They are highly poetic, elevated, and they do credit to a rich and colorful Oriental imagination. But they do not stem from the more ancient sources of popular legends, nor do they come from the widely current Messianic ideas which found their way into the Jewish apocalyptic literature of the last two pre-Christian and the first two post-Christian centuries. Therefore their historical importance is far less than that of the Messianic ideas from the time of the Tannaim, ideas whose time of origin coincides with the rise of the Jewish apocalyptic literature and the beginning of Christianity.

[27] Erubin 43*b*; Pesahim 13*a* (see above, p. 452).
[28] All these are summarized in Castelli, *Il Messia*, pp. 196-201. They are presented at more length in M. Friedmann, Introduction to Seder Eliyahu, pp. 2-44; Y. M. Guttmann, "Elijah the Prophet in Legends of Israel" [Heb.] (*He-Atid*, ed. S. I. Horowitz, V, 14-46); *idem, Key to the Talmud* [Heb.], III, 17-56.

CHAPTER VII

The Name and Personality of the Messiah

ATTENTION HAS already been called to the fact that the Biblical and post-Biblical Messianic passages differ fundamentally at one point. In the Biblical Messianic idea the point of emphasis is the redemption of Israel and the propagation of the idea of monotheism and divine righteousness. The Messiah himself is sometimes not even mentioned among the promises of redemption; and even if he is mentioned here and there he does not occupy the dominant place that he assumed later. The word *Messiah* ("anointed one") itself, in the sense in which it was used from the second century B.C.E. onward, does not occur in the Old Testament.[1]

It is entirely otherwise with the Messianic expectations of post-Biblical times. Here the Messiah stands in the foreground. He becomes the center of all events, from him proceeds almost everything, and the coming age itself is named after him "the Days of the Messiah" or "the generation of Messiah."[2] Even in the Tannaitic period this emphasis on the personality of the Messiah is already prominent.

But the signs of natural development must not be overlooked. When we survey the very detailed and exaggerated descriptions of the Messiah's every movement and characteristic that come from the post-Tannaitic period; when we take into account the innumerable legends relating to the personality of the Messiah that sprang up like mushrooms in the centuries between the Tannaim and the Cru-

---
[1] See on this above, pp. 7–8.
[2] See D. Castelli, *Il Messia*, pp. 202–203.

sades—we must admit that, in comparison with these exaggerated flights of fancy, the sayings about the personality of the Messiah transmitted to us in the name of the Tannaim are almost as scanty and as simple as those in the Old Testament. The reason for this is that the Tannaitic sayings are still for the most part close to the original conception. For at the beginning legendary conceptions are always simple and few in number. Only through a more or less lengthy development do they become richer, more poetic, more filled with flights of fancy; but they lose their originality and simplicity. In the Tannaitic period there was still no conception of a "suffering Messiah" or a "pre-existent Messiah." A noble king, a man of the highest moral quality, a political and spiritual leader of the Jewish people in particular and of the human race in general—this, and only this, was the Messiah of the Tannaim.

Before we proceed to a presentation of Tannaitic sayings concerning the name and personality of the Messiah, a remark must be made about one matter: concerning a kingdom of heaven on earth without the ideal king, that is to say, a Messianic kingdom without a Messiah, as sometimes found in the Old Testament and even in the Apocrypha and Pseudepigrapha,[3] the Tannaim know nothing at all. The remark of R. Johanan ben Torta to R. Akiba, "Akiba, grass will be growing up around your jawbones, and still the son of David will not come," is not, as James Drummond thought,[4] proof that R. Johanan ben Torta could imagine the future of Israel without a Messiah. It is simply, as the context shows,[5] a personal criticism of R. Akiba, who had made the mistake of believing in the messiahship of Bar-Cochba. The second saying which Drummond cites as proof of the possibility of the Messianic age without a Messiah, one from Rab Hillel,[6] is Amoraic and belongs to a time when there was a desire to weaken belief in the Messiah's coming as much as possible.[7] Against this it suffices to quote the rule of R. Judah the Patriarch:

[3] This was shown by James Drummond in a special chapter entitled "Conception of the Ideal Kingdom Without a Messiah" (*The Jewish Messiah*, pp. 226-273).
[4] *Ibid.*, pp. 272-273.
[5] Yerushalmi, Taanith 4:8.
[6] See *The Jewish Messiah*, p. 273.
[7] See above, pp. 404-405.

Whoever omits to mention . . . the kingdom of the house of David (that is, "And the throne of Thy servant David do Thou make ready therein speedily") [8] in "Who buildest Jerusalem" (the fourteenth of the Eighteen Benedictions) has not performed his obligation.[9]

The Messiah and his kingdom, a heritage from the house of David, are, therefore, an inseparable part of the Messianic expectations of the Tannaim.

We turn now to the *name* of the Messiah. This name receives rather strange treatment in the Talmudic literature. An unusual Baraitha reads:

Seven things were created before the world was created, and these are they: the Torah, repentance, the Garden of Eden, Gehenna, the Throne of Glory, the Temple, and *the name of the Messiah*. The Torah, for it is written. . . .[10] The name of the Messiah, as it is written (Ps. 72:17), "His name shall endure forever, *before the sun* his name shall exist." [11]

What this name is the Baraitha does not reveal. To conclude from this passage that the Messiah's name preceded the creation of the world (pre-existence) would be senseless. What need would there be for the Messiah's name if the Messiah himself did not yet exist? And that the Messiah himself existed before Creation is nowhere stated in Tannaitic literature. We have no recourse, therefore, but to accept the hypothesis of Maurice Vernes [12] and Meir Friedmann,[13] that "the name of the Messiah" is the *idea* of the Messiah, or, more exactly, *the idea of redemption through the Messiah*. This idea did precede Creation. Before Creation, Israel was predestined to produce from itself a Messiah, to be redeemed by him, and through him to redeem all

---

[8] Or, according to the Palestinian text of the *Shemoneh Esreh* found in the Genizah (Schechter, *JQR*, X [1898], 654–659): "Have mercy . . . upon the *kingdom* of the house of David, Thy righteous Messiah."

[9] Berakhoth 49a.

[10] Here are given Biblical verses appropriate to each one of the seven things; but the verses may not belong to the Baraitha, since they are introduced by the late (Aramaic) formula "for it is written" instead of the earlier (Hebrew) formula "as it is said."

[11] Pesahim 54a; Nedarim 39b. The same thing is said in the "Parables" of the Ethiopic Enoch, 48:3 (see above, Part II, p. 293). See also the Targum Pseudo-Jonathan on Zech. 4:7.

[12] See M. Vernes, *Histoire des idées messianiques*, pp. 268–269; p. 281, Note 1.

[13] Introduction to Seder Eliyahu, p. 114.

THE NAME AND PERSONALITY OF THE MESSIAH   461

mankind from the evil in the world. That this interpretation of the expression "the name of the Messiah" is not strange to the Talmudic writers is shown by a passage from Midrash Rabbah, a Palestinian work. In it "the name of the Messiah" is numbered among the things which were "contemplated for creation." [14] This existence before the creation of the world is apparently also alluded to in the following Baraitha:

The school of R. Ishmael taught: As a reward for the observance of the three "firsts" (that is, the first days of the three festivals mentioned in Lev. 23:7, 35, 40), they (Israel) merited three other "firsts": to destroy the seed of Esau, the building of the Temple, *and the name of the Messiah*. . . . as it is written (Isa. 41:27), *"First* unto Zion, behold, behold them." [15]

This can only be interpreted in the sense that the idea of the Messiah, like the destruction of the seed of Esau (that is, Edom-Rome), which still remained to be accomplished, and like the future rebuilding of the Temple,[16] had been predestined before Creation (the name of the Messiah is "first"); and by the keeping of the festivals the children of Israel had shown themselves worthy of this "idea" of the Messiah. We have here, in some measure, the Platonic doctrine of ideas.[17]

As to actual names, only a few are known to the Tannaitic period, in contrast to the following period, which knows them in great numbers. The one name that recurs most frequently (but much less in the pre-Hadrianic time) is "Son of David." This occurs frequently not only as a descriptive title but as an actual personal name. A late

[14] Gen. R., Chap. 1: "Six things preceded the creation of the world; some of them were actually created, while the creation of the others was already contemplated. The Torah and the Throne of Glory were created. . . . The creation of the Patriarchs . . . , of Israel . . . , of the Temple . . . [and] of the name of Messiah was contemplated." This passage militates against everything which Christian scholars have written on this subject (see, e.g., Schürer, *Geschichte*, II⁴, 616–619).

[15] Pesahim 5a.

[16] The Temple also, in the Baraitha in Pesahim and Nedarim, and in Genesis Rabbah, is numbered among the things that preceded the creation of the world.

[17] The identification of the name with the person of the Messiah, which Bousset-Gressmann (*Das Religion des Judentums,* pp. 262–263 and Note 1, p. 263) wish to make, is not correct, at least so far as the really early Jewish literature is concerned. In that literature the name, *but not the person,* precedes the creation of the world. The idea is perhaps based on the verse "Before the sun his name shall exist" (Ps. 72:17).

Palestinian Baraitha [18] calls him not "Son of David" but simply "David"; [19] but this occurs only once in the Tannaitic period. On the contrary, "Redeemer" was apparently a common designation, since it already occurs in the first benediction of the *Shemoneh Esreh* and in the "Thanksgivings" of Ben-Sira,[20] which are so similar to the *Shemoneh Esreh*. Indeed, this designation occurs in the Old Testament itself.[21]

The other names for the Messiah from the Tannaitic period come from individual Tannaim who, on the basis of their exposition of some Biblical verse, would apply to the Messiah a chance title current only among themselves and their disciples. The following is an example:

R. Jose the Galilean (pre-Hadrianic) says: Also, the Messiah's name is called Peace, for it is written (Isa. 9:5) "Everlasting Father, Prince (called) Peace." [22]

This name did not take root in Jewish literature or become current among common people or scholars; it remained the individual creation of R. Jose the Galilean.

Another name for the Messiah attained even less recognition:

R. Judah [23] expounded as follows: "The burden of the word of the LORD. In the land of Hadrach and in Damascus shall be his resting-place, for the

---

[18] Yerushalmi, Berakhoth 2:4 (f. 5a).

[19] This usage is also quoted in the name of the early Amora (semi-Tanna) Rab, Sanhedrin 99a; but see above, pp. 46-47.

[20] The "Thanksgivings" occur in the Hebrew text of 51:12. Supplementary Verse 5 reads, "Give thanks unto the *Redeemer* of Israel, for His mercy endureth forever"; here, however, the term is applied to God.

[21] Cf. Isa. 49:7 with 59:20.

[22] *Pereq ha-Shalom* (Chapter on Peace), which is a supplement at the end of Derekh Erets Zuta. See the texts published by M. Higger, *Massekhtoth Zeeroth*, New York, 1929, pp. 101, 104. [The Hebrew words *Sar-Shalom*, if joined together, may mean "Prince of Peace" (as usually translated) or "Prince (called) Peace," as interpreted here by R. Jose. The words may also be separated into two names, "Prince" (and) "Peace" as in San. 94a.]

[23] This is the younger disciple of R. Akiba, R. Judah ben Ilai, who taught after the time of Hadrian. But apparently he offered this exposition while still a student, since R. Jose ben Dormaskith was a pre-Hadrianic teacher (Bacher, *Agada der Tannaiten*, I, 293, Heb. trans., Vol. I, Part II, p. 113, Note 15). R. Jose roundly denounces the exposition and calls Judah *Berabbi* ["son (or pupil) of the master"(?), perhaps in sarcasm] (but see article BYRBY in Kohut, *Aruch Completum*, II², 183).

LORD's is the eye of man and all the tribes of Israel" (Zech. 9:1). This (the name Hadrach) is the Messiah, who will be *Had* ("sharp") toward the nations of the world, but *Rach* ("soft") toward Israel.[24]

But this artificial interpretation was immediately rejected by an older pre-Hadrianic Tanna named R. Jose ben Dormaskith,[25] who replied to R. Judah thus:

Son of the master! Why do you twist the Scriptures against us? I call heaven and earth to witness that I am from Damascus and that there is a place there and its name is Hadrach.[26]

This Rabbinic passage is important because it shows us how groundless and hypothetical a Messianic name may sometimes be, even if it comes from the Sages of the pre-Hadrianic period.

Still more so are the names applied by the Amoraim. A whole series of names from a well known Talmudic passage is based purely on paronomasia:

The school of R. Shila said: His name is Shiloh. . . . The school of R. Yannai said: His name is Yinnon. . . . The school of R. Haninah maintained: His name is Haninah. . . . Some say: His name is Menahem ("comforter"), son of Hezekiah. . . . The Rabbis said: His name is "the leper of the school of Rabbi." [27]

Thus each school chooses a name for the Messiah resembling in sound and meaning the name of that school or its head. Only one name found here is introduced by the formula "some say" and is not dependent on paronomasia; therefore this Messianic name is more important, and may come from an earlier period. It is the name "Menahem son of Hezekiah," and it may refer to Menahem, son of Judas the Galilean and grandson of Hezekiah, who played an important

---

[24] Siphre, Deut. 1 (ed. Friedmann, 65a).
[25] His mother was apparently a proselyte from Damascus; "Dormaskith" is a special form (similar to the Syriac) of the word meaning "Damascene woman."
[26] Siphre, *loc. cit.* In Pesiqta de-Rab Kahana, section on "Sing, O barren one" [Isa. 54:1] (ed. Buber, 143a), R. Nehemiah, the regular opponent of R. Judah, says: "The place is called Hadrach." And of course in the Aramaic inscription of Zakur [Zakar, Zakir], king of Hamath, the city of Ḥazrak (Assyrian Ḥatriku)—same as Hadrach in Hebrew—is mentioned. See H. Pognon, *Inscriptions sémitiques de la Syrie et de la Mésopotamie*, Paris, 1907, p. 156.
[27] Sanhedrin 98b.

part at the beginning of the First Revolt (*Wars* 2:17:8–9), and according to Graetz [28] considered himself the Messiah.

But the name can equally well be explained symbolically. The Messiah is *the comforter*, on the basis of Lamentations 1:16: "Because *the comforter* is far from me, even he that should refresh my soul." [29] The symbolic meaning of the name Menahem is obvious since the "redeemer" of the nation is also its "comforter" (on the basis of Isa. 40:1; 51:12). But why is he called "son of Hezekiah"? Here perhaps we may still recognize surviving traces of an earlier and truer understanding of the Messianic prophecies of Isaiah, according to which these prophecies were applied to Hezekiah, king of Judah.[30] We hear the last echoes of this once widely current view in the following exposition by a younger contemporary of R. Judah the Patriarch: [31]

"Of the increase [Heb. *leMarbeh*, with an unusual *m*] of his government and peace there shall be no end" (Isa. 9:6). R. Tanhum said: Bar Kappara expounded in Sepphoris, Why is every other *m* in the middle of a word open, while this one is closed? The Holy One, blessed be He, wished to appoint Hezekiah as the Messiah, and Sennacherib as Gog and Magog; whereupon the Attribute of Justice appeared before the Holy One, blessed be He, and said: 'Sovereign of the Universe! If Thou didst not make David the Messiah, who uttered so many hymns and psalms before Thee, wilt Thou appoint Hezekiah as such, who did not hymn Thee in spite of all these miracles which Thou wroughtest for him?' Therefore it (the *m*) was closed. Straightway the earth opened and said to Him: 'Sovereign of the Universe! Let me utter song before Thee instead of this righteous man (Hezekiah), and make him the Messiah.' So it broke into

---

[28] *Op. cit.*, Hebrew trans. by S. P. Rabbinowitz, II, 80, Note 1. See also J. Klausner, *History of the Second Temple* [Heb.], V, 147-149; idem, *When a Nation Fights for Its Freedom* [Heb.], 8th ed. (1952), pp. 169-170.

[29] Sanhedrin 98b; Yerushalmi, Berakhoth 2:4; Lam. R. on 1:16 (ed. Buber, f. 45). Menahem (ben Ammiel) as a name of the Messiah is frequently found in the later literature. Still later Nehemiah (of similar meaning) was used, as in Nehemiah ben Hushiel.

[30] In the time of Justin Martyr, the Jews still held strongly to the idea that some of the Messianic oracles of Isaiah (e.g., Chap. 11) refer to Hezekiah (*Dialogue with Trypho*, Chaps. 43, 67, 68, 71, 77). The opinion of the Amora Rab Hillel (quoted above, p. 404), "There shall be no Messiah for Israel because they have already enjoyed him in the days of Hezekiah," is of course also based on this older view.

[31] Sanhedrin 94a.

song before Him, as it is written (Isa. 24:16), "From the uttermost part of the earth have we heard songs: Glory to the righteous one." Then the Prince of the Universe [a special angel] said to Him: 'Sovereign of the Universe! Fulfill the desire [32] of this righteous man. But a heavenly voice cried out, "The secret is mine, the secret is mine" (Isa. 24:16, usual interpretation, "I waste away"; the secret here is that Hezekiah cannot become Messiah). To which the prophet rejoined (Isa. 24:16), "Woe is me, woe is me"; how long (must Israel wait for the Messiah)? The heavenly voice again cried out (Isa. 24:16), "The treacherous deal treacherously, yea the treacherous deal very treacherously." [33]

From this very interesting exposition it is to be seen that the truer interpretation of the Messianic passages in Isaiah was not wholly forgotten in the latter part of the Tannaitic period, even though it was somewhat obscured.[34] We may be fairly certain, therefore, that the saying of Rabban Johanan ben Zakkai, "Make ready a throne for Hezekiah, king of Judah, who is coming," [35] refers to the near approach of the Messiah and not to R. Gamaliel the Patriarch, as was thought by Jacob Levy.[36]

Now I turn from the idea and name of the Messiah to his personality.

In no trustworthy, authentic source of the Tannaitic period is to be found any description of the person and characteristics of the Messiah that goes beyond the bounds of human nature. To be sure, his qualities and his deeds surpass the ordinary standard of human powers. But other righteous and pious persons could also perform signs and wonders, and in the Messianic age the supernatural would become the usual, one might almost say, the natural. The miracles which Elijah had performed in his lifetime and would perform in the Messianic age would be in no wise inferior to those of the King-Messiah.

[32] Heb. *tsivyon*, from the Biblical *tsevi*, with the meaning of the Syriac *tsevyana*.
[33] That is to say, they must wait until woes are piled upon woes, and treacheries upon treacheries. So this passage is interpreted (in San. 94*a*) by the Amora Raba or R. Isaac. See also Kethubboth 112*b* (end of the tractate).
[34] See F. Weber, *System d. altsyn. palästin. Theologie*, p. 341.
[35] Berakhoth 28*b*; Yerushalmi, Sotah 9:16, and Abodah Zarah 3:1; Aboth de-R. Nathan, Recension A, Chap. 25 (ed. Schechter, p. 80). See above, Chap. I, p. 396.
[36] See *Neuhebr. Wörterbuch*, II, 362, where Levy wrongly attributes this saying to R. Eliezer.

Only as a mighty ruler and an exalted and unequaled moral personality would the Messiah be superior to all the rest of the saints and prophets of Israel. He might be "a moral superman," to use an expression of Ahad Ha-Am; but his kingdom is definitely *a kingdom of this world*. Of the *divine* nature of the Messiah, there are perhaps certain indications in the later Midrashim; [37] in the authentic writings of the Tannaitic period there is not a trace. Trypho the Jew says in the book of Justin Martyr: "All of us (Jews) expect the Messiah to come as a man from among men." [38] Thus, even if it were possible to prove that the post-Tannaitic literature does indeed ascribe divine nature to the Messiah (though Castelli and Drummond doubt it), we may assume that this feature was indirectly and unconsciously borrowed from Christianity. Or else we must conclude that the increasingly exaggerated and fantastic veneration of the Messiah did not shrink, from the seventh century C.E. onward, even from making him divine. *But in the earlier literature there is no trace of this.*

The following is an interesting Baraitha concerning the Messiah:

Nine persons entered into Paradise during their lifetime: Enoch son of Jared, Elijah, *the Messiah*, Eliezer the servant of Abraham, Hiram king of Tyre, Ebedmelech the Ethiopian, Jabez son of R. Judah the Patriarch, Bithiah daughter of Pharaoh, and Serah daughter of Asher.[39]

Here we have the supposition that the Messiah already exists in Paradise.[40] Yet it is worthy of notice that even in this Baraitha the Messiah is put on a level with mere human beings, distinguished only for their good deeds. Even certain Gentiles are included: Hiram king of Tyre, Ebedmelech the Ethiopian, and Bithiah daughter of the king of Egypt. This Baraitha is, to be sure, very late, since it mentions the son of R. Judah the Patriarch, the redactor of the Mishnah. There are, of course, variant texts of this Baraitha, in which other personages from the Bible are substituted for the Gentiles and R.

---

[37] Collected by Wünsche, *Die Leiden des Messias*, pp. 42, 76, 77–81. Against this opinion see Castelli, *op. cit.*, pp. 203–209; Drummond, *op. cit.*, chapter on "The Nature of the Messiah," pp. 290–295.
[38] See *Dialogue with Trypho*, Chap. 49, beginning (ἄνθρωπον ἐξ ἀνθρώπων).
[39] Derekh Erets Zuta, end of Chap. 1.
[40] Thus he exists also in Ethiopic Enoch 39:6–7; IV Ezra 12:32; 13:26, 52; 14:9. See Schürer, *op. cit.*, II⁴, 616–619; above, Part II, pp. 293, 358–359.

THE NAME AND PERSONALITY OF THE MESSIAH 467

Judah's son.[41] Yet the very fact that the Messiah could be put on the same level with persons like Eliezer and Serah (who occur in all the texts) proves that the Messiah is "a man from among men."

Another similar Baraitha says:

In the Age to Come the son of David will be in the middle, with Adam, Seth, and Methuselah on his right, and Abraham, Moses, and Jacob on his left.[42]

But this Baraitha is also very late and its text corrupt.[43] Perhaps simply "David" is to be read here instead of "the son of David." [44]

On *the characteristics* of the Messiah we have the following exposition from the time of R. Judah the Patriarch:

R. Tanhum said: Bar Kappara expounded in Sepphoris: Why is it written (Ruth 3:17), "These six [a word missing?] of barley gave he to me"? . . . He (Boaz) symbolically intimated to her (Ruth) that six sons were destined to come forth from her, who should each be blessed with six blessings: David, Messiah, Daniel, Hananiah, Mishael, and Azariah. David, for it is written, . . .[45] The Messiah, for it is written (Isa. 11:2), "And the spirit of the LORD shall rest upon him, the spirit of wisdom and understanding, the spirit of counsel and might, the spirit of knowledge and the fear of the LORD." [46]

The Messiah will inherit, therefore, the six "gifts of the Holy Spirit."

The next verse in Isaiah (11:3) reads:

And his delight [literally "smell"] shall be in the fear of the LORD, and he shall not judge after the sight of his eyes, neither decide after the hearing of his ears.

---

[41] See the *Haggahoth* (Critical Notes) of Elijah of Vilna, *ad loc.; Tosaphoth*, Yebamoth 16b, on *Pasuq;* M. Friedmann, Introduction to Seder Eliyahu, p. 15.

[42] Kallah Rabbathi, Chap. 7, near end (*Hamishshah Konterisim* [Five Tractates] by N. N. Coronel, Vienna, 1864, 13b.

[43] As is evident from the fact that here Jacob comes not after Abraham, but after Moses.

[44] See Sukkah 52b, where the reading is thus: "David in the middle, with Adam, Seth, and Methuselah on his right, and Abraham, Jacob, and Moses on his left." Cf. Midrash Shoher Tob (Tehillim), Ps. 18:29 end (ed. Buber, 79). See also J. Klausner, *Jesus of Nazareth*, 5th Heb. ed., p. 344, Note 2 [Eng. ed., p. 320, Note 12].

[45] Here is quoted I Sam. 16:18 as proof of the blessings which David had received; then follows the discussion of the Amoraim on this verse.

[46] Sanhedrin 93ab.

On this is based another attribute of Messiah, the lack of which caused Bar-Cochba to be recognized as a false Messiah:

> Bar Koziba reigned two and a half years, and then said to the Rabbis, "I am the Messiah." They answered, "Of Messiah it is written that he smells and judges (that is, he has an instinct for who is right and who is wrong); let us see whether he (Bar-Cochba) can smell and judge?" When they saw that he could not smell and judge,[47] they killed him.[48]

Thus the Messiah should possess a very deep feeling for what is just and right, and in his judgments he should reach the truth by instinct. But this whole passage seems to me rather late, since it is closely connected with a saying of the Amora Raba.[49] It is written in Aramaic, and *in the existing context* this also points to an Amoraic origin (though sometimes an Aramaic saying is quite early). Obviously the passage came into being many years after Bar-Cochba's failure, and served "after the fact," when the grandiose schemes of "the Son of the Star" had collapsed, as a justification of the frightful defeat which the Jews suffered at Bethar.

In connexion with the saying of R. Jose the Galilean quoted above, concerning Messiah's name, stands this further statement of the same Rabbi:

> Great is peace, for in the hour when the King-Messiah is manifested to Israel, he will begin speaking with words of peace, as it is written (Isa. 52:7), "How beautiful upon the mountains are the feet of him that bringeth good tidings, that proclaimeth peace."[50]

This is an important statement. The King-Messiah, who must at times be a mighty warrior, begins his glorious career with words of

---

[47] This is no doubt a reference to the slaying of the innocent R. Eleazar of Modi'im, whom Bar-Cochba put to death on mere suspicion. On this slaying see Graetz, *Geschichte der Juden*, IV, 175-176 (Heb. trans., II, 247); J. Klausner, "Simon Bar-Cochba" (*When a Nation Fights for Its Freedom* [Heb.], 8th ed., 1952, pp. 243-244).

[48] Sanhedrin 93*b*.

[49] *Loc. cit.*: "Raba said: He smells and judges, as it is written (Isa. 11:3-4), 'and he shall not judge after the sight of his eyes, . . . but with righteousness shall he judge the poor, and decide with equity for the meek of the land.'"

[50] Derekh Erets Zuta, Chap. 11 (the "Chapter on Peace"); M. Higger, *op. cit.*, p. 101, and note, p. 148; Lev. R., Chap. 9.

THE NAME AND PERSONALITY OF THE MESSIAH 469

peace. Below, in Chapter IX, we shall see again the importance of this idea.

It was mentioned in the preceding chapter that the Messiah will be anointed by Elijah, from a marvelous flask of anointing oil, from which have already been anointed the Tabernacle, Aaron and his sons, and many of Israel's high priests and kings. It was also mentioned that Aaron's rod, which budded miraculously in the wilderness, will serve the Messiah as a royal scepter.[51]

This virtually completes the Tannaitic descriptions of the personality of the Messiah. The Tannaim did not add much to the characteristics of the Messiah found in the Scriptures. They only emphasized and heightened his spiritual qualities by the addition of a few pleasing touches. The Amoraim and their still later successors made a greater attempt to glorify the personality of the redeemer, but their highly colored flights of fancy are no longer original and primary. But for the Tannaim, as for the prophets (and the Tannaim were the spiritual heirs of the prophets), the essential thing is not the Messiah, but *the Messianic age*. After all, it is God Himself who will bring redemption in the Messianic age. The Messiah is here in the Tannaitic literature only the instrument of God, albeit the most favored and glorious divine instrument that would ever take bodily form on earth.

[51] See above, in the preceding chapter, pp. 455–456.

CHAPTER VIII

The Ingathering of the Exiles and the Reception of Proselytes

A WIDESPREAD BELIEF, which already occupied a large place in the prophetic books, prevailed among the Jews in the Tannaitic period. This was the deep-rooted conviction that the dispersion of Israel would in the Messianic age return from the four corners of the earth to Palestine. If we remember that the dispersion of Israel, the "Diaspora," was extensive and widely scattered, and that both before and after the destruction of the Temple the number of Jews who lived outside Palestine (which during the whole Tannaitic period still remained not only the religious but also the national center of the Jewish people) was much greater than the number in the Holy Land,[1] we shall not be surprised that the Jews saw in the eagerly awaited ingathering of exiles a miraculous accomplishment that could only be brought about in the Messianic age.[2]

Who will accomplish this miracle? According to the *Shemoneh Esreh* it is God Himself who will "sound the great horn for freedom"[3] and "lift up the ensign to gather our exiles, and gather us quickly from the four corners of the earth" just before Messiah's coming.[4] But according to the Psalms of Solomon (17:26–28) and

[1] See on this J. Klausner, *From Jesus to Paul* [Heb.], I (1939), 30–31 [Eng. ed., pp. 32-33]; idem, "The Jewish Population of Palestine in the Period of the Second Temple" (*Ramat-Gan*, Jubilee Volume, Tel-Aviv, 1947, pp. 173-183).
[2] The Diaspora at the time of the rise of Christianity has been discussed at length by J. Juster, *Les Juifs dans l'Empire Romaine*, Paris, 1914, I, 179–212; Schürer, *Geschichte*, III⁴, 1–70; A. Causse, *Les Dispersés d'Israel*, Paris, 1929.
[3] Cf. Zech., 9:14 and Isa. 27:13.
[4] Benediction 10 [Singer, *The Standard Prayer Book*, enlarged American ed.,

the Targum Pseudo-Jonathan (on Deut. 30:4 and Jer. 33:13) the Messiah will bring back the dispersed nation to its own land. In the later Rabbinic literature occurs often the expression "the trumpet of Messiah"; but just as "the birth pangs of Messiah" does not mean personal sufferings of the Messiah, but the miseries of the Messianic age, so also "the trumpet of Messiah" is not a trumpet blown by the Messiah, but the trumpet of the Messianic age.

That God Himself will lead His chosen people to their promised land can be shown by many passages in the Tannaitic literature. In a post-Hadrianic Baraitha we read:

R. Simeon ben Yohai says: Come and see how beloved is Israel before the Holy One, blessed is He; for wherever they went into exile the Shekhinah was with them. They went into exile to Egypt, and the Shekhinah was with them, as it is written (I Sam. 2:27), "Did I indeed reveal myself unto the house of thy father when they were in Egypt?" They went into exile to Babylonia, and the Shekhinah was with them, as it is written (Isa. 43:14), "For your sake I was sent [usual reading, "I sent"] to Babylonia." Likewise, when they shall be redeemed in the future, the Shekhinah will be with them, as it is written (Deut. 30:3), "Then the LORD thy God will return with thy captivity." It does not say "will bring back thy captivity" but "will return with thy captivity"—teaching that the Holy One, Blessed is He, returns with them from the places of exile.[5]

This tender, poetic, and touching story, according to which God Himself, if we may speak thus, goes into exile with His beloved people and shares the sufferings of exile with them, shows again that in the view of the Tannaim, God Himself redeems His people, and is Himself redeemed, so to speak, with them. It is as though the divine Shekhinah had its feet encased in fetters. It cannot reveal itself in its fullness and in all its brightness and splendor so long as the oppressed and suffering nation has not become "a light to the Gentiles."

---

p. 142]. See also Megillah 17b and 18a. Of similar kind are the prescribed forms of Grace after Meals [Singer, *op. cit.*, pp. 424–431]. See also M. Friedmann, Introduction to Seder Eliyahu, pp. 140–141.

[5] Megillah 29a. A similar idea appears in the following anonymous saying: "'I am that I am' (Ex. 3:14). The Holy One, blessed be He, said to Moses: Go and say to Israel: I was with you in this [Egyptian] servitude, and I shall be with you in the servitude of the [other] kingdoms" (Ber. 9b).

The redemption itself will come suddenly.[6] The return of Israel from its exile will be like a triumphal procession; "in returning and rest" [Isa. 30:15], without haste or fear, will the hosts of the redeemed march forward.[7] Clouds of glory will be spread out over them, according to the Biblical verse (Isa. 4:6), "And there shall be a pavilion for a shadow in the day-time," and according to a further verse (Isa. 35:10), "And the ransomed of the LORD shall return, and come with singing unto Zion, and everlasting joy shall be upon their heads."[8] These elect of the LORD will sing new songs of praise. This is seen in an early pre-Hadrianic Baraitha dealing with the recital of the Hallel, the disputants being R. Eliezer ben Hyrcanus, R. Joshua,[9] R. Eliezer of Modiim, R. Eleazar ben Azariah, R. Akiba, and R. Jose the Galilean. The end of the Baraitha says: "And when they (the Children of Israel) are redeemed, they will recite it (the Hallel), because of their redemption."[10]

Another related question demands solution: Will all the Children of Israel return to Palestine or only a part of them?

R. Akiba answers this question by saying that the greater part of the Israelite people will not return to their land. His opinion, together with that of his opponent, R. Eliezer ben Hyrcanus (pre-Hadrianic), was important enough to be recorded in the Mishnah, thus:

The Ten Tribes shall not return again, for it is written (Deut. 29:27), "And he cast them into another land [11] like as this day." As this day goes and returns not, so do they go and return not. So R. Akiba says. But R. Eliezer says, "Like as this day": as the day grows dark and then becomes light, so also with the Ten Tribes; now they are in darkness, but in the future there shall be light for them.[12]

---

[6] Mekhilta, Pisha, Chap. 14 (ed. Friedmann, 15a).
[7] Ibid., Pisha, Chap. 7 (ed. Friedmann, 7b).
[8] Ibid., Beshallah, Chap. 1 (ed. Friedmann, 25a, beginning).
[9] Thus we should read instead of "R. Judah," who, as a younger disciple of R. Akiba, does not fit into this list of earlier Tannaim. The error arose from the use of the initials "R. J."
[10] Pesahim 117a.
[11] On these two words see in detail above, Part II, p. 362, Note 48.
[12] Mishnah, Sanhedrin 10:3. On the variant readings see Bacher, *Agada der Tannaiten*, I, 142-144 (Heb. trans., I, 100-101).

THE INGATHERING OF THE EXILES 473

In a Baraitha immediately following this Mishnah, R. Simeon ben Yohai, the younger disciple of R. Akiba, attempts to mediate between these two extreme views:

R. Simeon ben Judah of the village of Ikkos [13] says on the authority of R. Simeon (ben Yohai): If their deeds remain "like as this day," they will not return; but if otherwise, they will return.[14]

It is to be remarked that this Mishnah may not refer at all to a return to the Holy Land, but to a turning back from evil ways and a repentance for sins, by which the Twelve Tribes could have a share in the World to Come. For the verb *ḥazar* ("to return") is also used in the sense of "to repent," [15] and all of Chapter XI of the tractate Sanhedrin (the so-called "Chapter of the Share"), in which our Mishnah is found, is concerned with those who do or do not have a share in the World to Come. Indeed, in the other version of this controversy about the Ten Tribes, instead of "shall not return," there appear the words "shall not come to life and shall not be judged," that is, they shall not rise at the resurrection of the dead and shall not be judged on the day of the Great Judgment; [16] and in the Tosephta it says definitely, "The Ten Tribes have no share in the World to Come and shall not come to life in the World to Come." [17]

But in a Tannaitic Midrash this same opinion of R. Akiba appears in a version that leaves no doubt about the Messianic character of this whole controversy. This version reads:

"And ye shall perish among the nations" (Lev. 26:38). R. Akiba says: These are the Ten Tribes which went into exile to Media. Others say: "And ye shall perish among the nations" means not annihilation but only exile. Can it actually mean annihilation? Now when it says (in the same verse), "And the land of your enemies shall eat you up," annihilation is

---

[13] Thus we should read instead of "Acco" (Bacher, *op. cit.*, I, 95, Note 3; Heb. trans., I, 70, Note 5).
[14] Sanhedrin 110b. See above, Part II, pp. 362–364.
[15] Cf. "The wicked do not *repent* even at the gate of Gehenna" (Erub. 19a).
[16] Aboth de R. Nathan, Chap. 36 (ed. Schechter, p. 108). Also the Baraitha in Sanhedrin 110b begins, "The Ten Tribes have no share in the World to Come."
[17] Tosephta, Sanhedrin 13:12 (end of the chapter).

actually meant. Therefore it is as I maintain: "And ye shall perish among the nations" means not annihilation but only exile.[18]

If by "others," as the Talmud asserts in one place,[19] is meant R. Meir, then we have here the second post-Hadrianic disciple of R. Akiba who, like his colleague R. Simeon ben Yohai, was more charitable toward the Ten Tribes than was R. Akiba. This will be easy to understand if we remember what was pointed out in Chapter I of the present part of this book. R. Akiba held his opinion because he had proclaimed Bar-Cochba as Messiah and was expecting the redemption of Israel through him, while the remnants of the Ten Tribes at that time had not yet returned to Palestine and had no intention of doing so. The latter fact may have been discovered by R. Akiba on his long journeys to Gaul, Africa,[20] Arabia,[21] and particularly Media,[22] to which the Ten Tribes had been exiled according to Scripture (II Kings 17:6). Therefore he was forced to oppose the opinion that the Ten Tribes must return in the Messianic age.[23]

But his two disciples, who taught in the post-Hadrianic period and who had shared in their master's bitter disillusionment, had no reason to maintain his opinion about the Ten Tribes. This time the rest of the Tannaim were not on the side of R. Akiba in his controversy with R. Eliezer. Moreover, the famous third-century Amora R. Johanan expressed his protest against this opinion of R. Akiba in

[18] Siphra, Behuqqothai, Chap. 8, beginning (ed. Weiss, 112a). Cf. Makkoth 24a (near end of the tractate).

[19] Horayoth 13b. But it is not always possible to consider R. Meir as the author of sayings attributed to "others" (see I. H. Weiss, *Each Generation and Its Interpreters* [Heb.], II², 137, Note 3).

[20] According to Levy (*Neuhebr. Wörterbuch*, I, 150ab), this should be Phrygia.

[21] See for details Rosh ha-Shanah 26a.

[22] Abodah Zarah 34a says, "R. Akiba happened to come to Ginzak"; Gen. R., Chap. 33 [Sect. 5], says more explicitly: "Ginzak *in Media*" (Gazaka). [This is not true of all texts of Gen. R.; but see Note 3, p. 265, in the Soncino translation of Gen. R., and the critical apparatus in the Theodor-Albeck edition, p. 310, 1. 2. There seems to be no doubt that Ginzak was in Media.—TRANS.]

[23] See Castelli, *Il Messia*, pp. 252–253. Cf. S. M. Lazar, *The Ten Tribes* [Heb.], Drohobycz, 1908, p. 9, Note 2. But Isaac Halevy, author of *The Early Generations* [Heb.] (I⁵, 620–629), opposes this view of Graetz and S. J. Rapoport, and thinks that R. Akiba made his journeys not in the interest of the revolt, but for other purposes, e.g., the teaching of Torah (see above, p. 398). Actually, the point cannot be proved. The Talmud was not obliged to divulge that R. Akiba had gone to rouse Jews in distant lands to rebellion.

these words: "R. Akiba forsook his piety." [24] Likewise, the anonymous Baraitha quoted above (p. 409) says plainly and without controversy, "The land of Israel will in time to come be divided between thirteen tribes." [25]

All the tribes of Israel will, therefore [according to general Tannaitic opinion], return to their native country and have a share in the land of their fathers.

Now there follows naturally this question: Will "the sons of Abraham" alone benefit from the joy and prosperity of the Messianic age? The answer to this question is highly characteristic of the Tannaitic period.

An anonymous Baraitha says:

No proselytes will be accepted in the Days of the Messiah, just as no proselytes were accepted in the days of David or in the days of Solomon.[26]

Then follows an appeal to Isaiah 54:15, which the Amora Rab Eleazar [27] interprets thus: "Behold he shall be a proselyte who is converted while I am not with you," that is, the outsider must become a proselyte while I, God, am not with Israel [while Israel is still forsaken by God]; "whoever lives with you (Rashi: in the time of your adversity) shall be settled among you" (interpreting the verb *naphal*, "to fall," as "to be settled," as in Gen. 25:18).[28]

According to this Baraitha, the reason why proselytes will not be accepted in the Messianic age is clear: there would be the suspicion that the Gentiles were being converted not out of conviction, but out

---

[24] Sanhedrin 110b. This is proof that the reading in Aboth de R. Nathan, according to which R. Akiba is in favor of the Ten Tribes, is incorrect.

[25] Baba Bathra 122a. There will be thirteen tribes because Manasseh, Ephraim, and Levi will all be counted among the tribes. According to the Pentateuch, Levi would not have a portion of land, but according to Ezekiel 48:13, 22, 31 it will have a portion. In the opinion of the Amora R. Hisda, the thirteenth part will be for the Messiah (see the commentary of R. Samuel ben Meir [Rashbam] on Baba Bathra 122a).

[26] Yebamoth 24b; Abodah Zarah 3b (for the second half of the Baraitha cf. Yeb. 76a, end).

[27] Not R. Eliezer, as is erroneously given in Yebamoth 24b; for the simple name "R. Eliezer" means Eliezer ben Hyrcanus, and this early Tanna could not have concerned himself with the reason for a Baraitha. The interchange of Eleazar and Eliezer is frequent in the Talmud.

[28] See Rashi on Yebamoth 24b.

of desire for material or political advantage, or out of fear of the great power of the King-Messiah. In any case their conversion would not be wholehearted. That this explanation of the Amora is not a late interpretation irrelevant to the Baraitha is to be seen from the second half of the Baraitha itself, "just as no proselytes were accepted in the days of David or in the days of Solomon." It was precisely in the prosperous periods of Israel's history that proselytes were not admitted, because at such times there was ground for suspicion that the Gentiles were being converted out of fear of David's might, or because they hoped to obtain political positions in Solomon's splendid kingdom. Likewise, the Tannaim completely repudiated conversion from any motive other than deep religious conviction.

Typical of this attitude is the saying of R. Nehemiah that occurs in a late Mishnah,[29] and immediately precedes our Baraitha:

Both a man who became a proselyte for the sake of a woman and a woman who became a proselyte for the sake of a man, and similarly, a man who became a proselyte for the sake of the table of kings,[30] or for the sake of joining Solomon's servants,[31] are no proper proselytes. These are the words of R. Nehemiah, for R. Nehemiah used to say: Neither lion-proselytes,[32] nor dream-proselytes,[33] nor the proselytes of Mordecai

---

[29] See the Tractate Gerim 1:7.

[30] I.e., in order to become king of Israel. This is perhaps an allusion to the Herodian dynasty, which, although originating from Idumean proselytes, attained the kingship in Judea. The expression is also found in Yerushalmi, Kiddushin, beginning of Chap. 4, f. 65b.

[31] I.e., in order to be not a mere slave, but an important person in the kingdom of a powerful Israelite ruler such as Solomon (see Rashi, ad loc.). For according to I Kings 9:20-22, Solomon made those who were left of the former inhabitants of Palestine "a levy of bondservants," while the Israelites were made "men of war, and his servants, and his princes, and his captains, and the rulers of his chariots and of his horsemen." This expression explains that part of the Baraitha quoted above which says that "no proselytes were accepted in the days of David or in the days of Solomon." A group called "Solomon's servants" still existed in the early part of the period of the Second Temple (Ezra 2:55, 58; Neh. 7:60 and 11:3).

[32] "Lion-proselytes" is a regular designation of the Samaritans or Cutheans (Kidd. 75b; Baba Kamma 38b; San. 85b; Hullin 3b; Niddah 56b), because, according to II Kings 17:25-27, they became proselytes only from fear of the lions which threatened to kill them.

[33] I.e., Gentiles who became proselytes because they dreamed that they should forsake paganism. This is apparently a reference to Izates (Zotos), king of Adiabene. See Josephus, *Antiquities* 20:2-4; Gen. R., Chap. 46; J. Klausner, *History of the Second Temple* [Heb.], V, 44-49.

and Esther (such as "became Jews, for the fear of the Jews was fallen upon them," Esther 8:17) are proper proselytes unless they become converted at the present time (when there would be no advantage to a proselyte in embracing an oppressed and persecuted Judaism).[34]

Thus the Tannaim taught that even in their time, a time of oppression and persecution of the Jews, proselytes should not be hastily admitted, lest their intentions be not truly religious, but based on ulterior motives. An anonymous Baraitha says:

If at the present time a man desires to become a proselyte, he is to be addressed as follows: "What reason have you for desiring to become a proselyte? Do you not know that the Jews at the present time are oppressed, harassed, mortified,[35] rejected, and overcome by afflictions?" If he replies, "I know and yet am unworthy" (to share in this melancholy fate of Israel), he is accepted forthwith.[36]

The Tannaim were not opposed to proselytism on principle. If they had been, it would be incomprehensible how in their time entire provinces were converted and a whole network of proselyte congregations were spread over Asia Minor, Egypt, Italy, Mesopotamia, and other regions.[37] But they were afraid of "false proselytes."[38] As true Pharisees (in the correct sense of this word and not in its popular sense), the Tannaim rated the observance of the ceremonial laws as on the same plane with proper belief and purity of thought. Therefore, they were apprehensive about proselytes, for whom it was naturally difficult to forget inherited pagan practices, and thus impossible to carry out strictly the many burdensome requirements of the Jewish religion.

The Talmud is full of complaints against proselytes who do not

---

[34] Yebamoth 24*b*. Cf. Tractate Gerim 1:7, where the words of R. Nehemiah are followed by this general rule: "Whoever does not become a proselyte through religious conviction is not a proselyte."

[35] *Seḥûphîm* is corrupt for *segûphîm* (so in Tractate Gerim 1:1). See Levy, *op. cit.*, III, 477*a*, art. SGP.

[36] Yebamoth 47*a*. According to Tractate Gerim 1:1, a person proposing to become a proselyte should have the present condition of Israel presented to him in even darker colors, in order to remove from him any idea of material advantage.

[37] See on this in detail Schürer, *Geschichte*, III[4], 162–188; J. Juster, *op. cit.*, I, 179–212; J. Klausner, *From Jesus to Paul* [Heb.], I, 29–45 [Eng. ed., pp. 31–40].

[38] Yerushalmi, Baba Metsia 5:7, f. 10*c*.

comply properly with the ritual requirements, but "keep hold of the practices of their fathers." [39] Josephus says that many of the Greeks "have come over to our laws, and some of them have continued in their observance, although others of them had not courage enough to persevere, and so departed from them again." [40] One saying, cited in a late Talmudic tractate [41] as a Baraitha, but usually cited in the Talmud as from the Amora R. Helbo, runs thus: "Proselytes are as hard for Israel to endure as a sore" [42]—because they are not versed in the ceremonial laws.[43] Thus also is to be understood the anonymous Baraitha already quoted,[44] according to which "proselytes delay the coming of Messiah" [45]—obviously because they do not meticulously observe the ceremonial laws.

But this fear of ritualistic transgressions is not sufficient to explain all the harsh and bitter attacks on proselytes in the Talmud. In the Gospels [46] it is said of the Pharisees, "You range over land and sea to make one proselyte." In the *Shemoneh Esreh* the Tannaim included a special blessing "towards the proselytes of righteousness" (Benediction 13); [47] and although they argued over Ecclesiastes, Song of Songs, and other books, they received into Holy Scripture without argument the Book of Ruth, in which David and his dynasty, and hence the King-Messiah also, are traced back to a converted Moabitess. Hence the Pharisees and their successors, the Tannaim, could not have been at all opposed to proselytes in general.[48]

[39] E.g., Mishnah, Niddah 7:3; Baba Metsia 59*b*, end; Yebamoth 47*b* and 109*b*; Kiddushin 70*b*; Niddah 13*b*; Kallah Rabbathi, Chap. 4.
[40] *Against Apion* 2:10, Sect. 123.
[41] Kallah Rabbathi, Chap. 4.
[42] Yebamoth 47*b* and 109*b*; Kiddushin 70*b*; Niddah 13*b*.
[43] See Rashi on Niddah 13*b* and Levy, *op. cit.*, I, 354, top.
[44] See above, p. 430.
[45] Niddah 13*b* and Kallah Rabbathi, Chap. 4.
[46] Matt. 23:15. See on this in general, Juster, *op. cit.*, I, 255-337; A. S. Hershberg, "The Great Proselyte Movement in the Period of the Second Temple" [Heb.], *Ha-Tequphah*, XII, 129-143; XIII, 189-210.
[47] The Palestinian version has a special blessing; the Babylonian version includes "the proselytes of righteousness" [meaning "true proselytes"] with "the righteous and the pious"; to these are added, in the ordinary version, "the elders of Thy people the house of Israel, and the remnant of their scribes."
[48] An impression of antiquity (relative, of course) is made by the marvelous parable of the flock and the stag (Gen. R., Chap. 8): "The Holy One, blessed be He, greatly loves the proselytes. To what may this be compared? To a king who

But in the Tannaitic period there was a large group of "semi-proselytes" [or "half-proselytes"] who may well have aroused special dislike among the Pharisees. These persons were called variously "devout ones," "fearers," "God-fearers," "worshipers of God," and the like. They are mentioned a number of times in the Acts of the Apostles and also in the works of Josephus.[49] These "God-fearers" appropriated only the loftier ideas of Judaism, such as monotheism and the ethics of the prophets. Most of them kept the Sabbath and refrained from eating swine's flesh, but they did not observe the numerous ritual rules of Pharisaic Judaism.[50] In my opinion, it was against these semi-proselytes in particular that the hostile sayings of the Tannaim were directed. For, as Schürer has rightly observed,[51] these "devout ones" are called in the Talmud neither "proselytes of the gate" (*gere sha'ar*, an expression *never* found in the Talmud [and meaning little more than "aliens"]) nor "settler-proselytes" (*gere toshab*, an expression applied to Gentiles in Palestine who refrained from idolatry and observed "the seven commandments of the sons of Noah" [but were definitely not converts]).[52] Therefore, "God-

---

had a flock which used to go out to the field and come in at even. So it was each day. Once a stag came in with the flock." The king instructed the shepherd to look after the stag carefully, because the flock was accustomed to grazing in the field and returning to the fold, but "stags sleep in the wilderness" and this stag "has left behind the whole of the broad, vast wilderness" to join the flock. "In like manner, ought we not to be grateful to the proselyte who has left behind him his family and his father's house, aye, has left behind his people and all the other peoples of the world and has chosen to come to us?" (See J. Klausner, *From Jesus to Paul* [Heb.], I, 33–34 [Eng. ed., pp. 35–37].

[49] *Antiquities* 14:7:2; 20:8:11.
[50] *Op. cit.*, III⁴, 173–175.
[51] *Ibid.*, pp. 176–180.
[52] It may be that these "worshipers of God" ($\sigma\epsilon\beta\acute{o}\mu\epsilon\nu\text{o}\iota$ $\tau\grave{o}\nu$ $\theta\epsilon\acute{o}\nu$ in Greek) are found in the following saying, which occurs in several places: "'One shall say: I am the LORD's' (Isa. 44:5). He is the one who belongs wholly to God, with no admixture of sin in him. 'And another shall call himself by the name of Jacob' (*ibid.*). These are the righteous proselytes. 'And another shall subscribe with his hand unto the LORD' (*ibid.*). These are the repentant sinners. 'And surname himself by the name of Israel' (*ibid.*). These are *the fearers of heaven*" (Mekhilta, Nezikin, Chap. 18, ed. Friedmann, 95*b*; Tractate Gerim, end; Num. R., Chap. 8; and in a different version, Aboth de R. Nathan, Recension A, Chap. 36, ed. Schechter, 54*a*; Seder Eliyahu Rabbah, Chap. 18, ed. Friedmann, p. 105). See also Aboth de R. Nathan, Recension B, p. 40. In Midrash Tehillim 118:11 occurs this statement, "The fearers of the LORD—these are the proselytes," but it is lacking in ed. Buber, p. 482; see Notes and Corrections, p. 242. Also in Lev. R., Chap. 3,

fearers" are designated in the Talmud simply by the word *gerim* ("proselytes"). And the lax attitude of these semi-proselytes toward the ceremonial laws sufficiently explains why the Tannaim so strongly opposed the reception of proselytes, and why they not only imposed hard conditions upon proselytes in their own time, but were also unwilling to have them accepted in the Messianic age, when it would be *advantageous* for Gentiles to become Jews.

That the real reason for this rejection of proselytes is their light regard for the ceremonial laws can be seen clearly from the following Baraitha:

R. Jose (post-Hadrianic) says: In the Age to Come Gentiles will come and offer themselves as proselytes . . . ,[53] and will place phylacteries on their foreheads and on their arms, fringes on their garments, and a *mezuzah* on their doorposts. But when they see the war of Gog and Magog, they will say to Gog and Magog, "Why have you come here?" Gog and Magog will answer, "Against the LORD and against His anointed," as it is written (Ps. 2:1-2), "Why are the nations in an uproar, and why do the peoples mutter in vain," and so on. Then each of the proselytes will throw aside his religious tokens [54] and get away, as it is written (Ps. 2:3), "Let us break their bands asunder"; and the Holy One, blessed be He, will sit and laugh, as it is written (Ps. 2:4), "He that sitteth in heaven laugheth." [55]

The distrust which the Tannaim felt for those Gentiles who became proselytes and then found it hard to stand the test and keep

---

"Ye that fear the LORD" (Ps. 22:24) are [according to one Rabbi] "those that fear heaven" or [according to another Rabbi] "the righteous proselytes." To these "fearers of heaven," here set in contrast to "the righteous [true] proselytes," are rightly to be applied the words of Isa. 44:5, "And surname himself by the name of Israel." "Fearers of heaven" and "fearers of God" are, as is well known, the same; likewise "kingdom of heaven" and "kingdom of God," and "name of heaven" and "name of God." See J. Klausner, *Jesus of Nazareth*, 5th Heb. ed., pp. 199, 256, 432 [Eng. ed., pp. 196, 245, 398].

[53] At this point there is a discussion of the Amoraim, who explain the expression "offer themselves as proselytes" as meaning "self-made proselytes" [*gerim gerurim*, literally "dragged-in proselytes"]; on this expression see below, in this chapter. [See also Moore, *Judaism*, I, 337f.]

[54] Literally, "ceremonial rules"; the term is used here not in the abstract sense, but in the concrete sense of objects by means of which the ceremonial rules are observed, such as phylacteries, fringes, *mezuzoth*.

[55] Abodah Zarah 3b. This passage provides further evidence that in the Messianic age the Law will continue in force unchanged, including also all the ceremonial rules.

THE INGATHERING OF THE EXILES 481

the ceremonial laws like the Jews could hardly be shown more clearly than in this post-Hadrianic Baraitha. "The Holy One, blessed be He, will sit and laugh" at these light-minded Gentiles, who fail in their very first test, because the Law is for them a heavy yoke, and they are in haste to throw it off.

It is noteworthy that here again the Tannaim are not so far from the prophets—at least from the latest of them. Zechariah 9-14 (Deutero-Zechariah, as this section is usually called) stresses the participation of the Gentiles in the blessings of the Messianic age, speaks especially of their coming to Jerusalem to celebrate the Feast of Tabernacles, and tells us that the Gentile who does not come to celebrate this feast will suffer severe punishment.[56]

Thus the necessity for converted Gentiles to keep the ceremonial laws is something of which the Tannaim are sure. The only question is whether Gentiles will be admitted in the Messianic age as at present; in other words, whether then they will be rated equal in merit to Israelites. For at the present time a proselyte who "has been immersed and has come up again is deemed to be an Israelite in all respects." [57] According to R. Eliezer ben Hyrcanus (pre-Hadrianic), "All of them will become self-made proselytes (*Mitläufer* in German) in the Age to Come" [from ulterior motives].[58] That is to say, the Jews will not receive them willingly, from fear that they were converted only because they wished to take advantage of the good political and economic situation of the Jews in the Messianic age (a suspicion that did not apply to the pre-Messianic age); yet once they are proselytes, they have a share in everything belonging to Israel.[59]

A somewhat later Baraitha goes still farther:

If one sees a place [in Palestine] from which idolatry has been uprooted, he says, "Blessed be He who uprooted idolatry from our land; and as it has

---

[56] Zech. 14:16-19. See above, Part I, p. 205.

[57] Yebamoth 47b. The distinctions between Jews and proselytes enumerated by Schürer (*op. cit.*, III⁴, 186-187) are based solely upon the life of the proselyte while he was still a pagan, before he was converted.

[58] Abodah Zarah 24a.

[59] This follows from the fact that the opinion of R. Eliezer is based upon Zeph. 3:9, where it is plainly said that the Gentiles will not only forsake idolatry, but will serve the LORD "with one consent" [or "shoulder to shoulder"], along with Israel.

been uprooted from this place, so may it be uprooted from all places belonging to Israel; and do Thou turn the heart of those [Jews] that serve them [idols] to serve Thee." But outside Palestine it is not necessary to say, "And do Thou turn the heart of those that serve them to serve Thee," because most of them are Gentiles. R. Simeon ben Yohai [60] says: Even outside Palestine this should be said, because they are destined to become proselytes, as it is written (Zeph. 3:9), "For then will I turn to the peoples a pure language [that they may all call upon the name of the LORD, to serve him with one accord]." [61]

Here nothing whatever is said about special conditions for the admission of proselytes, or about invidious distinctions between proselytes and Israelites on racial grounds.[62] Israelites and proselytes "all" call upon the name of the LORD, and serve Him *"with one consent."* Even in this respect a number of the Tannaim rose to prophetic heights and dreamed of "perfecting the world under the kingdom of the Almighty" (the *Alenu* prayer)—a world without distinction of nationality or language.

[60] The Talmud (Ber. 57b) here has R. Simeon ben Eleazar. But Tosephta, Berakhoth 7 (6):2 (ed. Zuckermandel, p. 14, notes), reads simply "R. Simeon," which ordinarily means R. Simeon ben Yohai. In my opinion Simeon ben Yohai is the better reading, since from this younger disciple of R. Akiba we have a greater number of Messianic sayings of this kind.

[61] Berakhoth 57b; Tosephta, Berakhoth 7(6):2 (with Zuckermandel's notes to his edition of Tosephta).

[62] L. Freund, "Ueber Genealogien und Familienreinheit," etc. (*A. Schwarz-Festschrift*, pp. 179–182), argues convincingly that shortly after the Destruction, in the time of R. Eleazar ben Azariah and R. Akiba, there came about a change for the better in the attitude toward proselytes, a change based on the conditions of the times. But after the downfall of Bar-Cochba, this attitude again became more hostile, partly because of the attitude of the proselytes themselves during and after the revolt. E.g., Judah, the son of proselytes, betrayed R. Simeon ben Yohai to the Romans. See also the article by Israel Levi, "The Attitude of Talmud and Midrash toward Proselytism" [Heb.], *Ha-Goren*, ed. S. A. Horodetzki, IX, 5–30 = *Revue des études juives*, LI (1906), 1–29.

CHAPTER IX

Messiah ben Joseph and the War with Gog and Magog

THE PROBLEM of the source and nature of the idea of *a second Messiah* is a very difficult and complicated one. Rightly did the Italian Jewish scholar, David Castelli, call it "a matter which has led astray wiser men than I." The opinions about the origin of this belief in a Messiah who is not the son of David, but the son of Joseph (in later times also "son of Ephraim" and "son of Manasseh"), are so varied and contradictory that I am compelled, before I state my own opinion, to examine the more acceptable hypotheses of outstanding scholars of the Messianic idea.

It is not necessary to speak at all of the view of those Christian theologians who wish to see in "Messiah ben Joseph" a Messiah who makes atonement for the sins of Israel or of all mankind (a theme found later in the Kabbalistic books, for example, "The Two Tables of the Covenant" by Isaiah Horowitz). For Castelli has already conclusively proved that the death of the Messiah killed in battle has no atoning power whatever.[1] Likewise, it is nowhere said that the function of this Messiah is to restore the Ten Tribes to their own land.[2]

Much more worthy of attention is the original view by one of the

---

[1] See *Il Messia*, pp. 224-229. On p. 228 Castelli says: "In no stage of the tradition is it said that the Messiah son of Joseph must suffer as an expiator of sins; it is only said there that he will die in battle," etc.

[2] *Ibid.*, pp. 233-234, in opposition to W. Bousset, *Der Antichrist*, p. 65.

older Christian scholars, Bertholdt.[3] According to him, this second Messiah came to the Jews from the Samaritans, who, being Ephraimites, called their Messiah "son of Joseph" or "son of Ephraim." This Messiah, who was referred to by the Samaritans as Taëb (meaning "he who returns" [4] or according to others "he who causes to return," that is, one who brings about repentance or brings back better days), is in the later Samaritan sources regarded primarily as a prophet who will restore everywhere the true Law to its former validity and convert all peoples, especially the Jews, to the Samaritan religion. But at the same time he is also a warrior and king, who will overcome Gog and subdue eleven nations. He will not be slain in battle against his enemies, but will die a natural death after fulfilling his mission in the world.[5] According to Bertholdt, the Jews borrowed this Messiah from the Samaritans and changed him into their own "Messiah ben Joseph."

But this view has been opposed by de Wette, Gesenius, Gläsener, Castelli, and Dalman.[6] They rightly conclude that, if we remember how strong was the antagonism between the Jews and Samaritans from the time of Zerubbabel onward, we cannot believe that the Jews would have permitted themselves to add to their own Messiah ben David the Messiah of this detested sect, which Ben-Sira had called "that foolish nation that dwelleth in Shechem" and of which he had said that it was "not a people." [7] Dalman further points out that the course of the Samaritan Messiah's life is completely different from

---

[3] See Bertholdt, *Christologia Judaeorum Jesu apostolorumque aetate*, Erlangae, 1811, pp. 75-81. Cf. Castelli, *op. cit.*, pp. 232-233; Dalman, *Der leidende und sterbende Messias*, p. 16.

[4] So interprets Adalbert Merx, *Ein samaritanisches Fragment über den Taeb oder Messias*, Leiden, 1893, pp. 9, 16-17 ("Taeb can only mean 'the returner' "). But now most scholars translate "the restorer" (Bousset-Gressmann, *Die Religion des Judentums*, 3rd ed., 1926, pp. 224-225); see for details J. A. Montgomery, *The Samaritans*, Philadelphia, 1907, pp. 239-251: M. Haran, "The Conception of the 'Taheb' in the Samaritan Religion" [Heb.], *Tarbits*, XXIII (1942), 96-111.

[5] See Montgomery, *op. cit.*, pp. 243-245; Merx, *op. cit.*, pp. 11-12, 16-19. Bibliography on this Messiah in Schürer, *Geschichte*, II[4], 608, Note 33; Haran, *op. cit.*, pp. 97-100. H. Hammer, *Traktat vom Samaritanermessias*, Bonn, 1913, is not really concerned with the Samaritan Messiah, but with Jesus, who is represented by the author as a Samaritan Messiah.

[6] Cf. Castelli, *op. cit.*, pp. 232-233; Dalman, *op. cit.*, p. 16.

[7] Ben-Sira (Hebrew) 50:25-26.

that of Messiah ben Joseph. For, while the latter dies in battle, "the Messiah of the Samaritan dies only because he is a mortal man." [8]

David Castelli [9] thinks that the idea of this Messiah came into being because of a desire to placate the Ten Tribes by recognizing a Messiah of theirs, but only a temporary Messiah who would eventually fall in battle. Thus the implication would remain that true and final victory would come only through the Messiah of the house of David. Dalman [10] opposes this view and answers it rightly by saying that new and important doctrines, like that of a second Messiah, could not have arisen merely for the purpose of appeasing tribes which were far away and deemed as good as lost.[11]

According to James Drummond,[12] the belief in a second Messiah arose from Zechariah 12, because it was difficult to harmonize the defeat and death of the King-Messiah as described in this chapter with the Jewish Messianic idea as a whole. In this Drummond agrees with the opinion of Wünsche.[13] There was the possibility [according to Drummond] that the Jews would imagine a second Messiah; for "the northern tribes, as well as the Judahites, could have had a Messiah; and the legislator of the Age to Come could have been conceived to have, like Moses, someone to share in this work."

To this I reply that as a rule (with exceptions, of course) *a passage of Scripture* (unless it indicates a certain fact with complete clarity) *does not create a new idea; but the new idea, which is already emerging, finds proof and support in the Scriptural passage.* Therefore, Zechariah 12 is not the cause of the belief in a second Messiah; but, on the contrary, since a belief in Messiah ben Joseph was already current, the Tannaim were forced to interpret Zechariah 12 in a Messianic sense. The fact is to be noted that, according to Justin Martyr's *Dia-*

---

[8] See Dalman, *op. cit.*, p. 16, and Merx, *op. cit.*, p. 16.
[9] *Op. cit.*, pp. 234–236
[10] *Op. cit.*, p. 16.
[11] J. L. Katzenelson attempted to prove in various articles (e.g., his Russian article "Vavilonskoye Plyeneniye," *Voskhod*, March, 1902, pp. 126–139) that the Ten Tribes of the Assyrian exile came into closer contact with the Judahites after the destruction of the First Temple; and hence it is possible that these tribes influenced the Messianic belief of the Jews.
[12] *The Jewish Messiah*, I, 357.
[13] *Die Leiden des Messias*, pp. 109–110.

logue with Trypho the Jew, this chapter is not among the Biblical passages which were interpreted Messianically by the Jews in the time of Justin (*c.* 150 C.E.). And when Drummond imagines Messiah ben Joseph as assisting in the work of the "legislator," this is an unhistorical idea; for in all early Hebrew literature, prophetic and Tannaitic, there is no mention of any "legislative" work of the Messiah.

Jacob Levy [14] says of Messiah ben Joseph:

> The legend of the warrior Messiah probably owes its origin to the uprising of the Jews in the time of the Emperor Hadrian, under the leadership of the revolutionary chieftain, Bar-Cochba, to whose cause a large part of the Jews adhered, and whom R. Akiba expressly proclaimed as the expected Messiah. Then, in order that the Jews, because of their disillusionment and the ignominious downfall of that chieftain and his adherents, might not altogether reject belief in the Messiah, also partly to save the reputation of R. Akiba, the greatest Torah teacher of that time, it was asserted that the Messiahship of that chieftain had consisted in the fact that he, as the forerunner of the true Messiah, had waged these glorious wars, but himself should die a hero's death in battle; and that only after these preliminary events would the appearance of the Davidic Messiah be possible.

I have quoted Levy's words without abridgment because they contain truth and falsehood mixed and intermingled together. The kernel of truth is surrounded by a thick husk, which is hard to strip away. The artificiality in this opinion is easily recognized.[15] It is still the old rationalistic point of view, according to which an article of faith can be intentionally created *ad hoc*. Actually, belief in a second Messiah could have arisen in the consciousness of the people, or of their best representatives, only from a deep inner need, from religio-psychological motives; and not in order to save the Messianic faith or R. Akiba's reputation. Moreover, it cannot be imagined that Bar-Cochba, after the tragic fall of Bethar, could have been made into "the forerunner of the true Messiah"; rather, at that time the disillusionment was so dreadful that within a comparatively brief

---

[14] *Neuhebr. Wörterbuch*, III, 271 (article "Māshîaḥ"). Cf. Hamburger, *Realenzyclopaedie des Judentums*, II, 768; Supplement, pp. 123-136.

[15] Merx, *op. cit.*, p. 20, has already noticed this.

period he was branded as almost a blasphemer.[16] And why Bar-Cochba ("son of the star") should become ben-Joseph ("son of Joseph") is not explained by Levy at all. It is also possible to make the same objection against Levy which Dalman [17] has brought against Hamburger: Nowhere is there the slightest hint that the Jews continued to believe in the Messiahship of Bar-Cochba after he was slain.

Dalman himself [18] agrees with Drummond and Wünsche that it was Zechariah 12 that called forth belief in a second Messiah. But Dalman explains the fact that this second Messiah was depicted as the son of Joseph, as an Ephraimite, by connecting the Blessing of Moses with this Messiah; he calls particular attention to Deut. 33:17, where it is said of the tribe of Joseph, "His firstling bullock, majesty is his; and his horns are the horns of the wild-ox; with them he shall gore the peoples," and so on. For in various Midrashim this verse is applied to Messiah ben Joseph. According to Dalman, this verse, in conjunction with Zech. 12:10, 12 ("And they shall look unto him [19] whom they have pierced, and they shall mourn for him as one mourneth for his only son. . . . And the land shall mourn, every family apart"), must have brought into being the conception of a second Messiah, from the house of Joseph, a Messiah that would be slain.[20]

Against this can be raised the objection lodged above against the first part of the Drummond-Wünsche hypothesis: In Judaism, obscure Biblical verses have never brought into being completely new doctrines; it is only that *doctrines already in existence* are supported and confirmed by such verses. But, apart from this, all the Midrashim cited by Dalman as applying Deut. 33:17 to Messiah ben Joseph are late in time (not prior to the sixth century C.E.); and therefore they cannot solve the problem of the *origin* of the conception of a second Messiah—at least not in a decisive manner.

[16] Yerushalmi, Taanith 4:8; Lam. R. 2:2.
[17] *Op. cit.*, p. 21.
[18] *Ibid.*, pp. 17–18.
[19] Instead of "unto me" older editions of the Talmud read "unto him" (see *Dikduke Sopherim* on Sukkah 52a). Cf. Wünsche, *op. cit.*, p. 52, note. See above, p. 204.
[20] Dalman, *op. cit.*, pp. 19–20.

Somewhat akin to the opinions of Castelli, Drummond, and Levy, but much closer to the truth, is the view of Meir Friedmann [Ish-Shalom in Hebrew]. Friedmann repeatedly emphasizes that the belief in Messiah ben Joseph existed "among the remnants of the Ephraimite kingdom; and just as in Judah they hoped for Messiah ben David, so in the rest of the tribes they hoped for Messiah ben Joseph of the seed of Ephraim." [21] And at the time of Bar-Cochba this belief spread throughout all Israel. For out of the wars of Bar-Cochba arose among the Ephraimites the belief that this Messiah [Bar-Cochba] was ben-Joseph, and only after him could Messiah ben David come.

This opinion agrees most closely with that of Levy and Hamburger; except that Friedmann (likewise Merx) has the advantage over these two in that according to his view Bar-Cochba was not proclaimed Messiah ben Joseph for the specific purpose of saving a tottering Messianic faith or the reputation of R. Akiba. But some of the objections brought against Levy and Hamburger can also be directed against Friedmann. The disillusionment after the downfall of Bar-Cochba was so great that it cannot be imagined that his Messiahship was recognized after his untimely death. Nor is there any trace of such a belief in the whole Talmudic and Midrashic literature. Moreover, it still remains unproved that the Ten Tribes had a Messiah of their own. Friedmann makes no mention at all of the Samaritans and their "Taëb." Or does he perhaps refer to them when he speaks of "the remnants of the Ephraimite kingdom"? But how could a belief of these half-Jews have gained a foothold among the Jews in the very time of Bar-Cochba, when, as we know well, the hatred between Jews and "Cutheans" reached its height? [22]

[21] See Introduction to Seder Eliyahu, p. 9, note; p. 20, and p. 22, note. The view of Merx is very similar: "In order to explain the doctrine of two Messiahs, it must be supposed that there were two different Messianic genealogies, which belonged to different times, places, or schools, and were later combined" (*op. cit.*, pp. 20-21).

[22] Graetz, *Geschichte der Juden*, IV, 150-151 (Heb. trans. by S. P. Rabbinowitz, II, 229, 241, 246-247). See J. Klausner, "The Ethiopic Book of Baruch" [Heb.], *Ha-Shiloah*, VIII, 1901, pp. 242-243; *idem*, *When a Nation Fights for Its Freedom* [Heb.], pp. 181-183. This objection is also valid against the opinion of Merx. Before the time of Bar-Cochba no trace of a second Messiah can be found (see below). See also R. Eisler, *Iesous Basileus*, II (1929), 44-45, Note 7. Eisler found

Two further opinions about Messiah ben Joseph must be mentioned:

Hugo Gressmann [23] has tried to find this Messiah ben Joseph in Hyrcanus ben Joseph ben Tobias, who killed himself in the days of Antiochus Epiphanes.[24] But it seems to me that, except for the name "ben Joseph," the two have nothing in common.

Wilhelm Bousset [25] thinks that the material concerning Messiah ben Joseph was derived from the legends about Alexander the Great. But the points of similarity are very slight, and the Alexander legends themselves arose only at a very late date, most of them coming from late Arabic sources.[26]

Before I present my own opinion on this complex problem, I wish to examine Talmudic passages referring to Messiah ben Joseph that are of undoubted Tannaitic origin.

Unquestionably Tannaitic is, first of all, this Baraitha:

The Holy One, blessed be He, will say to the Messiah, the son of David (May he reveal himself speedily in our days!): "Ask of Me anything, and I will give it to thee, as it is said (Ps. 2:7–8), 'I will tell of the decree: the LORD said unto me: Thou art My son, this day have I begotten thee; ask of Me, and I will give the nations for thine inheritance.'" But when he (Messiah ben David) sees that Messiah ben Joseph is slain,[27] he will say to Him: "Lord of the Universe, I ask of Thee only the gift of life." He (God) will answer him: "Life?—Before you spoke, your father David has already prophesied of you, as it is written (Ps. 21:5), 'He asked life of Thee, Thou gavest it him, even length of days forever and ever.'" [28]

---

him in the Testaments of the Twelve Patriarchs; but the text which he quotes is an obvious Christian forgery and very peculiar.

[23] See H. Gressmann, "Die ammonitischen Tobiaden" (*Sitzungsberichte der Berliner Akademie*, July 1921, XXXIX, 670ff.).

[24] See on him in detail J. Klausner, "The Author of the Book of Koheleth" (*The Second Temple in Its Days of Glory* [Heb.], pp. 160–175).

[25] See Bousset-Gressmann, *op. cit.*, p. 231.

[26] See also G. Kittel, *Die Probleme des palästinischen Spätjudentums und das Urchristentum*, 1926, pp. 84–85.

[27] Wünsche (*op. cit.*, pp. 64–65) at this point wrongly exchanged subject and predicate, and so translated that Messiah ben Joseph *himself* saw that he would be slain; and from this erroneous translation he drew such far-fetched conclusions that finally he was forced to renounce them along with the erroneous translation.

[28] Sukkah 52a.

Messiah ben Joseph is referred to here only incidentally, but it is most interesting that his existence and his violent death are considered as matters known to all.

The next passage, which immediately precedes the above Baraitha, reads as follows:

"And the land shall mourn, every family apart; the family of the house of David apart, and their wives apart" (Zech. 12:12). . . . What is the cause of this mourning? R. Dosa and Our Teachers [*Rabbanan*] differ on the point. One said, The cause is the slaying of Messiah ben Joseph, and another said, The cause is the slaying of the evil inclination.—It is well with him who said the cause is the slaying of Messiah ben Joseph, for that agrees with the verse (Zech. 12:10), "And they shall look upon him [29] whom they have pierced, and they shall mourn for him as one mourneth for his only son." [30]

This passage is not a Baraitha. I strongly emphasize this point, since it has not been noticed by Castelli, Drummond, Wünsche, or Dalman. The general style of the passage, and also the Aramaic language of the introductory question, leave no doubt that we have here *an Amoraic transmission of a Tannaitic interpretation*. The Amora who transmitted the interpretation did not even know which of the Tannaim applied Zechariah 12:12 to Messiah ben Joseph and which applied it to the evil inclination; hence he took refuge in the vague expression "One said . . . another said." Thus we do not know whether R. Dosa applied the verse in Zechariah to Messiah ben Joseph or to the evil inclination.

It is quite possible that the Messianic interpretation of this verse came from the later Tannaim ("Our Teachers"). That there are grounds for this supposition is shown by the parallel passage in the Palestinian Talmud, which reads:

Two Amoraim (disputed on the matter). One said, This is the mourning over Messiah.— The other said, This is the mourning over the evil inclination.[31]

---

[29] See above, p. 487, Note 19.
[30] Sukkah 52a.
[31] Yerushalmi, Succah 8:2.

Here two Amoraim express exactly the same opinions which the Babylonian Talmud attributes to R. Dosa and "Our Teachers"; but the names of the Amoraim are not given.

It is very difficult in this case to find a means of fixing even an approximate date. For even if we seize, as other writers have done, upon the name of R. Dosa, and regard *him* as the author of the Messianic interpretation of the verse in Zechariah, it is still not easy for us to determine the date of this R. Dosa. On the one hand, it follows from one Talmudic passage that R. Dosa was much older than R. Joshua ben Hananiah, R. Eleazar ben Azariah, and R. Akiba.[32] According to this, he would still belong to the generation of R. Johanan ben Zakkai, who had known the Temple before its destruction.[33] On the other hand, one of R. Akiba's younger disciples, R. Judah ben Ilai, places R. Dosa in "the later generations" in contrast to the school of Shammai, which is referred to as "the earlier generations." [34] According to this, R. Dosa lived at a time much later than the school of Shammai, which still existed in the days of R. Joshua ben Hananiah, the disciple of R. Johanan ben Zakkai.[35] Finally, in two Talmudic passages are recorded disputes between R. Judah and R. Dosa;[36] and in another passage a R. Dosa transmits a ruling in the name of R. Judah.[37]

On the basis of all this, Zechariah Frankel [38] and Wilhelm Bacher [39] think that there were *two* Tannaim by the name of Dosa. The younger of these, according to Bacher, lived in the period immediately after the Hadrianic persecution, and was the author of the saying about "the slaying of Messiah ben Joseph" (or "of the evil inclina-

---

[32] Yebamoth 16a.
[33] Weiss, *Each Generation* [Heb.], I³, 173; Frankel, *Ways of the Mishnah* [Heb.], pp. 74-75.
[34] Gittin 81a; cf. Frankel, *op. cit.*, p. 75, Note 3.
[35] R. Joshua could still carry on a discussion with a student from the school of Shammai (Hagigah 22b). See Frankel, *op. cit.*, pp. 93-94.
[36] Yoma 12b; Baba Kamma 49a.
[37] Zebahim 88b. But in *Dikduke Sopherim* the words "in the name of R. Judah" are lacking; see A. Hyman, *History of Tannaim and Amoraim* [Heb.], London, 1910, section on R. Dosa, I, 323.
[38] *Op. cit.*, p. 75, Note 5.
[39] *Agada der Tannaiten*, II, 389-390 (Heb. trans., II, 84).

tion").⁴⁰ In my opinion, this is close to the truth; yet it is also possible that the R. Dosa in the disputes about Messiah ben Joseph *versus* the evil inclination is the Amora Rab Dosa (A Palestinian Amora of the third or fourth generation, in the fourth century C.E.).⁴¹ This would account for the fact that the Palestinian Talmud speaks of "two Amoraim" instead of "R. Dosa and Our Teachers." And "Our Teachers" would here refer to Amoraim and not Tannaim. In any case, even if this saying about Messiah ben Joseph is Tannaitic, it is not so early as Castelli supposed.⁴²

But even if we attribute this saying to the older R. Dosa (ben Hurkinas), we are still not forced to regard the idea of a second Messiah as pre-Hadrianic. For on one occasion, when the older R. Dosa saw R. Akiba, he said to him, "You are Akiba ben Joseph, whose name is known from one end of the world to the other!" ⁴³ R. Dosa was still living, therefore, at the time of R. Akiba's greatest fame. Akiba's name was "known from one end of the world to the other" only after he had visited the Jews in distant lands, arousing their enthusiasm in support of the revolt of Bar-Cochba.⁴⁴ If R. Dosa lived until that time, it is possible that he also witnessed the swift fall of Bar-Cochba and the Hadrianic persecution that followed. Thus the saying about Messiah ben Joseph, if it really came from R. Dosa (which seems doubtful), could still have been delivered after the Hadrianic persecution.

We hold, therefore, to the opinion that the Baraitha and the immediately preceding section concerning Messiah ben Joseph were delivered after the fall of Bethar. With this opinion Jacob Levy, Hamburger, and M. Friedmann are in agreement, as we have seen. Dalman ⁴⁵ also agrees on this point. The point of time, the "when," is established and agreed upon. Only this question remains: *How* did the idea of a twofold Messiah arise; and *why* is the second Messiah called "son of Joseph"?

---

⁴⁰ *Ibid.*, II, 389 (Heb., II, 84).
⁴¹ A. Hyman, *op. cit.*, I, 324–325.
⁴² See Castelli, *op. cit.*, p. 227.
⁴³ Yebamoth 16a.
⁴⁴ See above, pp. 474–475.
⁴⁵ *Op. cit.*, p. 23.

It seems to me that the idea of a twofold Messiah inevitably arose from the conception of *the twofold character of the essentially single Messiah*. I have already indicated above [46] that *the Jewish Messiah was never thought of as exclusively spiritual*. That is to say, he would never have been satisfied with a purely spiritual dominion. Even a person so deeply reflective and so thoroughly ethical as Philo of Alexandria cannot imagine a purely spiritual Messiah. Philo says of the Messiah:

For "there shall come forth a man" says the oracle (Num. 24:7, LXX), and leading his host to war he will subdue great and populous nations, because God has sent to his aid the reinforcement which befits the godly; and that is dauntless courage of soul and all-powerful strength of body, either of which strikes fear into the enemy, and the two if united are quite irresistible. . . . For the conduct of their rulers shows three high qualities which contribute to make a government secure from subversion: namely, dignity (or holiness), strictness (or might), and benevolence (σεμνότητα καὶ δεινότητα καὶ εὐεργεσίαν), which produce the feelings mentioned above. For respect is created by dignity, fear by strictness, and affection by benevolence; and these when blended harmoniously in the soul render subjects obedient to their rulers.[47]

Thus throughout the earlier periods of the Messianic idea, Israel's best minds thought of the Messiah as *a king and a warrior*. Like any ordinary king, the Messiah must lead his assembled people in the last battle and bring them to victory over foes who had afflicted and oppressed Israel as no other nation had ever been afflicted and oppressed. All this is so entirely natural throughout the periods of Assyrian, Babylonian, Persian, and Roman control, that we find the idea of a great and final Messianic battle in the prophetic books of Amos and Ezekiel as well as in the Targums. We shall see below that the war with Gog and Magog is already mentioned by the earliest Tannaim. The Messiah must, therefore, be a military hero in the fullest sense of the term.

In direct contrast to this view, with its marked political coloring, was another widespread conception, which found support in Isaiah

---

[46] See above, pp. 392–398.
[47] Philo, *On Rewards and Punishments*, Chap. 16, Sect. 95–97 (M., II, 423–424; C.-W., V, 357–358); [translation adapted from Colson, Loeb Library, Philo VIII. 371–373]. Cf. Schürer, *op. cit.*, II⁴, 601–603.

11 and Zechariah 12. According to this, there is only a spiritual and ethical Messiah, who is free from sin, full of wisdom, kindness and piety, humble and lowly in all his works, and saintly and pure in all his ways. This picture of a purely spiritual Messiah hovered not only before the eyes of the prophets, but also before the authors of the Psalms of Solomon and IV Ezra; also before the greatest of the Tannaim. All of these, with their high morality and exalted piety, had reached a spiritual height from which all political activity seemed of secondary importance, and war with its bloodshed as a gross evil. How could all these "humble of the earth" [Ps. 76:10] look upon the godly Messiah as a man of vengeance and a shedder of blood, as simply a military hero who would vanquish his foes with murderous weapons—they, who already regarded weapons of war as a disgrace to humanity! [48]

Thus this inner contradiction between the political and the spiritual Messiah was inherent in the Jewish conception of the Messiah from the earliest times. But as long as the political tendency dominated Jewish thought and feeling (that is to say, from the destruction of the Second Temple to the fall of Bethar,[49] this contradiction was not readily apparent. The unhappy people, robbed of freedom, persecuted and afflicted to the point of death by the Romans, longed for vengeance on their enemies and for political independence. Thus it came about that R. Akiba could join himself to a *purely political* Messiah who was distinguished for no spiritual qualities whatever; and could devote himself to Bar-Cochba with all the ardor of his great soul. Only after the bitter disillusionment that came with the fall of Bethar and the untimely death of both Bar-Cochba and R. Akiba, only after the political hope of redemption by war and weapons had been dashed by historical events themselves—only then was the contradiction described above felt with full force. Then the spiritual and religio-ethical tendency in the Messianic faith inevitably gained the upper hand. Consequently, this question was raised: How can sword and bow, which could bring death to the Messiah, as happened to

---

[48] Mishnah, Shabbath 6:4. For details on this see the beginning of the next chapter, p. 502.
[49] See above, pp. 392–399.

Bar-Cochba, R. Akiba's Messiah, be the instruments of God's Messiah? In other words, why must he, the Holy and Elect One, whose name preceded the creation of the world,[50] have recourse to the power of warlike weapons, like an ordinary military leader among the heathen?

Near at hand lay this idea: The *twofold character* of the Messiah should be transformed into a *twofold Messiah*. And this was achieved by transferring to a second Messiah the function of waging war in its entirety. Therefore this second Messiah is a warrior-Messiah exclusively, and is more frequently referred to in the later Midrashic literature as "the one anointed for war" (*meshuaḥ milḥamah*).[51] Dalman has rightly remarked: "The entire activity of the Messiah ben Joseph has a significance almost exclusively political." [52]

Once a second Messiah became necessary, he could come from no other tribe than from the tribe of Joseph. The first Messiah was regarded as the son of David, and thus as coming from Judah. What else, then, could the second Messiah be except a son of Joseph or of Ephraim? There is no need whatever to assume here any borrowing from the Ten Tribes (Friedmann) or from the Samaritans (Bertholdt). However, the possibility of such borrowing from the latter, once the psychological need for a second Messiah had been felt, cannot be ruled out; for we learn *consciously* only from our friends, but *unconsciously* from our enemies also. But we cannot assume a desire to placate the Ten Tribes (Castelli), who were either lost altogether or dispersed in distant lands. So, once the necessity of a second Messiah was admitted, he could not be described in any other way: there were only two predominant tribes in Israel, and if "the great redeemer" (as Messiah ben David is called in one place),[53] comes from the tribe of Judah, then his junior colleague must be "son of Joseph," that is, from the tribe of Ephraim.[54]

[50] See above, pp. 460–461.
[51] This is discussed by Levy, *op. cit.*, III, 270b–271a. There Levy has quoted the most important passages in Midrashic literature concerning "the one anointed for war." Cf. Dalman, *op. cit.*, pp. 6–7.
[52] *Op. cit.*, p. 23.
[53] Num. R., Chap. 14, beginning.
[54] Cf. Ezekiel's allegory of the Two Sticks (37:15–22), in which "the stick of Joseph, which is in the hand of Ephraim, and the tribes of Israel his companions," stands on a par with "the stick of Judah." See also Merx, *op. cit.*, pp. 20–22.

Likewise, it is not difficult to explain why this second Messiah must be slain. An early Talmudic maxim asks, "Is it possible for two kings to wear one crown?" [55] So the crown of the Messianic king could not be divided. And naturally the lesser had to give way to the greater.

Now it is highly probable that at this point the heroic death of Bar-Cochba in his struggle with the enemies of Israel, after a brief period as prince and conqueror, provided an example that gave rise to the conception of a Messiah from the tribe of Joseph, who at first is victorious, but later falls in battle. This is not to say that Bar-Cochba himself was ever thought to be Messiah ben Joseph (as supposed by Levy, Hamburger, and in part by Friedmann); for that we have no evidence. But it is not to be denied that the events of Bar-Cochba's time made a powerful impression on all Jews, especially on the Tannaim of R. Akiba's school (and most of the outstanding post-Hadrianic Tannaim had belonged to this school). Therefore it is likely that the Messianic thinking of these men was influenced by these depressing events; but it is of course not necessary to assume that the events were consciously or intentionally brought into connexion with Messianic speculation.

Tannaitic passages referring to Messiah ben Joseph are so few and brief that we can determine from them only the untimely death of this Messiah. Where and when this will occur, and what Messiah ben Joseph will do in general are not recorded. But in the relatively early Targum,[56] it is clearly asserted that Messiah ben Ephraim will, in the latter days, conquer Gog, the mighty enemy of Israel. In the post-Tannaitic literature this idea is found frequently.[57] A hint that the wars of the Messianic age are to be waged not by Messiah ben

---

[55] Hullin 60b.

[56] The Targum Pseudo-Jonathan, Ex. 40:11 (see also 40:2); Jerusalem Targum ("Fragment Targum"), Num. 11:23 (see also Targum Jonathan, *ibid.*).

[57] In the very late Midrashim (Midrash Wayosha, Sepher Zerubbabel, Secrets of R. Simeon ben Yohai, Signs of the Messiah—see *Minor Midrashim* [Heb.], ed. S. Asaf, Odessa, 1919; *Treasury of Midrashim* [Heb.] by J. D. Eisenstein, 2 vols., New York, 1915; Judah Ibn-Shmuel (Kaufman), *Midrashim of Redemption* [Heb.], Tel-Aviv, 1943), Messiah ben Joseph (or ben Ephraim—also called Nehemiah ben Hushiel) fights not against Gog and Magog (to be conquered by Messiah ben David), but against Armilus, who is the "Antichrist"; but since Armilus is not mentioned at all in Tannaitic sources, he can be ignored here.

David himself, but by a Messiah who precedes him, is already present in the Baraitha of R. Simeon ben Yohai quoted above:[58] "In the seventh (year of 'the week [seven-year period] when the son of David comes'), wars; and at the end of the seventh year, the son of David will come." Messiah ben David will come, therefore, *after* the wars. It likewise follows from another passage, also quoted above,[59] that the Messianic age itself comes after "the wars of the dragons" and after the war with Gog and Magog. The military commander in these great battles can be none other than Messiah ben Joseph.

On this basis it is easily possible to clarify the contradictions in the Talmudic literature with regard to the war with Gog and Magog—whether it comes at the beginning or at the end of the Messianic age.[60] It comes after the Messianic age has begun; for Messiah ben Joseph, the first in time but the second in rank of the two Messiahs, is already present at the time of this war. But the Messianic age reaches its *culmination* only *after* the war with Gog and Magog, when Messiah ben David appears in all his glory.

With regard to the war with Gog and Magog itself, it is to be noted that this legendary war is mentioned in the earliest Tannaitic literature. Gog and Magog (instead of "Gog of the land of Magog," as in Ezekiel 38:2) play the part of *a collective anti-Messiah*.[61] I have already had occasion to quote the two consecutive passages in Mekhilta, in which the pre-Hadrianic Tanna R. Eliezer ben Hyrcanus says that if Israel succeeds in keeping the Sabbath, they will be saved "from the day of Gog and Magog."[62] The following passage also appears to be pre-Hadrianic:

"I did not reject them" (Lev. 26:44)—in the days of Vespasian; "I did not abhor them"—in the days of the Greeks (that is, of Antiochus Epiphanes); nor "destroy them utterly . . . to break My covenant with them"—in the days of Haman; "I am the LORD their God"—in the days of Gog.[63]

---

[58] See above, p. 445.
[59] See above, p. 422.
[60] See F. Weber, *System der altsyn. palästin. Theologie*, pp. 369–371.
[61] See M. Friedländer, *Der Antichrist*, pp. 171-173.
[62] See above, p. 450, where is quoted a similar saying by the semi-Tanna Bar Kappara.
[63] Siphra, Behuqqothai, Chap. 2 (ed. Weiss, 112b). This passage appears to me

Note that the persecution by Hadrian is not mentioned.

Who will fight this war with Gog is stated neither here nor in the post-Hadrianic sayings of this kind. The following seems to indicate that *God Himself* will wage these battles:

> There are four "shinings forth": the first was in Egypt, as it is written (Ps. 80:2), "Give ear, O Shepherd of Israel, Thou that leadest Joseph like a flock, Thou that art enthroned upon the cherubim, *shine forth*"; the second was at the time of the giving of the Law, as it is written (Deut. 33:2), "He *shone forth* from Mount Paran"; the third will take place *in the days of Gog and Magog*, as it is written (Ps. 94:1), ". . . Thou God to whom vengeance belongeth, *shine forth*"; the fourth will be in the Days of the Messiah (ben David), as it is written (Ps. 50:2), "Out of Zion, the perfection of beauty, shall God *shine forth*." [64]

Another Baraitha says:

> Ten times did the Shekhinah descend upon the world . . . and in the future it will be so once *in the days of Gog and Magog*, as it is written (Zech. 14:4), "And His feet shall stand in that day upon the Mount of Olives." [65]

The prophet Elijah will also appear in the days of Gog and Magog,[66] but for what purpose is not known. We can conclude with reasonable certainty that in the pre-Hadrianic period it was believed that Messiah ben David would, with the aid of the Shekhinah, fight against and overcome the enemies of Israel; but in the post-Hadrianic period, the fighting was attributed to Messiah ben Joseph, who, after a great but not decisive victory, would have to be slain. The final and decisive victory, which God Himself would bring about, would give the crown to Messiah ben David alone, as sole king of the Davidic dynasty.

Interesting details about the war in the Messianic age are already found in the Tannaitic literature. But in the post-Tannaitic period everything concerning this war is so overlaid with the colored embroidery of imagination that the originality of the older tradition is

---

very old, since Megillah 11a gives it in expanded form, with an added explanation in the form of a Baraitha.

[64] Siphre, Deut., 343 (ed. Friedmann, 143a).

[65] Aboth de R. Nathan, A, Chap. 34, ed. Schechter, p. 102, and Note 32 (cf. B, Chap. 37, ed. Schechter, p. 49).

[66] Seder Olam Rabbah, Chap. 17.

lost. A relatively early and widely accepted Tannaitic view was that God had already revealed to Moses the defeat of Gog and Magog.[67] According to R. Nehemiah,[68] one of the younger disciples of R. Akiba, Eldad and Medad (Numbers 11:26) prophesied concerning the war with Gog and Magog,

as it is written (Ezek. 38:17), "Thus saith the LORD God: Art thou he of whom I spoke in old time by My servants the prophets of Israel, that prophesied in those days [for many] years that I would bring thee against them?" and so on. Read not *shanim* (years) but *shnayim* (two). And which two prophets prophesied the same thing at the same time? Eldad and Medad, of course.[69]

Another of R. Akiba's disciples, R. Simeon ben Yohai, compares the war with Gog and Magog with the worst evils that can come upon mankind:

Viciousness[70] in a man's own household is worse than the war with Gog and Magog. For it is said (Ps. 3:1), "A Psalm of David, when he fled from Absalom his son"; and next it is written (Ps. 3:2), "LORD, how many are mine adversaries become! Many are they that rise up against me." Now in regard to the war with Gog and Magog it is written (Ps. 2:1), "Why are the nations in an uproar? And why do the peoples mutter in vain?"— but it is not written, "How many are mine adversaries become!"[71]

This, however, is not even a tradition of the schools, but only a chance homily, delivered *ad hoc*.

More firmly founded on early tradition are, *first*, the saying of R. Akiba, which even found a place in the Mishnah, that "the judgment of Gog and Magog in the future to come shall endure twelve months";[72] *second*, the tradition, for which Scriptural support [Deut.

---

[67] Mekhilta, Amalek, Chap. 2 (ed. Friedmann, 55b and 56a); Siphre, Deut., 357 (ed. Friedmann, 149b, beginning).

[68] So we must read instead of "R. Nahman" (see Bacher, *op. cit.*, II, 235, Note 3 —Heb. trans., Vol. II, Part I, p. 162 and Note 43 on p. 165). This confusion of "Nehemiah" with "Nahman" occurs frequently: e.g., San. 12a; Lev. R., Chap. 18, end; Deut. R., Chap. 5, beginning; Pesiqta R., Chap. 3, end.

[69] Sanhedrin 17a. Cf. Jer. Targum, Num. 11:26; Num. R., Chap. 15; Tanhuma, Beha'alothekha, 12; Tanhuma, ed. Buber, Beha'alothekha, 22, f. 29.

[70] I.e., an untrained child, a son who is ill mannered. See Levy, *op. cit.*, IV, 667a.

[71] Berakhoth 7b.

[72] Eduyyoth 2:10. The conclusion of Schürer (*op. cit.*, II⁴, 622, also Note 35) from this Mishnah, that Gog and Magog will appear "only after the end of the Messianic kingdom as a last manifestation of the demonic powers," is not really

34:3] is claimed, that "Gog and all his multitude are destined to come up and fall in the valley of Jericho." [73] But before their fall, these strong and numerous foes will cast such terror upon the Jews who have returned from exile, that after the Jews have been saved from these foes they will no longer remember the deliverance from the bondage in Egypt—for the deliverance from Gog and Magog "and all his multitude" will seem to them much more marvelous. This is explained by R. Simeon ben Yoḥai, some of whose Messianic sayings have already been quoted, in a beautiful parable:

To what can it be compared? To a man who was traveling along the road. He encountered a wolf and was saved from him. So he kept on telling the story of the wolf. Then he encountered a lion and was saved from him. So he forgot the story of the wolf and kept on telling the story of the lion.

So it will be with Israel. After they have been delivered from the fearful battles with Gog and Magog, they will no longer remember their escape from the burdens of Egypt, but only their deliverance from the terrible agonies of the *last* wars.[74] For the miseries that will come upon Israel on account of the Messianic wars will be so terrible that the Talmud mentions them, as we have already seen above,[75] alongside "the Messianic birth pangs," of which these miseries will perhaps be only a part.

Who will stand at Israel's head as commander in these wars is, as was said before, not made clear in the authentic Tannaitic literature (apart from the Targum attributed to Jonathan, of about 300 C.E.,

---

based on this Mishnah. For the words "in the future to come" (*le'atid labo'*) refer simply to the Messianic age, as was shown above, pp. 415–418; moreover, in early editions of the Mishnah the word "to come" (*labo'*) is lacking (see *Dikduke Sopherim*, X, on Eduyyoth 2:10).

[73] Mekhilta, Amalek, Chap. 2 (ed. Friedmann, 55b and 56a); Siphre, Deut., 357 (ed. Friedmann, 149b, beginning). In Mekhilta this saying is introduced by the expression "And we have learned" (and in Siphre by "It is taught"); thus we have here a still earlier tradition.

[74] Cf. Mekhilta, Pisḥa, Chap. 16 (ed. Friedmann, 19a, beginning), with Berakhoth 13a, where this same parable occurs, with the addition of a third danger—an encounter with a serpent (likewise in Yer. Ber., end of Chap. 1, f. 4a [also in some Mekhilta texts; see Lauterbach's ed., *ad loc.*, I, 133]). The passage in Berakhoth 13a is introduced by the phrase "R. Joseph learnt"; hence it is to a certain extent a Baraitha, though only a late one.

[75] See above, p. 450.

and the still later Jerusalem Targum of about 650 C.E.). The older tradition wavers between God Himself and Messiah ben David as the conqueror of Gog and Magog. The later tradition wavers between Messiah ben David and Messiah ben Joseph; for it must be definitely borne in mind that belief in Messiah ben Joseph was not held by all of Israel's sages by any means, and that this belief was much less widely current among the people than the belief in Messiah ben David.[76]

This belief in Messiah ben Joseph arose from the logical contradiction between "redeemer" and "king." Hence those who saw God Himself as the military commander, or those who had not yet perceived the yawning gulf between "salvation" and "warfare" (note the modern self-contradictory name "Salvation Army")—such as these could get along very well without the fighting and dying Messiah. This was all the more possible for them because the Tannaim did not praise Messiah ben Joseph overmuch, and in general did not attribute to him any characteristics out of the ordinary. He was simply a great and noble warrior, who goes to death for the good of his people and is slain on the field of battle in the manner of Bar-Cochba. Such a hero could not be the ideal for a people which, after the fall of Bethar, no longer engaged in war and was far removed from political activity. Therefore Messiah ben Joseph could not for long occupy an equal position alongside the highly regarded and glorified Messiah ben David, who "shall smite the land with the rod of his mouth, and with the breath of his lips shall he slay the wicked" [Isa. 11:4]. Only such sanguinary events as the Arab wars of the seventh and eighth centuries and the Crusades of the twelfth century could revive the belief in a second Messiah.[77] In more peaceful times this Messiah holds no significant place in Judaism.

[76] See Dalman, *op. cit.*, p. 24.
[77] See Judah Ibn-Shmuel (Kaufman), *op. cit.*, pp. 50–55.

CHAPTER X

The Messianic Age and the Signs of the Messiah

AFTER THE destruction of Israel's last enemies, the actual Messianic age or Messianic kingdom (kingdom of heaven, kingdom of the Almighty) will begin. The political status of this kingdom will be splendid. The other peoples and kingdoms will continue to exist, but no nation or kingdom will any longer have authority over Israel.[1] For subjugation and war will cease entirely.

Such was the opinion of most of the Tannaim.[2] Nevertheless, in the pre-Hadrianic period, while political motives still occupied an important place in the life of the Jewish nation, there was a single Tanna who held an entirely different view on this subject. The controversy about this is extremely interesting. It found a place in the Mishnah and was further expounded in a Baraitha. In the Mishnah [3] we read:

A man may not go out (on the Sabbath) with a sword or a bow or a shield or a club or a spear; and if he went out (with the like of these), he must make a sin-offering. R. Eliezer (ben Hyrcanus) says: These are his ornaments (and it is permissible to go out on the Sabbath wearing ornaments). But the Sages say: They are naught save a reproach, for it is written (Isa. 2:4), "And they shall beat their swords into plowshares, and their spears into pruning-hooks; nation shall not lift up sword against nation, neither shall they learn war any more."

[1] Megillah 11a (Baraitha) and the passage quoted in the preceding chapter (above, p. 497) from Siphra, Behuqqothai, Chap. 2 (ed. Weiss, 112a); also Siphre, Deut., 315 (ed. Friedmann, 135a).
[2] Cf. Siphra, Behuqqothai, Chap. 2 (ed. Weiss, 111a).
[3] Shabbath 6:4.

MESSIANIC AGE AND SIGNS OF THE MESSIAH

In the Gemara this Baraitha follows:

They (the Sages) said to R. Eliezer: Since they are ornaments for him, why should they be eliminated in the Days of the Messiah? He said to them: Because they will not be required, as it is written, "Nation shall not lift up sword against nation. . . ."

There are some who give it this way: They said to R. Eliezer: Since they are ornaments for him, why should they be eliminated in the Days of the Messiah? He said to them: *Even in the Days of the Messiah they shall not be eliminated.*[4]

This isolated opinion is to be explained not only by the politically oriented and warlike spirit of the pre-Hadrianic period, but also by the pugnacious and uncompromising nature of R. Eliezer, whose opinions were almost always rejected by the other Tannaim,[5] and who was even severe enough to assert that if Israel did not repent, it would not be redeemed.[6]

R. Ishmael, son of R. Jose, transmits the following very interesting Messianic tradition in the name of his father, who was among the later disciples of R. Akiba:

Egypt is destined to bring a gift to the Messiah. He will think not to accept it from them, but the Holy One, blessed be He, will instruct him thus: Accept it from them; they furnished hospitality to My children in Egypt.—Immediately "nobles shall come out of Egypt" (Ps. 68:32). Then Ethiopia will draw an inference for herself, thus: If those (the Egyptians) who enslaved them (the Israelites) are thus welcomed, how much more will we, who did not enslave them, be welcomed?—At that the Holy One, blessed be He, will say to the Messiah, Accept from them.—Immediately "Ethiopia shall hasten to stretch out her hands [7] unto God" (*ibid.*). Then shall the Evil Kingdom [8] draw an inference for herself, thus: If those who are not their brethren are thus welcomed, how much more will we, their

---

[4] Shabbath 63a. The second version seems to me more in keeping with the spirit and inclinations of R. Eliezer.

[5] See the complete works of Ahad Ha-Am [in Hebrew], Jerusalem, 5707 [1947], pp. 59–60 (and particularly Note 2 on these pages).

[6] See above, pp. 428–429.

[7] "Hands" is no doubt used here, as in Deut. 32:36, in the sense of "powers" or "warriors." [The preceding verb ("hasten to stretch out") means literally "cause to run," and the author so interpreted it.–TRANS.]

[8] The ordinary Talmud editions read "kingdom of Ishmael," no doubt from fear of the censor. It is also possible that "Evil Kingdom" was substituted for "Edom" or "Rome" to avoid mentioning the kingdom by name.

brethren,[9] be welcomed?—But the Holy One, blessed be He, will say to Gabriel: "Rebuke the wild beast of the reeds (*qaneh*), the multitude [or, congregation] of the bulls" (Ps. 68:31); rebuke the wild beast and take possession (*qeneh*) [10] of the multitude (the congregation of Israel). Another interpretation is: "Rebuke the wild beast of the reeds," which dwells among the reeds,[11] as it is written (Ps. 80:14), "The boar out of the wood [12] doth ravage it, that which moveth in the field feedeth on it." [13]

Thus the foreign peoples and kingdoms will continue to exist in the Messianic age even though they voluntarily become proselytes, as thought this same R. Jose.[14] But they will attempt to curry favor with the King-Messiah by means of impressive deputations and rich gifts. The Messiah will be cordial and gracious to all the peoples. He will reject only the Romans, who in the very time of R. Jose, immediately after the fall of Bethar, had erected a marble image of a boar at the entrance to Jerusalem as a deliberate insult to the Jews, and thus had made "the boar out of the wood" a symbol of their control over Judea. At this time the political coloration of the Messianic kingdom had not been entirely eradicated; and even later it had not been entirely lost from the consciousness of the Tannaim.

Closely connected with this conception of the Messianic age expressed by R. Jose is the following saying of his contemporary, R. Simeon ben Gamaliel II:

---

[9] According to a common Talmudic formula, Rome is called "Edom" and Edom "Esau"; so Mal. 1:2 ("Was not Esau Jacob's brother?") can be applied to make the Romans brethren of the Jews.

[10] *Qaneh* (reeds) is here interpreted as *qeneh* (take possession)!

[11] An epithet for Rome (cf. Exod. R., Chap. 35) which no doubt comes from the legend of the founding of that city: "When Solomon married Pharaoh's daughter, Gabriel descended and stuck a reed into the sea, which gathered a sand-bank around it, on which was built the great city of Rome" (San. 21*b*).

[12] Rome is "the boar out of the wood" because after the defeat of Bar-Cochba the figure of a swine was engraved on one of the gates of Jerusalem ("Sus scalptus in marmore significans Romanae potestati subiacere Judaeos"—Eusebius-Jerome, Chronicle, ed. Schoene, II, 169). In modern times a Roman coin bearing a design with boars has been found in Jerusalem. See N. Krochmal, *The Guide* [Heb.], Sect. 13 (works of Krochmal, ed. Rawidowicz, Berlin, 1924, p. 203).

[13] Pesahim 118*b*; Exod. R., Chap. 35.

[14] See above, p. 480.

In Jerusalem all nations and all kingdoms are destined to be gathered together, as it is written (Jer. 3:17), "And all the nations shall be gathered unto it, to the name of the LORD." [15]

Therefore Jerusalem will need to be greatly enlarged. And not only Jerusalem, but the whole land of Israel as well. This had already been asserted by an earlier Tanna, whose career began before Hadrian (since he was a disciple of R. Eliezer ben Hyrcanus),[16] but whose Aggadic sayings belong mostly to the post-Hadrianic generation, since we find him in controversy with R. Judah, a younger disciple of R. Akiba. This Tanna was R. Jose ben Dormaskith.[17] His Messianic saying is as follows:

The land of Israel [18] is destined to be enlarged and spread out on all sides like this fig tree, which is small at the bottom (but broad at the top). And the gates of Jerusalem are destined to reach to Damascus, as it is written (Song of Songs 7:5), "Thy nose is like the tower of Lebanon, which looketh toward Damascus." And the exiles shall come and encamp therein, as it is written (Zech. 9:1), "And Damascus shall be his resting-place"; and as it is also written (Isa. 2:2), "And it shall come to pass in the end of days that the mountain of the LORD's house shall be established as the top of the mountains, and shall be exalted above the hills, and all nations shall flow unto it"; and as it is further written (Isa. 2:3), "And many peoples shall go and say: 'Come ye, and let us go up to the mountain of the LORD, to the house of the God of Jacob; and He will teach us of His ways, and we will walk in His paths.' For out of Zion shall go forth the law, and the word of the LORD from Jerusalem." [19]

This saying, in spite of the fact that it emphasizes the *spiritual* greatness of Israel in the time of the Messiah's rule (hence the long citations from Isaiah), still belongs with those Tannaitic sayings characterized by fantastic dreams of *material prosperity* in the Messianic age; for it greatly exaggerates the territorial extension of the land of Israel and particularly the size of Jerusalem.

---

[15] Aboth de R. Nathan, A, Chap. 35, end (ed. Schechter, p. 106).
[16] See Bacher, *Agada der Tannaiten*, I, 393 (Heb. trans., I, 2, 113).
[17] See on this Tanna above, pp. 462–463.
[18] Instead of "the land of Israel" one manuscript has "Jerusalem"; but this would make the word "Jerusalem" in the next sentence pleonastic.
[19] Siphre, Deut., end of Sect. 1 (ed. Friedmann, 65a).

The above saying leads us directly to the so-called "signs of the Messiah." This expression (which is not found in the Tannaitic literature) does not refer to miracles and wonders to be performed by the Messiah, but (like the "birth pangs of Messiah" and the "trumpet of Messiah") to marvels of the Messianic age to be accomplished by God Himself. *For the Messiah—and this should be carefully noted!— is never mentioned anywhere in the Tannaitic literature as a wonder-worker* per se.

These "signs of the Messiah" resemble the *Jewish* conceptions of the blessings of the Messianic age which we find in the Book of Enoch, in the earlier Sibylline Oracles, and especially in the Syriac Apocalypse of Baruch and IV Ezra; they also resemble the early *Christian* conceptions of the millennium (chiliasm). It may therefore be supposed that they also occur in the early Tannaitic literature. And, as a matter of fact, there is such a Messianic tradition from the Patriarch Rabban Gamaliel I, a contemporary of R. Johanan ben Zakkai, who knew the Second Temple before its destruction. This tradition is very similar to the marvelous descriptions found in the Baruch Apocalypse,[20] on the one hand, and in Papias,[21] one of the first of the Church Fathers, on the other hand:

Rabban Gamaliel sat and taught: Woman is destined to bear every day, as it is written (Jer. 31:7), "She shall conceive and immediately bear a child" [31:8 in English versions, which interpret otherwise]. But that pupil [also translated "a certain disciple"] scoffed at him, quoting (Eccl. 1:9), "There is nothing new under the sun." He (R. Gamaliel) replied, Come, and I will show you an example of this in the present age. He went out and showed him a hen.[22]

Again Rabban Gamaliel sat and taught: Trees are destined to yield fruit every day, as it is written (Ezek. 17:23), "And it shall bring forth twigs and bear fruit": just as there are twigs every day so shall there be fruit every day. But that pupil scoffed at him, saying, It is written, "There is nothing new under the sun." R. Gamaliel replied, Come, and I will show you an example of this in the present age. He went out and showed him a caper bush.

[20] Syriac Baruch 29:5-8. See above, pp. 342-344.
[21] His words are quoted in Irenaeus, *Against Heresies*, V 33. See J. Klausner, *Jesus of Nazareth*, 5th Heb. ed., p. 435 [Eng. ed., p. 401].
[22] Cf. Kallah Rabbathi, Chap. 2, where this short form occurs: "Woman is destined to bear every day, on the analogy of the hen."

Again Rabban Gamaliel sat and taught: The land of Israel is destined to bring forth Lesbian cakes (rolls of fine flour) and robes of Melat (garments of very fine wool from the city of Miletus), as it is written (Ps. 72:16), "There shall be an abundance (*pissath*) of grain (*bar*) in the land." [23] But that pupil scoffed at him, saying again, "There is nothing new under the sun." R. Gamaliel replied, Come, and I will show you an example of this in the present age. He went out and showed him morels and truffles [Palestinian edible fungi which resemble cakes]; and for robes of Melat, he showed him the bark of a young palm tree [which resembles wool].[24]

With these conceptions on the part of Rabban Gamaliel I, the Syriac Baruch, and Papias about the fabulous productivity of the earth in the Messianic age is to be compared a Baraitha that is in my opinion very early. It likewise is based on Ps. 72:16:

"There shall be an abundance of grain in the land upon the top of the mountains." From this it was inferred that there will be a time when wheat will rise as high as a palm tree and will grow on the top of the mountains. But in case you should think that there will be trouble in reaping it, it was specifically said in Scripture (Ps. 72:16), "Its fruit shall shake like Lebanon": the Holy One, blessed be He, will bring a wind from His treasure houses [25] which He will cause to blow upon it. This will bring down [26] its fine flour, and a man can walk out into the field and take a mere handful,[27] and that will be sufficient provision for himself and his household.

[23] The word *pissath* is applied by Rabban Gamaliel to "robes of Melat" from the expression *kethoneth passim*, "coat of many colors" (Gen. 37:3; II Sam. 13:18); see Rashi on Shabbath 30*b*. *Bar* is interpreted in the sense of "Lesbian cakes."

[24] Shabbath 30*b*. In Kethubboth 111*b* the last sentences are given in the name of the Amora Hiyya bar Joseph; he was no doubt only the transmitter of the Baraitha. But cf. Bacher, *op. cit.*, II, 96, Note 2 (Heb. trans., Vol. I, Part I, pp. 67–68). I am almost certain (in spite of the ill tempered attack on me on account of this on the part of Jewish apologists) that this is Rabban Gamaliel I (the Elder) and that "that pupil" is Paul, who sat "at the feet of Gamaliel" [Acts 22:3]. In like manner Jesus is called "that man." See J. Klausner, *From Jesus to Paul*, Heb. ed., II, 10–11, Eng. ed., pp. 310–311.

[25] Cf. Jer. 10:13 and 51:16; Ps. 135:7.

[26] *Mashshir* (cause to fall) is to be read instead of *Mashreh* (cause to rest). In Kallah Rabbathi, Chap. 2, the reading at this point is corrupt (see N. N. Coronel, *Five Tractates* [Heb.], Vienna, 1864, f. 4*a*); the reading of Siphre, Deut., 315 (ed. Friedmann, 135*b*) is quoted below (see Note 29).

[27] *Pissath yādō* is probably derived from *pissath bar;* the reading in Kallah Rabbathi must be corrected in the light of what we have here.

"With the kidney-fat of wheat" (Deut. 32:14). From this it was inferred that there will be a time when a grain of wheat will be as large as the two kidneys of a big bull. And you need not marvel at this, for a fox once made his nest in a turnip, and when they weighed it, they found it to be sixty pounds, according to the pound used in Sepphoris.[28]

The first part of this Baraitha also occurs in the following expanded form:

"And there was no strange god with him" (Deut. 32:12). This signifies that there shall not be among you any persons at all who occupy themselves with business enterprises. For it is written (Ps. 72:16), "There shall be a full abundance of grain"—signifying that wheat will produce Lesbian cakes that will make a good handful. "Its fruit shall shake like Lebanon." This means that the grains of wheat will rub against each other so that their fine flour will fall to the ground; then you can come and pick up the handful that will suffice for your sustenance.[29]

Wine also, like the wheat, will be the object of a supernatural blessing. I have already cited in another connexion [30] the early tradition (introduced by the expression "They said," that is, the preceding Sages said) in which it is foretold that in the Messianic age "a man will bring one grape on a wagon or a ship, put it in the corner of his house and use its contents as if it had been a large wine cask." [31] And the Baraitha goes on to say:

There will be no grape that will not contain thirty kegs of wine, for it is said in Scripture (Deut. 32:14), "And of the blood of the grape you shall drink foaming wine"; read not "foaming wine" (ḥemer) but ḥomer (a large liquid measure containing thirty seahs [kegs] and equivalent to a cor in dry measure).[32]

This last hyperbole agrees exactly with a description of material prosperity in the Syriac Baruch, which says, "Each grape shall pro-

---

[28] Kethubboth 111b; and with certain differences, Kallah Rabbathi, Chap. 2 (Coronel, *loc. cit.*). The last sentences and the story about the fox occur also in Siphre, Deut., 317 (ed. Friedmann, 135-136).

[29] Siphre, Deut., 315 (135ab).

[30] See above, p. 343 [see also Part III, Chap. II, pp. 409-410].

[31] The words which follow, "while its timber would be used to make fires for cooking," are doubtless a later addition, since they make poor sense and are lacking in Siphre, Deut., 317, end (ed. Friedmann, 136a, beginning).

[32] Kethubboth 111b.

duce a cor." [33] (The homer as a liquid measure corresponds to the cor as a dry measure, as was said.) But Papias [34] says, "Every grape when pressed will give twenty-five measures of wine." This estimate is much higher: a cor is equivalent to 360 litres, but the twenty-five measures of Papias amount to 800 litres! [35]

With that part of Rabban Gamaliel's exposition having to do with trees and grain, the following Baraitha is to be compared:

"And by the river upon the bank thereof, on this side and on that side, shall grow every tree for food, whose leaf shall not wither, neither shall the fruit thereof fail; it shall bring forth new fruit according to its months" (Ezek. 47:12). It is taught: [36] Rabbi Judah says, The fact is that [37] in this age grain yields its crop every six months, and a tree bears fruit every twelve months; [38] but in the Age to Come grain shall yield every month and a tree every two months. What is the proof?—"It shall bring forth new fruit according to its *months*" (plural number, at least two months required).

Rabbi Jose says, The fact is that in this age grain yields every six months and a tree every twelve months; but in the Age to Come grain shall yield every fifteen days and a tree every month. For we have found that in the days of Joel grain yielded every fifteen days and the Omer was offered from it. What is the proof?—"Be glad then, ye children of Zion, and rejoice in the LORD your God; for He giveth you the former rain in just measure, and He causeth to come down for you the rain, the former rain and the latter rain, on the first" (Joel 2:23).[39] And how does R. Jose interpret the words "It shall bring forth new fruit according to its months"?— "It shall bring forth new fruit *every* month." [40]

It is worthy of note that in nearly all of the passages quoted above, the Tannaim themselves sensed the exaggerated aspect of these predictions. Therefore, Rabban Gamaliel sought, by examples from

[33] Syriac Baruch 29:5 (see above, pp. 342-343).
[34] In Irenaeus, *Against Heresies*, V 33 (above, p. 344; *Jesus of Nazareth* [Eng. ed.], p. 401).
[35] See Hühn, *Die messian. Weissag.*, I, 160, Note 2.
[36] This introductory formula indicates a Baraitha. Cf. Yerushalmi, Taanith 1:2.
[37] These introductory words are superfluous here.
[38] See a similar saying by R. Meir, a fellow student of R. Judah and R. Jose, in Tosephta, Taanith 1:1 (beginning of the tractate).
[39] "On the first" means here, no doubt, the first day of the first month (Nisan), and so the fifteenth day before "the day of the waving of the Omer" on the day after the first day of Passover.
[40] Yerushalmi (also appended to Babli), Shekalim 6:2.

everyday life, to make his hyperbolic expositions more plausible to his incredulous and scoffing disciple (Paul, in my opinion). Likewise, the anonymous Baraitha which contains the characteristic words "And you need not marvel at this" seeks to make these wonders more natural and credible by reference to the story of the fox that made his nest in a turnip. R. Jose wished to do the same thing by recalling events in the time of the prophet Joel. But this earlier skepticism did not deter later Tannaim from the most extreme exaggeration in their predictions. Thus we find, for example, one opinion that not only will the earth produce a crop "on the same day wherein it is sown," but also trees "will bear fruit the same day they are planted." And not only will the *fruit* be edible, but even the trees themselves, for their very wood "is destined to be eaten." And not only fruit trees, but non-fruit trees also, will bear fruit.[41]

The Biblical words, "And the leaf thereof [shall be] for healing" (Ezek. 47:12), are explained by the semi-Tanna Bar Kappara thus: "to open the mouth (of the womb of) barren women."[42] For the *bodies* of mankind will be transformed in the Messianic age. On the verse (Lev. 26:13) "and I made [shall make] you go *at full height (qomemiyuth)*," R. Meir (post-Hadrianic) says:

It means (that the height of a man in the Messianic age will be) two hundred cubits, twice the height (*qomah*) of Adam.[43] R. Judah says: A hundred cubits, corresponding to the height of the Temple and its walls, as it is written (Ps. 144:12), "We whose sons are [shall be] as plants grown up in their youth, whose daughters are [shall be] as corner-pillars carved after the fashion of the Temple."[44]

According to another tradition:

R. Simeon says, Two hundred cubits. R. Judah says, One hundred cubits, like Adam. This applies to men only. How do we know it of women?

---

[41] Siphra, Behuqqothai, Chap. 1 (ed. Weiss, 110b). The last saying about "wild" trees bearing fruit is also found in Kethubboth 112b, near the end of the tractate, in the name of Rab, whose school is thought to have redacted Siphra ("Siphra debe Rab").

[42] Sanhedrin 100a; Menahoth 98a. In Yerushalmi, Shekalim 6:2, this saying occurs in the name of the Amora R. Hanina.

[43] Whose height was a hundred cubits, according to Hagigah 12a. Qomemiyuth is taken as the dual or plural ("the smallest plural is two") of *qomah*, "height."

[44] Baba Bathra 75a; Sanhedrin 100a.

Scripture says (Ps. 144:12), "Whose daughters are [shall be] as corner-pillars carved after the fashion of the Temple." And how high was the fashion of the Temple? A hundred cubits.—Another saying is, "And I made [shall make] you go *at full height*"; this means fully erect, because they will have no fear of any creature.[45]

This absence of fear of any creature includes security from the danger of wild beasts:

"And I will cause evil beasts to cease out of the land" (Lev. 26:6). R. Judah says, He will remove them from the world. R. Simeon says, He will cause them to cease from doing harm.[46] R. Simeon said, When does it redound more to the praise of God—when there are no harmful beasts or when there are harmful beasts yet they do no harm? When there are harmful beasts but they do no harm, of course. . . . For it is written, "And the wolf shall dwell with the lamb, and the leopard shall lie down with the kid; and the calf and the young lion and the fatling together, and a little child shall lead them. And the cow and the bear shall feed, their young ones shall lie down together, and the lion shall eat straw like the ox. And the suckling child shall play on the hole of the asp, and the weaned child shall put his hand on the basilisk's den" (Isa. 11:6–8).[47]

Thus in the Messianic age there will still be in the world wolves, leopards, lions, bears, asps, and basilisks, but "they shall not hurt nor destroy in all My holy mountain" (Isa. 11:9).

Man's material welfare will be increased not only by the productivity of the earth and security from danger, but also by *a juster distribution of land*. We have already seen [48] that in the Messianic age "there will be no single individual who will not possess land in mountain, lowland, and valley." [49] This means that each man will have a vineyard, an orchard, and a grain field.

An attractive, but also exaggerated, picture of the Messianic age is presented by R. Eliezer, the son of R. Jose the Galilean (post-Hadrianic). His words are few, yet striking:

---

[45] Siphra, Beḥuqqothai, end of Chap. 3 (ed. Weiss, 111a). This "other saying" is also found verbatim in Num. R., Chap. 13.
[46] This opinion of R. Simeon agrees exactly with that of Philo of Alexandria, *On Rewards and Punishments* 15 (M., II, 422; C.-W., V, 355-356, Sects. 88–90).
[47] Siphra, Beḥuqqothai, beginning of Chap. 2 (ed. Weiss, 111a).
[48] Above, p. 409.
[49] Baba Bathra 122a.

How can you prove that every Israelite is destined to have as many children as there were persons who came out of Egypt (600,000)? It is written (Ps. 45:17), "Instead of thy fathers shall be thy sons." But "sons" might mean wretched and afflicted ones. The verse, however, continues, "Whom thou shalt make princes in all the land." But "princes" might mean merchant-princes.[50] Scripture says, however, "a kingdom" (Ex. 19:6). But "a king" might mean one who goes about making conquests. The verse adds, however, "of priests." But "priests" might mean nonfunctioning priests, as it is written (II Sam. 8:18), "And David's sons were priests." Therefore Scripture says, "And a holy nation" (Ex. 19:6).[51]

The Messianic ideal here portrayed is very characteristic of the post-Hadrianic generation. The spiritual condition of the Jewish nation in the Messianic age and the function of that nation in the world are set forth in terms representative of the thought of the Sages of the Talmud. Israel will never again be persecuted and oppressed, nor be scattered among the Gentiles, nor be a nation of traffickers; rather, it will be "a kingdom of priests and a holy nation." But this kingdom will not seek conquest by war, nor will these priests be concerned with making proselytes as were Paul and the early Christians—though the Jews too were so concerned at the time of the appearance of the Sibylline Oracles.[52] The Gentiles will become proselytes of their own accord, without exhortation on the part of the Jews; for they will be irresistibly attracted by the model kingdom where all are priests and all combine to make a holy nation.[53] This is completely in accord with the conclusions reached above [Chapter VIII] with regard to the reception of proselytes in the Messianic age: the Gentiles will at that time become "self-made proselytes"—of their own accord.

[50] Doubtless on the basis of Isaiah 23:8, "whose merchants are princes." That Israel would not be concerned with business pursuits in the Messianic age we have already seen from Siphre, Deut. 315 (ed. Friedmann, 135a end. See above, p. 508).
[51] Mekhilta, Baḥodesh, Chap. 2 (ed. Friedmann, 63a, beginning). Friedmann corrected the text according to Yalqut on Exod. 19:2 (275) and Yalqut on Ps. 45. The reading of ed. Weiss, 71a, is less correct.
[52] This is the idea behind the phrase "priests that go around seeking" (*kohanim meḥazzerim*).
[53] See the commentary (*Me'ir 'Ayin*) in M. Friedmann's edition of Siphre, 63a, Note 34. Friedmann gives evidence against the idea of the "mission" of the Jewish people.

MESSIANIC AGE AND SIGNS OF THE MESSIAH 513

It remains to point out various wonders ("signs") that will occur in the Messianic age.

We have seen above [54] that the prophet Elijah will at that time restore "the jar of manna, the flask of water for purification, and the flask of oil for anointing; and some say, also Aaron's rod," which will blossom anew. I also discussed the question of whether the Law would be forgotten in the Messianic age;[55] and I showed that as a result of the Hadrianic persecutions there arose the idea that the Law could be forgotten—at least temporarily. But this was not a firmly fixed or widespread opinion. So when a new generation of Tannaim arose, who had not experienced the Hadrianic decrees, entirely different opinions prevailed. Thus R. Eliezer (Eleazar) ha-Kappar,[56] a contemporary of R. Judah the Patriarch, concludes in a late Baraitha:

> The synagogues and houses of learning that are in Babylonia will in the time to come be re-established in Palestine, as it is written (Jer. 46:18), "Surely like Tabor among the mountains, and like Carmel by the sea, so shall he come."[57] Now can we not draw an inference here *a fortiori?* Seeing that Tabor and Carmel, which came only on a single occasion to learn the Torah (that is, to demand that the Torah be given from them), were established in Palestine, how much more must this be the case with the synagogues and houses of learning, where the Torah is read and expounded![58]

Thus the Law will not be forgotten in the Messianic age. Even its ritual requirements will be in force as before. For the Temple will be rebuilt and the sacrifices will be offered therein as in former times. There is nothing to which the Tannaim hold more strongly than this.[59] It is specifically stated that the Temple and the sacrifices, along

---

[54] See above, pp. 455–456.
[55] See above, pp. 445–450.
[56] See Tosephta, Ahiloth [Oholoth] 18:18. Bacher, *op. cit.*, II, 496, 500–501 (Heb. trans., Vol. II, Part II, pp. 166–167, Note 45 on p. 174), attributes this and other sayings to Bar Kappara, the son of R. Eliezer ha-Kappar.
[57] This is apparently a reference to the strange legend that at the time of the giving of the Law by Moses, Mount Carmel came through the sea from Aspamea and Mount Tabor from Beth-Elim to the wilderness of Sinai, in order that the Law might be given on them (see Mekhilta, Baḥodesh, Chap. 5, ed. Friedmann, 66b). Cf. J. Renzer, *Die Hauptpersonen des Richterbuches im Talmud und Midrasch*, I, Simson, Berlin, 1902.
[58] Megillah 29a.
[59] Contrary to the opinion of Castelli, *Il Messia*, pp. 271–277.

with the Davidic kingdom and the oil for anointing, will endure "forever and ever and ever."[60] In many Mishnahs[61] and Baraithas[62] mention of the Temple is accompanied by the prayer, "May it speedily be rebuilt in our time!" Many ordinances which actually had no meaning after the Temple was destroyed were still accounted obligatory for one reason only: "The Temple will speedily be rebuilt," and its ritual restored.[63] This faith was so strong that we read in an anonymous Baraitha: "One who becomes a proselyte at the present time must set aside a quarter (of a denar) for his bird-offering"—so that he would be able to present the [minimum] offering of a pair of doves or pigeons if the Temple should be rebuilt in his lifetime.[64] According to I. H. Weiss,[65] this requirement originated with Rabban Johanan ben Zakkai, who, however, later annulled it "because it was a stumbling block."

R. Akiba very clearly expressed his strong faith in the rebuilding of the Temple and the restoration of the sacrifices in a benediction found in the Mishnah and quoted above.[66] And one of his younger disciples, R. Judah ben Ilai, who is well known to us through his traditions concerning the Second Temple, can even assert that the harp of the Messianic age will have eight strings.[67] The same R. Judah speaks of a high priest serving in the Messianic age as something to be taken for granted:

Can it be that Aaron and his sons will need the oil of anointing in the Age to Come? Scripture says (Lev. 7:35), "This is the portion of the anointing of Aaron and of the anointing of his sons." And how do I interpret the following: "These are the two anointed ones that stand by the Lord of the whole earth" (Zech. 4:14)? This means Aaron and David.[68]

---

[60] Siphre, Num., 92 (ed. Friedmann, 25b; ed. H. S. Horovitz, *Qobets Ma'ase ha-Tannaim*, Leipzig, 1917, III, 3, p. 92).
[61] E.g., Mishnah, Taanith 4:8; Tamid 7:3.
[62] E.g., Baba Metsia 28b, beginning.
[63] Sukkah 41a; Menahoth 25b; Rosh ha-Shanah 30a; Betsah 5b; Taanith 17b; Sanhedrin 22b; Bekhoroth 53b.
[64] Rosh ha-Shanah 31b; Kerithoth 9a (see Rashi on these two passages).
[65] *Each Generation and Its Interpreters* [Heb.], II², 37, Note 1.
[66] See above, p. 397.
[67] See above, p. 411.
[68] Siphra, Tsaw, Chap. 18 (ed. Weiss, 40a).

Much is said in the Talmudic literature about the high priest in the Messianic age. I have proposed above [69] the hypothesis that this high priest is none other than Elijah the prophet. According to another tradition,[70] this high priest will come in company with Elijah; he is called "the Righteous Priest" (*Kohen-Zedek*)—an appellation apparently identical with Melchizedek.[71] Here we have a significant point of contact of the Talmud with the Epistle to the Hebrews (wrongly attributed to Paul) in the New Testament.[72] But the Talmud also has many passages militating against the conclusion that Melchizedek and the Messiah are identical—of course, not without polemical tendency against Christianity.[73] Such an anti-Christian tendency may also be seen in the saying of the Patriarch Rabban Simeon ben Gamaliel II (post-Hadrianic) on Zechariah 4:14:

"These are the two anointed ones." This means the Righteous Priest and the Messiah. And I do not know which of them is the more beloved. But since it says (Ps. 110:4), "The LORD hath sworn and will not repent: 'Thou art a priest for ever [after the manner of Melchizedek],' " [74] we know that the King-Messiah is more beloved than the Righteous Priest.[75]

The high priest in the Age to Come, Melchizedek, who plays such an important rôle in the Epistle to the Hebrews, is here less beloved of God than the Messiah. But the *existence* of the high priest in the Messianic age is mentioned as something to be taken for granted by common consent.

If the high priest is to return to the Temple, then naturally his official garments and the breastplate and the Urim and Thummim

[69] See p. 456.
[70] Sukkah 52b (apparently Amoraic).
[71] Rashi on Sukkah 52b. Cf. Dalman, *Der leidende und sterbende Messias*, pp. 7-8 (especially Note **).
[72] Heb. 6:20; 7:1-17. Cf. Matt. 22:43-44; Mark 12:36; Luke 20:42-44 (these passages quote the Psalm [110] which also says, "Thou art a priest forever, after the manner of Melchizedek").
[73] This stands out clearly in the saying of R. Ishmael in Nedarim 32b (end of Chap. III).
[74] The words in square brackets were included in the commentary of Rabbenu Gershom (Meor ha-Golah) on Nedarim 32b. This is one more proof that "the Righteous Priest" and Melchizedek are identical.
[75] Aboth de R. Nathan, A, Chap. 34 (ed. Schechter, p. 100). See above, p. 456, Note 23.

will also be restored. And indeed, once in the Talmud the question is simply asked, "How will he put them on in the Age to Come?"[76] That is to say, how [or in what order] will the high priest in the Messianic age put on his special garments?

An interesting anonymous Baraitha says this:

When the first Temple was destroyed, the cities with pasture land (belonging to the Levites, according to Lev. 25:32-34) were abolished, the Urim and Thummim ceased, and there was no more a king from the house of David. And if someone whispers to you to quote "And the governor said unto them that they should not eat of the most holy things till there stood [should stand] up a priest with Urim and Thummim" (Ezra 2:63; Neh. 7:65), reply to him: [It is a phrase for the future] as if one man should say to another, "Until the dead come to life and Messiah ben David comes."[77]

But if there are to be Temple, priests, and sacrifices, there will surely also be sins and sinners. And as a matter of fact, we find a Tannaitic saying which reveals this plainly:

Thus you will find in the Days of the Messiah, that people are going to be rebellious only from too much eating, drinking, and ease. What is written about these things? "But Jeshurun waxed fat, and kicked" (Deut. 32:15).[78]

When one keeps the Messianic age separate from the subsequent "World to Come," as I have attempted to do in Chapter II, Part III, of the present work, the strong similarity between "the Messianic generation" and present generations appears entirely natural. The Tannaim also—like Judaism later and Christianity always—looked forward to a time when sin would vanish completely and the sacrifices, like all the rest of the requirements of the Law, would no longer be necessary. But that time without sin and without the Law is to come *after* the Messianic age. Only then "will the righteous sit with their crowns on their heads, basking in the brightness of the Shekhinah."[79]

---

[76] Yoma 5*b*. This passage, apparently Amoraic, is concerned with the resurrection of Aaron.

[77] Sotah 48*b*. A partially different version of this saying occurs in Yerushalmi, Kiddushin 4:1.

[78] Siphre, Deut., 318 (ed. Friedmann, 136*a*).

[79] See above, p. 412. All the sayings cited by Castelli (*op. cit.*, pp. 264-270) on this point either are concerned with the World to Come or are from a later,

The Jewish Messianic idea, in its authentic form, came forth from an essentially political aspiration—the longing of the nation to recover its lost political power and to see the revival of the Davidic kingdom, a kingdom of right and might alike. Hence this idea, in spite of its increasing spiritualization and the great ethical height to which it rose, necessarily remained in essence mundane and political. The kingdom of the Messiah is actually the kingdom of David, except that it is extended over a wider area, and possesses every worldly blessing; it also exemplifies a pure and refined morality, in so far as a rich Oriental imagination could conceive of this kind of spirituality without thereby obliterating the political side of the Messianic idea. For the kingdom of the Jewish King-Messiah was and remained— at least as far as the Tannaitic period is concerned—*a kingdom of this world.*

---

non-Tannaitic time. Hence the far-fetched explanations and the contradictions which he is forced to find too often in the post-Biblical literature (see especially pp. 269-270). Actually, the diverse views are to be explained from the different "ages" with which they are concerned and from the different historical periods from which they come.

APPENDIX

The Jewish and the Christian Messiah *

REMARK ONE:

The subject of this article would require a whole book for its elucidation. Within the limits of a short article I can only indicate the general outlines of the problem and restrict myself to certain important principles. Also, for the sake of brevity, I shall be compelled to cite from the extensive literature on matters pertaining to this subject only what is most relevant.

REMARK TWO:

The conception both of the Jewish Messiah and of the Christian Messiah has changed from period to period. The Jewish Messiah of Isaiah and Jeremiah is not the same as that of Daniel or the Ethiopic Enoch; nor is the conception of the Jewish Messiah in all these like that in the early Talmudic Aggadah, the *Mishneh Torah* of Maimonides, or the Kabbalistic books. It is likewise with respect to the conception of the Christian Messiah: Jesus himself understood his Messiahship very differently from the way in which Paul understood it. The later Church Fathers greatly modified what Paul taught; and the Catholics, Greek Orthodox, and Protestants differ greatly among themselves about how to conceive of the Messiah.

In this brief article I shall deal only with the conception of the Jewish Messiah as it has become crystallized in Biblical-Talmudic Judaism and accepted by most Jews; and with respect to the Christian

* Reprinted from *Sepher Magnes* [Heb.], Jerusalem, 1938.

conception of the Messiah I shall deal only with those features now shared by all three branches of the Christian faith. Then I shall attempt to present these two conceptions, the Jewish and the Christian, in contrast with each other, in order to show the difference between them.

I

The Jewish Messiah is a redeemer strong in physical power and in spirit, who in the final days will bring complete redemption, economic and spiritual, to the Jewish people—and along with this, eternal peace, material prosperity, and ethical perfection to the whole human race.

The Jewish Messiah is truly human in origin, of flesh and blood like all mortals. Justin Martyr in his time put this clearly into the mouth of Trypho the Jew, thus: "We Jews all expect that the Messiah will be a man of purely human origin."[1] This human conception of the Messiah remains normative in Judaism to this day. To be sure, a Talmudic Baraitha numbers the name of the Messiah among the seven things which "were created before the world was created";[2] there is also something of this sort in the "Parables" of the Ethiopic Enoch.[3] But no doubt what is intended is the *idea* of the Messiah or the idea of redemption through the Messiah.[4]

The Messiah is full of the spirit of wisdom and understanding, counsel and might, knowledge and the fear of the LORD. He has a special feeling for justice: he "smells and judges" [that is, he can almost tell a man's guilt or innocence by his sense of smell].[5] He "shall smite the land (or, the tyrant) with the rod of his mouth, and with the breath of his lips shall he slay the wicked."[6] For "the war against Gog and Magog," who come to destroy Israel, there is a special Mes-

---

[1] Ἄνθρωπον ἐξ ἀνθρώπων. See Justin Martyr, *Dialogue with Trypho the Jew*, Chap. 49, beginning.
[2] Pesahim 54a; Nedarim 39b.
[3] Ethiopic Enoch 48:3.
[4] See M. Friedmann, Introduction to Seder Eliyahu Rabbah, Vienna, 1902, p. 114; M. Vernes, *Histoire des idées messianiques*, Paris, 1874, pp. 268–269, 281, note.
[5] Sanhedrin 93b; see above, p. 468.
[6] Isa. 11:4.

siah—Messiah ben Joseph, who is slain in the war.[7] But Messiah ben David is the king of peace:

When the King-Messiah is revealed to Israel, he will not open his mouth except for peace, as it is written (Isa. 52:7), "How beautiful upon the mountains are the feet of the messenger of good tidings, that announceth peace."[8]

Also, "the Messiah shall be peaceful in his very name, as it is written (Isa. 9:5), 'Everlasting father, prince of peace.'"[9]

What in essence is the task of the King-Messiah?

He redeems Israel from exile and servitude, and he redeems the whole world from oppression, suffering, war, and above all from heathenism and everything which it involves: man's sins both against God and against his fellow man, and particularly the sins of nation against nation. For in the Messianic age all peoples will be converted to Judaism—some of them becoming "true proselytes" and some only "proselytes hanging on" (from self-interest).[10] In the *Alenu* prayer, which is offered by Jews three times daily, we find the hope that speedily

... the world will be perfected under the kingdom of the Almighty, and *all the children of flesh* will call upon Thy name, when Thou wilt turn unto Thyself all the wicked of the earth. Let *all the inhabitants of the world* perceive and know that unto Thee *every* knee must bow, *every* tongue must swear ... and let them *all* accept the yoke of Thy kingdom.[11]

And in the *Shemoneh Esreh* prayer for "Solemn Days" [New Year and Day of Atonement], Jews say: "And let all creatures prostrate themselves before Thee, that they may all form a single band to do Thy will with a perfect heart." In this prayer the Jew prays:

Give then glory, O LORD, unto Thy people, ... joy to Thy land (Palestine), gladness to Thy city (Jerusalem), a flourishing horn unto

---

[7] Sukkah 52a; see above, pp. 483–501.
[8] Derekh Erets Zuta, Chap. 11 (Section on Peace). See M. Higger, *Minor Tractates* [Heb.], New York, 1929, p. 101, and notes on p. 148; Lev. R., Chap. 9, end.
[9] Derekh Erets Zuta, Section on Peace, Text B (M. Higger, *op. cit.*, p. 104).
[10] *Gerim gerurim.* Cf. Berakhoth 57a and Tosephta, Berakhoth 7(6):2 (and Zuckermandel's notes *ad loc.*) with Abodah Zarah 24a. [See p. 481 above.]
[11] Singer, *Standard Prayer Book*, American ed., p. 94.

David Thy servant, and a clear shining light unto the son of Jesse, Thine anointed.

But at the same time he also prays that "all wickedness shall be wholly consumed like smoke, when Thou makest the dominion of arrogance to pass away from the (whole) earth." [12]

Along with redemption from servitude, from evil, and from heathenism, that is to say, from the evil in man, the Messiah will save man from the evil in nature. No longer will poisonous reptiles and beasts of prey exist; or rather, they will exist, but will do no harm.[13] There will be great material prosperity in the world: the earth will bring forth an abundance of grain and fruit, which man will be able to enjoy without excessive toil.[14] As to the Jewish people, not only will they freely dwell in their own land, but there will also be an "ingathering of exiles," whereby all Jews scattered to the four corners of the earth will be returned to Palestine. All nations will acknowledge the God of Israel and accept His revelation of truth. Thus the King-Messiah, the king of righteousness, will be in a certain sense also the king of all nations, just as the God of Israel will be King over all the earth because He is the One and Only God.

Not every book of prophecy mentions an individual human Messiah. In the books of Nahum, Zephaniah, Habakkuk, Malachi, Joel, and Daniel, God alone is the redeemer. In the books of Amos, Ezekiel, Obadiah, and in the Book of Psalms, there is only a collective Messiah: "deliverers" and "saints" redeem the world by their righteousness and piety. In the books of Haggai and Zechariah, the Messiah is none other than Zerubbabel, a person who is not out of the ordinary except that he is of the house of David. In Deutero-Isaiah and Daniel, the Messiah is not a person at all, but is the whole Jewish people. Likewise, in the Apocryphal books (as distinguished from the Pseudepigrapha), there is no individual Messiah. In the Talmud, Rabbi Hillel (to be distinguished from Hillel the Elder) makes bold to say: "There shall be no Messiah for Israel, because they have already enjoyed him in the days of Hezekiah." [15] To be sure, Rab Joseph rebelled against

---

[12] *Ibid.*, pp. 350–351.
[13] Siphra, Beḥuqqothai, Chap. 2, beginning (ed. Weiss, 111a).
[14] See on all this above, pp. 505–512.
[15] Sanhedrin 98b and 99a.

this opinion, saying: "May God forgive R. Hillel for saying this." [16] But the fact remains that it was possible for a Jew faithful to his nation and his religion to conceive of redemption without an individual human redeemer: God Himself would be the redeemer.[17]

This view did not prevail in Judaism. Belief in the coming of the Messiah is the twelfth in the thirteen "Articles of Faith" of Maimonides. But the fact that at one time Judaism could have conceived of redemption without a Messiah is not surprising. For redemption comes from God and through God. The Messiah is only an instrument in the hands of God. He is a human being, flesh and blood, like all mortals. He is but the finest of the human race and the chosen of his nation. And as the chosen of his nation, who is also the choicest of the human race, he must needs be crowned with all the highest virtues to which mortal man can attain.

As the Messiah, he exemplifies both physical and spiritual perfection. Even such an extremely spiritual and ethical person as Philo of Alexandria sees in the Messiah not only the spiritual and ethical side, but also finds in him "all-powerful strength of body" and "might" ($\delta\epsilon\iota\nu\acute{o}\tau\eta s$); for "leading his host to war he will subdue great and populous nations." At the same time Philo finds in the Messiah "holiness and beneficence" ($\sigma\epsilon\mu\nu\acute{o}\tau\eta s$ $\kappa\alpha\grave{\iota}$ $\epsilon\grave{\upsilon}\epsilon\rho\gamma\epsilon\sigma\acute{\iota}\alpha$).[18] Both with respect to holiness, righteousness, truth, and goodness, and with respect to might and authority, the Messiah is the "supreme man" of Judaism, which is very far from Nietzsche's "blond beast." But with all his superior qualities, the Messiah remains a human being. Within the limits of a constantly improving humanity, Judaism has devised the ideal man, or, if we may speak in the language of Kant, "the conception of the [upper] limit of man"—concerning whom we may say with the divinely inspired psalmist, "Thou hast made him but little lower than God." [19] But this "little" leaves the Messiah within the bounds of humanity and does not allow him to pass beyond.

[16] *Loc. cit.*
[17] See on this, James Drummond, *The Jewish Messiah*, London, 1877, pp. 226-277.
[18] See Philo, *On Rewards and Punishments*, Chap. 16, Sects. 95-97 (ed. M., II, 423-424; ed. C.-W., V, 357). See also J. Klausner, *Philosophers and Thinkers* [Heb.], I, 87-88; above, p. 493.
[19] Ps. 8:6.

The kingdom of the Jewish Messiah is definitely "of this world."

Judaism is not only a religion, but is also the view of life of a single nation that holds to this religion alone, while the other religions include various nations. It is absolutely necessary, therefore, that Judaism's ideal for mankind should require first of all the realization of the yearning of its oppressed, suffering, exiled, and persecuted nation to return to its own land and recover its former status. But this ingathering of exiles and this national freedom are closely linked with the emancipation of all humanity—the destruction of evil and tyranny in the world, man's conquest of nature (material prosperity and the elimination of natural forces of destruction), the union of all peoples into "a single band" to fulfill God's purpose, that is, to do good and to seek perfection, righteousness, and brotherhood. This is the "kingdom of heaven" or the "kingdom of the Almighty"; it is the Messiah's reign or the "Days of the Messiah." But the Messiah is not the primary figure, although he occupies a central place in this "kingdom of heaven"; "heaven," that is, God, is the primary figure. (The word "heaven" is used here as a surrogate for God, to avoid blasphemy; hence "kingdom of heaven" and "kingdom of God," or "kingdom of the Almighty," are used interchangeably in the literature of the end of the period of the Second Temple and later.)

Finally, the "kingdom of heaven" will come only "in the end of the days." The chief difference [on this point] between Judaism and Hellenism is that the Greeks and Romans saw the "Golden Age" *in the past*, at the beginning of history, while the Jews saw it *in the future*, at the end of history. Humanity is steeped in wickedness and injustice, and hence is incomplete, or lacking in fulfillment. This fulfillment will come "in the end of the days," when wrongdoing, insolence, and conflict will pass from the earth, when "the wolf shall dwell with the lamb" and "the earth shall be full of the knowledge of the LORD as the waters cover the sea." Then those national achievements for which Israel longs in its exile and bondage will be realized: the return of the banished, the recovery of the homeland, the revival of the Hebrew language,[20] and the restoration of the

---

[20] Testaments of the Twelve Patriarchs, Judah 25:3. See on this above, p. 316; I. Ostersetzer, *The Outside Books* [Heb.], ed. Kahana, I, 1, p. 180; R. H. Charles,

kingdom (the kingdom of the house of David or the kingdom of the Messiah).

This notion of perfection stems from the ardent progressivism that belongs to the very foundation of Judaism. Both present-day Judaism and present-day humanity require completion, that is, they demand and are prepared for development and progress. This completion, the fruition of improvement by means of repentance and good works, will be achieved in the Messianic age. To be sure, the Messiah is reckoned among "three things that come unexpectedly"; [21] but among the "seven things hidden from men" is included also this: "when the kingdom of David will be restored to its former position." [22] Therefore, "unexpectedly" is not to be interpreted to mean that the Messiah will come without preparation, but that it is impossible to know in advance when the preparation will be complete, so that the Messiah *will be able* to come. And therefore, "the advent of Messiah" is not to be contrasted with "the end of the days": "the Messianic time of the end" and "the end of the days" are one and the same. The elimination of imperialistic oppression, the cessation of wars, everlasting peace, the fraternity of nations in "a single band," the removal of evil in man and nature, economic abundance, the flowing of all peoples to "the mountain of the LORD's house"—this whole complex of material and spiritual well-being is the Messianic age or the "kingdom of heaven"; for "heaven" (God) will bring all these things to the world through the Messiah, the exalted instrument of the Divine Will.

This is the Jewish Messiah and these his characteristics and activities.

II

And now by contrast—the Christian Messiah.

Christianity is wholly based on the personality of the Messiah. This statement needs no proof. When the people of Antioch began to

---

Apocrypha and Pseudepigrapha of the Old Testament in English, Oxford, 1913, II, 324, Note 3.
[21] Sanhedrin 97a.
[22] Mekhilta, Wayyassa, Chap. 6 (ed. Friedmann, 51a; ed. Horowitz-Rabin, p. 171); Pesahim 54b, beginning.

make a distinction between the believers in Jesus on the one hand, and Jews expecting the Messiah along with pagan Greeks on the other hand, they could find no more fitting name than "Christians"—a term derived from the Greek translation (*Christos*) of the Hebrew word "Messiah" (*Māshiaḥ*).[23] For at first the only difference between Jews and Christians was that the former believed that the Messiah *was still to come*, and the latter that the Messiah *had already come*.

But because of the fact that the Messiah who had already come was crucified as an ordinary rebel after being scourged and humiliated, and thus was not successful in the political sense, having failed to redeem his people Israel; because of the lowly political status of the Jews at the end of the period of the Second Temple and after the Destruction; and because of the fear that the Romans would persecute believers in a political Messiah—for these reasons there perforce came about a development of ideas, which after centuries of controversy became crystallized in Christianity in the following form:

1. The Messiah did not come to redeem from political oppression and economic wrong, but to redeem from spiritual evil alone.

2. Political oppression is a special problem of the Jews, but spiritual evil is world-wide. Hence Jesus came to redeem the whole world; *not* to redeem the Jewish people and their land *first*, and *then as a consequence* to redeem the whole world, which will forsake idolatry and become like Israel in every respect. And hence the kingdom of the Christian Messiah is "not of this world."

3. Jesus was scourged and humiliated as a common rebel. But he was not a common rebel; he only preached repentance and good works. Therefore, he was a true Messiah and not a false Messiah. Then why did God allow His Chosen One, the Messiah, to undergo frightful suffering and even to be crucified—the most shameful death of all, according to Cicero[24] and Tacitus[25]—and not save him from all these things? The answer can only be that it was the will of God and the will of the Messiah himself that he should be scourged, humiliated, and crucified. But whence came a purpose like this, that

---

[23] Acts 11:26.
[24] See Cicero, *Against Verres*, V 64.
[25] See Tacitus, *Histories*, IV 3 and 11.

would bring about suffering and death without sin? The answer can only be that the suffering was *vicarious* and the death was an *atoning death*. Jesus the Messiah suffered for others, for many, for all humanity. With his blood the Messiah redeemed humanity from sin, *inherited sin*, the sin of Adam, sin which became a part of Adam's nature, bringing death upon him and upon all his descendants. The Messiah went willingly to a disgraceful death in order that humanity might be redeemed from evil, from sin, from suffering, from death, and from the powers of Satan that prevail in the world—that Satan who by his enticement to sin brought death to the world. Support for this belief that the Messiah suffers for the iniquity of others (vicarious suffering) was found in Isaiah 53, which was interpreted not as referring to the persecuted people Israel, but to the suffering Messiah: "Yet he bore the sin of many." [26]

4. But the Messianic suffering which Jesus took upon himself by his own will and by the will of God cannot end in a shameful death. After the Messianic age comes the resurrection of the dead, according to Jewish doctrine. Therefore, of course, the Messiah rose from the dead—the first of men so to rise ("the firstfruits of them that slept," "the firstborn from the dead").[27] And therefore, Jesus is not mortal like other men. The will of God has been revealed in the will of the Messiah, and hence the Messiah is related to God *in a special way*.

5. God says to the Messiah, "Thou art My son, this day have I begotten thee." [28] And Jesus during his lifetime spoke much of "my Father who is in heaven." For Jews this was a common poetic-figurative expression. But the Gentiles, who asserted that certain of their eminent men—Alexander the Great, Plato, Pythagoras—had been fathered by gods who had visited mortal women, saw in this expression an actual genetic relationship of Jesus to God. Saul-Paul of Tarsus, who was a Jew, but one steeped in Greek culture, began to employ the concept "son of God" in a sense close to but not identical with the pagan concept: as Messiah, Jesus is "son of God" in the sense

[26] Isa. 53:12.
[27] I Cor. 15:20; Col. 1:18.
[28] Ps. 2:7.

of a "heavenly man" not susceptible to sin nor even to death. By his *temporary* death he atoned for the sin of Adam, and in his resurrection for eternity he ascended into heaven and sits at the right hand of God because he is closer to God than are the angels. This was the first step toward deification. But Paul the Jew did not go so far as to call Jesus "God."

The second step was to identify Jesus with the "Word" by which the world was created according to Judaism,[29] or with the "Logos," which is a sort of angelic being according to Philo of Alexandria.[30] This identification we find in the Gospel of John.[31] But it was natural that the Gentiles whom Paul brought into Christianity should take the third and final step and make Jesus a "God-man"—"one person with two natures"—God and man at one and the same time. Thus Jesus' Messiahship was gradually obscured: Jesus the Messiah gave way to "Jesus the God-man," or "the God Jesus"; and matters finally reached such a pass that the name "Christ" became the essential cognomen of Jesus ("Jesus Christ" and not "Jesus the Messiah"). The Messiahship of Jesus became secondary to his deity.

6. Although Jesus has been elevated to a rank fully equal to that of "God the Father," he still remains "Redeemer," and hence is still Messiah also. He has already come once into the world in the form of a man and has redeemed the world from sin and evil and death and Satan. Yet sin and evil and death and Satan still prevail in the world; therefore we are to expect his second coming, his "Parousia," at which time the Day of Judgment will occur, and Jesus, having taken his seat at the right hand of "his Father," will judge all persons that have ever lived, and will deliver those who believe in him. Then will Satan be conquered, evil will come to an end, sin will cease, and death will pass away; all the powers of darkness will vanish, and the kingdom of heaven will be fully established, though it had already begun with the first appearance of Jesus in the world.

7. Meanwhile, in "this world," men may turn in prayer to Jesus *as* to God his Father *and instead of* God his Father. In this sense he is

---

[29] Aboth 5:1.
[30] See on this in detail J. Klausner, *op. cit.*, I, 78–83.
[31] John 1:1–14.

"mediator" and "Paraclete" between God and man, although actually he himself is God and the true mediator is none other than Mary his mother, the Holy Virgin, "the mother of God" (*Theotokos*) by the Holy Spirit.

This is what happened in Christianity to the Jewish conception of the Messiah. The Christian Messiah ceased to be only a man, and passed beyond the limitations of mortality. Man cannot redeem himself from sin; but the Messiah-God, clothed in the form of a man, is the one who by his own freely shed blood has redeemed mankind. And he will come a second time to redeem humanity, since his first appearance, and even his death on the cross, did not suffice to eradicate evil from the world and to convert all men to belief in him. The first Christians expected this "Parousia" in their own time, and hence would pray, *Marana Tha*—"Our Lord, come!" (and not *Maran Atha* —"Our Lord has come").[32] When their prayer failed to be answered, and the Messiah-God did not again appear, they began to hope for the "thousand-year kingdom" or millennium (chiliasm); and finally they postponed the "Parousia" to an indefinite time.[33]

III

The Christian Messiah is in essence only a further development of the Jewish Messiah. For from Judaism Christianity received the ideas of redemption, the redeemer-Messiah, the Day of Judgment, and the kingdom of heaven. And much of what was common to Judaism and Christianity with respect to Messianic thinking remained even after estrangement and separation between them took place. Nevertheless, the difference between the Jewish and the Christian Messiah is very great.

First of all, Jewish redemption can be conceived without any individual Messiah at all—something which is absolutely impossible in Christianity. Also, "the Redeemer of Israel" for Judaism can mean God alone; in Christianity the Redeemer is Jesus only. Without the

---

[32] I Cor. 16:22. Cf. Rev. 22:20.
[33] See on this J. Klausner, *History of the Second Temple* [Heb.], V³ (1952), 125–129; *idem, Jesus of Nazareth*, 5th Heb. ed., Jerusalem, 1945, pp. 432–441 [Eng. ed., pp. 398–407].

Jewish Messiah, Judaism is defective; without the Christian Messiah, Christianity does not exist at all.

Second, there is an irrational side even in the Jewish Messianic conception: where there is no mysticism at all there is no faith. But the irrational and mystical element in the Jewish Messiah is only unnatural, but not anti-natural, not opposed to nature. The unity of God is not affected in any essential way by the Jewish Messiah. In the last analysis, the Jewish Messiah is only, as said above, the instrument of deity—although of course a choice and superb instrument. But in Christianity monotheism is obscured by the Messiah, who is "Son of God," the "Logos," "the Lord," a "God-man," and "one person with two natures." And from this spring the rest of the marked differences between the Jewish and Christian Messiahs: one cannot pray to the Jewish Messiah, he is not a mediator between God and man, he is not a "Paraclete" for man, and so on.

Third, the Jewish Messiah is the redeemer of his people and the redeemer of mankind. But he does not redeem them by his blood; instead, he lends aid to their redemption by his great abilities and deeds. Even Messiah ben Joseph, who is slain, affords no atonement by his blood and his sufferings are not vicarious. Judaism is familiar with "the sin of Adam," but the Jewish Messiah does not with his blood redeem from "original sin," nor from death, nor from Satan. To be sure, Satan will be vanquished in the Messianic age—not by the Messiah, but by God. Man must redeem himself from sin *not by faith alone*, but *by repentance and good works;* then God will redeem him from death and Satan. (Generally speaking, Satan does not occupy in Judaism the central place that he takes in Christianity; Satan in Christianity is almost like the God of Evil of the Persians.) Each man is responsible for himself, and through his good deeds he must find atonement for his sins. He cannot lean upon the Messiah or upon the Messiah's suffering and death.[34]

Fourth and finally, since the Jewish Messiah is only "a righteous man ruling in the fear of God," and since he brings only ethical perfection to the world, the progress of humanity does not depend on him, but *on humanity itself*. Numberless times the Talmud returns to

[34] See A. Büchler, *Studies in Sin and Atonement*, London, 1928, pp. 375-461.

the idea that redemption depends on repentance and good works; well known is the interpretation of the verse "I the LORD will hasten it in its time": [35] "If they are worthy, I will hasten it [the redemption]; if not, it will come in its [own good] time." [36] And the Hebrew people, who were the first to acknowledge faith in One God, the God of goodness, and to whom came prophets of truth and righteousness, can and will be the first to "hasten the redemption" by repentance and good works. In other words, the Jews can and must march at the head of humanity on the road of personal and social progress, on the road to ethical perfection. This will be possible only when they have returned to their own land, have gathered in their exiles, have reestablished their own state, and are no longer under the oppression of foreigners; but the "kingdom of heaven" is their goal and their highest aspiration, and without this goal Israel would never be freed from "bondage to foreign powers"—cessation of which will be the obvious external sign that the Days of the Messiah are near.[37]

Therefore, we can say, without being suspected of undue bias toward Judaism, that the Jewish Messianic faith is the seed of progress, which has been planted by Judaism throughout the whole world.

[35] Isa. 60:22.
[36] Sanhedrin 98a; and Yerushalmi, Taanith 1:1 (63d) says, "If you are worthy, I will hasten it; if not, it will come in its [own good] time."
[37] "There is no difference between this age and the Days of the Messiah except bondage to foreign powers" (Ber. 34b and parallels).

Index

[This index is a combination and condensation of the author's two indexes, one an index of names and subjects in Hebrew, and the other an index of names in Latin characters.—TRANS.]

Aaron, 256-257, 313, 455-456, 469, 514
Abraham, 346, 466
Abramowitz, Shalom Jacob, 200
Abtalion, 392
Adam, 285, 346, 354, 356, 368, 467, 510, 528
Adiabene, 476
Agag, 31
Age to Come, 415-418, 425, 446-450, et passim
Ahab (king), 21, 135
Ahab (false prophet), 113
Ahad Ha-Am, 10, 466, 503
Ahasuerus, 225
Ahaz, 47, 53-54, 72
Ahikam son of Shaphan, 111
Ahmose (Amasis), 148
Akiba, R., 31, 250, 364, 394-403, 410-411, 423-424, 431-432, 435, 438-439, 441, 444-445, 459, 472-475, 486-488, 491-499, 503, 514
Albeck, C., 449
Albright, W. F., 162, 185, 303
Alexander Janneus. See Janneus Alexander
Alexander the Great, 176, 180, 222, 225, 228, 286, 489, 527
Alexandri, Rab (Amora), 407
Alexandria, Alexandrians, 330, 370, 379, 416, 493
Alroy, David, 11
Alt, A., 187
Amalek, 31, 312
Amasis. See Ahmose
Amaziah, priest of Bethel, 43
Ammon, 54, 84, 85, 187
Amon (king), 82, 87

Amoraim, *passim, especially Part III*
Amos, 28, 36-44, 210, 282, 374, 493
Amram, 367
Anan, 303
Ancient of Days, the, 229, 291
Anshan, 89
Antichrist, 373-375, 406-407, 496-497
Anti-Messiah. See Antichrist
Antinomians, 307, 434, 442, 446. See also Belial, Beliar
Antiochus I, 228
Antiochus II, 225, 228
Antiochus III (the Great), 229
Antiochus IV Epiphanes, 223, 225-233, 274, 326, 336, 399, 441-442, 489
Antiochus VII Sidetes, 267, 286
Antony, Mark, 371, 373, 374
Apocalyptic, 180-184, 227-228, 249, 272-273, 312, 325-328, 330, 379, 414, 457
Apollonius, 223
Apries. See Hophra
Aptowitzer, V., 412, 456
Arabia, Arabians, 37, 93, 406, 474
Archelaus, 325, 328
Aristagoras, 199
Aristeas, Letter of, 370
Aristobulus I. See Judas Aristobulus
Aristobulus II, 317
Armenia, Armenians, 181, 189, 277, 297
Armilus, 373, 407, 496
Artaxerxes III, 180, 218
Asenapper (Osnapper, Asnapper). See Ashurbanipal
Ashdod, Ashdodites, 187
Ashkelon, 202
Ashkenaz, 89, 127. See also Scythians
Ashkuza. See Ashkenaz

533

Ashurbanipal (Asenapper), 79, 88, 127, 173
Assi, Rab, 430
Assumption of Moses, 276, 325-329, 373, 393
Assyria, Assyrians, 31, 36, 40, 42, 50, 52-55, 61, 78, 80-81, 84, 87, 88, 156, 178, 181, 197-198, 200-202
Athenians, 199
Auerbach, E., 52
Augustus, 372
Azariah, 467
Azael, 279
Azazel, 279, 296
Azov, Sea of, 297

Baalis, 187
Babylon, Babylonia, Babylonians, *passim*
Bacher, W., 364, 396, 397, 398, 401, 414, 420, 425, 428, 433, 434, 436, 443, 444, 462, 491, 499, 505, 507, 513
Baer, J., 405
Balaam, 32, 368. See also Section on Balaam
Banias. See Pamias
Bar-Cochba (Ben-Coziba), 19, 31, 227, 250, 331, 360, 371, 394-395, 397-402, 407, 423-425, 434, 442, 459, 468, 482, 486-488, 492-496
Bardiya (Smerdis), 189
Bar-Kappara, 391, 436, 450, 467, 497, 510
Baruch, the Apocryphal, 248, 251, 267-269, 318, 330
Baruch, the Greek, 330, 382
Baruch, the Syriac, 227, 276, 299, 330-348, 349, 351, 354-355, 357, 359, 360, 364-365, 366, 380, 393, 414, 506-509
Baruch, the Slavonic, 383
Bastards (offspring of forbidden unions), 187, 454
Beer, G., 286, 299
Begrich, J., 52
Behemoth. See Wild ox
Belial, 316, 371, 373-374. See also Antinomians
Beliar. See Belial
Belshazzar, 148, 224-225, 227
Belteshazzar, 148
Benjamin of Tudela, 438
Ben-Koziba. See Bar-Cochba

Ben-Sira, 159, 180, 216-219, 226-227, 248, 252-258, 273, 284, 455, 484
Ben-Yehudah, E., 144
Ben Zoma, 410, 416-417
Bernfeld, S., 84, 117, 135, 145, 160, 180, 196, 198, 214, 218, 225, 318
Bertholdt, L., 484
Bertholet, A., 108
Bethar, 400-403, 435, 441, 450, 468, 486, 492-494, 504
Bethel, 43, 186
Bethlehem, 77
Bezold, C., 456
Biblical Antiquities ("of Philo"), 366-369, 432
Bickermann, E., 231
Birth pangs of Messiah, 34, 41, 83-84, 178-179, 208-209, 278-282, 297-300, 325-329, 335-339, 342, 350-354, 372-374, 400-401, 440-450. See also Day of the LORD and Day of Judgment
Bithiah (daughter of Pharaoh), 466
Blessing of Jacob, 29-30
Blessing of Moses, 487
Boettcher, J. F., 166
Bonwetsch, D., 383
Book of Enoch. See Enoch
Bousset, W., 13, 230, 406, 483, 489
Bousset-Gressmann, 13, 230, 292, 376, 379, 389, 414, 432, 461, 484, 489
Budde, K., 45, 48, 74-75, 79, 80, 84, 113, 117, 123, 135, 136, 145, 162, 198, 201, 207, 216, 227
Büchler, A., 302, 453, 530
Burkitt, F. C., 326
Buttenwieser, M., 406

Caesarea Philippi, 433
Calvin, J., 217
Cambyses, 181-182, 189
Canaan, Canaanites, 93, 136-138, 203, 205, 312
Cappadocians, 312
Carchemish, 90
Carmel, 456, 513
Castelli, D., 2-5, 18, 26, 30, 34, 48, 57, 64, 74, 77-79, 87, 97, 118, 126, 174, 210, 219-221, 234, 405, 406, 408, 414, 429, 443, 457, 458, 466, 484, 485, 492, 513, 516-517
Causse, A., 137, 470
Chajes, Z. P., 141-142, 218-219

Chaldeans, 87, 148-149, 158
Charles, R. H., 256, 267, 285, 311-316, 323, 326, 336, 347, 354, 371, 380, 524-525
Chebar River, 111
Cherub-Addan, 111, 172
Cheyne, T. K., 56, 165, 218
Chiliasm, Chiliasts, 10, 283-284, 414, 506, 529
Chwolsohn, D., 453
Cicero, 526
Circumcision, 172-173
Clement of Alexandria, 234
Cleopatra, 304, 371, 374
Cohen, Hermann, 415
Cohn, L., 366
Colani, T., 435
Conder, C. R., 250
Coniah. See Jehoiachin
Consolation of Zion, 144, 150-151, 158-160, 220, 228-229, 257-258, 345-346, 423
Cornill, C. H., 112, 126, 133, 136, 155, 160, 198
Cowley, A., 310
Croesus, 127, 147-148
Cyrus, 89, 108, 110, 127, 143, 147-149, 154-156, 185-186, 189, 228, 233

Daiches, S., 111, 172, 189, 214
Dalman, G., 2-3, 401, 405-406, 440, 456, 484-487, 490-492, 501, 515
Damascus, 40, 202, 463, 505
Damascus Covenant, 304, 311
Danel, 224
Daniel, 222-236, 239, 249, 284-285, 291, 358-360, 413, 467, 519
Darius I, 189-193, 208, 225, 227
Darius II (son of Ahasuerus), 225, 232
David, 19-21, 28-32, 42-44, 46-47, 101-102, 140, 305, 467, *et passim*
David Alroy. See Alroy, David
Day of Judgment, 38-41, 58-61, 92-93, 122, 126-127, 137, 178-179, 182, 208-209, 210, 211, 215, 220, 264, 278-282, 286-287, 296-298, 306-308, 312, 328-329, 335-339, 345, 356-358, 371-374, 379-380, 450. See also Day of the LORD; Birth pangs of Messiah
Day of the LORD. See Day of Judgment
Days of the Messiah (Messianic Age), 287-288, 294-301, 339-348, 354-365, 377-379, 408-419, 502-517, *et passim*
Dead Sea. See Sea of Sodom
Dead Sea Scrolls, 289, 302, 325, 326
Delitzsch, Franz, 217, 321
Delitzsch-Schnedermann, 414
Demetrius (historian), 233-234
Demetrius I (king), 229
Demons and devils, 279-280, 313, 316, 334
Deutero-Isaiah. See Isaiah (Second)
Deutero-Zechariah. See Zechariah (Second)
De Wette, W. M. L., 484
Dillmann, A., 448
Dosa, R., 355, 420-421, 490-492
Dougherty, R. H., 148
Drummond, J., 3, 9, 414, 424, 449, 456, 459, 466, 485-488, 523
Dudael, 279
Duhm, B., 145-146, 162
Dunedain, 298

Ebed-melech the Ethiopian, 111, 466
Ebeling, E., 111
Edom, 31, 75, 90, 135-139, 180-182, 187, 210, 286, 303, 340, 503-504. See also Rome
Egypt, 13, 15, 17, 63, 67-68, 74, 88, 93, 132, 176, 180-182, 189, 198, 201, 304, 371-374, 410, 425, 471, 503
Eichrodt, W., 14, 35
Eighteen Benedictions. See Shemoneh Esreh
Eisler, R., 379, 488-489
Eissfeldt, O., 28
Ekron, 202
Elbogen, I. M., 393
Eldad and Medad, 499
Eleazar, Rab (Amora), 475
Eleazar ben Azariah, R., 420, 448, 472
Eleazar ben Shammua, R., 401
Eleazar of Modi'im, R., 397, 415, 468, 472
Eliezer (servant of Abraham), 466
Eliezer ben Hyrcanus, R., 363-364, 397, 420, 425, 428-429, 448-450, 472, 475, 481, 497, 502-503, 505
Eliezer ha-Kappar, R., 513. See also Bar-Kappara
Eliezer, son of R. Jose the Galilean, R., 511

Elijah, 18, 215-216, 257, 260, 343, 451-457, 466, 469, 498, 513, 515
End, End of (the) Days, etc., 56, 68-71, 234-236, 297-301, 308-309, 312, 342-348, 352-358, 368, 378-380, 393, 403, 408-419, 420-426, 447, 456
Enoch, 466
Enoch, the Ethiopic, 227, 229, 272, 275, 277-301, 310, 325, 331, 332, 342, 344, 346, 351, 359, 365, 374, 393, 414, 506
Enoch, the Slavonic, 383
Ephraim, 95-96, 100, 138, 186, 197-200, 483-488, 495-496
Ephrathah. *See* Bethlehem
Epiphanes. *See* Antiochus IV
Epiphanius, 374
Epstein, J. N., 453
Essenes, 250, 275, 289, 309, 325
Esther, 477
Eternity (perpetuity) of Israel, 70, 95, 168, 174, 228-231, 255-258, 367-368, 512
Eternity (perpetuity) of the Law, 174, 367-368, 445-450, 513-514
Ethiopia, Ethiopians, 68, 84, 174, 375, 503
Euphrates (River), 183, 203, 258, 345, 362
Eve, 368
Evil-Merodach, 148-149, 224
Evil spirits, unclean spirits. *See* Demons and devils
Ewald, H., 136, 218
Ezekiel, 33, 108-134, 142, 146, 149, 186, 210-212, 220, 224, 226-227, 249, 287, 297, 353, 358, 375-377, 409, 493, 495-497
Ezra, 131, 146, 170, 200-201, 207, 211, 216, 222, 227
Ezra, the Aprocryphal (Third), 349
Ezra, the Pseudepigraphical (Fourth), 227, 272, 276, 299, 331, 333, 340, 343, 346, 349-365, 375, 380, 393, 396, 412, 414, 494, 506

Faitlowitch, J., 303
Feigin, S., 55
Flask of oil for anointing, 455-456, 469, 513
Flemming, J., 168, 290, 298
Flood, 298, 306
Flood of fire, 279

Forerunner of the Messiah, 80, 158, 215-216, 451-457. *See also* Elijah
Forgetting of the Law, 41, 334, 441, 447-450, 513
Fränkel, I. S., 248
Frankel, Z., 381, 406-407, 411, 436, 438, 448
Fravartish. *See* Phraortes
Freund, L., 454
Friedlaender, M., 273, 406, 434, 442, 445, 446, 497
Friedmann, M., 293, 397, 401, 421, 447, 451, 454, 455, 457, 460, 467, 471-472, 488, 492, 495-496

Gablan, 443-444
Gabriel (angel), 226, 296, 504
Gadd, C. J., 79
Galilee, 443-444
Gamaliel I, Rabban, 506-507, 509
Gamaliel II, Rabban, 396, 448, 451, 465
Garden of Eden, 14, 298, 460. *See also* Paradise
Gaumata, 181, 182, 189
Gaza, 53, 202
Gedaliah (son of Ahikam), 187
Gehenna, 272, 274, 281, 287, 296, 316, 348, 356, 367, 380, 408, 414, 460
Geiger, A., 309
Generation of Messiah, 420-426
Gershom Meor ha-Golah, Rabbenu, 515
Gesenius, W., 218, 484
Gfroerer, A. F., 5
Giesebrecht, F., 162
Gideon, 19
Ginzberg, Levi (Louis), 336, 379
Giving of the Law, 498
Glaesener, 484
God-fearers, 479-480
God of the Spirits, 290, 296, 298, 300
Gog and Magog, 11, 57, 89, 127-132, 201, 205, 297, 353, 361, 363, 375-376, 398, 401, 422, 450, 464, 496-501
Goldschmidt, E. (L.), 288, 292
Graetz, H., 142, 169, 170, 172, 187, 218, 279, 395, 424, 435, 442, 464
"Great Assembly," 260
Greece, Greeks, 137, 173, 198-199, 202, 207, 208, 225-226, 228, 230-231, 339, 377
Greenstone, J. H., 2-3, 250

INDEX

Gressmann, H., 13, 18, 22, 29, 30, 35, 62, 84, 164, 180, 203, 210, 230, 292, 338, 359, 389, 489
Grotius, Hugo, 31
Guf. *See* Treasury of souls
Gunkel, H., 22, 35, 349, 351, 353, 357
Guttmann, J. M., 447, 451, 457

Habakkuk, 87, 403
Hadrach, 463
Hadrian, 367, 371, 398, 399, 402, 420, 424-425, 430-434, 441-445, 461-463
Haggai, 147, 185-193, 201, 208, 212
Halevy, Isaac, 398, 435, 474
Haman, 429, 497
Hamburger, J., 486-488, 492, 496
Hammer, H., 484
Hanan, 53
Hananiah, Mishael, and Azariah, 467
Hananiah ben Teradion. *See* Hanina ben Teradion
Hanina ben Teradion, 432, 435
Hannah, 34, 367
Hasidim ("saints" or "the pious"), 218-219, 223, 250, 275, 311, 319, 325, 327
Hasmoneans, 176, 218-219, 256, 259-263, 384
Hebrew language in the Messianic age, 316, 386, 524
Helbo, Rab, 478
Heliodorus, 223
Hengstenberg, E. W., 30
Herald of good news, 80, 151, 158, 318, 451-457, 468
Heresy (*Minuth*) and heretics (*Minim*), 385, 443, 445-446
Herford, R. T., 250, 273, 304, 311, 386, 393, 445
Herod, 8, 325, 329, 336, 374, 392-393, 424, 434, 441, 476
Herodotus, 89
Herzfeld, L., 137
Hezekiah, 47, 52-57, 105, 143-144, 396, 463-465
Higger, M., 462, 468, 521
High priest (in the Messianic age), 456, 515-516
Hilkiah (chief priest), 89
Hillel the Elder, 392-393, 453
Hillel, Rab (Amora), 9, 57, 404, 459, 464, 522-523
Hillel, school of, 393-394, 448

Hiram, 466
Hisda, R., 409, 475
Histiaeus of Miletus, 199
Hitzig, F., 77, 217
Hiyya, R., 391, 436-437, 507
Hoelscher, G., 187
Holtzmann, A., 344
Holy Spirit, 65, 294, 467
Hommel, F., 32, 52, 89, 127, 154
Honor, L., 55
Hophra (Pharaoh), 90
Horowitz, Isaiah, 483
Hosea (prophet), 28, 45-51, 55, 101, 113, 119, 125, 255
Hoshea (king), 54, 362
Hühn, E., 2, 27, 34, 43, 45, 47-49, 61, 64, 95, 99, 103, 123, 125, 127, 196, 210, 225, 236, 329, 379, 383, 406, 421, 509
Hyman, A., 491-492
Hyrcanus. *See* John Hyrcanus
Hyrcanus ben Joseph ben Tobias, 489

Ibn-Ezra, Abraham, 143, 303
Ibn-Shemuel (Kaufman), Judah, 406, 496, 501
Immer, 111, 172
Individualism, religious, 124
Informers, 434-435
Ingathering of the exiles, 47, 74, 86, 95-96, 183, 220, 254, 265-269, 287, 297-298, 317, 363-364, 470-475
Ipsus, 198, 225
Irenaeus, 26, 283, 332, 343, 506, 509
Isaiah (First), 35, 52-71, 104, 147, 152, 155, 178, 180, 196, 198, 205, 251, 282, 294, 342, 378, 493-494, 519
Isaiah (Second), 143-184, 186, 199, 201, 204, 208, 212, 266, 268, 318, 345, 354-355, 379
Isaiah ("Third"), 145-147
Ishmael ben Elisha, R., 424, 431, 438, 455, 461
Ishmael ben Jose the Galilean, R., 503-504
Ish-Shalom. *See* Friedmann
Izates (Zotos), 476

Jabez (son of R. Judah), 466
Jackson-Lake, 389
James, M. R., 333, 366-369, 432
Jamnia (Yabneh), 396, 447-448

INDEX

Jampel, S., 185, 212
Janneus Alexander, 180, 199, 250, 259-260, 288-289, 292, 296, 302-304, 313, 318, 336-337
Jason, *See* Jeshua-Jason
Jehoahaz (Shallum), 90
Jehoash son of Ahaziah (king), 206
Jehoiachin, 90, 108-109, 149, 162, 185, 188, 192, 224
Jehoiada, 206
Jehoiakim, 90-92, 224
Jehoram, 135, 138
Jehu, 128
Jellinek, A., 5, 415
Jeremiah, 82, 88-107, 115, 136, 161, 171, 192, 195, 197, 205, 232-233, 237-242, 282, 286, 374, 519
Jeremias, A., 13-14, 53
Jericho, 187
Jeroboam son of Joash, 35, 36-37
Jerome, 227, 360, 504
Jerusalem—*throughout the book*
Jerusalem the heavenly, 287, 346, 361-362
Jeshua-Jason, 223, 234
Jeshua (Joshua) son of Jozadak, 133, 185, 186, 188, 190-191, 194-196, 212, 286
Jesus, 10, 162, 203-204, 230, 293, 310, 314, 332, 344, 350, 354, 371, 439, 519, 526-529; as Paraclete, 530
Jezreel, 47
Job, 224, 252
Joel, 206-211, 215, 329, 374, 509, 522
Johanan, R. (Amora), 404, 428, 430, 474-475
Johanan ben Torta, R., 459
Johanan ben Zakkai, R., 394-396, 428, 453, 465, 514
John (disciple of Jesus), 344
John (the Evangelist), 392
John Hyrcanus, 180, 199, 259, 260, 275, 289, 302-303, 311, 313, 319
John the Baptist, 314, 428
Jonah the Prophet, 81
Jonathan ben Uzziel, 405, 425
Jonathan son of Mattathias, 199, 275
Jose, Rab (Amora), 9, 404, 446, 522
Jose ben Dormaskith, R., 463, 505
Jose ben Halaphta, R., 401, 403, 425, 428, 430-432, 452, 454, 480, 504, 509
Jose ben Joezer, R., 392

Jose ben Johanan, R., 392
Jose ben Kisma, R., 397, 432-434, 450
Jose the Galilean, R., 407, 420-421, 428, 462, 468, 472
Josephus, 233, 328, 362, 374, 411, 476, 478-479
Joshua, 19, 325, 327, 328
Joshua ben Hananiah, R., 363, 397, 416, 425-426, 428-429, 438, 448, 452-455, 472
Joshua ben Levi, R., 406
Joshua ben Perahiah, R., 392
Josiah, 82, 87, 88-90, 104, 141
Jotham (king), 52, 72, 143
"Jozedek among the prophets," 103
Jubilees, Book of, 272, 276, 302-309, 366
Judah (Land of Promise), *passim*
Judah ben Baba, R., 401, 435
Judah ben Bathyra, R., 454-455
Judah ben Ilai, R., 401, 402, 411, 444, 452, 462-463, 509-510, 514
Judah ben Tabbai, 296, 392
Judah the Patriarch, R., 364, 391, 403, 406, 411, 417, 436-439, 459-460
Judas Aristobulus, 259
Judas Maccabeus, 223-225, 232, 234, 250, 260, 262, 275, 286
"Judges," 19, 138
Judith, 248, 264, 265, 273
Jülicher, A., 371
Julius Caesar, 373
Juster, J., 470, 477
Justin Martyr, 56-57, 407, 456, 464, 466, 485-486, 520

Kahana, Abraham, 136, 218, 219, 247, 267, 276, 325, 349
Kahana, David, 32, 219, 227
Kaminetzky, A. S., 218, 318, 326
Kaminka, A., 144-145, 180, 349
Kanbuzi. *See* Cambyses
Kant, E., 24, 118, 146, 523
Karaites, 303
Katz, Ben-Zion, 276
Katzenelson, J. L., 200, 485
Kaufman, Judah. *See* Ibn-Shemuel
Kaufmann, Ezekiel, 140, 217
Kautzsch, E., 42-43, 166, 234, 267, 299, 335, 349
Kedar, 175
Kingdom of Heaven (Kingdom of the

Almighty), 235, 372, 418, 482, 502, 504-507
Kingdom of priests, 512
Kittel, Gerhardt, 13, 489
Kittel, Rudolf, 13, 35, 52, 105
Klamroth, E., 111
Klein, S., 279, 453
Koenig, E., 2, 13, 29, 49, 206
Kohler, K., 311
Kohut, A. (H. J.), 279, 431, 443, 462
Kolbe, W., 262
Kosters, W. H., 185
Krauss, S., 132, 144, 147, 154, 162, 164, 169, 173, 338
Krenkel, M., 78
Krochmal, N., 143, 197, 218, 504
Kuenen, A., 216

Labashi-Marduk, 148
Lambert, M., 125, 226, 229
Law, 460. *See also* Forgetting of the Law; Eternity of the Law
Lazar, S. M., 474
Le 'Atid Labo.' *See* Age to Come
Leper of the House of Rabbi, 406, 463
Levi, House of Levi, 304-305, 311-316, 326, 409, 454
Leviathan, 182, 274, 298-299, 342, 343, 364-365
Levitas of Jabneh, R., 412
Levy, Jacob, 52, 423, 443, 465, 474, 477, 486-488, 492, 495, 499
Levy, Reuben, 145, 167
Lieberman, S., 405, 447
Lods, A., 42
Luther, Martin, 350
Luzzato, S. D., 64, 70, 166
Lydda, 187
Lydia, 127-128, 137, 144, 147-148, 173
Lysias, 260

Maccabees (First), book, 248, 251, 259-261, 276
Maccabees (Second), book, 248, 251, 262-263, 270
Maimonides, 415, 519, 523
Malachi, 147, 202, 211-216, 235
Manasseh (king), 87
Manna, 343, 345, 355, 421, 513
Mark, bishop of Jerusalem, 445
Marti, K., 42, 135, 145, 180, 196, 199, 207, 217, 225, 229, 234, 236

Martini, Raymundus, 405, 407
Mattaniah. *See* Zedekiah
Mattathias (Mattithiah) son of John Hasmoneus, 223, 260, 286, 326
Mattathias Antigonus, 433-434
Media, Medes, 89, 93, 144, 178, 181, 189, 225, 228, 277, 297, 473-474
Mediterranean Sea, 203
Meir, R., 402-403, 454, 474, 509
Meissner, B., 154
Mekhilta, 423-424, 450
Melchizedek, 456, 515. *See also* Righteous priest
Menahem son of Gadi, 53
Menahem son of Hezekiah, 463-464
Mendele the Bookseller, 200
Menelaus, 223
Merx, A., 484, 486, 495
Messel, N., 292
Messiah, Messiah ben David—*throughout the book*
Individual (personal) Messiah, 8-11, 47-48, 64, 74, 87, 101-106, 125-126, 138, 154-156, 192, 194-196, 230, 250, 254, 288-301, 323-324, 337, 340, 354, 358-362, 367, 376, 458-462
Messiah ben Joseph, 11, 129, 204, 343, 375, 400-401, 483, 501, 520-521
Messiah of the House of Levi, 304-305, 310-316, 326
Moses and the Messiah, 15-19. *See also* Moses
Name of the Messiah, 7-8, 288-289, 293-294, 358-359, 460-465
Personality of the Messiah, 358-362, 465-469, 520-521
Samaritan Messiah, 484-485, 488, 495. *See also* Taëb
Suffering Messiah, 204, 361, 405-407, 483-501
Twofold Messiah, 16-17, 163, 392, 400-401, 492-497, 517
Messianic age (Days of the Messiah), 287-289, 294-301, 340-348, 354-358, 376-379, 408-419, 502-517, *et passim*
Methuselah, 467
Meyer, E., 105, 185
Micah, 35, 51, 72-79, 113
Michael, 226, 235, 285, 296, 329
Midian, 54, 175
Migdal-eder, 77
Migdol, 89

INDEX

Miletus, 507
Minim, Minuth. *See* Heretics and heresy
Miracles, 465, 470-471, 509-517
Mishael, 467
Momigliano, A., 262
Montefiore, C. G., 349
Montgomery, J. A., 484
Mordecai, 476
Moses, 15-19, 74, 162, 325-328, 467, *et passim*
Mount of Olives, 205
Mourners for Zion, 169-170, 395-396, 437-439
Murashu, 111, 144

Nabateans, 180, 181, 187
Nabonidus (Nabunaid), 148, 225
Nabopolassar, 88
Nahum, 79-81, 87, 88
Name of the Messiah. *See under* Messiah
Nathan, R., 399, 403, 424
Nathan the Prophet, 20, 28, 30
Nebuchadrezzar II, 88, 90, 111, 112, 126, 135, 148, 149, 180, 182, 201, 207, 224, 227-228
Necho (Pharaoh), 89-90, 141
Nehemiah, R., 401-402, 444, 476-477, 499
Nehemiah ben Hushiel, 496
Nehemiah son of Hacaliah, 170, 200, 201, 207-209, 222-223, 349
Nehorai, R., 402, 444
Nephilim, 279-280, 282, 286, 296-297, 373
Nergal-sharezer (Neriglissar), 148
Nero (emperor), 371, 381
Nestle, E., 232
Neubauer, A., 443
Neumark, D., 173
New Covenant, 98, 176
New World, 306, 339-341, 347-348, 352-357, 378-381, 413-414, 417-418, 420
Nidintu-Bel, 189
Nietzsche, F., 523
Nineveh, 79-81, 88
Ninth of Ab, 403, 438-439
Nittai the Arbelite, 392
Noah, 224, 226-227, 298, 370

Nomocracy, 131
Noth, M., 105

Obadiah, 135-139
Octavian, 373
Oestreicher, T., 89
Oil for anointing, 455-456, 514
Olshausen, J., 217
Omri, 128
Onias, temple of, 371
Onias III, 223, 233, 286
Ostersetzer, I., 311, 314, 524

Pamias, 433
Paneas. *See* Pamias
Papias, 283, 332, 414, 506-507, 509
Paradise, 274, 354-356, 367, 408, 414, 466
Parthians, 277, 297, 432-434
Pass-Arendzen, 310
Passover, 397
Paul, 162, 389, 446, 507, 510, 512, 519, 527
Peace (in the Messianic age), 50-51, 63-71, 76, 78-79, 203, 283, 288, 296, 308, 314, 321, 340-342, 376-379, 468-469
Peace (as a name of the Messiah), 462, 521
Pekah son of Remaliah, 53
Perles, F., 318
Persia, Persians, 89, 127, 132, 143, 154, 170, 178, 181, 188-192, 199-202, 222, 224-225, 228, 233, 297, 339, 418, 433
Personality of the Messiah. *See under* Messiah
Phanuel (angel), 296
Pharisees, 250, 260, 267, 275, 277, 288-289, 292, 303, 309, 317, 336, 393. *See also* Mourners for Zion
Philistia, 75, 84, 93, 138
Philo, 366, 386, 493, 511, 523, 528
Phinehas, 255-256, 456
Phoenicia, Phoenicians. *See* Canaan, Canaanites
Phraortes, 189
Plato, 461, 527
Pliny, 362
Pognon, H., 463
Pompey, 289, 317, 319, 373
Porphyry, 227
Poznansky, A., 29
Primeval silence, 355

INDEX

Procreation (in the Messianic age), 412-413
Prophets, the (in relation to the Messianic idea), 21-25, 33-35, *et passim*
Proselytes. *See* Reception of proselytes
Prosperity, material, 43-44, 49, 62-63, 85-86, 99-101, 125, 130, 133, 154, 158-160, 175-177, 194, 203, 209, 283-284, 299, 312, 324, 342-345, 364, 367, 377-378, 381, 409-410, 505-512
Proverbs, 252
Psalms (Biblical), 140-142, 217-221, 222, 249
Psalms of Solomon, 218, 276, 317-324, 331, 392, 470, 494
Psamtik (Psammetichus) I, 89, 127
Ptolemy, Ptolemies, 222-225, 228, 286
Ptolemy II Philadelphus, 225
Ptolemy Lathyrus, 304
Ptolemy Physcon, 371
Pul. *See* Tiglath-pileser IV
Punishment, 38, 45, 58-60, 73, 83-84, 92-94, 119-120, 136-137, 149, 161-162, 171, 178-179, 181-182, 192, 220, 278-282, 305, 313, 331, 400-401. *See also* Day of Judgment; Birth pangs of Messiah
Pythagoras, 527

Rab (Abba Arikha), 404
Raba (bar Joseph), 468
Rabinsohn, M., 419
Raphael (angel), 279, 296
Rashi, 9, 29, 31, 206, 333, 416, 421, 423, 424, 426, 429, 431, 433, 436, 442, 475, 476, 507, 514, 515
Reception of proselytes, 106-107, 172, 214, 320-321, 475-482, 512
Red Sea, 203
Redeemer, 15-25, 74, *et passim*. *See also* Messiah
Redemption—*passim*
Reider, J., 372, 380
Remnant of Israel, the, 61-62, 76-77, 85, 95, 187
Renan, E., 20
Renzer, J., 513
Repentance, 40, 61-62, 96, 117-118, 120-122, 150, 171, 183, 209, 267, 295, 305, 307, 308, 315, 327, 346, 422, 427-429, 530-531

Rephaim ("Shades"), 183, 295, 355
Resch, A., 344
Resurrection of the dead, 125, 183, 235-236, 272, 295, 303, 313, 316, 339, 347-348, 350, 354-355, 368, 379, 408, 413-418, 420, 456, 473, 527
Return to Zion, 33, 115, 145, 156, 171-172, 185-186, 265-268, 470-475
Reuss, E., 217
Rezin (king of Syria), 53-54
Righteous priest, 456, 515
River of Egypt, 183
Rod of Aaron, 455, 469, 513
Rome, Romans, 275, 311, 317, *et passim*
Rome, "the boar out of the wood," 504
Romulus Augustulus, 423
Rosenthal, F., 327
Rowley, H. H., 225, 229
Ruth, 478
Ryssel, V., 335

Sabbath, the, 112, 172
Sacrifices (in the Messianic age), 173, 397, 513-517
Sadducees, 250, 259, 262, 303, 307, 309
Salome Alexandra, 277, 302, 453
Salvador, J., 131
Samaria, 33, 53, 54, 186, 374, 398
Samaritans, 186, 200, 201, 303, 434-435, 484-485, 488, 495
Sambation, 362
Samuel (Amora), 404, 454
Samuel (prophet), 19
Samuel the Little (Tanna), 412
Saoshyant, 13-14
Sarakos. *See* Sin-shar-ishkun
Sardis (Sardes), 137, 199
Sargon, 53-54
Satan, 279, 282, 329, 373-374
Saul (king), 19, 31
Schechter, S., 219, 460
Scheftelowitz, J., 14, 170
Schiller-Szinessy, S. M., 362
Schmidt, N., 13
Schmiedel, P., 2
Schurer, E., 8, 217, 225, 227, 234, 333, 359, 366, 370-371, 388, 394, 399, 407, 413, 418, 431, 436, 461, 466, 470, 479, 499-500
Scythians, 89, 127, 199, 206. *See also* Ashkuza and Ashkenaz

Sea of Sodom, 351
Sebaste, Sebastenes, 371, 373
Section on Balaam, 30-32
Segal, M. Z., 36, 144, 162, 207, 304, 311
Seleucus I, 228
Seleucus II, 228
Seleucus III, 228
Seleucus IV, 223, 229
Sellin, E., 13, 22, 31, 32, 35, 42, 62, 162
Sennacherib, 53-55, 464
Sepharad, 137, 199. *See also* Sardis
Sepphoris, 467, 508
Serah daughter of Asher, 466
Seraiah, 185
Servant of the LORD, 153, 157, 162-168
Seth, 467
Shabbatai Zevi, 11
Shadal. *See* Luzzato, S. D.
Shamhazzai, 279
Shallum. *See* Jehoahaz
Shalmaneser IV (V), 53, 362
Shammai, 392, 448
Shammai, school of, 448, 491
Sheba, Sabeans, 54, 154, 174, 175
Shechem, 15, 176, 484
Shelom-Zion. *See* Salome Alexandra
Shemaiah (Tanna), 392
Shemaiah the Nehelamite, 113
Shemoneh Esreh (prayer), 352, 460, 470, 478
Sheol, 295. *See also* Gehenna
Sheshbazzar, 158, 186, 188, 191
Shoot, righteous, 65, 102, 195-196
Sibylline Oracles, 276, 370-381, 506, 512
Sidon, 90, 137, 180, 197, 202, 207
Signs of the Messiah, 178-183, 207-208, 268-269, 278-280, 326-329, 332-336, 339-345, 350-354, 359-363, 378, 431-433, 439, 442-449, 503-517. *See also* Birth pangs of Messiah; Day of Judgment; Day of the LORD
Silver, A. H., 423
Simeon ben Eleazar, R., 449
Simeon ben Gamaliel II, Rabban, 431, 435, 438, 504, 515
Simeon ben Judah, R., 364
Simeon ben Shetah, R., 337, 393
Simeon ben Yohai, R., 401-403, 406, 427, 445, 448-449, 471, 474, 482, 497, 499-500, 510-511
Simeon son of Johanan (Simeon II, high priest), 255-256

Simhoni, I. N., 124, 133, 218
Simlai, Rab (Amora), 424, 435, 436
Simon (Simeon), "Prince of the Sanctuary," 223
Simon Magus, 371
Simon son of Mattathias, 260, 275
Sin-shar-ishkun (Sarakos), 127
Slouschz, N., 102
Smend, R., 43, 217
Smith, Robertson, 218
Socrates, 23
Solomon, 30, 32, 476
Son of David—*throughout the book*
Son of Man, 229-231, 291-292, 331, 358-360
Son of Zion. *See* Sons of Zion
Song of Songs, 222
Sons of Zion, 453
Stade, B., 29, 169, 188, 192, 198-199, 204, 214, 219
Staehelin, J. J., 413
Stein, M., 218, 318, 323
Steinberg, Joshua, 63, 371-375, 380
Steuernagel, C., 84, 145, 158, 180, 196, 198, 207, 216
Stoics, 23
Stourdzé, S., 296
Success, political. *See* Prosperity, material
Syria, 176, 198

Tabor, 513
Tacitus, 526
Taëb (Samaritan Messiah), 484, 488
Tanhum son of Hiyya, R. (Amora), 431
Tannaim—*throughout the book*
Tarphon, R. (Tanna), 407
Tattenai (governor of Syria), 193
Taxo, 326-327
Tel-abib, 111
Tel-harsha, 111, 172
Tel-melah, 111, 172
Temple, the—*in many places*
Ten Tribes, the, 345-348, 362-364, 398, 472-475, 488, 495
Testaments of the Twelve Tribes (Patriarchs), 275, 304, 310-316
Theocracy, 131
Thracians, 199
Throne of Glory, 460-461
Tiberius (emperor), 428

INDEX

Tiglath-pileser IV (III), 53-54
Tigranes, 277
Titus, 112
Tobiads, 222
Tobit, 251, 265-266, 268, 273
Torah. See Eternity of the Law; Forgetting of the Law; Law
Torrey, C. C., 108, 185
Trajan (emperor), 367
Treasury of souls, 332-333, 355, 367, 431
Trito-Isaiah. See Isaiah ("Third")
Trumpet of the Messiah, 183, 278, 318, 352, 470-471
Trypho the Jew, 407, 456, 466, 520
Tyre, 90, 197, 202, 207, 224

Universalism, 67-71, 86, 106-107, 139, 151, 159-167, 172-173, 185-186, 194, 209-210, 214, 220-221, 228-234, 377-379, 475-482, 512
Uriah son of Shemaiah, 161
Uriel (angel), 296
Utopia (Ezekiel's), 116, 130-134
Uzziah, 35-37, 52, 72-73, 143

Vahyazdata, 189
Valley of Jehoshaphat, 207
Varus, 325
Vergil, 14, 379
Vernes, M., 2, 185, 293, 435, 460, 520
Vespasian, 394
Vesuvius, 371
Vicarious suffering, 18, 161-167, 527-528
Volz, P., 2, 13, 42
Vulgate, 350

Walther, Franz, 38
Weber, Ferdinand, 396, 414, 449, 452, 465, 497
Weincoop, J. J. B., 136, 138, 206
Weiss, I. H., 393, 396, 403, 406, 408, 414, 446, 474, 491, 497, 514

Well-being, spiritual, 62, 64-71, 86-87, 97-98, 141-142, 152-154, 161-168, 197, 203-205, 210-211, 221, 229-236, 252-258, 284, 293-296, 318-324, 376-377, 502, 511-516
Wellhausen, J., 30, 42, 75, 77, 80, 112, 123, 127, 132, 149, 160, 186, 187, 188, 199, 217, 233, 361
Whitehouse, O. C., 267
Wild ox (Behemoth), 274, 298-299, 364-365
Wisdom of Solomon, 248, 251, 270-271
World to Come, 270-271, 274, 278, 331, 341-342, 347-348, 352-353, 356-358, 404, 408-419
Wuttke, G., 456

Yeivin, S., 31, 398
Yinnon, 463

Zabibe (queen), 53
Zadok, Zadokites, 256-257
Zadokite Work. See Damascus Covenant
Zarathustra. See Zoroaster
Zarephath (dependency of Sidon), 136-137
Zealots, 326, 393
Zechariah (First), 147, 169, 193-197, 208, 212, 215
Zechariah (Second), 169, 197-205, 208, 210, 258, 352, 481, 485-487, 490, 494
Zedekiah (false prophet), 113
Zedekiah (Mattaniah, king), 90, 103-106, 109-110, 113, 115-116, 126, 195
Zeitlin, S., 302-303
Zephaniah (prophet), 82-87, 113, 127, 134, 161, 208, 282, 329, 374
Zephaniah son of Maaseiah (priest), 111
Zerubbabel, 158, 162, 176, 185-196, 202-203, 212
Zoroaster, 14
Zotos. See Izates

www.ingramcontent.com/pod-product-compliance
Lightning Source LLC
Chambersburg PA
CBHW052044290426
44111CB00011B/1609